1963

HISTORY
OF THE
COMMUNIST
PARTY
OF THE
SOVIET
UNION

1883 - 1960

FOREIGN LANGUAGES PUBLISHING HOUSE

Moscow 1960

Published in Great Britain by
LAWRENCE AND WISHART LTD
81 Chancery Lane, London, W.C.2

TRANSLATED FROM THE RUSSIAN

EDITED BY ANDREW ROTHSTEIN

The History of the C.P.S.U. has been prepared by a group of authors: *B. N. Ponomaryov*, Corresponding Member of the Academy of Sciences of the U.S.S.R. (head); *V. M. Khvostov*, Corresponding Member of the Academy of Sciences of the U.S.S.R.; *A. P. Kuchkin*, Doctor of Historical Sciences; *I. I. Mints*, Academician; *N. I. Shatagin*, Doctor of Historical Sciences; *L. A. Slepov*, Candidate of Economic Sciences; *A. I. Sobolev*, Candidate of Philosophical Sciences; *A. A. Timofeyevsky*, Candidate of Historical Sciences; *M. S. Volin*, Candidate of Historical Sciences; Prof. *I. M. Volkov*; *V. S. Zaitsev*, Candidate of Historical Sciences.

CONTENTS

Chapter Four

THE BOLSHEVIK PARTY IN THE PERIOD OF REACTION
(1907-1910)

Chapter Five

THE BOLSHEVIK PARTY DURING
THE NEW UPSURGE OF THE REVOLUTIONARY MOVEMENT
(1910-1914)

Chapter Six

THE BOLSHEVIK PARTY IN THE PERIOD
OF THE IMPERIALIST WORLD WAR.
THE SECOND REVOLUTION IN RUSSIA
(1914-February 1917)

Chapter Ten

THE PARTY IN THE STRUGGLE TO REHABILITATE THE NATIONAL ECONOMY

(1921-1925)

Chapter Eleven

THE STRUGGLE OF THE PARTY FOR THE SOCIALIST INDUSTRIALISATION OF THE COUNTRY AND THE PREPARATION FOR THE SOLID COLLECTIVISATION OF AGRICULTURE

(1926-1929)

Chapter Fifteen

THE PARTY IN THE PERIOD OF THE GREAT PATRIOTIC WAR

(June 1941-1945)

Chapter Sixteen

THE PARTY'S STRUGGLE FOR THE RESTORATION AND DEVELOPMENT OF THE SOCIALIST NATIONAL ECONOMY AFTER THE WAR

(1945-1953)

INTRODUCTION

The Communist Party of the Soviet Union, founded and brought to maturity by the great Lenin, has travelled a historical road the like of which is unknown to any other political party in the world. Its history is a record of more than half a century of the heroic struggles, severe trials and epoch-making victories of the working class, the victories of Socialism.

At the end of the nineteenth and the beginning of the twentieth century the Party entered the historical arena and boldly led the working class and the peasantry into battle against the tsarist autocracy and Russian capitalism. The struggle against tsarism and capitalism in Russia was also a struggle against world imperialism. Russia became the centre of the world revolutionary movement. By arming the working class and the bulk of the labouring peasantry of Russia with the ideas of Marxism-Leninism, the Party ensured the victory of the people over the tsarist autocracy and the bourgeoisie.

Starting with small Marxist circles active in the working-class movement of Russia at the end of the nineteenth century, the Party developed into a great force which today directs a powerful Socialist State.

The Communist Party led the peoples of Russia through three revolutions: the bourgeois-democratic revolution of 1905-1907, the bourgeois-democratic revolution of February 1917 and the Great October Socialist Revolution, and brought the Soviet people to the victory of Socialism which opened a new epoch in world history. The Communist Party stood the test of two imperialist wars (the Russo-Japanese War of 1904-1905 and the first world war of 1914-1918). The Communist Party headed the heroic struggle of the Soviet people in two patriotic wars—the Civil War of 1918-1920 and the Great Patriotic War of 1941-1945—and successfully defended the Socialist Motherland against the assaults of a host of enemies.

At all stages of its development, the Party has elaborated and pursued a policy based on the theory of Marxism-Leninism, a policy answering the interests of the working class, the labouring peasantry, and all the nations inhabiting the country, the interests of the Motherland, the interests of the victory of Communism in the Soviet Union and of the cause of international Socialism.

The Communist Party has accumulated great and varied experience in the struggle for the victory of the dictatorship of the proletariat. In the years before the October Revolution, working underground in the hardest conditions, the Bolsheviks developed the theoretical solutions for complex ideological, political and organisational problems, which enabled them to achieve victory in the bourgeois-democratic and Socialist revolutions. These problems included: elaboration of the theory of a new type of party— a revolutionary Marxist party—and the creation of such a party; elaboration of a new theory of revolution applicable to the era of imperialism; elaboration of the strategy and tactics to be used in the bourgeois-democratic and the Socialist revolution; the struggle to win the hegemony of the proletariat for victory over tsarism and capitalism, to achieve unity of the working-class movement, to establish an alliance between the working class and the peasantry, to win over the oppressed nations to the side of the proletariat; the struggle against the enemies of Marxism in the ranks of the revolutionary and working-class movement in Russia and on the international arena, and other problems. The Party's activities provided a pattern of how legal and illegal, parliamentary and extraparliamentary forms of struggle and work should be combined.

The Communist Party's experience in conditions of the dictatorship of the proletariat has been even more rich and varied. Socialism was built for the first time in human history in a vast country with a comparatively underdeveloped economy, with a predominantly peasant population, and inhabited by many different nations and nationalities. The Party had to, and did, work out theoretically the most complicated problems of Socialist construction. The historical experience of the C.P.S.U. covers a vast range of problems relating to the transition from capitalism to Socialism, and to the development of Socialist society towards Communism.

Chief among these problems are:

implementation of the dictatorship of the proletariat and of Socialist democracy at different stages of development of Soviet society; realisation of the alliance between the working class and the peasantry under the leadership of the working class throughout the whole period of transition from capitalism to Socialism; solution of the national question, and formation of a commonwealth of Socialist nations in the Soviet State; elaboration of the basic problems of the transition from Socialism to Communism;

creation of Socialist forms of economy; industrialisation of the country and bringing into being of the material and technical basis of Socialism; collectivisation of agriculture and development of large-scale mechanised Socialist agriculture, elimination of the exploiting classes and abolition of the exploitation of man by man; the transition of formerly backward peoples to Socialism without passing through the capitalist stage of development;

working out of new principles of inter-State relations, in keeping with the interests of the Soviet people and of the working people throughout the world; consistent pursuance of a peaceable foreign policy—a policy of peaceful coexistence of countries with different social systems; consolidation and strengthening of the defensive capacity of the Socialist State; consolidation and extension of co-operation among the countries of the world Socialist system;

the affirmation of a Socialist ideology and the victory of a scientific, Marxist-Leninist world outlook; the carrying out of a cultural revolution; the flowering of Socialist science and the training of a large new people's intelligentsia; education of the new man in a Communist spirit;

transformation of the Communist Party from a force for overthrowing the system of exploitation into a force for building a new, Communist society; giving effect to the leading role of the Party in the system of the dictatorship of the proletariat; consolidation of the unity of the Party on the basis of Marxism-Leninism; development of inner-Party democracy; education and ideological tempering of the Party cadres and of all members of the Party; strengthening of ties with brother Communist and Workers' Parties, based on the principles of Marxism-Leninism.

Comprehensively elaborated in theory and tested in practice, all this can now be drawn upon, in their struggle for Socialism, by the peoples of different countries who are at various stages of social development, with due regard, of course, to the specific national features of each country.

Thus, as a result of the theoretical work and practical struggle of the Communist Party of the Soviet Union, which won the leadership of the working class and the mass of the people and based itself on the objective laws of social development, mankind has acquired the first Socialist society in history, and together with this the science of building Socialism, a science tested in practice.

Under the leadership of the C.P.S.U., the Soviet people and their armed forces have successfully maintained the freedom and independence of the Socialist Motherland.

At the same time, the Communist Party of the Soviet Union, true to the principle of proletarian internationalism, has consistently discharged its obligations towards the working class and the liberation movement of the peoples of other countries, and has done everything possible to secure the triumph of the ideas of Socialism. During the second world war the Soviet Union played the decisive part in securing victory for the anti-Hitlerite coalition and in delivering the peoples from the fascist yoke. The Soviet people, under the leadership of the Party, helped the peoples of South-East and Central Europe, as well as of China, Korea and Vietnam, in their struggle against German and Japanese occupation; and later it assisted them in the struggle to establish and consolidate the system of people's democracy in their countries.

As a result of the victory of the working class over the exploiting classes, and on the basis of the combined efforts and fraternal co-operation of the states which have taken the path of Socialism, a world Socialist system that embraces one-third of mankind has come into being. The Communist Party as it guides the Soviet Union, the core of the Socialist system, spares no effort to help accomplish the great and historic task of further strengthening and advancing the world system of Socialism. The Communist Party is the standard-bearer of peace and friendship among the peoples of all countries.

The Communist Party of the Soviet Union has always been guided by the revolutionary theory of Marxism-Leninism. It has defended Marxist theory against the attacks of its enemies, overt and covert, against opportunists of every hue, and has developed this theory further. Vladimir Ilyich Lenin, the founder of the Communist Party, enriched the theory of Marx and Engels in every respect and raised it to a new, higher level. Leninism is the continuation and development of Marxism: it is Marxism of the era of imperialism and proletarian revolutions, of the era of Socialist and Communist construction in the U.S.S.R., of the rise and development of the world Socialist system, of the era of the transition of human society from capitalism to Communism.

Marxism-Leninism is the banner under which the Great October Revolution was accomplished, a Socialist society built and the world system of Socialism founded. Marxism-Leninism is the banner under which millions of workmen and other working people in all countries are today waging their struggle.

The faithful disciples and followers of Marx, Engels and Lenin have ever upheld their great teachings, and have developed them further in keeping with the new, present-day conditions of the struggle for the building of Socialism and Communism, for the interests of the international proletariat and for the national liberation of the peoples.

In the course of the preparations for and during the revolution in Russia, the Communist Party waged a stubborn and uncompromising struggle against the hostile political parties and groups active in the country—the "Economists," the Mensheviks—the main variety of opportunism in the working-class movement in Russia—the Socialist-Revolutionaries, the Anarchists, and also against the monarchists, the Cadets (Constitutional Democrats) and the bourgeois-nationalist parties.

After testing all the political parties in practice, the working class, the masses of the people, became firmly convinced that the Communist Party was the genuine representative of their interests, and the sole party that could lead them.

Within the Party itself, a prolonged and bitter struggle was waged against various anti-Leninist groups—the Trotskyists, the "Workers' Opposition," the "Democratic Centralism" group, the Trotskyist-Zinovievite bloc, the Right opportunists, and nationalist and other groups.

Political victory over all hostile parties and anti-Leninist groups and their ideological defeat, were essential for the victory of the Socialist revolution and for the building of Socialism in the U.S.S.R.

The history of the Communist Party of the Soviet Union falls into two main periods. The first period covers the Party's struggle to overthrow the tsarist autocracy and the capitalist system and to establish the dictatorship of the proletariat. In the second period the Party is in power, directing the struggle for the building of Socialism and Communism in the Soviet Union. The tasks of the Party, its strategy and tactics, and the forms in which its activities were organised, varied in accordance with these periods.

The study of the history of the C.P.S.U., of the victorious path it has travelled, and of the theory of Marxism-Leninism arms the working people with a knowledge of the laws of social development, the laws of the class struggle and of the motive forces of revolution, with a knowledge of the laws governing the building of Socialist society and of Communism.

The study of the history of the Party inspires Communists and all Soviet people with legitimate pride in their great Party and in its epoch-making victories, with a desire to be worthy of their Party and their country in every way. It helps them to apply the rich experience of the Party in solving new problems, and engenders the creative energy required for building Communism.

The history of the Communist Party of the Soviet Union, which has achieved epoch-making victories of Socialism over capitalism, undermined the roots of the world imperialist system and ensured the triumph of Marxism-Leninism, inspires the Communists of other countries with legitimate pride in their victorious brother Party and strengthens the faith of the working people of the whole world in the victory of Socialism. The study of the history of the Party helps us to master Marxism-Leninism and assimilate the experience of the struggle to overthrow the exploiters' yoke and to build Communism.

This book gives a concise outline of the history of the Communist Party of the Soviet Union.

CHAPTER ONE

THE BEGINNING
OF THE WORKING-CLASS MOVEMENT
AND THE SPREAD OF MARXISM IN RUSSIA

(1883-1894)

1. Development of Capitalism and the Conditions of the Masses in Russia in the Second Half of the Nineteenth Century

Tsarist Russia was one of the particularly backward countries of Europe. Capitalism began to develop there comparatively late. Serfdom, under which the peasant could be bought and sold like chattel, existed in Russia as late as the middle of the nineteenth century. The productivity of the forced labour of the serfs was low, and agriculture based on such labour was extremely backward. There could be no real development of industry, which needed a free labour force and a home market. The development of capitalist commodity relations made the abolition of serfdom imperative, but the serfowning landlords stubbornly resisted this step.

The rottenness of the system of serfdom and its damaging effect on the country became increasingly evident. The Crimean War (1853-1856) most glaringly revealed this. In 1861 the tsarist government, pressed by economic necessity and frightened by mounting peasant disturbances, was compelled to abolish serfdom.

After the fall of serfdom the development of capitalism in Russia proceeded fairly rapidly, primarily in industry. Between 1866 and 1890, the number of factories was more than doubled, growing from 2,500-3,000 to 6,000. Machines were gradually superseding manual labour. What were in those days very large factories, equipped with machines and employing thousands of workers, made their appearance. By 1890 big enterprises, employing more than 100 workers each, comprised less than 7 per cent of all enterprises, but they produced more than 50 per cent of the total industrial output. The length of the railways increased more than sevenfold, from under 2,500 to over 18,000 miles. The large cities, centres of economic, political and cultural life, began to grow rapidly. New industrial regions came into being: the Donets coalfield and the Baku oil area. All these changes took place in the course of a quarter of a century, during a single generation.

The development of capitalism produced radical changes in the class composition of the population. Under serfdom there were two principal classes in Russia—the landlords and the peasants. With the development of capitalism, the bourgeoisie and the proletariat entered the arena of social life. The bourgeoisie, which had already come into being in the period of serfdom, grew rapidly, amassing wealth and acquiring great economic power.

The rise and development of large-scale capitalist industrial production was attended by the appearance and growth of a modern industrial proletariat. In 1890 the number of workers employed in the large factories alone, in the mining industry and on the railways had grown to 1,432,000 or double what it was in 1865. Nearly half the industrial workers (48.3 per cent) were concentrated in the bigger enterprises, each employing 500 workers or more. Factory workers constituted the backbone of the huge army of wage-labour. Altogether, according to Lenin's estimates, at the end of the nineteenth century there were in Russia about 10 million wage-workers employed in industry, on the railways, in agriculture, building, lumbering, navvying, and so on.

The appearance of large-scale machine industry and of an industrial proletariat was a progressive development; but Russia's transformation into a capitalist country was achieved, as everywhere else, through the intensified exploitation of the working people. The statistics showing the increased number of factories, the building of railways and the increased number of workers, concealed the misery of the people, their tears and blood. What made the conditions of the masses all the more unbearable was the fact that capitalist exploitation was combined with survivals of feudal oppression.

Serfdom was abolished in such a way as to preserve the privileges and the power of the serfowning landlords. In the process of their "emancipation," the peasants were robbed in the most unscrupulous manner. More than one-fifth of the best land previously cultivated by them was cut off by the landlords for themselves. These cut-off portions of land were called by the peasants *otrezki* (cuts). The tsarist authorities forced the peasants to pay exorbitant redemption prices for the rest of the land. Not surprisingly, the peasants reacted to their "emancipation" by mass actions, which were brutally suppressed by the tsarist authorities. Almost half a century after their "emancipation" the peasants were still paying off the landlords for their own land, land drenched with their sweat and blood. It was only under pressure of the revolution that the tsarist government abolished redemption payments in 1907.

The landlords retained vast estates and power. The first and biggest landlord was the tsar. In European Russia the imperial family alone owned nearly 19 million acres of land, which was more than the holdings of half a million peasant families. In the late seventies the landed nobility owned more than 197 million out of a total of 247 million acres of privately-owned land. The big landed estates formed the basis for semi-feudal exploitation. The peasants were obliged to rent land from the landlords on terms which put a noose round their necks: to cultivate the landlord's land with their own implements and horses, to give up one half of their crops to the landlord. The existence of *otrabotki* (labour service), *ispolu* work (share-cropping) and of redemption payments meant that survivals of serfdom were still strong in the countryside.

Capitalism was developing not only in the towns, but also in the countryside. Peasant farming turned more and more from natural economy to commodity production, and became ever more dependent upon the market. Competition was growing, the renting and purchase of land began to spread, and agricultural production was increasingly becoming concentrated in the hands of the more prosperous peasants. Under the influence of capitalism differentiation proceeded among the peasantry: there were emerging the kulaks (rural bourgeoisie) and the peasant poor (rural proletarians and semi-proletarians, as Lenin called them). By the end of the nineteenth century, of the 10 million peasant households in the country, approximately 6.5 million were poor peasant, 2 million middle-peasant and 1.5 million kulak households.

The landlords and the kulaks bled the peasants white, dooming them to poverty and extinction. Crop failure and famine were frequent visitations upon the countryside. About 40 million peasants were affected by the terrible famine of 1891. Poverty drove the peasants from their native villages in search of a livelihood. By the end of the nineties these peasants made up a vast mass, for 5-6 million people left their villages every year. A large proportion of them settled down in the cities permanently, went to work in the factories, became workmen.

The peasant's lot was a bitter one. Incredibly hard, too, were the conditions of the workers, who were entirely at the mercy of the capitalists and the tsarist authorities. The working day was not less than 12-13 hours, and as much as 15-16 hours in the textile mills. There was no labour protection. The terms of employment were of the hardest. The beggarly wages paid afforded no more than a bare subsistence. And even these miserly wages were cut in every possible way. The workers were cheated, wages were paid irregularly, at the employer's discretion. Workers were compelled to buy foodstuffs on credit in company stores and to pay exorbitant prices for stale goods. They were especially plagued by fines, which were imposed on any pretext and often swallowed up as much as one-third, or even 40 per cent, of wages. Female and child labour were widely employed. Although women and children worked the same hours as men, they were paid much less.

Most of the workers lived in factory-owned barracks, in common "dormitories" with double- or triple-decker berths. Three or four families huddled together in the corners of a small room. Miners as a rule lived in hovels or dugouts. Back-breaking toil and poverty bred disease on a mass scale. They led to the rapid exhaustion and early death of workers and to high child mortality.

The survivals of serfdom were particularly evident in the country's social and political life. Politically, Russia was an absolute monarchy, that is, full and undivided power was vested in the tsar, who decreed laws and appointed ministers and officials at his own discretion, levied taxes and spent the people's money entirely uncontrolled. Essentially, the tsarist monarchy was a dictatorship of the feudal landlords, who had all the political rights, enjoyed all the privileges, held all the important posts in the State and received huge subsidies out of the people's money. The tsarist government supported the big manufacturers, the financial and industrial magnates. The people in Russia had no political rights whatever. They were denied freedom to assemble, to voice their opinions and present their demands, freedom to form unions and organisations, freedom to publish newspapers, magazines and books. A huge army of gendarmes, secret police, jailers, constables, village police of different kinds and Zemsky Nachalniks (rural superintendents)[1] protected the tsar, the landlords and the capitalists from the people.

The tsarist government feared lest the spread of knowledge would make the people insubordinate. It therefore kept the people in darkness and ignorance. The Ministry of Public Education was in fact a department for befogging the minds of the people. The annual allocations for schools were paltry, amounting to only 80 kopeks a year per person. "Cooks' children," as young people of working-class and peasant origin were contemptuously called, were kept out of the secondary schools and universities. Nearly four-fifths of Russia's population were illiterate. Tsarism doomed the people not only to material, but also to intellectual poverty.

Tsarist Russia was a prison of the peoples. The exploiting classes, together with tsarism and its entire machinery of State, were responsible for national oppression in Russia. The non-Russian peoples, who constituted the bulk of the population (57 per cent), were denied all rights; they suffered countless humiliations and insults. Tsarist officials administered arbitrary justice and meted out punishment. The national culture of the non-Russian peoples was savagely persecuted. Many peoples were forbidden to publish newspapers and books and to instruct their children in their native language. The population in the East was totally illiterate. The tsarist government deliberately fomented national discord, officially referred to the non-Russian peoples as "aliens," and tried to foster in the Russians a contemptuous attitude towards these peoples as supposedly inferior races. The tsarist authorities incited one people against another. They engineered Jewish pogroms and provoked Armenians and Azerbaijanians to massacre each other. Tsarism was an executioner and torturer of the non-Russian peoples.

The survivals of serfdom hindered the country's progress. At the end of the nineteenth century about five-sixths of the population were engaged in agriculture, with inefficient small-scale peasant farming predominating. Notwithstanding the development of capitalism in Russia, she remained an economically backward agrarian country.

An approximate idea of Russia's class composition at that time is provided by the figures of the 1897 census. Altogether Russia had a population of 125.6 million. Of these the bulk were peasants, two-thirds of whom were poor peasants. Workmen and their families made up almost one-fifth of the population. Approximately as many belonged to the well-to-do strata: the kulaks, owners of small enterprises, bourgeois intellectuals, officials, etc. The big bourgeoisie, landlords and high officials accounted for about two per cent.

The working people—workers, the rural poor and middle peasants and artisans—made up nearly four-fifths of the population. And this vast majority of the people was oppressed and enslaved by a handful of landlords and capitalists, who had a faithful guardian in the tsarist government. The millions of indigent and enslaved working folk of town and country represented a powerful revolutionary force. But this force had to be *organised* and politically *enlightened*; it had to be given a clear understanding of its own interests and of the ways of fighting for its freedom from oppression; it had to be *rallied* around the working class.

The abolition of serfdom, without eliminating the contradictions between peasants and landlords, added new class contradictions, those between workers and capitalists. The development of capitalism aggravated all the class contradictions in Russia. The working masses suffered both from capitalist exploitation and from remnants of the yoke of serfdom. The interests of the people and of all social development demanded, first and foremost, the abolition of the survivals of serfdom and the overthrow of the tsarist autocracy.

At the end of the nineteenth century Russia was no longer what it had been before 1861. Here is how Lenin described the processes at work in Russia at that time:

"Capitalist Russia was succeeding serfowning Russia. A new generation of peasants, who had engaged in seasonal work, lived in the cities and learned a thing or two from their bitter experience as migratory wage-workers, was growing up to succeed the settled, downtrodden peasant serf who was tied to his village, believed the priests and feared the 'authorities.' The number of workers was growing steadily in the big cities, in the factories and mills. Associations of workers gradually began to be formed for joint struggle against the capitalists and the government. By conducting this struggle the Russian working class was helping millions of peasants to stand up, straighten their backs and discard the habits of bonded slaves" (*Collected Works*, Vol. 17, p. 66).*

These processes fostered the revolutionary movement in Russia.

2. Revolutionary Democrats and Narodniks. The First Workers' Organisations

The revolutionary movement in Russia has a rich and heroic history. The yoke of serfdom, which doomed the people to grinding toil and poverty, and stifled all that was alive in the country, roused discontent and protest among the masses. These sentiments flared up in revolts and disturbances. Revolutionary thought in Russia had its roots in the struggle of the peasant masses against serfdom. Already in the period of serfdom, in the forties and fifties of the nineteenth century, the rich soil of the class struggle nurtured such great revolutionary democrats as V. G. Belinsky, A. I. Herzen, N. A. Dobrolyubov and N. G. Chernyshevsky. Their work was permeated with a deep hatred of all the manifestations of serfdom in Russia's social life, and was dedicated to the ardent advocacy of progressive development of the country. They fought selflessly for the interests of the people, and played an outstanding part in the emancipation movement of the peoples of Russia. A particularly strong influence was exerted on advanced

---

* All references to Lenin's and other works are given according to the 4th Russian edition unless otherwise specified.—*Trans.*

Russian men and women in the latter half of the nineteenth century by N. G. Chernyshevsky, leader of the Russian revolutionary democrats and the most outstanding revolutionary thinker of the pre-Marxist period.

The revolutionary democrats persistently and critically sought for a sound theory, as the instrument for the emancipation of the people from the autocracy, from exploitation. They rightly thought the people to be the principal motive force of social development. But they did not see, nor could they have seen at that time, the historic role of the working class, its ability to transform society.

The revolutionary democrats were ideologists of the peasant revolution. They regarded militant democracy and utopian Socialism as being one inseparable whole. All over Europe protest against social oppression at first gave rise to utopian Socialist doctrines. The utopian Socialists condemned capitalism and dreamed of a better social system, but they could not show the real way out, because they did not see the social force that could become the builder of the new society, a society free from the exploitation of man by man. The utopian Socialists of Russia who, unlike the West European utopians, advocated the transformation of the country through a peasant revolution, dreamed of a transition to Socialism through the peasant commune. A characteristic of the village commune in pre-revolutionary Russia was common ownership of the land. Individual peasant households received land for temporary use; the land was periodically redistributed on an equalitarian basis. And it was this village commune that the utopian Socialists mistakenly regarded as the embryo of Socialism.

After the fall of serfdom the revolutionary movement in Russia grew stronger. In the seventies this movement was dominated by the Narodniks. The name "Narodnik" (from the Russian word *narod*, the people) owes its origin to the movement among the most advanced, revolutionary-minded intellectuals, especially students, who "went among the people," to the countryside, in the hope of rousing the peasants to a revolution against the tsarist autocracy. Revolutionary Narodism was a widespread social movement with different trends and shades. Its main trends were represented by M. A. Bakunin, P. L. Lavrov and P. N. Tkachov; but all the Narodniks held the same views on Russia's development. They were ideologists of a peasant democracy; they believed that the Russian way of life was a special one, and saw in the village commune the starting-point for Socialist development of the country. Hence their belief in the possibility of a peasant Socialist revolution in Russia. They were inspired by this idea, which roused them to a heroic and selfless struggle against the tsarist autocracy and the tyranny of the landlords. Among the Narodniks were such outstanding revolutionaries as A. I. Zhelyabov, I. N. Myshkin and S. L. Perovskaya. The tsarist hangmen dealt ruthlessly with the revolutionary Narodniks, hanged them, left them to rot in prison dungeons or made them suffer the horrors of penal servitude. Some of the revolutionary Narodniks were the first people in the history of the Russian emancipation movement to work among the factory workers, even though they did not understand the historic role of the proletariat. Lenin, who showed the complicated and contradictory nature of Narodism, highly appreciated its revolutionary peasant democratic spirit and its call to revolution.

The Narodism of the seventies played an important part in the development of the revolutionary movement in Russia. But the course chosen by the Narodniks for their struggle, and especially their guiding theory, were profoundly erroneous. Although the Narodniks were influenced by the revolutionary democrats, their views on many questions were a step back. Far from holding materialist views, they idealised the peasant and misunderstood the role of the masses in history. Their erroneous view of the peasant commune as the basis for Socialist development of the country became especially harmful in the new historical conditions, when capitalism began to develop in Russia and an industrial proletariat appeared. But the Narodniks failed to understand these new conditions. They asserted that capitalism in Russia was an "accidental phenomenon," and therefore denied the leading, revolutionary role of the working class in the development of society.

Real life proved the utter fallacy of the Narodnik ideas about the peasant's "Communist instincts." The peasants were mistrustful of the preachings of the Narodniks, which were remote from their interests. The tsarist authorities arrested the revolutionaries by the hundred. The unsuccessful "going among the people" did not however undermine the Narodnik illusions all at once. A Narodnik organisation, "Zemlya i Volya" (Land and Freedom), was formed at the end of 1876. It sent its supporters into the countryside to settle permanently there, in the hope of winning the confidence of the peasants and rousing them to revolution. But the Narodniks were no more successful here. Disputes over methods of continuing the struggle grew ever sharper. In 1879 "Zemlya i Volya" split up. A minority among the Narodniks clung to their old position: they rejected the struggle for political freedom, considering that such a struggle could only benefit the bourgeoisie. They preached redistribution of all the land, the landlords' estates included, among the peasants, and set up an organisation known as the "Chorny Peredel" (General Redistribution).

The majority of the Narodniks founded their own organisation, the "Narodnaya Volya" (People's Will). The "Narodnaya Volya" took a step forward by engaging in political struggle against the tsarist autocracy. However, the members of the "Narodnaya Volya" regarded the political struggle not as a struggle of the masses, but as a conspiracy by a small organisation of revolutionaries to overthrow the tsarist autocracy and seize power. They chose as their method of struggle individual terrorism, that is, the assassination of individual representatives of the tsarist autocracy and of the tsar himself, hoping to seize power by frightening and disorganising the government.' In this the "Narodnaya Volya" proceeded from the erroneous theory of active "heroes" and a passive "mob." According to this theory, history is made by outstanding individuals, while the masses, the people, the "mob," can only follow them blindly. The tactics of the "Narodnaya Volya" fettered the activity of the masses, and thereby injured the revolutionary movement, the injury becoming more and more palpable as the struggle of the masses developed.

Narodism doomed the revolutionary movement to defeat. Their erroneous theory directed the Narodniks along the wrong path. They did not see the historical force which was to take the lead of the struggle of the masses against the landlords and the bourgeoisie, and to bring it to victory. That force was the working class.

Rapacious exploitation and complete denial of political rights roused the protest of the workers. Disturbances and strikes took place already in the sixties. Their number increased in the seventies. According to incomplete data, there were 326 strikes and disturbances among workmen in ten years (1870-1879). But they were, as yet, only the spontaneous acts of people drivento despair, of people who, though they did not yet know why they were suffering such hardships or what they should be striving for, were looking for a way out of their intolerable situation.

The spontaneous struggle of the workers was a manifestation of class consciousness in embryonic form: the workers were beginning to realise that the existing social system which oppressed them was not something permanent; they would not any longer bear everything with servile submissiveness; they were beginning to feel the need of a common stand against their oppressors. In the course of the struggle there began to emerge from the mass of the workers more advanced and class-conscious workmen, who were becoming revolutionaries.

The Narodniks held undivided sway in the revolutionary movement of that time, and the revolutionary workers fell under their influence and joined them. But the more advanced workers were eagerly acquiring knowledge. They avidly sought for the root causes of the workers' miseries and ways of setting them free.

They already had some idea of the First International and of the activities of the European working-class parties. The first Russian translations of the writings of Marx and Engels began to reach them. They were contemporaries of the Paris Commune. The revolutionary worker pondered a great deal over the lessons of the mass actions of the Russian proletariat. He could no longer be satisfied with the Narodnik teachings, which assigned to the workers an auxiliary role in the revolution. The foremost workers were trying to find their *own* ways of struggle, to create an *independent* organisation.

The first organisation of this kind was the South Russian Workers' Union, formed in Odessa in 1875 by Y. O. Zaslavsky, a revolutionary intellectual. The Union had a membership of about 200 workers. It had supporters in Rostov-on-Don, Kharkov, Orel and Taganrog. The Union existed for about a year and was then broken up by the tsarist police. The aim of the South Russian Workers' Union was "to propagate the idea of emancipating the workers from the yoke of capitalism and the privileged classes," and to unite the workers for "the future struggle against the existing economic and political system." The influence of Narodism was still felt in the Union. It found expression, for example, in a decision to organise settlements in the countryside for work among the peasants. The historic service rendered by the Union lay in the fact that it spread in the working-class movement the idea of political struggle, and established an independent organisation of the proletariat.

In the middle seventies the advanced workers of St. Petersburg also proceeded to form their own organisation, which took final shape in 1878 as the North Russian Workers' Union. Its founders were Victor Obnorsky and Stepan Khalturin, outstanding working-class revolutionaries. The appearance of this Union was another important step in the development of the working-class movement. Its programme proclaimed the idea of the international class solidarity of the proletariat and stated that "in its aims it stands close to the Social-Democratic parties of the West." The ultimate aim of the Union was "the overthrow of the existing political and economic system of the State as extremely unjust." Its immediate aim was to win political liberty. The influence of Narodism was still felt in the programme of this Union, which saw the peasant commune as a factor of Socialism.

The membership of the Northern Union was about 200 workers. It took part in several strikes, issued leaflets and introduced an element of organisation into the struggle. The Union enjoyed great prestige among the workers. It was broken up by the gendarmes in 1879-1880, but the cause for which it fought was not lost. "And so, the final decision rests with you, workers.

On you depends the fate of the great Union and the success of the social revolution in Russia "—this impassioned appeal in the programme of the Union found a response among the foremost workers.

The Russian working class gradually began to set itself broad political tasks, to develop splendid militant, revolutionary qualities in the course of its struggle, to advance outstanding revolutionary leaders. The words of the Moscow weaver Pyotr Alexeyev at his trial in 1877 about the historic role of the Russian working class rang like a prophecy: "The muscular arm of millions of working men will be lifted and the yoke of despotism, guarded by soldiers' bayonets, will be smashed to atoms!" The first class organisations of the proletariat arose. But they were merely the initial steps of the working-class movement along its independent course. It required great effort on the part of the foremost workers to rid themselves of the dead weight of Narodnik ideas. A striking case in point is S. Khalturin. After the Northern Union had been broken up, he gave up systematic work among the masses to fight against the autocracy by the erroneous method of individual terrorism. The proletarian stream was still unable to break away from the general current of Narodism.

In order to emerge as an independent force from the general democratic movement the working class had to draw a distinct line of demarcation between itself and the other classes, *to determine its own position ideologically and politically*. The working-class movement had therefore to overcome the petty-bourgeois ideology of Narodism and adopt Marxism as the real ideology of the proletariat.

Marx and Engels, the great teachers of the proletariat, accomplished the greatest revolution in science in the middle of the nineteenth century. They converted Socialism from *a utopia into a science*. They made a study of capitalism, discovered the laws of its development and proved scientifically that capitalism was historically transient, just as the feudal order had been before it, and that capitalism itself prepares the conditions for its destruction. They showed that the development of capitalism is attended by concentration of the means of production: small and medium enterprises are continually being ousted and swallowed up by the big ones. Labour and production acquire an increasingly social character, but the product of social labour is appropriated by a handful of capitalists because they own the means of production. Thus capitalism itself creates the material prerequisite for the establishment of Socialism—large-scale production. If the capitalist mode of production is to be replaced by the Socialist mode, the means of production have to be converted from the private property of the capitalist class into the property of society as a whole.

But the dominant exploiting classes will not voluntarily relinquish their property, privileges and power. A social force is needed which is capable of sweeping away the old, exploiting society and creating a new society free of exploitation. Such a social force is the *proletariat*, the modern working class. Marx and Engels showed the historic role of the working class as the grave-digger of capitalism and the builder of a new, Communist society. Capitalism itself calls into existence the proletarians, people deprived of the means of production and obliged to sell their labour power in order to subsist. The proletariat grows and develops along with the growth of capitalism. It occupies a special position in capitalist society, as compared with the rest of the working people. The working class has no property in the means of production; it is not in the least interested in preserving a society based on exploitation; it has nothing to lose in a revolution but its chains. Joint work at the big factories in the large cities brings the workers together in masses, disciplines and unites them, teaches them to take common action. At every step the workers encounter their chief enemy, the capitalist class. The struggle between the workers and the capitalists grows ever sharper. Being the most oppressed class of capitalist society, the proletariat is interested in the radical reorganisation of society as a whole, in the complete abolition of private property, poverty and oppression. It cannot emancipate itself without at the same time freeing the remaining mass of the working people from all exploitation. The proletariat is therefore the most revolutionary, the most advanced, class of society.

Marx and Engels proved scientifically that the development of capitalist society and the class struggle within it will inevitably lead to the downfall of capitalism and the victory of the proletariat. This victory will be won in decisive and uncompromising struggle against capitalism. In order to convert capitalist property into social property and to replace capitalist by Socialist relations of production, the working class, taking the lead of all the oppressed, will have to carry out a Socialist revolution and establish its political supremacy, *the dictatorship of the proletariat*, to suppress the resistance of the exploiters and to build a new, classless, Communist society.

Marx and Engels taught that the strength of the working class lies in its organisation and class consciousness, in its having a clear understanding of its aims and tasks and of the ways and means of struggle. In order to be victorious, the working-class movement must be armed with the theory of scientific Socialism. Marx and Engels thus proved the need for fusing Socialism with the working-class movement, for only if they are fused does the class struggle of the workers become a conscious struggle of the proletariat for its emancipation from capitalist exploitation. The fusion of Socialism with the working-class movement is effected by *the party of the working class* which represents, not the particular interests of individual groups of workers united according to occupation or nationality, but the common interests of the proletariat as a whole. The party must point out to the working-class movement its political tasks and ultimate goal. Consequently, in order to overthrow capitalism and build Communism, the proletariat must have its own *independent* party, the Communist Party.

Marxism was an influential force in the West European working-class movement of the seventies. This fact exerted a certain influence upon the revolutionary movement in Russia. The founders of scientific Communism, Marx and Engels, were in contact with many Russian revolutionaries. They watched developments in Russia with unabating interest; they were deeply convinced of the world-wide impact of the coming Russian revolution, and they studied the Russian language in order to have a better knowledge of the country and its people. Marx and Engels struck the first blows against the Narodnik theory. In his work, *On Social Relations in Russia*, written in close collaboration with Marx, Engels criticised the basic tenets of Narodism—the conception of the special lines along which Russia must develop, the denial of the development of capitalism in Russia, the idealisation of the peasant commune, and failure to understand the bourgeois character of the coming Russian revolution.

Progressive Russians became acquainted with some of the writings of Marx and Engels as early as the forties and fifties, but it was only in the seventies that the writings of the founders of Marxism began to circulate among the Russian revolutionaries. Of special significance was the legal publication, in 1872, of a Russian translation of Volume I of *Capital*, actually the world's first translation of this fundamental work of Karl Marx.

"Almost immediately after the appearance of *Capital*," wrote Lenin, "'the destiny of capitalism in Russia' became the principal theoretical problem for Russian Socialists; the most heated debates raged around this problem, and the most important points of programme were decided accordingly" (*Collected Works*, Vol. 1, p. 249).

Thus, at a time when Narodism still held full sway in the revolutionary movement, the entire course of development of revolutionary thought and of the working-class movement had already prepared the ground for the appearance of Marxism in Russia. For Marxism to spread, and still more for Marxism to be victorious in the Russian revolutionary movement, Narodnik views had to be overcome and ideologically defeated.

3. Plekhanov and the Emancipation of Labour Group. Marxist Circles in Russia. Beginning of Lenin's Revolutionary Activity

A revolutionary situation developed in Russia in 1879-1880. The conditions of the masses had grown worse after the Reform of 1861. Their resentment was mounting against the most brutal oppression and utter lack of civil rights. According to very incomplete data, in 1877 peasant disturbances broke out in 11 gubernias,* and in 1880 they spread to as many as 34 gubernias of European Russia. The working-class movement was also growing. Big strikes occurred in St. Petersburg in the late seventies. The revolutionaries intensified their struggle against tsarism. Fear of revolution grew in the class, the landlords. The ruling clique began to dash from pillar to post, now intensifying police terror, now promising a constitution.

However, the workers and peasants were not yet mature enough to overthrow the tsarist autocracy by bold and resolute mass action. The peasantry could do no more than rise in isolated spontaneous revolts, while the proletariat was taking only its first steps in the revolutionary struggle. The bourgeoisie behaved in a cowardly manner; it humbly begged the tsarist government for petty reforms and in effect helped to bolster up the autocracy. There was no revolutionary party connected with the masses and equipped with the right revolutionary theory, a party capable of appraising the situation properly and advancing scientifically substantiated watchwords for the struggle. As for the "Narodnaya Volya," its members had chosen the profoundly erroneous course of individual terrorism. On March 1, 1881, they succeeded in assassinating Tsar Alexander II. But he was succeeded on the throne by Alexander III. The change of tsars did not alter the situation, while the autocratic regime intensified its oppression of the masses. The tsarist government took the offensive. Isolated from the people, the "Narodnaya Volya" was broken up. The tide of revolution began to ebb.

This defeat provoked a deep ideological crisis in Narodism. Some of the Narodniks tried in vain to revive the "Narodnaya Volya" organisation. Most of them, however, abandoned the revolutionary struggle altogether. Those revolutionaries who did not want to give up the struggle were confronted with a number of questions: Why did not the assassination of the tsar lead to a

---

* *Administrative divisions*: the biggest territorial division in tsarist Russia was the *gubernia* (literally—governor's province); each gubernia had its capital city which was the seat of the governor. The gubernia was divided into *uyezds* (counties), each with its administrative centre and these in turn were divided into *volosts* (rural districts) containing a number of villages.—*Ed.*

revolution in Russia? What were the prospects of the revolutionary movement? Where was the real force that could bring about Socialism? What should be the ways and methods of revolutionary struggle? It was only natural that the revolutionaries should continue their search for a new revolutionary theory with still greater energy. They were impelled primarily by disillusionment in Narodism. The development of the working-class movement in Russia and the successes of the West European proletariat had a considerable influence on revolutionary thought.

A small group of revolutionary Narodniks, the "General Redistributionists," who had been compelled to emigrate, began to make a careful study of Marxism and the West European working-class movement. Its members pondered seriously over the significance of the workers' strikes in Russia and, in particular, over the lessons of their own work among the advanced Russian proletarians. On September 25, 1883, the group issued a statement of programme, announcing its final break with Narodism and proclaiming the need to organise a separate party of the Russian working class. It declared as its principal aims to disseminate Marxism, to criticise the Narodism still prevalent among the revolutionaries, and to work out the crucial problems of Russian social life from the standpoint of Marxism and of the interests of Russia's working people. Thus there arose the first Russian Marxist organisation, the Emancipation of Labour group. Its members were G. V. Plekhanov, P. B. Axelrod, L. G. Deich, V. I. Zasulich and V. N. Ignatov. The founder and leader of the group was G. V. Plekhanov, a talented theoretician and propagandist of Marxism.

The Emancipation of Labour group accordingly began to disseminate Marxism in Russia. With this end in view, the group translated into Russian, published and secretly circulated in Russia a number of writings by Marx and Engels: *The Communist Manifesto, Wage-Labour and Capital, The Poverty of Philosophy, Ludwig Feuerbach, Development of Scientific Socialism, Address on Free Trade, On Social Relations in Russia (Frederick Engels on Russia)*. Marx and Engels prepared special prefaces to some of the Russian translations of their writings. Plekhanov wrote many books and articles in which he brilliantly expounded and defended Marxism. In Plekhanov's writings the Russian revolutionaries found the answers to many of the questions that had troubled them. His works of that period played an important part in educating the first generation of Russian Marxists.

The first work of the Russian Marxists was Plekhanov's pamphlet *Socialism and the Political Struggle* published in the autumn of 1883. On the basis of an analysis of the Russian revolutionary movement, Plekhanov showed the profound vitality of Marx's proposition that every class struggle is a political struggle. Far from contradicting each other, Socialism and the political struggle are inseparable; they must be closely linked, fused into one. The way to Socialism lies through the political struggle of the working class, through the conquest of political power by the proletariat. The revolutionary movement in Russia will lead to the fusion of Socialism with the working-class movement, and that will make it invincible.

In order to confute Narodism, it was necessary to make a study of the economic processes at work in Russia, which were little known at that time. Plekhanov's book, *Our Differences*, published in 1885, was the first attempt to give a Marxist analysis of Russia's economy.

Plekhanov refuted the views of the Narodniks, who asserted that capitalism was an "accidental phenomenon" in Russia because conditions for its development were lacking, and in general saw capitalism in Russia as a process of decline and retrogression. But facts such as the expansion of the home market, the number of workers, the position of the handicraftsmen and the number of factories, showed that Russia had already entered the path of capitalist development. It was therefore wrong to bemoan the fact and speak of the "ulcer of proletariatism," as the Narodniks were doing. It was the task of the revolutionaries, said Plekhanov, to use the development of capitalism in the interests of revolution and of the working people. It was therefore essential that the revolutionaries should understand that capitalism engenders a powerful revolutionary force, the proletariat, and that they should rely upon this force in the struggle against the autocracy and capitalism.

The Narodnik view that the peasant commune was a bulwark against capitalism and a bridge to Socialism was utterly untenable. The peasant commune had existed in many countries and had disintegrated under the blows of capitalism. There were obvious signs of the disintegration of the commune in Russia as well. Poor peasants and kulaks were emerging within the commune. Lacking the means for cultivating their land, the poor peasants were surrendering it to the kulaks and hiring themselves out to them as farm-labourers, or seeking a livelihood elsewhere. The poor peasants were already dependent upon the kulak and the usurer, and the commune was becoming a burden to them. To the tsarist government, however, the commune was a convenient means of exacting taxes on the basis of collective liability. A commune of this type was not and could not be the embryo or the basis of Socialism.

Plekhanov showed how deeply mistaken the Narodniks were in denying the leading, revolutionary role of the working class in the transformation of society. The vanguard, revolutionary role in the struggle belonged to the workers and not to the peasants. The peasants were engaged in small-scale production and were essentially dispersed. They were less capable of conscious political initiative, less receptive to Socialist theory, and lent themselves less easily to organisation than the proletariat, which was bound up with large-scale industrial production. The ranks of the proletariat were growing steadily, it was receptive to the ideas of Socialism and was capable of organisation. It was the task of revolutionaries to develop the class consciousness, initiative and organisation of the workers, to concentrate on the organisation of a workers' Socialist party. The prime task of the revolutionaries at the moment was Socialist propaganda among the workers.

Plekhanov also criticised the Narodniks' erroneous views of society. His writings enriched Marxist materialism. Of particular importance in this respect was his book, *The Development of the Monist View of History*, published in 1895. The Narodniks denied the existence of objective laws of the development of society; they held that history is made by outstanding individuals, by heroes, and that the world is ruled by ideas. They claimed that the intelligentsia exerts a decisive influence on society, and that the direction in which the wheel of history will be turned depends on its will. But the life and the development of society are determined, not by the wishes and ideas of outstanding individuals, but by material conditions, by changes in the mode of social production. The people is the real maker of history. Ideas become a material force only when they take hold of the minds of the masses. Outstanding individuals play an important part only in so far as they correctly express the pressing requirements of social development. The most outstanding individuals are doomed to defeat if they do not understand existing historical conditions, if their acts run counter to the requirements of society. A correct understanding of the laws governing historical development, with the object of transforming society, is provided only by Marxism. Plekhanov's book, *The Development of the Monist View of History*, was of great importance in spreading the scientific, materialist world outlook. Lenin noted that this book "served to rear a whole generation of Russian Marxists . . ." (*Collected Works*, Vol. 16, p. 243).

An important contribution to the Marxist working-class movement in Russia was the programme of the Emancipation of Labour group. In the main and for its time, the programme rightly defined the way forward and the tasks of the Russian Marxists. It emphasised that only the working class was an independent fighter for Socialism. The ultimate aim of the proletariat was to replace capitalism by a new social order, Communism. The precondition for the achievement of this aim was the conquest of political power by the working class. The programme proclaimed the need to form a revolutionary workers' party, whose primary political task was the overthrow of the autocracy.

The Emancipation of Labour group shattered the Narodnik illusion about the possibility of Russia passing at that time directly to Socialism. That idea was wrong both from the theoretical and the historical standpoint. The most urgent problem of the revolutionary struggle was the abolition of the survivals of serfdom, the overthrow of the autocracy; consequently, at the first stage the country faced a bourgeois and not a Socialist revolution. Herein lay the undoubted service rendered by the first Russian Marxist group.

However, the group had no clear idea of the alignment of classes in the coming bourgeois revolution, and was unable correctly to assess the place and role of the peasantry in the revolution; its attitude to this question was inconsistent and contradictory. In some of his writings, Plekhanov erroneously declared that in its policy the proletariat should take the bourgeoisie as its guide-star: he ignored the revolutionary role of the peasantry. He also expressed the view that it was inadvisable as yet to frighten the liberal bourgeoisie with the "red spectre" of Socialism, and that it was therefore necessary to have a programme to which the liberals would also subscribe. The future workers' party in Russia was conceived as something like the Social-Democratic parties then existing in Western Europe. All these erroneous views subsequently led the leaders of the group away from Marxism to the camp of opportunism.

Engels welcomed the appearance of the first Marxist organisation in Russia. Plekhanov took part in founding the Second International, and addressed its First Congress, held in 1889.

The Emancipation of Labour group played a prominent part in Russian history. Plekhanov's theoretical works enriched Russian culture. *Marxism became a trend of Russian social and revolutionary thought.* The period of the undivided domination of Narodism in the Russian revolutionary movement came to an end. The traditional Narodnik foundations of the revolutionary ideology of the time crumbled under the well-aimed blows of Marxist criticism.

The ideological defeat of Narodism however was still far from complete. Narodism was still very influential among the revolutionary intellectuals and advanced workers, and was the main ideological obstacle to the spread of Marxism. Marxism was battling its way forward, penetrating ever deeper into the revolutionary movement and also exerting ever greater influence on many

Narodniks. Evidence of that was the activity of the group led
by Alexander Ilyich Ulyanov (Lenin's elder brother). The influence of Marxism was evident in its programme, which regarded
Socialism as the inevitable result of capitalism, and attached
great importance to the workers as the core of a Socialist party.
But it continued to regard the political struggle as one of terrorist acts and conspiracies. The group called itself the "Terrorist
Wing of the 'Narodnaya Volya' Party." Its attempt to organise
the assassination of the tsar on March 1, 1887, ended in failure.
The leaders of the group, including A. I. Ulyanov, were executed.

Only by waging a struggle against Narodism could Marxism
develop and grow strong in Russia.

The activity of the Emancipation of Labour group cleared
the way for the creation of a Marxist workers' party in Russia.
But the group had no practical connections with the mass working-class movement. The place of this first Marxist organisation
in the history of the working-class movement and of the proletarian party in Russia was precisely defined by Lenin as follows:

"The Emancipation of Labour group only laid the theoretical
foundations for the Social-Democratic movement and took the
first step towards the working-class movement" (*Collected
Works*, Vol. 20, p. 255).

A critical reappraisal of the theory and practice of Narodism
was taking place also in Russia. There were heated debates at
secret meetings of revolutionary-minded youth, and the determined search for new ways continued. Considerable influence
on the revolutionary circles was exerted by the Emancipation
of Labour group, whose activities had greatly undermined the
influence of Narodism. Revolutionary thought was taking root
on the soil of the working-class movement, which continued to
grow in spite of the savage political reaction that had set in in
the country. Four hundred and forty-six strikes and disturbances
took place in the eighties, and 232 strikes in the early nineties,
involving 157,000 workers.

Particularly notable for its level of organisation was the strike
at the Morozov Mills in Orekhovo-Zuyevo, in January, 1885.
It was headed by talented leaders, Pyotr Moiseyenko and Vasily
Volkov. A former member of the Northern Union, Moiseyenko
had experienced prison and exile. At a secret meeting of the more
active workers, a number of demands were drawn up which were
to be presented to the mill-owner. These included the demand
to restore the old piece-prices and reduce fines. The steadfastness
and courage of the workers astounded public opinion and frightened the tsarist government. The strike was suppressed by
armed force. About 600 workers were exiled and 33 were committed
for trial. But the picture of outrageous maltreatment of the

workers disclosed at the trial was so shocking that even the jurors of the tsarist court were compelled to return a verdict of "not guilty" on all 101 points of the indictment. The reactionary newspaper *Moskovskiye Vedomosti* (*Moscow Recorder*) wrote with fury about the "salute of a hundred and one guns fired in honour of the labour problem having made its appearance in Russia." Notwithstanding the fact that Moiseyenko and Volkov had been acquitted by the court, the gendarmes did not release them from their clutches. They were exiled. Volkov died shortly after. Moiseyenko later became a Bolshevik.

The Morozov strike was indicative of the awakening class solidarity and class consciousness of the workers. They had come to realise the significance of leadership and organisation. When Volkov and Moiseyenko were brought into court, all the workers present rose and bowed deeply to them.

Soon afterwards the tsarist government was compelled to promulgate a law on fines which to some extent restricted the tyranny of the capitalists.

The Morozov strike became an important landmark in the Russian working-class movement. Lenin described it as a mass strike in which a few Socialists took part. The Morozov strike eloquently showed what a formidable force the working class could become when led by a strong organisation.

The struggle of the proletariat influenced revolutionary thought in a Marxist direction. Along with the Emancipation of Labour group abroad, Marxists appeared inside Russia as well, primarily in St. Petersburg. Here in the winter of 1883-1884 there arose a Marxist organisation, calling itself the "Party of Russian Social-Democrats," and known in history as the Blagoyev group. Its organiser was the Bulgarian D. Blagoyev, a student at St. Petersburg University, who subsequently became the founder of the Social-Democratic Party, and later of the Communist Party, of Bulgaria.

Contact was soon established between the Blagoyev group and the Emancipation of Labour group. The Blagoyev group began to disseminate Marxism among the workers and students of St. Petersburg. It organised about 15 workers' circles. In 1885 it secretly published two issues of the newspaper *Rabochy* (*Worker*), the first Social-Democratic workers' newspaper to appear in Russia.

Tracked down by the tsarist police, the Blagoyev group was broken up at the beginning of 1887. But the group's three years of activity had left their mark. The seeds sown by the group bore fruit. The group had initiated the systematic propaganda of Marxism among the workers in the country's political centre, St. Petersburg.

In the autumn of 1885 another Marxist organisation arose in St. Petersburg. It later adopted the name of "The Association of St. Petersburg Workmen." Its organiser was P. V. Tochissky. At that time the Blagoyev and Tochissky groups worked separately and had no contacts with each other. A great merit of the "Association" was that it established strong ties of organisation with the advanced workers. Among the remarkable revolutionary workers to come from its circles were Y. A. Afanasyev (Klimanov) and V. A. Shelgunov. Later Tochissky, Shelgunov and Klimanov became members of the Bolshevik Party.

In 1888 the "Association" was broken up by the police. Workers who escaped arrest provided the element of continuity with a new organisation formed in 1888-1889. It is known as M. I. Brusnev's group, after its organiser. Gradually the Brusnev group developed into a well-knit organisation, with circles in almost all the districts of St. Petersburg. Altogether there were about twenty circles, each composed of six or seven workers. Furthermore, the first Marxist circle of working women was organised.

The Brusnev group sought to establish closer contact with the workers. It issued appeals in connection with some strikes. In 1891 advanced workers marched in the funeral procession of the democratic writer N. V. Shelgunov. On the ribbon of the wreath they bore were the words: "To N. V. Shelgunov, who pointed the way to liberty and fraternity, from the workers of St. Petersburg." The same year, the Brusnev group organised the first May Day celebration in Russia. Between seventy and eighty workers gathered at a secret out-of-town rally. The speeches delivered by workers were secretly printed and later widely circulated. These were the first Social-Democratic demonstrations of the advanced workers, but there was no mass movement as yet.

Many members of the group later took an active part in the Social-Democratic movement. The worker F. A. Afanasyev subsequently became a prominent figure in the Party.

In 1892 the Brusnev group was broken up by the gendarmes, and only a small nucleus escaped destruction. It retained contact with some of the workers' circles.

The late eighties witnessed the spread of Marxism to a number of regions in Russia. Marxist circles appeared in Moscow. The Volga region—Kazan, Samara (now Kuibyshev) and Nizhni-Novgorod (now Gorky)—became one of the centres of Marxist propaganda. A big part in guiding the revolutionaries to Marxism was played by N. Y. Fedoseyev, a talented and devoted revolutionary. In after years he died in exile in Siberia. Marxist circles sprang up in Ukraine—in Kiev, Kharkov, Odessa and Yekaterinoslav (now Dnepropetrovsk). The organiser of the first Marxist circles in Ukraine was Y. D. Melnikov, a prominent revolutionary.

Among the first Russian Marxists was Vladimir Ilyich Lenin (Ulyanov), the founder and leader of the party of the Bolsheviks, the Communist Party. In 1887, at the age of seventeen, he was arrested and exiled for taking part in the revolutionary student movement in Kazan. This was Lenin's entry upon the path of revolutionary struggle. His bitter hatred of all tyranny and oppression and his ardent love for the ordinary working man made Lenin a revolutionary. He dedicated his whole life to the struggle for the emancipation of the working people from oppression and exploitation, to the struggle for mankind's happy future. Lenin absorbed the traditions of sublime heroism and supreme self-sacrifice of the Russian revolutionaries, his predecessors, but chose a different path, a path free from their mistakes—the path of revolutionary Marxism.

Lenin studied the writings of Marx and Engels and became a convinced Marxist. At the end of 1888 he joined a Marxist circle in Kazan. In 1889 he moved to Samara, where he organised a Marxist circle and established contact with the Marxists of Nizhni-Novgorod, Vladimir and St. Petersburg. At that time Lenin was already playing an important part in disseminating Marxism in Russia. In Marxism he saw a powerful weapon for the revolutionary transformation of the world, for the emancipation of the working people from economic, political and spiritual slavery.

A bookish, abstract conception of Marxist theory was utterly alien to Lenin. To him Marxism was always a living guide to revolutionary action, not a lifeless dogma. From the very beginning of his revolutionary activity Lenin, with his mastery of Marxism, set about solving the most important *theoretical* problem facing Russian Marxists, namely, to make a comprehensive study of the social and economic system of the Russia of that period, its economic development and class relations. Without that it was impossible to rout Narodism completely and work out scientifically the programme and tactics of a workers' party in Russia.

In the spring of 1893 Lenin set forth a number of important ideas in his article "New Economic Developments in Peasant Life," the earliest of his writings which have been preserved. He showed that deep economic discord and class antagonisms had matured among the peasantry, that the peasantry was splitting up into three basic groups—poor, middle and well-to-do—and that capitalism in Russia was developing irresistibly. This article reveals the great mastery with which the young Lenin was applying the Marxist method in his analysis of the most complicated problems of Russian life.

The years 1883-1894 were a period of the slow and difficult growth of a Social-Democratic movement in Russia. There were very few supporters of the new Marxist teachings. Throughout the vast country there were hardly more than a dozen small Marxist groups and circles in the big cities. And these circles conducted propaganda only among the advanced workers; they did not carry on any political work among the masses. The Social-Democratic movement, as Lenin wrote, was in the process of foetal development.

The first Russian Marxists became steeled in ideological battles with the Narodniks. The teachings of scientific Socialism brightly lit up the path of struggle ahead of them, and they carried their knowledge to the workers. A bitter struggle was being waged in the revolutionary circles between the Marxists and the Narodniks. More and more of the foremost workers and revolutionary intellectuals were becoming convinced Marxists. The generation of Marxists of the late eighties and early nineties advanced from their midst outstanding leaders of the Bolshevik Party: M. F. Vladimirsky, V. V. Vorovsky, L. B. Krasin, G. M. Krzhizhanovsky, V. K. Kurnatovsky, A. V. Lunacharsky, M. N. Lyadov, N. A. Semashko, P. I. Stuchka, M. G. Tskhakaya, A. D. Tsyurupa, V. L. Schantzer (Marat), A. G. Schlichter and many others. At that period A. M. Gorky and A. S. Serafimovich, the future proletarian writers, were developing under the influence of Marxist ideas. Marxism was becoming an appreciable factor in the country's intellectual and political life. The influence of Narodism was greatly undermined.

BRIEF SUMMARY

With the development of capitalism and the appearance of an industrial proletariat in tsarist Russia, in the second half of the nineteenth century, the revolutionary struggle grew in intensity. It manifested itself in the working-class movement, peasant unrest, and in the activities of the revolutionary organisations.

As in all other countries where a revolutionary struggle first began, Socialist theory and the working-class movement in Russia were not at first connected. Gradually the first Marxist organisations arose in Russia, on the basis of the Russian working-class movement, as a result of the defeat of Narodism and under the influence of the successes of the West European proletariat. The Emancipation of Labour group, founded by Plekhanov in 1883, dealt a serious ideological blow to Narodism and took the first step towards the working-class movement.

Marxism developed and gained strength in Russia in the struggle against Narodism. But old, obsolescent views never give way without stubborn and bitter resistance. It took Marxism years of determined ideological struggle against Narodism to gain the upper hand and to become the theoretical foundation of the Russian working-class movement.

The first Marxist groups and circles were not connected with the working-class movement. Until the mid-nineties, Marxism in Russia remained an ideological trend that had no contact with the working-class movement. The development of the struggle of the proletariat and the work of the Marxist organisations prepared the ground for combining scientific Socialism with the mass working-class movement, and for the appearance of a Marxist party in Russia. The task of founding such a party was accomplished by Lenin.

A new era was beginning in the history of the working class and of the revolutionary movement in Russia.

CHAPTER TWO

THE STRUGGLE FOR THE CREATION OF A MARXIST PARTY IN RUSSIA. FORMATION OF THE RUSSIAN SOCIAL-DEMOCRATIC LABOUR PARTY. THE RISE OF BOLSHEVISM

(1894-1904)

1. Beginning of the Leninist Stage in the Development of Marxism. Lenin's Struggle Against Narodism and "Legal Marxism." The St. Petersburg "League of Struggle for the Emancipation of the Working Class." First Congress of the R.S.D.L.P.

Capitalism in Russia continued to make headway in the nineties of the nineteenth century. It was a period of industrial boom. Railway construction was developing at a particularly rapid pace. More than 14,000 miles of new railway lines were laid between 1890 and 1900. This stimulated the rapid growth of the metallurgical and fuel industries. Foreign capital, attracted by high profits, flowed into the country. In the course of the decade the volume of production and the total number of workers doubled. Industry alone absorbed about 1,000,000 new workers. Fifty per cent of the industrial workers were hereditary proletarians, whose fathers had worked in factories before them.

The spontaneous strikes of the seventies and eighties helped to rouse the working-class masses to conscious struggle. In the autumn of 1893, on the eve of the upsurge of the working-class movement, Lenin arrived in St. Petersburg from Samara to take part in the revolutionary struggle. His very first speeches in the St. Petersburg groups showed that the revolutionary movement had acquired an outstanding figure, a profound theoretician and brilliant organiser, a staunch revolutionary of inexhaustible energy and iron will, one who had deep faith in the invincibility of the working-class cause and inspired others with this faith. Before long Lenin became the generally recognised leader of the St. Petersburg Marxists.

Lenin put forward before the Marxists the problem of founding an independent Marxist workers' party. This party had to be built up in the harsh conditions of illegality, under the fire of incessant police persecution. The Russian Marxists had to build up their party in bitter struggle not only against Narodism, but also against other political trends and against the opportunists in the working-class movement, who sacrificed the vital interests of the proletariat to gain for it temporary advantages. Formerly, the leading role in the struggle for Marxism had been played by the Emancipation of Labour group. Now the decisive part in this struggle was taken over by the serious Marxist cadres who had grown up in Russia itself.

Narodism still remained the main ideological obstacle to the establishment of Marxism. It had to be defeated completely if the victory of Marxism was to be assured and a proletarian party created. In an attempt to arrest the rapid growth of Marxist influence among the revolutionaries, the Narodniks started a campaign against it. This evoked numerous letters of protest from the Russian Marxists, notable among which were the letters of N. Y. Fedoseyev. These illegal letters were passed on from hand to hand; they were eagerly read in the underground revolutionary groups.

An outstanding role in the ideological war against Narodism was played by Lenin's book, What the "Friends of the People" Are and How They Fight the Social-Democrats, printed secretly in the summer of 1894. The book criticised the world outlook, economic views, political platform and tactics of Narodism.

Lenin opposed the idealist views of the Narodniks on history by the Marxist, materialist conception of social life. The course of history is conditioned, not by the subjective desires of individuals, but by the objective laws of development of society. Marxist science discloses all the forms of contradiction under capitalism and shows the proletariat the way to deliverance from capitalist exploitation. It was the task of the Russian Socialists to develop Marxist theory further, to disseminate it among the masses of the workers and organise the working class. The theoretical work of the Marxists must go hand in hand with their practical activity, theory must serve practice, it must supply the answers to the questions put forward by real life, and it must be tested in practice. Only on this condition would the Marxists become the real ideological leaders of the proletariat, free from dogmatism and sectarianism.

Lenin showed that Narodism had undergone profound changes, that it had turned from revolutionary into liberal Narodism and he completely exposed the Narodniks of the nineties. The Narodniks (Mikhailovsky, Vorontsov and others) had begun to assert that capitalism could "enter the life of the people" without ruining the peasants and without exploiting the working people. They lauded the hard-working "enterprising muzhik," that is, in effect extolled the development of kulak farms. The Narodniks slurred over the class contradictions in the countryside and the poor peasants' decline into bondage to the kulaks, representing all this as mere "defects" that could easily be remedied by a "people-loving" administration. They offered a paltry programme of petty reforms which, leaving the foundations of exploitation in the countryside intact, tended to divert the peasants from the revolutionary struggle and benefited only the rich, kulak households. The Narodniks abandoned the struggle against the tsarist regime. They now placed all their hopes in the tsarist government, which they claimed was above all classes and therefore capable of helping the working people.

Liberal Narodism differed fundamentally from revolutionary Narodism. The degeneration of Narodism was due to the profound social and economic processes which had taken place in the countryside. The revolutionary Narodniks of the seventies were active at a time when the differentiation in the countryside was just beginning, and they reflected the mood of the broad masses of the peasantry. The liberal Narodniks of the nineties were active in the period when the peasantry was splitting up under the influence of capitalist development, and they in fact expressed the interests of the kulaks. Consequently, the Narodniks were false friends of the people. The real representatives of the people were the Marxists, who called for the overthrow of tsarism, the abolition of the yoke of the landlords and of capitalist exploitation.

In his book, *What the "Friends of the People" Are and How They Fight the Social-Democrats*, Lenin charted the historical course of the Russian working class as the political *leader* of the people, advanced the idea of the *hegemony* (leading role) of the proletariat and dealt with the question of the *allies* of the proletariat in the revolutionary struggle. The ally of the working class in the struggle against the tsarist autocracy was the peasantry, the broad mass of the people. The working class was coming forward against capitalism, not as a solitary fighter, but together with other sections of the working and exploited masses of the country.

In order to accomplish its historic tasks, the proletariat needed a Marxist party which would impart class consciousness to and organise the working-class movement. The prime task of the Russian Marxists was therefore to form a united Socialist workers' party out of the scattered Marxist groups. Once the Marxists have created a strong organisation, a party capable of transforming scattered revolts and strikes of the workers into a politically conscious proletarian class struggle, "then," wrote Lenin, "the Russian WORKER, rising at the head of all democratic elements, will overthrow absolutism and lead the RUSSIAN PROLETARIAT (side by side with the proletariat of ALL COUNTRIES) *along the straight road of open political struggle to the* VICTORIOUS COMMUNIST REVOLUTION" (*Collected Works*, Vol. 1, p. 282).

Lenin was the first Russian Marxist to advance the idea of the *hegemony of the proletariat* and the idea of a *revolutionary alliance* of the working class and the peasantry as the principal means of overthrowing tsarism, the landlords and the bourgeoisie.

These ideas of Lenin's were a valuable contribution to Marxist theory. Lenin taught Marxists, the advanced workers, to understand the historic role of the proletariat as the leader of all the oppressed; he taught them to understand the tremendous revolutionary potentialities of the masses of the people, and, above all, of the peasantry.

In the nineties the revolutionary Marxists in Russia had another enemy to contend with besides the Narodniks—the so-called "legal Marxists." These were bourgeois intellectuals who used the banner of Marxism to expound their views in the legal press, that is, in newspapers and periodicals licenced by the tsarist government. Advocating the capitalist development of the country, the "legal Marxists" criticised the Narodniks in their own way as defenders of small-scale production. And it was for the purpose of such criticism that they tried to make use of Marxism—but Marxism stripped of all revolutionary content. P. B. Struve, the leader of the "legal Marxists," extolled capitalism, and instead of calling for a revolutionary struggle against the bourgeois system urged that "we acknowledge our lack of culture and go to capitalism for schooling." Thus the "legal Marxists" were spokesmen of bourgeois ideology. They sought to adapt Marxism and the working-class movement to the interests of the bourgeoisie.

In the struggle against Narodism, the revolutionary Marxists entered into a temporary agreement with the "legal Marxists," and began to publish articles in magazines edited by the "legal Marxists." At the same time, however, Lenin, in his work, *The Economic Content of Narodism and the Criticism of It in Mr. Struve's Book* (1895), sharply criticised "legal Marxism" for its revision of the principles of Marxism, namely, the theory of the Socialist revolution and the dictatorship of the proletariat. Describing "legal Marxism" as a reflection of Marxism in bourgeois literature, Lenin exposed the "legal Marxists" as ideologists of the liberal bourgeoisie. Lenin's characterisation of the "legal Marxists" was later completely confirmed: they became prominent Cadets (as the principal party of the Russian liberal bourgeoisie was called), and later diehard Whites.

The Narodniks were open enemies of Marxism. In the "legal Marxists," the Russian Marxists for the first time encountered disguised enemies who called themselves supporters of Marx's teachings, while in reality they deprived Marxism of its revolutionary content. Similar distortions of Marxism were current also in Western Europe. Lenin's fight against "legal Marxism" was of international significance; it was a model of ideological irreconcilability to distortions of Marxist theory.

Of outstanding significance in the development of Marxism and in the ideological and theoretical education of Marxists was Lenin's book, *The Development of Capitalism in Russia*, published in 1899. This book completed the ideological defeat of Narodism.

Basing himself on the study of a wealth of factual data, Lenin drew some very important conclusions. Russia had become a capitalist country. The contradictions between capitalism and the survivals of serfdom were growing increasingly acute. The development of capitalism was undermining the foundations of the autocratic system. Objective conditions for the abolition of this system were maturing in the country. The forces of revolution were taking shape in the country: the decisive role belonged to the working class, and the strength of the proletariat in the historical movement was immeasurably greater than its proportion to the general mass of the population. The ally of the working class was the peasantry, whose revolutionary spirit had deep-seated economic roots. Lenin's analysis of economic development and class relations in Russia was the basis on which the programme and tactics of the Marxist party were worked out.

The Russian Marxists introduced Lenin's ideas into the practical activity of the working-class movement. Lenin persuaded the St. Petersburg Marxists to undertake political agitation among the mass of the working class. In December, 1894, in connection with disturbances at the Semyannikov Works (now the V. I. Lenin Works), Lenin, in collaboration with I. V. Babushkin, a worker at this plant, wrote an appeal to the workers which was circulated in several copies in the plant. Social-Democrats also took part in the strikes in the New Port, at the Thornton Mill (now the Ernst Thaelmann Mill), the Putilov (now Kirov) Works and many other enterprises. The leaflets, in which economic and political demands were combined, greatly encouraged the workers and raised their revolutionary consciousness. The Marxists began to conduct regular and systematic political education and organisational work among the mass of the workers. In this way under Lenin's guidance they *changed over* from propaganda among small groups of advanced workers to agitation among the broad mass of the working class.

To develop their work among the masses, the Marxist groups in St. Petersburg united on Lenin's initiative into a single illegal Social-Democratic organisation, which at the end of 1895 adopted the name of "League of Struggle for the Emancipation of the Working Class." The League was organised on the principles of centralism, strict discipline and close contact with the masses. Its core was composed of fifteen to seventeen members assigned to three districts. The workers' circles in the factories and mills formed the basis of the League. Its leadership consisted of a central group headed by Lenin, who was at the same time the editor of all the League's publications. Among the League members were A. A. Vaneyev, P. K. Zaporozhets, G. M. Krzhizhanovsky, N. K. Krupskaya, Y. O. Martov, A. N. Potresov, S. I. Radchenko, V. V. Starkov and others.

Alarmed by the activities of the League, the tsarist government dealt it a severe blow. The leadership of the League, headed by Lenin, and about forty active members were arrested on the night of December 9, 1895. A number of other police raids, carried out in 1896, wrested more and more fighters from the ranks of the League. Lenin spent more than a year in prison. But even there he carried on his revolutionary activities, and continued to assist the League in its work: he wrote several leaflets for it and drafted a Party programme. In 1897 Lenin was exiled to distant Siberia. Many active members of the League were also exiled. Severe as these losses were, the League was able to withstand the blows of the tsar's henchmen, for it had deep roots in the working-class movement.

The year 1896 brought a major victory to the League. In the summer more than 30,000 St. Petersburg workers went on strike. The strike at the Yekaterinhof Textile Mill (Ravenstvo—Equality—Mill today) grew into a general strike of the textile workers of the capital. Notwithstanding the arrest of its leadership, the League directed the strike. It issued thirteen leaflets in the course of one month. The tsarist government arrested more than 1,000 workers, attempted not only to break the strike by brutal repressions, but also to demoralise the movement ideologically by the false assurances that the government had "equally at heart the interests of the employers and of the workers." The League of Struggle immediately exposed this manoeuvre in a leaflet. The news of the strike spread throughout the country and far beyond its borders. Terrified by the extent of the strike movement, the tsarist government was compelled in 1897 to issue a law limiting the working day to $11^1/_2$ hours.

The St. Petersburg strikes of 1895-1896, and especially the strike of 1896, ushered in a new period in Russian history, the period of preparation for a people's revolution. For the first time the working-class masses had risen to fight *under the leadership of a Social-Democratic organisation.*

The action of the proletariat created a new situation in the revolutionary struggle. As Lenin noted, there were three distinct periods in the Russian revolutionary movement in the nineteenth century, depending on which social class left its distinguishing mark on the movement. In the serf period, from the Decembrist revolt to the fall of serfdom, it was revolutionary noblemen that predominated in the revolutionary movement. From 1861 and up to the mid-nineties, the leading force in the movement were the democratic intellectuals of non-noble origin. The development of capitalism, the growth of the working-class movement and the activities of the Marxists prepared the ground for a radical change, for the third, proletarian period of the revolutionary movement, which began about 1895. The working class emerged as a major political force, a powerful revolutionary factor. With the rise of a mass Social-Democratic working-class movement, the question of who was to lead the peasantry, whether the working class or the liberal bourgeoisie, acquired paramount importance in Russia's political life.

The League of Struggle produced a group of advanced proletarians, builders of the Party, who worked tirelessly among the masses. Among the leading members of the League were workers employed in big factories, such as V. A. Shelgunov at the Obukhov (now Bolshevik) Works, I. V. Babushkin at the Semyannikov Works, N. G. Poletayev (subsequently a member of the Third State Duma), M. I. Kalinin and others at the Putilov Works.

Under Lenin's guidance, the St. Petersburg League of Struggle for the Emancipation of the Working Class was the first organisation in Russia that began to *unite* Socialism with the working-class movement, linking up the struggle of the workers for economic demands with the political struggle against tsarism and capitalist exploitation. That was, as Lenin wrote, the *first* real *rudiment* of a revolutionary party, finding its strength in the working-class movement and leading the class struggle of the proletariat.

The St. Petersburg League of Struggle had a powerful impact on the development of the Social-Democratic movement in Russia. It served as a model for similar leagues organised in other cities. A "Workers' Union" was formed in Moscow. Social-Democratic groups were organised at Tula, Ivanovo-Voznesensk (Ivanovo), Yaroslavl, Kostroma, Vladimir, Rostov-on-Don and other cities. Social-Democratic organisations arose in Ukraine and in Transcaucasia. Many of them adopted the title of "League of Struggle." One of their main tasks was the organisation of strikes. They sought to convert every strike into a school of class struggle for the proletariat. In this way it became a tradition for the Social-Democratic organisations to take an active part in strikes. The Social-Democrats began to live the life of the workers.

The Social-Democratic movement spread to the western non-Russian border regions. The Social-Democratic Party of Poland was founded in 1893, and the General Jewish Workers' Union in Russia and Poland (the Bund) in 1897. In the second half of the nineties, the first Social-Democratic organisations were formed in Latvia.

The advance from propaganda circles to agitation among the mass of the workers was not accomplished without a struggle within the organisations. Some stubbornly clung to the obsolete forms of study-circle propaganda and organisation. Others favoured the advance to agitation, but neglected the political tasks of the proletariat. They proposed to confine themselves to economic agitation, to set up mutual benefit funds and similar organisations which would meet the economic needs of the workers, and to leave the political struggle to the liberals.

Thus at the very dawn of the Social-Democratic movement in Russia, there arose a dangerous tendency: to build a narrow trade union organisation of the proletariat rather than a political one, to make the working-class movement purely economic in character. The supporters of such views were called "Economists." They based themselves on the ideas of the "legal Marxists" in Russia and the reformists in the West, and in practice subordinated the working-class movement to the liberal bourgeoisie.

Lenin and his supporters launched a vigorous struggle against these first manifestations of opportunism in the Russian working-class movement. Lenin considered Marx's conclusion that the proletariat must have its own independent party an enduring principle of the international working-class movement. He began to form such a party in Russia, and waged an uncompromising struggle against the slightest encroachments upon its independence. That struggle was of great significance for training cadres for the future Bolshevik party and for the birth of Bolshevism. That was just how Lenin appraised its historic significance when he wrote later: "The Bolsheviks are no 'freak,' they *grew up* out of the struggle against opportunism in 1894-1914!!" (*Lenin Miscellany*, XIV, p. 317).

Lenin's activities in the nineties, the ideas he advanced, his uncompromising struggle against distortions of Marxist theory, the education of Party cadres and the working-class masses in a revolutionary spirit—all this marked the beginning of a new stage, *the Leninist stage, in the development of Marxism.*

The Social-Democratic movement was making appreciable progress, and the revolutionary Marxists were confronted with the task of uniting the Social-Democratic organisations into a party. The ideological ground for this unification had been prepared by Lenin's "League of Struggle." Practical steps were also taken to hold a congress. To this end, in the summer of 1896, N. K. Krupskaya, a member of the League, negotiated with Social-Democrats in other cities. Lenin, who was in exile at that time, wrote his pamphlet, *The Tasks of the Russian Social-Democrats*, in which he outlined, on the basis of the experience of the "St. Petersburg League of Struggle," the Marxist platform for a workers' party.

The First Congress of local Social-Democratic organisations met secretly in Minsk, from March 1 to 3, 1898. It was attended by only nine delegates, representing the St. Petersburg, Moscow, Kiev and Yekaterinoslav Leagues of Struggle, the Bund and the *Rabochaya Gazeta* (*Workers' Gazette*) group of Kiev. The Congress resolved to form the Russian Social-Democratic Labour Party (R.S.D.L.P.) and elected a Central Committee of three members. The Party emphasised from the outset that it was uniting the foremost workers of all the peoples of Russia.* The manifesto issued in the name of the Congress played a positive part as an open declaration of the aims of the Party. On behalf of the Party, it declared that:

"The Russian proletariat will throw off the yoke of the autocracy in order to continue, with still greater energy, the struggle against capitalism and the bourgeoisie until the complete victory of Socialism" (*The C.P.S.U. in Resolutions and Decisions of Its Congresses, Conferences and Plenary Meetings of the Central Committee*, Part I, Gospolitizdat, 1954, p. 13).

But the manifesto did not express clearly enough the basic ideas formulated by Lenin with regard to the conquest of political power by the proletariat, the leading role of the working class, and its allies in the struggle against tsarism and capitalism.

The Congress proclaimed the formation of the Party, a fact of great political and revolutionary-propagandist importance. The announcement was received with great satisfaction by Social-Democrats everywhere. The news of the Congress encouraged and heartened the Party cadres in the difficult conditions of illegal revolutionary work and opened wide prospects before them. The local Social-Democratic organisations began to call themselves committees of the R.S.D.L.P. The Party gained increasing recognition and popularity among the mass of the workers.

---

* It did so by calling itself, not *Russkaya* ("Russian" in the national sense) but *Rossiiskaya* (a term used in the title of the Empire, and implying in everyday usage both Russian and non-Russian peoples).—*Trans.*

49

In reality, however, no party had as yet been formed. The Social-Democratic organisations still had no common programme, rules or tactics, they had no single leading centre, and there was no ideological and organisational unity. Soon after the First Congress the tsarist police arrested two members of the Central Committee and many prominent Social-Democrats. Ideological vacillations increased, and so did the influence of opportunist elements. The absence of the strong core of revolutionary Marxists headed by Lenin, who were in exile, began to tell.

It was in these difficult conditions that the Marxist party began to take shape in Russia.

2. Lenin's Plan for Building a Marxist Party. The Struggle of the Leninist *Iskra* for the Creation of the Party

The need for a workers' party was becoming increasingly acute. By the beginning of the twentieth century enough inflammable material for a revolutionary explosion had accumulated in tsarist Russia.

In 1900-1903 the world was in the grip of an economic crisis. Russia was particularly hard hit. Small and medium enterprises crumbled under its blows. About 3,000 factories were closed down. The concentration of industry increased, and capitalist monopoly associations grew rapidly, gaining control of the mining, metallurgical, engineering and other important industries. Capitalism in Russia was becoming imperialist.

The crisis heightened the tension in the country. Unemployment grew. The unemployed returned "home" by the thousand to villages stricken by crop failure and famine. The workers began to adopt new forms of struggle, passing from economic to political strikes and demonstrations. In February and March 1901, in response to the call of the local committees of the R.S.D.L.P., thousands of demonstrators came out in the streets of St. Petersburg, Moscow, Kharkov, Kiev and other big cities with the slogan: "Down with the autocracy!" May Day demonstrations and strikes took place in many cities. The strike at the Obukhov Works developed into a clash with the police and troops. The workers offered stiff resistance, but the odds against them were too heavy, and the tsarist authorities retaliated with savage reprisals. The heroic "Obukhov defence" raised the militant spirit of the proletariat.

The year 1902 witnessed a further upsurge in the working-class movement. Strikes and demonstrations took place in St. Petersburg, Moscow, Kiev, Baku, Batum (Batumi), Nizhni-Novgorod, Sormovo, Odessa, Saratov, Tiflis (Tbilisi) and other cities. Of particular importance was the big strike in Rostov-on-Don. It was led by the local committee of the R.S.D.L.P. Meetings were held several days in succession, with many thousands of workers listening eagerly to Social-Democratic speakers. The police were powerless to disperse these open-air meetings and rallies, and only by summoning troops were they able to get the better of the workers.

In 1903 the tide of the working-class movement rose still higher. May Day strikes and demonstrations were held in many cities. Political general strikes under the leadership of the R.S.D.L.P. committees took place in the summer of that year in the South: in Transcaucasia (Baku, Tiflis, Batum, Chiatury, on the Transcaucasian Railway) and in Ukraine (Odessa, Kiev, Yekaterinoslav, Nikolayev, Yelisavetgrad). More than 200,000 workers took part in these strikes. The proletariat of Russia was rising for a revolutionary struggle against the tsarist regime.

Frightened by the growth of the working-class movement, the tsarist government tried to arrest it by all possible means. More and more often it responded to the revolutionary actions of the proletariat with the bullet and the Cossack whip, prison and exile. An especially brutal act was the shooting of the Zlatoust workers in March 1903. At the same time the tsarist government tried to divert the workers from the revolutionary struggle. Through its agents the Okhrana (tsarist secret police) set up in several cities organisations which tried to persuade the workers that the tsarist government itself was prepared to help them to secure the satisfaction of their economic demands, so long as they kept out of politics. These tactics, designed to mislead the workers, became known as "police socialism," or Zubatovism (after the name of its initiator, Zubatov, a colonel of the gendarmes). But the growing revolutionary movement of the working class swept these police organisations out of its way.

Under the influence of the revolutionary struggle of the proletariat, other classes and social strata began to rouse themselves to action. Driven to despair by hopeless want, the peasantry rose to fight. Its struggle manifested itself most forcefully in 1902 in the Poltava, Kharkov and Saratov gubernias, where peasants began to set fire to landlords' mansions, seize their land and offer resistance to the police and troops. A movement developed among the students. In answer to savage police attacks, the students in a number of cities went on strike in the winter of 1901/02.

The liberal bourgeoisie also began to stir. But inasmuch as it was economically linked with tsarism and feared the movement of the masses, it was incapable of taking any sort of decisive action. The liberals confined themselves to sending petitions to the tsar to introduce minor reforms.

The approach of revolution was felt everywhere. "Let the storm break in full fury!"—this impassioned appeal of Gorky's "Song of the Stormy Petrel" splendidly reflected the revolutionary sentiments then prevailing. It was necessary that the proletariat should meet the revolution fully prepared, with a militant Marxist party capable of leading the struggle of the working people.

The Social-Democratic movement had considerably developed by the end of the nineteenth century. It had its committees and groups in St. Petersburg, Moscow, Tula, Tver (now Kalinin), Ivanovo-Voznesensk, Yaroslavl, Kostroma, Nizhni-Novgorod, Saratov, Kiev, Yekaterinoslav, Odessa, Kharkov, Nikolayev, Baku, Tiflis, Batum, Gomel, Vitebsk, Ufa and other cities, in the Donets coalfield and in Siberia.

But all these organisations were not yet connected with each other. The committees had no well thought-out plan of action; they confined themselves to narrow, practical activities on a local scale, and did not set themselves political tasks on an all-Russian scale. Owing to their amateurish methods of work and their poor observance of conspiratorial practice, the Social-Democratic organisations were often broken up by the police. There was therefore no continuity in their work. This lack of organisational cohesion was aggravated by ideological confusion among the Social-Democrats, who had as yet no common understanding of the tasks of the working-class movement, or of the ways and means of fulfilling them. The Social-Democratic organisations were clearly lagging behind the spontaneous movement of the masses. Russian Social-Democracy was in a state of disunity and vacillation. The ideological confusion and lack of organisational integration were so great as to make it extremely difficult to form a united and centralised party.

A special danger was represented by the "Economists." They had their own press—the newspaper *Rabochaya Mysl* (*Workers' Thought*) in Russia and the magazine *Rabocheye Dyelo* (*Workers' Cause*) abroad. They urged the workers to confine themselves exclusively to the struggle for economic demands—wage increases, a shorter working day, etc. The "Economists" declared: "A struggle on economic grounds, the struggle against capital for daily vital interests, with strikes as the method of this struggle—such should be the motto of the working-class movement." Some "Economists" advocated this opportunist idea in more veiled form, preaching a "theory of stages." According to this "theory," the working class should begin its economic struggle by advancing the demand for the right to strike, then pass to the demand for the right to organise trade unions, and only then cautiously approach the idea of political liberty in general.

The views of the "Economists" were most vividly expressed in the document known as the "Credo" (confession of faith). Its authors, Kuskova and Prokopovich, subsequently became Cadets, and in the Soviet period White émigrés. "The economic struggle is for the workers, and the political struggle for the liberals," was the view they advocated. The "Economists" denied the independent political role of the proletariat and the need for an independent political party of the working class. There was the danger that the spread of these opportunist ideas would convert the proletariat into a political appendage of the bourgeoisie.

At the end of the nineteenth century the "Economists" were predominant in the Social-Democratic committees. "Economism" in Russia originated from the same source as opportunism in any other capitalist country, namely, the penetration of bourgeois influence into the working-class movement and the mixed composition of the proletariat. The predominance of the petty bourgeoisie in the population* was another factor contributing to the spread of opportunism in Russia. Furthermore, the "Economists" were able to gain ground because a great many leading Marxists were in prison or in exile at that time, and the young intellectuals who streamed into the Social-Democratic organisations under the influence of the victory of Marxism over Narodism lacked the necessary Marxist training and political experience.

"Economism" was the Russian variety of international opportunism. In the nineties Marxism had already become the leading force in the West European working-class movement, and the enemies of Marxism began to camouflage themselves. They put forward the slogan of "freedom to criticise" Marx, and demanded the revision of his teachings. The revisionists denied that the need for and inevitability of Socialism could be scientifically proved, and declared that the very idea of an "ultimate goal" for the working-class movement, that is, Communism, was untenable. They denied the growing impoverishment of the masses and the intensification of capitalist contradictions. They insisted on rejecting the basic propositions of Marxism—the theory of the class struggle, the Socialist revolution, and the dictatorship of the proletariat. The German Social-Democrat Bernstein, the leader of revisionism, declared: "The ultimate goal is nothing, the movement is everything." In other words, the main thing so far as the opportunists were concerned was to get the ruling exploiting classes to grant reforms, minor improvements for the

---

* Here "petty bourgeoisie" means chiefly the peasantry, which at that time made up the overwhelming majority of the population.—*Trans.*

workers, without touching the foundations of capitalism. The opportunists strove to turn Social-Democracy from a party of social revolution into a party of social reforms. The "Economists" were reformists of precisely this kind, people who betrayed the fundamental interests of the proletariat.

Lenin came out vigorously against the "Economists."

In answer to the "Credo," he wrote in 1899 "A Protest by Russian Social-Democrats," which was approved at a meeting of seventeen Marxists then in exile in Siberia. In their programme statement, the revolutionary Marxists called for an uncompromising war on the whole range of "Economist" ideas. The Protest was widely circulated among the Social-Democratic organisations; it played a tremendous part in the building of a Marxist party in Russia. A movement against the "Economists" started in a number of local Social-Democratic organisations. Abroad, the struggle against the "Economists" was taken up by Plekhanov.

It was necessary to unite all revolutionary Social-Democratic forces to combat such evils as amateurish methods, ideological vacillations and "Economism." While still in exile, Lenin came to the conclusion that the decisive role in the formation of a Marxist party would be played by an all-Russian political newspaper. In 1900, as soon as he returned from exile, Lenin energetically set about organising such a newspaper. He visited a number of cities, where he held talks with many Social-Democrats, enlisting and uniting the supporters of the future newspaper. After preparing the ground in Russia, Lenin went abroad to make arrangements for the publication of the paper. *Iskra (The Spark)*, as the paper was called, was the first all-Russian political newspaper of the revolutionary Marxists. Its editorial board consisted of representatives of the Social-Democratic organisations in Russia—Lenin, Martov and Potresov—and of members of the Emancipation of Labour group—Plekhanov, Axelrod and Zasulich. The real inspirer, organiser and director of *Iskra* was Lenin.

The first issue of *Iskra* appeared abroad, on December 11, 1900. It bore the epigraph "The spark will kindle a flame," taken from the reply of the Decembrists to Pushkin's message. The Russian Marxists abided firmly by the great slogan proclaimed by Marx: "Workers of all countries, unite!", and regarded themselves as one of the detachments of the international working-class movement. At the same time they openly declared that the Russian working class would carry on the work of the preceding generations of revolutionaries, and voiced the deep conviction that it would be the proletariat that would accomplish the task bequeathed to it by the history of the revolutionary struggle in Russia.

The editorial "The Urgent Tasks of Our Movement," written by Lenin in the paper's first issue, stated that *Iskra*'s main task was the formation of a Marxist party in Russia. Without such a party, wrote Lenin, the proletariat would be incapable of rising to the level of conscious class struggle, the working-class movement would be doomed to impotence, and the working class would never succeed in discharging its great historic mission of emancipating itself and all the working people of Russia from political and economic slavery.

"An enemy fortress towers before us, in all its strength," wrote Lenin. "It is raining shot and shell upon us, and mowing down our best fighters. We must capture this fortress, and we shall do so if we unite all the forces of the awakening proletariat and of the Russian revolutionaries into one party that will attract all that is alive and honest in Russia" (*Collected Works*, Vol. 4, p. 346).

It was to the building of this party that *Iskra* dedicated its efforts.

How to begin the building of the party in the conditions obtaining at that time? The answer to this question was given by Lenin in the article "Where to Begin?" published in *Iskra* in May, 1901. This article outlined Lenin's famous plan for building a Marxist party. The important thing, wrote Lenin, was that the broad masses were rushing into battle, but the revolutionaries lacked a staff of leaders and organisers. And his answer to the question "Where to begin?" was with the establishment of an all-Russian political newspaper. This newspaper would clear the way for the ideological defeat of the enemies within the working-class movement and would uphold the purity of the revolutionary theory. It would help to establish a common understanding of the programme, aims and tactical tasks of the party, and of its practical methods of work. The newspaper would also be a powerful instrument for organisationally uniting local committees and groups into a single party. Around the newspaper, being the affair of the whole party, a network of agents would come into being, who would supply it with information, circulate it, and bring it into contact with the workers. The organisation of the paper's supporters would form the core, or skeleton, of the future party.

Iskra launched its activities at a time when wide sections of society were up in arms against the autocracy. There were many different groups in the Social-Democratic movement, and each insisted that the course it recommended was the only right one. This movement also involved petty-bourgeois intellectuals, who in essence had nothing in common with the Socialist aims of the proletariat but who for the time being were fellow-travellers of the working class in so far as the struggle against tsarism was concerned. All the revolutionary Marxist forces had to be united, and to achieve this they had to dissociate themselves from all sorts of fellow-travellers and opportunist elements, and give a clear-cut definition of their own position. And *Iskra* proclaimed:

"Before we can unite, and in order that we may unite, we must first of all draw firm and definite lines of demarcation" (Lenin, *Collected Works*, Vol. 4, p. 329).

What had to be done in the first place was to draw a line of demarcation from the "Economists," who constituted the principal obstacle to the founding of a Marxist party. *Iskra* launched an energetic offensive against them.

An outstanding part in the struggle for a revolutionary Marxist party was played by Lenin's book, *What Is To Be Done?*, published in March, 1902.

The idea that runs through Lenin's book is that of *the Party as the revolutionising, leading and organising force of the working-class movement.*

Lenin showed that "Economism" was a most vicious caricature of Marxism. The "Economists" maintained that since everything in history was governed by immutable laws, the role of the conscious element in social development was insignificant. More than this. All conscious, planned activity was superfluous and even harmful, because it was almost an act of violence against the objective course of history. That is why, the "Economists" argued, the Party should not consciously guide the spontaneous working-class movement, but should wait passively for the proletariat itself to come gradually to Socialism.

Marxism, however, has nothing in common with the opportunist philosophy of spontaneity, which depreciates theory and consciousness in the eyes of the workers. On the contrary, Marxism attaches vast importance to the consciousness, energy and determination of the leaders of the people. The right theory is a powerful weapon that helps us to understand the present and foresee the future; it facilitates and hastens the proletariat's achievement of its aims. Lenin wrote:

"*The role of vanguard fighter can be fulfilled only by a party that is guided by the most advanced theory.*" (*Collected Works*, Vol. 5, p. 342).

This advanced, revolutionary theory, a reliable guide to revolutionary action, is Marxism.

The proletariat fights the bourgeoisie not only in the sphere of politics and economics, but also in that of theory, of ideology. The ideological struggle is of exceptional, vital importance for the working class. The point is that there are two ideologies in capitalist society: bourgeois and Socialist. By virtue of its social position, the working class is drawn towards Socialism; but the bourgeoisie, as the ruling class, does its utmost to inoculate the proletariat with its own ideology. The "Economists" helped the bourgeoisie in this by denying the necessity of imparting a Socialist consciousness to the working class and declaring that the Socialist ideology springs of its own accord from the spontaneous working-class movement. But Socialist ideology, that is, Marxism, arises in the process of the development of science, and is introduced into the working-class movement by the political party of the proletariat.

"*All* worship of the spontaneity of the working-class movement," wrote Lenin, "all belittling of the role of 'the conscious element,' of the role of Social-Democracy, *means, quite irrespective of whether the belittler wants it or not, strengthening the influence of bourgeois ideology on the workers*" (*ibid.*, p. 354).

The Socialist and bourgeois ideologies are engaged in a life-and-death struggle; Lenin emphasised:

"The *only* choice is: either the bourgeois or the Socialist ideology. There is no middle course. . . . Hence to belittle the Socialist ideology *in any way, to turn away from it in the slightest degree*, means to strengthen the bourgeois ideology" (*ibid.*, pp. 355-56).

It is therefore imperative to wage constant and resolute struggle against bourgeois ideas which penetrate into the ranks of the proletariat. This struggle is waged by the Marxist party, one of whose most important tasks is to guard the ideological independence of the proletariat, to disseminate Socialist ideology among the working class. The party is *the class-conscious section of the proletariat, which imparts a Socialist consciousness to the spontaneous working-class movement.*

Lenin explained that the worship of spontaneity converts the working-class party into a passive force, that such a party trails behind the working-class movement and bears no resemblance whatsoever to the guiding staff of this movement. In fact, it leaves the proletariat without a party and thus disarms it in the face of its class enemies.

The "Economists" preached profoundly erroneous and harmful views on the political struggle of the proletariat in general, and on the political tasks of Russia's working class in particular. They advised the Social-Democrats to confine themselves exclusively to organising the "economic struggle of the workers against their employers and the government" and thus "lend the economic struggle itself a political character." But the economic struggle against the employers and the government restricts the working-class movement to questions of better terms for the sale of labour power, whereas the proletariat is interested in the complete abolition of the exploiting system and replacement of it by Socialism.

In order to wage a successful struggle for Socialism, the proletariat must have a high level of class political consciousness. This consciousness is fostered in the proletariat by the Marxist party, which teaches it to observe and properly appraise all classes in every aspect of their life, and to react against every case of tyranny and oppression from its own standpoint, no matter what class is affected.

The working class of Russia, wrote Lenin, must act as the vanguard fighter for democracy, as the organiser and leader of the nation-wide struggle against tsarism. For this the proletariat needs a party that is really the vanguard of its class. In order that the party may in fact become this vanguard, it must organise the political exposure of the autocracy from every angle and utilise every manifestation of protest against this, the bitterest enemy of the people. It must be in the forefront of the struggle to solve all common democratic problems, while unswervingly defending the interests of the proletariat and its Socialist aims. Therein lies one of the most important tasks of the Marxist party as the *political leader* of the working class in the struggle for its emancipation.

"The Social-Democrat's ideal," stated Lenin, "should not be a trade union secretary, but a *tribune of the people*, able to react to each and every manifestation of tyranny and oppression, no matter where it takes place, no matter what stratum or class of the people it affects; he must be able to generalise all these manifestations to produce a single picture of police violence and capitalist exploitation; he must be able to take advantage of every event, however small, to explain his Socialist convictions and his democratic demands *to all*, to explain *to each* and everyone the world historic significance of the proletariat's struggle for emancipation" (*Collected Works*, Vol. 5, p. 393).

It was this famous definition by Lenin of the real revolutionary as a tribune of the people that guided the Party in educating its members and demanding that they should become political leaders. The Party organisations learned how to organise the masses, explaining to them the Socialist convictions and democratic demands of the working class.

The "Economists'" servile worship of spontaneity caused no less harm in the sphere of working-class organisation. The "Economists" sought to justify amateurish methods and to create organisations of a narrow trade union type. Lenin wrote bitterly that the activity of the Social-Democratic organisations of that period reminded one of a march of peasants armed with cudgels against a modern army. To win the war against tsarism and capitalism, the working class needed a strong organisation of its own.

"Give us an organisation of revolutionaries, and we shall overturn Russia!" declared Lenin (*ibid.*, p. 435).

Lenin pointed out that the working class of Russia could fulfil its historic tasks only if it had a militant, centralised, revolutionary Marxist party, inseparably linked with the masses. Such a party would ensure the strength and stability of the revolutionary working-class movement. Completely devoted to the revolution, it would enjoy the equally absolute confidence of the widest sections of the working class. To build such a party, professional revolutionaries were needed who would devote themselves wholly to revolutionary work, perseveringly and systematically cultivating in themselves the necessary qualities. In this way a well-knit team of leaders would be built up, tested and trained in a long school of political activity, without whom "no class in modern society can wage a determined struggle" (*ibid.*, p. 430).

The Marxist party, wrote Lenin, is "the highest form of the Socialist working-class movement." A specific feature of the working-class movement in Russia was that in it there first developed a political organisation of the working class, and that at that time the proletariat had no organisations other than the Social-Democratic Party. Lenin, however, foresaw the appearance of various organisations in the working-class movement. He pointed out that the party of the working class should be surrounded by the latter's other organisations: trade unions, cultural and educational societies, etc. The Party, as the *highest form of class organisation*, had the mission of leading all the other organisations of the proletariat.

Lenin showed that great historic tasks confronted the revolutionary Marxist party of the working class of Russia. He wrote prophetically:

"History has now confronted us with an immediate task which is the *most revolutionary* of all the *immediate* tasks that confront the proletariat of any country. The fulfilment of this task, the destruction of the most powerful bulwark not only of European, but also (it may now be said) of Asiatic reaction, would make the Russian proletariat the vanguard of the international revolutionary proletariat" (*ibid.*, p. 345).

Lenin's book *What Is To Be Done?* played an outstanding part in the ideological defeat of "Economism," in uniting the Party cadres on the basis of Marxism, in preparing for the Second Congress of the R.S.D.L.P. and in founding a revolutionary Marxist party in Russia. In this book, Lenin dealt a telling blow at the revisionists in the West European Social-Democratic parties as represented by Bernstein and his followers, and exposed their opportunism and betrayal of the interests of the working class.

In the new period of history, when revolutionary battles of the proletariat against the bourgeoisie were approaching, Lenin raised the question of the working-class party from a new angle. The West European Socialist parties were not directing the various forms of the class struggle of the proletariat. They confined themselves to parliamentary activity. Their opportunism was becoming increasingly evident, they were not preparing the Party cadres and working-class masses for revolution.

Lenin was the first Marxist to see that the working class needed a party of a *new type*. He expounded his views on this party, on its character and its role in the working-class movement, and the basic principles that should underlie its activities, in his book *What Is To Be Done?*

The historic significance of *What Is To Be Done?* lies in the fact that in it Lenin, developing the ideas of Marx and Engels on the proletarian party, worked out foundations of the theory of the revolutionary Marxist party as a party of a new type.

He substantiated the fundamental Marxist proposition that a Marxist party is a fusion of the working-class movement with Socialism.

He brought out the supreme importance of the theory of scientific Socialism for the spontaneous working-class movement and for the entire activity of the Party.

He elaborated the conception of the Party as the political leader of the proletariat, as the guiding force of the working-class movement, a force which unites and directs the class struggle of the proletariat.

He proved that it was necessary completely to reorganise the whole work of the Party along the lines of educating and preparing the masses for revolution.

He showed that the ideological roots of opportunism lie primarily in worship of spontaneity in the working-class movement and in belittling the role of Socialist consciousness in that movement.

The Leninist *Iskra* raised aloft the banner of struggle for the revolutionary theory of Marxism. In the international battle of the revolutionaries against the opportunists, the Russian Marxists were in the front ranks. In defending the purity of Marxism, Lenin laid special emphasis on the necessity of developing theory further, of enriching it with the experience of the practical movement. At the time when preparations were still being made for the publication of *Iskra*, Lenin wrote:

"We do not at all regard Marxist theory as something completed and inviolable; on the contrary, we are convinced that it has only laid the corner-stone of the science which Socialists *must* extend in all directions if they wish to keep pace with life" (*Collected Works*, Vol. 4, p. 191).

Lenin explained that the general principles of Marxism must be applied in each country with due regard to its specific features, and that it was the duty of the Russian Socialists to elaborate Marxist theory independently. The work of Lenin himself was a brilliant example of this creative approach to Marxism.

Narodism, which had revived under the influence of the revolutionary upsurge, was a great danger to the creation of a revolutionary Marxist party. At the end of 1901 the remnants of various Narodnik groups united under the high-sounding title of Socialist-Revolutionary Party (SRs). In 1901-1902, the SRs carried out several terrorist acts, and, in particular, assassinated two tsarist ministers. The "Narodnaya Volya" traditions of conspiracy and terrorism, and a certain, purely outward revolutionism of the Socialist-Revolutionaries appealed to the revolutionary intelligentsia, to a section of the workers and even to less stable Social-Democrats.

Iskra came out most sharply against the Socialist-Revolutionaries. By denying the class distinctions between the proletariat, the peasantry and the intelligentsia, the Socialist-Revolutionaries made it difficult for the working class to realise its own leading role in the revolutionary struggle. By preaching that the intelligentsia should fight the autocracy single-handed, they were diverting the revolutionary forces to futile terrorist acts and undermining the organisation of the revolutionary struggle of the masses. In advancing the demand for the "socialisation of the land," they deceived the workers and the peasants by arguing that Socialism could be introduced in the countryside even under capitalism, by abolishing private property in land and dividing the land equally among the peasants.

One of the most important achievements of *Iskra* was the drafting of a programme for the Party. Defining the aims and tasks of the Party, the programme was to cement the scattered Social-Democratic organisations ideologically into a single party. The draft programme was published in June, 1902. It specified clearly and precisely that the ultimate goal of the working-class movement was the replacement of capitalism by Socialism; that the way to this goal was through Socialist revolution and the dictatorship of the proletariat; and that the immediate tasks of the working-class party in Russia were the revolutionary overthrow of the autocracy and the establishment of a democratic republic.

Iskra put forward a broad political plan for organising a nation-wide struggle against tsarism at a time when the tide of revolution was mounting in the country. Its activities greatly facilitated preparations for the approaching revolution.

Iskra considered one of its main tasks to be the transformation of the existing Social-Democratic committees into real headquarters of the leaders and organisers of the class struggle of the proletariat. Unlike the West European Socialist parties, which confined themselves to peaceful parliamentary activities, *Iskra* called for revolutionary struggle and stressed the importance of revolutionary methods, such as political strikes and demonstrations. The role of the committees in the working-class movement siding with *Iskra*, their influence and leadership, grew steadily. Working in the very heart of the working-class movement, the R.S.D.L.P. committees strengthened their contacts with the masses, and trained genuine leaders of the masses.

Iskra consistently championed proletarian leadership of the revolutionary struggle of the masses. It set before the Social-Democrats the task of "going among all classes of the population." Under its influence the Social-Democratic organisations broadened the scope of their work.

Iskra devoted special attention to the peasantry as the ally of the proletariat. It called on the working class to give all possible support to the peasant movement. And when peasant disturbances began in the spring of 1902, the Social-Democrats reacted to them with a clear understanding of their tasks. In the nineties, Social-Democratic ideas had been carried to the countryside by workers who had been banished from the cities for taking part in "disorders." Now the R.S.D.L.P. committees established direct contact with the countryside: leaflets addressed to the peasants appeared and Social-Democratic propaganda groups were organised among the peasants. Modest as those early successes may have been, they were of tremendous fundamental importance, for they marked the beginning of the regular dissemination of the ideas of the class struggle and of political consciousness among the many millions of peasants.

In his pamphlet, *To the Rural Poor*, published in 1903, Lenin expounded, in popular language comprehensible to the peasantry, the policy of the workers' party, and explained to the village poor what their position should be in the revolutionary struggle.

"All Russian workers and all the rural poor," wrote Lenin, "must *fight with both hands and on two sides*: with one hand, *against all the bourgeois*, in alliance with all the workers; and with the other hand, *against the rural officials, against the feudal landlords,* in alliance with all the peasants. . . .

"The first step in the countryside must be the complete emancipation of the peasant, full rights for him and the establishment of peasant committees for the purpose of restoring the *otrezki.* And our last step will be the same in both town and country: *we shall take all the land and all the factories from the landlords and the bourgeoisie and set up a Socialist society"* (*Collected Works,* Vol. 6, pp. 370, 379-80).

The Social-Democratic organisations were also active in the army. A revolutionary military organisation, closely associated with the R.S.D.L.P., was formed in December 1902. The influence of Social-Democracy among the students increased. Social-Democratic groups were formed in the universities and colleges. At the beginning of 1902, the All-Russian Students' Congress resolved to establish the closest possible relations with the R.S.D.L.P.

Iskra encouraged expressions of dissatisfaction with the existing order in tsarist Russia in every part of society. That also determined its attitude towards the opposition movement of the liberal bourgeoisie. So long as the liberals did not constitute an organised political group, *Iskra* encouraged their protests against the arbitrary rule of the tsarist autocracy, at the same time, however, criticising their half-heartedness and cowardice. But in 1902, following the appearance of a political group of liberals headed by P. Struve, with its own organ *Osvobozhdeniye* (*Emancipation*), which was published abroad and laid claim to leadership of the liberation movement, what became most important for *Iskra* was the exposure of the anti-revolutionary nature of liberalism.

The militant newspaper of the Russian Marxists consistently defended the right of every nation to shape its own fate. It vigorously criticised all manifestations of national oppression. *Iskra* took up the defence of the legitimate rights of the Finnish people, indignantly denouncing the violence of the tsarist gang. It exposed the policy of colonial conquest in the Far East, and branded as a crime the war against the Chinese people organised by Russian tsarism and the European imperialists. The Leninist *Iskra* did much to inspire the working masses of the oppressed nations with confidence in the Russian proletariat, and to make them see that it was a steadfast and indomitable fighter against all forms of national oppression. At the same time *Iskra* waged an uncompromising struggle against the Jewish, Polish and other petty-bourgeois nationalists who sowed national discord among the workers. Lenin tirelessly conducted propaganda for the principle of proletarian internationalism. He explained that only a close alliance of the workers of the oppressed nations with the Russian proletariat, only the militant unity of the entire working class of Russia, irrespective of nationality, would lead them to victory over tsarism and ensure the complete political and economic emancipation of the working people.

Thus, by steadily and consistently spreading the influence of the working class to all spheres of the country's social life, the Leninist *Iskra* awakened political discontent in the various strata of the population. *Iskra* was building a party that would fight against all economic, political, social and national oppression; it was educating the working class to be the leader of the struggle of the whole nation against tsarism.

Iskra persistently put into effect Lenin's plan of organisation. In his *Letter to a Comrade on Our Organisational Tasks*, Lenin proposed the following pattern for building the local organisations of the R.S.D.L.P. There should be one Party committee in every city to lead the local movement. An end should be put to the abnormal and harmful division of the local organisations into two separate committees, one for the workers and the other for the intellectuals, as practised by the "Economists." The committee should include all the chief leaders of the working-class movement, with the widest contacts and the greatest prestige among the masses. It should have two types of organisation subordinated to it. First, district groups and factory subcommittees. Every factory should become our stronghold, Lenin demanded. These district and factory groups would link the committee with the working-class masses. Secondly, groups attached to the committee itself, serving the various requirements of the Party: groups for propagandists; groups for transport, printing, the provision of clandestine quarters, shadowing spies; youth groups; groups of officials assisting the Party, etc. Some of these groups would be part of the Party organisation, while others would be closely associated with it and work under its influence. In this way each local Party organisation was to consist of leading Party workers, chiefly professional revolutionaries, and of a wide network of circles and groups around them. This structure of the organisation would ensure centralism, discipline, close contact with the masses, manoeuvrability and flexibility. The reconstruction of the Social-Democratic organisations began on the basis of Lenin's plan.

A strong organisation of professional revolutionaries was built up around *Iskra*. A Russian organisation of *Iskra* and "The League of Russian Revolutionary Social-Democrats Abroad" were formed. A body of professional revolutionaries, people selflessly devoted to the cause of the proletariat, men and women of high principle and well-disciplined, irreconcilable in their attitude towards all opportunist scum and inseparably linked with the masses, was tempered in the severe conditions of underground work, in the struggle against numerous enemies. Among these professional revolutionaries were I. V. Babushkin, N. E. Bauman, M. I. Kalinin, N. K. Krupskaya, M. M. Litvinov, G. I. Petrovsky, O. A. Pyatnitsky, S. G. Shaumyan, J. V. Stalin, Y. D. Stasova, Y. M. Sverdlov, R. S. Zemlyachka and many other *Iskra*-ists. The *Iskra*-ist organisation of professional revolutionaries played a signal part in the creation and development of the Party.

Iskra appeared as a united force in the struggle to found the Party. But during the drafting of the programme and tactics of the Party Lenin had to overcome serious waverings and vacillations on the editorial board of *Iskra*. Differences made their appearance over the question of the attitude towards the liberal bourgeoisie. Lenin favoured severe criticism of the political flabbiness and cowardice of the liberals and held that their anti-revolutionary nature should be exposed. Plekhanov and Axelrod regarded the liberals as allies in the revolution.

Sharp disputes arose over the programme. Plekhanov vacillated on the question of the dictatorship of the proletariat. It was only thanks to Lenin that the basic proposition of Marxism regarding the dictatorship of the proletariat was formulated clearly in the draft programme. Plekhanov dissolved the proletariat in the general mass of the working people; he failed to emphasise that the working class could and should unite around itself all those oppressed by capital. The idea of the leadership of the Party in the class struggle of the proletariat was likewise lacking in his conception. At Lenin's instance, the proletarian character of the Party and the idea of the hegemony of the working class were clearly expressed in the draft programme, and the vanguard, leading role of the Party in the working-class movement precisely indicated.

A sharp struggle developed over the agrarian programme. Lenin put forward the demand for the abolition of the survivals of serfdom in the village, and, in particular, for the return of the "cut-off" lands (*otrezki*) to the peasants. At the same time Lenin held that, as the revolutionary peasant movement developed, the demand for the restoration of the "cut-off" lands to the peasants would have to be replaced by a programme of nationalisation of the land. Lenin's proposition on the nationalisation of the land was opposed by Plekhanov, Axelrod and Martov, which showed that they underestimated the importance of an alliance of the workers and peasants in the revolution.

In the disputes on the editorial board two political lines already became evident: the revolutionary Marxist and the opportunist trends. The sharp clashes over basic questions of principle threatened at times to cause a complete rupture in the leadership of *Iskra*, but matters were not carried to a split at that time.

Thanks to Lenin's leadership, *Iskra* adopted a revolutionary Marxist position on all questions concerning the working-class movement. Lenin later described the old *Iskra* as having been fully Bolshevik in its trend.

"During the three years 1900-1903," wrote Lenin, "Bolshevism led the old *Iskra* and emerged for the struggle against Menshevism as an integral trend" (*Collected Works*, Vol. 16, p. 41).

Iskra began its work in an atmosphere of ideological vacillations and organisational chaos. As a result of its work over a period of almost three years, the ground was prepared in ideology and organisation for the foundation of a revolutionary Marxist party. In the second half of 1902 and the beginning of 1903 all the committees (with the exception of the Voronezh Committee, where the "Economists" were still in control) joined *Iskra*. It was necessary to consolidate the victory of *Iskra* at a party congress.

3. Second Congress of the R.S.D.L.P. Founding of the Bolshevik Party

The Second Congress of the R.S.D.L.P. met secretly at first in Brussels and later in London, from July 17 to August 10, 1903. It was attended by 43 delegates representing 26 organisations, with 51 votes between them. For the thoroughness with which it was prepared, its wide representation and the range of questions it had to decide, the Second Congress of the R.S.D.L.P. was an event unprecedented in the whole history of the Russian revolutionary movement. Immediately before and during the Congress, a great wave of general strikes swept over the South of Russia. The delegates brought to the Congress the breath of the approaching revolutionary storm.

The principal task of the Congress, Lenin pointed out, was to create a real revolutionary workers' party according to the principles and on the organisational lines proposed and worked out by *Iskra*. This task was accomplished in a bitter struggle against opportunism.

With 33 votes, *Iskra* commanded a majority at the Congress. The opponents of the *Iskra*-ists had 8 votes (3 "Economists" and 5 Bundists). The Southern Worker group, which was supported by the vacillating elements, the centrists, or the "quagmire," as Lenin called them, had 10 votes. Although the majority of the delegates considered themselves supporters of *Iskra*, they were not all real Leninist *Iskra*-ists. The firm and consistent *Iskra*-ists, the supporters of Lenin, commanded 24 votes; the so-called "mild" *Iskra*-ists, the future Mensheviks, who followed Martov, commanded 9 votes. The opponents of the *Iskra*-ists tried to exploit the disagreements among the *Iskra*-ists to their own ends.

When founding the Party, the Congress had to overcome an obstacle such as the existence of separate "circles." The existence of separate "circles," each with its own conception of the fundamental principles of the Party's policy, was a specific feature of the development of the Social-Democratic movement in Russia. The task of the Congress was to replace the narrow study circle connections by a single wide Party connections, to set up a party in which all units would be firmly welded together ideologically and organisationally. The process of drawing all these "circles" into the Party was a painful one, and at the Congress the principles of party organisation came into conflict again and again with the protagonists of the "circle" principle.

The Congress opened with a discussion of the place of the Bund in the Party. That was not accidental. *Iskra* upheld the idea of uniting the foremost workers of all the nations inhabiting Russia in one centralised party. The Bund, however, wanted a party based on the principles of federation, regarding it as a formal union of national organisations independent of the general leadership of the Party. Such organisations would have been loosely linked with one another, and would not have constituted a united proletarian party.

Lenin and his followers waged an uncompromising struggle against the organisational nationalism of the Bund, explaining the harmfulness of federation, which sanctioned estrangement in the internal life of the Party and contradicted the principle of centralism. The Congress rejected the nationalist principle of federation in building the party. Lenin's idea of a party based on the principles of centralism and proletarian internationalism triumphed.

The Congress then proceeded to consider the question of the draft Party programme.

A sharp struggle developed around the clause on the dictatorship of the proletariat. The opportunist leaders—the Bundist Lieber and the "Economists" Akimov and Martynov—furiously opposed the inclusion of the clause on the dictatorship of the proletariat in the programme; here they referred to the programmes of the West European Socialist parties, which did not raise the question of establishing the dictatorship of the proletariat. They alleged that class contradictions were growing less sharp, and that a gradual improvement in the standard of living of the working class would automatically lead to Socialism, without the dictatorship of the proletariat. The Congress delivered a decisive blow to the opportunists and voted for the inclusion in the programme of the fundamental Marxist principle of the dictatorship of the proletariat.

The "Economists" objected to the inclusion in the programme of a clause on the leading role of the Party in the working-class movement, and proposed a number of amendments along the lines of the "theory of spontaneity." The Congress rejected all their amendments.

The opportunists objected with particular vehemence to the programme's demands on the peasant question. By assertions that the peasantry was not revolutionary they sought to cover up their unwillingness, and even fear, to rouse the masses to revolution. Essentially, the opportunists were bitterly opposed to the proletariat being the leading force in the revolution and to an alliance between the workers and peasants.

Speaking in defence of the agrarian programme, Lenin emphasised that the demand for the abolition of the survivals of serfdom was revolutionary in character.

"We are confident," said Lenin, "that since the Social-Democrats have now taken up the struggle for the interests of the peasants, we shall in the future have to reckon with the fact that the peasant masses will learn to look upon Social-Democracy as the defender of their interests" (*Collected Works*, Vol. 6, p. 452).

Serious disputes arose over the national question. For a multinational country like Russia it was exceptionally important to have a correct programme and policy on the national question. Lenin elaborated the theoretical principles and practical demands of the Marxist national programme. In his work, *The National Question in Our Programme*, and in other articles published in *Iskra*, he substantiated the consistently internationalist principles of the programme: the demand for the full equality of all citizens irrespective of nationality, recognition of the right to self-determination for all nations forming part of the State, the principle of uniting the workers of all nations in common class organisations (party, trade unions, etc.).

The programme slogan of the right of nations to self-determination was a powerful weapon for the Party in its revolutionary struggle, for it drew the oppressed nationalities of Russia to the side of the proletariat as the consistent fighter against national oppression, and helped to educate the working class in the spirit of proletarian internationalism. To this slogan, the Bundists opposed the utterly opportunist and nationalist demand for national cultural autonomy. This demand divided the workers according to their various national cultures, and destroyed the international class unity of the proletariat; it limited the interests of the working people of different nations to cultural matters and diverted them from the struggle for revolution, for the democratic reorganisation of the State as a whole. An incorrect position on the national question was also taken up by the representatives of Polish Social-Democracy. They wrongly held that the demand for the right of nations to self-determination would play into the hands of the Polish nationalists, and proposed that it be withdrawn.

Lenin's ideas and the Party programme on the national question, adopted by the Second Congress of the R.S.D.L.P., represented a blow at nationalism. They enriched Marxist theory and helped the Party to pursue a correct national policy.

All the attacks of the opportunists were beaten off by the *Iskra*-ists. The Congress approved the *Iskra* programme which consisted of two parts: a maximum programme and a minimum programme. The maximum programme dealt with the ultimate aim of the Party, namely, the building of a Socialist society, and with the conditions necessary for achieving this—a Socialist revolution and the establishment of the dictatorship of the proletariat. The minimum programme dealt with the immediate aims of the Party, namely, the overthrow of tsarism, a bourgeois-democratic revolution, the establishment of a democratic republic, the introduction of an 8-hour working day, complete equality and the right to self-determination for all nations, and the abolition of the remnants of serfdom in the countryside.

The programme adopted by the Second Congress was a truly Marxist programme of a revolutionary proletarian party. Unlike the programmes of the West European Social-Democratic parties, it was the only programme of a working-class party in the world which formulated the idea of the dictatorship of the proletariat. The programme of the R.S.D.L.P. was a result of the theoretical work of the Russian Marxists, and it enriched Marxism considerably. The programme defined the consistently Marxist policy of the Party and helped to educate the proletariat in a spirit of revolutionary struggle for power. The Party could legitimately be proud of this programme. It was the foundation on which the Bolshevik Party took shape and gained strength. Guided by it, the Party fought successfully for the victory of the bourgeois-democratic and Socialist revolutions in Russia.

The Congress noted the outstanding services of *Iskra* in the fight against opportunism, in the defence and development of Marxism and in building the Party, and declared *Iskra* to be the central organ of the Party. The Congress thereby recognised the *Iskra*-ist trend as that of the entire Party.

Discussion of the Party rules, and, especially, of the first paragraph, dealing with Party membership, revealed two sharply-opposed approaches to the question of the Party. Lenin proposed the following formulation for the first paragraph: "A Party member is one who recognises the Party programme and supports the Party financially, as well as by personal participation in one of its organisations." In opposition to Lenin, Martov proposed his formulation, according to which a Party member could be "one who accepts its programme, supports the Party financially, and renders it regular personal assistance under the guidance of one of its organisations." Thus, when the definition of membership was discussed, Lenin insisted on "personal participation in one of the Party organisations," while Martov proposed simply "regular personal assistance."

Lenin regarded the Party as an organised whole. Every Party member must belong to one of the Party organisations. That ensured both a Marxist training and high discipline for every one of its members, and real control and firm guidance of his activities by the Party. This made the Party an ordered system of organisations functioning according to a single plan, and an embodiment of discipline and organisation.

Martov proposed admitting to the Party all who wanted to join, without binding them to membership of one of its organisations or submitting them to Party discipline. Martov and his followers supported the "open-door" policy of the Social-Democratic parties of the Second International, which weakened strict adherence to principle in the Party organisation of the proletariat. In the opinion of the Martovites, any striker or intellectual had the right to regard himself as a member of the Party, even if he did not belong, and did not want to belong, to one of the Party organisations. Thus the Party would have lost its clearly defined organisational boundaries, and would have become a heterogeneous, loose and amorphous body.

Lenin's conception of membership safeguarded the firmness of the Marxist party line and the purity of its principles, and made it difficult for unstable elements to get into the Party.

"It is our task," said Lenin, "to safeguard the firmness, consistency and purity of our Party. We must strive to raise the title and significance of a Party member ever higher, and that is why I am opposed to Martov's formulation" (*Collected Works*, Vol. 6, p. 459).

Lenin warned against the danger of cluttering up the Party with all kinds of unstable, vacillating and opportunist elements. This danger, which threatens a workers' party in any country, was particularly great in Russia, a country which was on the eve of a bourgeois-democratic revolution, in consequence of which petty-bourgeois elements were seeking to join the Party. Lenin's advice to be discriminating when admitting members into the Party and to be most exacting as regards the title of Party member became one of the basic principles of organisation of the Bolshevik Party.

The cardinal issue in the struggle over the first paragraph of the draft rules was the question of what the nature of the Party should be. The Leninists fought for a monolithic, militant and disciplined revolutionary proletarian party with a clearly-defined organisational structure, whereas the Martovites wanted an amorphous and heterogeneous, loose, petty-bourgeois, opportunist party. Lenin fought for such internal Party structure as would ensure its consistent revolutionary character. That is why Martov's formulation was solidly backed by all the opportunist elements: the Bundists, the "Economists," the centrists and the "mild" *Iskra*-ists. The opportunists, from Akimov to Trotsky, joined forces, and the Congress adopted, by a majority of 28 votes to 22 with one abstention, Martov's formulation of the first paragraph of the rules.

The Leninists were not discouraged by the opportunists' temporary victory. A sharp struggle developed over the question of the role of the Party's leading bodies. The opportunists tried their utmost to limit the leading role of the Central Committee. They proposed restricting the right of the Central Committee to dissolve local committees, and considering only those decisions of the Central Committee which concerned the whole Party as binding on Party organisations. These proposals were rejected by the Congress. It was clearly stated in the rules that the Central Committee "unites and guides all the practical activities of the Party," allocates the Party's forces and funds, organises the various Party institutions and guides their work, and that "all the decisions of the Central Committee are binding on all Party organisations . . ." (*C.P.S.U. in Resolutions*, Part I, p. 46). These provisions remained in all the later rules of the Party. The firm *Iskra*-ists thus successfully upheld the principle of centralism in the structure of the Party, as against the opportunist principle of autonomy and federation.

The struggle for the Party rules which the *Iskra*-ists waged under Lenin's leadership was of tremendous significance. Lenin and his supporters won the day for *Iskra*'s organisational plan at the Congress. It was on the foundation of this plan that there arose and was consolidated a revolutionary Marxist party in Russia—the Bolshevik Party.

In connection with the adoption of the rules, the Congress adopted a number of decisions aimed at strengthening Party organisation. It resolved to put an end to the abnormal situation abroad created by the existence of two organisations, the "Economist" "Union of Russian Social-Democrats Abroad" and the *Iskra*-ist "League of Russian Revolutionary Social-Democrats Abroad," and recognised the latter as the only organisation of the R.S.D.L.P. abroad. In protest, the two "Economists" representing their "Union" left the Congress.

At the Congress, the Bund demanded to be recognised as the sole representative of the Jewish proletariat. That would have meant dividing the workers in the Party organisations according to nationality, and renouncing common class organisations of the proletariat. The Bund was a Jewish nationalist organisation. The Congress rejected its demands, whereupon the five Bundists also left the Congress, declaring that the Bund was withdrawing from the R.S.D.L.P. The departure of these seven opportunists altered the balance of forces in favour of the firm *Iskra*-ists.

It was necessary to consolidate the victory of *Iskra*-ist principles in the spheres of the programme, tactics and organisation by taking decisive steps to do away with the narrow study circle principle and electing a leadership which would ensure a consistently revolutionary direction of the Party's entire activity. The Leninists demanded the election of a Central Committee which would be composed of staunch and consistent revolutionaries. The Martovites strove to secure the predominance of unstable, opportunist elements in the Central Committee. The firm *Iskra*-ists proposed electing Lenin, Martov and Plekhanov to the editorial board of *Iskra*. The Martovites insisted on all the six former editors remaining there.

Lenin's plan for consolidating the victory of the *Iskra* principle of Party organisation had the firm support of the majority of the delegates. Lenin, Martov and Plekhanov were elected to the *Iskra* editorial board. Krzhizhanovsky, Lengnik and Noskov were elected to the Party's Central Committee. Martov, however, refused to join the editorial board, and his supporters did not take part in the elections to the Central Committee.

By its vote on the question of the central bodies the Congress confirmed the victory of Lenin's principles in the Party. From that time on, Lenin's supporters, who obtained a majority of votes in the elections to the leading organs of the Party, have been called the Bolsheviks (from the Russian word *bolshinstvo*, majority), and Lenin's opponents the Mensheviks (from the word *menshinstvo*, minority). The word *Bolshevik*, born in the battles at the Congress, became synonymous with the conception of "a consistent Marxist revolutionary, who is utterly devoted to the cause of the working class, to the cause of Communism."

The victory of the Bolsheviks at the Congress was prepared

by the entire development of the Social-Democratic movement. Represented at the Congress were the Party cadres who had waged a bitter struggle of principle against the opportunists. The intention of the Martovites to turn the leadership of the Party over to unstable, vacillating elements was bound to alienate consistent supporters of the *Iskra* line. The interests of the Party were staunchly defended, against the alliance of heterogeneous opportunist elements that took shape at the Congress, by the representatives of the biggest committees: A. V. Shotman of St. Petersburg, N. E. Bauman of Moscow, B. M. Knunyants of Baku, S. I. Gusev of the Don Committee, P. A. Krasikov of Kiev, R. S. Zemlyachka of Odessa, L. M. Knipovich and A. M. Stopani of the "Northern League," S. I. Stepanov and D. I. Ulyanov (Lenin's brother) of Tula.

At the Congress Lenin's outstanding role in the struggle for the Party became increasingly evident. All those who consistently fought for the formation of a Marxist party united around Lenin.

The creation of a revolutionary Marxist party, the Bolshevik Party, was the principal result of the Second Congress of the R.S.D.L.P. The working-class movement in Russia had travelled a long and thorny path before it evolved its highest form, namely, an independent political party. This Party was based on the ideological and organisational principles elaborated by the Leninist *Iskra*; its core was made up of professional revolutionaries tempered in battle, and its leaders were Leninist Bolsheviks.

The appearance of a working-class revolutionary party was a most important landmark in the history of Russia. Since the middle of the nineties the proletariat had been a major political force in the life of the country. And with the formation of its own party it began to be transformed into the leader of all the working people. In the programme of the R.S.D.L.P., the working class, the dispossessed peasant masses and the oppressed nationalities found expression for their innermost aspirations. While the liberals confined themselves to wishes for a moderate constitution, under which the tsarist monarchy would be retained, and the Socialist-Revolutionaries went no further than the vague demand for political liberty, the workers' party called the masses to the overthrow of the tsarist autocracy and demanded the complete democratisation of all public and social life with the aim of fighting for the Socialist revolution, the dictatorship of the proletariat, and the fundamental reconstruction of society on Socialist principles. The R.S.D.L.P. proved to be the only party in Russia whose activities wholly accorded with the interests of the country and the people.

The Second Congress was an event of historic importance for the world. It marked a turning-point in the international working-class movement. In Western Europe the working-class parties had taken shape in the conditions of a comparatively peaceful development of capitalism, when the era of bourgeois revolutions had in the main come to an end, and the era of Socialist revolution had not yet begun. In this situation there gradually developed parliamentary parties that were corrupted by bourgeois legality and reconciled to opportunism in their midst. In Russia the workers' party took shape in a situation of approaching revolution. It was faced with the task of preparing the masses for that revolution. The Party became steeled and tempered as a completely revolutionary force in conditions of savage police persecution and in bitter struggle against various manifestations of opportunism.

In Russia, the Marxist party appeared at the beginning of a new era in history, the era of imperialism, when the proletariat was on the threshold of revolutionary battles. The parties of the Second International were incapable of solving the new problems correctly, in a Marxist way; they did not prepare the working class for revolutionary battles aiming at the overthrow of the capitalist yoke and the establishment of the dictatorship of the proletariat. After the death of Engels (1895) the leadership of the Second International drifted more and more towards opportunism. The very first battles against revisionism at the opening of the twentieth century ended in the leaders of the West European Socialist parties virtually submitting to the enemies of Marxism, who preached renunciation of Socialist revolution and agreement with the bourgeoisie. The revolutionary elements in the Second International were too weak to change the situation.

Only the Russian Marxists, the Bolsheviks headed by Lenin, proved equal to the challenge of the new era and supplied the right answer to the fundamental problems of the working-class movement. They defined the role of the party as that of political leader of the proletariat, and set themselves the task of winning over the masses of the working people to the side of the working class, in order to carry out the Socialist revolution and establish the dictatorship of the proletariat. They declared one of the most urgent tasks of the working-class movement to be a resolute struggle against opportunism, and they set an example of uncompromising attitude towards it. The Russian Marxists founded a party which systematically educated the working class in a revolutionary spirit, and which trained in its ranks leaders who were closely connected with the masses and able to influence them.

Bolshevism became the most revolutionary and consistently Marxist trend in the international working-class movement. As a result of the activities of Lenin and of the Marxists guided by him there arose in Russia, for the first time in history, a party of a new type, irreconcilable in its attitude towards opportunism and revolutionary with regard to the bourgeoisie, a party standing for social revolution and the dictatorship of the proletariat, the Bolshevik Party.

"As a trend of political thought and as a political party," said Lenin, "Bolshevism has existed since 1903" (*Collected Works*, Vol. 31, p. 8).

4. Development of the Struggle Against the Mensheviks, for the Consolidation of the Party

The situation in the Party after the Second Congress was complicated by the split that had taken place in the ranks of the *Iskra*-ists themselves. The "Economists" had been completely exposed as opportunists and defeated. In the Mensheviks the Party had to deal with new opportunists, but the truly opportunist nature of the Mensheviks had not yet been laid bare. Every *Iskra*-ist had yet fully to realise the grave danger which the Mensheviks represented to the Party.

A bitter and stubborn struggle which was to last many years began between the revolutionaries (Bolsheviks) and the opportunists (Mensheviks). It was to have tremendous significance for the destiny of the Party, for the development of the revolution and the country. Lenin and the Bolsheviks sought to get the Party to act on the basis of the revolutionary Marxist programme approved by the Congress, and that this programme be put into practice. The Mensheviks, on the contrary, tried to direct the Party into opportunist ways. They refused to submit to the decisions of the Congress; but they did not venture to call upon their followers openly to break with the Party: they did not openly proclaim the formation of another party. Soon after the Congress the Mensheviks, in secret from the Party, formed their own anti-Party factional organisation, headed by Martov, Trotsky and Axelrod. They set out to capture the leadership in the Party by boycotting the central Party institutions and disorganising the work of the Party. The Mensheviks, in the words of Martov, "rose in revolt against Leninism."

They chose as the base for their struggle against the Party the "League of Russian Revolutionary Social-Democrats Abroad," where traditions of the old "circles" were particularly strong, where intellectuals predominated and there was no direct contact with the masses of the workers. Gradually the Mensheviks captured all the central institutions of the Party: *Iskra* in November, 1903, and the Central Committee in July, 1904. They succeeded in doing so, not because they were able to win over the Party ideologically and convince it that they were right, but because of help received from conciliators in the central Party institutions.

Plekhanov came forward as the advocate of conciliation. He had supported Lenin at the Congress, but soon after it he demanded that the four former Menshevik editors of *Iskra* be included in the editorial board. Lenin could not agree to this breach of the Congress decision and resigned from the editorial board. Co-opted into the Central Committee, Lenin from this position launched an attack against the opportunists. Acting by himself, Plekhanov "co-opted" all the former editors to the editorial board of *Iskra*. Explaining his action in an article entitled "What Should Not Be Done," Plekhanov wrote that it was necessary to make concessions to the opportunists for the sake of peace in the Party. That amounted to surrendering positions of principle to the opponents of the Party. Plekhanov's article was received with jubilation by all those who were opposed to a revolutionary Marxist party. The bourgeois liberal Struve described it as a "momentous turning-point."

The activity of Plekhanov himself was a glaring example of what "should not be done." Starting out with his statement on the need to make concessions to the Mensheviks, even though they occupied a mistaken position, Plekhanov soon ended up by becoming a rabid Menshevik himself. The Party members were able to see for themselves that concessions to opportunism on questions of principle enabled opportunism to gain the upper hand.

Plekhanov's departure from Marxism was due primarily to the fact that he did not understand the new tasks of the working class in the new historical era. His many years of isolation from the Russian working-class movement were also telling. Plekhanov's vacillations and mistakes in the past, even before the Second Congress, accounted in large measure for his fall.

Beginning with issue No. 52, *Iskra* ceased to be a militant newspaper of revolutionary Marxism, of struggle for the Party. The Mensheviks who had captured *Iskra* converted it into a newspaper fighting against the Party and a forum for the advocacy of opportunism, primarily in the field of organisational questions. The Mensheviks themselves had to admit that "a gulf has formed between the old and the new *Iskra*." A campaign aimed at undermining the fundamental principles of the Party began. The demand for absolute compliance with all the decisions of the Party was declared to be "bureaucracy" and "formalism"; subordination of the minority to the majority was considered a "grossly mechanical" suppression of the will and freedom of the Party member, and Party discipline was denounced as "serf-dom." The Mensheviks were trying to drag the Party back to organisational disunity and looseness, to the parochial outlook of the old "circles" and to amateurish methods.

It was necessary to give decisive battle to the Mensheviks, to expose the opportunist nature of their views on questions of organisation, to show the full extent of the danger of Menshevism to the Party. This task was accomplished by Lenin in his book, *One Step Forward, Two Steps Back*, published in May, 1904. In it, the Marxist doctrine of the Party was developed further. Proceeding from the view that the Marxist party is the political leader of the proletariat, Lenin elaborated the following organisational principles of the Bolshevik Party.

The Marxist party is a part of the working class, its vanguard detachment. The Party must not be confused with the entire class. It is formed by admitting to its ranks the finest members of the working class, the most class-conscious and best organised, those who are selflessly devoted to the cause of the revolution.

The proletariat is not homogeneous. It consists of strata with varying degrees of class consciousness and practical experience. More than that. Under capitalism, the ranks of the working class are being constantly swelled by ruined peasants and small handicraftsmen. Distinctions between the advanced elements and the remaining mass of the workers are inevitable. What would become of the Party if it indiscriminately admitted to its ranks all those who desired to join? Clearly, it would be incapable of performing its role as the vanguard detachment.

The basic mistake in the Mensheviks' views on the Party was that they confused party and class. By demanding that every striker be allowed to call himself a member of the Party, the Mensheviks were obliterating every distinction between the advanced elements and the remaining mass of the workers. That would have meant converting the Party into an organisation which would be dragging at the tail of unprogressive moods among the least advanced strata, instead of elevating the entire working class to the level of the class consciousness of its most advanced detachment. That would inevitably have led to the Party losing its vanguard role.

The Party is the highest expression of the class consciousness of the proletariat; it absorbs the most rich experience and the revolutionary traditions of the working class. The Party is armed with advanced revolutionary theory, with a knowledge of the laws of social development and of class struggle: that is what gives it the ability to lead the working class.

The Party is not only the vanguard, but also an *organised detachment* of the working class. It can carry out its role of advanced detachment if it is organised as a single and general detachment of the working class, welded together by unity of will, unity of action, and unity of discipline.

In order to secure unity of action, the proletariat needs unity of will, and unity of will is inconceivable without organisation. As a class-conscious contingent of the working class, the Party is an embodiment of its organisation. Only as a solidly united organisation can the Party successfully guide the struggle of the working class.

The Mensheviks tried to frighten the Party by saying that many intellectuals would remain outside the Party because they found Party discipline irksome, and did not want to join any of the Party organisations. But the Party of the working class has no use for intellectuals with individualist inclinations. The proletariat does not fear organisation and discipline. The whole life of the workers accustoms them to organisation. Large-scale capitalist production unites and disciplines the proletariat; the class struggle helps them to understand the need for organisation and discipline. That is why the advanced worker appreciates organisation and realises its importance for the struggle.

The proletariat is heterogeneous not only as regards level of class consciousness, but also as regards degree of organisation. Organisation and class consciousness are closely interdependent. The higher the level of class consciousness, the greater the degree of organisation. The ranks of the workers include both quite backward, unorganised elements and those less politically developed strata to whom the trade union is the height of organisation. The Party, as the vanguard detachment of the working class, is the highest form of class organisation of the proletariat.

The Party will be strong and united only if it is organised on the principle of *centralism*. The principle of centralism implies the building and functioning of the Party on the basis of one set of rules, its guidance by one leading body—the Party Congress and, in the intervals between congresses, the Central Committee; it implies uniform discipline, the submission of the minority to the majority and of the lower units to the higher.

In view of the fact that the Party existed illegally under the tsarist autocracy, the Party organisations could not in those days be built up on the elective principle and had therefore to work in strict secrecy. But Lenin believed that when the Party became legal, its organisations would be based on the principle of *democratic centralism*.

The Mensheviks demagogically alleged that centralism would transform the Party into a "factory" and its members into "cogs and wheels." In reality the Mensheviks were opposed to Party discipline; they wanted to drag the Party back to the times when every Party organisation acted at its own discretion and did not recognise any authority in the shape of higher Party bodies.

"*Previously*," Lenin wrote, "our Party was not a formally organised whole, but a mere sum of separate groups, and, therefore, no other relations except those of ideological influence were possible between these groups. *Now* we have become an organised Party, and this implies the establishment of authority, the transformation of the power of ideas into the power of authority, the subordination of lower Party bodies to higher ones" (*Collected Works*, Vol. 7, pp. 338-39).

Without leadership from a single centre, the party of the working class cannot be a really revolutionary party, cannot guide the class struggle of the proletariat.

A united and centralised Party is inconceivable without *discipline*. Organisation and discipline are closely interconnected; there can be no strong organisation without strict discipline. Freedom of discussion and criticism, unity of action—that is how Lenin defined discipline in the workers' party. Once a decision has been adopted, all the members of the Party must act as one man, for organisation is unity of action.

By boycotting the resolutions of the Congress and the decisions of the Central Committee, the Mensheviks were in practice undermining discipline in the Party. They advocated that the Congress resolutions should not be binding on Party members, especially on the "chosen few," the leaders. But the party of the working class cannot establish a procedure which would make its decisions binding on the rank-and-file members but not on the leaders. Such a "procedure" would create a grave threat to the unity of the Party.

"It seems to intellectual individualism, which has already manifested itself in the dispute over Par. I, revealing its weakness for opportunist argument and anarchist phrase-mongering, that *any* proletarian organisation and discipline *are serfdom*," wrote Lenin (*ibid.*, p. 329).

Real Party unity is not only ideological unity; it is also unity of organisation, unthinkable without a uniform discipline binding on all Party members.

The Marxist party is *the embodiment of the connection* between the vanguard of the working class and the working-class millions.

Lenin exposed the fallacy of the Menshevik assertion that the union of the advanced elements in a centralised and disciplined organisation would weaken their contact with the masses, and that a party built up on these principles would lose contact with the masses.

"On the contrary," replied Lenin, "the stronger our Party organisations consisting of *real* Social-Democrats are, and the less wavering and instability there is *within* the Party, the broader, more varied, richer and more fertile will be the influence of the Party on the elements of the working-class *masses* surrounding it and guided by it" (*Collected Works*, Vol. 7, p. 239).

The Party must ever be concerned with multiplying and strengthening its contacts with the non-Party masses, and with winning the confidence of its class. The Marxist party cannot develop unless it strengthens its contacts with the working-class masses, unless it has their support.

The Party gains strength and multiplies its contacts with the masses if it practises *inner-Party democracy* and *self-criticism*.

All the members of the Party should be encouraged in every possible way to be more active, to take part in discussing all major questions of Party life.

"In order to become a party of the masses not in words alone," wrote Lenin, "we must draw ever broader sections of the masses into participation in all Party affairs . . . " (*ibid.*, p. 100).

The Marxist party considers its duty to carry on "self-criticism and ruthless exposure of its own defects" (*ibid.*, p. 190), and regards this as one of the best ways of eliminating shortcomings in its own work and in educating Party cadres.

The Marxist party is the *highest form* of class organisation of the proletariat.

Lenin explained that by effacing the distinction between the Party as a political organisation and the working class, the Mensheviks were actually denying the significance of the Party as the leading organisation of the working-class movement.

The Marxist party unites the most class-conscious and organised elements of the working class. It is armed with a knowledge of the laws of social development, and has a clear programme and flexible tactics. Such a party is the best school for training working-class leaders; in its ranks the advanced workers acquire the theoretical knowledge and political experience that are essential in order to guide the class struggle of the proletariat in all its forms. By taking part in the daily struggle of the proletariat, and firmly defending its fundamental interests, the Party, its committees and its leaders win the confidence of the working-class masses. All this enables the Party as a political organisation to ensure leadership of all the other organisations of the proletariat, to map out their friendly and concerted action, and to guide their activities towards the common goal—the overthrow of the system of exploitation and the establishment of a Socialist system.

Lenin showed that the views of the Mensheviks, which found expression in the discussion on the first paragraph of the rules, had grown into an entire system of opportunism. The principal features of the organisational opportunism of the Mensheviks were their hostile attitude towards centralism, hatred of discipline, defence of organisational backwardness, their opening of the doors of the party of the working class to petty-bourgeois, opportunist elements, and their denial of the role of the Party as the principal weapon of the working class in the struggle for the dictatorship of the proletariat, for Socialism.

The fundamental difference between the Bolshevik and the Menshevik approach to questions of organisation was an expression of two opposite tendencies in building the Party. The Bolsheviks represented proletarian organisation and discipline, while the Mensheviks supported bourgeois-intellectual individualism.

This was the first time in the history of Marxism that an exhaustive criticism had been made of opportunism in matters of organisation and the great danger which the belittlement of the importance of organisation represented to the working-class movement. In his book, Lenin emphatically stressed the immense importance of a Marxist party in the struggle of the working class, especially in the new period of history when the tide of a great people's revolution was rising in Russia and the capitalist world was ripe for a Socialist revolution.

"In its struggle for power, the proletariat has no other weapon but organisation. Disunited by the rule of anarchic competition in the bourgeois world, ground down by forced labour for capital, constantly thrust back to the 'lower depths' of utter destitution, savagery and degeneration, the proletariat can, and inevitably will, become an invincible force only when its ideological unification by the principles of Marxism is consolidated by the material unity of an organisation welding millions of toilers into an army of the working class. Neither the decrepit rule of Russian tsarism, nor the ageing rule of international capital will be able to withstand this army" (V. I. Lenin, *ibid.*, p. 383).

"In its struggle for power, the proletariat has no other weapon but organisation"—this Leninist proposition became one of the corner-stones of Bolshevism.

In the struggle for the Party, its cadres displayed political maturity and a thorough understanding of Lenin's ideas of organisation. Many committees levelled sharp criticism at the Menshevik *Iskra*. The committees in the Urals linked the question of the Party and of its organisational principles directly with the tasks of the fight for the dictatorship of the proletariat. "The preparation of the proletariat for its dictatorship," wrote the Ural members, "is so important an organisational task that all other tasks should be subordinated to it. This preparation consists, among other things, in creating a sentiment in favour of a strong and powerful proletarian organisation, and in fully explaining its importance" (*Third Congress of the R.S.D.L.P.*, *Collection of Documents and Materials*, Gospolitizdat, 1955, p. 146).

Lenin had to wage the struggle for the Party without the support, and even in face of the outright hostility, of the leadership of the West European Social-Democratic parties. The leaders of the Second International came out against Lenin, who had made a new contribution to Marxism on the role of the Party, its character and principles of organisation, and on the training of Party cadres in decisive and uncompromising struggle against opportunism. The Mensheviks in their struggle against the Bolsheviks could rely for support on such recognised authorities of the time as August Bebel and Karl Kautsky.

The Bolsheviks gave a fitting reply to the leaders of the Second International. In a number of statements, and in particular at the Amsterdam Congress of the Second International in 1904, the Bolsheviks plainly declared that Lenin's formulation of the first paragraph of the Party rules took into account the sad experience of the German Social-Democrats. The rules of the German Social-Democratic Party did not demand that a Party member should belong to one of the Party organisations, and the opportunist elements took full advantage of this to the detriment of the Party.

The Bolsheviks refused to build the Party after the pattern and image of the parties of the Second International. Carefully studying and critically assimilating the experience of the international and Russian working-class movement, they, under Lenin's guidance, boldly set about building a party of a new type.

In the summer of 1904 the Party was in a very difficult position. The Menshevik leaders had captured its central bodies and proceeded to split the local Party organisations. The disruptive activities of the Mensheviks were undermining working-class unity of action. This situation was all the more intolerable since the revolutionary situation in the country called for the consolidation of the Party forces and for militant unity of the proletariat.

An important part in uniting the Party was played by the conference of 22 Bolsheviks, which met in Switzerland in August, 1904, under Lenin's leadership. In its appeal "To the Party," the conference called on the Party organisations to start a campaign for the convocation of the Third Congress, which would put a curb on the Mensheviks and constitute a new leadership, one that would conform to the will of the Party.

Between September and December, 1904, three conferences, the Southern, Caucasian and Northern, met. Thirteen committees of the R.S.D.L.P. were represented at them. They set up a Bureau of Committees of the Majority under the leadership of Lenin. On December 22, 1904, the first issue of the newspaper *Vperyod* (*Forward*) appeared; it was a worthy continuator of the cause of the old *Iskra*. Its editors were V. I. Lenin, V. V. Vorovsky, A. V. Lunacharsky and M. S. Olminsky.

The Bolsheviks had the support of the big industrial areas and leading centres: St. Petersburg, Moscow, Riga, Baku, Yekaterinoslav, Odessa, the Donets coalfield, the Central Industrial Region and the Urals. Lenin had the full support of the bulk of professional revolutionaries. New Party forces developed in the struggle for Bolshevism. Having put such leaders as Plekhanov, Axelrod and Martov to the test, the Party, in its overwhelming majority, turned away from them and rallied around Lenin as its leader.

BRIEF SUMMARY

The decade preceding the first Russian revolution (1894-1904) was marked by major changes in the life of the people. Lenin noted that with the appearance of the working class as the most powerful revolutionary force in Russia, a new era had begun in the country's history.

The Russian revolutionaries' search for a correct, and truly scientific revolutionary theory over half a century, was completed by the middle of the nineties. At the cost of countless sacrifices, and by testing various theories in practice and critically comparing them, Russian revolutionary thought and the Russian working-class movement arrived at Marxism. There arose a mass working-class movement connected with Social-Democracy. Two trends emerged in Social-Democracy—the revolutionary Marxist and the opportunist trends. Lenin raised the banner of uncompromising struggle for Marxism, and formed in St. Petersburg the League of Struggle for the Emancipation of the Working Class, the embryo of a Marxist party in Russia. A new, Leninist stage in the development of Marxism had begun.

At the beginning of the twentieth century revolution was maturing in Russia; the working class was forging its ideological and political weapons for the coming battles. Under Lenin's direction, *Iskra* waged a victorious struggle against the "Economists" and prepared the ground for the founding of a Marxist party. The Second Congress of the R.S.D.L.P. served as the beginning of the existence of the Bolshevik Party, the party of social revolution and of the dictatorship of the proletariat.

The Bolsheviks waged a decisive struggle against the Mensheviks at the Second Congress and after it. The struggle of Bolshe-

vism against Menshevism was of the greatest historical significance. It was a struggle for a Marxist party of a new type, for
the leading role of the working class in the revolutionary battles
against the autocracy and capitalism. It was a struggle against
opportunism in the international working-class movement.

In the fire of this struggle, Lenin worked out the theory of
the Party as the principal weapon of the working class in the
struggle for the dictatorship of the proletariat, for the victorious
Communist revolution. In the person of Lenin there appeared
a great leader of the proletariat, a worthy continuator of the
teachings of Marx and Engels. Lenin's writings constituted an
enormous ideological treasure-store for the Party, and formed
its unshakable theoretical foundation.

The appearance in Russia of a revolutionary Marxist working-
class party was to be of momentous significance for the future
destiny of the country and of the international working-class
movement. For the first time in history the most oppressed and
most revolutionary class, the proletariat, entered a revolution
possessing its own independent Marxist party.

CHAPTER THREE

THE BOLSHEVIK PARTY IN THE REVOLUTION OF 1905-1907

1. The Revolutionary Movement in Russia on the Eve of 1905. The Russo-Japanese War. January 9. Beginning of the First Russian Revolution

Revolution in Russia had been maturing for many years. The economic and political situation in the country at the beginning of the twentieth century clearly showed that a revolutionary explosion was imminent. By that time capitalism in Russia, as everywhere else in the world, had entered its highest and last stage of development, imperialism, which is characterised by the extreme sharpening of all the social and political contradictions within the capitalist system.

Imperialism in Russia had its specific features. There existed a highly concentrated large-scale industry, in which capitalist monopolies were coming to play an increasingly powerful role. A small group of capitalists dominated the entire industrial and financial life of the country. This highly developed capitalism was interwoven with strong survivals of serfdom in the social and economic system. The chief of these were tsarism and landlord proprietorship, which left a feudal (serfowning) impress on the entire social life of the country. They gave rise to particularly brutal forms of exploitation of the proletariat, extreme poverty of the peasantry and gross oppression of the non-Russian nationalities.

The Russian proletariat was experiencing all the horrors of capitalist exploitation. The economic crisis of 1900-1903 added to the hardships of the labouring people. A large army of unemployed appeared, their number exceeding 200,000. During the years of crisis the wages of the workers were further reduced and their working day lengthened. Although, under the law of 1897, the working day was restricted to $11\frac{1}{2}$ hours, it was in fact not less than 12 to 14 hours at most of the factories.

In the crisis years the food, housing and living conditions of the workers grew still worse. Most of the workers continued to be crowded together in basements and factory-owned barracks. Even the bourgeois press was compelled to admit that "life in them differs little from that of convicts."

Lenin described the conditions of the working class at that time as follows:

"Thousands and tens of thousands of people, who have toiled all their lives to create wealth for others, are perishing from hunger and constant malnutrition, are dying prematurely from sickness caused by appalling labour conditions, wretched housing and lack of rest" (*Collected Works*, Vol. 5, p. 13).

Exceedingly hard was the lot of the working peasantry. A large part of the land, and the best at that, was concentrated in the hands of the landlords, the privileged nobility. In 1905, 10,500,000 peasant households, ruined and crushed by feudal exploitation, possessed in all just over 200 million acres of land while almost as much land—nearly 190 million acres—was held by 30,000 big landlords. The land shortage compelled the peasants to lease land from the landlords on most onerous terms. The peasantry paid about five hundred million gold rubles in money rent annually.

To bondage under the landlord was added bondage under the kulak. The kulaks concentrated in their hands half the total area of peasant land and more than half the total number of draught animals. The kulaks grew rich while the mass of the peasants were falling into pauperism. In the closing decade of the nineteenth century alone, the number of peasant households possessing no horses, or only one horse, increased from 5,700,000 to 6,600,000. Crop failures and famine were the constant lot of the bulk of the peasantry. Every year 8,000,000 to 9,000,000 peasants quit their villages to earn a livelihood elsewhere: at factories, on building railways, on lumbering and timber-floating, as unskilled workers in the towns and ports, or as kulaks' farm-hands or day-labourers.

For the slightest "offence" against the authorities or for tardy payment of taxes, the peasants were flogged and their property sold. Right up to 1903 officially, but actually even later, peasants were subjected to corporal punishment.

Describing the life of the peasantry on the eve of 1905 Lenin wrote:

"The whole forty years that have elapsed since the Reform have been one constant process of 'depeasantisation,' a process of slow and painful extinction of the peasantry. The peasants were reduced to beggary. They lived together with their cattle, they were clothed in rags and fed on weeds. . . . The peasants were in a state of chronic starvation, and died in tens of thousands from famine and epidemics during the bad harvests, which recurred with increasing frequency" (*Collected Works*, Vol. 4, p. 396).

Landlord and capitalist oppression was intensified by the arbitrary rule of the tsarist autocracy which crushed everything living and progressive. Standing guard over the interests of the exploiters were the army, the police, the courts—in a word, the entire machinery of the tsarist State.

The various forms of oppression—landlord, capitalist and national—combined with the police despotism of the autocracy, made the plight of the masses intolerable and particularly aggravated class antagonisms. The fundamental needs of social development and the vital interests of the workers and peasants imperatively demanded, above all, the abolition of landlord domination and the tsarist monarchy. Only a revolution could accomplish these tasks.

In the years immediately preceding the revolution the political activity and revolutionary inclinations of the working class and peasantry grew rapidly. The proletariat began to come out openly against all the exploiting classes and the tsarist government, and put forward demands that rallied all the country's democratic forces. In 1904 political strikes and demonstrations took place in several industrial cities. In December of that year a big strike broke out in Baku, led by the Bolshevik Committee. It ended in a victory for the workers. The action of the Baku workers set off solidarity strikes in St. Petersburg and other Russian cities.

By its revolutionary activity the working class set an example to the peasantry. The peasants in various regions of Russia began to rise up more and more often. The actions of the working class and the peasantry influenced other sections of society. A student movement developed, which demanded political liberties.

The Bolsheviks taught the proletariat to utilise, in the interests of the revolution, all elements opposed to tsarism, but at the same time they consistently exposed the policy of the liberal bourgeoisie and its striving to come to terms with the tsarist government.

The national bourgeoisie of Poland, the Baltic provinces, Finland, Transcaucasia and other regions were at that time more oppositionally inclined than the Russian bourgeoisie, for the tsarist monarchy was the vehicle not only of political and feudal oppression, but also of national oppression. The bourgeoisie of the oppressed nationalities would have liked to throw off the yoke of Russian tsarism in order to become masters of the situation and have a free hand themselves to exploit the working masses. But the development of capitalism within these nations was also bringing with it the development of a working class that was waging a class struggle not only against tsarism but against its "own" national bourgeoisie as well. The bourgeoisie of the non-Russian areas was therefore extremely inconsistent in its opposition, and only too ready to make common cause with tsarism. Thus, in Poland the big bourgeoisie, nobility and clergy, while seeking petty reforms for Poland, reconciled themselves to Russian tsarism because it protected their class interests. In Finland the bourgeoisie and landlords, for all that the Finnish people were oppressed, paraded their allegiance to tsarism. In Latvia and Estonia, the German landlord-barons were a bulwark for the tsarist government. Many of them, like the representatives of the landlord-bourgeois upper crust in Georgia and Finland, held important posts in the tsarist government.

The working class was the only force that fought consistently against all forms of national oppression, and for the complete self-determination of the nations oppressed by tsarism. Following the example of the Russian workers, the proletariat of the oppressed nationalities rose more and more often to fight against tsarism, against feudal, class and national oppression.

Under pressure of the rising revolutionary movement the tsarist government sought to enlist the support of the liberal bourgeoisie by making slight concessions to it. At the end of 1904 there began the so-called "liberal spring," the expression current at that time. The government allowed the bourgeoisie and the Zemstvo[2] bodies to hold congresses and banquets; at these the representatives of the liberal bourgeoisie and landlords made speeches about the need for a constitution, saying that it would be a good idea to have representatives of the bourgeoisie in the government.

The Mensheviks came forward with a plan for a "Zemstvo campaign." They urged the workers to go to these banquets in order to get the bourgeoisie to plead their cause with the tsarist government. The workers were thus assigned the role of trailing behind the liberal bourgeoisie.

The Bolsheviks, on the contrary, called on the workers not to attend the banquets of the liberals, but to go out into the streets and head all the militant, revolutionary forces in demonstrations against the autocracy. Thus, on the eve of 1905, the differences between the Bolsheviks and the Mensheviks had sharply intensified. Added to the differences over questions of organisation that had arisen at the Second Congress, and that continued to grow sharper, there were now differences over tactical questions, differences in defining the Party's policy in the rising revolutionary movement.

The outbreak of war with Japan in January, 1904, further aggravated social contradictions within the country and accelerated revolutionary events. The Russo-Japanese war was one of the first in the era of imperialism. Its underlying cause was the clash of interests between Japanese and Russian imperialism. For many years already the Japanese ruling classes had been plundering China. Japan was seeking to lay her hands on Korea and Manchuria, to entrench herself on the Asian continent. Tsarism, which Lenin described as "military-feudal imperialism," was, for its part, pursuing an annexationist policy in the Far East, where concessions were being secured in the selfish interests of the tsar and his immediate entourage. The Russian bourgeoisie was seeking new markets.

Foreseeing a clash with other imperialist States, Japan began vigorous war preparations. She enjoyed the financial and diplomatic support of American and British imperialism, which encouraged her to attack Russia, calculating that a war would weaken both Russia and Japan. Russia was not prepared for war. The tsarist government, however, continued to pursue its adventurist policy, thinking that war would help to check the approaching revolution. It reckoned that an "easy" victory over Japan would bring with it new colonies and new markets, would enhance the prestige of the autocracy and would help to smash the revolutionary movement in the country.

The tsarist government miscalculated. The Japanese imperialists, well informed of the unpreparedness of the tsarist army and navy, treacherously attacked the Russian Pacific fleet and the fortress of Port Arthur without declaring war, and struck a sudden and heavy blow at Russia's armed forces in the Far East.

The Russian troops fought bravely. But the tsarist army, unprepared for war and commanded by stupid and ignorant generals like Kuropatkin and admirals like Rozhdestvensky, suffered defeat after defeat. The rout of the First and Second Pacific squadrons, the defeat of the army near Mukden, and the fall of Port Arthur showed that Russia had lost the war. The tsarist autocracy was ignominiously defeated.

The war confronted the R.S.D.L.P. for the first time with the question of the attitude that the working class should adopt towards an imperialist war waged by the government of its own country. Lenin and the Bolsheviks gave a clear answer to this question. They showed that the war was being waged, not in the interests of the peoples of Russia and Japan, but in behalf of the tsarist autocracy and Russian imperialism on the one hand, and of Japanese imperialism and the ruling classes of Japan on the other. The Bolsheviks, therefore, agitated against it. They explained its unjust character to the people and called upon them to fight against the autocracy that was waging it.

The Bolsheviks were the only Social-Democratic Party to advance the slogan of the defeat of their own government in war. They maintained that the defeat of tsarism in the war would not signify the defeat of the people, that, on the contrary, the people stood to gain by it. The defeat of tsarism would lead to a revolutionary upsurge in Russia: it would help to overthrow tsarism and promote the victory of a people's revolution.

"The cause of Russian freedom," wrote Lenin, "and the struggle of the Russian (and world) proletariat for Socialism depends to a very large extent on the military defeats of the autocracy" (*Collected Works*, Vol. 8, p. 37).

In conformity with this line of Lenin's, the local Bolshevik organisations conducted explanatory work among the workers, peasants and intellectuals, as well as among the soldiers. They put out proclamations and leaflets in which they explained the real aims of the war and exposed the tsarist autocracy. The Bolsheviks called on the people to fight against the war and tsarism. The revolutionary Marxist position taken by the Bolsheviks in the Russo-Japanese war prepared the way for the correct policy which they adopted in the imperialist war of 1914-1918.

The Mensheviks' attitude was different. They advocated the slogan of "peace at any price," without linking this slogan with the revolutionary struggle against the autocracy. They thereby prepared the ground for the openly defencist platform which they were to take up in the war of 1914-1918.

The war was unpopular in Russia from the very outset. The revolutionary and democratic strata of the population all realised that the Russian army had been defeated because of the rottenness, not only of the war machine but also of the entire autocratic regime. Defeat in the war with Japan greatly undermined the prestige of the tsarist government.

The war brought new hardships for the working masses. It undermined the economy, dislocated transport, and drained the treasury; the cost of living soared. Real wages dropped by nearly 25 per cent. But the ruling bourgeois upper crust and commissariat officials were raking in enormous profits. In the countryside, mobilisation was depriving peasant families of their breadwinners, arousing resentment and discontent.

The war was the last drop that filled the people's cup of patience to overflowing. A profound revolutionary crisis matured in the country.

The tsarist government did everything it could to stem the revolutionary tide. With this end in view, it resorted to all kinds of measures, including the most unscrupulous. Thus, in 1904 a priest by the name of Gapon, on the instructions of the Okhrana, set up an organisation of St. Petersburg workers on the pattern of the Zubatov organisation. At the beginning of January, 1905, when a strike broke out at the Putilov Works, which was joined by other factories, Gapon provocatively proposed to the workers that they march to the Winter Palace and present a petition to the tsar.

The Bolsheviks could not prevent this. As a result of the splitting activities of the Mensheviks after the Second Congress of the R.S.D.L.P. there were three Social-Democratic organisations in St. Petersburg at that time: the St. Petersburg Committee of the Bolsheviks, the St. Petersburg group of the Mensheviks and a group of conciliators. This state of affairs in the Social-Democratic organisation was injurious to the working-class movement in the capital.

The Bolsheviks exposed the provocative Gapon venture and warned the workers that the tsar might resort to bloody reprisals against them. A leaflet issued by the St. Petersburg Committee in this connection read:

"Liberty is bought with blood, it is won arms in hand, in bitter battle. Do not beg anything of the tsar, do not even demand anything of him, do not humble yourselves before our sworn enemy. Cast him off the throne. . . . The emancipation of the workers must be the act of the working class itself. Don't expect to be given your liberty by the priests or the tsars. . . . Down with the war! Down with the autocracy! Long live the armed uprising of the people! Long live revolution!"

Under the influence of the Bolsheviks, who spoke at workers' meetings, the petition was supplemented by demands for a political amnesty, political liberty, responsibility of Ministers to the people, the equality of all before the law, the right of labour to fight capital, freedom of conscience, an 8-hour working day, and a number of other demands which coincided with the Social-Democratic programme. The petition ended with words that expressed the wretched lot of the working people: "Our patience is exhausted. The dreaded moment has arrived when we would rather die than bear these intolerable sufferings any longer. . . . There are only two ways open to us: to liberty and happiness, or to the grave. . . ."

However, at that time a large part of the workers still believed in the tsar. On Sunday, January 9, more than 140,000 St. Petersburg workers carrying church banners, icons and portraits of the tsar set out in peaceful procession for the Winter Palace.

The Bolsheviks' warning proved right. The unarmed workers, and their wives and children who came with them, were met, on the orders of the tsar, with rifle fire, sabres and whips. Over a thousand people were killed and about five thousand wounded.

A storm of indignation swept over the working people of the capital. "We no longer have a tsar," shouted thousands of people staggered by the brutal massacre. Workers began to arm. There, in the very streets of St. Petersburg, they heroically beat off the attacks of the soldiers and Cossacks.

Since then January 9 has been known as "Bloody Sunday." That day was a momentous one in the political awakening of the workers of Russia. On that day they realised whose interests the tsar and the tsarist government were defending. On that day their faith in the tsar was riddled by bullets. In answer to the shootings at the Winter Palace, a wave of protest strikes swept the country. On January 10 armed clashes between the workers and the troops continued in St. Petersburg. On the same day a general strike broke out in Moscow. On January 13 the proletariat of Riga went on strike and marched in a political demonstration. Seventy people were killed and some 200 wounded in ensuing clashes with the police. On January 14 a general strike broke out in Warsaw, and on January 18 in Tiflis, starting off a series of political strikes in Transcaucasia.

On learning of the events of January 9, Lenin wrote:

"The working class has received a momentous lesson in civil war; the revolutionary education of the proletariat made more progress in one day than it could have made in months and years of drab, humdrum, wretched existence. The slogan of the heroic St. Petersburg proletariat, 'death or liberty!', is reverberating throughout Russia ..." (*Collected Works*, Vol. 8, p. 77).

The events of January 9, 1905 roused the working masses throughout the country to a struggle against tsarism. In January alone 440,000 workers went on strike, that is, more than during the whole preceding decade.

After January 9 events developed rapidly. *Revolution had begun* in the country.

On May 1, 1905, political strikes under the slogan of "Down with the autocracy!" took place in nearly 200 towns of Russia. May Day strikes and demonstrations in the towns of Poland ended in big armed clashes with the troops. The strike in Baku lasted two weeks.

The struggle of the proletariat spread to the countryside, awakening a revolutionary ferment among Russia's one hundred million peasants. In February peasant revolts broke out in the Orel, Voronezh and Kursk gubernias. The peasant movement swept one gubernia after another. In the spring the peasants, taking the law into their own hands, began to till the landlords' lands, pasture their cattle on them and seize the meadows. The peasant movement was particularly powerful in the Volga region, the Baltic provinces, Transcaucasia and Poland. Meetings and demonstrations took place in the villages. Strikes of agricultural labourers, organised by the Social-Democrats, occurred in many places in the spring of 1905.

2. Bolshevik Appraisal of the Character, Motive Forces and Tasks of the Revolution. Third Party Congress

The strengthening of the Party and its policy in the revolution were of the first importance if it was effectively to lead the revolutionary struggle of the workers and peasants. But owing to the disorganising activities of the Mensheviks, the Russian Social-Democratic Labour Party was at that time split into two groups. Since its Second Congress the Party had been going through a serious crisis caused, as Lenin pointed out, by "the stubborn refusal of the minority of the Second Congress to submit to the majority" (*ibid.*, p. 409).

Lenin worked to secure the speediest possible convocation of a Third Congress, which should elaborate the tactics of the Party in the revolution already in progress and rally the Party on the basis of the R.S.D.L.P. programme.

All the Party organisations were invited to the Congress, but the Mensheviks refused to take part in it and met separately in Geneva. Since the number of delegates attending was very small (only nine committees were represented), the Mensheviks did not venture to call their gathering a congress, and described it as a conference of Party workers.

The Third Congress met in London from April 12 to 27, 1905. It was attended by 38 delegates representing 20 Bolshevik committees, chiefly of the big industrial centres. The work of the Congress was guided by Lenin. Among its delegates were A. A. Bogdanov, V. V. Vorovsky, R. S. Zemlyachka, N. K. Krupskaya, M. M. Litvinov, A. V. Lunacharsky, and M. G. Tskhakaya.

The Congress discussed the cardinal problems of the developing revolution and specified the tasks of the proletariat as the leader of the revolution. It dealt with the questions of armed insurrection, the attitude to be taken towards the tactics of the government on the eve of the revolution, a provisional revolutionary government, the attitude to be taken towards the peasant movement, the section that had split away from the Party (the Mensheviks), the question of open political action by the R.S.D.L.P., etc.

"The Russian proletariat," stated the announcement about the Third Congress which was written by Lenin, "will be able to do its duty to the end. It will be capable of taking the lead of the people's armed insurrection. It will not be daunted by the difficult task of participating in a provisional revolutionary government if it has to tackle this task. It will be able to repel all attempts at counter-revolution, to crush all enemies of freedom ruthlessly, staunchly uphold the democratic republic and achieve, in a revolutionary way, the realisation of the whole of our minimum programme. The Russian proletarians should not fear such an outcome, but passionately desire it. Our victory in the coming democratic revolution will be a giant stride forward towards our Socialist goal; we shall deliver all Europe from the oppressive yoke of a reactionary military Power and help our brothers, the class-conscious workers of the whole world, to advance to Socialism more quickly, boldly and decisively . . ." (*Collected Works*, Vol. 8, p. 405).

The strategic plan worked out by the Third Congress laid down that in the first stage of the revolution, the proletariat, in alliance with the entire peasantry, and with the bourgeoisie isolated, should fight for the *victory* of the bourgeois-democratic revolution, that is, for the overthrow of the autocracy and the establishment of a democratic republic, and for the abolition of all survivals of serfdom. The working class must not merely take a direct and active part in the revolution, and fight selflessly for its triumph; it must also take the lead. In the next stage, the proletariat must fight for the immediate development of the bourgeois-democratic revolution into a Socialist revolution.

The Russian bourgeoisie was incapable of heading the revolution and bringing it to a victorious finish, because it was not interested in overthrowing the autocracy: it sought only to restrict the power of the tsar and come to terms with tsarism. It was to its advantage to preserve the monarchy and the survivals of serfdom, on which it could rely in its fight against the proletariat. Only the peasantry could be an ally of the working class, for it sought to do away with the survivals of serfdom in the countryside, obtain the land of the landlords and get rid of tsarist and landlord bondage. And the peasantry could achieve this only with the complete victory of the revolution.

In keeping with this strategic plan, the Congress also worked out the tactical line of the Party, recognising the organisation of *armed rising* as the chief and most urgent task of the Party and the working class. Proceeding from the thesis of the leading role of the proletariat in the general democratic revolutionary movement, the Congress pointed out that "the task of organising the proletariat for direct participation in the struggle against the autocracy through armed insurrection is one of the main and most urgent tasks of the Party at the present stage of the revolution" (*C.P.S.U. in Resolutions*, Part I, p. 77). All Party organisations were called upon to explain to the proletariat not only the political significance of the impending armed insurrection, but also the practical aspects of its organisation.

The Congress noted the special role of mass political strikes on the eve of insurrection and during its course. It recommended adopting the most energetic measures to organise the fighting forces of the proletariat, drawing up a plan of armed uprising in advance, and taking steps to give direct leadership in it, setting up special groups of Party workers for the purpose.

One of the main tactical questions discussed at the Congress was that of the provisional revolutionary government which was to be formed following the overthrow of tsarism and the victory of the people's revolution. The Bolsheviks held that the provisional revolutionary government must be a government of the dictatorship of the victorious classes, that is, a *revolutionary-democratic dictatorship of the proletariat and the peasantry.*

The Congress defined the attitude of the Party towards the peasant movement in conditions of the rising tide of revolution. It put forward the demand for confiscation (that is, expropriation in favour of the peasants without compensation) of all lands belonging to the landlords, the treasury, the church, the monasteries and the tsar's family. This demand was a concrete expression of the Bolshevik Party's policy of an alliance of the working class with the entire peasantry in the bourgeois-democratic revolution. It promoted the development of the struggle of the peasantry against the autocratic and landlord system. The Congress called for the immediate establishment of revolutionary peasant committees throughout the country and for the implementation of revolutionary-democratic reforms from below. All Party organisations were instructed also "to strive for the independent organisation of the rural proletariat, for its fusion with the urban proletariat under the banner of the Social-Democratic Party and for the election of its representatives on the peasant committees" (*ibid.,* p. 81).

In this way the Bolsheviks were setting in motion the huge peasant reserves which were to fight, together with the urban proletariat and under its leadership, against the autocracy.

The resolution "On the section that has split away from the Party" condemned the opportunist views of the Mensheviks on questions not only of organisation but also of tactics. However, taking into account the vital necessity of uniting the forces of the proletariat in the developing revolution, the Congress at the same time considered it permissible for members of the Party who supported the Mensheviks, especially workers, to take part in the activities of Party organisations, provided they abided by the decisions of the Party congresses and by the rules and submitted to Party discipline. The Central Committee was instructed to dissolve those Menshevik organisations which refused to recognise the decisions of the Third Congress.

The Third Congress annulled the first paragraph of the rules as formulated by Martov at the Second Congress, and adopted Lenin's formulation of the first paragraph. This was to be of very great importance in the continuing struggle to cement the party of a new type. One of Lenin's basic organisational principles was thus incorporated in the rules of the R.S.D.L.P.

The Congress put an end to the existence of two central bodies in the Party (the Central Committee and the Central Organ) and elected one directing body—the Central Committee. In view of the fact that *Iskra* had fallen into the hands of the Mensheviks and was pursuing an opportunist line, the Third Congress instructed the Central Committee to establish a new central organ, *Proletary*. Lenin was elected editor of the paper.

At their conference in Geneva the Mensheviks made a different evaluation of the character, motive forces and tasks of the revolution. They maintained that the revolution in Russia, like earlier bourgeois revolutions in Western Europe, should be carried out under the leadership of the bourgeoisie and, in the event of victory, should place the bourgeoisie in power.

The Mensheviks denied that the proletariat had any independent tasks in the revolution. They held that the job of the workers was to support the bourgeoisie and not allow it to be frightened away from the revolution by determined revolutionary actions of the masses. They refused to recognise the leading role of the proletariat in the revolution and denied the revolutionary role of the peasantry.

The Mensheviks opposed an armed rising with particular zeal, an attitude which was fully in accord with their "theory of spontaneity" in the working-class movement and their negation of the active, leading role of the Party in the revolution. Insurrection, they said, is a spontaneous process and cannot be prepared in advance. Plekhanov, Axelrod, Martov and the other Menshevik leaders argued that an insurrection could only frighten away the bourgeoisie and that the Party of the working class should not prepare for it. In this, as in all other questions, the Mensheviks occupied essentially the same position as the opportunists of the Second International.

The Third Congress of the R.S.D.L.P. worked out the Party's policy in the revolution which had begun without the Mensheviks and in opposition to them. The Bolsheviks existed in effect as an independent party with its own programme, rules, and tactical line, with its own organisations, press and Central Committee. Two congresses—two parties: that is how Lenin summed up the situation in the Russian Social-Democratic Labour Party in 1905.

The Third Congress decisions, the Party's strategic plan and its tactics found comprehensive theoretical substantiation in Lenin's book *Two Tactics of Social-Democracy in the Democratic Revolution*. This work, a major contribution to the theory of scientific Socialism, was written in June-July, 1905.

In his book, for the first time in the history of Marxism, Lenin elaborated the question of the specific features of the bourgeois-democratic revolution in the era of imperialism, its motive forces and prospects. He subjected to devastating criticism the anti-Marxist, opportunist standpoint of the Mensheviks in questions of theory, strategy and tactics of the Party in the revolution, and also the reformist views of the leaders of the Second International, whose support the Mensheviks enjoyed.

In its character and aims, the revolution which had begun in Russia was a bourgeois revolution, that is, one aimed at abolishing the tsarist autocracy and eliminating the survivals of serfdom. It did not immediately raise the question of abolishing the capitalist system. Yet the bourgeois revolution in Russia, said Lenin, had a number of new features and peculiarities which fundamentally distinguished it from the bourgeois revolutions in Western Europe in the period of rising capitalism.

As distinct from the bourgeois revolutions in the West, the principal motive force and leader of the Russian revolution was the proletariat. Though bourgeois-democratic in character, the revolution in Russia was a proletarian one in respect of the leading role played in it by the proletariat, and the methods employed in the struggle against the autocracy (strikes and armed uprising).

The Russian revolution was at the same time a peasant revolution, since its chief aim was the abolition of landlord proprietorship. The peasantry was one of the motive forces of the revolution and the proletariat's immediate ally, for it could obtain possession of the landlords' land and achieve its emancipation from oppression by the autocracy and the landlords only under the leadership of the working class.

As for the bourgeoisie, its interests were closely intertwined with those of tsarism. Frightened by the revolutionary spirit of the proletariat, it was not, and could not be, a motive force of the revolution. With the advance of the revolution it lost more and more of its opposition spirit, made outright deals with tsarism and went over to the camp of the counter-revolution. By coming to terms with tsarism it sought to put an end to the revolution. "The victory of the bourgeois revolution is impossible in our country *as the victory of the bourgeoisie*," wrote Lenin.

"This sounds paradoxical, but it is a fact. The preponderance of the peasant population, its terrible oppression by feudal (semi-feudal) big landowning, the strength and class consciousness of the proletariat already organised in a Socialist party— all these circumstances impart to *our* bourgeois revolution a *specific* character" (*Collected Works*, Vol. 15, p. 41).

Proceeding from a scientific Marxist analysis of the basic and distinctive features of the Russian revolution, Lenin in his book discussed and elaborated the following questions:

the hegemony of the proletariat in the bourgeois-democratic revolution;

the alliance of the working class and the peasantry in the bourgeois-democratic revolution, and the alliance of the proletariat with the poorest peasants, and with all the semi-proletarian masses of town and country, in the Socialist revolution;

armed insurrection as the principal means of overthrowing the autocracy and achieving the victory of the revolution;

the revolutionary-democratic dictatorship of the working class and the peasantry, and the provisional revolutionary government as its political organ;

the development of the bourgeois-democratic revolution into a Socialist revolution;

the political party of the proletariat as the decisive condition for the latter fulfilling its role as leader of the people's revolution.

The fate of the revolution depended on whether the working class would play the part of leader of the people's revolution or that of a subsidiary of the bourgeoisie. Lenin foresaw two possible outcomes of the revolution: either a decisive victory over tsarism and the establishment of a democratic republic, or, if the forces were inadequate for a decisive victory, a deal between the tsar and the most inconsistent and most self-seeking elements of the bourgeoisie. The working class and the broad masses of the people were interested in complete victory over tsarism. But such an outcome was possible only if the proletariat became the leader of the revolution.

Lenin pointed out that in Russia the working class suffered not so much from capitalism as from insufficient capitalist development. The preservation of the survivals of serfowning relations hampered the development of the productive forces, and was an obstacle to the development of the struggle of the working class for a Socialist revolution and the victory of Socialism. The working class, therefore, was vitally interested in ridding the country of all survivals of serfdom as soon as possible.

In order that the proletariat might actually become the *leader of the revolution* it needed, first, to have an *ally* who was interested in the decisive victory of the revolution, and, secondly, to force out of the arena and *isolate* the liberal bourgeoisie, which was trying to end the revolution by a deal with the tsar at the expense of the workers and peasants.

"Only the proletariat can be a consistent fighter for democracy," wrote Lenin. "It can become a victorious fighter for democracy only if the peasant masses join its revolutionary struggle" (*Collected Works*, Vol. 9, p. 44).

Contrary to the Mensheviks, who asserted that the peasantry was reactionary, Lenin held that the basic interests of the peasantry made it a natural ally of the proletariat and a supporter of a radical democratic revolution. Landlord proprietorship could be abolished and democratic liberties won only by revolutionary means. And only the proletariat was capable of supporting the peasantry to the end in this struggle.

The peasantry was heterogeneous: besides the poor peasants, who constituted the bulk, it included the middle peasants and the rural bourgeoisie (the kulaks). This was one of the reasons for its instability. But the instability of the peasantry differed radically from the instability of the bourgeoisie. The peasantry was vitally interested in abolishing landlord proprietorship and completely eliminating the remnants of serfdom. Lenin scathingly criticised the opportunist policy of the Mensheviks, aimed at ensuring the liberal bourgeoisie the hegemony in the revolution and the substitution of petty reforms for revolution.

It was of greater advantage to the bourgeoisie, wrote Lenin, if the necessary changes in the direction of bourgeois democracy took place by means of reforms rather than revolution, ". . . if these changes develop as little as possible the independent revolutionary activity, initiative and energy of the common people, i.e., the peasantry and especially the workers, for otherwise it will be easier for the workers, as the French say, 'to hitch the rifle from one shoulder to the other,' i.e., to turn against the bourgeoisie itself the arms which the bourgeois revolution will place in their hands . . ." (*ibid.*, pp. 34-35).

In his book Lenin conclusively substantiated the proletarian forms and means of struggle which would ensure the victory of the revolution. Contrary to the Mensheviks, who clung to reformist methods, Lenin considered that the most decisive means of overthrowing the autocracy was *armed insurrection*. Tsarism relied on armed force: the army and the police. Only by force of arms, through a victorious armed rising, could this force be crushed, tsarism be overthrown and a democratic republic established. The revolutionary movement, Lenin pointed out, had already brought about the *necessity* for an armed insurrection.

7*

Lenin was the first since Marx and Engels to raise the question of organising armed insurrection as a practical task, to which all other Party activities must be subordinated during the revolution.

To rouse the revolutionary energy of the masses, to draw them into open armed struggle against tsarism, it was necessary for the Party to issue political slogans that particularly appealed to the people, and would be understood by them. The following, the Bolsheviks considered, were such slogans: immediate introduction, in a revolutionary way, of an 8-hour working day; the setting-up of revolutionary peasant committees in order to carry out democratic changes in the countryside, including the confiscation of the landlords' estates; mass political strikes; the arming of the workers and the formation of a revolutionary army.

Lenin considered it of exceptional importance that *an 8-hour working day* be introduced everywhere from below, by the workers themselves, and that democratic changes in the countryside be carried out by the peasants. These were new tactics, which called into play all the activity and creative initiative of the masses. Application of these tactics paralysed the State machinery, rendering it powerless to combat the revolution.

The use of the *mass political strike*, a specifically proletarian method of struggle that played a most important part in mobilising the masses for the struggle against tsarism, was a new and very important weapon.

Lenin treated the question of *State power*, the basic question of revolution, in a new way. He showed that a victorious bourgeois-democratic revolution in which the proletariat was the guiding force must lead not to the winning of power by the bourgeoisie, as had been the case in bourgeois revolutions of the past, but to a revolutionary-democratic dictatorship of the proletariat and the peasantry.

"A decisive victory of the revolution over tsarism," wrote Lenin, "is *the revolutionary-democratic dictatorship of the proletariat and the peasantry. . . .*

"And such a victory will be precisely a dictatorship, i.e., it must inevitably rely on military force, on the arming of the masses, on insurrection, and not on institutions, of one kind or another, established in a 'lawful' or 'peaceful' way" (*Collected Works*, Vol. 9, p. 40).

The achievement of revolutionary changes in the interests of the workers and peasants would call forth the desperate resistance of tsarism, the landlords and the big bourgeoisie. In order to break down this resistance, to repel attempts at counter-revolution, complete the bourgeois-democratic revolution, defend its gains and completely clear the arena for the struggle for Socialism, a dictatorship was essential. But it would be as yet a democratic, not a Socialist, dictatorship.

The political organ of the revolutionary-democratic dictatorship of the proletariat and the peasantry would be *a provisional revolutionary government*, relying on the armed people. Its task would be to consolidate the gains of the revolution, crush the resistance of the counter-revolution and give effect to the minimum programme of the Russian Social-Democratic Labour Party, i.e., establish a democratic republic, introduce an 8-hour working day and confiscate the landed estates.

Lenin held that it was permissible for, and under favourable circumstances incumbent upon, the Social-Democrats to take part in a revolutionary government. That would enable them to wage a relentless struggle against the counter-revolution, defend the independent interests of the working class and promote the further development of the revolution. At the same time it was necessary to organise pressure upon the provisional revolutionary government from below, by the working class and the broad masses of working people. Participation in the government and pressure from below would help to consolidate and extend the gains of the revolution, to put into effect the minimum programme of the Social-Democratic Party, and to prepare the ground for the bourgeois-democratic revolution passing into a Socialist revolution.

Exposing the harmful standpoint of the Mensheviks, who were opposed to participation in a revolutionary government, Lenin pointed out that it in fact implied yielding leadership of the revolution to the bourgeoisie.

In his book Lenin worked out *the theory of the bourgeois-democratic revolution developing into a Socialist revolution*. Marx's ideas on uninterrupted (permanent) revolution and on the alliance of the proletariat and the peasantry as an indispensable condition for such a revolution were consigned to oblivion by the opportunists of the Second International. To Marx's revolutionary ideas they opposed an opportunist scheme, according to which a long interval would separate the bourgeois revolution from the proletarian revolution. This anti-revolutionary scheme was based on a denial of the leading role of the proletariat in relation to the peasantry, a denial of the hegemony of the proletariat in the bourgeois-democratic revolution.

Lenin developed Marx's idea of permanent revolution into the consistent theory of the bourgeois-democratic revolution developing into a Socialist revolution. According to this theory, the hegemony of the proletariat in the bourgeois revolution, the proletariat being in alliance with the peasantry, would develop into the hegemony of the proletariat in the Socialist revolution, the proletariat now being in alliance with the poor peasants and the other semi-proletarian elements. The democratic dictatorship of the proletariat and the peasantry would be destined to prepare the ground for the Socialist dictatorship of the proletariat.

"The proletariat must carry the democratic revolution to completion, allying to itself the mass of the peasantry in order to crush by force the resistance of the autocracy and to paralyse the instability of the bourgeoisie. The proletariat must accomplish the Socialist revolution, allying to itself the mass of the semi-proletarian elements of the population, in order to crush by force the resistance of the bourgeoisie and paralyse the instability of the peasantry and the petty bourgeoisie" (Lenin, *Collected Works*, Vol. 9, p. 81).

In substantiating the theory of the bourgeois revolution developing into a Socialist revolution, Lenin showed that the objective conditions for this existed in the social and economic system in Russia. The numerous survivals of serfdom and the relatively high development of capitalism in Russia produced contradictions of two kinds. The contradictions between the development of the productive forces and semi-feudal relations of production created the prerequisites for a bourgeois-democratic revolution. The contradictions between the growth of the productive forces and capitalist production relations created the necessary objective conditions for the bourgeois-democratic revolution developing into a Socialist revolution.

Hence there arose social strife of two kinds. One was the struggle of the entire people against the tsar and the landlords, for a democratic republic; the other was the struggle of the proletariat against the bourgeoisie, for the dictatorship of the proletariat, for a Socialist structure of society. In 1905-1907, the nationwide struggle for the overthrow of the autocracy was the paramount task. The mission of the proletariat was to fight "at the head of the entire people, and particularly of the peasantry, for complete freedom, for a consistent democratic revolution, for a republic! At the head of all the toilers and the exploited—for Socialism!" (*ibid.*, p. 94).

Lenin repeatedly emphasised the necessity for the uninterrupted development of the revolution right up to the victory of the Socialist revolution. In his article, "The Attitude of Social-Democracy Toward the Peasant Movement," Lenin wrote:

"From the democratic revolution we shall at once, and in precise accordance with the measure of our strength, the strength of the class-conscious and organised proletariat, begin to pass to the Socialist revolution. We stand for uninterrupted revolution. We shall not stop half-way" (*ibid.*, p. 213).

The West European opportunists and the Russian Mensheviks held that in the Socialist revolution the proletariat would stand alone, without allies, against all the non-proletarian classes and strata. They denied the revolutionary potentialities of the semi-proletarian masses of town and country, who were exploited and downtrodden by the capitalists and who for that very reason could become true allies of the proletariat in the struggle against capitalism. Hence their wrong conclusion that the conditions for a Socialist revolution could be considered ripe only when the proletariat, as a result of the economic development of society, became a majority in the nation.

Lenin's theory of Socialist revolution confuted these exceedingly harmful opportunist dogmas, which doomed the proletariat to inaction.

Lenin considered that the existence of an independent political party of the working class, with the mission of leading and organising the revolutionary struggle, was one of the main prerequisites for the victory of the bourgeois-democratic revolution and its development into a Socialist revolution. The proletariat could play the role of leader in this revolution, Lenin pointed out, only if it were united into a solid, independent political force under the banner of a revolutionary Marxist party which guided the proletariat in its struggle, not only ideologically but in the practical sense as well.

Lenin's theory of Socialist revolution confuted not only the theories of the Russian Mensheviks and the reformists of the Second International, but also Trotsky's theory of "permanent revolution." Falsifying Marx's idea of permanent (uninterrupted) revolution, Trotsky denied the hegemony of the proletariat in the bourgeois-democratic revolution and the revolutionary role of the peasantry; he rejected the revolutionary-democratic dictatorship of the proletariat and the peasantry. He advanced the slogan: "No tsar, but a workers' government," which was Left in form but opportunist in essence. Such a skipping of the bourgeois-democratic stage of the revolution would only have led to the isolation of the proletariat from the many millions of peasants and to the defeat of the revolution.

Lenin's theory of revolution, worked out in 1905, armed the Bolshevik Party with a scientifically substantiated strategy and tactics. It already contained nearly all the basic elements for the conclusion that Socialism could triumph at first in a single capitalist country: the conception of the hegemony of the proletariat in the revolution, of the alliance of the working class and the peasantry, of the leading and guiding role of the party of a new type in the revolution, and of the bourgeois-democratic revolution developing into a Socialist revolution. In 1915 Lenin arrived at the conclusion that Socialism could be victorious in one country. Lenin enriched Marxism with a new theory of Socialist revolution, which became a powerful ideological weapon for the proletariat in the struggle for the victory of its cause.

3. Upsurge of the Revolution. All-Russian Political Strike. Formation of the Soviets. December Armed Uprising

The course of revolutionary events proved the decisions of the Third Congress correct. The tide of revolution mounted rapidly. The strikes assumed a more stubborn and aggressive character, and were marked by a high level of organisation.

In May 1905 a strike broke out in Ivanovo-Voznesensk. It lasted 72 days. It was an example of the staunchness of the workers, and was a rich political schooling for the masses. A Council of Workers' Representatives (deputies) was elected to direct it. In the course of the revolutionary battles it became one of the first Soviets of Workers' Deputies. The strike was led by the Ivanovo-Voznesensk Bolshevik organisation headed by F. A. Afanasyev and M. V. Frunze, actively assisted by the Bolshevik workers S. I. Balashov, Y. A. Dunayev and F. N. Samoilov. Workers came together openly at meetings to draw up and discuss their demands and their answers to the factory owners, and outline plans for further action. At these meetings Bolsheviks delivered reports and lectures on the tasks of the working-class movement. These meetings were a veritable "Socialist university" for the workers. The strike of the Ivanovo-Voznesensk workers was joined by the textile workers of Shuya, Orekhovo-Zuyevo and other towns. The tsarist authorities carried out a bloody massacre of the workers.

The shooting down of Ivanovo-Voznesensk workers roused a storm of protest throughout Russia. In June, 1905, the workers of Lodz erected barricades in the streets and for three days battled against the police and the troops. They were, wrote Lenin, "not only setting a new standard of revolutionary enthusiasm and heroism, but also showing examples of superior forms of struggle" (*Collected Works*, Vol. 8, p. 502). In the Urals, the metal-workers of Perm and Yekaterinburg (Sverdlovsk), the gunsmiths of the Zlatoust Works, the iron and steel workers of Nadezhdinsk and Nizhni Tagil, and the railwaymen of Chelyabinsk, Ufa and Yekaterinburg were at the head of the strike movement. As the revolution developed, the Councils of Workers' Representatives (deputies) that were set up in the spring of 1905 at Alapayevsk, Nadezhdinsk, Motovilikha, Nizhni Tagil, and other industrial centres of the Urals were transformed from strike organisations into organisations for revolutionary struggle.

The working class of Lativa fought heroically. In Nikolayev, Yekaterinoslav, Kharkov, Lugansk, Mariupol, Gorlovka and other towns, political strikes developed into clashes with the police and troops. In June a general strike took place in Tiflis. It was followed by others at Kutais, Batum and Chiatury. In June and July strikes spread to three quarters of the Baku oilfields and other enterprises. The general strike of the Baku proletariat in August was accompanied by armed clashes with the troops.

The working class of Russia emerged from these strikes politically more and more mature and steeled, gathering its forces for the decisive struggle against tsarism.

In the summer of 1905 semi-legal trade union organisations began to spring up everywhere. Even then, while defending the economic interests of the workers, the trade unions advanced a number of important political demands. The Bolsheviks took an active part in establishing the trade unions and in their work. This was to have an important bearing on the subsequent development of trade unions in Russia as militant class organisations of the proletariat.

By its consistent revolutionary struggle the proletariat was teaching the peasantry how to fight the tsarist system. The rising tide of the working-class struggle was followed by a wave of peasant movements. By the spring and summer of 1905 this movement had spread to nearly a fifth of all the uyezds, and by the autumn to more than half. Strikes of agricultural labourers broke out in Ukraine and the Baltic provinces. The peasant movement was on a particularly large scale in the Volga region, in many parts of Ukraine, in the Baltic provinces and in Georgia.

The combination of the proletarian movement with peasant revolts shook the tsarist army and navy. The Bolsheviks developed self-sacrificing activity in the army and navy in 1905. Many leading Party functionaries, among them I. F. Dubrovinsky, Y. M. Yaroslavsky and R. S. Zemlyachka, were sent to work among the armed forces by the Central Committee of the R.S.D.L.P.

The Bolsheviks employed diverse forms and methods of revolutionary work among the soldiers and sailors: they issued newspapers and leaflets, arranged meetings, set up study-groups. As a result, the influence of the Bolshevik organisations among the soldiers and sailors grew considerably. Contacts were established between them and the workers. The defeat of the tsarist army in the Far East intensified revolutionary feeling in the armed forces.

The first instance of mass discontent among the soldiers and sailors was the revolt on the battleship *Potemkin* in June, 1905. For the first time in history, the crew of a battleship raised the banner of revolution and revolted against the existing regime. The insurgent battleship came to Odessa. But the Bolshevik committee in the city, weakened by arrests, was not united at that time, while the Mensheviks did not organise any rising of the workers of Odessa in support of the insurgent sailors.

Despite the heroism of the sailors, the revolt ended in defeat, for it lacked proper leadership. It was but the first attempt at revolutionary action in the tsarist armed forces. But the very fact that a revolt had occurred was of the utmost importance. It made the idea of the necessity and possibility of the army and navy joining forces with the working class in the struggle against tsarism more comprehensible and acceptable to the workers and peasants, and especially to the soldiers and sailors themselves. The question of the formation of a revolutionary army was now on the order of the day.

After the revolt of the *Potemkin* the Bolsheviks increased their revolutionary activities in the armed forces. The summer and autumn of 1905 witnessed dozens of revolutionary actions by soldiers and sailors. The individual actions of workers, soldiers and peasants were growing into a general Russian revolutionary conflagration.

The tsarist government tried to divert the people from the revolutionary struggle by concessions and promises. On August 6, 1905, it issued its manifesto convening a State Duma (called the Bulygin Duma after the tsarist minister Bulygin, who drew up the project for it). The tsarist government also hastened to end the Russo-Japanese War. At the end of August, 1905 it signed peace with Japan.

The Duma was an attempt by the tsarist government to put an end to the revolution by diverting it to a monarchist-constitutional path. In convening a Duma, tsarism also sought to put an end to oppositionist ferment among the liberal bourgeoisie which, itself fearing the revolution, tried nevertheless to use it to frighten the tsar. The Bulygin Duma was intended to be an assembly of landlords, capitalists and a negligible number of rich peasants. It was to be no more than an advisory body, that is, it could discuss certain questions and give advice on them to the tsar. It was a flagrant travesty of popular representation.

The Bolsheviks called upon the workers and peasants actively to boycott the anti-popular Duma. They conducted their campaign around the slogans: an armed insurrection, a revolutionary army, and a provisional revolutionary government. The Mensheviks, upholding a parliamentary, reformist line of action, hailed the Duma as "a turning-point in the liberation movement" and advocated collaboration with the liberals in the farce of Duma elections. The tactics of the Mensheviks in regard to the Duma actually played into the hands of the liberal bourgeoisie, helping it to deceive the masses of the people and side-track them from the revolutionary struggle.

A conference of the Social-Democratic organisations of Russia, which met in Riga in September, 1905 to work out their tactics towards the State Duma, approved the Bolshevik policy of active boycott of the Bulygin Duma and condemned the Menshevik policy of participating in it. The tactics of active boycott were supported not only by the workers, but also by the peasants and the progressive section of the intelligentsia. The Bolsheviks utilised the boycott campaign to mobilise all the revolutionary forces for mass political strikes and preparations for armed uprising.

In the summer and autumn of 1905 preparations proceeded apace for a general political strike. The tremendous organisational and agitational work carried on by the Bolsheviks facilitated the progress of the revolution. At the end of September a printers' strike broke out in Moscow. It was supported by the workers of other plants and factories, and was accompanied by meetings and demonstrations. The workers had armed clashes with the police and troops in the streets of Moscow.

The September strike of the Moscow workers was a rich political schooling for the proletariat. The mass political strike, accompanied by revolutionary meetings, demonstrations and armed clashes with the police, became the most widespread form of working-class action. In the course of the struggle a Soviet of workers of five trades was formed: printers, metal-workers, tobacco workers, joiners and railwaymen. New sections of the working class were drawn into the political struggle under the leadership of the Bolsheviks.

On October 6 the Moscow Committee of the R.S.D.L.P. decided to call a general political strike in Moscow. The strike spread rapidly to all industrial centres and grew into an all-Russian strike. The railways came to a standstill. The factories closed down. The post and telegraph stopped operating.

The October strike grew into a powerful political demonstration on the part of the proletariat. It was carried out under the slogans: overthrow of the autocracy, active boycott of the Bulygin Duma, convocation of a Constituent Assembly and the establishment of a democratic republic. The strikers were joined by clerks, students, lawyers, doctors, engineers, etc. Over two million people took part in the strike. The All-Russian political strike conclusively revealed the Bolshevik Party's close ties with the masses and the vitality of its slogans.

It also revealed the strengthening ties between the workers of the different nationalities inhabiting Russia. Lettish, Polish, Ukrainian, Azerbaijanian, Georgian and Byelorussian workers, together with the workers of other nationalities, fought side by side with the Russian proletariat against their bitterest enemy, the tsarist autocracy.

Lenin explained the paramount importance of mass proletarian actions such as political and economic strikes and demonstrations. Such actions, he noted, play a big role in the defence of the vital interests of the working class and the masses generally, and also in the preparation for higher forms of struggle—the general strike, armed insurrection, and, hence, the struggle for power. The political and the economic strike, Lenin wrote subsequently, "mutually support each other, the one constituting a source of strength for the other. Unless these two forms of strike action are closely interlinked, there can be no really broad mass movement—one, moreover, that will be of *national* importance" (*Collected Works*, Vol. 18, p. 67).

In the course of political strikes the working class not only advances political demands that express its own vital interests, but also champions the common interests of the mass of the people. In political strikes the working class acts as the vanguard class of the entire people, as the leader of the popular movement.

Economic strikes likewise play an important part in the working-class movement. By taking part in them and securing better economic conditions, the masses are also drawn into the political movement.

The All-Russian October strike demonstrated the might of the working class as the vanguard fighter, organiser and leader of the struggle of the whole people against the autocracy. The strike paralysed the forces of the government. The sweep of the revolution grew ever more powerful. The tsarist government, frightened by the growing tide of the revolution, hastened to make certain concessions to save the autocracy. On October 17 the tsar issued a manifesto containing many false promises. The manifesto proclaimed freedom of speech, assembly and association and the inviolability of person. It promised to convene a "Russian parliament"—a State Duma with legislative functions.

The promulgation of the tsar's manifesto, Lenin noted, was caused by the establishment of a certain temporary equilibrium of forces: the workers and the peasants, having wrung the manifesto from the tsar, were still not strong enough to overthrow tsarism, while tsarism was no longer able to rule by the old methods alone.

The bourgeoisie gladly accepted this sop from the tsar. The big capitalists and the landlord magnates who ran their estates on capitalist lines backed the tsarist government, although they still continued to argue with it about the division of power. The tsar's manifesto suited them perfectly. They united into the "League of October Seventeenth," the party of Octobrists, that is, supporters of the tsar's October manifesto. Part of the capitalists, landlords, Zemstvo leaders and bourgeois intellectuals united into the Constitutional-Democratic Party (Cadets), the leading party of the liberal-monarchist bourgeoisie. The Cadets wanted the tsar and the landlords to share power with the bourgeoisie. To deceive the working masses, they falsely called themselves the "Party of People's Freedom." Their programme, however, did not even contain the demand for a republic.

Characterising the Cadet Party, Lenin wrote:

"The liberal bourgeoisie vacillates between the people and the government of pogrom-makers. In words they are against the government; in reality, they most of all fear the struggle of the people; in reality they want to come to terms with the monarchy, that is, with the pogrom-makers, against the people" (*Collected Works*, Vol. 11, p. 272).

The bourgeois parties saw in the tsar's manifesto an opportunity to direct the revolution into peaceful, constitutional channels, and to save the autocracy and the feudal system from downfall. They therefore extolled the manifesto of October 17 in every possible way.

The Bolsheviks called on the workers and peasants to place no faith in the paper "constitution" and to continue the struggle until they had overthrown tsarism. They declared that the government was deceiving the people. Instead of the promised liberties, the government, with the help of the police-sponsored organisations which demagogically called themselves the "Union of the Russian People" and the "League of Michael the Archangel"—and which the people christened the "Black Hundreds"—was beating up and murdering revolutionaries and advanced workers, and breaking up meetings. In order to disunite the forces of the people, the tsarist authorities were kindling enmity among the different nationalities, engineering bloody pogroms of Jews, provoking massacres between Azerbaijanians and Armenians.

After the first victory, wrested by the political general strike, the struggle had to be continued for the overthrow of tsarism. The workers, inspired by the Bolsheviks, energetically set about forming fighting squads.

The October upsurge of the working-class movement gave an impetus to the revolutionary struggle of the peasants.

The peasantry in Russia had no party of its own. The "All-Russian Peasant Union" and the "Trudovik group," which arose during the revolution, were not real political parties. The Socialist-Revolutionaries and Popular Socialists posed as the spokesmen of the peasantry, but in reality they expressed the class interests of the kulaks in the countryside. Reviving the old Narodnik theory about the supposedly Socialist character of the peasant movement, the Socialist-Revolutionaries denied the leading role of the working class in the revolution. Lenin and the Bolsheviks exposed the pseudo-Socialist character of the Socialist-Revolutionary programme, and criticised the vacillations and inconsistency of the peasant organisations. At the same time the Bolsheviks concluded temporary agreements with them in the fight against tsarism.

As the advanced detachment of the proletariat the Bolsheviks also championed the interests of the peasantry, both political (overthrow of the autocracy and the entire semi-feudal system which was the enemy of the peasantry) and economic (abolition of landlord proprietorship and the transfer of the land to the peasants). The fact that it was the Bolsheviks who upheld the interests of the masses of the peasantry was to have tremendous significance in the further struggle for the victory of the revolution.

The local Bolshevik organisations worked energetically to win the peasantry over to the side of the proletariat. Beginning with the summer of 1905 agrarian groups were set up by the Moscow, Kazan, Nizhni-Novgorod, Simbirsk, Saratov, Samara, St. Petersburg, Vladimir, Kostroma, Ivanovo-Voznesensk and other committees in central Russia, and by the Vitebsk, Minsk, Vilno, Poltava, Lugansk, Odessa and other committees in Byelorussia, Lithuania, Ukraine and Latvia.

The Bolshevik organisations conducted political work in the countryside: they distributed proclamations and leaflets, and set up revolutionary study-groups among the peasants. The Moscow Committee issued special instructions for Party members working among the peasantry. Most popular with the peasants was Lenin's pamphlet, *To the Rural Poor*, which was reprinted several times by local Bolshevik organisations.

The Bolsheviks intensified their activities among the soldiers and sailors. By the autumn of 1905 they had set up a number of Party organisations in the armed forces. The biggest of them were the St. Petersburg, Moscow, Finland and Riga organisations. Many more leaflets and appeals, addressed to the soldiers and sailors, began to be published. That autumn there were revolutionary outbreaks by the soldiers garrisoned in Kharkov, Kiev, Tashkent, Warsaw and other cities. Revolts broke out among the sailors in Kronstadt, Vladivostok and in Sevastopol.

It was during that rapid rise in the tide of revolution that the *Soviets of Workers' Deputies* first arose. They were brought into being through the revolutionary creative effort of the working class. Formed originally to direct economic and political strikes, and as organs of the delegates or representatives of workers of various factories, the Soviets became organs for preparing insurrection; they were the embryo of a new public authority. In defiance of all the institutions of the tsarist government, they issued their own decrees, orders and instructions and introduced on their own authority the 8-hour working day and democratic liberties.

Lenin, with his usual perspicacity, saw in the Soviets organs of struggle for the victory of the revolution, for Socialism, *organs of the dictatorship of the people*, and highly appraised their significance. Lenin theoretically elaborated the question of the Soviets. In this way the combination in practice of the revolutionary creative activity of the working class, which gave rise to the Soviets, and of the theoretical substantiation of the latter provided by Lenin and the Party produced a remarkable form of political organisation of the working class and labouring peasantry, a form that played an historic role in the struggle for the victory of the revolution, for Socialism. The Soviets of 1905, one of the greatest historic gains of the working class, served as the prototype for the Soviet power set up in 1917.

The Bolsheviks entered the Soviets everywhere, and wherever they succeeded in winning a dominant influence the Soviets became militant headquarters for mobilising the revolutionary forces and for preparing and carrying out armed insurrection; they became embryonic organs of a new authority. As for the Mensheviks, they regarded the Soviets simply as strike committees or organs of local self-government. The St. Petersburg Soviet, which was headed by Mensheviks (Trotsky, Khrustalyov), did not perform its main task: it did not become an organ of armed insurrection for the overthrow of the autocracy. The Moscow Soviet and the ward Soviets in the city, on the other hand, where the leadership was in the hands of the Bolsheviks, played an outstanding part in the revolution.

At the beginning of November, 1905 Lenin returned to Russia from abroad illegally. Immediately on his arrival in St. Petersburg he threw himself into vigorous activity. He directed the activities of the Central Committee of the Party, took charge of the editorial committee of the legal Bolshevik paper *Novaya Zhizn* (*New Life*) which at that time was in effect the central newspaper of the Party, addressed meetings of the Executive Committee of the St. Petersburg Soviet of Workers' Deputies, and took part in various Party meetings.

The October All-Russian political strike had brought the working class to the threshold of the highest form of class struggle, armed insurrection.

The Bolsheviks, giving effect to the decisions of the Third Congress of the Party, combined agitation and propaganda work with practical preparations for the insurrection. The fighting squads formed by the Bolsheviks became most active. Their members were trained in street fighting and musketry, and workshops for the manufacture of bombs, arms depots, etc., were organised. Fighting detachments and squads were formed in St. Petersburg, Moscow, Sormovo, Yaroslavl, Ivanovo-Voznesensk, the Urals, Ukraine, Siberia, the Caucasus and the Baltic provinces. The military and technical preparation for the insurrection was directed by the Fighting Group of the Central Committee of the Party.

The Moscow proletariat was the first to raise the banner of armed insurrection against tsarism. On December 5, a conference of the Moscow Bolsheviks, voicing the will of the workers, declared in favour of calling a strike and starting an armed insurrection. The Moscow Soviet declared a political general strike as from December 7 with the object of turning it into an insurrection.

More than 150,000 workers went on strike in Moscow in the very first two days. There were numerous meetings at factories, and street demonstrations. The first clashes with the Cossacks and the police occurred. Hurriedly mobilising their forces, the authorities launched an offensive. The proletariat of Moscow replied by putting up barricades. On December 10, the strike developed into an armed revolt. Bitter fighting ensued. The Presnya, Zamoskvorechye and Rogozhsko-Simonovsky districts, and the vicinity of the Kazan Railway, became the centres of the insurrection. About a thousand barricades appeared in the streets of Moscow. For nine days the workers waged a heroic battle.

Maxim Gorky, an eyewitness of the armed fighting, wrote: "I have just come in from the streets. Fighting is in progress near the Sandunov Baths, near the Nikolayevsky Station, on the Smolensk Market and in the vicinity of Kudrino. Good fighting! . . . Everywhere on the streets the gendarmes and the police are being disarmed. . . . The workers are behaving splendidly!"

Exceptional heroism and tenacity were displayed by the workers in the Presnya District, where the best of the workers' fighting squads of Moscow were concentrated.

The Moscow workers fought heroically. The whole world tensely followed the course of the insurrection, which was shaking the very foundations of one of the biggest monarchies. The tsarist government realised that the entire autocratic-feudal regime was in danger of collapsing, and dispatched large forces to crush the uprising. The arrival of fresh military units in Moscow fundamentally changed the balance of fighting forces in favour of the counter-revolution.

The insurgent workers lacked experience in armed struggle, they were short of arms, and their contact with the troops was inadequate. When, at the beginning of December, the Rostov Regiment, quartered in Moscow, revolted and the Moscow garrison was wavering, the organisers of the insurrection delayed too long, and failed to take advantage of the garrison's vacillation to win it over to the side of the insurgent workers. The tsarist government succeeded in keeping the Moscow garrison under control and in isolating it from the insurgents. It was also able to retain control of the St. Petersburg-Moscow Railway. The St. Petersburg Soviet, which was headed by the Mensheviks, did not raise the banner of revolt in the capital, nor did it paralyse the actions of the government. The Moscow insurrection did not develop into an all-Russian one.

The leadership of the insurrection as a whole lagged behind the growing spontaneous movement of the masses. At the beginning of the insurrection the leading workers of the Moscow Bolshevik Committee and organisers of the rising—V. L. Schantzer (Marat), M. I. Vasilyev-Yuzhin and others—were arrested. The Moscow insurrection turned into isolated revolts in separate districts, and followed defensive instead of offensive tactics. This doomed it to defeat.

The Mensheviks and Socialist-Revolutionaries brought disorganisation into the ranks of the insurgents. Soon after signing, under pressure from the workers, the call for a general strike and an armed insurrection, they announced the disbanding of their squads. On December 14, even before the arrival of troops from St. Petersburg, the Mensheviks demanded that the Soviet call off the insurrection immediately. The capitulationist attitude of the Mensheviks and Socialist-Revolutionaries contributed to its defeat.

In order to preserve the revolutionary forces, the Moscow Bolshevik Committee and the Moscow Soviet called for the cessation of the armed struggle as from December 19. Unshakable faith in the coming victory of the working class is expressed in the last appeal issued by the headquarters of the Presnya fighting squads: "We began. We finish. . . . Blood, violence and death will dog our footsteps. But that does not matter. The future belongs to the working class. In all countries, generation after generation will learn tenacity from the experience of Presnya. . . . Long live the struggle and victory of the workers!"

Following Moscow, insurrections flared up in December, 1905 and January, 1906 in other cities. On December 12, the proletariat of Nizhni-Novgorod rose in armed revolt at the call of the R.S.D.L.P. Committee. On December 13, an insurrection broke out at Rostov-on-Don. A political strike in Novorossiisk that started on December 8 grew into an armed insurrection. Power passed into the hands of the Soviet of Workers' Deputies, whose leadership consisted mainly of Bolsheviks. The Soviet was the organ not only of the uprising, but also of a new people's authority. The Novorossiisk of those days has gone down in history as the "Novorossiisk Republic." The proletariat of Ukraine took up arms against the autocracy. Particularly extensive armed actions occurred in the Donets coalfield and in Yekaterinoslav.

The revolutionary struggle of the Urals workers was best organised at Perm (at the Motovilikha Works) and at Ufa.

A bitter armed struggle was waged by the workers of Siberia, particularly at Krasnoyarsk and Chita, where strong Bolshevik organisations existed. There the insurgent workers were joined by the soldiers. In Krasnoyarsk a united Soviet of Workers' and Soldiers' Deputies was set up which became the organ of revolutionary power. The Soviet proclaimed freedom of the press, assembly and association, introduced an 8-hour working day, and disarmed the police and gendarmerie. In Chita the garrison went over to the workers. The Soviet of Soldiers' and Cossack Deputies, formed there at the end of November, was the virtual organ of power in the town. The so-called "Chita Republic" came into being.

In Poland and the Baltic provinces the armed struggle of the workers, farm-labourers and peasants reached vast dimensions. A wave of risings swept over Transcaucasia, where the Bolshevik organisations skilfully linked up the struggle of the workers with the peasant movement. The revolt of the peasants in Guria, where whole districts were in the hands of the insurgents, assumed a particularly stubborn character. In Finland the armed struggle against tsarism was widespread.

But all these insurrections were crushed with incredible ferocity by the tsarist government. The tsar earned the nickname of "Nicholas the Bloody," and it stuck.

The December armed insurrection, started on the initiative of the Moscow workers and headed by the Bolsheviks, was the climax of the revolution.

The Bolsheviks and the Mensheviks differed fundamentally in their appraisals of the insurrection. The Mensheviks condemned the heroic struggle of the Russian proletariat which had taken to arms. "They should not have taken to arms," declared Plekhanov. On the contrary, replied the Bolsheviks, they should have taken to arms more resolutely; it should have been made clear to the masses that tsarism could not be defeated by strikes and other peaceful means alone, and that the victory of the revolution could be achieved only through armed struggle. Lenin thought very highly of the December insurrection. He made a profound analysis of its positive aspects and the causes of its defeat, and called on all class-conscious workers to study its lessons and prepare for new battles.

The December uprising revealed the unprecedented growth of the political consciousness and organisation of the working class. A tremendous distance had been travelled since January 9. The working class had fought heroically, arms in hand, for the overthrow of the autocracy and for the victory of the revolution. The idea that the tsarist monarchy must be overthrown and the feudal system abolished was taking firm root in the minds of the working class and the millions of labouring people of Russia.

The December events proved conclusively that "freedom cannot be won without the greatest sacrifices, that the armed resistance of tsarism must be broken and crushed with an armed hand" (Lenin, *Collected Works*, Vol. 8, p. 504).

4. Building the Bolshevik Party in Conditions of the Revolution. Fourth Congress of the R.S.D.L.P.

Unlike the Social-Democratic parties in most countries, which had developed legally, the Bolshevik Party up to 1905 took shape and grew in conditions of underground, illegal work. Revolutionaries paid with years of imprisonment or penal servitude for the slightest attempt to organise workers' groups or to publish appeals or leaflets. Members of the Party and Party committees could not hold meetings openly. The local Party committee was appointed by the Central or the regional Committee of the R.S.D.L.P. Revolutionary newspapers, pamphlets and books were mostly printed abroad and brought into Russia secretly.

The conditions of illegality demanded the strictest secrecy on the part of all members of the Party, but this did not result in the Party becoming an exclusive organisation. In all its work it maintained close contact with the workers and other sections of the working people, and led many actions of the proletariat.

The rising tide of revolution created new conditions for Party work. The revolutionary struggle of the masses had won them freedom of assembly, association and the press. Meetings, conferences and congresses of representatives of various public organisations were being held throughout the country. Halls and auditoriums for mass meetings were being seized without legal authority. The summer and autumn of 1905 witnessed huge open-air meetings. They were openly addressed by Bolshevik speakers and by representatives of other parties, who stated the platforms of their respective parties and called on the masses to support them. The ideas of the Bolshevik Party were spread far and wide, and were winning an ever larger number of active adherents.

"In the spring of 1905," wrote Lenin, "our Party was a league of underground circles; in the autumn it became the Party of the *millions* of the proletariat" (*Collected Works*, Vol. 15, p. 132).

Taking advantage of the relative liberties won by the people, many Bolshevik organisations began to issue legal workers' papers: *Borba* (*Struggle*) and *Vperyod* (*Forward*) in Moscow, *Kavkazsky Rabochy Listok* (*Caucasian Workers' Sheet*) in Transcaucasia, *Krasnoyarsky Rabochy* (*Krasnoyarsk Worker*) in Krasnoyarsk, *Zabaikalsky Rabochy* (*Transbaikal Worker*) in Chita, etc. The Bolsheviks also began to put out in the Tatar language the paper *Ural*, which propagated Lenin's ideas among the oppressed peoples of the Volga region and Central Asia. The publication of leaflets and proclamations was considerably increased. During the period of the revolution the Bolshevik organisations issued more than two thousand different leaflets, the monthly circulation of which exceeded one million copies. On the initiative of the Bolsheviks, a considerable quantity of Marxist literature was published in St. Petersburg, Moscow, Kiev, Odessa, Rostov-on-Don, Tiflis, Baku, Tomsk, Irkutsk, Krasnoyarsk and other cities, in 1905-1907.

The new conditions necessitated changes in the structure of the Party and in its organisational work. In his article, "Reorganisation of the Party," Lenin outlined the programme for such a reconstruction. He proposed making every possible use of legal opportunities, setting up legal and semi-legal Party bodies, as well as a network of organisations close to the Party, but at the same time preserving the illegal apparatus of the Party. Lenin raised the question of drawing a mass of new members into the ranks of the R.S.D.L.P., first and foremost from among the workers. "Let the new spirit of young revolutionary Russia be infused through them," wrote Lenin. Wherever possible, election of leading Party bodies was to be introduced, and in place of the "circles" which had existed underground Party nuclei were to be formed, as the principal primary organisations of the Party.

The Party rearranged its work in conformity with the new conditions. The principle of democratic centralism began to be put into practice.

In the course of the revolution the Party grew, being joined by the best, advanced workers. Towards the end of 1905 the St. Petersburg organisation had a membership of nearly 3,000, the Moscow organisation 2,500, the Ivanovo-Voznesensk organisation nearly 900, the Baku and Kharkov organisations 1,000 members each.

More than 50 Bolshevik committees and groups functioned in Russia at that time, predominantly in the industrial centres. As for the Mensheviks, they enjoyed influence among the handicraftsmen, intelligentsia, students, urban petty bourgeoisie and the less class-conscious workers.

With the influx of many new workers into its ranks during the upsurge of revolution, the R.S.D.L.P. was becoming a mass party. Its young members only gradually learned of the existence of Bolsheviks and Mensheviks, with different views and platforms. They strove to understand what these differences were. The existence of separate local Bolshevik and Menshevik organisations using one and the same name—R.S.D.L.P.—caused confusion among the workers. Their class feeling told them that such a state of affairs could only weaken the working class, the Party and the revolution. But at that time the Mensheviks still regarded themselves as Social-Democrats; they did not openly reject the programme of the R.S.D.L.P., and worked to draw new members into their organisations. Some time was needed before the Party members could convince themselves, from their own experience, of the treachery of the Mensheviks and realise that the Bolsheviks were the sole spokesmen of the interests of the working class and of Socialism.

Soon after the Third Congress of the R.S.D.L.P. many members of the Party began to demand the unification of the Party. The movement from below of the Party masses and the advanced workers for Party unity was an expression of their desire to strengthen the Party and increase its prestige in the working class, to consolidate all forces for a successful struggle to win the revolution. The Central Committee of the Party, elected at the Third Congress, supported this demand. Lenin and the Bolsheviks were firmly convinced that in the end revolutionary Marxist principles would triumph in the R.S.D.L.P. and the Mensheviks would be isolated.

Describing the history of the struggle inside the R.S.D.L.P., Lenin noted:

"It should be said that the formal breaks with the Mensheviks in the spring of 1905 and in January, 1912, alternated with partial and complete unification in 1906 and 1907, and then in 1910, not only owing to the vicissitudes of the struggle, but also under the pressure of the rank and file, who insisted on testing matters by their own experience" (*Lenin Miscellany*, Vol. 35, p. 303).

Lenin and the Bolsheviks held that it was necessary to ensure that the entire R.S.D.L.P. take a revolutionary Marxist stand and guide the working-class and revolutionary movement in Russia. The Bolsheviks sought to win over the widest possible sections of the Social-Democratic workers to their side. Lenin put before them the task of inducing the entire R.S.D.L.P. to accept the platform of the Third Congress. He pointed out that victory of the Bolsheviks over the Mensheviks in those circumstances called for tactics of manoeuvre and compromise "but such manoeuvres and compromises, of course, as would assist, accelerate, consolidate and strengthen the Bolsheviks at the expense of the Mensheviks" (*Collected Works*, Vol. 31, p. 56).

A unity Congress was made imperative not only by these considerations. There were in Russia at that time, besides the Bolsheviks and Mensheviks, some other Social-Democratic parties, among them the Social-Democracy of Poland and Lithuania and the Lettish Social-Democratic Labour Party. These parties were not affiliated to the R.S.D.L.P., and acted separately. The interests of the struggle against tsarism, particularly at a time of revolution, demanded the unification of the efforts of all the nationalities inhabiting Russia, and the international consolidation of the workers of the whole country.

The next Congress of the Party was to decide the question of unification. The Bolsheviks did not succeed in holding the Congress at the appointed time, on account of the railway strike, and of the armed insurrection that had begun in Moscow. Having assembled in Tammerfors, the Bolshevik delegates held a conference of their own there, from December 12 to 17, 1905.

The Conference expressed itself in favour of Party unification, of "the immediate and simultaneous amalgamation of the practical (centres) and literary central organs on a basis of equality ..." (*C.P.S.U. in Resolutions*, Part I, p. 98). In its resolution on "Reorganisation of the Party," the Conference recommended the wide application of the elective principle and the principle of democratic centralism. Departures from this principle were considered permissible only in the event of insurmountable practical obstacles. In its "Agrarian Resolution" the Conference, enlarging on the decisions of the Third Congress, proposed that the provision of the Party's agrarian programme concerning the *otrezki* be replaced by the demand for the confiscation of all State, landlord and church lands.

At the end of December a joint Central Committee of the R.S.D.L.P. was formed. It was entrusted with convening the Fourth Congress of the Party.

Lenin considered it necessary that the Bolsheviks should come to the Congress with their own platform on all the major questions of the revolution, so that the workers might see clearly what the attitude of the Bolsheviks was and be able to choose between the Bolsheviks and the Mensheviks. In the second half of February 1906 Lenin drew up the platform of the Bolsheviks—a draft of the main resolutions of the Congress. The resolutions of the Bolsheviks called for preparations for a new revolutionary onslaught on the autocracy. The armed struggle of the broad masses of the people was recognised as the main form of struggle. The Mensheviks put forward their own tactical platform, which in essence rejected the revolutionary struggle. As a result of the discussion of the two platforms, a majority of the Party organisations supported the Bolshevik platform.

The Fourth (Unity) Congress of the R.S.D.L.P. met in Stockholm from April 10 to 25, 1906. It was attended by 112 delegates with the right to vote, representing 57 local organisations, and 22 delegates with voice but no vote. There were three representatives each from the Social-Democratic Party of Poland and Lithuania, the Bund, the Lettish Social-Democratic Labour Party, and one each from the Ukrainian Social-Democratic Labour Party and the Labour Party of Finland.

The Bolshevik delegates included V. I. Lenin, Artem (F. A. Sergeyev), M. V. Frunze, M. I. Kalinin, N. K. Krupskaya, A. V. Lunacharsky, S. G. Shaumyan, I. I. Skvortsov-Stepanov, J. V. Stalin, K. Y. Voroshilov, V. V. Vorovsky, and Y. M. Yaroslavsky. The Bolsheviks at the Congress were supported by F. E. Dzerzhinsky, a delegate from the Social-Democratic Party of Poland and Lithuania.

Among the delegates with the right to vote were 46 Bolsheviks and 62 Mensheviks. A small group of the delegates held an indefinite position. The numerical predominance of the Mensheviks was due to the fact that many Bolshevik Party organisations which had headed the armed uprising were unable to send delegates. Central Russia, the Urals, Siberia and the North —strongholds of the Bolsheviks—were represented by only a small number of delegates. The Mensheviks, who had the most numerous organisations in the non-industrial regions of the country, were able to send more delegates. The composition of the Congress determined the Menshevik character of most of its decisions.

The Congress discussed the agrarian question, the current situation and the class tasks of the proletariat, the attitude to be taken towards the State Duma and other questions.

Lenin delivered a report on the agrarian question for the Bolsheviks. He defended the demand for confiscation of all the landed estates and the nationalisation of the land, that is, the abolition of the private ownership of land and the handing over of all land to the State. The Bolshevik agrarian programme called upon the peasants to fight the landlords and the tsar. Nationalisation of the land, stated Lenin, like the solution of the agrarian-peasant question as a whole, was possible only with the overthrow of the tsarist autocracy, the seizure of power by the people and the establishment of a revolutionary-democratic dictatorship of the proletariat and the peasantry. Nationalisation of the land would not only destroy the survivals of serfdom. It would also sharpen the class struggle within the peasantry, and in this way help to rally the poor peasants around the proletariat; it would hasten the development of the bourgeois-democratic revolution into a Socialist revolution.

Some of the Bolshevik delegates (J. V. Stalin, S. A. Suvorov and others) supported the demand that the landed estates be divided and transferred to the peasants as their private property. Lenin criticised this demand of the "divisionists," noting that it was a mistake, though not a harmful one. The mistake stemmed from the premise that a long interval would elapse between the bourgeois-democratic and the Socialist revolutions, and failed to take into account the prospect of the bourgeois-democratic revolution developing into a Socialist revolution.

The Mensheviks advocated a programme of municipalisation of the land. According to this programme the landed estates were to be placed at the disposal of the municipalities, from which the peasants were to rent the land. The political harmfulness of this programme lay in the fact that instead of calling for revolutionary action it sowed harmful illusions about the possibility of solving the agrarian question in a peaceful way while preserving the reactionary central authority. Instead of the idea of an alliance of the working class and the peasantry, the Mensheviks actually preached a policy of peasant-landlord agreement. Lenin sharply criticised the Menshevik programme of municipalisation, and exposed its erroneousness and the damage it would cause to the revolutionary movement. The Menshevik agrarian programme received a majority of votes at the Congress. The Bolsheviks, however, secured the inclusion of their slogan of confiscation of the landed estates in the resolution, in place of the opportunist formula, "alienation," proposed by the Mensheviks.

The report on "the current situation and the class tasks of the proletariat" was also made by Lenin. The Bolsheviks were for exposing the parties of the liberal bourgeoisie and for an alliance with the democratic forces in the fight against the tsarist autocracy and the political parties supporting it. The Mensheviks, on the other hand, were ready to place the leadership of the revolution in the hands of the bourgeoisie.

The Bolsheviks put forward the task of combating the constitutional illusions about the Duma spread among the people by the liberal bourgeoisie, destroying confidence in the promises and laws of the tsarist government and exposing the hypocrisy and instability of the Cadet majority in the Duma. The Mensheviks, on the other hand, regarded the Duma as a "national political centre," capable of uniting and "co-ordinating" the struggle against the old regime. They advocated a course directed towards liquidating the revolution, seeking to switch it over to a parliamentary or Duma path. The role of the Mensheviks as the vehicles of bourgeois influence on the working class was particularly evident in this question.

The Fourth Congress adopted Party rules. The first paragraph of the rules was given in Lenin's formulation. The Bolshevik formulation on democratic centralism was introduced in the Party rules for the first time. It has been included in the rules ever since.

The Congress decided on unity with the Polish and Lettish Social-Democracies which had joined the R.S.D.L.P. as territorial organisations working among the proletariat of all the nationalities of their region. The Congress also adopted a draft laying down the conditions on which the Bund could join the R.S.D.L.P., but in a separate resolution emphatically opposed the organisation of the proletariat according to nationality. The question of admitting the Ukrainian Social-Democratic Labour Party into the R.S.D.L.P. was deferred and later became superfluous in view of that party's petty-bourgeois, nationalist character. The workers of Ukraine united and carried on the struggle in the all-Russian organisations of the R.S.D.L.P., where they were educated in a spirit of class struggle and proletarian internationalism.

The Fourth Congress of the R.S.D.L.P. thus demonstrated the triumph of the principles of proletarian internationalism proclaimed by Lenin and upheld by the Second Congress of the Party. One of the major achievements of the Fourth Congress was the merging of the Social-Democratic parties of the various nationalities of Russia with the R.S.D.L.P. This unity secured the Bolsheviks ideological influence on broad sections of the workers of all the nationalities in the country, promoted the internationalist education and close rallying of all the genuinely revolutionary forces of the proletariat, and facilitated the exposure and isolation of the opportunists, chauvinists and nationalists.

"A big practical undertaking of the Congress," wrote Lenin, "is the planned (and partly accomplished) fusion with the non-Russian Social-Democratic parties. This fusion will strengthen the Russian S.D.L. Party. It will help to eradicate the last vestiges of the narrow study circle principle. It will introduce a fresh current into the work of the Party. It will increase the power of the proletariat of all the peoples of Russia to a tremendous degree" (*Collected Works*, Vol. 10, pp. 344-45).

The Central Committee elected at the Fourth Congress consisted of three Bolsheviks and seven Mensheviks. The editorial board of the central newspaper, *Sotsial-Demokrat* (*Social-Democrat*), was formed entirely of Mensheviks.

The sharp struggle at the Congress between the Bolsheviks and the Mensheviks on all the fundamental questions of the revolution was of great importance in educating the proletariat, in exposing the Mensheviks and in advancing the struggle to build a Marxist party, a party of a new type. The cardinal questions of the revolution demanded an answer. In the course of the revolution the differences between the Bolsheviks and the Mensheviks grew deeper. The Mensheviks slipped lower and lower, revealing themselves more and more as agents of the bourgeoisie in the working-class movement.

Immediately after the Congress Lenin, on behalf of the Bolshevik delegates, addressed an appeal to the Party, making a fundamental criticism of the Menshevik decisions adopted by the Fourth Congress despite the protests of the Bolsheviks. He sharply criticised the programme of municipalisation of the land, and called on all Social-Democrats to secure at the next Congress a decision cancelling that programme. The Bolsheviks began to work within the R.S.D.L.P. to ensure that the next Party Congress should adopt correct, revolutionary, Marxist decisions and thereby reject the incorrect, Menshevik resolutions of the Fourth Congress.

Since the central newspaper of the Party was in the hands of the Mensheviks, the Bolsheviks began in August, 1906 to publish their own illegal paper, *Proletary*. It was edited by Lenin, and, in fact, became the central newspaper of the Bolsheviks. They also organised the publication of the legal papers *Volna* (*The Wave*), *Vperyod* and *Ekho* (*The Echo*).

Only formal unity was effected at the Fourth Congress. In reality, the Bolsheviks and the Mensheviks retained their own views and platforms on the vital issues of the revolution. The Bolsheviks continued to carry on a profoundly principled struggle against the Mensheviks and against opportunism in the working-class movement. They preserved their organisational independence and leading centre. The Mensheviks, for their part, had their own independent organisations. Lenin wrote later:

"Between 1903 and 1912, there were periods of several years in which we were formally united with the Mensheviks in one Social-Democratic Party; but we *never* ceased our ideological and political struggle against them as opportunists and vehicles of bourgeois influence on the proletariat" (*Collected Works*, Vol. 31, p. 53).

The Bolsheviks were guided by Lenin's proposition that the policy of unification must not be taken to mean mixing up Bolsheviks and Mensheviks, or confusing their ideological and political standpoints. Lenin and the Bolsheviks, taking into account the great harm caused by the increasingly opportunist line of the Mensheviks (support for the Cadet Duma, capitulation to the liberal bourgeoisie, and a policy of liquidating the revolutionary struggle), intensified their fight against this line.

5. Tactics of the Bolsheviks in Relation to the First and Second State Dumas. Fifth Congress of the R.S.D.L.P. Causes of the Defeat of the Revolution

After the defeat of the December armed insurrection the tide of revolution gradually subsided. But the causes which had given rise to the revolution had deep roots, and the revolutionary sentiments of the masses were strong both in town and country. The revolutionary struggle continued right up to the middle of 1907. The working class and the masses of Russia generally, who had risen in revolution, made a fighting retreat.

Tsarism intensified its onslaught on the forces of the revolution. Punitive expeditions and courts-martial were at work everywhere, the Black-Hundred pogrom-makers were rampant. The tsar's hangmen smashed up the Soviets of Workers' Deputies, the trade unions and other mass organisations of the workers, peasants and soldiers. Particularly savage was the persecution of the foremost representatives of the working class, the Bolsheviks. Thousands of them were sentenced to death, or shot without trial or investigation.

The tsarist government, in combating the revolution, did not confine itself to repressive measures. It also had recourse to reforms. On December 11, 1905, at the height of the armed insurrection in Moscow, a law on elections to the State Duma was promulgated. Tsarism hoped in this way to sow among the masses the illusion that they could achieve their demands peacefully, through a "Russian parliament." The government sought to deceive the peasants, who still believed that they could obtain the landlords' land through the Duma, to wrest them from the working class and thus to deal the revolution a final blow.

The electoral law deprived over half the population of the suffrage. Elections to the Duma were neither universal, nor equal, nor direct, nor by secret ballot. The electoral law ensured the overwhelming preponderance of the representatives of the land-lords and capitalists in the future Duma. The electorate was divided into categories known as curias, accoiding to property and class qualifications (landowner, urban, peasant and work-er). Electors were elected in every curia, but not on an equal basis. Thus, the landlords elected one elector for every 2,000 voters, the peasants one foi every 30,000 and the workers one for every 90,000 voters.

The stubborn struggle waged by the working class and peas-antry in 1906 raised hopes of a new revolutionary upsurge. In these circumstances, the Bolsheviks could not abandon their policy of the further deepening and extension of the revolution. In accordance with the decision of the Tammerfors Conference, therefore, they called on the masses to boycott the Duma, and made wide use of election meetings to carry on agitation for armed insurrection. As for the Mensheviks, they advocated semi-boy-cott tactics (participation in the election of delegates and elec-tors, but not in the election of members to the Duma). This inde-terminate and unprincipled attitude of the Mensheviks split the ranks of the workers and fostered harmful constitutional illusions.

The Bolshevik and Menshevik tactics towards the Duma were widely discussed in the R.S.D.L.P. in January and February, 1906 on the basis of the respective platforms. Most local Party organisations declared in favour of the tactics of active boycott. The more class-conscious and revolutionary workers, and a sec-tion of the democratic intelligentsia, boycotted the elections. The boycott, however, was unable to frustrate elections to the Duma. The principal reason for this was the absence of a mass revolutionary upsurge capable of preventing the convocation of the Duma. Another reason was the disorganising policy of the Mensheviks and the strong constitutional illusions of the peas-antry, a large section of which succumbed to the overtures of the Cadets. Analysing the experience of the revolution, Lenin admitted later that the boycott of the First Duma in 1906 had been a mistake, reality showing that the revolution had by then passed its peak.

The Cadet Party won a majority in the First State Duma. The Bolsheviks set themselves the task of exposing the activi-ties of the Duma, which was no more than a fig-leaf for the autoc-racy. Lenin considered the struggle against the constitutional illusions prevalent among the peasantry to be one of the Party's most important political tasks at that period. With the object of strengthening the alliance of the working class and the peas-antry, the Bolsheviks supported the Trudoviks—the peasant deputies in the First Duma who reflected the aspirations of the peasant masses in their fight for land.

The Mensheviks, proceeding from an opportunist appraisal of the motive forces and prospects of the revolution, regarded the Duma as the "rallying centre" of the revolutionary forces. The Menshevik Central Committee elected at the Fourth Congress called for support of the Duma in its intention to form a Cadet government. This sort of appeal could only bolster up constitutional illusions and engender false hopes of the possibility of a peaceful transfer of power to the people.

The Central Committee did not voice the will of the Party on questions concerning the State Duma. Most local Party organisations, proceeding from Lenin's appraisal of the Duma and the Bolshevik criticism of the Menshevik position, condemned the opportunist line of the Central Committee.

The convocation of the First Duma did not halt the revolutionary movement. The proletariat fought heavy rearguard battles against the onslaught of reaction, drawing its deepest reserves into the revolutionary movement. Taking into account the experience of the December insurrection, the Party intensified its work among the peasants, and particularly among the soldiers. At the end of 1905 and the beginning of 1906 a number of Party organisations in the armed forces began to publish newspapers for the soldiers and sailors: *Kazarma* (*Barracks*) in St. Petersburg, which was actually the central newspaper of the Bolshevik organisation in the armed forces, *Soldatskaya Zhizn* (*Soldier's Life*) in Moscow, *Soldat* (*The Soldier*) in Sevastopol, *Golos Soldata* (*The Soldier's Voice*) in Riga, *Zhizn Kazarmy* (*Barracks Life*) in Voronezh, etc.

In the summer of 1906 the peasant movement flared up with fresh vigour. Peasant unrest spread to 215 uyezds in the European part of Russia, i.e., to half the uyezds in that part of the country. Revolutionary actions continued in the armed forces. The biggest revolts of soldiers and sailors in 1906 broke out in the Baltic Fleet—at Sveaborg, Kronstadt and Revel (Tallinn).

The tsarist government took new steps to crush the revolution completely. On July 8, 1906, the First State Duma, from whose rostrum the tsarist government had often been criticised, mainly on the agrarian question, was dissolved. The counter-revolution then intensified its onslaught.

The revolution having begun to recede, the Bolsheviks changed their tactics. They decided to take part in the Second State Duma in order to use it as a platform for revolutionary agitation and for exposing the autocracy and the counter-revolutionary bourgeoisie.

The Bolsheviks launched an election campaign, using it to organise the proletariat and educate it politically. They advanced the idea of a "Left bloc" with the Trudoviks, stressing the revolutionary-democratic character of the agrarian demands of the Trudoviks who, as Lenin noted, in spite of their narrow petty-bourgeois outlook, "expressed something real and *progressive* at the present historical moment" (*Collected Works*, Vol. 13, p. 213).

The principal aim of the Bolshevik Duma tactics was to rid the peasantry of the influence of the liberal bourgeoisie and to form a revolutionary bloc of representatives of the working class and the peasantry in the Duma.

The Mensheviks advocated a bloc with the Cadets during the election campaign and in the Duma itself. By taking this stand they helped the bourgeoisie to spread among the people false hopes of the possibility of winning liberty without an armed insurrection.

The opportunist position of the Menshevik Central Committee on the principal questions of tactics aroused the indignation of the overwhelming majority of the local Party organisations, which demanded that an extraordinary Party Congress be convened as speedily as possible. In September, 1906 the St. Petersburg Committee, the Regional Bureau of the Social-Democratic organisations of Central Russia, the Central Board of the Polish and Lithuanian Social-Democracy, and the Central Committee of the Lettish Social-Democracy adopted an appeal for the calling of a Party Congress. This appeal was supported by many Party organisations.

The Fifth Congress of the R.S.D.L.P. met in London from April 30 to May 19, 1907. It was attended by 336 delegates representing 147,000 members of the Party (46,000 Bolsheviks, 38,000 Mensheviks, 25,000 Bundists, 25,000 Polish Social-Democrats, and 13,000 Lettish Social-Democrats). Among the delegates were 105 Bolsheviks, 97 Mensheviks, 44 members of the Polish and Lithuanian Social-Democracy and 29 members of the Social-Democracy of the Lettish territory. The remaining delegates represented the Bund and the other organisations of the Party.

As a result of the resolute struggle waged by the Bolsheviks under Lenin's leadership against opportunist trends and against a conciliatory attitude to them, and as a result of the day-to-day explanatory work conducted among the Party membership, a majority of the delegates from the big industrial centres (St. Petersburg, Moscow, the Urals, Ivanovo-Voznesensk, etc.) were Bolsheviks, while the Menshevik delegates represented, in the main, districts where peasants or artisans predominated.

The Congress was attended by a solid group of Bolshevik delegates: V. I. Lenin, A. S. Bubnov, I. F. Dubrovinsky, M. N. Lyadov, S. G. Shaumyan, J. V. Stalin, M. G. Tskhakaya, K. Y. Voroshilov, Y. M. Yaroslavsky and others.

Maxim Gorky, the great proletarian writer, took part in the work of the Congress. A true friend of the people, closely linked with the working-class movement and the Bolshevik Party, Gorky sympathised whole-heartedly with the revolution and rendered the Bolsheviks tremendous assistance. Lenin thought very highly of Gorky, with whom he maintained close contact over many years. Gorky more than once took issue with the Mensheviks, and openly condemned their opportunist line. He castigated the Cadets and the liberals, and waged a resolute struggle against tsarism.

The Polish and Lettish Social-Democrats supported the Bolsheviks at the Congress. However, the representatives of these parties occasionally vacillated and voted for the Mensheviks.

On the basic questions the Congress adopted the Bolshevik resolutions, which determined the Party's long-term policy.

The main question discussed was that of the attitude towards the bourgeois parties. Lenin delivered the report on this question.

The various parties in Russia expressed the interests of specific classes. The different attitudes of the Bolsheviks and the Mensheviks towards the non-proletarian parties also determined their attitude towards the fundamental questions of the revolution. Lenin held that a relentless struggle must be waged against the parties of the Black Hundreds ("Union of the Russian People," the "Council of the United Nobility," and others) and against the parties of the big landlords and the bourgeoisie ("League of October Seventeenth," the Commercial and Industrial Party, and others). As regards the Cadet Party, the party of the liberal-monarchist bourgeoisie, Lenin stressed that in fighting this party it was particularly necessary to expose its sham democracy and thus prevent the Cadets from leading the peasantry and urban petty bourgeoisie in its wake. The Mensheviks, on the contrary, proposed forming a bloc with the Cadets in the State Duma. At the Congress, Lenin exposed these capitulationist tactics of the Mensheviks.

Lenin took a different view of the Trudoviks, the name then given to representatives of the petty-bourgeois democracy in the Duma. The group consisted of deputies from the peasantry—non-party people, Socialist-Revolutionaries, and Popular Socialists. They wavered between submitting to the hegemony of the liberals and carrying on a resolute struggle against landlord proprietorship and the feudal State. Lenin proposed exposing the reactionary aspect of the Trudovik group, but at the same time considered it advisable, in particular circumstances, to conclude agreements with the Trudoviks, as representatives of petty-bourgeois democracy in the common struggle of the working class and peasantry against the landlords and the autocracy.

The Congress approved the Bolshevik resolution on the policy to be adopted towards the bourgeois parties.

The Mensheviks suffered a complete defeat on their idea of calling a so-called "labour congress." The idea was suggested by the Menshevik Axelrod and supported by other prominent Mensheviks. They proposed holding a congress of representatives of various workers' organisations, and forming at this congress a "broad labour party" representing the Social-Democrats, Socialist-Revolutionaries and Anarchists. Actually this would have meant the liquidation of the R.S.D.L.P. On the proposal of the Bolsheviks the Congress condemned the idea of a "labour congress" as being definitely prejudicial to the working-class movement. The Polish Social-Democrats (headed by Rosa Luxemburg) and the Lettish Social-Democrats supported the Bolsheviks on this issue.

The Bolsheviks won a big victory over the opportunists on the Party's tactics in the State Duma. The Congress declared that the activities of the Social-Democrats in the Duma should be subordinated to the struggle outside the Duma, that the Duma should be utilised pre-eminently as a platform for exposing the tsarist autocracy and the conciliatory policy of the bourgeoisie, and for proclaiming and popularising the revolutionary programme of the Party.

This was a new, revolutionary-Marxist course of action for the representatives of the proletariat in parliamentary bodies. It provided a model for the entire international working-class movement. It acquired particular significance in view of the fact that the West European Social-Democrats were sinking deeper and deeper into opportunism, renouncing revolutionary struggle and sowing illusions in the working class as to the possibility of power being won by parliamentary means.

The Congress also adopted the Bolshevik resolution on the relations between the Party and the trade unions. The trade union movement in Russia had been growing rapidly as a result of the revolution. By 1907 there were nearly 650 trade unions in the country. The further course of the revolutionary struggle greatly depended upon whom the trade unions would follow. The Mensheviks advocated "neutrality" of the trade unions. The Bolsheviks, on the contrary, held that the workers must be educated in a spirit of class struggle and the Socialist aims of the proletariat. The Fifth Congress decided accordingly that all members of the R.S.D.L.P. must help to induce "the trade unions to recognise the ideological leadership of the Social-Democratic Party . . ." (*C.P.S.U. in Resolutions*, Part I, p. 170).

The Congress elected a Central Committee in which the supporters of Lenin's line were in the majority. The C.C., however, also included Mensheviks and representatives of the non-Russian Social-Democratic organisations, who often vacillated between the Bolsheviks and the Mensheviks. In view of the unreliability of the Central Committee leadership, made up as it was of representatives of various trends, the Bolsheviks formed their own Bolshevik Centre at a conference that they held at the time of the Congress.

The Bolsheviks did not let their victory at the Congress turn their heads. Lenin stressed that they must not rest on their laurels in the fight against the opportunists, that many battles and trials still lay ahead.

The first Russian revolution continued for nearly two and a half years. It actually began to recede after the defeat of the December armed uprising. It retreated slowly, continuing to fight. By the middle of 1907 it was clear that the workers and peasants lacked the forces necessary to defeat tsarism. Reaction passed to an all-out offensive.

On June 3, 1907, the tsarist government dissolved the Second State Duma. The members of the Social-Democratic group in the Duma were arrested. A new law on elections to the Third State Duma was promulgated which ensured undivided sway in the Duma for the representatives of the feudal landlords and the big bourgeoisie.

The working-class organisations were smashed. Particularly savage was the persecution of the Bolshevik Party. The police authorities began a zealous search for Lenin in order to wreak vengeance on him. Forewarned by friends, Lenin managed, at the risk of his life, to cross the ice of the Gulf of Finland and to make his way abroad. In emigration for the second time, he remained there until April, 1917.

The first people's revolution in Russia had ended in defeat. One of the causes of its defeat was that the working class of Russia had not yet succeeded in forming a stable alliance with the peasantry in the fight against tsarism; the peasants' actions were scattered, they were not sufficiently organised and resolute. The major revolutionary actions of the peasantry occurred when tsarism had succeeded in crushing the strongholds of the revolution in the industrial centres of the country. The bulk of the peasants, extremely backward politically, still had faith in the tsar. Being under the influence of the Socialist-Revolutionaries and Cadets, they placed their hopes in the tsarist State Duma. Nor was there a sufficiently concerted revolutionary onslaught on tsarism by the working masses of the oppressed nationalities, whose forces were being undermined by the bourgeois and petty-bourgeois nationalist parties.

All this had an adverse effect on the conduct of the army, which consisted largely of peasants' sons clad in soldiers' uniforms. Even though some military units came out against the autocracy, most of the soldiers remained loyal to the tsarist government and executed its orders.

The working class acted as the leading force of the revolution. But the action of the workers, too, was insufficiently concerted; some sections of the workers entered the struggle when the vanguard of the working class had already been considerably weakened. Owing to the absence of a single all-Russian centre to direct the insurrection, the armed struggle assumed the character of scattered local uprisings.

Because of the splitting, disorganising activities of the Mensheviks, the R.S.D.L.P. was not united. The Bolsheviks fought to extend the revolution in every possible way, for the overthrow of tsarism by armed insurrection, for strengthening the alliance of the working class and the peasantry, for the isolation of the Cadet bourgeoisie, and for the formation of a provisional revolutionary government consisting of workers and peasants. The Mensheviks stubbornly opposed the revolutionary line of the Bolsheviks and acted as agents of the bourgeoisie in the working-class movement. The absence of unity inside the R.S.D.L.P. split the ranks of the working class and thus weakened its onslaught. For these reasons, the proletariat proved unable fully to play its leading part in the revolution to the end and to bring the revolution to a victorious conclusion.

A counter-revolutionary role was played by the Russian liberal bourgeoisie, which came to terms with tsarism.

Another factor contributing to the defeat of the revolution in Russia was the financial assistance received by the tsarist government from foreign imperialists, who feared the loss of their investments in Russian industry and the possible spread of the revolution to other countries. World imperialism had been the sworn enemy of the Russian revolution from the very beginning.

The conclusion of peace with Japan in August 1905 also served to bolster up the position of tsarism.

Despite the fact that the first Russian revolution ended in defeat, *the first breach had been made in the autocratic system.* By its heroic struggle, the proletariat won a number of political and economic gains for itself and for the entire people. For the first time freedom of speech, association and assembly was won in Russia, if only for a short time: a legal workers' press, educational and cultural societies, and trade unions came into being.

The revolution compelled tsarism to establish the first representative body, the State Duma. Even though the State Duma, whose composition was packed and whose rights were curtailed, was no more than a powerless appendage of tsarism, the Bolsheviks used it as a platform for revolutionary agitation and for exposing tsarism and the political parties of the bourgeoisie.

The proletariat won some improvement in its working conditions. Wages were raised in many industries. The peasantry as a result of the revolution secured the abolition of redemption payments, and a reduction of rentals and sale prices of land.

But the principal aim of the revolution, namely, the overthrow of tsarism, was not attained. The revolution conclusively showed the mass of the people that it was not enough merely to undermine tsarist rule; this rule had to be completely destroyed.

6. International Significance of the Revolution

The Russian revolution of 1905-1907 ushered in a new era, one of most profound political upheavals and revolutionary battles. The first blow delivered by it to tsarism, whose interests were interwoven with those of Western imperialism, weakened the imperialist system as a whole.

The revolution began a new stage in the international working-class movement, and exercised a powerful influence on the development of the national liberation struggle of the peoples of the colonies and semi-colonies.

The revolution produced a tremendous impression. It aroused the warm sympathy and received the support of the proletariat of Germany, France, Italy, Austria-Hungary, Rumania, Bulgaria, and other countries. "The working people of Paris, the city of revolution," stated a manifesto addressed to the proletariat of Russia, "are heart and soul with you, and address these words to you: Count on us! Our help is assured! Down with tsarism! Down with the exploiters! Long live social revolution!"

The Russian revolution was enthusiastically hailed by the representatives of French Socialist thought: Jules Guesde, Paul Lafargue, Jean Jaurès; by the leading figures of German Social-Democracy: August Bebel, Rosa Luxemburg, Karl Liebknecht, Franz Mehring, Clara Zetkin. "The liberty that Russia will gain will also mean liberty for Prussia, for Saxony, for Germany," said Liebknecht, calling upon the German workers "to rally under the banner of the Russian revolution."

The revolutionary events evoked a warm response among the working people of the Slav lands of Austria-Hungary, especially of Bohemia, Moravia and Galicia; the Slovenes and Croats began to rise up in a national liberation struggle. In November, 1905 mass demonstrations of working people, which in some cases were accompanied by open clashes with the police, took place in the major industrial centres of Austria-Hungary—Vienna, Budapest, Prague and Lvov. Under the pressure of the sweeping strike movement, the Austrian Government was compelled to introduce universal suffrage.

In Bulgaria under the influence of the Russian revolution a stubborn economic and political struggle developed under the leadership of the Tesnyak Socialists.[3]

In Rumania, the working people enthusiastically greeted the revolutionary sailors of the battleship *Potemkin* and, through them, the people of Russia risen in revolution. In 1907 a powerful peasant movement started in Moldavia and Wallachia.

In Germany, Italy, Austria-Hungary and other countries the workers, in defiance of the will of the Right Social-Democratic and trade union leaders, had recourse to political strikes more and more often.

The Russian revolution was of particularly great significance to the national liberation movement in the countries of the East. Between 1905 and 1912 bourgeois revolutions took place in the major countries of the East—Iran, Turkey and China. There began an upsurge of the national liberation movements in India, Afghanistan, Indonesia and other countries. Lenin noted that the mighty uprising of 1905 had left deep traces and that its influence, to be seen in the progressive movement of hundreds of millions of people, was not to be eradicated.

In 1912 the monarchical regime was overthrown in China. Describing the Chinese revolution, Lenin prophetically spoke of a great people "capable not only of bemoaning its age-long slavery, and dreaming of liberty and equality, but of *fighting* the age-long oppressors of China" (*Collected Works*, Vol. 18, p. 144).

The democratic revolutions that began in the countries of the East after 1905 shook the colonial system of imperialism.

The struggle of the Bolsheviks for a revolutionary solution of the fundamental problems of the Russian revolution, namely, the leading role of the party of the working class, the alliance of the working class and the peasantry, the hegemony of the proletariat, the revolutionary-democratic dictatorship of the proletariat and the peasantry, the development of the bourgeois-democratic revolution into a Socialist revolution, the leadership of the national liberation movement, forms and means of revolutionary struggle, dealt a telling blow to the opportunists of the Second International. The Bolsheviks disproved the views current in the parties of the Second International about the inevitability of the hegemony of the bourgeoisie in bourgeois revolutions, the reactionary character of the peasantry, and the inevitability of a long interval between the bourgeois and the Socialist revolutions.

The struggle of the Bolsheviks against opportunism facilitated further demarcation between the revolutionary and reformist trends in the Social-Democratic parties of Europe, and the crystallisation and development of Left trends (the German Left Social-Democrats, the Lefts in the British Socialist Party and others). The experience of the first Russian revolution helped the Bulgarian Social-Democratic Labour Party of Tesnyak Socialists to take a firm revolutionary position. By their example the Bolsheviks showed how opportunism should be combated and stable positions among the masses won.

Lenin and the Bolsheviks also exposed the centrists in the Second International. Among them were its official leaders, who were pursuing a policy of conciliation with and concessions to the opportunists. Lenin insistently urged the Lefts in the German Social-Democratic movement to break not only with the reformists, but with the centrists as well.

BRIEF SUMMARY

The first Russian revolution was an outstanding event which had a tremendous influence on the entire subsequent development of the country and the international revolutionary movement. It roused the broadest masses of the people in Russia to conscious revolutionary action, and enriched them with great political experience.

"So far as teaching the fundamentals of political science—both to masses and leaders, both to classes and parties—was concerned," wrote Lenin, "each month of this period was equivalent to a whole year of 'peaceful,' 'constitutional,' development" (*Collected Works*, Vol. 31, p. 11).

The revolution conclusively proved that the tsarist autocracy, and then the capitalist yoke, could only be overthrown by a revolutionary struggle of the masses, by the joint fight of the oppressed peoples of Russia.

The revolution showed the various classes and parties in action; it revealed their aims, role and significance in the life of the country. It showed the masses of the people what the different parties were fighting for, whose class interests they were defending.

The revolution graphically confirmed that working-class unity was an essential condition for the victory of the revolution.

The labouring peasantry, despite its vacillations, came forward as the ally of the working class. True, this alliance was still in the making, and as yet something spontaneous, formless and often unconscious. The forces of the workers and peasants were still scattered and insufficiently organised.

The proletariat, for the first time in history, came forward as the leader of the bourgeois-democratic revolution, having wrested the leadership of the masses of the people from the liberal bourgeoisie. It thus confirmed that the proletariat was capable of becoming the leader of the revolution, even if, owing to the inadequate development of capitalism, it numerically constituted a minority of the population. The revolution also proved the ability of the democratic masses of the peasantry to help the proletariat to win. The revolution clearly revealed the counter-revolutionary character of the bourgeoisie.

The first Russian revolution showed that the centre of the world revolutionary movement had shifted to Russia, and that the heroic Russian proletariat had become the vanguard of the revolutionary proletariat of the whole world.

The first Russian revolution advanced new forms and methods of struggle, unknown to previous revolutions. For the first time a mass political strike had been held which developed into armed insurrection. The Soviets of Workers' Deputies that were set up in the course of the revolution were not only organs of insurrection. They were also the embryo form of the revolutionary-democratic dictatorship of the proletariat and the peasantry. They were the prototype of the Soviet power that was established in our country as a result of the victory of the Great October Socialist Revolution.

Throughout the revolution the workers and peasants of Ukraine, Byelorussia, Poland, the Baltic provinces, Transcaucasia, Central Asia and other outlying regions of tsarist Russia heroically fought side by side with the Russian workers and peasants against tsarism and the landlords. The experience of the revolution confirmed the necessity for, and possibility of, a militant alliance of the working people of all the nationalities inhabiting Russia, under the leadership of the proletariat, for a joint struggle for national and social emancipation.

During this period Lenin elaborated the basic questions of the revolution and the course to be followed by the party of the working class in the struggle for the victory of the revolution.

The years of the revolution were a test for two political lines—Bolshevik and Menshevik. The course of the revolutionary struggle bore out the soundness of the strategic plan and the tactics of the Bolsheviks.

A most important landmark in the life of the Party was the Third Congress, which gave a Marxist-Leninist definition of the character and motive forces of the revolution. The Congress armed the Party with a revolutionary-Marxist strategic plan and tactical policy, which differed fundamentally from the opportunist policy of the Mensheviks. The Congress adopted Lenin's formulation of the first paragraph of the Party rules, which was to be of great importance in strengthening the Party.

At the Fourth (Unity) Congress, a number of non-Russian Social-Democratic parties merged with the R.S.D.L.P. in the interests of the revolution and of working-class unity, on the principles of proletarian internationalism worked out by Lenin. As regards unification with the Mensheviks within the R.S.D.L.P. only formal unity was achieved owing to fundamental differences of principle.

The Fifth Congress of the R.S.D.L.P. adopted Bolshevik resolutions on such important questions as the Party's policy towards the bourgeois parties, the trade unions and the so-called "labour congress." The Congress decisions and the relation of forces at the Congress reflected the successes achieved in disseminating Lenin's ideas, and the headway made by the Bolsheviks in winning over the masses.

During the years of the revolution the Bolshevik Party received a rich political schooling, and gained tremendous experience as an organiser of the masses. Prior to 1905 only a comparatively small circle of people had heard of the Bolsheviks, but after the revolution they became known to the broad masses. The Party became a mass party. The Bolsheviks battled selflessly for the interests of the people; they were always to be found in the forefront of the struggle, where the fighting was most dangerous. All this left a profound impression on the minds of the masses of the people, and later bore fruit during the Great October Socialist Revolution.

"Without the 'dress rehearsal' of 1905, the Revolution of 1917—both the bourgeois February Revolution and the proletarian October Revolution—would have been impossible" (Lenin, *Collected Works*, Vol. 29, p. 284).

CHAPTER FOUR

THE BOLSHEVIK PARTY
IN THE PERIOD OF REACTION

(1907-1910)

1. The Stolypin Reaction

Having dissolved the State Duma on 3 June, 1907, the triumph of tsarism was complete. The country was in the grip of a reign of terror—the terror of the Black Hundreds. The workers and peasants were put down without mercy. Punitive expeditions and courts-martial were at work everywhere, and meted out savage sentences to everyone suspected of association with the revolutionary movement. Thousands were executed for having taken part in the revolution, and tens of thousands sentenced to penal servitude. The jails were filled to overflowing. The exploiting classes were visiting cruel reprisal upon the working people for having dared to rise up in revolt. Stolypin, the tsar's Prime Minister, was dubbed "Stolypin the Hangman," and the people called the gallows he set up throughout the country "Stolypin neckties." The government's assault on the working class was especially brutal. Workers' organisations were hounded by the police with particular zeal. During the years from 1906 to 1910 the tsarist authorities banned 497 trade unions and refused registration to 604. Trade union membership dropped from 245,000 at the beginning of 1907 to 13,000 at the close of 1909. The tsarist secret police honeycombed revolutionary organisations with agents-provocateurs, who spied on the revolutionaries and betrayed them.

Police terror went hand in hand with a capitalist offensive. With industry stagnant (a slight recovery began only in 1909), unemployment increased. The employers' federations furiously attacked the workers. Factory owners proclaimed lockouts, closed down factories and laid off workers in masses. Militant workers were blacklisted, and could not find work in any factory belonging to members of the employer federations. Many of the pre-revolutionary practices were re-established: the workday was lengthened, wages reduced and fines imposed on the slightest pretext. "Our day has come, we're back in the saddle," employers brazenly told the workers.

However, the tsarist government could not fully re-establish the pre-revolutionary order of things. Russia was not the same as before 1905: the revolution had affected all classes and each drew its own conclusions from it.

The tsarist government and the feudal landlords realised that if they were to retain their power and profits they would have to adjust themselves to the capitalist development of Russia. Accordingly, they sought allies among the urban and rural bourgeoisie. The government launched a new policy associated with the name of Stolypin. The "Third of June" political regime and the new agrarian policy were its most distinctive features.

Tsarism needed the State Duma to consolidate the counter-revolutionary alliance of landlords and bourgeoisie and to mislead the backward sections of the population. But it needed a docile Duma. The new electoral law curtailed the rights of the people still further: in the gubernia assemblies of electors, at which the deputies were chosen, there was a standing landlord and capitalist majority, since the landlords and capitalists, through their respective curias, controlled more than three quarters of the votes, while the workers and peasants controlled less than one quarter. Representation of the oppressed nationalities was likewise drastically cut; the indigenous population of Central Asia was denied the franchise altogether, and the number of Duma members from Poland, the Caucasus and other national-minority areas reduced by nearly two-thirds. This monstrous electoral law produced the results the ruling clique desired. Nearly half the seats in the Third Duma were held by landlords, and together with the tsarist officials and the clergy they commanded a two-thirds majority.

The tsarist government also tried to find its own solution for the land problem, one that would enable it to grant land not to all the peasants and not at the expense of the landlords. The revolution had made it clear to the ruling clique that it could no longer rely on the peasants' blind loyalty to the "Little Father, the tsar," and it decided to build up a solid base of support for itself in the rural bourgeoisie, the kulaks. This found expression in Stolypin's agrarian policy, made formal in the tsar's edict of November 9, 1906, and the law of June 14, 1910.

Both were designed to further the interests of the landlords and the kulaks. The landed estates were not affected at all. The peasants were given the right to withdraw from the village communes and take possession of their allotments as private property. When a peasant left his commune, the latter was obliged to allot him land in a single tract (*khutor, otrub*).* The commune was thus being forcibly broken up, with the kulaks obtaining the best peasant allotments. No wonder the peasants dubbed the government land adjustment commissions "land-grabbing commissions" and the whole Stolypin scheme "misadjustment."

In the nine years 1907-1915 some 2,500,000 peasant householders withdrew from the communes, and nearly 46,000,000 acres of land became private property. Those most interested in this arrangement were the village bourgeoisie, for it enabled them to build up their farms. But part of the poor peasants, especially those working in the towns, also withdrew from the communes, sold their allotments and thus severed all connection with village life. The kulaks were able to buy these plots cheaply with advances from the Peasant Bank. However, the bulk of the peasants did not see a way out of poverty and exploitation in the new system, and despite strong pressure by the tsarist authorities, only about a quarter of the peasant farms in European Russia withdrew from the communes.

Stolypin's agrarian policy led to the further impoverishment of the peasant population and aggravation of class contradictions in the countryside. Weighed down by want, the peasant's farm remained as backward as ever. He had, as before, to eke out a miserable existence on a tiny plot of poor and exhausted soil, using old, primitive implements and obsolete methods. In 1910 there were about 10,000,000 primitive wooden ploughs on peasant farms.

Stolypin's policy was the second step, after the 1861 Reform, towards converting tsarism into a bourgeois monarchy. It was, in the words of Lenin, an attempt to open the last safety valve in order to prevent revolution and retain the power, property and privileges of the feudal landlords. But Stolypin did not succeed in turning tsarism into a bourgeois monarchy. In actual fact the tsarist autocracy remained a dictatorship of the diehard landlords, who ruled the country in close alliance with the big bourgeoisie. Stolypin's reform, far from removing the basic contradiction between the peasantry and the landlords, only sharpened the struggle within the peasant commune. Tsarism remained the chief enemy of the entire people.

---

* *Khutor*—a form of land tenure under which the peasant with his household moved out of the village to a single piece of land allotted to him from the village commune's holdings.

Otrub—a form of land tenure under which the peasant was allotted his main piece of land in one place, his household remaining in the village.—*Ed.*

The position of the various parties in the Third Duma was indicative of the class struggle after the revolution. The 429 seats were distributed as follows: Rights—144, Octobrists—148, Cadets and kindred groups—104, Trudoviks—14 and Social-Democrats—19.

The interests of the feudal landlords were upheld by the Rights, who openly supported the tsarist autocracy. It was they who organised the bloody massacres of workers and peasants, the Jewish pogroms, the persecution of non-Russian nationalities and the assassination of revolutionaries and progressives. The people rightly called them the Black Hundreds.

The bourgeoisie, tied to the landlords and the tsarist bureaucracy by a thousand economic links, and frightened by the leading role of the proletariat in the revolution, took up a counter-revolutionary position.

This determined the conduct of the Octobrist and Cadet members of the Duma. The Octobrists, who spoke for the big bourgeoisie and the landlords running their estates on capitalist lines, zealously supported Stolypin's policy, and were one of the government parties. The Cadets, who championed the interests of the liberal monarchist bourgeoisie, played the role of an opposition party and occasionally criticised individual government measures.

The Cadets tried to bring the masses under their ideological and political sway by fraudulent propaganda. But in reality the Cadets were counter-revolutionary liberals, kowtowing to the reactionaries. The Cadet members of the Duma supported the tsarist government on all cardinal political issues—its fiscal policy, allocations for the preparation of a new war, the agrarian policy that was ruining the peasants, and the measures it took to strangle the revolution. In 1909 a group of prominent Cadet writers put out a volume of articles entitled *Vekhi* (*Landmarks*) in which they declared: "We should bless the government which alone, with its bayonets and jails, protects us from the ire of the people."

The peasantry was anxious to get rid of the landlords and abolish landlord proprietorship. It had learned much from the revolution, but had not yet fully realised that victory was possible only under the leadership of the proletariat, and that the so-called "Party of People's Freedom," was really a party of traitors to the people's freedom. The Trudoviks, the petty-bourgeois democrats who represented the peasants in the Duma, were poorly organised, lacked adequate political understanding and were prone to swing from one policy to another. Their class status as small proprietors determined their vacillation between Cadets and Social-Democrats.

The working class was represented in the Duma by the Social-Democrats, among whom were both Bolsheviks and Mensheviks. Only the Bolsheviks voiced the interests of Russia's working folk consistently and unswervingly in the Duma. Lenin said that the task of the party of the working class in the Duma was to help the weak petty-bourgeois democrats, wrest them from the influence of the Cadets, and, in the struggle against tsarism, rally the democratic forces not only against avowed supporters of the autocracy, but also against the counter-revolutionary liberals—thereby influencing the peasant masses.

The reaction was manifest in every realm of public life, in science, philosophy and the arts. Tsarism carried on a rabid chauvinist (jingo) propaganda campaign. Aggressive clericalism was active. Counter-revolutionary sentiments, renegade ideas, mysticism and religion gained wide currency among intellectuals. The purpose was to erase all memory of the revolution from the minds of the people.

With the defeat of the revolution and the triumph of counter-revolution, the mass struggle abated. The tide of the working-class movement receded: the number of strikers declined drastically, from 740,000 in 1907 to 46,500 in 1910. The sharp agrarian struggle likewise subsided for a time. Fatigue after several years of extreme revolutionary tension was making itself felt, and time was needed for this to pass. But the workers and peasants had not forgotten those heroic years; there was an undercurrent of ferment among the masses. In reply to the Black-Hundred government terror and the tyranny of the employers, the workers used to say: "Wait, there will be another 1905!"

2. Struggle of the Bolsheviks for the Party Against the Liquidators, "Otzovists" and Trotskyists

The Black-Hundred government concentrated its fiercest attacks on the revolutionary party of the working class. Wholesale arrests began, several members of the Central Committee were sent to prison. The workers' press was throttled. Publication of *Sotsial-Demokrat*, the central Party organ, was resumed only in 1909. Not a single local Party committee escaped the police raids. The St. Petersburg Committee was arrested no less than ten times in these years. Many prominent Party functionaries found themselves in convict camps, prison and exile. Petty-bourgeois intellectuals deserted the Party. Membership fell considerably: in St. Petersburg, where the Party had nearly 8,000 members in 1907, there were only about 3,000 in 1908; in Yekaterinburg the figure dropped from 1,070 to 250, and in Ivanovo-Voznesensk the drop was from 2,000 to about 600. Contacts between Party organisations were weakened.

Working underground in this period of reaction was much more difficult than in the pre-revolutionary period. At that time Party organisations had worked in conditions of maturing revolution: now they worked in conditions created by its defeat. Conducting an offensive was one thing, forced retreat quite another: it called for particular staunchness and stamina. The organisational weakening of the R.S.D.L.P. was attended by serious ideological differences within its ranks. The gulf between Bolsheviks and Mensheviks became still wider.

The Mensheviks were utterly demoralised by the defeat of the revolution. They retreated in panic, proclaiming more and more loudly that there could be no question of a new revolution. They disgracefully renounced the Party's revolutionary programme and revolutionary slogans. Instead, they urged the working class to come to an agreement with the bourgeoisie, or, in other words, to accept in effect Stolypin's Black-Hundred regime. They were thus betraying not only Socialism but democracy as well. They pressed for liquidation of the illegal Party organisations and cessation of all illegal revolutionary activity. They were working for the abolition (liquidation) of the revolutionary party of the working class, the party of revolutionary Marxism. By renouncing the Party's programme, tactics and revolutionary traditions, the liquidators hoped to secure police permission for a legal party. No wonder they were dubbed the "Stolypin Labour Party."

Some Menshevik leaders, notably Dan and Martov, in an effort to conceal their liquidationist policies, began to publish abroad a new Menshevik paper, *Golos Sotsial-Demokrata* (*The Voice of the Social-Democrat*). There was thus a curious division of labour; the liquidators in Russia were entrenched in legal organisations and would not hear of an illegal party; the Menshevik paper abroad did its utmost to whitewash their anti-Party activities.

There were dangerous vacillations at this time among some unstable Bolsheviks. Resorting to revolutionary phraseology, they declared that only those who summoned the workers to the barricades were true revolutionaries, and that it did not befit revolutionaries to sit in the Black-Hundred Duma. Accordingly, they urged the Party to renounce legal forms of work and to recall the Social-Democrats from the Duma. The "otzovists," as they were called (*otozvat* means to recall), formed a group of their own, led by A. A. Bogdanov, which began an attack on Lenin and the Party's Leninist policy. But they proved to be an insignificant minority within the Bolshevik ranks. Whereas the liquidators openly advocated abolishing the illegal Party, the "otzovists" endangered its existence in another underhand way: by refusing to utilise legal opportunities for work among the masses, the Party would be cut off from the latter which would mean that it would degenerate into a sectarian organisation with little or no influence. That is why Lenin described the "otzovists" as "liquidators inside out."

Liquidationism and "otzovism" had their class roots. Numerous petty-bourgeois fellow-travellers joined the Party during the revolution. Its defeat led to confusion and demoralisation among the petty bourgeoisie, and this found expression within the Party. The Mensheviks were obediently following the liberal bourgeoisie, and under the direct influence of counter-revolutionary bourgeois liberalism, Menshevik opportunism developed into liquidationism. Both liquidators and "otzovists" were petty-bourgeois fellow-travellers of the proletariat and its party, agents of the bourgeoisie within the working-class movement.

With the revolution defeated and the masses tired out by struggle, ideological waverings were especially harmful. They represented a grave danger to the Marxist party and the working class. The liquidators were implanting a defeatist philosophy of surrender to tsarism. The "otzovists" were impelling the movement towards rash and adventurist actions. Both were instilling disbelief in the revolutionary potentialities of the masses and in the victory of the working class. They were challenging the very existence of the Party.

In these trying times Lenin's voice resounded as a clarion call to the Party. In the very first article written on his arrival abroad, Lenin foretold that victory lay ahead. He addressed these words to the Party:

"We knew how to work during the long years preceding the revolution. Not for nothing do they say that we are as firm as a rock. The Social-Democrats have built a proletarian party which will not be disheartened by the failure of the first armed onslaught, will not lose its head, nor be carried away by adventures. This party is marching to Socialism without tying itself or its destiny to the outcome of any particular period of bourgeois revolutions. That is precisely why it is also free of the weaker aspects of bourgeois revolution. And this proletarian party is marching to victory" (*Collected Works*, Vol. 13, p. 409).

Lenin gave the Party a clear perspective for its continued struggle, defined its objectives and tactics in the new conditions.

The fundamental causes of the revolution remained: the people still had no rights, the peasants were still under the landlord yoke and the workers under the double yoke of employer and gendarme. A new revolutionary upsurge was inevitable. The Bolsheviks' basic political objectives remained the same as in 1905, namely, the complete triumph of the bourgeois-democratic revolution and its development into a Socialist revolution. The demands of the Party's revolutionary programme retained all their validity: a democratic republic, confiscation of the landed estates and their distribution among the peasants, the 8-hour day, the right of nations to self-determination, up to and including secession, and other demands that accorded with the interests of the people.

But the revolutionary struggle had to be continued in new and changed conditions, in a situation when reaction had triumphed and the mass movement was on the decline. This meant that the Party's tactics during the revolution—appeal to the masses for the direct attack on the tsarist monarchy—had to be altered. It was necessary to retreat, to pass from direct revolutionary struggle to outflanking methods. A new revolution had to be prepared, by perseverance in training and organisation of the working class and the working people generally. To do that the illegal Party would have to make maximum use of every available legal opportunity—the State Duma, the trade unions, co-operatives, workers' clubs and other legal bodies. The Bolsheviks would have to learn to combine illegal work with legal, under the direction of the illegal Party organisations. Lenin worked out and substantiated these flexible tactics, designed to preserve and muster the Party's forces for the starting of a new revolutionary offensive when conditions were favourable.

The revolutionary Marxist party was faced with a problem which it had never yet had to solve—to carry out an orderly retreat and, at the same time, utilise all legal forms of work and organisation in the interests of the revolution. This required the preservation and strengthening of an illegal Party closely linked with the masses. And the Bolsheviks, led by Lenin, carried out this policy in a fight on two fronts—against the liquidators and the "otzovists."

The turning-point in the Party's development in these years of reaction was the Fifth All-Russian Conference of the R.S.D.L.P. held in Paris in December, 1908, and at which Bolsheviks, Mensheviks, Polish Social-Democrats and the Bund were represented. The Conference was attended by delegates from such major Party organisations as those of St. Petersburg, Moscow, the Central Industrial Region, the Urals and the Caucasus. The main report was delivered by Lenin. On the basis of this report, and after a sharp struggle against the Menshevik liquidators, the Conference adopted resolutions, which determined the Party's revolutionary line and organisation policy for the entire period of reaction.

A new revolutionary crisis was inevitable, the Conference declared, and the Party would continue to pursue its old revolutionary objectives. The first task to be undertaken was sustained work on training, organising and uniting the proletariat, peasantry and soldiers and utilising such legal opportunities as existed. On Lenin's proposal, the Conference condemned liquidationism as an anti-Party trend and called on all Party organisations to wage an implacable struggle against it. At the same time, the Conference resolutely dissociated itself from "otzovism."

The Conference signified a big victory for Bolshevism over Menshevism; its decisions guided the Party throughout the difficult years of reaction.

The fight against "otzovism" was of great importance for the Bolshevik Party. A section of the workers of Moscow, St. Petersburg, Odessa and several other industrial centres felt that the Party should not participate in the Black-Hundred Duma; but Lenin pointed out that their resentment of the Black-Hundred Duma and the activity of the Social-Democratic group within it should be clearly distinguished from "otzovism" as a political trend. "We will not allow this justified resentment to lead us into a wrong policy," he said (*Collected Works*, Vol. 15, p. 272). These workers' sentiments, Lenin pointed out, would soon pass; experience would show, and the Bolsheviks would explain, the need for making use of the Duma. As for "otzovism" as a political trend, a relentless ideological fight must be carried on against it. Lenin taught the Bolsheviks to abhor "revolutionary phrase-mongering" and to realise that a genuine revolutionary must be able to perform his duty even in the most difficult, inconspicuous and prosaic everyday activities.

A conference of the enlarged editorial board of the Bolshevik newspaper *Proletary* (which in fact was the Bolshevik centre) was held in Paris in June, 1909, to work out policy for the new conditions and to rally the Bolshevik forces for struggle against the "otzovists." Attended by delegates from St. Petersburg, the Moscow Region and the Urals, it expelled the "otzovists" from the Bolshevik organisation, declaring that "otzovism" was incompatible with Bolshevism, and urged all Bolsheviks resolutely to combat this defection from revolutionary Marxism. The "otzovists" began the publication of a paper of their own, *Vperyod*, and came to be known as the *Vperyod*-ist faction.

In connection with the new developments in the life of the Party, the conference mapped out the new tasks facing the Bolsheviks in their struggle for the Party. In a number of organisations (the Vyborg District of St. Petersburg, Moscow, Yekaterinoslav, Kiev, Baku, Ufa, etc.), Menshevik workers had declared against the liquidators; they began to be called pro-Party Mensheviks. Plekhanov also criticised the liquidators. In view of this, the conference, without obscuring the fundamental differences between the Bolsheviks and the Mensheviks in any way, called for a tactical bloc of Bolsheviks and pro-Party Mensheviks in the struggle to preserve and strengthen the illegal Party.

At that time there were many workers who did not clearly realise what divided the Bolsheviks and the Mensheviks, and were still under Menshevik influence. But there was a growing realisation that the liquidators had betrayed Socialism and democracy and were out to destroy the illegal Party, into the building of which the working class had put its best forces. As time went on, these workers became more and more convinced that it was only the Bolsheviks who, in the hard years of reaction, were staunchly and unswervingly upholding the interests of the Party in a determined and uncompromising struggle against the liquidators. The workers rallied around the Bolsheviks.

Meanwhile the struggle against the Mensheviks grew more and more acute. The liquidators were supported by the centrists. Centrism, a trend in the Second International, represented the ideology and policy of subordinating the proletarian to the petty-bourgeois elements in one common party. The centrists in words professed their loyalty to Marxism, but in practice they distorted it. They refused to combat opportunism, thereby facilitating its triumph in the West European Social-Democratic parties. Lenin trenchantly criticised Kautsky's centrist stand on the cardinal problems of Marxism and the international working-class movement. In Russia, centrism was being spread by Trotsky. Through his newspaper *Pravda*, published in Vienna, he tried to instil the pernicious and harmful "theory" that revolutionaries and opportunists could coexist in one common party, and advocated unity on an unprincipled basis. Trotsky called himself an "extra-factional" Social-Democrat, but his advocacy of conciliation was merely a screen for his liquidationism. He was exposed by Lenin, who showed that Trotsky's claim to stand above factions was a form of liquidationism and support for the Mensheviks. Lenin branded him "Judas Trotsky," declaring: "Trotsky behaves like a most despicable careerist and factionalist.... He pays lip service to the Party, and behaves worse than any of the other factionalists" (*Collected Works*, Vol. 34, p. 349).

The Trotskyists found an ally in the conciliators, who tried to convince Party members that joint work with the liquidators was possible. Two members of the Party Central Committee, Dubrovinsky and Nogin, inclined towards that view. But especially great damage was done by Zinoviev, Kamenev and Rykov, who tried to come to an agreement with Trotsky behind Lenin's back. In opposition to Lenin's plan for a bloc of Bolsheviks and pro-Party Mensheviks against the liquidators, the conciliators demanded that the Bolsheviks join forces with the liquidators and Trotskyists. This in fact would have meant winding up the Bolshevik Party. These developments complicated the efforts of Lenin and his followers to purge the Party of liquidators.

A plenary meeting of the Party Central Committee was held in Paris in January, 1910, at which the conciliators, working hand in glove with Trotsky, put through their resolutions against Lenin's wishes. It was thus decided to bring Menshevik liquidators, not pro-Party Mensheviks, into the central bodies, give financial support to Trotsky's *Pravda* and appoint Kamenev Central Committee representative on its editorial board. The conciliators' obvious aim was to make Trotsky's centrist paper the organ of the Central Committee. However, on Lenin's insistence, the plenary meeting condemned liquidationism and "otzovism" as manifestations of bourgeois influence on the proletariat. But here, too, the Trotskyists and conciliators insisted that "both deviations" be condemned indirectly, without referring to the liquidators and "otzovists" as such.

These conciliatory decisions did much damage to the Party. As Lenin had foretold, the conciliators (Zinoviev, Kamenev and others) played into the hands of the liquidators. They agreed to close down the Bolshevik newspaper, *Proletary*, but the Mensheviks refused to close down their factional organ, *Golos Sotsial-Demokrata*. The liquidators started publication of a legal newspaper in Russia, *Nasha Zarya (Our Dawn)*, to which Axel-Dan, Martov and other Mensheviks associated with the contributed. It required intensive efforts by Lenin to re- the damage done by the conciliatory decisions of the ple- meeting.

the position within the R.S.D.L.P. in these years of reaction extremely grave. The various opportunist factions and groups—liquidators, "otzovists," Trotskyists, etc.—sought to inculcate into the working class disbelief in the possibility of a new revolution, and to prove that there was no point in continuing the revolutionary struggle. They all did everything they could to destroy the illegal revolutionary party of the proletariat. In those troubled times only the Bolsheviks, led by Lenin, proved to be resolute and uncompromising revolutionaries, and courageously upheld the Party principle. Experience was to prove to Party members and class-conscious workers the correctness of Lenin's line.

The Bolsheviks championed the interests of the Party in an irreconcilable struggle against opportunists of every hue. In doing so, they had the authority of the decisions of Party conferences and plenary meetings of the Central Committee which were binding on all members of the R.S.D.L.P. to rely upon. The Bolsheviks' policy was a correct one: to unite all the forces capable of fighting to preserve the illegal Party against its disrupters. This enabled them to gain new positions in the battle for the Party and for winning over the whole of the R.S.D.L.P. to revolutionary Marxism.

3. Lenin's Defence and Development of Marxist Philosophy; His Further Elaboration of the Theory of the Party

The Bolsheviks worked to strengthen the proletarian party on the firm ideological basis of Marxism, enriched by the experience of the revolution.

In the years of reaction, defence of the Marxist philosophy, the theoretical foundations of the Party and its world outlook assumed prime importance in the ideological struggle. This was due to a number of reasons.

The reactionary offensive was being waged on the ideological front as on all others. Bourgeois scientists, writers and journalists were "refuting" Marxism in every possible way, particularly its philosophical foundations. Dialectical materialism was declared to be old-fashioned and obsolete, and religion was proclaimed the "supreme achievement" of the human spirit. The bitterest attacks against Marxism came from many former fellow-travellers of the revolution, bourgeois intellectuals who were now vilifying the revolution and extolling those who abjured it. They ridiculed defence of the people's interests as "idolatry of the people" and proclaimed betrayal of the people to be an act of supreme courage. In an effort to dupe the people and divert them from revolutionary struggle, these bourgeois intellectuals preached clericalism and mysticism, sang the praises of pessimism and decadence, and cultivated sexual depravity.

Ideological demoralisation penetrated the revolutionary ranks as well. A section of Party intellectuals, who considered themselves Marxists but had a very poor knowledge of Marxism, abandoned it and took up a revisionist position in philosophy. Menshevik writers (Valentinov, Yushkevich) and several intellectuals who had been in the Bolshevik ranks (Bogdanov, Bazarov), attacked the fundamental tenets of the Marxist philosophy. But the attack was not conducted openly and directly; it was waged in a veiled and hypocritical form under the guise of "defending," "improving" and "correcting" Marxism.

Some Social-Democrats even went so far as to advocate the combination of Marxism with religion. Their contention was that "Socialism is a religion" (Lunacharsky), and that they were building the new and superior religion of the future. Such preachers, who wanted to turn scientific Socialism into a religious faith, came to be known as "God-builders."

Bourgeois scientists and their revisionist echoers endeavoured to use the achievements of natural science—giving them their own perverted interpretation—against Marxist philosophy and for the preaching of idealist or religious views.

They took advantage of the fact that many recent discoveries in physics and other natural sciences had demolished traditional conceptions and notions. Hitherto scientists had considered the atom to be the final, indivisible particle of matter and that the chemical elements were immutable. The discovery of the electron and radioactivity showed that the atom was divisible, while chemical elements were mutable. The old concept of mass as something constant and not dependent on motion was likewise disproved. Studying the electron, physicists established that its mass depended on the speed of motion. There were also other important discoveries that radically changed the existing conception of the structure and motion of matter.

Many scientists, however, could not assess the new discoveries properly. It seemed to them that matter was being destroyed, that science itself was perishing, and that the very foundations of knowledge were being undermined. There was talk of a "crisis in natural science." The supporters of clericalism and the idealists of diverse schools decided to take advantage of this. They gave their own, idealistic interpretation of these discoveries and on this basis opened an attack on Marxist philosophy.

The revisionists, both in Western Europe and Russia, who were followers of the Austrian bourgeois philosopher Mach, sought to prove that the new scientific discoveries were evidence of the "disappearance" of matter. From this they concluded that philosophical materialism was obsolete and dialectics sheer "mysticism." The Machians furthermore claimed that their idealistic philosophy was a "neutral" one, standing above the two warring camps of materialists and idealists. Actually, in the Machian doctrine idealism was adopting a particularly subtle and streamlined form.

In this situation, the absence of a correct, materialist generalisation of the latest developments in science threatened the very fundamentals of the Marxist outlook.

It was all the more necessary to fight for the purity of Marxist theory because the revolution had awakened vast sections of the people to political life. Many workers who had fought in the revolution had joined the Party and made their first acquaintance with Marxism. The preaching in the Party's ranks, and among the workers generally, of philosophical views that rejected materialism and dialectics, the dissemination of Machism represented a grave danger. It might have done irreparable damage to the political education of the masses and the ideological tempering of Party members. Machian philosophy, and particularly "God-building," merged with reactionary views in politics. The views of the revisionist philosophers led to acceptance of the existing order of things in Russia, renunciation of the struggle and faith in the "divine will." In other words, revisionism in questions of philosophy doomed the masses politically to docility and inaction.

Furthermore, the need to defend and develop Marxist philosophy was dictated by the situation in the international working-class movement. The West European opportunists maintained that Marxism in politics was fully compatible with idealism in philosophy. Karl Kautsky, the leading theoretician of the Second International, declared that philosophical controversies were a "private matter" in which the Party should not interfere. The struggle against apostasy from Marxism in Russia was, therefore, also a struggle against revisionism in the international Social-Democratic movement.

The party of the working class considered it to be its duty resolutely to rebuff these attacks on Marxism and provide a genuinely scientific, philosophical generalisation of the new developments in natural science. That important and responsible task was undertaken by Lenin.

Lenin had always devoted much attention to the development of Marxist philosophy. His exposure of the Narodniks, the "Economists" and the Mensheviks in *What the "Friends of the People" Are and How They Fight the Social-Democrats, What Is To Be Done?* and many other works, had enriched Marxist philosophy. In the period of reaction, when philosophical problems acquired great acuteness, Lenin wrote his *Materialism and Empirio-Criticism*, specially devoted to philosophical problems. Published in 1909, it represented a whole epoch in the development of Marxist philosophy.

Its historic significance lies in the following:

Lenin beat off all the attacks of bourgeois ideologists and revisionists on the philosophy of Marxism. He demonstrated that all the idealistic schools of philosophy were contrary to science and based on fallacious theories. He marshalled an immense amount of scientific and historical evidence to demonstrate convincingly that only one philosophy—*dialectical materialism*—offered a scientific explanation of the world we live in, and armed the working class with a knowledge of the most general laws of development in nature, society and thought. Only Marxist philosophy enables us correctly to understand and refashion the world around us. Lenin thus accomplished what no other Marxist before him had undertaken—*a Marxist generalisation of the latest discoveries in natural science*. He demolished the attempts of the foes of Marxism to give these discoveries a wrong, idealist interpretation in the interests of reactionary ideology. Lenin showed that the radical break in science did not nullify the materiality of the world or materialism, as the Machians maintained, but changed and deepened our conceptions of matter and its properties. Only dialectical materialism offered a way out of the "crisis in natural science." Lenin's analysis of the essence of this "crisis" and the way out of it has been fully vindicated His *Materialism and Empirio-Criticism* retains all its validity today as the methodological basis of advance in the natural sciences.

Lenin upheld and developed *Marxist philosophical materialism*, which has indicated to the proletariat the way out of spiritual slavery, and provided a new scientific basis for this theory. Drawing on the latest discoveries in natural science, he further developed the Marxist conception of matter and substantiated the view that the world is material.

Lenin upheld and developed the theory that the material world is fully knowable, disclosed the complexity of the process of cognition and the path its development has followed. Gradually, step by step, man's cognition provides a correct and exact understanding of the phenomena and laws of the objective material world. Thus, the unknown becomes known, incomplete and inexact knowledge becomes more and more complete and exact. Whereas idealistic philosophy maintained, in effect, that science could not unravel the secrets of nature, Marxist philosophy proclaimed that science is all-powerful, and there is no limit to its development.

"Human reason," Lenin wrote, "has discovered many amazing things in nature, and will discover still more, thereby increasing its power over nature" (*Collected Works*, Vol. 14, p. 268).

Lenin developed and substantiated the Marxist view that practice is the basis of cognition and the criterion of truth. Science, knowledge stem and develop from human practice, from experience, from man's productive and social activities. Only conclusions of science tested by practice are authentic knowledge, having the validity of objective truth. Practice constantly enriches science and advances it.

Lenin upheld and developed *Marxist materialist dialectics*, which is of primary importance for the revolutionary activity of the proletariat and its party.

In *Materialism and Empirio-Criticism*, and in a number of other works, Lenin demonstrated that materialist dialectics is the most comprehensive, rich and profound theory of development. It has proved that the world is neither static nor immutable, but undergoes a constant process of development and renewal. The source of this development is the contradictions intrinsic in every thing, every process and phenomenon; and these contradictions arise, reach a definite degree of sharpness and are subsequently resolved. The ability to perceive and resolve these contradictions in good time is the great art of dialectics, an art taught by Lenin.

This most important proposition of materialist dialectics— the contradiction, the unity and struggle of opposites in every process of development—constitutes the basic law, or "kernel," of dialectics.

"Briefly, dialectics can be defined as the study of the unity of opposites," Lenin wrote (*Philosophical Notebooks*, Gospolitizdat, 1947, p. 194).

Materialist dialectics gives us a correct understanding of how the gradual but continuous changes in the processes at work in nature and society lead to abrupt turns, to fundamental changes, to leaps in development.

Lenin upheld and developed *historical materialism*, the science of the laws of social development. He demonstrated that behind the verbal trickery of the Machian Bogdanov about being and consciousness was concealed denial of the objective laws governing the development of society. He demonstrated, too, the scientific untenability of the Machians' contention that the evolution of human society follows the laws of physiology or some other biological science, and not its own intrinsic laws. Once it knows these laws, the Party can foresee what course social development will take over a long period, scientifically define the tasks maturing in the revolutionary struggle, and mobilise the masses of the people to accomplish them.

Lenin developed and substantiated the principle of *partisanship in philosophy*. His exhaustive critical analysis of the various attempts to revise Marxist philosophy revealed their class roots. He demonstrated that the struggle of philosophical trends was essentially an expression of the conflicting ideologies of the antagonistic classes of modern society. The Machians, like all other supporters of idealism, objectively served clericalism and reaction.

Lenin proved, further, that there was a direct connection between a party's philosophy and its policy. "The political line of Marxism," he wrote, "... is inseparably bound up with its philosophical principles" (*Collected Works*, Vol. 15, p. 374).

There was a similar connection also between defection from Marxist philosophy and opportunism. That was particularly apparent from the example of the revisionists in philosophy—the Mensheviks who were liquidators in politics, and the Bogdanovites who turned out to be "otzovists" in politics and slipped into Menshevism.

Lenin's *Materialism and Empirio-Criticism* enriched Marxist philosophy and raised it to a new, higher stage, in accordance with the new developments in science—thereby advancing social thought as a whole.

The book played a tremendous part in the ideological growth of the Bolshevik Party, the theoretical tempering of its membership, and the defence and development of its theoretical principles. It has served, and still serves, as a guide for the training of revolutionary fighters.

The conference of the enlarged editorial board of the Bolshevik newspaper *Proletary* in 1909 rebuffed the revisionists in the sphere of Marxist philosophy and condemned "God-building" as an anti-Marxist trend. This conference decision on a matter of principle was of vast importance. The Bolsheviks emphatically declared that the Party could not be neutral on philosophical issues and must carefully safeguard Marxism, its great ideological treasure. The Bolsheviks saw unremitting defence of the Marxist outlook against attack from any quarter whatsoever as a cardinal task of the Party.

Lenin's defence and further development of the Marxist concept of the Party played an exceptional part in the Party's ideological life. The first Russian revolution had conclusively confirmed the outstanding importance of the Party. For the first time in history, a Marxist party had laid a powerful imprint on the course of revolution and had led millions of workers into battle. That is why the bourgeoisie and its liquidator yes-men were making such desperate efforts to destroy the working-class party.

In his writings during the period of reaction, Lenin elaborated the Marxist conception of a party's *leading role* in the mass struggle. Experience had clearly proved that the masses do not at once come to understand the need for the Party and its role in the class struggle. Appreciation of the Party and Party allegiance grow as the masses become more class-conscious and see more clearly the alignment of class forces in society. The bourgeoisie, anxious to dull the political consciousness of the masses, preaches in every possible way a negative attitude towards partisanship and extols non-partisanship. To this bourgeois concept of non-partisanship the Marxists oppose proletarian partisanship.

"Politics, in the serious sense of the term, can be made only by the *masses*," Lenin wrote, "but the mass that is non-party and does not follow a strong party is a disintegrated, politically unconscious mass, incapable of sustained effort and a plaything in the hands of the adroit politicians of the ruling class, who always appear on the scene 'at the right time' in order to take advantage of 'opportune' situations" (*Collected Works*, Vol. 19, p. 393).

Lenin upheld the Marxist concept of the party as the highest form of class organisation possessed by the proletariat, and taught the Party to value the outstanding importance of organisation for the working-class movement.

"The strength of the working class lies in organisation. Without mass organisation the proletariat is nil; organised, it is everything" (*Collected Works*, Vol. 11, p. 286).

Diverse proletarian organisations, embracing different sections of the working class and catering to its various needs, emerged during the revolution. The question of the Party's relations with them became one of the vital problems of the Russian working-class movement.

The bourgeoisie tried to tear these workers' organisations away from the Marxist party and set them against it. Its agents within the working-class movement advocated "neutrality" of the trade unions and co-operatives, the "right" of a Party writer to contribute to the capitalist press in whatever way he saw fit, and demanded the "independence" of the Duma group, or even its domination of the Party. To follow that path would have been tantamount to eliminating class consciousness from these organisations—that consciousness of which the Marxist party is the supreme expression. Organisation without class consciousness, Lenin pointed out, was meaningless, if not worse, for it played into the hands of the enemy. To the bourgeois idea of "independence" of the Party, the Bolsheviks opposed the Marxist principle of the Party's ideological and political leadership of all other working-class organisations.

Lenin developed the Marxist views on the question of the *social roots* of opportunism and the Marxist views on the *nature and significance* of the struggle within the working-class movement and the Party. In the early 1900's, and more particularly after the revolution of 1905-1907, the struggle between revolutionary and opportunist elements within the Russian and international working-class movement became more acute. That struggle had deep class roots. For the sharpening of the conflict between labour and capital and the successes of the working-class movement intensified the struggle of the bourgeoisie against the proletariat. The bourgeoisie seeks for ways and means of penetrating the working-class movement and subjecting it to its influence. Against the idea of class struggle and Socialist revolution it counterposes ideas of class harmony and social reform. The opportunists spread these bourgeois ideas within the working class.

The proletariat is not isolated from other classes. It comes into contact with the petty bourgeoisie, and its ranks are constantly swelled by petty-bourgeois elements ruined by big capital. Furthermore, the bourgeoisie systematically bribes and corrupts the top stratum of the working class, whose way of life approximates to that of the petty bourgeoisie. The growth of the working-class movement attracts supporters from among the petty bourgeoisie. All these petty-bourgeois elements are channels for bourgeois influence in the labour movement. This is what leads to the struggle between the revolutionaries and the opportunists.

The struggle against opportunism is one of the *laws of development* of the working-class movement. It is an essential pre-condition for the preparation and victory of the Socialist revolution. The development of the proletarian party is impossible without a resolute struggle of the revolutionary Marxists against the opportunists. The policy of peaceful "cohabitation" of revolutionaries and opportunists in one common party leads in practice only to the victory of opportunism. That is why the Party must be irreconcilable in relation not only to the opportunists, but also to those who, like the centrists, advocate reconciliation with the opportunists. *The Party becomes strong by cleansing itself of opportunist elements.* Lenin pointed out that "the social revolution of the proletariat is inconceivable without this struggle, without a clear demarcation of principle" between revolutionaries and opportunists prior to the revolution, "without a complete break between the opportunist petty-bourgeois elements and the proletarian revolutionary elements of the new historic force *during* this revolution" (*Collected Works*, Vol. 17, p. 200).

Drawing on the vast experience of the pre-revolutionary and revolutionary years, Lenin explained the cardinal importance of the Party's work in *preparing* for a revolution. He pointed out that the Party should not lose heart because it again consisted of small illegal organisations, conducting seemingly unimportant, inconspicuous work among the masses. That work would not be wasted. For the revolution in Russia had shown that the years of persevering effort in organising the masses and enlightening them politically had greatly facilitated the maturing of the revolution.

Summarising the experience of the revolution, Lenin wrote:

"The long period during which the forces of the proletariat were prepared, and during which it was trained and organised, preceded those actions of hundreds of thousands of workers which dealt a mortal blow to the old Russian autocracy. The sustained and imperceptible work of guiding all the manifestations of the proletarian class struggle, the work of building a strong and seasoned Party, preceded the explosion of the truly mass struggle and provided the conditions necessary for the transformation of that explosion into a revolution. Now, too, the proletariat, as the people's fighting vanguard, must strengthen its organisation, scrape off all the green mould of intellectual opportunism and gather its forces for a similar sustained and stubborn effort" (*Collected Works*, Vol. 13, pp. 102-03).

In the dark night of Stolypin reaction Lenin's ideas were a vivid beacon, lighting up the great objective and guiding the Bolsheviks in their self-sacrificing effort.

4. Struggle of the Party to Win Over the Masses and Prepare Them for a New Revolution

The Party saw the two possible paths of development before post-revolutionary Russia quite clearly: complete democratic transformation, or a bourgeois evolution that would preserve the monarchy and the rule of the landlords. The tsarist government, the landlords and the bourgeoisie employed every means available to prevent a new revolution, and in this they had the ready assistance of the Mensheviks and Socialist-Revolutionaries. The Bolsheviks, on the other hand, advocated the revolutionary path of development, one that fully conformed with the people's vital interests. And it was only the people who could make the choice. Stolypin was aware of that when he declared that he needed "twenty years of quiet," that is, twenty years of meek submission and no mass struggle—to carry out his plan. But the people, who had gone through the crucible of revolution, were not prepared to grant the Black-Hundred government these "twenty years of quiet."

The Bolsheviks were the only organised revolutionary force in the country. The illegal Menshevik organisations had fallen apart. The Socialist-Revolutionaries were in a state of ideological and organisational disintegration. The defeat of the revolution had not broken the Bolsheviks. Marxist seasoning, unshakable confidence in the coming triumph of the revolution, supreme devotion to the interests of the proletariat, and irreconcilable opposition to opportunism, all helped the Bolsheviks to surmount the great difficulties that faced them, to retreat in full order, and to preserve the Party's fighting core. Despite incessant police raids and persecution, Party organisations continued to function nearly everywhere, and Party committees were at work in all the major towns and industrial centres. In the big factories the Party retained its groups or its contacts with the workers. Leaflets and illegal Party newspapers were issued in many localities. Regional Party conferences were held in the Central Industrial Region, the Volga region and the Urals, and local Party conferences in St. Petersburg, Moscow, Ivanovo-Voznesensk, Nizhni-Novgorod and other towns.

The desertion of wavering petty-bourgeois elements was at the same time a cleansing of the Party. It helped to rid the Party of unstable adherents and fellow-travellers. Every crisis breaks some and steels others. The severe crisis of the years of reaction steeled the Bolshevik Party organisations. New forces drawn from among the advanced workers came to the fore, and on them fell the whole burden of Party work in the localities.

The stern school of underground activities, the fires of revolution, the days of defeat, the battles against tsarism and the bourgeoisie, the clashes with many other opponents, were the training-ground that produced the remarkable qualities of the Bolshevik, an unyielding and courageous fighter for the working people's interests of whom Lenin said: "Not for nothing have they called us rock-hard." It was of such fighters that a famous revolutionary poet wrote:

"Were nails made of these men, there would be no tougher nails in the world."

Though hounded by the police, the Bolsheviks never abandoned their work of training, organising and mustering the forces of the proletariat. Nor did they abandon their activities among the peasants, patiently explaining that the only way out of poverty and misery was through a joint struggle with the working class, and under its leadership, to overthrow tsarism.

The preservation and strengthening of its contacts with the masses was of vital importance to the Party, and the chief guarantee that Russia would follow the revolutionary and not the Stolypin path of development. And to extend contact with the masses it was necessary to utilise every legal opportunity of working among them, from the rostrum of the Black-Hundred Duma to temperance societies.

It was important for the Party to make use of the Duma rostrum for educating and organising the proletariat in the revolutionary Marxist spirit, and for winning over the peasantry. The elections to the Third State Duma showed that the proletariat had remained true to its Party. Despite police terror, the working class elected only Social-Democrats.

The Bolsheviks had to go their own way in working out their parliamentary tactics. The parliamentary experience of the West European Socialists had to be approached critically, for it was weighed down with opportunism. During the revolution itself, on the basis of the experience gained in the First and Second Dumas, Lenin worked out the fundamental principles of the Party's tactics in the Duma; and he developed them and made them more concrete in the period of reaction. Much attention was paid to proper relationships between the Duma group and the Party leadership. The Duma group was considered one of the organs of the Party, directly subordinated to the Central Committee. Criticising the Mensheviks, who urged the Social-Democratic deputies to share in the Duma's so-called legislative activities, Lenin insisted that they should consistently champion the interests of the people, and speak from the Duma rostrum of what was disturbing the masses. The Social-Democratic deputies, he emphasised, should not confine themselves to work within the Duma; they must extend their activities beyond the Duma, contact the workers and participate in the Party's illegal activities.

The Bolshevik deputies were guided by these propositions.

Their position was extremely difficult. Of the 19 Social-Democrats elected to the Third Duma, one, the Bolshevik V. Y. Kosorotov, representing the Urals workers, had been handed over by the Black-Hundred majority to the police and sent to prison; five Menshevik deputies had deserted to the enemy. The Mensheviks, who were mostly elected by petty-bourgeois votes, had a majority in the group. At first the group committed a number of serious mistakes. It failed to emphasise its class, Socialist character, it did not champion democratic demands consistently nor expose the counter-revolutionary policy of the Cadets. But gradually criticism of these mistakes by the Party and the workers' organisations had its effect, and the activities of the group improved.

The militant voices of the Bolsheviks rang out in the musty atmosphere of the Black-Hundred Duma. An important part in the Social-Democratic group was played by the Bolshevik N. G. Poletayev, representative of the St. Petersburg workers. The workers' deputies criticised the government's home and foreign policy, its part in suppression of the Persian revolution, the shackling loans it received abroad to maintain the police and army, the police terror, the heavy tax burden laid on the labouring population, the oppression of the Finnish people. The Bolshevik deputies vigorously opposed the offensive of the tsarist government and the Black-Hundred Duma against the vital interests of the workers. They drew up bills providing for an 8-hour day, trade union freedom, the right to strike, opposed the Stolypin agrarian reform and demanded the transfer to the peasants of all the landed estates without compensation. The Bolsheviks made use of the Duma to expose the government's reactionary policy and the treacherous conduct of the Cadets, to further the political education of the masses and to win the peasantry over to the side of the working class.

The various legal congresses, which the tsarist government was obliged to permit, played no small part in the situation of prevailing reaction. The Bolshevik delegates, representing diverse workers' organisations at such congresses, were able to expound the Party's views on many vital issues. At the congress of people's universities, a resolution tabled by the workers' group demanding abolition of police control of education, and the right of the workers' organisations themselves to approve study programmes and select the tutors, received wide support and was defeated only by a very slight majority. At the women's congress, the delegates of women workers declared that the emancipation of working women could be won only through participation in the working-class movement. At the factory physicians' congress, the workers' group, representing trade unions in St. Petersburg, Moscow, the Central Industrial Region, Ukraine and Transcaucasia cited numerous facts and figures to show the unbridgable gap between the interests of labour and capital. The workers' delegates and part of the physicians left the congress in protest against police persecution, after which the conveners of the congress had to close its proceedings. The firm stand taken by the workers' group at the temperance congress, and the adoption of several resolutions tabled by it, infuriated the tsarist government. The reactionary press wrote: "This is no congress for fighting drunkenness: it is a congress for fighting the government." The tsarist officials and church representatives hurriedly left the congress, and nearly all the workers' delegates were arrested. The Duma group immediately tabled a question in which it exposed the actions of the tsarist authorities.

The Duma, the legal organisations and the congresses provided a wealth of material for the Party's political work, which the illegal Bolshevik organisations directed along revolutionary lines. What the Party's spokesmen could not say from the legal platform, the illegal Party organisations said in their leaflets, at illegal gatherings and in talks with the workers, always driving home the need for uniting in an organised force and for the revolutionary overthrow of tsarism.

Party work was making good headway in St. Petersburg, Moscow, Baku and other industrial centres. Here many tried and tested revolutionaries worked, whenever they succeeded in escaping from prison or exile. In St. Petersburg I. F. Dubrovinsky, M. I. Kalinin, V. V. Kuibyshev were active; in Moscow—A. S. Bubnov, D. I. Kursky, I. I. Skvortsov-Stepanov, Y. M. Sverdlov. Among the leaders of the Baku organisation were such prominent figures as Meshadi Azizbekov, P. A. Japaridze, G. K. Orjonikidze, S. G. Shaumyan, S. S. Spandaryan, J. V. Stalin. The St. Petersburg and Moscow Bolsheviks bore the main burden of organising the activities of the Duma group and of the workers' groups at legal congresses. The Bolsheviks had strong positions also in the trade unions where there were Party groups. At Baku the Oil Workers' Union was under Bolshevik leadership, and so were the trade union newspaper, *Gudok* (*Whistle*), the Workers' Educational Society "Znaniye—Sila" (Knowledge is Strength) and the People's House. The revolutionary use of legally existing organisations was no easy matter, but the Party had many achievements in this sphere. Gradually the Bolsheviks were ousting the liquidators, and becoming an influential force in the legal organisations.

An important aspect of Party activity was acquainting the masses with the experience of the revolution. The Cadets and liquidators were anxious to erase the very idea of revolution from the minds of the people. They tried to discredit revolutionary traditions and to divert the masses from revolutionary methods of struggle to "the constitutional path." For the liberals and the Mensheviks, Lenin wrote, the revolution was an example of what should not be done; for the working-class party it was an example of what should be done. The Party used the historic examples of mass struggle during the Russian revolution to train new generations of fighters.

Much of what Lenin wrote in this period was devoted to generalising the experience and popularising for the masses the lessons of the revolution. Thus, in *The Agrarian Programme of Social-Democracy in the First Russian Revolution of 1905-1907*, Lenin analysed a number of theoretical problems of the revolution. He elaborated the concept of peasant revolution under proletarian leadership, proved the need for the programme of revolutionary break-up of the remnants of serfdom in the countryside, and the Bolshevik slogan of land nationalisation, and indicated the ways and means of strengthening the alliance of workers and peasants in the revolutionary struggle.

The liquidators maintained that the idea of the hegemony of the proletariat was dead and buried. But events disproved this; they showed that the working class was exerting an increasing influence on the broad mass of the people. The Party's consistent defence of the interests of the working people and its unfaltering struggle for democracy won the masses over to its side. By exposing the Cadets and criticising the waverings of the Trudoviks, the Bolsheviks helped to dispel the peasants' illusions. Under the Party's influence, the Trudovik Duma members frequently dissociated themselves from the Cadets and joined forces with the Social-Democrats. In a Duma by-election in the second

St. Petersburg curia (which was composed of petty bourgeoisie, intellectuals, shop assistants and worker-houseowners) in 1909, the Social-Democrat candidate polled a bigger percentage of the vote than in the 1907 elections. At the legal congresses the workers' group usually had the support of all the democratic elements. Throughout the whole of this period of reaction, in the face of incredible difficulties, Russia's working-class party successfully fought for the hegemony of the proletariat and paved the way for a new revolutionary upsurge in the country. The symptoms of this upsurge had become unmistakable towards the end of 1910.

BRIEF SUMMARY

The defeat of the revolution ushered in a difficult period in the life of Russia and her people. All the parties that had styled themselves oppositionist and revolutionary failed to withstand the grim test. They all capitulated to reaction, renounced the revolution and betrayed the people. Only the Bolshevik Party stood firm, did not lose heart, and steadfastly continued to strengthen its ranks and stubbornly gathered its forces for fresh revolutionary battles. By their actions the Bolsheviks proved their devotion to the people and their loyalty to the revolution. They gave the proletariat a revolutionary perspective and, at the same time, fought for the day-to-day needs and interests of the working people. In those trying times the working class rallied closer to the Bolsheviks, for in them it saw staunch friends and reliable leaders.

In the years of reaction the working-class party was subjected to bitter attacks by renegades and degenerate elements of every shade. The liquidators, "otzovists," Trotskyists and other opportunist factionalists tried to destroy the illegal Marxist party and discredit it in the eyes of the working class. These enemies of Marxism levelled their bitterest attacks at the theoretical foundations of the Party, its dialectical-materialist philosophy. The Bolsheviks proved to be the only force that successfully defended the Party, its revolutionary theory, its revolutionary principles and traditions in uncompromising struggle against the opportunists of every hue. In this struggle the Bolsheviks ideologically routed the traitors to the revolution and the enemies of Marxism, and won unchallengeable prestige and complete predominance in the Party organisations, which rallied around Lenin and the Leninists.

The revolutionary struggle in the years of reaction enriched the Party with new political experience, new methods of struggle and new forms of organisation. During the revolution the Bolsheviks learned how to advance; the defeat of the revolution taught them how to conduct an organised retreat and preserve their main forces. From direct revolutionary methods of struggle the Party passed to roundabout ones. The Bolsheviks systematically and persistently mastered the art of doing legal work in a revolutionary way, in a country under a Black-Hundred regime. That experience was of inestimable importance for the subsequent victory of the revolution. As Lenin pointed out, victory could not be won without mastering the art of organised advance and organised retreat. The Bolsheviks set the international proletariat an example of how a Marxist party should utilise bourgeois legality for its revolutionary aims.

In the dark days of the Stolypin reaction, the Bolsheviks preserved their illegal Marxist party, the main revolutionary force of the working class. Headed by Lenin, the Bolsheviks held the banner of revolution firmly aloft, training and organising the masses for further struggle.

CHAPTER FIVE

THE BOLSHEVIK PARTY
DURING THE NEW UPSURGE
OF THE REVOLUTIONARY MOVEMENT

(1910-1914)

1. Collapse of the Stolypin Policy. Growth of Revolutionary Sentiments Among the Masses

A new economic and political situation arose in Russia in 1910-1911. Beginning with 1910, industrial stagnation was succeeded by a boom. Coal output rose from nearly 26 million tons in 1909 to nearly 36 million in 1913, pig-iron from under 3 million tons to over $4\frac{1}{2}$ million, steel from just over 3 million tons to nearly 5 million, with increases in the output of textiles and sugar.

The post-revolutionary years saw the rapid development of imperialism in Russia. There was a marked increase in the concentration of production and capital, with monopoly concerns dominating nearly every branch of industry and transport. In iron, for instance, the Prodamet syndicate controlled more than 80 per cent of total output, and in coal another syndicate, Produgol, controlled three-quarters of the Donets coalfield output. Over 80 per cent of the assets of the joint-stock banks were concentrated in 12 big banks. The financial oligarchy was steadily extending its domination over the country's economic life and merging more closely with the bureaucratic upper levels of the government machine.

There was a greater inflow of foreign capital. By 1914, approximately one-third of all industrial shares, and over two-fifths of the capital of the principal banks, were held by the West European bourgeoisie. Foreign capitalists held sway in such key industries as coal, oil and metalworking, and their annual profits from investments and loans ran into hundreds of millions of rubles. Tsarist Russia was becoming more and more dependent upon West European imperialism.

A handful of European and Russian capitalist magnates were growing richer, while the people were growing poorer. The landlords, capitalists and kulaks appropriated about three-quarters of the national income. Hundreds of thousands of people were forced to emigrate in search of work. Over one and a half million left the country in the first ten years of the century.

The cost of living was rising, and the position of the worker was deteriorating. An official industrial survey revealed that while annual wages averaged 246 rubles, annual profit per worker averaged 252 rubles. The greater part of the working day was thus passed in work for the capitalist. The workers' life and health were cheap in tsarist Russia. The "Accident Compensation Table" at the big Obukhov shipbuilding and engineering works in St. Petersburg allowed 100 rubles' compensation for complete blindness, 35 rubles for loss of one eye, 50 rubles for total loss of hearing, and 40 rubles for loss of speech.

Incredible poverty reigned in the countryside. Stolypin's agrarian policy had, as its direct result, the mass impoverishment of the peasants and enrichment of the kulak blood-suckers. The number of farms with one horse or no horse at all increased by nearly two million between the turn of the century and 1912. The Russian countryside presented a picture of omnipotent feudal landlords, bigger and richer kulak farms, the impoverishment of a vast mass of middle peasants, and a substantially increased mass of landless peasants or rural proletarians. The tsarist government had attempted to remove some of these contradictions by settling several million peasants from European Russia in Siberia; but this policy failed completely. The peasants would sell all their property and move to Siberia, only to return penniless and rebellious.

Contradictions within the rural community became sharper. The peasant's chief enemy was still the feudal landlord. But there was also sharper conflict between the kulak and the poor peasant. Cases of peasants setting fire to manor houses and kulak farmsteads became more frequent after 1910. On top of this came the terrible famine of 1911, which affected some 30 million peasants. The situation left no doubt whatever that the Stolypin policy had collapsed.

Its collapse brought out more saliently than ever the profound contradictions throughout Russia's social and political system. It demonstrated anew that the tsarist government was incapable of solving the country's basic social and economic problems.

The remnants of serfdom were an intolerable obstacle to national development. Though Russia had taken the capitalist path, every year that passed saw her lagging further and further behind the advanced capitalist countries. Lenin wrote in 1913 that, though in the half century since the emancipation of the peasants iron consumption had increased fivefold, Russia still remained a backward country, equipped with modern machinery four times worse than Britain, five times worse than Germany and ten times worse than the United States. In 1900 Russia led the world in oil production; some ten years later she was behind other countries. Poverty, oppression, lack of human rights, humiliating indignities imposed on the people—all this, Lenin emphasised, was in crying contradiction to the state of the country's productive forces and to the degree of political understanding and demands of the masses, awakened by the first Russian revolution. Only a new revolution could save Russia.

No amount of savage Stolypin repression could eradicate the people's urge for freedom and a better life. The fatigue of the masses was passing; hatred of the oppressors was coming to the surface with ever greater force.

The working class was the first to take the offensive. The years of revolution and reaction had taught the workers much and had raised their class consciousness. They had grown considerably in numbers since the beginning of the century. In 1913, there were already about 3,500,000 workers in industry alone, and they were more highly concentrated than in any other country. Over half (53.4 per cent) worked in factories employing 500 workers or more, whereas in the United States the proportion was about one-third.

In the summer of 1910 strikes broke out in Moscow. They gave an impetus to the movement, and towards the end of the year there were political demonstrations in St. Petersburg, Moscow and other towns, followed by student rallies and strikes. The movement continued to mount throughout 1911, with over 105,000 workers, or double the number as compared with the preceding year, involved in strike stoppages. The year ended with powerful demonstrations at St. Petersburg factories in support of the Social-Democrats' Duma interpellation on the frame-up trial of the Social-Democrat members of the Second Duma. The Bolshevik demand for their release was supported by the workers.

The Bolsheviks' prediction that a new revolutionary upsurge was inevitable proved to be true. Everywhere there was growing discontent and indignation among the people. The workers saw in the Bolshevik revolutionary slogans a clear-cut expression of their own aspirations. An important part in bringing these slogans home to the masses was played by the Bolshevik weekly legal newspaper *Zvezda* (*Star*), which began publication in St. Petersburg towards the end of 1910.

The opportunists played a particularly harmful and ignominious role in this new revolutionary revival. Instead of revolutionary struggle, the liquidators and Trotskyists called for a "petition campaign," urging the workers to sign a petition to the Duma requesting "freedom of coalition" (freedom of association, assembly, strikes, etc.). The Bolsheviks explained to the workers that there could be no freedom as long as the country remained in the hands of the Black-Hundred landlords. Freedom for the people could be won only with the overthrow of the monarchy. The clamorous "petition campaign" proved a fiasco: the liquidators collected barely 1,300 signatures, whereas the Bolshevik slogans had the solid support of hundreds of thousands of workers.

These strikes, political demonstrations and rallies, together with the peasant actions against the landlords and kulaks, were the harbingers of a new revolution. Could the proletariat perform its role as leader in this maturing revolutionary struggle of the mass of the people? That depended, to a decisive extent, on the state of the Marxist party of the Russian working class.

2. The Prague Party Conference

The new revolutionary struggles posed the urgent need to strengthen the Party and formulate the new tasks in leading the mass revolutionary movement.

The formal uniting of Bolsheviks and Mensheviks within a single R.S.D.L.P. during the revolution had led to a peculiar situation and had predetermined what the Bolsheviks had to do within the Party. The Bolsheviks had set themselves the task of cleansing the Party of opportunist elements through ideological struggle. They had accomplished much in that respect. Nearly all the illegal Party organisations were Bolshevik. The Menshevik betrayal of the proletariat had gone so far that the Party membership was coming to realise more and more the need for a complete break with the liquidators and their expulsion from the Party.

The Bolsheviks began to prepare energetically for a Party conference. The liquidators, Trotskyists and conciliators made frenzied but futile attempts to prevent a conference taking place, and thereby block the consolidation of the Party on Bolshevik principles. In the summer of 1911, G. K. Orjonikidze, I. I. Schwarz (Semyon) and other Party workers were sent to Russia. At a conference of leading Party committees, a Russian Organisation Commission (R.O.C.) was set up. It carried out a vast amount of organising and propaganda work in preparation for the conference.

The Sixth All-Russian Conference of the R.S.D.L.P. was held in Prague on January 5-17, 1912, and was attended by delegates from more than twenty Party organisations, among them St. Petersburg, Moscow, the Central Industrial Region, Kazan, Saratov, Tiflis, Baku, Nikolayev, Kiev, Yekaterinoslav, Dvinsk and Vilno. Police persecution and other obstacles prevented the participation of delegates from the Urals, Samara, Nizhni-Novgorod, Sormovo, Lugansk and Rostov-on-Don.

The "Announcement" on the Conference issued by the Central Committee declared that, notwithstanding the trying years of reaction, political persecution and opportunist betrayal, the Russian proletariat and its Party were prepared for new class battles against tsarism, the landlords and the capitalists. The statement said:

"Not only have the banner of the Russian Social-Democratic Party, its programme and its revolutionary traditions survived, but so has its organisation, which persecution may have undermined and weakened, but could never utterly destroy" (*C.P.S.U. in Resolutions*, Part I, p. 267).

Considering that practically all the Party organisations active in Russia were represented, the Conference was fully justified in declaring, in a special resolution, that it "constitutes itself a general Party Conference of the R.S.D.L.P., the supreme body of the Party." The Conference in effect had the significance of a Party congress.

A most important task was to *cleanse the Party of opportunists*. Of vast theoretical and practical significance were its resolutions on "liquidationism and the group of liquidators," and on "the Party organisation abroad." The Conference declared that the liquidators, grouped around the legal magazines *Nasha Zarya* (*Our Dawn*) and *Dyelo Zhizni* (*The Cause of Life*), had, "by their behaviour, *definitely placed themselves outside the Party*." The Conference expelled them from the Party.

But in addition to the avowed liquidators, there were the under-cover liquidators with their various supporters. They banded themselves together in small émigré groups abroad that had no contact with the workers, and were not supported by even a single illegal Party organisation in Russia. To this category belonged the Mensheviks grouped around the newspaper *Golos Sotsial-Demokrata*, the Trotskyists, the *Vperyod* group and others. With regard to all these groups, the Conference adopted the following decision:

"The Conference declares that the groups abroad which have refused to submit to the centre directing Social-Democratic work in Russia, i.e., the Central Committee, and are introducing disruption by setting up their own communications with Russia which bypass the Central Committee, have no right to use the name of the Russian Social-Democratic Labour Party" (*ibid.*, p. 286).

All these groups demonstrated their anti-Party attitude by refusing to accept the Conference decisions.

The final result was that the opportunists found themselves outside the Party. Their expulsion only strengthened its ranks, heightened its discipline and fighting capacity, and thus helped to create genuine Party unity. Like the sturdy oak that becomes stronger when dead branches are cut off in good time, the working-class party became stronger and more solid with the expulsion of the Mensheviks. The Bolsheviks carried their struggle against opportunism to its logical conclusion, i.e., the expulsion of the Mensheviks from the Party. This was of the utmost importance for the triumph of the democratic and Socialist revolution in Russia.

The Conference devoted much attention to tactics. It noted the rise of a revolutionary mood among the masses, and in this connection adopted a number of decisions on the next tasks in building up the new type of proletarian party and leading the revolutionary upsurge. The proletariat should be the leader of the peasantry in a democratic revolution. The demands of the Party's minimum programme were put forward as the main slogans of the hour: a democratic republic, an 8-hour working day, confiscation of all landed estates. It was the task of the Party to make these "three pillars" the common demand of all the democratic forces, the slogans of the people's revolution. It was under these slogans that the Party fought the elections to the Fourth State Duma.

In a special resolution on the Party's tasks in combating the famine, the Conference called on all Party organisations to explain to the peasants the connection between the famine and the tsarist policy, and to direct the mass unrest caused by the famine into an organised struggle against the tsarist monarchy. The Conference urged the Party organisations to strengthen and extend the number of illegal nuclei, and to surround them with a ramified network of diverse legal workers' societies.

Of all the political parties then active in Russia only the Bolsheviks had a platform that fully accorded with the interests of the working class and the people generally.

The Conference also discussed international questions. A special resolution emphasised the world-wide significance of the Chinese people's revolutionary struggle, which was bringing freedom to Asia and undermining European bourgeois domination. The Conference denounced the predatory policies of British imperialism and Russian tsarism in Persia. It addressed a message of greeting to the German Social-Democrats on the occasion of their signal victory in the Reichstag elections. Expressed in all these resolutions were the principles of proletarian internationalism.

Of major importance was the election of a Central Committee, for the Central Committee elected at the Fifth R.S.D.L.P. Congress had virtually ceased to exist as a result of Menshevik disruption. There had been no Central Committee meetings since January, 1910, and the Party was without an official directing centre.

As the supreme Party assembly, the Conference elected an authoritative Central Committee, headed by Lenin and including representatives of local Party organisations, men steeled in the difficult years of reaction and known for their revolutionary courage and staunchness. Among those elected, besides Lenin, were F. I. Goloshchokin, G. K. Orjonikidze and S. S. Spandaryan. The Central Committee co-opted J. V. Stalin and appointed A. S. Bubnov, M. I. Kalinin, S. G. Shaumyan and Y. D. Stasova as alternate members to replace the C.C. members arrested. Subsequently the Central Committee also co-opted G. I. Petrovsky and Y. M. Sverdlov.

The Prague Conference played an outstanding part in building the Bolshevik Party, a party of a new type. It *summed up* a whole historical period of Bolshevik struggle against Menshevism, and *consolidated the victory* of the Bolsheviks, retaining the banner of the Russian Social-Democratic Labour Party firmly in their hands. Factionalism was thus eliminated within the Party and its leadership, the Central Committee, and this was of exceptional importance for the Party's continued growth and for enhancing its role in the revolutionary struggle. Assessing the Prague Conference decisions, Lenin wrote in 1914:

"Since 1912, for over two years, there has been *no* factionalism among the organised Marxists in Russia, no controversies over tactics in *united* organisations, at united *conferences* and congresses. There is a *complete* break between the Party— which in January, 1912, formally announced that the liquidators *did not* belong to it—and the liquidators" (*Collected Works*, Vol. 20, pp. 304-05).

The Conference was of tremendous importance for the life of the Party. Party organisations were built up in various parts of the country on the basis of its decisions, and it strengthened the Party as an all-Russian organisation. Now that it was free of the dead weight of opportunism, the Party could provide effective leadership for the new and powerful rise of the revolutionary mass struggle.

Lenin wrote to Maxim Gorky at the beginning of 1912, on the results of the Prague Conference:

"At last we have succeeded, in spite of the liquidator scum, in restoring the Party and its Central Committee. I hope you will rejoice at this with us" (*Collected Works*, Vol. 35, p. 1).

The Prague Conference also holds an important place in the history of the international working-class movement.

The degeneration of the parties of the Second International was becoming increasingly obvious. The struggle between revolutionary and opportunist elements within the international labour movement became more acute with the approach of the first world war. The Bolsheviks played a very active part in that struggle. Lenin resolutely fought the opportunists at the congresses of the Second International at Stuttgart (1907) and Copenhagen (1910), at meetings of the International Socialist Bureau, and in the press. The Bolsheviks supported the Left wing of the Socialist parties in Germany, Italy, the Netherlands and other countries and worked to unite and strengthen them.

But the revolutionaries in the parties of the Second International did not fully appreciate the dangers of opportunism, and they lacked consistency and determination in combating the opportunists as agents of the bourgeoisie in the labour movement. The Bolshevik victory over the Mensheviks was, for that reason, of international importance. The expulsion of the Mensheviks set an example, for the revolutionary elements in other Social-Democratic parties, of how an uncompromising struggle against opportunism should be carried on, up to a complete organisational rupture.

3. The Bolshevik Newspaper *Pravda*. The Bolshevik Group in the Fourth State Duma

The declaration of the Prague Conference that a new revolutionary upsurge was on the way was confirmed within three months. The event that converted the revolutionary temper of the masses into a revolutionary upsurge was the bloody drama at the Lena goldfields in Siberia.

The goldfields belonged to British capitalists and their partners, Russian capitalists, members of the imperial family and high-ranking tsarist officials. The owners made an annual profit of some seven million rubles. In remote Siberia the capitalists and their underlings acted entirely without restraint. The workers were paid beggarly wages for their back-breaking toil, and supplied with rotten food. Their wives and daughters were subjected to all manner of insult. Unable to endure this monstrous oppression any longer, the workers struck in protest. They stood together firmly, and presented their demands in an organised manner. But all the demands were insolently rejected. Even the demand for decent treatment was considered a "political offence." On April 4, 1912, on the order of a gendarme officer, troops fired on a peaceful demonstration of workers proceeding to negotiate with the management. More than 500 were killed or wounded.

News of the Lena massacre flashed throughout the country and aroused a storm of indignation. Mass protest strikes, demonstrations and meetings began. The Bolshevik newspaper *Zvezda* (*Star*) provided the slogans for the movement, and by its truthful account and interpretation of events dispelled the fog of foul lies behind which the bourgeois press was trying to conceal this bloody tsarist crime. Every issue of *Zvezda* was confiscated by the police, but many copies none the less found their way to the workers. The Social-Democratic Duma group interpellated the government on the shooting. The insolent reply of the tsar's Minister, Makarov: "So it was, so it will be!" only further aroused the anger of the workers. Some 300,000 workers participated in the protest strikes, and about 400,000 in the May Day strikes that followed. The scope of the strike movement in 1912, Lenin pointed out, was comparable to that of 1905.

The days following the Lena massacre emphasised how important it was for the working class to have a legally published newspaper. The *Zvezda* was a weekly, intended for advanced workers. What the Party needed now was a daily paper for the widest mass of the workers. And the workers readily responded to the Bolshevik appeal to subscribe their coppers so that one might be started.

The first issue of the Bolshevik paper *Pravda* (*The Truth*) appeared in St. Petersburg on May 5 (April 22, old style*), 1912. It was a daily mass workers' Marxist paper. Since 1914, the day it first appeared—May 5—has been celebrated as Workers' Press Day. *Pravda* was the Party's all-Russian legal organ, and played an immense part in the life of the working class.

With the rise of the revolutionary tide and the appearance of *Pravda*, the Foreign Bureau of the Central Committee, headed by Lenin, moved to Cracow in Galicia (then part of Austria) in order to be nearer to Russia. *Pravda* was a legal workers' paper of a new type. To found such a paper was no easy task. Lenin devoted exceptional attention to *Pravda*, seeing to it that it was written in a militant revolutionary spirit, and criticising it trenchantly for publishing articles that did not present the Party's policy on fundamental issues clearly. More than 250 articles by Lenin appeared in the pre-revolutionary *Pravda*; they were a guide to the Party in its work and policy. At various times its editorial board and active contributors included N. N. Baturin, Demyan Bedny, N. K. Krupskaya,

---

* The "old style," or Julian calendar, was thirteen days behind the more modern, or the Gregorian calendar; but Russia still retained it until the October Revolution.—*Trans.*

V. M. Molotov, M. S. Olminsky, N. I. Podvoisky, N. G. Poletayev, K. N. Samoilova, N. A. Skrypnik, Y. M. Sverdlov, J. V. Stalin, K. S. Yeremeyev. The Party's best forces wrote for *Pravda*; contributions by Maxim Gorky appeared in its columns.

The Bolshevik *Pravda* kept the Party in daily contact with the broad mass of the workers. Every issue contained dozens of items from worker correspondents, describing the appalling conditions in the factories and citing instances of police terror and employer tyranny. These were damning indictments of the tsarist regime and the capitalist system. More than 17,000 such items appeared in the paper in a little over two years. Rallied around the paper was a veritable army of worker correspondents, staunch and courageous propagandists of Leninist ideas and Bolshevik slogans.

The paper played an especially big part in organising the strike movement. Each issue carried one or more items of strike actions. All told, there were some 10,000 strike reports in *Pravda*—daily communiqués from the battle fronts of the class war. They did much to unite the workers and spur them on to greater effort. *Pravda* formulated the workers' demands, organised support for the strikers by workers in other factories and towns, and brought ever new sections of the workers into action. It developed a spirit of class solidarity among the mass of the workers. It was the heart and soul of the fighting proletariat.

Pravda enjoyed tremendous authority among the workers. They regarded it as their own paper, one that unfalteringly stood up for their interests. From every part of Russia came messages of warm affection and gratitude. The workers were eager to support their paper. *Pravda*'s circulation reached about 40,000, whereas the liquidationist *Luch* (*Ray*) sold a bare 16,000 copies. Four-fifths of the donations to the labour press made by workers' groups went to *Pravda*, which by the summer of 1914 had subscribers in 924 localities. They carried its message to the masses.

Pravda devoted much space to peasant problems and ran a special section called "Peasant Life." The numerous peasant letters it published, from practically every gubernia of European Russia and from many of those in Siberia, described in plain and simple language the unending misery of the peasants, the tyranny of the landlords and the exploitation by the kulaks.

Lenin contributed many articles dealing with various aspects of peasant life. The position of the peasant, Lenin wrote, was approximately as follows: for every landlord with over 5,000 acres there were about 300 peasant families, tilling their poor and exhausted land with hopelessly obsolete implements and methods. In this system of big landownership lay the root of peasant poverty and recurrent famines. *Pravda* demonstrated to the peasants that the only way out of their bondage was to fight the tsar and the feudal landlords under the leadership of the working class.

A large share of the Party's organisational work was concentrated in the *Pravda* editorial offices. Here meetings were arranged with representatives of local Party nuclei. Here reports were received of Party activities in the mills and factories, and from here were transmitted the instructions of the St. Petersburg and Central Committees of the Party. *Pravda* helped to found new Party organisations in the factories.

The tsarist government was, of course, alive to the formidable revolutionary influence exerted by *Pravda*, and used every conceivable method to stop its publication. But the workers gave their newspaper unfailing support. When it was confiscated, they would see to it that a large part of the issue did not fall into the hands of the police, but found its way to the factory districts. When heavy fines were imposed on it, they collected the money—kopek by kopek—needed to pay them. The tsarist government then resorted to periodical bans. *Pravda* was suppressed eight times, but each time reappeared under a new but similar name—*Rabochaya Pravda (Workers' Truth), Severnaya Pravda (Northern Truth), Pravda Truda (Truth of Labour), Za Pravdu (For Truth), Proletarskaya Pravda (Proletarian Truth), Put Pravdy (The Path of Truth), Rabochy (The Worker), Trudovaya Pravda (Labour Truth)*. Each time the Bolshevik *Pravda* was born again and each time its voice rang out anew in the working-class districts.

Pravda was a genuine workers' paper. Only with the workers' support were the Bolsheviks able to carry out their bold plan of publishing—in the heart of the police-ridden Black-Hundred regime—a legal daily newspaper that spoke for an illegal party, and educated the workers in a consistently revolutionary spirit.

Pravda holds a place all its own in the history of the Bolshevik Party and the revolution. In those days the Bolsheviks were called *Pravdists*. Their paper resolutely fought the opportunists, those agents of the bourgeoisie in the working-class movement, exposed their treacherous role and trained the workers in a spirit of revolutionary Marxism. *Pravda* reared a whole generation of revolutionary workers, hundreds of thousands of self-sacrificing vanguard fighters for the revolution, for the cause of the working class and the interests of the people. It helped considerably to swell and strengthen the Party's ranks and cement its ties with the masses.

Another legally functioning all-Russian organ of the Party was the Bolshevik group in the Fourth State Duma.

The Duma elections were held in the autumn of 1912, in a situation that was extremely difficult for the working class.

The police furiously hounded militant workers and resorted to the most shameless fraud to deprive the working class of Duma representation. The Black Hundreds and liberals frequently joined forces against the Social-Democrat candidates. The liquidators attempted to split the ranks of the working class.

The electoral law allowed for a deputy to be elected from the workers' curia only in six industrial gubernias: St. Petersburg, Moscow, Vladimir, Kostroma, Yekaterinoslav and Kharkov. The election procedure was as follows: meetings of the workers* elected delegates, who, in turn, chose the electors to nominate the candidate from the workers' curia. But the actual nomination and voting took place in the gubernia electoral colleges, and here the landlords and capitalists had a majority. If the Party's representative was to be elected, only one candidate had to be nominated from the workers' curia. An turncoat would, of course, obtain the Black-Hundred vote and thereby defeat the man nominated by the worker electors. To avoid this, the Bolsheviks sought to persuade the delegate conferences to adopt decisions obliging all worker electors to withdraw their own nominations in favour of the single Party candidate.

Despite numerous police obstacles, the Party developed a mass political campaign around its basic minimum-programme demands, presenting them as part of the struggle for Socialism. The Bolshevik position was explained in the Party's election platform, drawn up by Lenin. Taking this as a basis, local Party committees drew up "mandates" (lists of demands) for the workers' deputies. *Pravda* appealed to all workers to vote for "consistent and staunch labour democrats," and the workers knew that this referred to the Bolsheviks. The paper exposed the Cadets and the liquidators.

The success of the Bolshevik campaign alarmed the tsarist government. It tried to break the workers' will, primarily in the capital, St. Petersburg, where it cancelled the elections of workers' delegates at many of the big factories. In reply, 100,000 workers, responding to the call of the St. Petersburg Bolshevik Committee, went on strike. The tsarist government was forced to retreat: not only did it withdraw its decision, but actually extended the list of factories sending delegates to the workers' curia. This victory greatly stimulated the movement in other parts of the country.

All of the six major industrial gubernias, accounting for about four-fifths of the Russian working class, returned Bolshevik deputies from the workers' curia. This brilliant victory was conclusive proof that the majority of the working class was with the

---

* Only in factories employing 50 or more workers; in other factories the workers were disfranchised.—*Ed.*

Bolsheviks. The six Bolshevik Duma members were A. Y. Badayev, M. K. Muranov, G. I. Petrovsky, F. N. Samoilov, N. R. Shagov and R. V. Malinovsky (subsequently exposed as a police agent). Seven Mensheviks were elected from non-industrial gubernias.

The Bolshevik deputies boldly expounded the Party's policy on pressing issues of the life of the people. From the Duma platform they told the truth about the appalling conditions of the workers, the needs of the peasants, the oppression of the non-Russian nationalities, the urgent need of the working people for an educational system uncontrolled by the tsarist government, the latter's feverish preparations for war.

The Bolshevik interpellations became in the Fourth Duma an even more effective weapon than they had been in the Third. A minimum of 30 signatures was required to table a question, and, as a rule, the Social-Democrats could obtain the signatures of the Trudoviks and some of the progressive-minded deputies of other parties. Every question dealt with some definite fact—the suppression of a trade union, persecution of a workers' newspaper, a pit disaster, a fatal accident at a mill, the arrest of strikers, the murder of a peasant by the police, etc. These interpellations enabled the Bolshevik deputies to present the country with a true picture of arbitrary police rule and the monstrous exploitation of the working people. The speeches of the Bolshevik deputies reached the masses, and fanned the popular resentment against tsarism, the landlords and the capitalists.

The worker deputies framed three bills: on the 8-hour working day, on social insurance and on national equality. They were published in *Pravda*.

The Bolshevik deputies did not confine themselves to work in the Duma. They were very active outside it as well, visiting mills and factories, touring the chief industrial centres, reporting back to the workers at meetings, conferring with individual workers, contributing to *Pravda* and organising strike relief and solidarity actions. They also took an active part in illegal work, addressing underground Party meetings, helping local Party organisations and carrying out various assignments for the Central Committee.

The small group of Bolshevik deputies were incessantly harassed in the Duma by the Black-Hundred representatives. Their speeches exposing tsarist misrule were constantly interrupted by the infuriated reactionaries, and were often cut short by the Duma President. But their courageous stand won them the confidence of the working class. The Bolshevik Duma group enjoyed tremendous authority and prestige, and played an important part in the country's political life. The peasant masses and the oppressed nationalities, too, regarded the workers' deputies as the champions and defenders of their cause. The following letter is typical of this attitude: "We, a group of peasants of Kazino village, having learned from the workers' press of the situation in the State Duma, find that only the six workers' deputies are living up to their high calling, and that they alone uphold the interests of the toiling masses staunchly and consistently. To them we say: 'We are with you and whole-heartedly wish you every success in your difficult work!'"

The Duma group was guided by the Party Central Committee. The deputies frequently visited Lenin to consult with him. He drafted many of the speeches they made in the Duma. Party leadership, close contact with the masses, skilful combination of legal and illegal work, helped to train a *new type* of parliamentarian—a *revolutionary parliamentarian* who faithfully championed working-class interests.

Pravda, the Bolshevik deputies and the illegal Party organisations worked in the closest contact with one another. In December, 1912, the Bolsheviks in the Duma tabled a question on the persecution of the trade unions. *Pravda* and the St. Petersburg Party Committee organised a mass campaign in support of the question. *Pravda* published reports showing how the trade unions were being hounded by the police, and the St. Petersburg Committee put out a leaflet (illegally) calling for a one-day stoppage in support of the Duma group. While Badayev was exposing the tsarist authorities from the Duma tribune, the workers of several big factories downed tools in support of their deputy.

In March, 1914, many women workers were poisoned at the Provodnik factory in Riga and the Treugolnik factory in St. Petersburg. The St. Petersburg Committee immediately circulated an illegal leaflet calling for a protest strike. *Pravda* published numerous reports exposing the monstrous exploitation of working women. The Bolshevik deputies interpellated the government on the subject, and one of them made a speech in the Duma. About 120,000 people took part in the protest strikes against the inhuman treatment of women workers.

These are examples of how the Bolsheviks skilfully combined the activities of *Pravda* and the Duma deputies with illegal work.

4. The Party at the Head of the Revolutionary Struggle of the Masses

The workers' movement continued to grow in scope and strength. There were over one million strikers in 1912, and 1,272,000 in 1913. Economic struggles were intertwined with political ones, and culminated in mass revolutionary strikes. The working class went over to the offensive against the capitalists and the tsarist monarchy.

The strikes were of national importance: they aroused wide masses of the people and spurred them on to action. In 1910-1914, according to patently minimised figures, there were over 13,000 peasant outbreaks, in which many manor houses and kulak farmsteads were destroyed, and grain, cattle and farm equipment confiscated. The unrest spread to the tsarist army. In July, 1912, a sapper unit stationed in Turkestan mutinied; in January, 1913, there was unrest in the Kiev garrison; mutiny was brewing in the Baltic and Black Sea fleets.

A new revolution was maturing in Russia.

Practical experience was fully confirming the correctness of the policy mapped out by the Prague Conference. It was now necessary to sum up the experience accumulated by the Party in these new conditions, and chart its next tasks in preparing for revolution. This was done at two conferences of the Central Committee with Party functionaries. The first was held in Cracow in December, 1912, and the second at Poronin, a village near Cracow, in September, 1913. They were attended by the Bolshevik Duma deputies and delegates from the Party organisations of St. Petersburg, Moscow, the Central Industrial Region, Ukraine, Urals and the Caucasus. Under Lenin's guidance, the conferences worked out decisions on major aspects of Party activity. They emphasised that Party organisations, combining illegal and legal activities, should develop and organise revolutionary mass actions, notably revolutionary mass strikes and street demonstrations, and draw the peasants into broad revolutionary actions, co-ordinated to the utmost possible extent with those of the workers.

The illegal Party, a sum-total of illegal nuclei surrounded by a network of legal and semi-legal workers' societies, was recognised as the only correct form of organisation. Party committees made up of the most active workers should be set up in every factory; and Party groups, conducting their activities in strict accordance with the Party spirit, should be formed in all legal workers' societies.

In its statement on the Poronin Conference the Central Committee wrote the following to all Party organisations:

"The path has been mapped out. The Party has devised its basic forms of work in the present transition period. Loyalty to the old revolutionary banner has been tested and proved in a new situation and under new conditions of work. The most difficult times are past, comrades. We are entering a new stage. Events of the utmost importance are on the way, and they will decide the fate of our country. To work, then, comrades!" (*C.P.S.U. in Resolutions*, Part I, p. 308.)

Militant unity of the proletarian ranks was a prerequisite of victory. The Cracow Conference regarded the fight for *unity of the working-class movement* as one of the Party's basic tasks. It called for unity from below, forged by the workers themselves and based on recognition of the illegal Party and acceptance of revolutionary tactics.

This slogan fully accorded with working-class sentiment. The 1905 Revolution had shown the workers how injurious a split within the movement could be, and now, in preparation for new revolutionary battles, there was an insistent demand for unity. No one understood or appreciated all the significance of the great principle of proletarian unity better than the Bolsheviks. "Disunited the workers are nil. United they are everything," Lenin declared (*Collected Works*, Vol. 19, p. 470). The basis of proletarian unity lay in the community of class interests and aims, in class discipline, and in the acceptance of the will of the majority. Explaining the Marxist conception of working-class unity, Lenin wrote:

"The working class needs unity. Unity is feasible only within a united organisation whose decisions are faithfully, and not just formally, carried out by all class-conscious workers. The discussion of an issue, stating **and** hearing diverse opinions, ascertaining the views of the *majority* of organised Marxists, expressing those views in a decision taken elsewhere, scrupulously carrying out that decision—that is what intelligent people throughout the world regard as *unity*. And such unity is supremely prized by the working class, is supremely important to it" (*ibid.*, p. 470).

Working-class unity implies, first and foremost, ideological and political unity. It is impossible without unity of the workers' organisations, and primarily the political organisation of the proletariat, the Party. The liquidators and Trotskyists were using the false slogan of "unity" as a screen for their activities to cause a split within the Party. It was therefore necessary to expose their unscrupulous exploitation of this great slogan and pillory them as destroyers of unity.

The liquidators were attacking the illegal Party more and more openly, maligning the revolutionary "underground" and advocating the formation of an "open" party. They ridiculed the heroic strike struggle of the workers as "strike fever." They had their own newspapers and, in several localities, notably St. Petersburg, Moscow and Yekaterinoslav, their own organisations, or so-called "initiative groups." Actually, they had set up—with police permission—their own party, though it had not taken definite organisational shape. And they still had a foothold in various legal organisations, where they did what they could to prevent united action.

The formation of an independent Bolshevik Duma group was of outstanding importance in the struggle against the liquidators for unity of the labour movement. The workers naturally wanted to see their parliamentary representatives united in a single group, and it was therefore necessary to explain to the masses that in forming a group of their own, the Bolsheviks were guided solely by working-class interests.

At first the Bolsheviks and Mensheviks formed a joint Social-Democratic group in the Duma; but an extremely abnormal situation prevailed within it. The six Bolsheviks had been elected from industrial gubernias with over a million workers, while the seven Menshevik liquidators represented non-industrial gubernias with only 136,000 workers. Using their accidental majority of one vote, the liquidators violated the elementary rights of the Bolshevik deputies. The result was that the liquidators, representing an insignificant minority of the working class, ignored the will of the vast majority of workers. The Party decided to submit the issue to the workers. There was a heated debate in the press, in Party organisations and at workers' meetings. Over two-thirds of the class-conscious workers pronounced in favour of the Bolshevik six. When the latter constituted themselves into an independent Duma group, in the autumn of 1913, they had the overwhelming support of the workers. The seven liquidators were left without worker contacts. This was an important victory for the Bolsheviks.

The Bolsheviks were successful in getting liquidators removed from responsible positions in legally functioning organisations, especially the trade unions. In St. Petersburg nearly all the unions were under Bolshevik leadership, the liquidators retaining the support only of the clerks, draughtsmen and pharmaceutists. In Moscow, all unions were either under the leadership of the Bolsheviks or closely associated with them. A particularly important victory was won in the St. Petersburg Metal-Workers' Union, where the liquidators polled only 150 votes out of a total of 3,000 in the elections to the Union Executive.

Another big victory was won in the insurance campaign, that is, in the elections to the sick-benefit societies organised under the social insurance law which the Duma had had to pass as a result of mass pressure. There was a keen contest between Bolsheviks and liquidators in the elections to the All-Russian and St. Petersburg insurance committees, with over 80 per cent of the elected delegates supporting the list of Bolshevik demands and candidates whose names were published in *Pravda*.

The working class was rallying to the Bolshevik banner. The campaign against the illegal revolutionary party was meeting with no support among the workers, and the enemies of Bolshevism.

decided on a new manoeuvre. Under the guise of "unity" Trotsky began building up a motley bloc of anti-Bolshevik groups. By posing as "non-factionalists" the Trotskyists were unscrupulously misleading the workers and thereby hampering the exposure of the liquidators. They were therefore much more dangerous than the avowed liquidators.

This anti-Bolshevik bloc was formalised at a conference called by Trotsky in August, 1912. Its opportunist character was clearly revealed by the platform the conference endorsed. Conspicuously absent were the demands for a democratic republic, confiscation of the landed estates and their transfer to the peasants, and the right of nations to self-determination. This attempt to start a centrist—in fact liquidationist—party in Russia was not supported by the workers. The Polish Social-Democrats and Plekhanov's group refused to have any part in the scheme, and the *Vperyod* group and Lettish Social-Democrats withdrew from the bloc shortly after its formation. All the others soon followed suit. Attacked by the Bolsheviks, the August bloc actually fell apart less than eighteen months after its formation.

The liquidationist Stolypin "Labour Party" dragged out a miserable existence, while Trotsky's anti-Bolshevik bloc ended in complete failure. This was due primarily to the fact that the Bolsheviks, led by Lenin, were indefatigable in combating opportunism, constantly explaining the great harm the opportunists were causing to the workers' interests, and instilling a spirit of implacable hatred for opportunism in all its ugly manifestations. The long years of hard struggle against the police tyranny of tsarism and capitalist oppression had developed splendid militant revolutionary traits in the Russian proletariat. Now that a new revolutionary crisis was maturing, and the workers were preparing for a new revolution, they indignantly turned their backs on the liquidators and their Trotskyist henchmen, who were preaching renunciation of the revolutionary struggle. No less than four-fifths of the class-conscious workers, the vast majority of the proletariat, were as a result won over to the Bolshevik side. The Bolsheviks were able to bring about working-class unity primarily because they upheld the unity of the Party, cleansed of opportunists.

In this period of revolutionary upsurge the question of *international unity* of the working-class movement acquired especial significance. The bourgeoisie was also seeking to divide the working class along national lines. In a multi-national country such as Russia, it was extremely important that the class struggle of the workers of the oppressing nation should merge with that of the workers of the oppressed nations. A characteristic feature of the post-1905 period was the spread of Black-Hundred chauvinism and the growth of nationalism among the bourgeoisie o all the nations of Russia. Nationalist tendencies became mor pronounced in the working-class movement too. The liquidator and Trotskyists vehemently attacked the Party's nationalities pro gramme. All this created a definite threat to the consisten class nature and militant unity of the movement.

Naturally, the national question occupied a prominent plac in the Party's activities. Both the Cracow and the Poronin con ferences adopted special resolutions on the subject. The Marxis programme on the national question and the Party's policy o nationalities were developed and substantiated by Lenin in hi articles "Critical Remarks on the National Question" and "The Righ of Nations to Self-Determination." A prominent contribution to Marxist literature was also Stalin's *Marxism and the Nationa Question*.

Lenin explained that *bourgeois nationalism* and *proletariar internationalism* were irreconcilably hostile philosophies. The nationalist holds narrow national interests above all others, while for the internationalist the most important consideration is the international class solidarity of the workers.

The national question, Lenin wrote, is part of the general question of revolution. National peace under capitalism is possible only under a consistent and fully democratic republican regime. The victory of the bourgeois-democratic revolution is essential for the complete democratisation of Russia. The demands of the Bolshevik programme in that revolution were: the right of nations to self-determination, i.e., the right of secession and formation of independent States; regional autonomy for nations which, for one reason or another, choose to remain part of a given State; complete equality of all nations and languages, with constitutional provisions that would rule out privileges of any kind whatsoever for any one nation and prevent violation of the rights of national minorities.

Such a nationalities programme would help the workers' effective struggle for Socialism. The interests of the proletariat in the battle against capitalism required the closest unity of the workers of all nations and their association in united proletarian organisations. In order to eliminate all national distrust, the working class must seek complete equality for all nations, for only on that basis could fraternal unity in the class struggle be achieved. The fundamental slogan of the right of nations to self-determination was a powerful instrument for the internationalist education of the workers, and one that would rally the masses of the oppressed nationalities around the proletariat. The substance of the Party's national programme, Lenin wrote, was:

"Complete equality of rights for all nations; the right of na-

ions to self-determination;-the amalgamation of the workers of
all nations—this is the nationalities programme that Marxism, the
experience of the whole world, the experience of Russia, teaches
the workers" (*Collected Works*, Vol. 20, p. 423).

The theoretical elucidation by the Bolsheviks of the national
question was a crushing blow to nationalism in Russia.

Lenin's programme on the national question had international
significance, for it was directed against the fallacious theory and
practice of the parties of the Second International, which held
the oppressed peoples in contempt and supported more and more
openly the predatory colonial policy of the imperialist Powers.

By relentlessly combating even the smallest manifestation of
national oppression and every variety of nationalism, the Bolsheviks were able to unite the workers of all the nationalities
of Russia around the Russian workers, who formed the core and
leading force of the working-class movement. The Party drew
the finest sons of the non-Russian peoples into its ranks. The
Bolshevik organisations conducted their revolutionary work in
many of the national minority areas. In Transcaucasia, they set
an example of proletarian internationalism by uniting in their
ranks Russians, Georgians, Armenians and Azerbaijanians.

Appreciable headway was also made by the Bolsheviks in the
national Social-Democratic organisations. The Polish Marxists
were represented at Poronin and supported the Bolsheviks. The
Lettish Social-Democratic Congress condemned the liquidators. The legal newspapers published by the Estonian and
Lithuanian Marxists followed the *Pravda* line.

Together with the rise of the working-class movement, the
party of the working class, the Bolshevik Party, grew and gained
in strength. After the hard years of reaction, and amidst the difficulties created by their illegal status, the Bolsheviks *re-established a mass party*, firmly led and guided by its Central Committee and the latter's Russian and Foreign Bureau. The Party published a widely-read daily newspaper, had a parliamentary group,
several regional, and a number of city committees, nuclei in
many factories and mills, and Party groups in workers' legal
organisations. The Central Committee maintained contact with
nearly 100 organisations and groups throughout the country,
from Vladivostok to Warsaw and from Vologda to Tashkent.
The Central Committee and local organisations reacted with
leaflets to every major development in the life of the country.
Despite continuous police persecution, the Party was able to
publish, in addition to *Pravda*, the legal magazines *Prosveshcheniye*
(*Enlightenment*), *Voprosy Strakhovaniya* (*Social Insurance*), *Rabotnitsa* (*Woman Worker*) and conduct a number of trade union
journals in a Bolshevik spirit.

The Party led every form of proletarian struggle. It organised the fight for the "partial demands" of the workers, integrating the economic needs and political interests of the proletariat. I taught the workers to react to every major manifestation and every crime of tsarist tyranny.

Of special importance for the revolutionary and class education of the proletariat were the annual illegal May Day meetings and the commemoration of Bloody Sunday (January 22 [9], 1905), and the Lena shootings. In recalling these memorable stages of the struggle, the Party conducted its campaign beforehand, calling on the workers to strike and demonstrate on these days. The police, for all its skill in repression, was powerless to prevent the workers responding to the Bolshevik appeals. On January 22, 1913, about 200,000 workers went on strike, and the following year the number was 250,000. The May Day gatherings in 1913 were attended by 420,000 workers, and by more than half a million in 1914.

Everywhere—in mass strikes, street demonstrations, factory gate meetings—the Bolsheviks emphasised that revolution was the only way out, and put forward slogans expressing the people's longings: a democratic republic, an 8-hour working day, confiscation of the landed estates in favour of the peasants. News of these revolutionary strikes and revolutionary demands of the workers reached peasant huts and army barracks. In the revolutionary struggle of the workers the peasants, driven to despair by the exploitation of the landlords, and the soldiers, furious at the tyrannous conditions to which they were subjected, saw an example for themselves to follow.

The working class thus became the leader of the revolution, its standard-bearer, training and organising the masses for victory.

Meanwhile the waves of the working-class movement rose higher and higher. In the first half of 1914 about 1,500,000 workers were involved in strikes. One strike followed another. The strikes on the anniversary of Bloody Sunday were followed by stoppages in protest against the mass poisoning of women workers at a number of St. Petersburg factories. After May Day came the general strike in Baku, a courageous struggle supported by the workers of St. Petersburg, Moscow and other cities. On July 3 the police opened fire on a workers' meeting at the Putilov Works in St. Petersburg. A wave of indignation swept over the country. The St. Petersburg Bolshevik Committee called for immediate strike action. On July 4, 90,000 workers downed tools, on the 7th, 130,000, and on the 11th, 200,000. Demonstrations began in protest against the actions of the tsarist authorities and the war, which everyone felt was about to break out. The strike wave spread to Moscow; barricades were thrown up in St. Petersburg, Baku and Lodz.

Russia was faced with a revolutionary crisis. The landlords and capitalists were accusing each other of inability to put out the flames of revolution. One Black-Hundred newspaper came out with the eloquent headline: "Badayev to the Gallows!" and called for the physical extermination of the working-class leaders. The tsarist government adopted "emergency" measures, the capital was turned into a veritable military camp. *Pravda* was closed down on July 8; wholesale arrests of Bolsheviks began.

The advance of the revolution was interrupted by the outbreak of the world war.

BRIEF SUMMARY

During the years of the new rise of the revolution (1910-1914) the Bolshevik Party was a cardinal factor in the political life of the country.

The Bolsheviks' uncompromising fight against the Mensheviks on all key issues of the working-class movement culminated in the Prague Conference, which expelled the Mensheviks from the Party as traitors to the working-class cause. This complete break with the opportunists played an important part in forging victory over the autocracy and capitalism in Russia and in shaping the destinies of the international working-class movement. The Prague Conference laid down the Party's policy and tactics in conditions of the new rise of the revolutionary movement.

By defeating the liquidators, Trotskyists, national-deviators and other opportunists, and by skilfully combining illegal with legal work, the Bolsheviks won over the majority of the working class. This made for unity of the working-class movement and represented a momentous victory for the Party. It was made possible by the resolute struggle to cleanse the workers' movement of bourgeois influences, and by the correct policy of gathering together all the revolutionary forces of the proletariat.

The Bolshevik newspaper *Pravda* widened and strengthened the Party's ties with the working class. The generation of front-rank workers trained by *Pravda* subsequently played an outstanding part in the Great October Socialist Revolution and in building Socialism. In this period of revolutionary upsurge, the Bolshevik Party made masterly use of the legal press and parliamentary platform for the revolutionary enlightenment of the masses.

The national question figured prominently in the Party's theoretical and practical work. With the labour movement subjected to intensified nationalist propaganda, the Bolsheviks set a shining example of proletarian internationalism. The Party built up its organisations on the principle of proletarian internationalism, and fought indefatigably against nationalism. The Bolshevik organisations in the non-Russian regions combated nationalist parties and trends, and educated the masses in a spirit of proletarian internationalism. Lenin's programme on the national question and the Party's nationalities policy convinced the peoples oppressed by tsarism that only the Bolsheviks were the true defenders of their rights and interests.

The Party mastered and skilfully applied every form of working-class struggle and organisation. It took the lead in the battles of the proletariat at a time of mounting revolutionary crisis. Headed by the Bolsheviks, the working class came forward as the leader of the whole people's revolutionary struggle for freedom.

By all its revolutionary and genuinely internationalist activity the Bolshevik Party was prepared for the great ordeals of the imperialist world war.

CHAPTER SIX

THE BOLSHEVIK PARTY
IN THE PERIOD OF THE IMPERIALIST WORLD WAR.
THE SECOND REVOLUTION IN RUSSIA

(1914-February 1917)

1. Outbreak and Causes of the First World War. Collapse of the Second International

The imperialist world war broke out on August 1 (July 19, old style), 1914. It was the cumulative result of the course of development of imperialism.

The distinctive feature of imperialism, the highest and last stage of capitalism, is the domination of monopolies—syndicates, trusts and similar organisations of a handful of millionaires controlling vast amounts of capital. Not content with exploitation of the home market, they sought to penetrate the colonies and economically underdeveloped countries. By the beginning of the century the whole world had already been divided among a small group of leading capitalist Powers.

But under capitalism even development is impossible. Individual enterprises, industries, countries overtake and outstrip others, which have to give way to their more successful competitors; or the latter themselves yield place to others, still more successful. Imperialism, with its domination of giant monopolies, accentuates this unevenness, both in the economic and political fields. The development of capitalism becomes more spasmodic, and this constantly upsets the international equilibrium, changing the relative economic and military strength of the Powers. And the greater their strength, the more insistent becomes their demand for new markets and colonies, because in a society based on private ownership of the means of production, division of spoils is always in accordance with strength or capital. But with the world already divided up among the biggest capitalist States, its redivision could only take place at the expense of one or another of these States, that is, through war.

Lenin pointed out that the emergence of powerful capitalist monopoly associations and their struggle for an economic redivision of the world which was already divided territorially was bound, in the era of imperialism, to lead to wars.

The imperialists had, in fact, long been preparing for a war to redivide the world. The most bellicose in this respect were the German militarists, who considered that they had been cheated out of their share of colonies. By the close of the last century, Germany had overtaken Britain in industrial development and was ousting her from her traditional markets. Germany's aim was a radical redivision of the world in her favour. This contradiction between British and German imperialism was in fact the root cause of the war. But a big part was also played by other imperialist contradictions, between Germany and France, Russia and Germany, etc. Long before the war, in 1879-1882, Germany had formed an alliance with Austria-Hungary and Italy against Russia and France. The latter retaliated by forming an alliance of their own, and the British imperialists, fearing Germany's advance to world domination, concluded an agreement (Entente) with France. In 1907, Russia concluded a treaty with Britain, as a result of which Russia joined the Entente. The two mutually opposed blocs in Europe thus took final shape.

Economically dependent, mainly on French and British capital, Russia was drawn into the war on the side of the Entente. But the tsarist government had its own reasons for taking part in the imperialist war. The Russian capitalists strongly resented German competition in the domestic market. The dominant classes of Russia wanted new markets in which there would be no competition. The Russian imperialists were out to gain possession of Constantinople and the straits leading from the Black Sea to the Mediterranean; they wanted to seize Turkish Armenia and thereby bring the whole of Armenia under Russian rule. This clashed with German imperialist plans in the Near East: Germany was penetrating into Turkey and Iran and had secured a concession for a railway from Berlin to Baghdad. Russo-German contradictions in the Near East became especially keen at the beginning of the twentieth century.

Another major cause of the war was the imperialist desire to hamstring the mounting revolutionary movement, which in the past ten years had grown to powerful dimensions in every country. The Russian revolution of 1905-1907 had greatly stimulated the working-class struggle in Europe and America and set off a national liberation movement in the East. The governments of the leading Powers—and the tsarist government first and foremost—feared a further spread of the revolution, and believed that war would sidetrack the masses from revolutionary struggle.

The imperialists hoped that by instigating the workers of different countries against each other they could drive a wedge into the international proletarian movement, poison it with the venom of chauvinism, physically annihilate a big section of the advanced workers and in this way crush, or at any rate weaken, the revolutionary pressure of the masses.

The war grew into a global conflict, with 28 countries of an aggregate population of over 1,500 million gradually drawn into its vortex. About 74 million people were mobilised.

The bourgeois parties of every country urged the people to support the war. In Germany, the people were told that Russian tsarism would destroy all their democratic gains. In France, the argument was that Prussian militarism would trample down French democracy. In Russia, the people were told the Germans had attacked their country with the object of enslaving it. In short, the bourgeois parties tried to condition the people to the belief that the war was being fought for national salvation and that everyone had to take up arms in defence of the bourgeois fatherland. There was the propaganda figment that this was to be the last war. The petty-bourgeois parties also supported the capitalists and sought to justify the war.

Following in the wake of the bourgeois parties, nearly all the parties of the Second International, which considered themselves to be the representatives of the proletariat, disregarded the class interests of the workers and came out in support of the war. The German Socialists, for many years regarded as the foremost party of the Second International, voted in parliament for war credits. The French Socialists, and their colleagues in Britain and Belgium, went a step further and joined the reactionary capitalist governments in order to facilitate prosecution of the war.

In Russia, the Menshevik Duma members at first voted against war credits, so strong were anti-war sentiments among the workers. But that proved only a manoeuvre, motivated by fear of losing whatever influence they still enjoyed within the working class. Thereafter the Mensheviks accepted the bourgeois slogan of defence of the fatherland. The Socialist-Revolutionaries were divided on the war issue. The bulk of them supported the tsarist government; the Left wing at first came out against the war and even shared in international Socialist anti-war conferences, but flatly refused to break with the party's jingo majority.

The Second International collapsed and fell to pieces: the Socialists of the Entente countries (including the Russian Mensheviks and Socialist-Revolutionaries) held a conference in London in 1915, while the Socialists of the German bloc met in Vienna. Both conferences voted for defence of their bourgeois fatherlands.

This was outright betrayal of the interests of the working class, and outright treachery to the Socialist cause, all the more so since the Social-Democratic leaders had time and again adopted resolutions against war and had given a pledge to the workers of their countries, and to the international labour movement generally, to launch a struggle against an imperialist war. Moreover, the Stuttgart (1907) and Basle (1912) congresses of the Second International had solemnly, in the name of all the Socialist parties, appealed to the workers not only to fight against the outbreak of war and for its cessation if it did break out, but also to take advantage of the crisis created by the war in order to hasten the overthrow of the bourgeoisie. Now, by betraying the proletariat and supporting their own bourgeoisie, the parties of the Second International were assuming political responsibility for the long and devastating war into which the imperialists had plunged mankind.

How did it come about that the Socialist parties went back on their own Basle manifesto and betrayed Socialism?

The imperialists shared part of their profits from colonial rapine with other sections of the population. This led to the emergence in the capitalist countries, over several decades, of a labour aristocracy, a trade union officialdom, Social-Democrat parliamentarians and numerous other functionaries. These were the elements that made up the petty-bourgeois opportunist component of the Second International and spread bourgeois influence within the working class. Lenin had good reason to describe the opportunists as agents of the bourgeoisie in the working-class movement. They advocated class collaboration and repudiated the class struggle; they renounced revolutionary methods and helped the bourgeoisie and the government of their particular country. The Bolsheviks had vigorously opposed the opportunists at congresses of the Second International where they united the Left-wing forces in the struggle against opportunism. Lenin repeatedly warned that the Social-Democratic leaders only talked of being opposed to opportunism, but that they would in practice side with the bourgeoisie.

The opportunists had got the upper hand in most Socialist parties, and with the outbreak of the war their secret compact with the bourgeoisie became an open alliance. Their approval of war credits and participation, in a number of countries, in bourgeois governments, meant open class collaboration with the imperialist bourgeoisie, a policy of preserving "civil peace" and supporting the imperialist governments in their predatory war. In Russia that policy was followed by the Mensheviks (Plekhanov, Potressov, Chkheidze and others) and by the Socialist-Revolutionaries. Opportunism had developed into chauvinism, into direct betrayal of internationalist principles and open support of the bourgeoisie. Obedient to the will of the bourgeoisie, the social-chauvinists called on the workers of their own country to defend the bourgeois fatherland, incited them to fight the workers of other countries, called on the working people to exterminate one another.

Besides the Right wing, which had come out openly in defence of the bourgeoisie, there was another form of opportunism in all the parties of the Second International, namely, the centrist trend. It had manifested itself even before the war, when the centrists had urged that avowed opportunists be allowed to remain in the Social-Democratic parties. Through these opportunists, the centrists maintained the alliance with the bourgeoisie. Kautsky, Trotsky, Martov were representatives of that trend. Lenin considered centrism to be the most harmful and dangerous variety of opportunism, for the centrists were disguised opportunists. They were "a hundredfold more harmful and dangerous to the working-class movement" than the avowed opportunists, for they masked their betrayal of the workers and their alliance with the bourgeoisie under Left-wing phraseology. The Trotskyists' slogan "neither victory nor defeat" could only mean that everything, including the tsarist regime, should be retained intact. This was a patently chauvinist slogan, for it implied defence of the tsarist government, protection of tsarism. Lenin wrote:

"Those who support the slogan 'Neither victory nor defeat,' are conscious or unconscious chauvinists, or at best conciliatory petty bourgeois; in any case they are *enemies* of proletarian policy, supporters of the existing governments and existing ruling classes" (*Collected Works*, Vol. 21, p. 251).

In the whole of the Second International *only one party* had worked out a consistently revolutionary Marxist policy on war and peace and was heroically fighting for its application. That party was the *Bolshevik Party*. The war was also opposed by the Bulgarian Workers' Social-Democratic Party (Tesnyaks) led by Dimitr Blagoyev, Georgi Dimitrov and Vasil Kolarov. It conducted active propaganda in the army and in the rear, rousing mass sentiment against the war. The Serbian Social-Democratic Party likewise came out against the war. The Italian Socialist Party at first took an internationalist stand, but subsequently, in common with other Social-Democratic parties, slid into defencism. In Germany, the imperialist war was actively opposed by Karl Liebknecht, Rosa Luxemburg, Clara Zetkin and Franz Mehring. But even they did not support the slogan advanced by Lenin and the Bolsheviks, that of the defeat of one's own government and the transformation of the imperialist war into a civil one.

For the war and, consequently, for imperialism, or against the war and, consequently, for revolution—such was the dividing line between the parties. The basic position of the overwhelming majority of the parties in the Second International was to support the war, their own bourgeoisie and their own government, for victory over other nations.

Lenin and the Bolsheviks went "against the stream." Led by Lenin, the Party called for a struggle against the imperialist war and for converting it into a civil war; he called on the peoples to fight against their own governments, against the capitalists and the landlords. Above the strident chorus of imperialist toadies, who were glorifying war, rose the courageous voice of the fighters for Socialism and for the people's interests. Amidst the flood of opportunism which, it seemed, had drowned the whole international working-class movement for a long time to come, Lenin and the Bolshevik Party raised aloft the banner of Marxism, of internationalism, and set an example of devotion to the cause of international proletarian solidarity.

2. The Party's Revolutionary Activities Among the Masses During the Imperialist War

The outbreak of the war found Lenin at Poronin, in Austria-Hungary, where he was arrested by the Austrian police. After his release Lenin went to Berne, in Switzerland, where, in the closing days of August, 1914, he acquainted the local Bolshevik group with his theses on the war. These were then sent to Russia through F. N. Samoilov, a Bolshevik Duma member. They were discussed and approved with some amendments by the Petrograd (former St. Petersburg), Moscow, Kharkov, Kiev and other leading Party organisations. In October, 1914, the Party's central organ, *Sotsial-Demokrat*, published the Central Committee manifesto, "The War and Russian Social-Democracy."

The nature of the war was differently assessed by different parties. For most parties the criterion was: who had begun the war? They accordingly divided wars into offensive and defensive ones. For other parties the criterion was: on whose territory was the war being fought? Bourgeois pacifists called for opposition to all wars, because, they argued, every war involves violence, rapine and the seizure of foreign territory. They dreamed of everlasting peace without the overthrow of capitalism.

The Bolsheviks maintained that the historical background and nature of the war should be concretely examined in each individual case. They rejected as incorrect the division of wars into offensive and defensive, for both elements are likely to occur in every war. The aggressor is at times obliged to take the defensive, and offensive operations are widely employed in wars of liberation. In defining the nature of a war, the important thing is likewise not who started it, who attacked whom. All the imperialists had prepared the first world war; but Germany had unleashed it at what she believed to be the most opportune moment.

The whole question was, *what class* is waging the war, *what policy* is the war continuing, *what political aims* is the ruling class pursuing in the war. From that standpoint, revolutionary Marxists divide wars into just and unjust. Wars waged by an oppressed class against its oppressors, by slaves against slave-owners, by serfs against feudal landlords, by wage-workers against the bourgeoisie, wars for national liberation, peoples' wars against the menace of national enslavement, wars of the victorious proletariat in defence of Socialism, against imperialist Powers—such wars, in the Marxist view, are just wars.

The imperialist world war, like all wars generally, was the continuation of the pre-war policy of the ruling classes. The policy of the imperialists at home had been to strengthen their own position and intensify the exploitation of the working people. The continuation of that policy on an international scale meant a struggle for world domination, for the redivision of the world in favour of the stronger Powers, the drive for new markets and colonies, and the intensified plundering of dependent countries. The world war was therefore imperialist on both sides.

And from this imperialist nature of the war followed the Bolshevik attitude towards it. True to the interests of the working class and the ideas of Socialism, the Party called not only for fighting against the war and for its immediate termination, but also for utilising all the difficulties created by the war to hasten the overthrow of tsarism. In opposition to the slogans of "civil peace" and class collaboration, upheld by the Mensheviks and other social-chauvinists, the Party's fundamental slogan was *the conversion of the imperialist war into a civil war*, into revolution against the ruling classes. The Party recommended a number of concrete measures to attain that goal: 1) unconditional refusal to vote for war credits, and immediate withdrawal of all Socialists from bourgeois governments; 2) rejection of any agreement with the bourgeoisie and of "civil peace"; 3) establishment of illegal organisations in countries where they did not exist and where work in legal organisations was difficult; 4) support of fraternisation by the soldiers at the front; 5) support for all revolutionary mass actions of the proletariat.

The reverses of tsarism at the front made the revolutionary mass struggle easier. In opposition to the Socialist-Revolutionary and Menshevik slogan of defence of the bourgeois-landlord fatherland, the Bolsheviks called *for the defeat of the tsarist government in the war*. This did not, of course, imply that the Party called on the people to blow up supply depots or commit other acts of sabotage. What it did imply was that the proletarian party should under no circumstances support measures designed to strengthen the tsarist government. The policy of the defeat of one's own government in the imperialist war was a continuation of the revolutionary struggle. The reverses suffered by the tsarist government weakened tsarism and thereby helped the revolutionary movement, making it easier to overthrow tsarism and carry the revolution to its victorious conclusion. The opponents of these Bolshevik tactics sought to attribute to Lenin the conclusion that the policy of the defeat of tsarism would lead to the victory of Germany. They were careful, however, not to mention the fact that Lenin applied the slogan concerning the defeat of one's own government not only to Russia, but to all the warring countries, thereby emphasising the internationalism of the Bolshevik tactics.

The third and last slogan advanced by the Party during the war was for *a complete break with the bankrupt Second International*, since continued unity with the opportunists would have been tantamount to continued alliance with the bourgeoisie. Lenin called for the creation of a new, Third International.

The bourgeois and petty-bourgeois parties accused the Bolsheviks of indifference to the interests of their country, of treason and lack of patriotism because they opposed the bourgeois slogan of defence of the fatherland in the imperialist war. The very men whose policies were inimical to the people and were converting a great country into a pawn of the imperialist Powers, Britain and France, were now slanderously accusing the Bolsheviks of lack of national pride. Lenin indignantly refuted that calumny. He wrote in his article "The National Pride of the Great Russians":

"Is the sense of national pride alien to us, Great-Russian class-conscious proletarians? Of course, not! We love our language and our country, we are doing more than anybody to raise *her* toiling masses (i.e., nine-tenths of *her* population) to the level of conscious democrats and Socialists. It pains us, more than anybody else, to see and feel the outrage, oppression and humiliation inflicted on our splendid country by the tsarist hangmen, nobles and capitalists. We are proud of the fact that these outrages have roused resistance in our midst, the midst of the Great Russians; that from *this* midst came Radishchev, the Decembrists and the revolutionary commoners of the seventies; that in 1905 the Great-Russian working class created a mighty, revolutionary mass party;

that at the same time the Great-Russian muzhik began to become a democrat, and began to overthrow the priest and the landlord" (*Collected Works*, Vol. 21, p. 85).

The Bolsheviks were opposed not to the fatherland as such, but to the landlord-bourgeois fatherland, to the attempt to present tsarist Russia, whose landlords and capitalists were ruthlessly exploiting the labouring people, as the fatherland. The Party exposed the false, bourgeois interpretation of the concept of fatherland.

The Bolsheviks represented a genuine patriotic force precisely because they called for the defeat of their government in the imperialist war, for the overthrow of the anti-popular government. Lenin explained how the Marxists understood the relation between proletarian internationalism and patriotism. He was not a patriot who supported this predatory war, a war fought in the interests of the landlords and bourgeoisie, and sought to preserve the privileges of the ruling classes. He alone was a patriot who fought for the interests of the people, who wanted a "free and independent, democratic, republican, proud Great Russia, building her relations with her neighbours on the humane principle of equality, and not on the feudal principle of privilege, degrading to a great nation" (*ibid.*, p. 86). In rousing the people to overthrow tsarism, and in fighting for Socialism, the Russian proletariat—"the principal driving force in the Communist revolution"—was fighting for a free, independent and democratic fatherland.

"The interests (not as some lackey would understand them) of the national pride of the Great Russians," Lenin wrote, "coincide with the *Socialist* interests of the Great-Russian (and all other) proletarians" (*ibid.*, p. 87).

A conference of Bolshevik organisations abroad held in Berne, Switzerland, in February, 1915, discussed the Party's tactics and approved its slogans on the war issue.

On the basis of Lenin's conceptions, the Bolsheviks developed their revolutionary work among the masses.

The tsarist government tried to crush the Party by unprecedented repressions and wholesale arrests. Every local Party Committee was raided by the police. Members of the St. Petersburg Committee were arrested on more than thirty occasions during the war; the Moscow organisation was kept in a state of constant tension by police raids, and several attempts to re-establish the Moscow Committee failed. In Samara successive committees were arrested six times in one year.

All the Bolshevik publications were closed, including the legal journal *Voprosy Strakhovaniya*. Most of the trade unions were dissolved by the government. Even such cultural associations as the "Wholesome Recreation Society" in Samara, the "Enlightenment" club in Moscow and the "Self-Education Society" in Petrograd were banned, out of fear that they might become centres of revolutionary propaganda and meeting-places for Party functionaries.

No other revolutionary party had ever had to work in such conditions. An employer had only to give the police a list of "undesirable" workers for them to be clapped in jail immediately.

But neither police terror, nor frame-ups, nor victimisation could break the Party's will or prevent its activities. In the very first week of the war, anti-war leaflets were issued by the Party organisations in Petrograd, Yekaterinoslav, Kharkov, Kiev, Moscow, Ufa, Tula and Samara.

The Bolshevik Duma members toured a number of industrial areas, re-establishing Party committees and organising new ones, and arranging numerous workers' meetings at which anti-war resolutions were adopted. The Bolshevik Duma members called a conference of representatives from Petrograd, Ivanovo-Voznesensk, Kharkov and Riga at Ozerki, a village near Petrograd, on November 2-4, 1914. It discussed Lenin's theses on the war and endorsed them unreservedly.

Acting on information supplied by agent-provocateurs, the police arrested all the participants. The Duma members were searched and released, only to be re-arrested on the night of November 5, and committed for trial. The trial was held on February 10-13, 1915, and the Bolshevik deputies took advantage of it to explain the Party's anti-war slogans. The tsarist court sentenced them to life exile in Turukhansk Territory (Eastern Siberia).

Tried together with the courageous Duma deputies was Kamenev, who had attended the Ozerki Conference. Unlike the Duma deputies, however, he renounced the Party's slogan that called for the defeat of one's own government in the war, declaring that he disagreed with Lenin and the Party. To prove this he requested that a Menshevik chauvinist be summoned as witness.

The Party branded Kamenev's behaviour at the trial as treachery.

The trial was of vast political significance. It showed the world proletariat the stand that a genuinely internationalist party should take in an imperialist war. At a time when the opportunists of the Second International had disgraced themselves by joining bourgeois governments, the Bolshevik deputies remained loyal to Socialism, though this meant penal servitude.

The arrest of the Duma members left the Party with less legal facilities for directing the revolutionary struggle. This made things more difficult, but it could not halt Party activities. The St. Petersburg Committee issued over 90 leaflets during the war (an average of three leaflets a month) in a total of more than 300,000 copies, and they found their way to every part of Russia. According to incomplete data, over 40 Party organisations issued leaflets during the war. In addition to those mentioned above, they included the Yekaterinburg, Zlatoust, Ivanovo-Voznesensk, Krasnoyarsk, and the Donets coalfield, Kronstadt, Nizhni-Novgorod, Rostov, Riga, Baku and Tiflis Party committees. All in all, over 400 different leaflets were put out in the war years.

The Party made use of every opportunity to conduct revolutionary propaganda. Its members were active in the illegal trade unions, in the workers' co-operatives, sick-benefit societies and cultural organisations that had so far escaped the police ban. In all these bodies the Party fought to win the masses over from the social-chauvinists. The Menshevik defencists were helped by the police; quite often the Mensheviks arrested at a meeting would be set free, while the Bolsheviks would be sentenced to penal servitude. None the less, in the teeth of ceaseless persecution, the Bolsheviks were able in the course of the war to gain a dominant influence in the trade unions and other labour organisations. The Party was the recognised leader of the workers.

This was most clearly demonstrated by the development of the strike struggle. The war brought the working people hunger, cold and incalculable sacrifice. The economy was dislocated; the transport system could not cope even with food shipments; the people were left without bare necessities, even bread. Prices soared, but wages remained the same or increased only slightly. The capitalists were making enormous profits out of the war, while all its burdens were borne by the people.

The early victories of the tsarist army at the front were followed by one reverse after another. The Germans overran Poland, part of the Baltic provinces and Byelorussia. Millions of refugees fled to the interior provinces. Their position was even more difficult than that of the rest of the population.

There was growing popular discontent with the war and with the policy of the tsarist government. The industrial workers were the first to translate this resentment into action; they set a fighting example to all the working people. The number of strikes grew rapidly—from about 70 in 1914 (after the outbreak of the war), involving about 35,000 workers, to more than 1,000 (according to minimised official figures) in 1915, involving over 500,000 workers. The strikes were brutally suppressed: in June, 1915, the police fired on a strikers' demonstration at Kostroma, killing and wounding more than 50, in August over 100 were killed and wounded at a meeting of strikers in Ivanovo-Voznesensk. The St. Petersburg Party Committee organised a protest strike.

Frightened by the surging wave of strikes and the government's inability to crush it, the capitalists resorted to a skilful manoeuvre in an attempt to placate the workers and bring them under their influence. War Industry Committees were set up in 1915, by permission of the authorities. Their purpose was to support the tsarist government, boost munitions production, step up exploitation and give factory owners a bigger say in the allocation of immensely profitable war contracts. The next step was to set up "worker groups" in these War Industry Committees, in order to create a semblance of "class truce." The Mensheviks helped in this, urging the workers to take part in the "groups." The Mensheviks were, in effect, following in the footsteps of their West European counterparts who had joined bourgeois governments, for the War Industry Committees were semigovernmental bodies.

The Bolsheviks vigorously opposed participation in the committees, and explained the position to the workers in the factories. Though the Party had to face the combined forces of the tsarist government, the bourgeoisie, the Socialist-Revolutionaries and the Mensheviks, it was able to foil the attempts of the bourgeoisie to bring about "class truce." The overwhelming majority of the working class declared against participation in the War Industry Committees: out of the 239 regional and local committees, elections of workers' representatives were held in only 70, and representatives were elected in only 36, or in 15 per cent of the total. The Russian proletariat had not succumbed to jingoism.

The Party developed extensive activities among the soldiers. Industrial workers had been mobilised for the army, including tens of thousands who had taken an active part in the revolutionary struggle. These were the Party's chief support in the army.

This work acquired immense significance. Concentrated in the army were millions of peasants, chiefly poor peasants; and the Bolsheviks took advantage of this to promote worker and peasant unity in the revolutionary struggle. Bolshevik leaflets called not only for peace, but also for the confiscation of the landed estates.

The Party committees in Petrograd, Moscow, Kharkov, Kiev, Yekaterinoslav, Riga and many other industrial centres issued special leaflets for distribution among the soldiers, telling them about the workers' strike struggles, the mounting revolutionary sentiment among the people and the need for a joint struggle against tsarism. They called for fraternisation at the front. There had been individual cases of fraternisation towards the close of 1914; in the spring of 1915, more and more instances were reported from the Austrian front, and in 1916, they became a common occurrence. Party organisations were founded in a number of army units. M. V. Frunze, N. V. Krylenko, A. F. Myasnikov (Myasnikyan) and other prominent Bolsheviks were active in the army and navy.

The Party conducted extensive political work in the navy, which was recruited largely from skilled workmen. Party groups were formed on every major vessel of the Baltic Fleet. Their activities were co-ordinated by the "Central Collective of the Kronstadt Military Organisation," which maintained connections with the military branch of the St. Petersburg Party Committee.

In October, 1915, a mutiny broke out on the battleship *Gangut*. The vessel was surrounded by destroyers and submarines and forced to surrender. In December, about a hundred of her crew were court-martialled, and 26 sentenced to penal servitude.

The St. Petersburg Committee made this trial the occasion for a special appeal to the army and navy, calling for unity of the revolutionary army with the revolutionary proletariat and the entire people. In October, 1916, when another group of Bolshevik sailors was court-martialled, the committee issued a strike appeal, to which some 130,000 Petrograd workers responded by a three-day stoppage. This and other mass actions frightened the government and the court did not dare pass any death sentences. The close connection between the working-class movement and these actions in the army and navy was a clear indication of the strengthening alliance of the proletariat and peasantry.

The Party's self-sacrificing and heroic work in the face of tsarist terror and provocation showed the working class that in the Bolsheviks it had a party fully capable of leading the people to victory in the revolution, and ready to do so.

The Party availed itself of every opportunity to make known the ideas of Bolshevism to the international proletariat and thereby help Social-Democratic workers to break free of opportunist influence.

In March, 1915, the Bolsheviks participated in the International Women's Socialist Conference in Berne, at which eight countries were represented by 25 delegates. The conference was convened on the initiative of Bolshevik women's organisations, and the Party's representatives, I. F. Armand and N. K. Krupskaya, played a prominent part in its proceedings. They drafted a resolution condemning social-chauvinism and urging acceptance of the slogan of converting the imperialist war into a civil war. Lenin and the Bolsheviks also rendered valuable assistance to the revolutionary youth movement. The Party took part in the International Socialist Youth Conference (Berne, March, 1915), at which ten countries were represented and at which International Youth Day was inaugurated.

Though neither of these conferences fully accepted the Bolshevik proposals, the speeches of the Party representatives exerted a powerful influence on the development of the international revolutionary movement.

An International Socialist Conference was held at Zimmerwald, a village near Berne, in the latter part of August, 1915. It was attended by 38 delegates from 11 countries. Most of the delegates were centrists, followers of Karl Kautsky. The conference manifesto, though emphasising the need to campaign for peace, did not advance the slogan of converting the imperialist war into a civil war, nor that of the defeat of one's own government and a complete break with opportunism.

Though the Zimmerwald Conference was dominated by inconsistent and vacillating elements, the Party took part in its work, believing that closer contact with them was both possible and necessary to further the struggle against social-chauvinism. But Lenin suggested that the Party should not confine itself to what was acceptable to these elements; it must criticise their vacillations, underline their half-heartedness and explain that a democratic peace was possible only by converting the imperialist war into a civil war.

On Lenin's initiative a Zimmerwald Left group of eight delegates was formed at the conference. It proposed a draft resolution which, basically, adhered to Lenin's slogans, and in a special statement pointed out the inadequacy of the manifesto and the refusal of its authors to break with opportunism. But the group voted for the manifesto, since it represented a first step in the fight against the war.

After the conference the Zimmerwald Left held a meeting of its own and elected a bureau. The group declared that, while remaining within the Zimmerwald organisation, it would conduct an independent international campaign in conformity with the draft resolution and draft manifesto it had brought before the conference. The Zimmerwald Left published a magazine in German, *Vorbote (Herald)*. The Bolsheviks, the only group to take a consistent stand, were the guiding force in the Zimmerwald Left.

It soon became the kernel of a broader internationalist movement that spread to every country. The success of the Zimmerwald Left made itself felt at the second International Socialist

Conference at Kienthal, Switzerland, in April, 1916. This time there were 43 delegates, 12 of them adherents of the Zimmerwald Left, which on a number of issues obtained as much as 45 per cent of the total vote.

The Bolsheviks fulfilled their international duty. Their courageous stand and activity contributed to the subsequent formation of Communist parties in all the capitalist countries.

3. Lenin's Theory of Socialist Revolution

Imperialism had brought mankind up to the threshold of Socialist revolution, and had made the latter an immediate and practical task. The war had accelerated the maturing of the prerequisites of revolution. The new conditions in which the proletarian class struggle was taking place required a new approach on the part of Marxist parties to the problems of revolution, and the ability creatively to apply the basic principles of Marxism in the new situation.

The founders of Marxism had disclosed the laws governing the rise, development and doom of the capitalist system. But in the days of Marx and Engels Socialist revolution was not yet an immediate goal; and Lenin was the first Marxist to give a profound analysis of the new era. This he did in his *Imperialism, the Highest Stage of Capitalism*, written in 1916 and based on a searching study of a vast amount of factual and historical data. From this analysis Lenin concluded that towards the beginning of the century capitalism had entered a new stage, imperialism, that it had "grown into a world-wide system of colonial oppression and financial strangulation of the overwhelming majority of the population of the world by a handful of 'advanced' countries" (*Collected Works*, Vol. 22, p. 179).

Imperialism rendered all the contradictions of capitalism extremely acute, above all its basic contradictions: production was becoming increasingly social in character, while appropriation remained private, the means of production being the private property of a handful of monopolists. It was the latter, and not the working people, who benefited from the gigantic development of the productive forces. Having concentrated immense wealth in their hands, the monopolies were all-powerful and, in fact, controlled the whole power of the State. Political reaction was becoming more pronounced everywhere. Monopoly rule brought with it a drastic rise in living costs, more unemployment and excessive taxes to maintain the army and government machine. Oppression and exploitation were carried to unprecedented extremes. This greatly aggravated the contradiction between labour and capital, between the bourgeoisie and the prole tariat.

At the same time, the contradictions between individual impe rialist countries and between groups of countries over redivision of the world became ever sharper, culminating in the world war

Lastly, there was an extreme sharpening of contradictions between the handful of imperialist States and the numerous colonial and semi-colonial areas where hundreds of millions of people were enslaved. The development of capitalist relations in the colonies led to the emergence of a national proletariat capable of leading the masses.

Such unparalleled accentuation of all the contradictions of capitalism was a distinctive feature of imperialism as the last stage of capitalism. Lenin defined imperialism as "moribund capitalism."

From the very outset of his revolutionary activity Lenin con centrated on a study of such vital theoretical problems of the revolution as that of the hegemony of the proletariat; its alliance with the whole of the peasantry and their revolutionary-democrat ic dictatorship in the bourgeois-democratic revolution; the de velopment of the latter into a Socialist revolution, and the al liance of the proletariat with the poorest peasantry; proletarian dictatorship, and the leading role of the Party in the revolution. Now, in the war years, on the basis of his analysis of imperial ism, Lenin developed the theory of Socialist revolution, and en riched it with new propositions, which in the main amount to the following:

1. Imperialism had created the objective prerequisites for carrying out a Socialist revolution. "Imperialism is the eve of the social revolution of the proletariat," is how Lenin defined the last stage of capitalism (*Collected Works*, Vol. 22, p. 182). But revolutions do not come of their own accord; nor can they be artificially induced or imported. Revolution matures within society itself, it grows out of objectively matured crises. Revo lution is inconceivable without a general political crisis embrac ing all strata of the population. Such a crisis was created by the imperialist war of 1914-1918.

For the war was the product of an age in which capitalism had reached the apex of its development—a stage characterised by the domination of monopoly and finance capital, when the ex port of capital rather than commodities had acquired paramount importance, when the territorial division of the world among the leading capitalist Powers was complete and its economic divi sion among the international monopolies had begun. The war had been engendered by imperialism, a system characterised by accentuation of all the contradictions of capitalism. But in its turn, the war had greatly aggravated all the contradictions latent in imperialism, and brought them to the surface. It was thus the beginning, and a clear manifestation, of the *general crisis of capitalism.* In most countries it had brought about a revolutionary situation. The imperialist war accelerated the development of capitalism. Lenin demonstrated that in the course of the war monopoly capitalism was being converted into State-monopoly capitalism, with the monopolists gaining increasing control over the State. But, on the other hand, the war had placed such a strain on the working people that they were faced with the choice of either perishing under imperialist rule, or entrusting the guidance of society to the proletariat for the transition to Socialism.

2. The three basic features of a revolutionary situation are: first, the ruling classes can no longer continue to govern as before. "For a revolution to break out," Lenin wrote, "it is not enough for the 'lower classes not to want' to live in the old way; it is necessary also that the 'upper classes should be unable' to live in the old way" (*Collected Works*, Vol. 21, p. 189). Second, acute worsening of the poverty and misery of the labouring masses as a result of the crisis. Third, discontent with the policy of the ruling classes, expressed in active popular movements.

Such are the objective conditions (that is, conditions not dependent on the will of individuals, parties or classes) that create a revolutionary situation.

However, not every revolutionary situation results in revolution. For a revolutionary situation to translate itself into revolution subjective, as well as objective, factors are needed, namely, the ability and readiness of the advanced class to fight for the overthrow of the ruling classes. And that, as Lenin already emphasised in his early works, is a quality that has to be forged, fashioned, by the revolutionary Marxist party of the working class.

3. For a Socialist revolution to take place, it is not at all necessary for the proletariat to become the majority of the population, as the Kautskyites maintained. The Socialist revolution is not a single act nor a single battle. It is a whole era of class battles, economic, political and ideological. Lenin showed that the revolution would consist of a series of battles waged against the ruling classes by all the oppressed and discontented classes, groups and elements of the population, but first and foremost by the proletariat and its ally, the peasantry. It would consist, also, of a movement of the semi-proletarian masses against landlord, bourgeois, national and other forms of oppression, of revolts of the colonial peoples and of other forms of mass struggle. The task of the proletariat is to lead all these battles, and direct

them towards a single goal—the overthrow of imperialism and the accomplishment of a Socialist revolution. Lenin wrote: "Whoever expects a 'pure' social revolution, will *never* live to see it. Such a person only pays lip service to revolution without understanding what revolution really is" (*Collected Works*, Vol. 22, p. 340).

4. The national liberation movement against imperialism weakens and undermines it, thereby facilitating its overthrow by the workers of the more advanced countries. On the other hand, the workers' revolutionary struggle makes for the success of the national liberation struggle of the oppressed nations.

The leaders of the bankrupt parties of the Second International refused to recognise the national liberation movement as a component of the Socialist revolution, and in this way condemned the revolution to defeat. The Trotskyists, like all the centrist elements, maintained that national liberation wars were impossible in the imperialist era. Bukharin and Pyatakov likewise believed that national liberation wars were impossible in the conditions of imperialism, and opposed the Party's programme demand for the self-determination of nations.

Lenin proved that this non-recognition of national liberation wars under imperialism actually amounted to a defence and justification of imperialism; it meant refusing to take into account such an important reserve of revolution as the anti-imperialist struggle of oppressed nations. He declared, in 1916, that the Party was "*for* utilising *all* national movements against imperialism for the purposes of the Socialist revolution" (*ibid.*, pp. 327-28).

5. Imperialism was a world-wide system, and it was therefore by no means obligatory that the revolution should take place in the most advanced capitalist country. Given the necessary objective and subjective factors—a certain level of capitalist development, the existence of a proletariat and a proletarian party capable of leading the peasantry and the other non-proletarian masses—the imperialist chain would be broken at its weakest link. A Socialist revolution could take place in a country where the contradictions were acutest and where the necessary forces had been prepared.

6. Imperialism and the imperialist war had created a new situation. Lenin, basing himself on Marxist theory, accordingly reviewed the proposition formulated by Marx and Engels that Socialism would triumph simultaneously in all or most capitalist countries. From that proposition, by which all Marxists had been guided before the war, it followed that the victory of Socialism in one separate country was impossible. That was true of *pre-imperialist* capitalism, in the period when capitalism was on the upgrade, and when the success of a Socialist revolution

could be ensured only by the simultaneous revolutionary action of the proletariat in all or the majority of capitalist countries against the domination of capital. This proposition, however, did not hold good in the era of imperialist capitalism; it had become obsolete and had to be replaced.

Lenin proved, by his study of imperialism, that the unevenness of the economic and political development of capitalism in its imperialist stage had assumed a particularly catastrophic and spasmodic character. Proceeding from this law, Lenin came to the conclusion that in the imperialist period Socialism could not triumph simultaneously in all countries, but that its victory was possible first in one country alone, or in a few countries. That view was set forth in two of his articles, "The United States of Europe Slogan" (1915) and "The War Programme of the Proletarian Revolution" (1916).

"Uneven economic and political development," Lenin wrote, "is an absolute law of capitalism. Hence, the victory of Socialism is possible at first in a few capitalist countries, or even in one, taken singly" (*Collected Works*, Vol. 21, p. 311).

Reverting to the question in his "War Programme of the Proletarian Revolution," Lenin emphasised:

"The development of capitalism proceeds extremely unevenly in the various countries. It cannot be otherwise under the commodity production system. From this it follows irrefutably that Socialism cannot achieve victory simultaneously *in all* countries. It will achieve victory first in one or several countries, while the others will remain bourgeois or pre-bourgeois for some time" (*Collected Works*, Vol. 23, p. 67).

7. After the victorious Socialist revolution, the proletariat will establish its dictatorship, without which the abolition of classes and the building of Socialism are inconceivable. The form of transition to Socialism may vary in different countries, depending upon the economic level, the relation of classes, and historical tradition. Lenin wrote in this connection:

"All nations will arrive at Socialism—this is inevitable, but all will do so in not exactly the same way, each will contribute something of its own to some form of democracy, to some variety of the dictatorship of the proletariat, to the varying rate of Socialist transformations in the different aspects of social life" (*ibid.*, p. 58).

While noting that the transition from capitalism to communism was bound to produce a vast abundance and diversity of political forms, Lenin emphasised that the substance of all these transitional forms would be one and the same, namely, proletarian dictatorship. He wrote:

"Dictatorship of the proletariat, the only consistently revolutionary class, is necessary to overthrow the bourgeoisie and beat off its attempts at counter-revolution" (*Collected Works*, Vol. 23, p. 57).

8. The victory of Socialism in one country will move the imperialists to try to crush the Socialist State. The proletariat will therefore have to defend its Socialist State, arms in hand.

"This must create not only friction," Lenin wrote in "The War Programme of the Proletarian Revolution," in reference to the victory of Socialism in a single country, "but also a direct striving on the part of the bourgeoisie of other countries to crush the victorious proletariat of the Socialist State. In such cases a war on our part would be legitimate and just" (*ibid.*, p. 67).

This theory of armed defence of the Socialist State, of just wars in defence of victorious Socialism, is thus an integral part of Lenin's theory of Socialist revolution, and follows directly from the possibility of Socialism emerging victorious in one country.

This was a new theoretical concept, *a new theory of Socialist revolution formulated by Lenin*.

It represented a further step in the creative development of Marxism and elaborated the ideas expounded in *Two Tactics of Social-Democracy in the Democratic Revolution* and other of Lenin's works. Lenin's theory took account of the new situation created by imperialism and the new experience gained by the world proletariat in the revolutionary struggle.

It armed the working class in all countries with a clear understanding of the motive forces of the revolution, the conditions necessary for its victory and the prospects of its development. The supreme value of Lenin's theory lies in the fact that it unfetters the initiative of the workers in their fight against their national bourgeoisie, and shows the working class of each country the path to salvation from the innumerable calamities engendered by imperialism.

4. The February Bourgeois-Democratic Revolution. Formation of Soviets of Workers' and Soldiers' Deputies. Dual Power

The objective course of history fully confirmed Lenin's view that the war had created a revolutionary situation. Backward Russia, the weakest link in the world imperialist chain, experienced the impact of the war more heavily than the other countries. Two years of war were enough to break the strength of tsarist Russia. In 1916 famine had begun in the towns. The government lacked money to finance the war, and was compelled to borrow nearly 8,000 million rubles abroad. This made tsarism even more dependent on British and French imperialism, and created the threat of Russia losing her national independence. The landlords and capitalists sought the support of foreign imperialists against their own people. It fell to the proletariat to save the country from ruin and from the danger of being converted into a semi-colony of foreign imperialists.

The Bolshevik Party realised that the country was on the threshold of a revolution. In 1915, in his article, "A Few Theses," Lenin made a profound analysis of the coming revolution. He showed that it would be bourgeois-democratic in character—its immediate task being, as previously, the overthrow of tsarism and elimination of all the survivals of serfdom. Much had changed during the ten years since the first bourgeois-democratic revolution of 1905-1907. Differentiation of classes in the countryside had become much more pronounced; the proletariat had grown in numbers and strength; the imperialist war had aggravated all the contradictions of Russian life, and laid them bare. Favourable conditions had been created by the course of history for a more rapid development of the bourgeois-democratic revolution into a Socialist revolution. That was the chief difference between the second and the first Russian revolutions.

The labour movement had grown considerably: in 1916 there were 1,500 strikes involving over one million workers, or double the 1915 figure.

Influenced by the working-class movement, action by the soldiers grew more frequent and widespread: cases of entire regiments refusing to obey combat orders were more frequent. Thousands of soldiers abandoned the front, preferring punishment for desertion to death in war for interests that were alien to them. Fraternisation became more frequent on many sectors of the front.

Peasants began to seize the landlords' grain stocks and farm implements, and often to set fire to manors—the detested "nests of the nobility."

There was unrest among the oppressed nations too. In mid-1916 a rising flared up in Central Asia and Kazakhstan, involving millions of people. It was obvious that a revolutionary crisis was maturing.

Alarmed by the approach of revolution, the ruling classes began to take measures to arrest its development. The tsarist government decided to dissolve the Duma and vest power in a military dictator. In order to have a free hand in suppressing the revolution, the tsarist government began secret negotiations with Germany for a separate peace.

This alarmed the Entente and the Russian imperialists. The Entente was afraid of losing the help of the Russian army; the

Russian bourgeoisie was afraid of losing its war profits and seeing its imperialist plans come to naught. Supported by the Anglo-French and American imperialists, it decided, in its turn, to avert revolution by deposing the tsar. The plan was to arrest Nicholas II, force him to abdicate in favour of his son, a minor, and appoint the Grand Duke Michael, the tsar's brother, regent.

Both plots were directed against the revolution, and both proved ineffectual. The strike movement spread with every passing day—250,000 workers were out in January, 1917, and over 400,000 in February. The situation was reaching its flash-point; a major strike could easily develop into revolution.

The situation was particularly tense in the capital. On February 17 a strike broke out in one of the shops of the Putilov Works, and the management decided to close the plant on the 22nd. On February 23 (March 8) there were demonstrations to celebrate International Women's Day. The St. Petersburg Committee of the Bolsheviks called for a political strike and nearly 90,000 workers in fifty factories responded. The Putilov workers marched to the centre of the city and were joined en route by workers from other factories and by women from the food queues. The demonstrators carried placards bearing the slogans: "We want bread!", "Down with the war!", "Down with the autocracy!"

The next day the demonstration was resumed with even greater vigour. About 200,000 workers were out on strike. The Bolsheviks decided to continue the strike and turn it into a general strike and then into an insurrection. On February 25 the strike became general. There were clashes with the police and many were killed and wounded. The government called in reinforcements from the front. Nicholas II wired from General Headquarters: "I command that the disorders in the capital be stopped not later than tomorrow...." In the early hours of February 26, the Okhrana raided the working-class districts and made wholesale arrests. Five members of the St. Petersburg Bolshevik Party Committee were arrested.

On the following morning, February 26, in response to the Bolshevik appeal, the workers passed from political strike to armed revolt. The police opened fire on the demonstrators, killing about forty people on Znamenskaya Square alone. The workers disarmed the police and took possession of their weapons.

Influenced by the revolutionary events, the troops began to waver. The St. Petersburg Party Committee called on them to join the revolution. Its leaflet said: "Only a fraternal alliance of the working class and revolutionary army can free the enslaved people and put an end to this senseless fratricidal war." Many Petrograd workers in the reserve regiments stationed in the capital had kept in touch with the factories they had worked at. Workers came to the army barracks to persuade the soldiers to support the revolution. A company of the Pavlovsky Regiment refused to fire on the people.

On the following day, February 27, the whole city was in the grip of the uprising. The insurgent workers took possession of the arsenal and armed themselves. Soldiers began to go over to the revolution. Towards the evening, over 60,000 men of the Petrograd garrison had joined the insurgent people. This was an alliance of workers and peasants clad in soldiers' uniform. The jails were seized and political prisoners released. The Bureau of the Party Central Committee issued a manifesto calling on the people to put an end to tsarism and to demand the formation of a Provisional Revolutionary Government which would establish a democratic republic, introduce an 8-hour working day, confiscate the landed estates in favour of the peasants and, together with the workers of the whole world, secure the immediate cessation of the imperialist war.

The Bolsheviks were the only party to offer the people a revolutionary programme, and to call on the masses to overthrow tsarism once and for all. The Romanov monarchy collapsed under the shattering blows of the people inspired by the Bolshevik Party.

On the day of the victorious insurrection the Bolsheviks called on the workers to set up Soviets of Workers' Deputies, declaring in their leaflet:

"Victory requires organisation, a centre to guide the movement.

"Begin immediately to elect strike committees at the factories. Their representatives will make up the *Soviet of Workers' Deputies*, which will organise and direct the movement and establish a Provisional Revolutionary Government."

On the evening of February 27 the first delegates elected at factories and military units appeared at the Taurida Palace. The militant unity of workers and soldiers, born in the streets of Petrograd, was now continued by the formation of a united revolutionary organisation, the Soviet of Workers' and Soldiers' Deputies. This was different from the 1905 Revolution, when there had been separate Soviets of workers and soldiers.

From Petrograd the revolution spread to every part of the country. Soviets of Workers' and Soldiers' Deputies were set up in all the gubernias and in most uyezd towns. In many industrial areas—the Central Industrial Region, the Urals and the Donets coalfield—the Soviets introduced an 8-hour working day by direct action, disbanded the police and formed Red Guards to protect the factories and defend the revolution, discharged tsarist judges and elected people's judges in their stead. In a number of places the Soviets dismissed factory managements notorious for their cruel exploitation of the workers and instituted workers' control. The army garrisons took their orders from the Soviets. In the non-industrial regions, too, the Soviets assumed power, took measures to combat the food shortage and supported workers in conflict with their employers. The Soviets were the embodiment of the workers' and peasants' alliance: they were organs of insurrection and organs of power of the workers and peasants, victorious in the revolution.

But side by side with the Soviets, which embodied the revolutionary-democratic dictatorship of the proletariat and peasantry, there arose a Provisional Government representing the dictatorship of the bourgeoisie. At the very first news of the victorious revolution in the capital, the State Duma decided to elect a Provisional Committee with instructions to "restore order" in the city. The committee had no intention of assuming power. Its first step was to dispatch a delegation to Nicholas II, then at General Headquarters, to persuade him to abdicate in favour of his son. That demand was supported by all army commanders, who informed the tsar that they could not vouch for the troops. Nicholas II signed a manifesto abdicating, on his own behalf and on behalf of his son, in favour of his brother, the Grand Duke Michael.

This attempt on the part of the bourgeoisie to preserve the monarchy failed. The question of State power was being decided not in the Duma, but by the insurgent workers and soldiers. When Milyukov, a Cadet member of the Duma Provisional Committee, appealed at a public meeting for the retention of the monarchy, he was shouted down by an angry crowd. The bourgeoisie decided to take power into its own hands so as to prevent the further development of the revolution.

The Duma's Provisional Committee decided to open negotiations with the Petrograd Soviet of Workers' and Soldiers' Deputies, where, especially in the Presiding Committee, the Socialist-Revolutionaries and Mensheviks had a majority. They feared the development of the revolution no less than the bourgeois parties, and were anxious to put an end to the revolutionary struggle of the people as quickly as possible. They did not discuss the matter at a meeting of the Soviet, but decided secretly, among their own adherents, to support the bourgeois government being formed by the Duma Provisional Committee. They refrained, however, from joining the government out of fear of losing the confidence of the masses.

In accordance with this agreement, a bourgeois Provisional Government under Prince Lvov was set up on March 2, with most of the ministers drawn from the Octobrist and Cadet parties.

One of the ministers was Kerensky, a member of the Trudovik group. No one had delegated him to the government—he had been included by the bourgeoisie in an attempt to mislead the masses; the capitalist press described him as a "hostage of democracy." Provincial governors and local police chiefs deposed by the people were replaced, at the orders of the Provisional Government, by chairmen of the Zemstvo boards, elected under the old tsarist laws, and commissars drawn, as a rule, from the Cadet and Octobrist parties. The government was anxious to preserve as much as it could of the old machinery of State.

The result was a *dual power*: the Provisional Government and the Soviet of Workers' and Soldiers' Deputies. The latter's Socialist-Revolutionary and Menshevik leaders voluntarily surrendered power to the bourgeoisie, pledging support for the bourgeois Provisional Government. The result was a peculiar *interlocking of two dictatorships—the dictatorship of the bourgeoisie, and the revolutionary-democratic dictatorship of the proletariat and peasantry.*

The seizure of State power by the bourgeoisie was due to several factors.

The February Revolution came as an abrupt change from the lawlessness and terrorism of tsarism to broad political freedom. Tens of millions who had previously taken no part in politics and were not versed in them, were now suddenly drawn into political activity. The petty bourgeoisie, which made up the bulk of Russia's population, wavered between the bourgeoisie and the proletariat, and this exerted a decisive influence on broad sections of the workers. Lenin wrote in this connection:

"A gigantic petty-bourgeois wave has swept over everything and overwhelmed the class-conscious proletariat, not only by force of numbers but also ideologically, that is, it has infected and imbued very wide circles of workers with the petty-bourgeois political outlook" (*Collected Works*, Vol. 24, p. 41).

This petty-bourgeois wave, in its turn, determined the composition of most of the Soviets, giving the petty-bourgeois parties a predominant influence. With the emergence of millions of petty bourgeois on the political scene, the Socialist-Revolutionaries and Mensheviks were able to gain a temporary majority in the Soviets. That explains why the victorious workers and peasants, represented by their Soviets, voluntarily surrendered power to representatives of the bourgeoisie.

While the Bolsheviks were fighting tsarism at the head of the masses, the Socialist-Revolutionaries and Mensheviks hastened to take advantage of the people's victory and rise to power on the crest of the revolutionary wave.

Another reason for the seizure of power by the bourgeoisie was the inadequate organisation and political understanding of the proletariat and peasantry. Tsarist repression had played havoc with the workers' organisations. Most of the Bolshevik leaders were in prison, in exile or abroad. Lenin had been compelled to emigrate and had great difficulty in communicating with Russia. Bourgeois political organisations, on the other hand, had not been persecuted at all. The bourgeoisie had grown stronger economically and politically during the war, and was now better organised than the masses, while the proletariat, as a result of the tsarist repression, was less organised. The most politically advanced workers were serving in the army. Many had been killed at the front. Their place in the factories was taken by raw peasants, and some time had to pass before their outlook could change.

The assistance provided by foreign capitalists also played its part in the victory of the bourgeoisie.

BRIEF SUMMARY

The imperialist world war of 1914-1918 was brought about by the contradictions of imperialism. It was the result of the uneven development of capitalism, the struggle between the monopolists for redivision of the world and their attempts to suppress the revolutionary movement.

The war was a test for all the parties of the Second International. During its course, social-opportunism developed into social-chauvinism. Most of the parties of the Second International betrayed Socialism, came out in defence of imperialism and thereby assumed responsibility before mankind for all the terrible consequences of the murderous war. The Second International collapsed. Only the Bolshevik Party set an example of devotion to Socialism and of revolutionary mass activity—a pattern of struggle to prepare the masses, including the army, for revolution. Only the Bolshevik Party put forward the right slogans for struggle against the imperialist war, and called for the overthrow of the government by the working class in each of the belligerent countries. The Party developed Marxism further, enriching it with Lenin's theory of imperialism and the theory of Socialism being able to triumph in one separate country.

The war brought incalculable calamities to the peoples: ten million were killed and twenty million wounded. It aggravated all the contradictions of imperialism, and was a clear manifestation of the general crisis of capitalism. It demonstrated graphically where the rule of imperialism was leading the world. It accelerated the development of capitalism and the growth of monopoly capitalism into State-monopoly capitalism. It thus intensified the objective prerequisites of revolution. Lenin said war was a powerful "stage manager" of revolution.

The February bourgeois-democratic revolution confirmed the correctness of the Party's slogans as formulated by Lenin. It marked the beginning of the conversion of the imperialist war into a civil war. It showed how correct the Party's policy of encouraging people to work for the defeat of their own governments had been. The defeat of tsarism facilitated revolutionary action by the masses and their overthrow of the autocracy. The revolution confirmed the correctness and timeliness of the Bolsheviks' organisational break with the Mensheviks, and of the latter's expulsion from the Party.

In the course of the February Revolution the masses themselves created the Soviets of Workers' and Soldiers' Deputies, organs of the revolutionary-democratic dictatorship of the proletariat and peasantry. But the Mensheviks and Socialist-Revolutionaries, who held sway in most of the Soviets, betrayed the interests of the workers and peasants and surrendered State power to the Provisional Government, the organ of bourgeois dictatorship. The result was a dual power. The Party was now faced with the task of securing the transfer of all power to the Soviets.

The February bourgeois-democratic revolution achieved the Party's immediate goal—the overthrow of tsarism—and opened the way to the abolition of capitalism and the establishment of Socialism.

CHAPTER SEVEN

THE PARTY INSPIRES AND ORGANISES THE VICTORY OF THE GREAT OCTOBER SOCIALIST REVOLUTION

(March-October 1917)

1. **International and Domestic Situation of the Country After the Overthrow of Tsarism. The Party Ceases to be Illegal**

The February Revolution of 1917 altered Russia's position in the international arena. The working people of the world enthusiastically hailed the Russian working class, the first to raise the banner of revolt during the imperialist war. Under the influence of the Russian revolution, the working-class and anti-war movements spread in other countries, especially in the belligerent States.

The ruling classes of the two imperialist blocs—the Entente on one hand and Germany and her allies on the other—viewed the revolution with deep alarm. The imperialists feared that the example of the Russian revolution might influence the working people of the world. They were not mistaken.

The position of the belligerent Powers was not the same. Although Germany had won some major victories at the front she had overstrained herself: her industry could hardly cope with supplies for the front, and her people were starving. Continuation of the war on two fronts—both against Britain and France and against Russia—was fraught with the threat of utter defeat for Germany. The governments of Germany and her allies therefore decided to take advantage of the revolution in Russia to force a separate peace on her and then to throw the whole weight of their forces against the Entente. The rulers of Germany wanted to conclude peace with the Provisional Government because they feared that the further development of the revolution would lead to the overthrow of the bourgeois government in Russia, and would thus strengthen the revolutionary movement all over the world.

Great Britain and France were in a somewhat better position than Germany and her allies. In April 1917 the United States, pursuing its own imperialist ends, joined forces with the Entente, and brought its vast industrial might into play. The Entente, however, feared that the development of the revolution would influence the working-class movement in its rear, lead to the withdrawal of Russia from the war and, consequently, make victory over Germany difficult. The Entente imperialists therefore decided to back the Provisional Government and get Russia to continue the war. At the same time the imperialists of the United States, Great Britain and France hoped to take advantage of Russia's position, weakened by the war, to tighten their economic stranglehold on the country and intensify the capitalist exploitation of her peoples.

Thus, the bourgeoisie of all the belligerent countries strove to help the Provisional Government to crush the revolution in Russia, and in this way to avert revolution in their own rear.

In carrying out the revolution, the working people of Russia hoped to secure peace, land, bread and liberty. The bourgeois government, however, had not the slightest intention of terminating the war. It planned, on the contrary, to take advantage of the revolution to further its own predatory designs. The Provisional Government confirmed the old tsarist treaties, which tied Russia to the Entente. The bourgeoisie hoped that the continuation of the war would help to destroy the dual power in the country, and that all power would then pass into its hands. Hence its slogan: "War to a victorious finish."

The Provisional Government had no intention of settling the agrarian question, either. To give the land to the peasants would have meant striking a blow not only at landlord property but also at capitalist property, for the greater part of the landed estates was mortgaged to capitalist banks. To confiscate this land would have meant losing many thousands of millions of banking capital. Not daring openly to refuse to give the peasants land, the Provisional Government tried to hoodwink them by shelving the question, pending the convocation of a Constituent Assembly. Meanwhile, it suppressed every attempt of the peasants to take away the land from the landlords.

The bourgeoisie had no intention of improving the conditions of the working people. Having secured power it did everything possible to increase its profits. The bourgeois government annulled all the old laws that hampered the development of the banks, the establishment of joint-stock companies and the growth of monopoly. Throwing aside all restraint, the bourgeoisie began to pile up profits which far surpassed the scandalous profits it had made in the past, under tsarist rule.

The Provisional Government had no intention of putting an end to national oppression. Imperialist in character, it continued to pursue the tsarist colonialist policy. The machinery of oppression remained intact in the national-minority areas.

Since the revolution was in progress, however, the Provisional Government could not venture any open opposition to the Soviets, which had the support of the masses. It therefore waged its struggle against the revolutionary movement of the masses covertly, trying to gain time to marshal its forces for an open assault.

In its fight for undivided power, the bourgeoisie reckoned on the support of the Socialist-Revolutionaries and Mensheviks, who held that the revolution was completed, that its aims had been achieved with the overthrow of tsarism and transfer of power to the bourgeoisie, and that there could be no question of a further development of the revolution, of going on to a Socialist revolution. The Socialist-Revolutionaries and Mensheviks assured the people that with the victory of the revolution the nature of the war had changed, that it had ceased to be an imperialist war, and called for the defence of the bourgeois fatherland. To deceive the people, they called themselves "revolutionary defencists." The greater part of the masses, only recently drawn into politics, did not see through the fraud immediately and believed the Socialist-Revolutionaries and Mensheviks.

Lenin differentiated strictly between the "defencist" feelings that gripped millions of peasants and workers and the defencism of the Menshevik and Socialist-Revolutionary parties. The workers and labouring peasantry had no interest in the war. The "defencist" sentiments of the masses were due, as Lenin noted, to the people being honestly mistaken. Not so in the case of the Socialist-Revolutionaries and Mensheviks. Their defencism was an expression of the interest of a certain section of the petty bourgeoisie, whom they represented, in receiving some share of the superprofits secured by the capitalists from the war and from plundering the oppressed peoples.

In an attempt to disguise their treacherous desertion to the bourgeoisie, the Socialist-Revolutionaries and Mensheviks promised to establish control over the Provisional Government. They advanced the "in so far as" formula, which meant that in so far as the government would deal with the problems of the revolution, it should be supported; but should the government want to go back to the old order of things, it should be criticised, though under no circumstances overthrown. This was nothing but hoodwinking the people, for there can be no control without power. In reality, such control implied agreement with the bourgeois government, confidence in and support of it.

Like the bourgeois Provisional Government, the Socialist-Revolutionaries and Mensheviks tried to persuade the people to wait for a Constituent Assembly to settle the questions of peace, land and bread, although they themselves were in no hurry to convene it. They came into the open as parties of compromise with the bourgeoisie. They sought to preserve and consolidate the capitalist system.

After the February Revolution the Bolshevik Party had emerged from its "underground" status, and for the first time was in a position to develop its activities openly and freely. On March 5 the first issue of *Pravda*, the newspaper of the Central and St. Petersburg Committees of the Bolshevik Party, appeared.

Armed with Lenin's theory of Socialist revolution, the Party fought to consolidate the victory won in the February days and to extend the revolution. It opposed confidence in the bourgeois Provisional Government. On March 4 the Bureau of the Central Committee adopted a resolution against any agreement whatsoever with the government, comprised as it was of representatives of the big bourgeoisie and the nobility. The Party exposed the Socialist-Revolutionary and Menshevik slogan of control over the government. "Control over the Provisional Government?" wrote *Pravda* on March 9, 1917. "What will it give them?" (that is, the workers). "It is quite obvious that the bourgeoisie, even when controlled by the workers, cannot undertake the fulfilment of proletarian programmes, and the workers have no right to count on making a cat's paw of other people, as the bourgeoisie does, but must take action themselves."

The Bolshevik Party waged a struggle for peace and against the war, which under the new government still continued to be an imperialist war. The Bolsheviks called on the workers to continue the revolution and form a workers' guard. "The proletariat must remember," wrote *Pravda*, "that only arms in hand can it consolidate its gains and carry the revolution through to completion."

The Party committees were reorganised on the principle of democratic centralism. All Party bodies, from top to bottom, were made elective. Bolshevik newspapers began to appear in Moscow and other industrial regions. Bolsheviks who had been arrested by the tsarist authorities were released from prison. Members of the Central Committee and leading Party workers began to return from exile, prison and abroad; among them were F. E. Dzerzhinsky, P. A. Japaridze, V. V. Kuibyshev, G. K. Orjonikidze, S. G. Shaumyan, J. V. Stalin, Y. M. Sverdlov, and Y. M. Yaroslavsky, and State Duma deputies G. I. Petrovsky, M. K. Muranov, A. Y. Badayev and others.

The overthrow of tsarism marked the end of one period in the country's history and the beginning of another. The new situation demanded a new orientation of the Party, a new strategic plan, different tactics and different slogans. Lenin supplied the solution for these problems. In the very first days of the revolution, while still abroad, Lenin wrote a series of articles which he called "Letters from Afar," and in which he indicated the line the Party should follow after the February Revolution. He wrote that the revolution was not yet over, that only its first stage had been completed, and that the workers must display heroism to achieve victory in the second stage of the revolution. He put forward the task of forming a workers' militia or workers' home guard, so as to prevent the bourgeois government from restoring the police and saving the monarchy. He insisted on the following tactics, outlined in a special telegram to the Bolsheviks in Russia:

"Absolute distrust of the new government, no support for it. Particularly suspicious of Kerensky. Arming of the proletariat the only guarantee; immediate elections to the Petrograd Duma; no rapprochement with other parties" (*Collected Works*, Vol. 23, p. 287).

Lenin particularly sharply castigated any attempt whatever to unite with the Mensheviks. Sentiments in favour of unification, which had spread, it is true, to only a small section of the Party organisations, constituted a grave danger to the development of the revolutionary struggle.

The Bolsheviks developed work on a vast scale among the masses.

The Party focussed its attention on organising and rallying the vanguard force of society—the proletariat. The Bolsheviks called for the formation of Soviets throughout Russia, and played an active part in organising Soviets of Workers' and Soldiers' Deputies, committees in the armed forces, and peasant organisations in the countryside. At many enterprises in Petrograd, Moscow, the Urals, the Donets coalfield and other industrial regions, the Bolsheviks formed Red Guard workers' detachments, the fighting forces of the revolution.

The Party urged the formation of trade unions as being the mass organisations which united the greatest possible number of workers. The Bolsheviks strove to ensure that the trade unions worked in close unity with the Party, the ideological and political leader of the proletariat.

The factory committees, formed on the initiative of the Bolsheviks, embraced all the workers in the factory concerned, irrespective of the union they belonged to (at that period there were several trade unions in each factory; the metal-workers, for example, had their own union, the carpenters were members of the Wood-workers' Union, and so on). In Petrograd, Moscow and other cities and industrial districts, the factory committees were under the leadership of the Bolshevik Party from the very beginning of the revolution.

A military organisation of the Central Committee and Petrograd Committee, headed by N. I. Podvoisky, was set up in the very first days of the revolution to guide political work in the armed forces.

Considerable work was carried on also among women. Publication of the Bolshevik magazine *Rabotnitsa* was resumed. Work was started on the establishment of a youth organisation.

Thus the Party was true to its principle of carrying on its activities wherever the masses of the people were to be found.

After the February Revolution the Party was confronted by a situation rarely met with in history, that of a dual power. The class significance and role of the Soviets were not understood all at once, or by all the people. Millions of the people had to be organised, the policy of the Provisional Government and the treacherous role of the compromisers had to be exposed. The magnitude of the tasks ahead was not at once clearly understood by the whole of the Party.

In the new situation some of the Bolshevik committees and several leading Party members adopted an incorrect attitude towards the Provisional Government. They called for the establishment of "control by the masses" over the activity of the Provisional Government, implying by such control the organisation of campaigns, demonstrations, public statements against the attempts of the Provisional Government to drag out the settlement of the issues involved in the revolution; they did not raise the question of all power passing to the Soviets. This meant that power continued to remain in the hands of the bourgeois Provisional Government, and created the false impression among the masses that this government could act in the interests of the revolution.

Stalin at first took up an erroneous position, suggesting pressure on the Provisional Government to begin peace talks immediately, but he soon abandoned this view and associated himself with Lenin.

"This was a profoundly mistaken position," said Stalin subsequently, "for it gave rise to pacifist illusions, brought grist to the mill of defencism and hindered the revolutionary education of the masses. At that time I shared this mistaken position with other Party comrades and fully abandoned it only in the middle of April, when I associated myself with Lenin's theses" (*Works*, Eng. ed., Vol. 6, p. 348).

Upon his return from exile, Kamenev took up a semi-Menshevik position. In his articles in *Pravda*, he defended the "in so far as" formula. Without saying a word about the fact that the war continued to be an imperialist one under the Provisional Government as well, he called upon the soldiers "to return bullet for bullet and shell for shell," that is, to continue the war. Kamenev's position was a continuation of his earlier opportunist line.

His position was vigorously rejected by the Bolsheviks, and no more defencist articles appeared in *Pravda*.

On April 3 Lenin arrived in Petrograd. He was given a rousing welcome by the masses. Numerous workers' delegations, appointed by all the districts of the capital, and headed by Red Guard detachments, came to meet him. Soldiers' delegations had been sent from the regiments of the garrison and men of an armoured car unit brought their vehicles with them. Sailors had come from Kronstadt. The square in front of the Finland Railway Station was crowded that evening with the workers, soldiers and sailors who had come to welcome their leader, returning after nine weary years of exile. Mounting an armoured car, Lenin delivered a speech in which he greeted those who had taken part in the revolution, and called upon them to fight for the victory of the Socialist revolution.

2. Lenin's April Theses. Seventh (April) All-Russian Conference. The Party's Policy of Developing the Bourgeois-Democratic Revolution into the Socialist Revolution

Lenin's arrival was of tremendous importance for the fate of the revolution. On April 4, 1917, Lenin delivered a report "on the tasks of the proletariat in the present revolution" at a meeting of members of the Central Committee and the St. Petersburg Party Committee and of the Bolshevik delegates to the All-Russian Conference of Soviets of Workers' and Soldiers' Deputies. On April 7 the theses of the report were published in *Pravda*. These were the brilliant April Theses, in which was defined the *Party's policy of the development of the bourgeois-democratic revolution into the Socialist revolution.*

In his theses Lenin elaborated the Party's political and economic platform at the new stage of the revolution. The basic question in any revolution is the question of power. Against what class is the revolution directed, and which class is taking over power—these are the cardinal features by which the character of the revolution is determined. After the February Revolution, dual power was established in Russia. But history teaches that two dictatorships of two classes, whose position in society makes them hostile and antagonistic to each other, cannot exist simultaneously for long. Dual power must inevitably end either in the dictatorship of the bourgeoisie or in the dictatorship of the proletariat. The class struggle will decide which. Lenin insisted that no confidence should be placed in the Provisional Government and no support be given to it. He called upon the Party to head the struggle of the masses and direct it towards the Socialist revolution.

"The specific feature of the present situation in Russia," wrote Lenin in his theses, "is that it represents *a transition* from the first stage of the revolution—which, owing to insufficient class consciousness and degree of organisation of the proletariat, placed power in the hands of the bourgeoisie—*to the second* stage, which must place power in the hands of the proletariat and the poorest strata of the peasantry" (*Collected Works*, Vol. 24, p. 4).

The new stage of the revolution brought with it a new relation of classes. The motive forces of the Socialist revolution, that is, the classes interested in completing the revolution, were the proletariat and the poorest peasantry. As a toiler, the middle peasant inclined to the peasant poor, while as a property owner he supported the kulak. Owing to the duality of his position, he wavered. The Party advanced a new slogan for the peasantry, one that corresponded to the tasks of the new strategic stage. Already in his work, *Two Tactics of Social-Democracy in the Democratic Revolution*, Lenin had shown the need for such a slogan in the new stage. He showed that in a Socialist revolution the proletariat advances together with the peasant poor against the bourgeoisie in town and country, winning the neutrality of the middle peasant.

And it was understood that winning the neutrality of the middle peasant in a Socialist revolution was not at all the same as neutralisation of the bourgeoisie in a bourgeois-democratic revolution. Neutralisation of the bourgeoisie in the first Russian revolution meant exposing its collusion with tsarism, isolating it, so as to prevent it from using the bogus title of the "People's Freedom Party" to deceive the peasantry. Winning the neutrality of the middle peasant in a Socialist revolution by no means implied alienating him from the revolution. On the contrary, the Party did everything to win over the middle peasant, to draw him away from the compromisers, to detach him from the kulak and make him an ally of the proletariat—but it always bore in mind his dual nature and the possibility of his wavering.

Charting the Party's course for the development of the bourgeois-democratic into the Socialist revolution, and describing the motive forces of the new revolution, Lenin in his April Theses also defined the political form which the organisation of power should take. Marx, proceeding from the experience of the Paris Commune, had spoken of a new form of State power "of the type of the Paris Commune." But the leaders of the Second International, Kautsky, Plekhanov and others had distorted Marx's idea of the State, and advocated the parliamentary republic as the best form of State for the transition to Socialism. Lenin, on the basis of the experience of the Paris Commune and the 1905 Revolution, exposed the opportunists, and showed that practical experience had brought into being a new, "higher type of democratic State" as compared with the parliamentary democratic republic; that the Paris Commune and the Soviets were the embryo of this new State. On the basis of a study of the experience of the 1905 and 1917 revolutions, Lenin proposed a Soviet republic as the political form the dictatorship of the proletariat should take.

"Not a parliamentary republic," said Lenin, "for to return to a parliamentary republic from the Soviets of Workers' Deputies would be a retrograde step, but a republic of Soviets of Workers', Agricultural Labourers' and Peasants' Deputies throughout the country, from top to bottom" (*Collected Works*, Vol. 24, p. 5).

This was how Lenin, in the new conditions prevailing, elaborated the Marxist teachings concerning the forms of political organisation of society in the period of transition from capitalism to Communism. It was a momentous scientific discovery, one that played a tremendous part in the victory of the Socialist revolution in Russia. "All power to the Soviets!" was the slogan advanced by the Party.

This slogan did not simply imply removing the bourgeois ministers from the government and replacing them by representatives of the parties that were in the majority in the Soviets—the Socialist-Revolutionaries and Mensheviks. Such an interpretation of the slogan would have meant that the entire old State machinery would remain intact, only a change in ministers being effected. But the retention of the old machinery of State, whoever the Minister at its head—even one appointed by the Soviet—meant in practice the retention of power by the bourgeoisie. Lenin's slogan "All power to the Soviets!" did not mean a mere reshuffling of personalities, the replacement of Cadets in the Provisional Government by Socialist-Revolutionaries and Mensheviks. It meant abolishing the dual power and establishing the undivided and full power of the Soviets, organising a new type of State, abolishing the old State machinery that stood over the people, and establishing a new machinery based, from top to bottom, on the Soviets—one wholly in conformity with the interests of the people.

In the circumstances then prevailing the slogan "All power to the Soviets!" did not mean a call for the immediate overthrow of the Provisional Government, for an armed insurrection. At that time the overthrow of the Provisional Government by force would have meant coming out against the Soviets too, because they had entered into an agreement with the bourgeois government and supported it. Like Marx, Lenin regarded revolution, or armed uprising, the general rule, for no class that has outlived its day surrenders its power to another class voluntarily, without armed struggle. But in the concrete historical situation obtaining in Russia after the February Revolution, the possibility arose— "by way of exception," to quote Lenin—of a peaceful transition of all power to the Soviets. The bourgeoisie did not dare as yet to use violence against the masses. Force was on the side of the people. The Bolshevik Party could work unhampered among the masses. As distinct from all previous revolutions, the people were in possession of a ready-made apparatus of power—the Soviets of Workers' and Soldiers' Deputies. Had the Soviets, representing the workers and peasants, the overwhelming majority of the people, declared that they were taking over all power, nobody would have dared to oppose them.

At the first stage the slogan "All power to the Soviets!" meant the transition of all power to the Soviets, the undivided rule of the Soviets of that period, in which the Socialist-Revolutionaries and Mensheviks were in the majority. What is more, the peaceful development of the revolution signified not only a peaceful transition of power to the Soviets in question. With the Soviets holding undivided and full power, the struggle of classes and parties within the Soviets, and a change of the parties in power, could proceed peacefully. The transition from the bourgeois-democratic to the Socialist revolution could proceed by peaceful means.

The Bolshevik Party realised that, with the transfer of power to Soviets controlled by the Socialist-Revolutionary and Menshevik parties, these parties essentially would not change. They would continue to vacillate and compromise—but now this would take place in Soviets which had broken with the bourgeoisie, and under the eyes of the broad masses of the working people, who had the right to recall from the Soviets deputies that had not justified their confidence. The waverings of the petty-bourgeois parties which were in power but were incapable of giving peace, land, bread and liberty to the peoples would discredit the Socialist-Revolutionaries and Mensheviks. The Bolsheviks in the Soviets, non-members of the government and remaining an opposition party, would criticise and unmask the Socialist-Revolutionaries and Mensheviks, and demand of the Menshevik-S.R.

government that it settle all the basic questions of the revolution. But the Mensheviks and Socialist-Revolutionaries were incapable of settling these questions. The masses by their own experience, and as a result of the explanatory work of the Bolsheviks, would outlive their illusions about the Mensheviks and Socialist-Revolutionaries, convince themselves of the treacherous part played by these parties and hand over the direction of the State to the Bolshevik Party, which alone was capable of securing peace, land, bread and liberty for the working people. The change of government would take place by a peaceful struggle within the Soviets, once the latter had become the sole and sovereign organs of State power. In this way the revolutionary-democratic dictatorship of the proletariat and peasantry would develop into the Socialist dictatorship of the proletariat.

Lenin considered the possibility of the peaceful development of the revolution as something *"extremely* rare in history and *extremely* valuable."* But the situation making this possible might change, and the Party would find itself confronted with the necessity of having to take power by armed action, as subsequently was the case. While insisting that the fullest use be made of every possibility of peaceful development, Lenin did not, however, forget for a minute that the revolution might develop differently, in which case the dictatorship of the bourgeoisie would have to be overthrown by armed insurrection.

Lenin urged the formation of a Red Guard, unity of the proletariat, organisation of the proletarian and semi-proletarian elements in the countryside, and winning over the soldiers to the Bolsheviks. The Party worked tirelessly, even when the development of the revolution was proceeding peacefully, to prepare its forces for an armed struggle for the victory of the Socialist revolution.

Recognition of the fact that a peaceful development of the revolution was possible, that is, that power could be transferred to the Soviets and the further struggle for the dictatorship of the proletariat carried on within the Soviets, meant that the Party was for the time being withdrawing the slogan it had advanced during the war of turning the imperialist war into a civil war. To have retained this slogan would have run counter to the Party policy of encouraging a peaceful development of the revolution. The main problem was to win a majority in the Soviets over to the Party. At that period of the revolution, wrote Lenin, "this civil war, so far as we are concerned, turns into peaceful, prolonged and patient class propaganda" (*Collected Works*, Vol. 24, p. 206).

In his April Theses Lenin showed what the attitude of the Bolsheviks to the war should be after the overthrow of tsarism.

he war continued to be an imperialist one on Russia's part even nder the new government, because it was bourgeois in character nd predatory in its aims. The Bolsheviks must therefore fight gainst the continuation of this predatory war and strive for a eally democratic peace, without annexations or indemnities. After the February Revolution, however, the Bolsheviks ceased o be defeatists, for the autocracy had been overthrown in Russia nd Soviets set up representing the workers and peasants, who vere not interested in the war. Once having taken power, the Soviets could put an end to the war. The Party, however, did not adopt a defencist position either, for that would have meant upport for the imperialist war and defence of bourgeois-landlord rule. The Party's slogan on the question of the war called for he transfer of all power to the Soviets. Only they, as the representatives of the masses of the people, could ensure the conclusion of peace in the interests of the people, and not of the capitalists. It was necessary patiently to explain to the "honest defencists" the indissoluble connection between capital and the imperialist war, that it was impossible to end the war by a democratic peace without the overthrow of the rule of capital. It was necessary to conduct the most extensive work in the army, showing the nature of the war, and encourage in every way fraternisation among the soldiers at the front, for it was revolutionising the minds of the soldier masses of the belligerent countries.

The economic platform in Lenin's theses advanced the following demands in the industrial field: introduction of controls by the Soviets over the social production and distribution of products, and immediate amalgamation of all the banks in the country into one national bank, under the control of the Soviets. On the agrarian question, Lenin proposed the confiscation of all the landlord estates, and on this basis the nationalisation of all land in the country, the disposal of the land to be vested in the Soviets of Peasants' and Agricultural Labourers' Deputies.

In the field of Party life, Lenin's theses proposed the immediate convening of a Party congress and the revision of the Party programme in the light of the changes that had come about since 1903. Lenin further proposed that the Party's name be changed from Social-Democratic to Communist Party, since the Social-Democratic leaders in nearly all countries had betrayed Socialism and gone over to the bourgeoisie. The name *Communist* correctly described the Party's ultimate aim, that of establishing Communism. Lenin called for the creation of a new International, the Third Communist International, which would be free of opportunism and social-chauvinism.

Lenin's theses covered all aspects of the struggle for the transition from the bourgeois-democratic revolution to the Socialist

revolution. They defined the motive forces of the proletaria
revolution, indicated the stages of transition, set forth the eco
nomic and, in particular, the agrarian platform of the Party
They specified that the political form of the dictatorship of th
proletariat should be a Soviet republic. The theses supplied th
Party with a concrete, well-grounded plan for advance to th
Socialist revolution.

Lenin's theses were received with violent hostility by all th
bourgeois and compromising parties. The bourgeoisie tried t
persuade the people that Lenin was ignoring the history and th
interests of the country. In its hatred of Lenin and his idea o
a Socialist revolution, the bourgeoisie, supported by the Men
shevik and Socialist-Revolutionary leaders, went so far as t
spread the monstrous slander that Lenin was connected with th
German General Staff. The Mensheviks shouted that Lenin wa
rendering "a service to reaction," that the revolution was bein
"threatened by undoubted danger," and that it was "essentia
to give the most determined rebuff to Lenin and his followers.
Plekhanov went to the point of calling the April Theses the rav
ings of a madman. As for Trotsky, he upheld his old slogan "n
tsar, but a workers' government," even after the February Revo
lution. This slogan would have led to the defeat of the revolution
for it would have broken the alliance of the workers and peasants
In his *Letters on Tactics*, Lenin stressed in particular that hi
theses were levelled against Trotsky, who in his scheme for "per
manent revolution" skipped the process of the development o
the bourgeois-democratic revolution into a Socialist revolution
Within the Party, the April Theses were opposed by Kamenev
Rykov, Pyatakov and a handful of their followers, who claime
that Russia was not ripe for a Socialist revolution.

In the course of two to three weeks the whole Party rallie
round Lenin's theses. Its entire history, all its resolute struggl
against opportunism, made this possible. The Bolsheviks wer
armed with Lenin's theory of the growth of the bourgeois-demo
cratic revolution into a Socialist revolution. The Party base
itself on Lenin's doctrine of the victory of Socialism in one coun
try, taken singly.

The ideological unity of the Party was vividly demonstrated
by the Petrograd City Conference of the Bolsheviks, which opened
on April 14, ten days after Lenin had proposed his theses.
The overwhelming majority of the delegates, after hearing Lenin's
report, voted for the resolution which he had drawn up in the
spirit of the theses.

The rallying of the Party round Lenin's theses on a country-
wide scale was completed by the Seventh (April) All-Russian
Conference of the Bolshevik Party, which met in Petrograd from

pril 24 to 29, 1917. The Conference was attended by 133 delegates with the right to vote and by 18 consultative delegates, epresenting 80,000 members of the Party. The Conference discussed the following questions: the current situation (the war nd the Provisional Government, etc.); the attitude to the Soviets f Workers' and Soldiers' Deputies; revision of the Party programme; the situation in the International, and the tasks of the Party; the agrarian question; the national question, etc. Lenin eported on the main questions: the current situation, the agrarian question, and revision of the Party programme. All his reports were based on the April Theses. The unanimity displayed by he All-Russian Conference in adopting the resolutions proposed by Lenin attested the political unity and cohesion of the Party.

Lenin was opposed by Kamenev, who asserted that the bourgeois-democratic revolution in Russia was not ended and that the country was not yet ripe for a Socialist revolution. Kamenev declared his opposition to a break with the Provisional Government, and supported the Menshevik proposal for "controlling" the government, which meant leaving power in the hands of the bourgeoisie. Kamenev stood for removing the question of Socialist revolution from the order of the day, denying the possibility of Socialism being victorious in Russia alone. He was supported by Rykov, who declared that the objective conditions for a Socialist revolution did not exist in Russia, and that the impetus for a Socialist revolution must come from the West. Lenin exposed the capitulatory position of Kamenev, Rykov and their small following, and vigorously denounced their denial of the possibility of the victory of Socialism in Russia.

"Rykov says that Socialism must come from other countries with a more developed industry. But that is not the case. Nobody can say who will begin it and who will end it. That is not Marxism; it is a parody of Marxism" (*Collected Works*, Vol. 24, p. 215).

The Conference unanimously adopted a resolution on Lenin's report regarding the current situation. After noting that the development of capitalism throughout the world had posed the question of the transfer of State power to the proletariat for the building of Socialism, the resolution stressed the leading role of the Russian proletariat in explaining to the people "the urgency of taking a number of practical steps towards Socialism for which the time is now ripe." Such steps were the nationalisation of the land, the establishment of State control over all the banks and their amalgamation into a single central bank, the establishment of controls over the insurance agencies and big capitalist syndicates. Parallel with the implementation of the above measures, the Soviets should be able to introduce universal labou service.

"All the above-mentioned and similar measures," said th resolution, "can and should not only be discussed and prepare for application on a national scale, in the event of all powe passing to the proletarians and semi-proletarians; they shoul also be put into effect by the local revolutionary organs o power of the whole people when the opportunity arises (*C.P.S.U. in Resolutions*, Part I, p. 351).

The Conference resolution confirmed Lenin's teachings on th possibility of the victory of Socialism in one country, Russia This resolution was directed both against the semi-Menshevil position of Kamenev and his followers, who repudiated Socialis revolution, and Trotsky's adventurist policy, which would hav doomed the revolution to defeat.

The April Conference also adopted the resolution, drafted by Lenin, on the attitude to the war. The Conference noted that the transfer of power in Russia to a government of landlords and capitalists had not changed the imperialist character of the war. The proletarian party should therefore not support the war, the government, or its war loans. The Conference voiced its protest against the calumny spread by the capitalists to the effect that the Bolsheviks favoured a separate peace with Germany. "We regard the German capitalists," stated the resolution, "as being the same kind of brigands as the Russian, British, French and other capitalists; for us, the Emperor Wilhelm is the same kind of crowned brigand as Nicholas II or the British, Italian, Rumanian and all other monarchs" (*ibid.*, p. 337). The war could only be ended in one way—by the transfer of the entire State power to the Soviets of Workers', Soldiers' and Peasants' Deputies.

In his report on the agrarian question, Lenin specifically dwelt on the class significance of the demand for the confiscation of the landlords' estates and the nationalisation of all the land. The confiscation of the landlords' land without compensation would, before all else, meet the age-old aspirations of the peasantry. At the same time it would undermine the foundations of the rule of the landlords and bourgeoisie. Property in land was the mainstay of the feudal landlords, and as such a guarantee of the possible restoration of the monarchy. The confiscation of the landed estates was a guarantee against the monarchy being restored. Since, moreover, these estates were mortgaged to the banks, their confiscation would also be a heavy blow at bourgeois property. The nationalisation of all the land would free the use of land of all feudal survivals.

Moreover, as was noted in the resolution proposed by Lenin, ". . . the nationalisation of the land, representing as it does the abolition of private ownership of land, would in practice deal such a mighty blow to the private ownership of all means of production in general that the party of the proletariat should assist such a reform in every possible way" (*C.P.S.U. in Resolutions*, Part I, p. 340). The Party vigorously attacked the attempts of the Provisional Government and the compromisers to postpone settlement of the agrarian question pending the convocation of the Constituent Assembly, and advised the peasants to take over the land immediately, in an organised way.

The victory of the Socialist revolution depended largely upon whether the proletariat could secure the support of the working people of the oppressed nations. At the Conference, Stalin made a report on the national question. He outlined the Party's nationalities policy, based on Leninist principles. He showed that the consistent fight of the Party for the right of nations to self-determination, up to and including secession, was a decisive condition for securing the support of the oppressed nations for the Party. After exposing the Bundists' nationalist slogan of national cultural autonomy, Stalin outlined the following principles of the Party's nationalities policy: (1) recognition of the right of nations to secession; (2) regional autonomy for peoples remaining within the boundaries of the given State; (3) special laws guaranteeing free development for national minorities; (4) a single, indivisible proletarian organisation, a single party, for the proletarians of all the nationalities of the given State.

The nationalities policy of the Party was opposed by Pyatakov who repeated the same arguments he had advanced against Lenin during the war years. He asserted at the Conference that the slogan of self-determination of nations up to and including secession was reactionary, for the national State was a thing of the past and was impossible under imperialism; that a struggle should be waged against national movements. Lenin scathingly criticised this standpoint, which actually meant refusal on the part of the proletariat to utilise the revolution's reserve forces represented by the various nationalities, and doomed the revolution to defeat.

The Conference adopted the resolution drawn up by Lenin. Its basic point was recognition of the right of all the nations forming part of Russia to secede freely and to form independent States. Only recognition of this right would ensure solidarity among the workers of the various nations concerned. At the same time the resolution spoke of the inadmissibility of confusing the *right to self-determination* with the question of the *advisability* of a given nation seceding. This question must be decided by the Party in each particular case from the standpoint of social development as a whole, as well as from that of the interests of the struggle of the proletariat for Socialism.

For all nations who wished to remain within the boundaries of a single State, the Party demanded the broadest autonomy and the enactment of special laws guaranteeing the free development of the national minorities, declaring invalid any privileges whatever enjoyed by any nation and prohibiting any infringements whatever of the rights of national minorities.

The Conference condemned the Menshevik and Bundist slogan of "national cultural autonomy" as one which artificially divided the workers living in one locality, and even working in the same industrial enterprise, and which strengthened the ties between the workers and the bourgeois culture of individual nations. The resolution noted that the interests of the working class demanded the unification of the workers of all nationalities in common proletarian organisations: political, trade union, co-operative-educational, and so forth.

"Only such common organisations of the workers of the various nationalities," stated the resolution, "will make it possible for the proletariat to wage a victorious struggle against international capital and bourgeois nationalism" (*C.P.S.U. in Resolutions*, Part I, p. 346).

On the basis of a report by Lenin, the Conference deemed it necessary to revise the Party programme, and indicated along what lines it was to be revised. It was necessary to give an evaluation of imperialism and the era of imperialist wars in connection with the impending Socialist revolution; to alter the section in the programme dealing with the State; to insert the demand for the establishment of a Soviet republic; to delete or correct the outdated sections of the programme, and in particular to alter the agrarian programme in conformity with the resolution adopted on the agrarian question; to insert the demand for the nationalisation of the monopolies where this was already possible, etc.

On the question of the International, Lenin proposed breaking with the Zimmerwald organisation and to start founding a new International immediately; as a last resort, Lenin considered it possible to remain in the organisation only for purposes of information. Zinoviev opposed this proposal, and insisted on retaining a bloc with those Zimmerwaldites who had not severed their ties with the defencists.

The Conference decided that the Bolsheviks should remain in the Zimmerwald bloc and uphold the tactics of the Zimmerwald Left. Lenin considered this decision to be a wrong one. Subsequently his viewpoint was recognised as correct. At the beginning of May the Central Committee unanimously resolved to send delegates to the forthcoming Zimmerwald Conference, authorising them to leave the Conference immediately and withdraw from the Zimmerwald organisation should it declare itself in favour of any contact or discussions with the social-chauvinists.

The Conference instructed the Central Committee to take the initiative in forming a Third International. It elected a Central Committee headed by Lenin.

The April Conference was the first legal conference of the Bolshevik Party to be held in Russia. In importance it was equal to a Party congress. The Conference equipped the Party with a plan of action for the struggle to develop the bourgeois-democratic revolution into a Socialist revolution. It exposed and rejected the opportunist line of Kamenev, Pyatakov and others, which would have doomed the revolution to defeat. The decisions of the April Conference showed the working class and all the working people the only way out of the war and of ruin for Russia, the way to deliverance from exploitation. It showed how the threat of the enslavement of Russia by foreign imperialists could be averted, and the victory of the Socialist revolution in Russia ensured.

3. The Party's Fight for the Masses in the Period of Dual Power. The July Days

Armed with the decisions of the April Conference, the Party launched activities on a great scale among the masses. It went to the people with a clear and integral programme which showed how peace, land and bread could be secured.

The Bolshevik Party came forward as the leader and champion of the interests of the exploited and downtrodden. The Bolsheviks roused all sections of the working people to action and directed the diverse revolutionary streams into a single channel for the fight against capitalism, for Socialism.

In the struggle for the transfer of all power to the Soviets, the bourgeoisie, as Lenin stressed, was the outright and principal class enemy of the working people. It was propped up by the support of the compromisers, who were predominant in the Soviets. The Socialist-Revolutionaries and Mensheviks were the chief social mainstay of the bourgeoisie. The problem was to knock this mainstay from under the feet of the bourgeoisie. It was necessary to wrest leadership in the Soviets and other mass organisations from the Socialist-Revolutionaries and Mensheviks, and isolate them from the masses. In order, therefore, to defeat the bourgeoisie, the Bolsheviks directed their main blow at its social support, the compromisers, the "immediate enemy," as Lenin put it.

The Party carried on its main work in the mass organisations, primarily in the Soviets of Workers' and Soldiers' Deputies, the Soviets of Peasants' Deputies and in the soldiers' committees. During March, Soviets of Workers' Deputies were established practically throughout the country, in all industrial centres and cities. About 400 Soviets were formed in gubernia and uyezd towns and industrial centres, not counting the Soviets at many Donets mines and in several other regions. The Soviets of Peasants' Deputies appeared later than the Soviets of Workers' Deputies, but by the summer of 1917, they numbered about 400. Soldiers' committees were formed in the army in all companies, regiments and in bigger formations, both at the front and in the garrisons. The newspapers *Soldatskaya Pravda* (*Soldiers' Truth*) and *Okopnaya Pravda* (*Trench Truth*) were published for the army. Work was carried on in the trade unions, factory committees and in other mass organisations. Thus, step by step, the Party built up the political army for an assault on capitalism.

The Party sought to convince the working people of the correctness of the Bolshevik ideas. Developments in the country, already on the eve of and during the April Conference, showed that the Bolsheviks were right.

On April 18 (old style) the working people of Russia celebrated May Day. For the first time on this day the workers and soldiers demonstrated freely. Most of the banners and posters bore slogans demanding a democratic peace. On that same day, Milyukov, the Minister for Foreign Affairs, sent a note to the Allied Powers in which he assured them that the Provisional Government would fully observe all treaties signed by the tsarist government and that Russia would continue the war to a victorious finish. On April 20 the workers and soldiers, who only two days previously had demonstrated under slogans demanding peace, learned about Milyukov's note. That day the soldiers of the Petrograd garrison marched to the Mariinsky Palace, where the Provisional Government was sitting, carrying posters demanding: "All power to the Soviets!", "Down with the war!", "Down with Milyukov!", "Down with Guchkov!" They began to be joined by workers. Meetings began in the city.

In reply to the action of the workers and soldiers, the supporters of the Provisional Government organised a counter-demonstration under the slogan of confidence in the government.

That same day, April 20, the Central Committee of the Bolshevik Party met. In a resolution drawn up by Lenin, the Central Committee pointed out that owing to its class character the bourgeois Provisional Government could not end the imperialist war. At the same time the Central Committee issued a warning against such slogans as "Down with Milyukov!" or "Down with Guchov!" The bourgeoisie and its Socialist-Revolutionary and Menshevik allies might resort to a manoeuvre: they could reshuffle the government somewhat, and then tell the people that the government's policy had changed as a result. Only the revolutionary proletariat, by assuming State power with the support of a majority of the people, would set up a government, in the form of the Soviets, which the workers of the world would believe in and which alone would be able to end the war quickly.

On April 21, in response to the call of the Bolshevik Party, the workers of Petrograd downed tools and demonstrated. More than 100,000 people took part in the demonstration demanding peace.

The entire bourgeois and petty-bourgeois press started accusing the Bolsheviks of preparing civil war. But the boot was on the other foot, for the initiators of civil war were accusing those whom they were preparing to attack. On April 21 the Central Committee of the Bolshevik Party adopted a resolution in which it emphatically refuted the calumny of the bourgeois and Socialist-Revolutionary and Menshevik press to the effect that the Bolsheviks were threatening to start a civil war. The Central Committee called on all the workers to hold new elections of delegates to the Soviets, to drive out the compromisers, and to send real representatives of the people in their place.

During the demonstration of April 21 a small group of members of the St. Petersburg Committee (S. Bagdatyev and others) issued, without the agreement of the committee, the slogan "Down with the Provisional Government!" On April 22 the Central Committee adopted Lenin's resolution condemning this slogan as an incorrect and adventurist one, for it was nothing less than a call to revolt and ran counter to the Party line of encouraging a peaceful development of the revolution and a peaceful conquest of the majority in the Soviets for the cause of the proletariat.

Demonstrations also took place in Moscow, the Urals, Ukraine and in other cities and parts of the country.

The April events were no ordinary demonstration. April witnessed simultaneous action by the proletariat and the bourgeoisie; the broad sections of the people were thus confronted with the question: with whom shall we go along? Many of those who had been "honestly mistaken," and had believed in the compromisers, now saw for themselves that only the proletariat, by taking power, could end the war. The April demonstration brought about, as Lenin put it, the "washing away" of the middle-class elements, that is, it hastened the transition of the waverers to the side of the revolutionary proletariat. The April events thereby speeded up the development of the bourgeois-democratic revolution to a Socialist revolution.

The April demonstration marked the beginning of a crisis of authority. The Provisional Government, which had hoped to secure absolute power by a conspiracy, proved to be powerless. It decided on the new manoeuvre, suggested by the foreign imperialists, of broadening the composition of the government by including Socialist-Revolutionaries and Mensheviks in it, and thus deceiving the people. On May 5 an agreement was reached between the Provisional Government and the Socialist-Revolutionary and Menshevik Executive Committee of the Petrograd Soviet to include representatives of the Socialist-Revolutionary and Menshevik parties in the government. A so-called coalition government was formed, which included the compromisers V. Chernov (from the Socialist-Revolutionaries), I. Tsereteli and M. Skobelev (from the Mensheviks) and others. The Mensheviks who in the first Russian revolution had declared it impermissible to take part in a revolutionary government, now thought nothing of entering a counter-revolutionary government of the bourgeoisie. This coalition consolidated the bloc between the big and the petty bourgeoisie which had in fact already taken shape at the beginning of the revolution. The bourgeois government was saved by the Socialist-Revolutionaries and Mensheviks, who went openly over to the side of the bourgeoisie.

The coalition government did not remove the causes of the crisis, nor did it solve a single problem of the revolution. The dislocation that had begun long before the revolution continued to spread. Throughout May strikes broke out in all the industrial areas, the workers demanding better economic conditions. In defiance of the resistance of the capitalists, the workers themselves introduced an 8-hour working day. The strike wave was accompanied by growing agrarian unrest. In the countryside the peasants, without waiting for the convocation of the Constituent Assembly, were themselves fixing the rents for land leased from the landlords, taking away from the latter their uncultivated land and sowing crops on it. By July the peasant movement had spread to 43 gubernias. The peasants were rising up against the landlords in defiance of the Socialist-Revolutionary leaders entrenched in the Soviets. Of tremendous significance for winning over the peasant masses was Lenin's speech on May 22, at the First All-Russian Congress of Peasants' Deputies, in which he outlined the Bolshevik platform on the agrarian question. The workers' and peasants' movement influenced the army; the continuation of the war was arousing indignation among the soldiers and heightening their revolutionary sentiments.

The work of the Bolsheviks in the army was facilitated by the All-Russian Conference of Bolshevik Army Organisations, convened by the Central Committee in June, 1917. The Conference was attended by delegates from 60 military organisations at the front and in the rear, uniting about 26,000 Party members. Lenin addressed the Conference, speaking on the current situation and the agrarian question. He called for the greatest energy to be displayed in preparing the forces of the proletariat and the revolutionary army for the transition of power to the Soviets.

The more far-reaching the revolution became, the more the bourgeoisie sought to save itself in the only way it considered possible, namely, by driving the soldiers at the front to take the offensive. The calculations of the bourgeoisie were simple. In the event of success, the offensive would strengthen the authority of the government and enable it to attack the Bolsheviks and disband the Soviets. In the event of failure, the entire blame could be thrown on to the Bolsheviks. They could be accused of having undermined army morale, and the activities of the Party could be prohibited and, later, the Soviets could be disbanded as well.

But the bourgeoisie realised that they would not be able to compel the soldiers to continue the war by force alone. Kerensky, who had by then been appointed Minister for War, had drawn up in advance the order for an offensive, without, however, indicating when it was to be launched. He wanted first to have this decision approved by the First All-Russian Congress of Soviets, which met on June 3. The Congress was attended by over 1,000 delegates, only 105 of whom were Bolsheviks. The bulk of the delegates consisted of Socialist-Revolutionaries and Mensheviks. The most important question on the agenda was that of the attitude towards the Provisional Government. The Socialist-Revolutionaries and Mensheviks declared in favour of retaining the bloc with the bourgeoisie. Speaking in defence of the coalition, Tsereteli, the Menshevik leader, declared that there was not a single political party in Russia that was prepared to assume all power. To this Lenin replied: "There *is* such a party!" When he was given the floor, Lenin outlined the Bolshevik programme, and called for the transfer of all power to the Soviets.

The compromisers mobilised all their forces in an attempt to prove that the slogan "All power to the Soviets!" was not feasible. They carried a resolution approving the coalition with the bourgeoisie, and endorsing the Provisional Government's policy.

The Bolsheviks decided to show the Congress how utterly at variance the position of its majority was with the views of the advanced sections of the proletariat and the army. The Central Committee of the Bolshevik Party called on the workers and soldiers of Petrograd to demonstrate on June 10 under the slogans: "All power to the Soviets!", "Down with the ten capitalist ministers!", "Workers' control over production!", "Against the policy of an offensive!"

But on June 9, the eve of the demonstration, the Socialist-Revolutionaries and Mensheviks decided to prevent it, and the Congress, which they dominated, adopted a resolution banning the demonstration.

To call it off was difficult. However, not to abide by the Congress decision meant setting oneself against the Congress. Late at night on June 9, the Central Committee of the Bolshevik Party decided to submit to the Congress decision, and called on the workers and soldiers not to demonstrate. The members of the C.C., the P.C. and Party functionaries spent the whole night making rounds of the districts, factories and army barracks, explaining the Party decision to the workers and soldiers. As a result, not a single factory or regiment came out to demonstrate. This spoke of the growth of the Party's influence, of its ability to maintain contact with the masses and to retreat at the right moment.

On the following day all the newspapers started a campaign of Bolshevik-baiting. At the Congress, the Menshevik leaders accused the Bolsheviks of conspiracy, and demanded that they be disarmed. Having cancelled the demonstration, the Congress instructed its delegates to visit the factories and barracks. When they did, they saw that it was not a question of a Bolshevik "conspiracy" but of the temper of the entire proletariat and the garrison of the capital. Fearing that it might completely lose its influence among the masses the Congress presidium decided to hold a demonstration, but under its own leadership. The demonstration was fixed for June 18. It was no accident that the Congress leaders chose that particular day. Having assured himself of the support of the Congress, Kerensky had given the order for an offensive to be launched on the South-Western front on June 18. The demonstration was designed to screen the plans of the bourgeoisie, and express approval for the offensive at the front.

On the appointed day, June 18, Petrograd was the scene of a mass demonstration, in which about half a million people took part. The Bolsheviks decided to participate in it under their own slogans. The overwhelming majority of the demonstrators carried banners bearing the slogan "All power to the Soviets!" Only a small group displayed slogans calling for confidence in the Provisional Government.

The tremendous scale of the demonstration and the predominance of Bolshevik slogans in it showed that the proletariat and the garrison of the capital supported the Bolsheviks. The demonstration showed that the masses had no confidence either in the Provisional Government or in the policy of compromise with the bourgeoisie pursued by the Socialist-Revolutionaries and Mensheviks.

The offensive of the Russian troops at the front failed and the counter-revolution immediately began to put into effect its premeditated plan in the event of failure, that is, to throw all the blame on to the Bolsheviks.

On July 2, as soon as news of the failure of the offensive reached Petrograd, the Cadets announced their withdrawal from the government. In doing so, they calculated that the Socialist-Revolutionary and Menshevik leaders would be afraid to remain in power alone and would agree to the terms of the Cadets, who demanded the disarmament of the workers, the withdrawal of revolutionary troops from Petrograd and, above all, the banning of the Bolshevik Party.

But the Cadets failed to take into account the mood of the people. They had hoped to create a government crisis, but overlooked the political crisis that had already come to a head, first in the capital and then throughout the country. On the morning of July 3, at a meeting of company and regimental committees of the First Machine-Gun Regiment in Petrograd, held to elect delegates to the Executive Committee of the Soviet, the soldiers spoke indignantly of the fact that the hated war was being continued, that the people were starving, while the bourgeoisie was amassing fortunes, and that the government was leading the country to catastrophe. Demands were made that the question of armed action and of the overthrow of the Provisional Government be discussed. The soldiers sent delegates to other regiments and to factories, suggesting that they take part in such action. The delegates met with support everywhere.

The Party supported the revolutionary sentiments of the masses, but it was opposed to immediate action. The workers and soldiers of Petrograd were strong enough to overthrow the Provisional Government and assume State power, but they would have been unable to retain this power, for the majority of the people in the country at that time still followed the Socialist-Revolutionaries and Mensheviks. Therefore the Central Committee decided on July 3 to refrain from any action or demonstrations. But it was no longer possible to restrain the masses. At the factories, in the regiments and aboard the ships of the Baltic Fleet, they listened to what the representatives of the Party had to say, yet continued to insist on action. There arose a danger that the masses would go out on to the streets and that the bourgeois government would have their demonstration shot down, declaring it to be an armed uprising.

The Central Committee of the Party annulled its decision and resolved to take part in the action of the masses, with the purpose

of turning it into a peaceful and organised demonstration, unde
the slogan "All power to the Soviets!" On the following day a
huge demonstration took place, in which more than 500,000 peo
ple took part. The workers marched under the protection of the
armed Red Guard, while the soldiers carried arms. Several thou
sand sailors from Kronstadt also took part in the demonstration

The demonstrators appointed 90 representatives to present to
the Central Executive Committee of the Soviets, in session at
the Taurida Palace, the demand that all power be taken by the
Soviets. But the Socialist-Revolutionaries and Mensheviks had
other plans. They had arranged with the government to smash
the demonstration. The order was given to summon troops loyal
to the Provisional Government from the front. In several districts—at the corner of Nevsky Prospekt and Sadovaya Street
on Liteiny Prospekt, and elsewhere—officer cadets and Cossacks
opened fire on the demonstrators.

The troops summoned from the front having arrived in Petrograd, the bourgeois government proceeded to repressive measures.
Wholesale searches began in the working-class districts. The
counter-revolutionaries disarmed the workers. The regiments which
had taken part in the demonstration began to be disarmed. The
counter-revolution fell upon the Bolsheviks with particular hatred. On July 6 the Trud printing plant, which had been purchased with money contributed by the workers to the Bolshevik
Party, was wrecked. *Pravda* was banned. The same day counter-
revolutionaries killed the worker Voinov merely because he had
removed from the printing plant copies of *Listok Pravdy* (*Pravda
Bulletin*) published by the Party in place of *Pravda*, which had
been suppressed.

The counter-revolutionary authorities began to arrest active
Party workers. The order was given to find Lenin and detain him
at all costs. In their search for him, the Provisional Government, which included Socialist-Revolutionaries and Mensheviks
who posed as revolutionaries, had no scruples about using the
services of agents of the former tsarist Okhrana. The slanderous
fabrication, prepared long in advance, that the Bolsheviks had
connections with Germany, was circulated. The Procurator issued
an order for the arrest and trial of Lenin, and several other Bolsheviks, on a charge of "high treason" and the organisation of
an armed uprising. General Polovtsev, the Commander-in-Chief
of the Petrograd Military Area, ordered the commander of the
unit specially formed for the purpose, to carry out a search for
Lenin and to shoot him immediately he was found.

The Party arranged for a safe hiding-place for its leader. At
first Lenin went into hiding in Petrograd, and later outside the
city, near Lake Razliv. The bourgeoisie tried to set a trap. The

entire Cadet and Socialist-Revolutionary-Menshevik press demanded that Lenin appear for trial. The counter-revolution, supported by the Socialist-Revolutionaries and Mensheviks, sought to decapitate the Bolshevik Party. Counter-revolution was rampant all over the country. The War Minister, Kerensky, re-introduced the death penalty at the front. With the help of the Socialist-Revolutionary and Menshevik committees, the authorities began disarming revolutionary units not only at the front, but also in the rear. Repressive measures were intensified with the appointment of General Kornilov as Supreme Commander-in-Chief.

The July events changed the situation and the relation of class forces in the country. The Mensheviks and Socialist-Revolutionaries rounded off their policy of compromise with the bourgeoisie by final desertion to the camp of the counter-revolution. Once parties of compromise with the bourgeoisie, the Socialist-Revolutionaries and Mensheviks had now become parties of accomplices of the counter-revolution. The dual power had come to an end. The bourgeoisie had achieved undivided authority. All power had passed into its hands. The Socialist-Revolutionary and Menshevik Soviets became an appendage of the bourgeois government.

But the bourgeoisie did not succeed in crushing the revolutionary masses. The Bolsheviks had been able to retreat in good time and withdraw their main forces from under the blow.

4. Sixth Party Congress. The Party Adopts the Policy of Preparing for Armed Insurrection. Rout of the Kornilov Revolt

With the change in the situation and in the relation of forces in the country, the Party had to alter its tactics and slogans. In an article entitled "On Slogans," Lenin showed that the political situation in Russia after July 4 differed radically from that of February 27 to July 4. The stage of peaceful development of the revolution, which would have then been possible and most desirable, had ended. By their treachery, the Socialist-Revolutionaries and Mensheviks had wrecked the peaceful course of development. Now that all power had passed into the hands of the counter-revolution, the working class could only take power by an armed insurrection.

At the same time Lenin gave warning that immediate action against the government would be a mistake. A decisive assault was possible only when a new revolutionary upsurge affected the very widest masses.

Lenin proposed the temporary withdrawal of the slogan "All power to the Soviets." This did not mean the renunciation of a

Soviet republic as a new type of State. The point was that the Soviets as they were then composed, and led as they were by the Socialist-Revolutionaries and Mensheviks, who had openly deserted to the camp of the counter-revolutionary bourgeoisie, and whose hands were stained with the blood of the people, could not be organs of people's power.

"Soviets can spring up in this new revolution, and are indeed bound to do so," wrote Lenin. "They will *not* be the present Soviets, which are organs of compromise with the bourgeoisie, however, but organs of a revolutionary struggle against the bourgeoisie. It is true that we shall be, then too, in favour of building the whole State on the model of the Soviets. It is not a question of Soviets in general, but of combating the *present* counter-revolution and the treachery of the *present* Soviets" (*Collected Works*, Vol. 25, p. 170).

Questions of the revolution, including the new tactics required to meet the changed situation, were dealt with by the Sixth Congress of the Party. The Congress met in Petrograd from July 26 to August 3, 1917. It had to work in semi-illegality. The campaign of Bolshevik-baiting in the bourgeois and petty-bourgeois press had intensified. The Provisional Government empowered the Ministers for War and Internal Affairs to prohibit all congresses, in other words, virtually gave the order to ban the Sixth Congress. Matters went so far that the foreign imperialists openly demanded that the Congress be dispersed and its delegates arrested.

But the plans of the counter-revolution were frustrated. The workers carefully guarded their Party's Congress.

Although Lenin was unable to attend, he guided its work through the members of the Central Committee who visited him while he was in hiding at Lake Razliv. Lenin drafted the theses "On the Political Situation," and his articles "On Slogans," "Lessons of the Revolution" and others, served as the basis of the Congress resolutions.

One of the first questions discussed by the delegates was whether Lenin should appear for trial. The Congress declared against Lenin appearing in court, and protested against the outrageous attacks on the leader of the revolutionary proletariat. The Congress sent a message of greeting to Lenin.

The chief items discussed at the Congress were the political report of the Central Committee and the political situation. Stalin made the reports on both these questions. They were on the lines indicated by Lenin.

"At the present time," stated the resolution adopted by the Congress on the report on the political situation, "peaceful development and a painless transition of power to the Soviets are no longer possible, for power has in fact already passed into the hands of the counter-revolutionary bourgeoisie.

"The right slogan at the present time can only be the complete abolition of the dictatorship of the counter-revolutionary bourgeoisie. Only the revolutionary proletariat, provided it is supported by the poorest peasantry, can fulfil this task, the task of a new upsurge" (*C.P.S.U. in Resolutions*, Part I, p. 376). The Sixth Party Congress thus showed that only by armed insurrection and by overthrowing the dictatorship of the bourgeoisie, could the proletariat and poorest peasantry assume power.

The Party's course towards a Socialist revolution was opposed by Bukharin, who asserted that the peasants had formed a bloc with the bourgeoisie and would not follow the working class. Stalin rejected this opportunist assertion, and showed that Bukharin, by approaching the peasantry without a class analysis, had abandoned the Marxist position. There were different kinds of peasants: the rich peasants supported the imperialist bourgeoisie, while the poor peasants supported the proletariat in its struggle for the victory of the revolution. Stalin also rejected the view of Preobrazhensky, who proposed an amendment denying that a Socialist revolution could be victorious in Russia and stating that the country could be directed towards Socialism only in the event of a proletarian revolution in the West.

"The possibility is not excluded," said Stalin, "that Russia will be the country that will lay the road to Socialism. . . . We must discard the antiquated idea that only Europe can show us the way" (*Works*, Eng. ed., Vol. 3, pp. 199, 200).

The Congress rejected the Trotskyist amendments of Preobrazhensky and Bukharin. The resolution was unanimously approved with four abstentions.

The report on the organisational work of the Central Committee was delivered by Y. M. Sverdlov. In the three months since the April Conference, the Party's membership had increased threefold: at the April Conference 78 organisations, with a membership of 80,000, had been represented; at the Sixth Congress, 162 organisations with a membership of 240,000 were represented. The Central Committee had succeeded in welding the whole Party together in this short period. An active part in the proceedings of the Congress was taken by representatives of the Polish, Lettish and Lithuanian Bolsheviks, who were carrying on revolutionary activity among the working people, sometimes as members of local Party organisations, and frequently as sections attached to the local Party committees.

The Congress declared against any unification whatsoever with the defencists, noting that unity was possible only with those

Menshevik-Internationalists who were really prepared to break with the Menshevik-defencists.

The Sixth Congress admitted the "Mezhrayontsy" and their leader, Trotsky, into the Party, on their declaration that they agreed with all the tenets of Bolshevism. The "Mezhrayontsy" were a small group that had already been formed before the war and consisted of Bolsheviks who had wavered and adopted a conciliatory attitude towards the opportunists, and of Trotskyist-Mensheviks. During the war the "Mezhrayontsy" had occupied a centrist position, vacillating between the Bolsheviks and the Mensheviks. They recognised the war to be an imperialist war, they were against defencism, but at the same time would not agree to a complete break with the Mensheviks. Now, however, they severed relations with the defencists. As events showed, some of the "Mezhrayontsy"—Volodarsky and Uritsky, for example—actually discarded their centrist vacillations, whereas Trotsky and a small group of his followers only temporarily suspended their fight against Bolshevism, and joined the Party so as, once inside, to fight Leninism and foist their opportunist, anti-Socialist policy upon it.

The changed conditions in which the Party had been working after coming out of illegality, and its rapid growth, made some additions to the Party rules essential. The first paragraph of the rules stated that anybody who accepted the Party programme, was a member of one of the Party organisations and paid membership dues, was considered to be a member of the Party. In the new rules the clause "and who submits to all decisions of the Party," was added. Another clause introduced in the rules was that new members should be accepted into the Party by local Party organisations, on the recommendation of two Party members and the approval of a general membership meeting of the local organisation. The rules stressed that all Party organisations should be built on the principle of democratic centralism, and that all Party organisations should be grouped on a district and regional basis. The rules provided for the regular convocation of congresses once a year, and for plenary meetings of the Central Committee at least once every two months.

The Congress heard a report and adopted a resolution on relations between the Party and the trade unions. After endorsing the Party's decisions condemning the Menshevik theory that the trade unions should be neutral, the Congress resolved: that everything possible should be done to organise all workers in trade unions; that all Party members should join the unions and form groups within them; that work should be started to establish an international organisation made up of unions refusing to support the imperialist war and accepting the standpoint of the class struggle.

The Congress dwelt separately on work among the youth. It declared itself in favour of establishing youth leagues not subordinate to the Party as organisations, but led by it ideologically. The Congress stressed that the Party should aim to make these leagues Socialist from the very outset. Their task would be to foster class consciousness among young working men and women, and lead them in step with the revolutionary vanguard of the proletariat.

The Sixth Congress discussed the Party's economic platform. In its resolution on this subject, the Congress noted that the country was passing through a profound economic crisis and was "sliding into a gulf of utter economic dislocation and ruin." The crisis was being deliberately aggravated by the bourgeoisie, which sought to use it against the revolution. The only way out of the critical situation was for power to pass into the hands of the proletariat and the poorest peasantry. Only these classes, on assuming power, could save the country by taking the following revolutionary measures: nationalisation and centralisation of the banks; nationalisation of a number of monopolies (oil, coal, sugar, metallurgical and transport); repudiation of foreign and internal debt, with due consideration for the interests of small owners; establishment of real workers' control, which should gradually develop into the complete regulation of production; organisation of proper exchange between town and country with the help of co-operatives and food committees, with a view to supplying the towns with the necessary agricultural products, and the countryside with manufactured goods, agricultural implements and machinery. The resolution called on all workers' organisations—the trade unions, factory committees and Soviets—to encourage the application of these measures, to display initiative in the matter, and to secure their implementation on a national scale.

Underlying all the Congress decisions was Lenin's idea of the alliance of the proletariat and the peasantry as a condition for the victory of the revolution. Meeting as it did on the eve of a new upsurge of the revolution, the Sixth Congress set itself one principal aim in all its decisions—to prepare the proletariat and the poorest peasantry for armed insurrection, for the triumph of the Socialist revolution. The Congress addressed a manifesto to all working people, to all workers, soldiers and peasants, calling on them to rally under the banner of the Bolshevik Party for the decisive battle with the bourgeoisie.

Having secured for itself undivided rule, the bourgeoisie set out to complete its plans for crushing the revolution and restoring the monarchy. One of the ways in which it hoped to achieve this was by further disorganising industry. This policy was brazenly expressed in the statement of the millionaire Ryabushinsk that "the gaunt hand of famine" should seize the revolution b the throat and strangle it. The capitalists closed down factor after factory, throwing tens of thousands of workers on to th streets. Business speculation reached incredible proportion Prices soared rapidly. The working people were starving. Econom ic catastrophe and enslavement by foreign capital threatene the country.

Not confining itself to economic measures, the counter-revolu tion made preparations for setting up a military dictatorship By agreement with the American, British and French government the role of military dictator was assigned to General Kornilov the Commander-in-Chief. To cover up the preparations for counter-revolutionary coup, it was decided to convene a Coun cil of State, composed of representatives of all the propertie strata of the population. Fearing the revolutionary workers o Petrograd, the bourgeoisie decided to hold the Council of Stat in Moscow, where it thought the situation was more tranquil

The Central Committee of the Bolshevik Party requested th Moscow Committee to organise a one-day protest strike agains the conspiracy of the bourgeoisie. On August 12, the day the Coun cil of State opened, over 400,000 Moscow workers downed tools By their unanimous strike action, they frustrated the design of the counter-revolution. It became obvious that the counter revolution would be able to carry out its plan only by armed force. The bourgeoisie decided to draw the people into a civil war Kornilov began to mobilise the necessary armed forces. The representatives of the United States, Britain and France promised him their help. He negotiated with the generals about with drawing troops from the front. The traitors did not hesitate to open the road to the enemy into the heart of Russia. They consid ered the working people of their own country a more dangerous enemy than the foreign invaders.

On August 25 Kornilov moved the Third Mounted Corps from the front against Petrograd. The situation was complicated by the fact that Kornilov had started the revolt supposedly against the Provisional Government. And that is how the Socialist-Rev olutionaries and Mensheviks tried to present the matter. They called for defence of the Provisional Government. Lenin suggest ed a wise course to the Party. While rousing the masses against Kornilov, it explained that it was not calling for defence of the Provisional Government, which was an accomplice in the Korni lov affair. The Party conducted the struggle against the would be military dictator without ceasing to expose the Provisional Government and its Socialist-Revolutionary and Menshevik aiders and abettors. The masses responded to the call of the Bolsheviks

y rising against Kornilov. The workers of the capital took to
rms. New Red Guard detachments were hurriedly formed.
'he Kornilov revolt was crushed by the workers and peasants
rganised by the Bolshevik Party. At the instance of the people,
Kornilov and his fellow-conspirators were arrested. The attempt
f the bourgeoisie and the landlords to crush the revolution had
ailed. The only way out of the situation that had arisen was to
verthrow the Provisional Government by armed insurrection
nd to establish the dictatorship of the proletariat.

5. Preparations for Armed Insurrection. Victory of the Great October Socialist Revolution

Taking into account the great danger the Kornilov revolt represented for the revolution, and bearing in mind the rising tide
of the mass movement and the fact that many Soviets had opposed
Kornilov, Lenin proposed to the Socialist-Revolutionaries and
Mensheviks, who were still predominant in the Soviets, that power
be assumed by the Soviets. The Party wanted to utilise this last
opportunity for a peaceful development of the revolution. But
the Socialist-Revolutionaries and Mensheviks, who had aligned
themselves firmly with the bourgeoisie, rejected the only possibility still open for a peaceful transfer of power to the Soviets.
The rout of the Kornilov revolt radically changed the situation
in the country. The workers discovered the real nature of the
compromisers, who had in fact screened and defended the bourgeoisie and the landlords. The peasants realised that behind the generals stood the landlords, who had no intention of giving up their
land. The soldiers at the front became convinced that the intention was to compel them to spend a fourth winter in the trenches,
and that the bourgeois and landlord government meant to pro-
long the bloody war. The working people of the oppressed nations now saw clearly that had the Kornilovites won, there would
have been no question of the abolition of national oppression.
The overwhelming mass of the people were now convinced from
their own experience of the correctness of the Bolshevik ideas.
The working people began to recall Socialist-Revolutionary and
Menshevik deputies from the Soviets and to replace them by
Bolsheviks. Non-Party deputies in the Soviets began to support
the Bolsheviks. On August 31 the Petrograd Soviet, for the first
time since its establishment, adopted a Bolshevik resolution
for the transfer of power to the Soviets.
On September 5 the Moscow Soviet adopted a similar resolution.
Following the two capitals, the Soviets of Kiev, Kharkov, Kazan,
Ufa, Minsk, Revel, Tashkent, Samara, Bryansk, Krasnoyarsk

and many towns in the Urals and the Donets coalfield also adop
ed Bolshevik resolutions. There began a rapid bolshevisatio
of the Soviets.

The slogan "All power to the Soviets!" was again placed o
the order of the day by the Party. By that time the compositio
of the Soviets in the key centres of the country had changed
they had become Bolshevik Soviets. This time the slogan "Al
power to the Soviets!" was a slogan calling for armed insurrectio
against the bourgeois government, and for the establishmen
of the dictatorship of the proletariat. More than 250 Soviet
declared for the Bolshevik slogan "All power to the Soviets!

By September, 1917, the Bolsheviks had, by their indefatig
able work, convinced the people that the salvation of the coun
try lay in the overthrow of the anti-popular government. The
country was in the grip of a universal crisis. The national econo
my was heading for catastrophe. The ruling classes were incapabl
of averting disaster. If anything, they were rapidly bringing i
closer by their policy. The masses refused to live in the old way
and to let the bourgeoisie and its hangers-on go on running the
country. In a word, all the signs of a revolutionary situatior
which Lenin had indicated were in existence. Graphic evidence
of the crisis was the people's resort to more and more vigorous
forms of struggle. The workers began to remove factory managements, arrest directors and take over the management of production. The working-class movement had come face to face
with the problem of power. As the leader and guiding force of
the revolution, the proletariat was rousing the whole people to
struggle.

"We have the following of the majority of a *class*, the vanguard of the revolution, the vanguard of the people, which is
capable of carrying the masses with it," wrote Lenin in September, 1917 (*Collected Works*, Vol. 26, p. 6).

A change had also taken place in the character of the peasant
movement. The peasants began to drive out the landlords, seize
the land and implements and distribute them among themselves,
and set fire to the manor houses. The peasant movement throughout the country was growing into insurrection. More than half
the European part of Russia was in the grip of peasant revolts.
"We have the following of the *majority* of the people . . ." noted
Lenin (*ibid.*).

After the defeat of the Kornilov revolt, new forms of struggle
appeared in the army as well. The soldiers were driving out the
reactionary commanders and electing new ones in their place.
The men refused to go on fighting. Discontent among the soldiers
threatened to turn into insurrection. On the fronts closest to
Petrograd and Moscow—the Northern and Western fronts—the

majority of the soldiers followed the Bolsheviks; and there were over 1,700,000 armed men on these two fronts alone. All the reserve regiments, of which there were over 100, supported Bolsheviks. The overwhelming majority of garrisons all over the country, in their turn, backed the Bolsheviks. The soldiers of the Moscow garrison, for example, during the elections to the ward Dumas held at the end of September, voted solidly for the Bolsheviks. There were nearly four million soldiers in the reserve and rear units. They consisted, in the main, of the most advanced and militant section of the poor peasantry. The sailors of the Baltic Fleet also fully supported the Bolshevik Party.

A change had also taken place in the character of the movement among the oppressed nations. Despite the resistance of the bourgeois organisations, the struggle of the working people in the national-minority regions began to merge in a united front with the general movement of the workers and peasants throughout Russia. The Bolshevik Party was active not only among the working people of all the nations of Russia, but also among the refugees from Poland and the Baltic provinces, and also among German, Hungarian, Polish, Czech, Slovak and Croat prisoners of war. The Bolsheviks helped to form Communist groups among them.

The international situation, too, had changed. Faced with the threat of a mounting revolutionary movement in their rear, the British and French imperialists tried to come to terms with the German imperialists about the conclusion of peace, with a view to waging a joint struggle against the revolution. The Russian counter-revolution was ready to conclude a separate peace with Germany so as to have its hands free within the country. The ruling classes of Russia surrendered Riga to the Germans; they were prepared to give up Petrograd and part of the country in exchange for assistance in strangling the revolution. This was a glaring instance of the unpatriotic spirit of the bourgeoisie, of their treacherous attitude towards their native land. The true patriots were the Bolsheviks, fighting to save Russia from defeat by German imperialism, and from enslavement by foreign states. The treacherous plan of the bourgeoisie could be frustrated only by overthrowing the government of betrayal.

The national crisis also affected the situation in the Menshevik and Socialist-Revolutionary parties. Disintegration set in in both parties. The Menshevik party broke up into several groups. A Left wing formed within the Socialist-Revolutionary Party, and declared itself to be an independent party. The Left Socialist-Revolutionaries tried to win over those sections of the peasantry that were disillusioned by the Socialist-Revolutionaries and had swung towards the proletariat.

Lenin closely followed the situation in the country from h hiding-place. The leader of the revolution responded to eve change, to the slightest alteration in the mood of the people a in the relation of classes. During the 110 days that Lenin was "u derground," he wrote more than 60 articles and letters, throug which the Party received advice and guidance. Among the works the book, *The Impending Catastrophe and How to Combat I* is particularly notable. It was the Bolshevik Party's platfor which answered the question raised by the masses: how could t country be saved from ruin? After drawing a picture of the di want and famine to which the people were doomed by the ru of the bourgeoisie and landlords, Lenin indicated the revol tionary measures which could save the people from the war an from famine, namely: workers' control over production, n tionalisation of the banks, syndicates and so forth, parall with the confiscation of the landlords' estates and the national sation of all the land. These measures for combating catastroph and famine were quite feasible, wrote Lenin, and the only reaso they were not put into effect was that they infringed "the sanctit of bourgeois property." The ruling classes tried to persuade th people that ruin and destruction threatened the country shoul the people set about putting these measures into effect.

"If, instead of a 'coalition' with the bourgeoisie, which i hampering every measure of control and sabotaging production, wrote Lenin, "the Socialist-Revolutionaries and Menshevik had in April effected the transfer of power to the Soviets . . Russia would now be a country completely transformed eco nomically, with the land in the hands of the peasants and th banks nationalised, that is, she would *to that extent* (and thes are extremely important economic bases of modern life) b *superior* to all other capitalist countries" (*Collected Works* Vol. 25, p. 335).

Putting into effect the Bolshevik platform would immediately ease the lot and improve the life of the labouring masses. Lenir showed that the material basis for Socialism existed in Russia not only because Russia was one of the links in the imperialist chain, but also because capitalism in Russia, though it lagged behind by comparison with the advanced capitalist countries, was still sufficiently developed. Lenin described Russia as a country of medium-developed capitalism. In Russia, too, capi talism was growing into State-monopoly capitalism. The start ing-point of the Bolshevik platform on the eve of the great prole tarian revolution was Lenin's basic principle of the possibility of Socialism being victorious at first in one country alone.

"One cannot mark time—in history in general, and during a war in particular," wrote Lenin. "One must either go forward or backward. To go forward in twentieth-century Russia, which has won a republic and democracy by revolutionary means, *is impossible* without *a d v a n c i n g* to Socialism, without taking *s t e p s* towards it . . ." (*ibid.*, p. 333).

In his work Lenin set a momentous task before the proletariat, once it was victorious:

"The result of the revolution has been that in its *p o l i t i-c a l* system Russia has in a few months caught up with the advanced countries.

"But that is not enough. The war is inexorable, it puts the alternative with ruthless severity: either we perish or we catch up with the advanced countries and outstrip them *e c o n o m-i c a l l y a s w e l l. . . .*

"Either we perish or advance at top speed. That is the alternative with which history has confronted us" (*ibid.*, p. 338).

In his work, *The Impending Catastrophe and How to Combat It*, Lenin substantiated the measures outlined in the programme for the transition to Socialism. In their sum-total, they signified a gradual transition to new, Socialist relations of production.

During this period Lenin completed his brilliant work, *The State and Revolution*, which constituted a further development of Marx's teaching on the State. Lenin restored those of Marx's views which had been forgotten or distorted by the opportunists, and on the basis of new revolutionary experience, especially of the work of the Soviets, developed further the Marxist theory of the State. The dominant idea that runs through Lenin's book is that a resolute and uncompromising struggle must be waged on two fronts—against the opportunist traitors and against the Anarchists. Lenin showed that they all were kindred in their rejection of the dictatorship of the proletariat. The Right-wing Socialist leaders, who refused to recognise the need for the victorious working class to break up the bourgeois State, had sunk to an undisguised defence of that State. The Anarchists, who were opposed to the revolutionary proletariat using State power to build Socialism, thereby rejected the dictatorship of the proletariat.

The victorious proletariat must completely break up the bourgeois State machinery of violence—the organ of exploitation of the working people—and establish the dictatorship of the proletariat for the entire period of transition from capitalism to Communism.

"The essence of Marx's teaching on the State," wrote Lenin, "has been mastered only by those who understand that the dictatorship of a *single* class is necessary not only for every class society in general, not only for the *proletariat* which has overthrown the bourgeoisie, but also for the entire *historical period* which separates capitalism from 'classless society, from Communism. . . . The transition from capitalism to Communism certainly cannot but yield a tremendous abundance and variety of political forms, but the essence will inevitably be the same: *the dictatorship of the proletariat"* (*Collected Works*, Vol. 25, pp. 384-85).

In the bourgeois States, democracy is utterly hypocritical and spurious, for even in the most democratic of them it is democracy for an insignificant minority, for the rich, for the exploiters and parasites. The proletarian State, on the contrary, is one that is "democratic *in a new way*," because democracy here is democracy for the vast majority of the working people, for the proletarians, for the broad masses of the peasantry, for all the poor, and "dictatorial *in a new way*," because it is a dictatorship directed against the bourgeoisie, a dictatorship of the majority of the people against the minority, against the exploiters. The proletariat uses State power not only to suppress the exploiters, but chiefly to lead the working people in building a Communist society.

"The proletariat," wrote Lenin, "needs State power, the centralised organisation of force, the organisation of violence, both to crush the resistance of the exploiters and to *lead* the enormous mass of the population—the peasantry, the petty bourgeoisie, the semi-proletarians—in the work of organising a Socialist economy" (*ibid.*, p. 376).

Defining the role and significance of the dictatorship of the proletariat in the transformation of society, Lenin stressed that the Communist Party is the leading and directing force in establishing and exercising the dictatorship of the proletariat. He was relentless in unmasking the opportunists, dominant in the Second International, who distorted the role of the Party, turning it into an organisation for members of the top stratum of the better-paid workers, men isolated from the masses, who sell and betray the interests of the people.

"By educating the workers' party," wrote Lenin, "Marxism educates the vanguard of the proletariat which is capable of assuming power and *leading the whole people* to Socialism, of directing and organising the new system, of being the teacher, the guide, the leader of all the toilers and exploited in the task of building up their social life without the bourgeoisie and against the bourgeoisie" (*ibid.*).

Lenin wrote his book at a turning-point in history, on the eve of the advent of the proletariat to power. It brings out in bold relief a characteristic feature of Marxism-Leninism, namely, the direct connection between theory and practice. Lenin himself noted in the preface that the question of the relationship of the Socialist revolution to the State acquires "not only practical political importance, but also the importance of a most urgent problem of the day, the problem of explaining to the masses what they will have to do in the very near future to free themselves from the yoke of capitalism" (*ibid.*, p. 356).

Between September 12 and 14 Lenin wrote a letter to the Central, Petrograd and Moscow committees of the Bolshevik Party ("The Bolsheviks Must Take Power"), and a letter to the Central Committee ("Marxism and Insurrection"), in which he called on the Party to organise the insurrection. Equipped with a profound knowledge of the laws of the development of society, and possessing a wealth of experience in revolutionary struggle, Lenin in these letters summed up his analysis of the situation, and explained with the utmost clarity why the Bolsheviks could and should take power at that particular time. The leadership of the Soviets in both capitals had passed into the hands of the Bolsheviks. They had the support of the people, who had convinced themselves that the Bolshevik Party alone represented and defended their interests. The Soviets, having assumed power, would immediately proceed to conclude a democratic peace, would deprive the landlords of their estates without compensation and hand them over to the peasants, and restore the liberties trampled underfoot by the government. All these measures would receive the full support of the masses.

Power must be taken now, noted Lenin, for the bourgeoisie was preparing to surrender Petrograd to the Germans, while the British and French imperialists were discussing a separate peace with Germany against, and at the expense of, Russia. Only by assuming power could the Bolshevik Party frustrate this criminal plot. The situation was quite ripe for an insurrection. It was the Party's task to treat insurrection as an art, to make thorough preparations for it, to think out all the measures necessary for its success, and not let things drift.

In his letters Lenin also worked out an approximate plan for the armed insurrection. He proposed the immediate organisation of a headquarters of the insurrectionary detachments, distribution of forces, concentration of the most reliable units at the most important points, preparations for surrounding government buildings, occupation of the central telephone exchange and telegraph office. Lenin recommended that strong detachments be formed such as would be ready to die rather than let the enemy reach the centre of the city, that the workers be given arms, and that measures be taken to guarantee the city's defence against a possible attack by officer cadets and other counter-revolutionary units.

Lenin called his plan an approximate one, but the actual course of the insurrection showed how profoundly and thoroughly this plan had been worked out. Lenin had further developed the ideas

of the founders of Marxism on insurrection, and turned them int
an integral doctrine.

No other party in history had ever been so thoroughly prepared
for launching an armed insurrection as was the Bolshevik Party
Thanks to Lenin, the Party had a most detailed plan for organising
the rising, and a well-thought-out, integral programme of economic
and political measures to be carried out on the very next day
after victory.

Lenin's letters were discussed at a meeting of the Central Committee on September 15. Kamenev, continuing his fight against
the Socialist revolution, opposed Lenin's proposals regarding
the organisation of the insurrection and insisted that the letters
be destroyed. A capitulatory resolution proposed by this
defender of capitalism was rejected. Stalin proposed that copies of
Lenin's letters be sent for discussion to the more important Party
organisations.

The Central Committee began to prepare for the insurrection.
The Military Organisation of the Central Committee was instructed
to speed up the formation of new Red Guard detachments. Special
courses for training military instructors were started in the capital. Workers were trained in the use of arms. The Bolsheviks in
the Baltic Fleet were instructed to get the fleet ready to take part
in the insurrection. On all big ships, special fighting squads were
formed, ready to come to the capital the moment the Party called.
The Bolshevik organisations at the front selected combat units
to assist the insurgents in Petrograd. The leaders of the biggest
Party organisations were forewarned of the preparations for
insurrection.

Meanwhile, the counter-revolution was taking measures against
the rising tide of the revolution. Cossack units were moved up
to the capital. It was decided to withdraw the revolutionary-minded
units of the garrison from Petrograd, so as to weaken the Bolsheviks. At the front, units were moved with the purpose of
surrounding and disarming the pro-Bolshevik regiments. Kornilov and his confederates were considered to be in prison, but were
in fact in communication with the generals at the front and were
mapping out a new plan for counter-revolutionary action. The
Provisional Government was preparing a second Kornilov affair.

The Socialist-Revolutionaries and Mensheviks were a party to
this conspiracy against the people. Sensing that the insurrection
was near, they made one more attempt to check the mobilisation
of the revolutionary forces: they decided to convene an All-Russian Democratic Conference in Petrograd. The social-Kornilov-
ites had lost their majority in the Soviets, and so were afraid to
convene a new congress, although they had promised to do so in
three months' time. The leaders of the compromisers resorted to a

subterfuge: they decided to substitute a Democratic Conference for a Congress of Soviets. The purpose of this manoeuvre was to retain leadership of the masses by deceit and uphold the Provisional Government.

The Democratic Conference opened on September 14. It was clearly a packed conference: the city Dumas, Zemstvos and co-operatives representing a small section of the population received more votes than the Soviets of Workers' and Soldiers' Deputies or the military organisations, which united the overwhelming majority of the people. The entire army of 10,000,000 men had only twice as many seats as the small Cossack force, which the Provisional Government considered as its mainstay. The Bolsheviks took part in the conference to expose the designs of the Socialist-Revolutionaries and Mensheviks.

At the conference, the compromisers set up a Provisional Council of the Republic, or, as they put it, a Pre-parliament, in an attempt to create the impression that a parliamentary system had been established in Russia. Kamenev, Rykov and Ryazanov supported this fraud on the part of the Socialist-Revolutionaries and Mensheviks, trying thus to divert the workers from the uprising. Lenin considered the whole Democratic Conference affair to be a trap set by the Socialist-Revolutionaries and Mensheviks, and categorically insisted on a boycott of the Pre-parliament. To participate in it, he said, would create the illusion that this institution could solve the problems of the revolution. The Central Committee discussed Lenin's proposal and, despite the opposition of Kamenev and other capitulators, resolved to withdraw from the Pre-parliament. The Central Committee proposed that gubernia and regional congresses of Soviets be held and that a struggle be waged for the convocation of the Second Congress of Soviets.

On October 3 the Central Committee resolved that Lenin should move to Petrograd so as to ensure regular and close contact with him and to enable him directly to lead the uprising. On October 7, Lenin arrived in the capital secretly and settled in an apartment in the Vyborg District, the most revolutionary in the city. On October 10 a meeting of the Central Committee took place at which Lenin reported on the current situation. He emphasised that the political situation was fully ripe for the transition of power to the proletariat and the poor peasantry. It was now a question of the insurrection itself. Lenin considered it necessary for the whole Party to place the question of the armed uprising on the order of the day.

"The Central Committee recognises," read the resolution drawn up by Lenin, "that the international position of the Russian revolution (the revolt in the German navy, which is an extreme manifestation of the growth throughout Europe of the world Socialist revolution; the threat of peace between the imperialists with the object of strangling the revolution in Russia), as well as the military situation (the indubitable decision of the Russian bourgeoisie and Kerensky and Co. to surrender Petrograd to the Germans) and the fact that the proletarian party has gained a majority in the Soviets—all this, taken in conjunction with the peasant revolt and the swing of popular confidence towards our Party (the elections in Moscow), and, finally, the obvious preparations being made for a second Kornilov affair (the withdrawal of troops from Petrograd, the dispatch of Cossacks to Petrograd, the encirclement of Minsk by Cossacks, etc.)—all this places armed insurrection on the order of the day.

"Considering therefore that an armed insurrection is inevitable, and that the time for it is fully ripe, the Central Committee instructs all Party organisations to be guided accordingly, and to discuss and decide all practical questions (the Congress of Soviets of the Northern Region, the withdrawal of troops from Petrograd, the action of our people in Moscow and Minsk, etc.) from this point of view" (*C.P.S.U. in Resolutions*, Part I, pp. 397-98).

Only Zinoviev and Kamenev opposed this resolution. They asserted that the working class was incapable of carrying out a Socialist revolution; they sank to the position of the Mensheviks, who were championing the bourgeois republic.

This was a betrayal of Socialism. The capitulatory position of Zinoviev and Kamenev was no accident. Their treachery was the direct outcome of all their opportunist vacillations.

At that meeting of the C. C., Trotsky did not vote against the resolution on the insurrection. But he insisted on its being postponed until the Second Congress of Soviets was convened. This was tantamount to wrecking the insurrection, for the Socialist-Revolutionaries and Mensheviks might postpone the Congress, and that would have enabled the Provisional Government to concentrate its forces by the time the Congress opened, so as to smash the insurrection.

The Central Committee adopted Lenin's resolution, and it became the Party's directive to *prepare for armed insurrection immediately*. The meeting elected a Political Bureau headed by Lenin.

A Revolutionary Military Committee of the Petrograd Soviet was set up, on the Party Central Committee's proposal, to direct the rising in the capital. It consisted of representatives of the C.C. and the P.C., of the Petrograd Soviet, factory committees, trade unions, garrison, Baltic Fleet and other organisations. The Revolutionary Military Committee operated under the direct leadership of the Central Committee of the Party.

Systematic preparations for armed action proceeded in all the key areas of the country. In Petrograd the Third City Conference of the Bolsheviks met, representing nearly 50,000 Party members. On October 11 it adopted Lenin's resolution on the insurrection. The same resolution was adopted by the Moscow City Conference of the Bolsheviks. The Moscow Regional Bureau, representing as many as 70,000 Party members, declared in favour of insurrection. During September and October more than 30 regional, gubernia, town and area conferences were held, representing the bulk of the Bolshevik Party. The overwhelming majority of the members were ready for decisive events.

Workers' Red Guard detachments were being rapidly formed everywhere. In October they numbered about 200,000 advanced workers, who were ready to give their lives for the revolution and could carry the masses of the working people with them.

On October 16 an enlarged meeting of the Central Committee was held, with representatives of the Petrograd Committee, the Military Organisation, the Petrograd Soviet, the Petrograd Area Committee, factory committees and trade unions. The meeting reaffirmed Lenin's resolution on the insurrection. At the end of the meeting a Revolutionary Military Centre was elected to direct it; the members were A. S. Bubnov, F. E. Dzerzhinsky, J. V. Stalin, Y. M. Sverdlov and M. S. Uritsky. It was decided that the Revolutionary Military Centre of the Party Central Committee would be part of the Revolutionary Military Committee of the Petrograd Soviet.

Defeated in the Central Committee, Zinoviev and Kamenev committed an unheard-of piece of treachery: they published a statement in the non-Party, semi-Menshevik paper *Novaya Zhizn* (*New Life*), in which they stated their disagreement with the decision on armed insurrection, and thereby betrayed the decision of the Central Committee to the enemy. Lenin indignantly denounced these strike-breakers of the revolution and demanded their expulsion from the Party. The Central Committee prohibited Kamenev and Zinoviev from making statements on behalf of the Party.

Forewarned by the traitors, the Provisional Government took immediate steps to crush the revolution. Special units were summoned from the front, the whole of Petrograd was divided into districts, and these were patrolled by mounted detachments. But the counter-revolution was now powerless to halt the mustering of the revolutionary forces. The Party had roused and organised vast masses of the people to fight for the Socialist revolution.

The entire work of organising the insurrection was directed by Lenin. He summoned members of the Revolutionary Military Committee, heard reports of the steps taken, and kept a check to see that everything was being done to ensure the victory of the insurrection.

He gave instructions regarding the detailed plan of insur rection and the strengthening and arming of the Red Guard. Le nin was visited by Bolsheviks active in the army and navy, wh received instructions on the use of the Baltic Fleet and on th summoning of revolutionary units from the front. Representative came to him from Moscow with reports on the situation in tha city and in the Moscow Region.

The Central Committee of the Party followed the basic instruc tion of Marxism to treat insurrection as an art. Representatives o the Central Committee were sent to various parts of the country to help the local Party organisations prepare for armed insurrec tion: G. I. Petrovsky was sent to the Donets coalfield and Ukraine and G. K. Orjonikidze to Transcaucasia. Representatives o local Party organisations came to the Central Committee fo instructions. Letters and directives were sent from the C.C. t the localities. The biggest Party organisations were not only in formed of the insurrection, but also received practical instructions on how to organise it. The Central Committee closely followed the work of the All-Russian Bureau for Military Organisations under the C. C. of the Bolshevik Party, helped it, gave instructions to the trade unions and drew them into the work of preparing the insurrection. The enlarged meeting of the Party Central Committee, held on October 16, was attended by representatives of the biggest unions. The work of the Central Committee during that period was a splendid example of collective leadership. In the three months alone, preceding the October Revolution, more than 30 meetings of the C.C. were held, including two plenary and two enlarged meetings.

Lenin insisted that the insurrection be begun without fail before the Second Congress of Soviets, scheduled for October 25. It was essential to forestall the enemy, who had been forewarned by the traitors and who expected action to be taken on the day the Congress opened.

"Under no circumstances," wrote Lenin in a letter to the Central Committee on October 24, "should the power be left in the hands of Kerensky and Co. until the 25th—not under any circumstances; the matter must be decided without fail this very evening or this very night.

"History will not forgive revolutionaries for procrastinating, when they can—and certainly will—win today, while they risk losing much, in fact everything, tomorrow" (*Collected Works*, Vol. 26, p. 204).

On Lenin's proposal, the insurrection was launched on October 24, before the Congress opened. The headquarters of the insurrection was in the Smolny Institute, where Lenin arrived late in the evening of the 24th to direct operations personally. On the intructions of headquarters, Red Guards occupied the objects previously decided on. They mounted guard over the factories. All approaches to the capital were guarded by revolutionary units, to prevent reinforcements for the Provisional Government passing through from the front. Sailors of the Baltic Fleet were summoned to the capital. In the course of the night all government institutions were occupied, and the Winter Palace, where the Provisional Government had taken refuge, was surrounded. The workers' Red Guard detachments formed the principal fighting force of the insurrection, the sailors of the Baltic Fleet sharing the glory of victory with them. Side by side with the Red Guard detachments and the sailors, fought the regiments of the Petrograd garrison. The insurrection enjoyed such wide support among the masses, and had been so thoroughly planned, that it was carried out with rare speed. By the morning of October 25 the Provisional Government had been deposed. At 10 o'clock in the morning appeared the manifesto "To the Citizens of Russia!" written by Lenin, the genius who had inspired and led the revolution.

"The Provisional Government has been deposed. State power has passed into the hands of the organ of the Petrograd Soviet of Workers' and Soldiers' Deputies—the Revolutionary Military Committee, which heads the Petrograd proletariat and garrison.

"The cause for which the people have fought, namely, the immediate offer of a democratic peace, the abolition of landlord ownership of land, workers' control over production, and the establishment of Soviet power—this cause has been secured.

"Long live the revolution of workers, soldiers and peasants!" (*Ibid.*, p. 207.)

The government which had been overthrown remained in possession only of the Winter Palace, garrisoned by officer cadets and a women's shock battalion. Lenin gave orders for this last stronghold of the bourgeois government to be taken by storm. From the Neva, the cruiser *Aurora* fired a shot, giving the signal for attack. That shot heralded the birth of a new world. On the night of October 25 the Winter Palace fell; the Ministers of the last government of the dictatorship of the bourgeoisie were arrested.

In the evening of October 25 the Second Congress of Soviets opened. It represented over 400 of the country's Soviets. Of the 650 delegates present, about 400 were Bolsheviks. The rest of the delegates were, in the main, Left Socialist-Revolutionaries. The Mensheviks and Right Socialist-Revolutionaries, who had till then dominated the Soviets, comprised a small group of 70 to 80. At the Congress itself, this group continued to dwindle, its members deserting either to the Left Socialist-Revolutionaries or to the Menshevik-Internationalists. The miserable remnants of the bankrupt parties of compromise with the bourgeoisie left the Con gress.

On the very first day of its labours the Second Congress of So viets adopted the proclamation "To the Workers, Soldiers and Peasants," written by Lenin.

"Backed by the will of the vast majority of the workers, soldier and peasants," read the proclamation, "and by the victorious insurrection of the workers and garrison which has taken place in Petrograd, the Congress takes power into its own hands. . .

"The Congress decrees: all power in the localities is transferred to the Soviets of Workers', Soldiers' and Peasants' Deputies which must duly ensure genuine revolutionary order" (*Collected Works*, Vol. 26, p. 215).

The workers and peasant poor had overthrown the dictatorship of the bourgeoisie and established the dictatorship of the prole tariat.

October 25 (November 7), 1917, has gone down in history as the day of the victory of the Great October Socialist Revolution in Russia.

At the second session of the Congress, on October 26, Lenin delivered two reports. The first was devoted to the question of peace. The Congress unanimously adopted the Decree on Peace, which proclaimed the Soviet Government's total renunciation of all predatory treaties and proposed to all the belligerent nations and their governments immediate negotiations for the conclusion of a general, just and democratic peace. The first thing the people did after seizing power was to begin a fight for peace, inspiring the whole of mankind by their example.

The Decree on Peace declared the war to be "the greatest of crimes against humanity" and solemnly proclaimed the Soviet Government's determination to sign peace immediately on terms equally just for all peoples, without annexations and indemnities.

For the first time in history new principles of international relations were proclaimed, principles which condemned war as a means of settling disputes and made peace the corner-stone of the foreign policy of the Socialist State. That first Soviet decree already proclaimed Lenin's idea of the possibility of coexistence of two systems differing in their social structure.

On Lenin's second report, the Congress adopted the Decree on Land, which proclaimed the confiscation of all the landlords' estates without compensation, and the transfer of all the land to the people.

The Bolshevik Party thus fulfilled the promises it had made to the people in its programme. The Decree on Land gave effect to the age-old hopes of the peasantry. In all, over 360 million acres of land passed to the people. For the first time in history the peasants were released from their land debts: they had been owing the Peasant ank alone nearly 1,500 million rubles (£ 150 millions), not ounting private debts to landlords, usurers and kulaks. The Decree on Land released the peasants from annual payment of rent for he land and from expenditure on the purchase of new lots, mounting to 700 million gold rubles (over £ 70 millions). In his way the land was nationalised. It became the property of the tate.

The Decree on Land included the peasant instructions, compiled y the Socialist-Revolutionaries on the basis of 242 local instructions by the peasants to their delegates. While in power, the Socialist-Revolutionaries had done nothing to put the instructions nto effect. The Bolsheviks made the peasant instructions law on he very day they assumed power—although in addition to the demand for the abolition of private property in land and the confiscation of the landlord estates without compensation, the instructions called for an equalitarian use of land, a point with which he Bolshevik Party did not agree. Replying to those who accused he Party of adopting the instructions, Lenin said:

"As a democratic government, we cannot ignore the decision of the rank and file of the people, even though we may disagree with it. In the fire of experience, in putting the decree into practice and carrying it out locally, the peasants will themselves realise where the truth lies" (*ibid.*, p. 228).

This act expressed the wisdom of the Party, the flexibility of its tactics, its ability to take the interests of the masses into account, and its profound confidence that the peasants would solidly support the Bolshevik line on the agrarian question.

That same day, October 26, the Second Congress of Soviets formed the Council of People's Commissars, headed by V. I. Ulyanov-Lenin. The people had entrusted the direction of the country to the Bolshevik Party.

Following Petrograd, Soviet power was, after several days of fighting, established in Moscow as well, and then throughout the country.

In a number of places the fight to establish Soviet power was complicated by the action of the whiteguards and the bourgeois nationalist counter-revolution (the Central Rada in Ukraine, Ataman Kaledin on the Don, and Ataman Dutov in Orenburg).

But, notwithstanding the diversity of conditions in the country (the different degrees of the Bolshevik Party's influence, the big differences in industrial development and in the numerical strength of the proletariat, national peculiarities, and so forth), Soviet power was established over the vast territory of Russia in a comparatively short space of time.

6. Reasons for the Victory of the Revolution. International Significance of the Great October Socialist Revolution

1. The chief reason for the victory of the October Socialist Revolution was that it was led by the working class of Russia. No other detachment of the international army of labour had gained such tremendous experience in so short an historical period. The proletariat of Russia, led by Lenin, was the first of all the classes in the country to form its own party. The working class led the struggle of the whole people against the autocracy and against the dictatorship of the bourgeoisie. The other sections of the working people had convinced themselves that in the proletariat they had a champion of the interests of the whole people, who were languishing under the yoke of the landlords and bourgeoisie. The proletariat of Russia was the principal motive force of the entire social and political development of the country.

2. The October Revolution was victorious because a social force had been created in Russia—the alliance between the proletariat and the peasantry—that broke the resistance of the moribund classes. In the course of the revolution the Bolsheviks had exposed the traitors to the working-class cause, the opportunists, who had maintained that the proletariat could assume and retain power only where it constituted a majority of the population. The Russian proletariat had secured the full backing of the poor peasantry, which constituted the overwhelming majority of the rural population—as much as 65 per cent. The broad masses of the peasantry had realised from their own experience, and as a result of the extensive work carried out by the Bolshevik Party, that only under the leadership of the proletariat could they secure land, peace, bread and liberty. By winning a majority of the labouring peasantry over to the proletariat, the Bolsheviks won the peasant reserves away from the bourgeoisie.

3. The October Revolution differed from all other revolutions in that the workers created their own organs of power. It was in the very midst of the Russian proletariat that a new form of revolutionary authority had arisen—the Soviets of Workers' Deputies. The Soviets of Workers', Soldiers' and Peasants' Deputies were organs of the alliance of the proletariat and the peasantry, a form of organisation that embodied the alliance of the workers and peasants under the leadership of the workers.

"Had not the creative effort of the revolutionary classes given rise to the Soviets," wrote Lenin, "the proletarian revolution in Russia would have been a hopeless cause" (*Collected Works*, Vol. 26, p. 80).

4. The October Revolution was victorious because it was confronted with a comparatively weak enemy, the Russian bourgeoisie.

The entire course of historical development of Russian capitalism, its backwardness as compared with that of the leading capitalist countries, and its dependence on foreign capital explain the political flabbiness, cowardice and inadequate experience of the Russian bourgeoisie. The compromisers, too — the Socialist-Revolutionaries and Mensheviks—proved powerless to help the Russian bourgeoisie. In a struggle that had gone on for many years, they had been exposed by the Bolsheviks as agents of the bourgeoisie. On the eve of the October Revolution these parties openly deserted to the camp of the counter-revolution, they championed the capitalist system.

5. A decisive circumstance that made the victory of the revolution possible was the fact that the masses of the people were headed by the well-tried, militant and revolutionary Bolshevik Party, a party guided by the advanced theory of the working class, the theory of Marxism-Leninism.

While the revolution was being prepared and carried out, the Party did an enormous amount of work in the theoretical field, and enriched Marxism with new propositions. The resolutions of the April Conference and the Sixth Party Congress, the resolutions and decisions of the Central Committee and, most important of all, the works of Lenin, contain the theoretical substantiation and elaboration of a concrete plan for the development of the bourgeois-democratic revolution into the Socialist revolution.

In its fight against the opportunists the Party worked out and upheld the theory that Socialism could be victorious in Russia. It showed that the development of capitalism in this country had created objective conditions in it for the establishment of Socialism, and that the particular acuteness of the contradictions in Russia had made it the weakest link in the chain of imperialism. Lenin developed the Marxist theory of Socialist revolution, discovered, in a republic of Soviets, a political form for the dictatorship of the proletariat, substantiated that view, and further elaborated Marxist views on armed insurrection, developing them into a full-fledged theory.

The Great October Socialist Revolution is a splendid example of the practical application and implementation of Lenin's theory of Socialist revolution.

The toiling masses had seen all the other parties in power, separately and in various combinations. They had seen the Cadets, who represented the bourgeoisie as a whole; they had experienced the rule of a coalition of Cadets, Socialist-Revolutionaries and Mensheviks; they had tested the Socialist-Revolutionaries and Mensheviks by their deeds, when they were in a majority in the Soviets. In the course of the revolution, all the bourgeois and compromising parties had discredited themselves, had revealed their counter-revolutionary essence. The working people turned away from the parties of compromise with the bourgeoisie and, using their right to recall deputies, proceeded to oust from the Soviets those who had betrayed their confidence, electing in their place Bolsheviks, people who had proved by their deeds that they were the only consistent defenders of the people's interests and genuine fighters for freedom and independence. In this way the Mensheviks and Socialist-Revolutionaries were isolated from the masses. The Bolshevik Party was the only party to lead the revolutionary struggle of the proletariat and the working people, as a whole, and do so undividedly.

The Bolshevik Party succeeded in uniting all the diverse revolutionary movements and in directing them towards a single goal, that of overthrowing imperialism. The Party merged into a single revolutionary torrent the movement of the whole people for peace, the peasants' fight for the land and against landlord oppression, the struggle of Russia's oppressed nations against national oppression, and the fight of the proletariat, the leading force in society, for Socialism. Under the leadership of the Bolshevik Party, the workers and poor peasants overthrew the government of the bourgeoisie and established Soviet power.

Such were the chief reasons of a domestic character that ensured the victory of the revolution.

Among the reasons of an international character that ensured the success of the Great October Socialist Revolution was the fact that the revolution began during the imperialist world war. Neither the Anglo-French nor the German bloc was able to give direct armed assistance to the Russian bourgeoisie. They helped it materially and by organising plots, but were unable to provide it with any considerable armed forces. The Russian bourgeoisie, left face to face with the Russian proletariat at the head of all the working people, could not withstand the onslaught of the masses.

The support of the international proletariat was also of enormous significance to the revolution. Under the influence of the October Revolution, the revolutionary mass movement grew stronger in all capitalist countries. The action of the international proletariat tied the hands of the imperialists and thereby facilitated the triumphal march of the Great October Revolution through the country.

Defining the international significance of the Great October Socialist Revolution, Lenin wrote that it manifested itself in two forms: in its influence on the revolutionary movement in other countries, and in the inevitability of a repetition of the basic features of the Russian revolution on an international scale.

All the cardinal questions of the Great October Socialist Revolution are of international importance, in the broad sense of the word. Under the direct influence of the October Revolution, the exploited people throughout the world, languishing under the yoke of imperialism, were moved to action. A number of revolutions—in Germany, Austria-Hungary and several other countries—together with revolutionary mass actions of the workers in Europe and America, shook the capitalist world to its foundations. The enslaved peoples of the colonial countries awoke to action. The Russian revolution began the uniting of the revolutionary actions of the workers and the national liberation struggle into a single force, capable of overthrowing imperialism.

The October Revolution was the clearest manifestation of the sharpening of the general crisis of capitalism. The Russian revolution broke the chain of imperialism and cleared the way for the establishment of a new, Socialist society. It put an end to the undivided rule of imperialism. The banner of Socialism was raised over one-sixth of the globe. The world was split into two camps: the camp of moribund capitalism and the camp of rising Socialism. The October Revolution ushered in a new era in the history of mankind, the era of the abolition of all forms of exploitation, the era of the victory of Communism.

The great international significance of the October Revolution lies not only in the fact that it advanced the entire course of world history, but also in its demonstration that its basic features must inevitably reappear in the Socialist revolution of any other country. It showed that without an alliance of the proletariat and the peasantry, led by the workers, without the dictatorship of the proletariat as a specific class alliance of the proletariat and the peasantry, the victory of revolution was impossible. The October Revolution was a classic realisation in Russia of Lenin's proposition regarding the dictatorship of the proletariat. Lenin described the dictatorship of the proletariat as an alliance of the Russian workers not only with the Russian peasants, but also with the working people of all the nationalities of Russia, as an alliance of the proletariat of an advanced country with the oppressed peoples of the colonies. These fundamental tenets of Lenin's theory of Socialist revolution are applicable to all countries.

The great, world-wide significance of the October Revolution lies in its having been the first revolution in history to give the people not only political rights, but also the material conditions necessary for a prosperous life.

Of enormous significance for the international proletariat are the theory and practice of Socialist construction in the U. S. S. R. that begun after the victory of the Great October Revolution. To the land of Soviets fell the task of first blazing the trail from capitalism to Socialism.

The October Revolution demonstrated to the whole world, and primarily to the dependent and colonial peoples, who comprised more than half of the human race, the only correct way to solve the national question.

The victory of the Socialist revolution in Russia strikingly confirmed the vitality of the ideas of Marxism-Leninism, the correctness of the Bolshevik Party's strategy and tactics, and in this way made easier the struggle of all working people for peace, democracy and Socialism.

BRIEF SUMMARY

The October Revolution of 1917 showed all working people that the Bolshevik Party was the only force that could abolish the capitalist system, avert national disaster and put the country on the path to independent development. In Lenin's April Theses and in the decisions of the Seventh All-Russian Conference, the Party provided the people with a concrete plan for transition from the bourgeois-democratic revolution to the Socialist revolution, and called on the masses to fight for the transfer of all power to the Soviets, which would secure peace, bread, land and liberty. Lenin discovered in the Soviets a political form for the dictatorship of the proletariat.

In advancing the slogan "All power to the Soviets!" the Party proceeded from the assumption that a peaceful development of the revolution was possible, that a bloodless transfer of all power to the Soviets could take place, and that the revolutionary-democratic dictatorship of the proletariat and peasantry could grow peacefully into the Socialist dictatorship of the proletariat.

After the July events, however, when the counter-revolutionary bourgeoisie succeeded in securing undivided power, a peaceful development of the revolution was no longer possible. The slogan "All power to the Soviets!" was temporarily withdrawn at the Sixth Party Congress, for the Mensheviks and Socialist-Revolutionaries had converted the Soviets into an appendage of the counter-revolutionary Provisional Government. They had finally deserted to the camp of the counter-revolutionary bourgeoisie.

With the new revolutionary upsurge, stimulated by the Kornilov revolt and its defeat, the Soviets revived, and became once again militant, revolutionary organs of the masses. The period of bolshevisation of the Soviets began. The Party again put forward the slogan "All power to the Soviets!", but this time it meant a call for insurrection against the dictatorship of the bourgeoisie and for the establishment of the dictatorship of the proletariat.

By its selfless work among the masses and flexible tactics, which ook into account the specific situation, the Party rallied the proletariat under its banners, and succeeded in convincing the masses of the correctness of its ideas and in rousing the people to decisive action against the Provisional Government. The Communist Party acted in the revolution as the wise and tested leader of the working people, ably directing all forms of the working people's struggle along the only right path—the path leading to liberty and a classless society.

The Provisional Government was not saved by the Socialist-Revolutionaries and Mensheviks. On the eve of the October Revolution these parties completed the cycle of their development, turning into outright defenders of counter-revolution, upholders of the capitalist system. In the course of the revolution and as a result of the explanatory work of the Bolsheviks, the people came to realise the essentially counter-revolutionary nature of the Socialist-Revolutionaries and Mensheviks. The masses convinced themselves that the Bolshevik Party was the only party whose words were never at variance with its deeds, that it alone would abolish all forms of exploitation and save the country from disaster. The workers, labouring peasants and soldiers convinced themselves of the Party's devotion to the interests of the people, of the heroism of its members, and of the Communists' readiness to face death in order to secure the triumph of the Socialist revolution. The masses entrusted their fate to the only revolutionary and fully consistent defender of their interests—the Bolshevik Party. Responding to its call, they overthrew the bourgeois Provisional Government and set up a Socialist republic of Soviets.

The October Socialist Revolution was a people's revolution. It overthrew the yoke of the exploiters. It established the dictatorship of the proletariat which, with the support of the poorest strata of the peasantry, set about laying the foundations of a Communist society. The October Revolution ushered in a new era in the history of mankind, the era of the triumph of Socialism and Communism.

CHAPTER EIGHT

THE PARTY'S FIGHT
TO DEVELOP THE SOCIALIST REVOLUTION
AND CONSOLIDATE SOVIET POWER

(October 1917-1918)

1. The Party's Fight to Establish the Soviet State. Firs Socialist Changes

The victory of the Great October Socialist Revolution and the establishment of the dictatorship of the proletariat brought about radical changes in the position of all classes and strata of the population in Russia. *The proletariat became the ruling class.* Around it rallied the working masses of town and country, primarily the poor peasants. The Soviets had the backing of the vast majority of the people—the workers, soldiers and working peasants. This powerful camp of the working people was headed by the Bolshevik Party. The camp of the enemies of Soviet power was made up of the defeated landlords, capitalists and kulaks, and those who voiced their interests: the monarchists, Cadets, Socialist-Revolutionaries, Mensheviks, Anarchists and bourgeois nationalists.

The October Revolution fundamentally changed the position of the Communist Party and the nature of its activities. It became the *governing party* in the world's first Socialist State of workers and peasants. It was confronted with new historical tasks—the building up and consolidation of the Soviet State, the reorganisation of society along Socialist lines, the organisation of the country's defence against the hostile capitalist encirclement, the strengthening of contacts with the proletarians of other countries.

The proletariat of Russia began to build Socialism in an extremely complex and difficult situation. The Socialist revolution had triumphed in one country, while capitalism continued to exist in the others. Russia's working class was the first in history to pave the way to Socialism. Economically, Russia was a comparatively backward country, with a predominantly small-holding peasant population. The war still continued. It had ruined and exhausted the country and created unprecedented chaos. The proletariat had practically no trained personnel to administer the State and manage the economy. The defeated exploiters—the landlords and capitalists—were offering furious resistance to the proletarian dictatorship. They still had an economic basis in the country in the form of small-scale production. They had the support of international capitalism, with which they were closely connected.

Russia's proletariat had resolutely to suppress the resistance of its numerous enemies, who, in their fight against Soviet power, engineered conspiracies and revolts, resorted to sabotage, calumny and provocation, and to the bribing of vacillating and unstable elements. In the very first days after the victory of the October Revolution, the Bolshevik Party had to deal with attempts by the counter-revolution to overthrow Soviet power. Kerensky, who had fled from Petrograd to the Northern front, mustered Cossack units and dispatched them against the capital under the command of General Krasnov. After capturing Gatchina, Krasnov launched an attack on Petrograd on October 28. On October 29, a counter-revolutionary organisation formed by the Right Socialist-Revolutionaries and the Mensheviks under the demagogic name of "Committee for the Salvation of the Fatherland and the Revolution," raised a mutiny of officer cadets in Petrograd. White officers and cadets mutinied simultaneously in Moscow. The counter-revolution started an armed struggle against Soviet power.

The Soviets had to crush the resistance of their enemies by force of arms. The Party and the Soviet Government acted with dispatch and resolution. With the support of the Petrograd workers, the sailors of the Baltic Fleet and soldiers of the Petrograd garrison, the anti-Soviet mutiny of the cadets was suppressed the same day. Two days later, on October 31, General Krasnov's Cossack detachments were routed at Pulkovo. In the early hours of November 3 the fighting in Moscow against the White rebels ended in victory for the workers. The first attempts of the counter-revolution to overthrow Soviet power by armed force were crushed.

When the anti-Soviet Kerensky-Krasnov mutiny was at its height, the Executive Committee of the All-Russian Railwaymen's Union (the Vikzhel), which was headed by Socialist-Revolutionaries and Mensheviks, demanded the formation of a so-called "all-Socialist government," to include, in addition to Bolsheviks, representatives of the counter-revolutionary Menshevik and Right Socialist-Revolutionary parties. The enemy hoped in this way to end Soviet power.

In order to unmask the Right Socialist-Revolutionaries and the Mensheviks, the Central Committee of the Bolshevik Party agreed to negotiate with them on condition that they recognised Soviet power and all the gains of the October Revolution. The negotiations with the Vikzhel were to serve, in Lenin's opinion, as diplomatic cover for military operations against Kerensky and to enable the Party to gain time in which to muster the forces of the revolution and defeat the enemies of the Soviets. The Central Committee appointed a delegation headed by Kamenev to conduct the negotiations. During the negotiations Kamenev violated the Party's instructions. He yielded to the demands of the Mensheviks and Socialist-Revolutionaries, and agreed to the formation of an "all-Socialist government" in which the Bolsheviks were to be assigned a minor role; he did not object to the demand that Lenin be replaced as head of the Government.

Kamenev's conduct during the negotiations with the Vikzhel roused the indignation of most of the Central Committee members. But Kamenev found several sympathisers. He was supported in the Central Committee by Zinoviev, Rykov, Nogin and Milyutin. The capitulatory position of Kamenev and Zinoviev was a continuation of the treacherous line they had followed prior to October. Kamenev, Zinoviev, Rykov and their supporters had no faith in the success of the Socialist revolution or in the possibility of Socialism being victorious in Russia. They proposed capitulating to the defeated counter-revolutionary parties, the Socialist-Revolutionaries and Mensheviks, which was tantamount to renunciation of Soviet power and a return to bourgeois parliamentarism, to capitalism.

The negotiations with the Vikzhel proved that Lenin was right. What the Mensheviks and Socialist-Revolutionaries were aiming at was the overthrow of Soviet power. While professing neutrality, the Vikzhel was actually supporting Kerensky and sabotaging the revolutionary measures of the Soviet Government. Representatives of the Vikzhel could not be admitted into the Soviet bodies. The Vikzhel had no support among the masses. The continuation of negotiations with it could cause damage to the Party and Soviet power.

At the beginning of November, 1917, the Central Committee of the Party adopted a resolution categorically rejecting any agreement with the Right Socialist-Revolutionaries and Mensheviks on the basis of the formation of an "all-Socialist government." The Central Committee demanded of the Kamenev-Zinoviev group that it cease its criminal activities. But the opposition group refused to submit to the will of the Central Committee majority, and at a meeting of the All-Russian Central Executive Committee (of Soviets) voted openly against the Party Central Committee decision to discontinue negotiations, thus committing a flagrant breach of Party discipline. Thereupon the Central Committee, eaded by Lenin, presented an ultimatum to the opposition, demanding that it stop its disruptive work. In reply, Kamenev, Zinoviev, Rykov, Nogin and Milyutin announced their disagreement with the policy of the Party and their resignation from the Central Committee. At the same time Nogin, Rykov, Milyutin and Teodorovich announced their resignation from the Government.

The desertion of a handful of capitulators and cowards from responsible Party and government posts caused jubilation in the enemy camp. The enemies of the Soviets forecast the collapse of Soviet power, but their hopes were not justified. The desertion of the capitulators was emphatically condemned by the Central Committee of the Party. On the proposal of the Bolshevik group, Kamenev was removed from the post of Chairman of the All-Russian Central Executive Committee. Y. M. Sverdlov was elected to this post. The Party Central Committee strengthened the Council of People's Commissars by appointing to it steadfast Bolsheviks who were veteran Party members. These were G. I. Petrovsky (People's Commissar for Internal Affairs), A. G. Schlichter (People's Commissar for Food), P. I. Stuchka (People's Commissar of Justice), and M. T. Yelizarov (People's Commissar of Railways). The local Party organisations unanimously supported the energetic measures of the Central Committee of the Party with regard to the capitulators. In a message to all Party members and to all the labouring classes of Russia, the Central Committee firmly declared: "There must be no government in Russia other than the *Soviet Government*" (Lenin, *Collected Works*, Vol. 26, p. 269).

The months immediately following the victory of the October insurrection were a period of supreme triumph for the Socialist revolution. Soviet power became more firmly established with every day that passed. After the failure of the Kerensky-Krasnov campaign against Petrograd, the counter-revolution renewed its attempts to overthrow Soviet power. But the more desperate the resistance of the bourgeoisie, the more energetic were the actions of the Soviet Government. In the latter half of November, 1917, revolutionary detachments of sailors and soldiers, acting on orders from the Soviet Government, liquidated the General Headquarters of the old army at Mogilev. At the end of November, a counter-revolutionary plot organised in Petrograd by the Cadets was foiled. The revolts of the Cossack upper strata in the Don area and the South Urals were successfully put down. The counter-revolution had no support among the masses. The Soviets suppressed the resistance of the exploiters with comparative ease, and were victorious on the home front. Lenin called the victorious march of the Socialist revolution across the vast territory of the country "the unbroken triumph of Soviet power."

While crushing the counter-revolutionary revolts and routin
the capitulators, the Party did an enormous amount of work t
build up the new Soviet State. It was a difficult and complicate
job. The old State machinery of the bourgeoisie and the landlord
had to be demolished and a new, Soviet State machinery set u
in its place; all the Soviets had to be united from top to bottor
into one well-knit State organisation, and the broad mass of th
working people drawn into the work of administering the State
The difficulties were all the greater since the Party did not knov
the practical shape which the organisation of the administrative
economic, military and other machinery of a Soviet State shoul
take. There was no experience it could draw upon, for it was th
first State of its kind to be set up in history.

Gathering all its energy, the Party set about overcoming th
difficulties involved in building the Soviet system. It was th
only force in the country capable of taking the lead in the struggl
for the establishment of a Soviet State. Party organisations exist
ed in all the gubernia centres, in most uyezd towns, at big fac
tories and in some of the volosts and villages. The Party sen
its best people to work in the Soviet governmental machine
Communists headed the central and local organs of Sovie
government, the People's Commissariats and other governmen
departments.

During the October Revolution and in the period when the
Soviet State was being built up, Lenin's genius for organisatior
manifested itself most strikingly. As head of the Council of People's
Commissars, Lenin personally directed the establishment of the
central machinery of the Soviet State and guided the Soviets in
their constructive activities throughout the country. Lenin per-
sonified a new type of statesman. He had deep faith in the creative
power of the masses and maintained close contact with them.
"The creative activity of the masses," he said, "is the basic factor
in the new public life" (*Collected Works*, Vol. 26, p. 254).

The October Revolution awakened broad sections of the people
to independent political activity. The revolutionary activity of
the masses was vividly expressed in numerous meetings and conferences, and at all-Russian, gubernia and uyezd congresses of
Soviets. Lenin described this democracy of the working people,
expressed in meetings which swept the country like a spring torrent, as the initial form of their discussion of the new conditions
of life, their first step in building and governing their State. At all-
Russian, gubernia and uyezd congresses of Soviets, at meetings
and conferences of workers, soldiers and peasants, the Bolsheviks
explained the historic significance of the October Revolution,
the essence of the Soviet State and its policy and decrees.

The Party channelled the revolutionary energy and creative

nitiative of the masses into building the Soviet machinery of State. The old, bourgeois-landlord machinery (police, bureaucratic, military and judicial) was destroyed and a new one created in its place, that of the proletarian State. The Ministries of the bourgeois Provisional Government were abolished in the very first days of the revolution, and replaced by People's Commissariats. The agents of the Provisional Government were removed and the local organs of bourgeois-landlord rule abolished. The city Dumas and Zemstvo boards, which had represented the interests of the bourgeoisie and the landlords, were disbanded. The Soviets of Workers', Soldiers' and Peasants' Deputies became the sole organs vested with full political power all over the country. Soviet People's Courts and a workers' militia were set up in place of the old courts and police. A special body, the All-Russian Extraordinary Commission with F. E. Dzerzhinsky at its head, was formed to combat counter-revolution and sabotage.

The monarchists, Cadets, Right Socialist-Revolutionaries, Mensheviks and other counter-revolutionary elements did their utmost to frustrate the building of the Soviet State and the work of the apparatus of the Soviets. They engineered sabotage by officials of the old machinery of State (former Ministries, banks, postal service, telegraph, etc.). Officials and higher-paid office workers, bribed by the bourgeoisie and closely connected with it, refused to obey the Soviet authorities. Their sabotage created additional difficulties. The Party appealed to the masses, sent thousands of the best workers, sailors and soldiers to work in government offices, and set up the machinery of the People's Commissariats. The sabotage of the officials was broken.

A most difficult task was the creation of new armed forces. The old army, notwithstanding the fact that the soldiers had gone over to the side of the Soviets, could not ensure the defence of the State against the foreign foe. Exhausted by the protracted war, it had long since lost its fighting capacity. The soldiers were eager to go home. To ensure the maintenance of revolutionary order among the troops, and the stability of the front until peace was concluded, the Soviet State democratised the army: all ranks and titles were abolished, election of all officers by soldiers was introduced, etc. In January, 1918, the Soviet Government started the gradual demobilisation of the old army. On January 15, 1918, the Council of People's Commissars adopted a decree "On the Workers' and Peasants' Red Army." The Red Army was formed on a voluntary basis. War-weariness being general among the masses, the core of a new, revolutionary army could only be formed from members of the working class and the poor peasantry, who were prepared to defend Soviet power selflessly. The most class-conscious elements of the working people joined the ranks of the Red Army. Its organisation and formation wa effected by an All-Russian Board, headed by N. V. Krylenk and N. I. Podvoisky. The entire work of building the armee forces of the Soviet Republic was directed by the Party heade by Lenin.

The October Revolution while accomplishing strictly Social ist tasks, at the same time carried the bourgeois-democratic rev olution to its conclusion. No bourgeois revolution has ever abol ished the feudal order of things so completely and decisivel as the October Socialist Revolution in Russia. On assuming pow er, the proletariat, led by the Bolshevik Party, eradicated th remnants of medievalism with exceptional speed and boldness The Decree on Land uprooted the survivals of serfdom and land ownership. All the divisions of society into "estates" with their ti tles (nobility, clergy, merchants, middle classes, etc.) were abol ished, and one common name was established for the entire pop ulation of the country, namely, citizen of the Russian Repub lic. The Soviet Government proclaimed freedom of conscience The church was separated from the State, and the school from th church. Women acquired equal rights.

The October Revolution put an end to the oppression and ine quality of the non-Russian nationalities. A People's Commissaria for the Affairs of Nationalities was set up within the Soviet Govern ment, and J. V. Stalin was placed at its head. "The Declaration of Rights of the Peoples of Russia," proclaimed by the Soviet Government on November 2, 1917, gave legal confirmation tc the free development and full equality of all the nationalities of Russia. All nations inhabiting the country were guaranteed the right of self-determination, up to and including secession and formation of independent States. In December, 1917, the So viet Government recognised the independence of Ukraine and Fin land. In its appeal "To All the Working Moslems of Russia and the East," the Council of People's Commissars proclaimed the freedom and inviolability of the national and cultural institu tions, customs and faith of the Moslems, and guaranteed them full freedom to arrange their own way of life.

The bourgeoisie and its accomplices, the Mensheviks and Socialist-Revolutionaries, claimed at the time that the Bolshe viks were destroying the Russian State, and that all the nationali ties were forsaking them. That was downright slander of the Bolshevik Party. The Soviet State was being founded by the Par ty as a voluntary union of free national republics. It was the bour geois nationalists, who were the bitterest enemies of the working people and of the Soviet State, who wanted to see Russia dismem bered, and sought to provoke discord among the peoples inhabit ing Russia. The workers and peasants of all the nationalities of Russia, however, welcomed the October Revolution. As soon as they took power into their own hands, they immediately addressed messages of solidarity to the Soviet Government, declaring their readiness to support it.

In December, 1917, the First All-Ukrainian Congress of Soviets met in Kharkov, and proclaimed Ukraine a Soviet republic. The bourgeois Central Rada was outlawed. The Congress of Soviets solemnly announced the establishment of a close union between Soviet Ukraine and Soviet Russia. The Ukrainians were the first to form their Soviet national republic. Between October, 1917, and the end of March, 1918, power passed to the Soviets in Byelorussia, Estonia, the part of Latvia not occupied by the Germans, Crimea, Moldavia, the city of Baku, the Volga national minority areas, Turkestan and the greater part of Kazakhstan.

Bolshevik organisations directed the working people's struggle in the areas inhabited by non-Russian nationalities. The Bolshevik Party drew into its ranks the best elements of the working people of all the nationalities of Russia, and from among them trained revolutionaries, devoted to the cause of Socialism and proletarian internationalism. Such were F. A. Sergeyev (Artem), G. I. Petrovsky, V. Y. Chubar and A. G. Schlichter in Ukraine; M. Azizbekov in Azerbaijan; A. F. Myasnikov (Myasnikyan) and S. G. Shaumyan in Armenia; P. A. Japaridze, F. I. Maharadze, G. K. Orjonikidze and M. G. Tskhakaya in Georgia; P. I. Stuchka in Latvia; V. S. Mitskevichius-Kapsukas (Mitskevich-Kapsukas) in Lithuania; A. T. Jangildin in Kazakhstan; V. E. Kingisepp in Estonia; U. D. Buinaksky in Daghestan, and many others. They were all Party leaders who had been tested in struggle and who enjoyed the deep confidence of the working people.

One of the main tasks confronting the Party and the Soviets was that of satisfying the people's most urgent economic and cultural needs. Everything possible was done to improve the living conditions of the workers and peasants by expropriating the capitalists and landlords. The Soviets took charge of food distribution, and ensured that the workers and their families were supplied first of all. They took over the municipal services. Hundreds of thousands of working-class families were moved from damp basements and congested barracks into well-appointed houses formerly owned by the bourgeoisie and the landlords. The workers, peasants and their children were given full access to education. Tuition fees in the schools were abolished and medical services were made free of charge. The palaces of the tsars and the mansions of the rich became the property of the people, and were turned into public meeting halls, sanatoria and museums. Working conditions and labour protection in industry were improved. An 8-

hour working day was introduced in industry and a decree was issued providing for the insurance of industrial and office workers against sickness, disability and unemployment.

The Bolshevik Party proved to the labouring peasants by its deeds that the working class was their most dependable ally and leader, the defender of their interests. On winning power, the proletariat fulfilled the peasants' most pressing economic demands with revolutionary dispatch and energy. The peasants received the landed estates for their own free use, and were liberated from the yoke of the landlords and capitalists. The peasant masses came to realise that the Decree on Land could only be implemented if they resolutely supported Soviet power in alliance with the urban workers, and by co-operating with them in the Soviets.

All these measures taken by the Party and the Soviet Government had a tremendous influence on the masses of the people. The alliance of the working class and the poor peasantry grew stronger. Soviet power was winning the increasing sympathy and support of the vast majority of the working people of Russia.

In November and December, 1917, the Extraordinary and Second All-Russian Congresses of Soviets of Peasants' Deputies met in Petrograd. At these congresses, the Right Socialist-Revolutionaries conducted a desperate struggle against the Bolsheviks, and tried to set the peasant delegates against them. But they failed: the Bolshevik Party exposed them completely as betrayers of the interests of the labouring peasantry. The peasant congresses endorsed the decrees and the policy of the Soviet Government, and declared in favour of uniting the Soviets of Peasants' Deputies and the Soviets of Workers' and Soldiers' Deputies. The unification of the workers, soldiers and peasants in common Soviets most effectively ensured the political leadership of the non-proletarian working masses by the proletariat, and the further consolidation of Soviet power. On the proposal of the Bolsheviks and at the instance of the delegates of the peasant congresses, representatives of the party of Left Socialist-Revolutionaries (Kolegayev, Proshyan, Steinberg) entered the Council of People's Commissars. The Party was aware of the instability of the Left Socialist-Revolutionaries, but it brought them into the Government because they still enjoyed the confidence of a considerable section of the peasantry and because they declared their support of Soviet power. This step weakened the forces of the enemies of Soviet power and struck a blow at the anti-Soviet parties, the Right Socialist-Revolutionaries and the Mensheviks.

The Party frustrated the designs of the counter-revolution to overthrow Soviet power with the aid of the Constituent Assembly. Elections to the Constituent Assembly were held in Noember, 1917, on the basis of the lists of party candidates drawn up before the October Revolution. They took place at a time when large sections of the people had not yet grasped the significance of the Socialist revolution. The Right Socialist-Revolutionaries took advantage of this, and managed to poll a majority in the regions and gubernias far removed from the capital and from the industrial centres. The counter-revolutionary forces tried to exploit this situation in order to seize power.

On the eve of the opening of the Constituent Assembly, the All-Russian Central Executive Committee adopted a "Declaration of the Rights of the Toiling and Exploited Peoples" drawn up by Lenin. The declaration stated that all power in the country belonged to the Soviets; it confirmed the Decrees on Peace and on Land and other acts, and endorsed the foreign policy pursued by the Soviet Government. The All-Russian Central Executive Committee proposed to the Constituent Assembly, which opened on January 5, 1918, that it adopt the declaration. But the counter-revolutionary majority of the Constituent Assembly evaded a discussion on it, and refused to recognise the Soviet Government and its decrees. The bourgeois Constituent Assembly thereby openly set itself against Soviet power and the will of the majority of the people, and exposed its counter-revolutionary nature. On January 6, by decree of the All-Russian Central Executive Committee, it was dissolved. The dissolution of the bourgeois Constituent Assembly was approved by the people.

The policy of the Party and the Government with regard to the Constituent Assembly was supported by the Third All-Russian Congress of Soviets of Workers' and Soldiers' Deputies, which opened on January 10, 1918, and which was joined by all the delegates to the Third All-Russian Congress of Soviets of Peasants' Deputies. The Joint All-Russian Congress of Soviets endorsed the policy of the Soviet Government and adopted the "Declaration of the Rights of the Toiling and Exploited Peoples." The Third Congress of Soviets consolidated the achievements of the October Socialist Revolution and the establishment of the Soviet system. The declaration stated: "Russia is hereby proclaimed a Republic of Soviets of Workers', Soldiers' and Peasants' Deputies." The Russian Soviet Republic was instituted as a voluntary union of free nations, as a federation of Soviet national republics.

The revolution spread in breadth and depth. Parallel with building the Soviet State system, the Party directed the struggle of the working class for the Socialist reorganisation of society. As a result of the October Revolution, all enterprises owned by the landlords' and capitalists' State became the property of the people. A Socialist form of economy came into existence. But in the early period following the establishment of Soviet power the greater part of the means of production remaine in the hands of the bourgeoisie. In order to become the rulin class in the full sense of the term, the proletariat, having wo State power, had to dispossess the bourgeoisie of the banks railways, factories and mines, and to convert them into publi property.

In the middle of November, 1917, the Soviet Government too over the administration of the *State Bank*, and then *national ised the private banks* and declared banking a State monopoly These measures greatly undermined the economic power of th bourgeoisie. At the same time the Soviet Government annulle all the foreign loans contracted by the tsar and the Provisiona Government. Russia's debt to other States amounted to abou 16,000 million gold rubles. The working people of Russia wer freed from the financial stranglehold of international capital.

The most difficult task was the transformation of capitalist int Socialist property. The bourgeoisie offered furious resistance t the economic measures taken by the Soviet State. The capital- ists closed down factories, concealed stocks of raw materials and finished goods, and delayed the payment of wages. The manu- facturers tried to disorganise production and cause economic disas- ter. The capitalists had to be curbed and their sabotage broken. That could have been done by expropriating them immediately. But when the proletariat came to power, it had neither experi- ence in economic management nor any economic bodies that could immediately take over the management of the country's economic life. The Soviet Government therefore did not decree the nation- alisation of the whole of industry at once, but instituted *work- ers' control* at capitalist-owned enterprises.

On November 14, 1917, the Soviet Government issued "Regu- lations on Workers' Control," which introduced workers' con- trol at all industrial, commercial, agricultural, transport and co-operative enterprises. The implementation of the regulations was entrusted to factory and other committees. This law unfet- tered the initiative of the working masses. By the beginning of 1918 workers' control had been introduced at nearly all industri- al enterprises.

Workers' control helped to break the sabotage of the bourgeoi- sie and to frustrate its attempts to convert the factories into strongholds of counter-revolution. The workers gradually ac- quainted themselves with the economic affairs of their enterprises and learned management of production. Organisers and execu- tives emerged from among the workers' ranks. In organising work- ers' control, the factory committees interfered more and more in the administrative and business activities of the employers, re- moved them from management and took it over themselves.

At the end of November, 1917, the Soviet Government began the *nationalisation of large-scale capitalist industry*. There began a radical break-up of capitalist relations. The nationalised enterprises became the property of the Soviet State, they became Socialist. By the middle of 1918, a considerable part of such large-scale capitalist industries as coal, metallurgy, oil, chemicals, engineering and textiles, and the whole of the sugar-refining industry were nationalised. Transport, the merchant marine and foreign trade were also nationalised. That, as Lenin aptly put it, was a "Red Guard attack on capital." The economic power of the bourgeoisie was torn up at its very roots. The Soviet State gained control of the *key positions* in the national economy.

To direct the socialisation of production on Socialist lines, and for State management of the national economy, a Supreme Council of National Economy was set up under the Council of People's Commissars on December 1, 1917. Beginning with December, 1917, economic councils began to be set up in the regions, gubernias and uyezds. Gradually concentrating in their hands the management of the economy, they performed the function of the Soviet State in the sphere of economic organisation. With the establishment of the Supreme Council of National Economy, and the nationalisation of the banks, railways and large-scale industry, the Soviet State was able to turn to the work of building the new, *Socialist* national economy.

The Communist Party raised the many millions of working people to the conscious making of history by giving them full freedom of initiative. The months immediately following the victory of the October Revolution showed what inexhaustible reserves of strength and revolutionary energy were latent in the masses, once they had freed themselves from the yoke of the landlords and capitalists. The whole country throbbed with new life. The absurd notion that only the rich could govern the State, implanted by the exploiters through the ages, was completely disproved. Having founded the new Soviet State, the workers and peasants began assiduously to learn how to govern it. The workers drove out the capitalists, and organised accounting and control. The peasants expropriated the landlords and arranged their life in a new way. The alliance of the working class and the labouring peasant masses, which constitutes the basis of Soviet power, was strengthened and tempered in the fire of the revolution. The Party inspired the masses with confidence in their own strength. In December, 1917, Lenin wrote:

"Victory will be on the side of the exploited, for on their side is life, numerical strength, the strength of the mass, the strength of the inexhaustible sources of all that is selfless, true to ideas, and upright, all that is surging forward and awakening

to the building of the new, all the gigantic reserves of energ
and talent latent in the so-called 'common people,' the worker
and peasants" (*Collected Works*, Vol. 26, p. 364).

2. The Struggle to Withdraw from the War. The Peace of Brest Litovsk. Seventh Congress of the R.C.P.(B.)

The profound revolutionary changes in all spheres of the coun
try's public life had considerably strengthened the Soviet system
However, its stability depended not only on the relation of clas
forces within the country, but also on the international positior
of the Soviet State. The biggest obstacle to the consolidation o
the Soviet power was the state of war with Germany.

From the very first day that Soviet power was established the
Party launched an active *fight for peace*. In the Decree on Peace
the Soviet State proposed to all the belligerent countries the
conclusion of a universal democratic peace, a peace without annexations and indemnities. The Entente countries (Britain, France,
the U.S.A. and others), however, refused to conduct peace negotiations, thus making the conclusion of universal peace impossible. Thereupon the Soviet Government, in compliance with the
will of the people, decided to start peace negotiations with Germany and her allies.

The negotiations with Germany began on November 20, 1917,
at Brest Litovsk (Brest). On December 2 an armistice was
signed, after which negotiations for a peace treaty began. In the
course of the negotiations it became clear that the German imperialists intended to impose a predatory and humiliating peace on Soviet Russia. They wanted to enslave Poland, Lithuania and the
part of Latvia and Byelorussia, wh:ch had been seized by their troops.
The German imperialists also had annexationist designs on Ukraine.
Acting in secret collusion with the delegation of the Ukrainian
Rada which had arrived in Brest Litovsk, they hoped, with the help
of the bourgeois national:sts, to sever Ukraine from Soviet Russia
and enslave the Ukrainian people.

The internal and international situation at that time dictated the
advisability of retreating before so strong and dangerous a maraud-
er as German imperialism, and of accepting onerous peace terms
in order to save the young Soviet Republic. The national economy
was in a state of chaos. Worn out and exhausted by the long war, the
old army could not have withstood a German offensive. The necessary enthusiasm for conducting a revolutionary war was lacking
among broad strata of the working class and the peasantry. In
order to save the country and the revolution, it was necessary
to secure a peaceful breathing-space in which to consolidate Soviet

power and to create a new army, the Red Army, which would be able to defend the country against imperialist invaders. It was mainly the bourgeoisie and the landlords, the White generals and officers, and also the Mensheviks and Socialist-Revolutionaries, who were interested in continuing the war. And the counter-revolutionaries of every shade, from the monarchists and Cadets to the Socialist-Revolutionaries and the Mensheviks, conducted a frenzied campaign against the peace negotiations. By impelling the Soviet Republic towards war with German imperialism, the bourgeoisie was setting a trap for Soviet power, hoping to take advantage of its defeat to strangle the revolution and restore the old regime.

The Party had to decide the issue of war and peace without delay.

On January 8, 1918, Lenin submitted to a conference of members of the Central Committee of the Party and the Bolshevik delegates to the Third Congress of Soviets, his theses regarding the immediate conclusion of a separate and annexationist peace. He showed that an objective appraisal of the social, economic and political situation in the country, and the fact that the Soviet Republic lacked an efficient army, dictated the necessity of concluding an *immediate* peace. But Lenin's viewpoint did not receive the support of a majority at the conference. The situation was aggravated by the fact that a number of local Party committees (the Moscow and the Urals regional committees, the Petrograd and other committees) proposed stopping the peace negotiations with the Germans. Many Party workers were carried away by revolutionary phrases, and insisted that a revolutionary war be declared on imperialist Germany. Their mood strongly smacked of intoxication with the initial successes of Soviet power in the struggle against the internal counter-revolution. Neither did Lenin have a majority on the question of a peace treaty in the Central Committee. Trotsky, Bukharin and their followers were opposed to accepting the German peace terms; they asserted that the German troops would not be able to conduct an offensive and that a revolution was at hand in Germany.

An extremely difficult situation arose in the Party. It required Lenin's tremendous perseverance and firmness to prove to the Party cadres the necessity of accepting severe terms of peace in order to win a breathing-space, and to expose the adventurist tactics of Trotsky and Bukharin, which spelled disaster for the Soviet Republic. Lenin explained that the essence of the question lay in the fact that

"the fundamental change now lies in establishing a Russian republic of Soviets, and that both from our own *and from the international Socialist standpoint* it is all-important to preserve this republic, which has already started the Socialist rev olution; that at the present moment the slogan calling for revolutionary war by Russia would mean either phrase-mon gering and an empty demonstration, or would objectively be tan tamount to walking into the trap being set for us by the im perialists, who want to *draw* us into continuing the *imperialis* war as a still weak particle, and to *smash* the young Soviet Re public as cheaply as possible" (*Collected Works*, Vol. 26, pp 409-10).

To avert the breaking-off of the peace negotiations, and t prevent Trotsky and Bukharin from pursuing their adventur ist tactics, Lenin secured a decision by the Party Central Com mittee in favour of dragging out the peace negotiations in every possible way, and the adoption by the Third Congress of Soviets of a decision to invest the Soviet Government with unlimited pow ers in deciding the question of war and peace. Lenin's position in the Central Committee was supported by F. A. Sergeyev (Ar tem), J. V. Stalin, Y. M. Sverdlov and others.

On January 27, 1918, the German delegates presented an ul timatum to the Soviet delegation, demanding that it sign the terms of a peace treaty which provided for the severance of the German-occupied territories from Russia. The Soviet peace delegation at Brest Litovsk was headed at that time by Trotsky, who had specific instructions from Lenin to drag out the negotiations and to sign a peace treaty immediately should the Germans present an ultimatum. On January 28, Lenin in a special telegram, signed by Stalin as well, re-emphasised the necessity of concluding a peace treaty. But Trotsky violated the directives of the Chairman of the Council of People's Commis sars. In spite of Lenin's insistent demand, he informed the Ger man representatives on January 28 (February 10; from here on wards, all dates will be given in the new style) that the Soviet Government refused to sign the peace treaty on the terms presented by Germany. Trotsky also informed the Germans that the Soviet Republic was ending the state of war with Germany and demobilising its army. This was a treacherous statement, fraught with disastrous consequences for the Soviet Republic.

The German Government took advantage of Trotsky's statement. Breaking the armistice, the German Command on February 18, 1918, launched an offensive all along the Russo-German front. The remnants of the old army could not withstand the onslaught of the enemy hordes. Encountering no serious resistance, the Ger man troops within a few days occupied the whole of Latvia and Estonia, a considerable part of Ukraine, captured Dvinsk, Minsk, Polotsk, Pskov and other towns. They threatened Petro grad.

Lenin's forecast that this would be the course of events proved right. The offensive of the German troops showed that the object of the German imperialists was to overthrow the Soviet power and turn Russia into their colony. Mortal danger threatened the Soviet land. On February 21, 1918, the Council of People's Commissars issued a call to the people written by Lenin: "The Socialist Fatherland Is in Danger!" The Central Committee and the Soviet Government called on all Party members, on all workers and peasants to defend the Soviet Republic against the invasion of the German imperialists.

The call of the Party and the Soviet Government evoked a surge of revolutionary energy among the working people. Advanced workers and demobilised soldiers volunteered in tens of thousands for service in the Red Army. Its detachments were sent forward against the enemy as soon as they were formed, and staunchly repulsed the onslaught of the German troops, which were armed to the teeth. Stiff fighting took place at Pskov, Revel (Tallinn) and Narva. Heroic resistance was offered to the German invaders at Pskov by Red Guard detachments and revolutionary units of the old army, which included Lettish riflemen. Sailors of the Baltic Fleet and Estonian Red Guard detachments took part in the fighting at Revel. Red Guard units of Petrograd workers, Red Army detachments and sailors of the Baltic Fleet fought in the battle of Narva.

The days of the Red Army's heroic defence of the gains of the October Socialist Revolution against the invasion of the hordes of German imperialism marked the birth of that army. In commemoration of this great exploit on the part of the Soviet people's armed forces, February 23 is observed annually in the Soviet Union as Red Army Day.

During the German offensive Lenin exerted tremendous efforts to secure a decision by the Central Committee of the Party in favour of the conclusion of peace. The principal opponents of the conclusion of peace were Trotsky and Bukharin; the latter at that time headed the anti-Party group of "Left Communists." Despite the fact that the offensive of the German troops showed quite patently the very great danger it presented to the Soviet Republic, the "Left Communists," masking their policy with leftist phrases, demanded continuation of the war. Lenin waged a relentless struggle against the "Left Communists" and against their policy, which was ruinous to the Soviet power. On February 18, 1918, on Lenin's insistence, the Party Central Committee had passed a resolution that the Soviet Republic was ready to sign a peace treaty. A telegram was sent to the German Government informing it of the Soviet Government's readiness to conclude an immediate peace. But imperialist Germany, in addition to

its original demands, presented new, still more onerous term
She laid claim to the whole of Latvia and Estonia; the Sovi
Republic was to pay an enormous indemnity to Germany and
demobilise its army. Ukraine was to become a vassal State
Germany, and fall under the yoke of the German imperialist

On February 23, when the new ultimatum of the German Go
ernment was discussed, the Party Central Committee adopte
Lenin's proposal for signing an immediate peace treaty on th
new terms presented by Germany. The advocates of a "revolu
tionary war" from among the group of "Left Communists" (Bu
kharin, Uritsky, Lomov and Bubnov) found themselves in a mi
nority on the Central Committee. Defeated there, Bukharin an
his followers adopted a policy of disorganising the entire worl
of the Party and the Government. In an attempt to split the Par
ty, they won over some of the local Party organisations an
tried to oppose them to the Central Committee. The Moscow Re
gional Bureau, which was composed of "Left Communists" (Lo
mov, Osinsky, Sapronov, Stukov and others), passed a resolu
tion containing the monstrous statement that it would be expe
dient in the interests of the international revolution to consent
to the possible loss of Soviet power, which, they alleged, would
become purely formal with the conclusion of peace. Lenin branded this resolution as "strange and monstrous." He attacked the
"Left Communists" most vigorously; in his impassioned articles, he exposed their adventurist policy which would have been
fatal to the Soviet Republic. He wrote: "Whoever is opposed
to an immediate, even if most onerous, peace, is destroying the
Soviet power" (*Collected Works*, Vol. 27, p. 22).

On March 3, 1918, the peace treaty with Germany was signed.
Meanwhile the "Left Communists," far from discontinuing their
attacks on the Party, intensified them. They openly called for
the wrecking of the Brest Litovsk peace. The disruptive anti-
Party activities of the "Left Communists" encouraged the Left
Socialist-Revolutionaries to hope that there would be a change
in the composition of the Soviet Government. They approached
Bukharin with the proposal that Lenin be removed from the post
of Chairman of the Council of People's Commissars and that a
new government of Left Socialist-Revolutionaries and "Left
Communists" be formed.

Lenin unmasked the "Left Communist" group as accomplices
of the German imperialists and the Russian bourgeoisie.
"And if the new terms are worse, more onerous and humiliating than the bad, onerous and humiliating Brest terms," wrote
Lenin, "it is *our would-be 'Left wingers'* Bukharin, Lomov,
Uritsky and Co. who are *guilty of it* before the great Russian Soviet Republic" (*ibid.*, p. 60).

Lenin showed that the differences which the "Left Communists" and Trotsky had with the Party went much deeper than appeared at first sight. The leaders of the "Left" opposition, along with Trotsky, denied that the victory of Socialism was possible in one country alone, and declared that the dictatorship of the proletariat and the gains of the October Revolution in Russia could only be preserved in the event of a victorious world Socialist revolution, which should be speeded up by war against world imperialism.

Exposing the "Left Communists," Lenin explained that their theory of "speeding up" the international revolution had nothing in common with Marxism. Marxism teaches that the development of revolution depends on the intensification of class contradictions within the capitalist countries. Lenin maintained that the victory of Socialism was possible in a single country and held that the working class of Soviet Russia, the first country in which the dictatorship of the proletariat had been victorious, would discharge its international duty best of all if it preserved and strengthened its dictatorship to defend the gains of the revolution and build Socialism.

Lenin also exposed another absurd argument of the "Left" opposition, namely, that the interests of the international revolution did not allow the Soviet State to conclude peace, or indeed any agreements, with the imperialists, and that the Soviet Republic could not exist in a capitalist encirclement. He wrote: "From this point of view, a Socialist republic surrounded by imperialist Powers could not conclude any economic treaties, and could not exist at all, without flying off to the moon" (*ibid.*, p. 49). The Party believed that by putting its economy in order and building up its armed forces, the Soviet Republic could withstand the onslaught of international imperialism, uphold its sovereignty and independence, win a peaceful breathing-space and ensure the building of Socialism.

The "Left Communists'" policy of wrecking the Brest Litovsk peace treaty suffered a fiasco. It needed Lenin's foresight, persistence and passion in the fight against the "Left Communists," his unshakable faith in the masses, to save the Soviet land from impending disaster. The Party membership and the advanced workers came out emphatically in support of the peace which had been concluded. In March, 1918, the policy of the Central Committee of the Party and the Soviet Government on the peace treaty was endorsed by the Moscow and Petrograd city Party conferences, as well as by other local Party organisations.

To take a final decision on the question of peace, the Seventh Congress of the Party was called. It was held in Petrograd on

March 6-8, 1918. It was the first Congress to be held after the Party had assumed leadership of the State. It was attended by 46 full delegates and 58 consultative delegates. The Congress represented approximately 170,000 members. Actually, the membership of the Party at that time was about 300,000, but owing to the urgency with which the Congress was convened, and to the fact that part of the territory of the country was occupied by German troops, many Party organisations were unable to send delegates.

The Congress discussed the following questions: the report of the Central Committee; the question of war and peace; and the question of revising the programme and changing the name of the Party. Lenin delivered the political report of the Central Committee and spoke on the revision of the programme, on the alteration of the name of the Party and on other questions. In the political report, Lenin dealt comprehensively with the question of war and peace.

A sharp struggle developed at the Congress between the supporters and the opponents of the Brest Litovsk peace. The "Left Communists" were defeated. The Congress confirmed the correctness of Lenin's line on the issue of the Brest peace, and deemed it necessary to approve the peace treaty with Germany signed by the Soviet Government. Lenin's resolution on war and peace was adopted by 30 votes to 12, with 4 abstentions. The Congress declared that it was the prime task of the Party and the Soviet Government to take the most energetic measures to strengthen discipline and self-discipline among the workers and peasants, and to give full scope to the initiative of all the working people's organisations in consolidating and defending the gains of the Socialist revolution. Stress was laid on the need to intensify the building up of the Red Army and to introduce universal military training for the working people.

Subsequent developments showed that Lenin's line in the fight for peace was the only correct one. His policy enabled the Soviet Republic to carry out an orderly retreat at a time when its forces were greatly outnumbered by those of the enemy, and to prepare with the utmost energy to repel fresh attacks by the imperialists.

The Seventh Congress adopted a resolution changing the name of the Party and altering its programme. A commission was elected to draw up a new programme, based on the draft programme prepared by Lenin. On Lenin's proposal, the Party's name was changed to the Russian Communist Party (Bolsheviks)—R.C.P.(B.). In his speech at the Congress, Lenin said that the name "Communist" was the only correct one, for

"In starting on Socialist changes, we must clearly set before ourselves the goal to which they are directed in the final analysis, namely, the creation of a Communist society . . ." (*Collected Works*, Vol. 27, p. 103).

During the elections to the central bodies of the Party, the Congress again came up against the disorganising conduct of the "Left Communist" group. Even before the Congress, Bukharin, Lomov, Uritsky and Bubnov had announced their resignation from the Central Committee. At the Congress itself, they declared that they would neither take part in the elections nor enter the Central Committee. Lenin sharply criticised the unworthy behaviour of the "Left" opposition leaders, and the Congress demanded that the "Left Communists" stop their splitting activities, which were jeopardising the unity of the Party.

The Seventh Congress of the R.C.P.(B.) accomplished a task of great historic importance. It succeeded in withdrawing the Soviet Republic from the war and securing peace for the peoples of Russia. It approved the basic principles of the foreign policy of the Party and the Soviet State elaborated by Lenin, and specified the immediate tasks of the Party in building Socialism. The Congress defeated those who tried to disorganise the Party— the "Left Communists" and Trotsky, who sought to wreck the unity of the Party and were undermining the dictatorship of the proletariat. It united the ranks of the Party on the basis of Lenin's policy.

Soon after the Seventh Congress, the Soviet Government and the Central Committee moved to Moscow, which became the capital of the Soviet State. On March 14, 1918, the Fourth Extraordinary All-Russian Congress of Soviets met there. It ratified the Brest Litovsk peace treaty. The Left Socialist-Revolutionaries at the Congress opposed ratification of the treaty, and announced their resignation from the Council of People's Commissars. The agreement with the Left Socialist-Revolutionaries, based on co-operation in the Soviet Government, was abrogated.

The conclusion of the Brest Litovsk peace was of tremendous international significance. The working people of the whole world had before them the example of the Soviet Republic, which had withdrawn from the imperialist war in spite of incredible difficulties.

The conclusion of the Brest Litovsk peace strengthened Soviet power. It won a breathing-space in which to normalise the country's economy, to build up the Red Army and to strengthen the alliance of the proletariat and the labouring peasant masses. A new stage in the development of the Soviet State was opening.

3. Lenin's Plan for Laying the Foundations of a Socialist Economy. The First Soviet Constitution

Thanks to the conclusion of peace, the Soviet Republic was able, in the spring of 1918, to concentrate on restoring the national economy and launching Socialist construction. The Communist Party was confronted with a new task, that of organising the country's administration. The main difficulty lay in the economic field, in the need to reorganise the whole economic life of the country on a Socialist basis. In April, 1918, Lenin, on the instruction of the Central Committee of the Party, drew up theses the profound import of which was shown in his celebrated work *The Immediate Tasks of the Soviet Government*. In this work and in several others, Lenin outlined a plan for laying the foundations of a Socialist economy. Summing up the results of the Communist Party's activities, he wrote:

"We, the Bolshevik Party, have *convinced* Russia. We have *won* Russia from the rich for the poor, from the exploiters for the working people. Now we must *administer* Russia" (*Collected Works*, Vol. 27, p. 214).

Further developing Marx's teachings, Lenin substantiated most important propositions concerning the economy of the period of transition from capitalism to Socialism. The State at this stage is that of the dictatorship of the proletariat. The economy in the transition period combines elements of Socialism and capitalism. The forms and methods of transition from capitalism to Socialism depend upon the specific conditions in the different countries in which the movement towards Socialism begins.

In Soviet Russia, the transition to Socialism was being effected at a time when the country's economy contained the elements of five economic formations, namely, (1) patriarchal (i.e., largely natural, peasant economy); (2) petty commodity production (production by those peasants who sold their grain); (3) private capitalism; (4) State capitalism, and (5) Socialism. Russia was a country of small peasants, with a predominantly petty commodity production, which provided the basis for the preservation and revival of capitalism. Millions of small proprietors and traders in town and country were engaged in speculation. This was particularly true of the kulaks, who speculated in grain and profited from the people's want. This petty-bourgeois element constituted the main danger to Soviet power and Socialism. Lenin pointed out that it was the task of the Party and the Soviet State to overcome this petty-bourgeois element, to strengthen the Socialist economic formation, and to convert it into the dominant and, later, the sole and all-embracing form.

The Party and the Soviet Government set about laying the foundations of Socialist economy amid incredible dislocation caused by the war and bourgeois management. It required colossal effort on the part of all the class-conscious workers and peasants to restore the country's productive forces and introduce some elementary order into the national economy. Only the proletariat could relieve the sufferings and privations which had fallen to the lot of the working people. Only the proletariat could overcome the petty-bourgeois element, normalise economic life and ensure the country's advance to Socialism. To that end, it was necessary that the broad working-class masses should have a clear understanding of the historic tasks set them by the revolution. A certain section of the workers, however, could not immediately adjust themselves to the new situation, and did not understand what being the ruling class meant. Their attitude to work in the factories which had become the people's property was the same as of old; they tried to avoid any extra responsibilities, to dodge work, and lived according to the principle: "Grab as much as you can and be off." Such sentiments were especially widespread among those workers who had come to the factories during the war. The Party helped the advanced workers to establish Socialist order, to combat the parasites, shirkers and self-seekers. Lenin taught the workers the Soviet way of running the economy. He called for a careful and conscientious handling of money, for economical management, for opposition to shirking and for observance of the strictest labour discipline. These were the *immediate and main slogans of the moment*. Their putting into effect was an essential condition for overcoming economic dislocation, restoration of normal economic life and the transition to Socialism.

The organisation of *accounting and control* over the manufacture and distribution of products was put forward as the foremost task in the field of the economic construction of Socialism. Without this, Lenin emphasised, it would be impossible to proceed to the management of production, and to ensure the smooth working of all branches of the national economy. While continuing to expropriate the capitalists, the Soviet State had to shift the main emphasis to the organisation of accounting and control. Responsibility for the implementation of accounting and control was placed upon the Soviets of Workers', Soldiers' and Peasants' Deputies, the consumers' co-operative societies and the factory committees. To curb the petty-bourgeois element and introduce accounting and control on a country-wide scale, Lenin proposed overhauling the State monopolies, especially the grain monopoly, strengthening State control over currency circulation and making use of the co-operative societies.

In the transition to Socialism Lenin attached special im portance to *State capitalism*. He considered State capitalism economically superior to the then existing peasant economy and not dangerous to the Soviet State. In Lenin's view, the sys tem of State capitalism was to include various Soviet joint stock companies, to participate in which private individual possessing their own capital, State-controlled manufacturers an bourgeois co-operators were invited. The Soviet authorities wer to exercise control over their activities. State capitalism facil itated the struggle of the Soviet Government against the petty bourgeois element; it enabled the Soviet State to receive a por tion of the output of State-capitalist enterprises for improving economic ties with petty-commodity peasant production, and i helped to step up the growth of the country's productive forces The consumers' co-operative societies were to serve the sam ends. With the aid of the co-operatives, the Soviet State could regulate the exchange of products and effectively control thei sale. Bourgeois influence was still strong in many co-operativ bodies at that time. But this circumstance, said Lenin, should not frighten the Party and the working class. With power in the hands of the proletariat, the use of bourgeois co-operators by the Soviet State enabled it to consolidate the position it had wor and gradually overcome the bourgeois elements in the co-op erative bodies.

One of the fundamental tasks of the Socialist revolution, Lenin explained, was to achieve a higher *productivity of labour* than exist ed under capitalism. Russia was an industrially backward coun try. In order to ensure high productivity of labour, it was nec essary first of all to develop heavy industry—the production of fuel and metal, the engineering, chemical and electrical in dustries. Lenin noted that the Soviet Republic possessed every thing necessary for "Russia to cease to be impoverished and weak, and become mighty and abundant in the full meaning of the word" (*Collected Works*, Vol. 27, p. 134). For this the country possessed adequate natural and enormous manpower resources, and the tremendous popular initiative released by the great revolution. Another highly important condition for raising the productivity of labour, in Lenin's opinion, was the cultural advancement of the population.

Lenin elaborated the principles on which the proletarian State should direct the national economy. He substantiated the prin ciple of *democratic centralism in the organisation of Soviet econom ic management*. Large-scale machine industry cannot function properly without the strictest order, created by the unity of will which directs the common labour of hundreds and thousands of people. The interests of Socialism, Lenin taught, demanded that the mass should implicitly obey the will of the manager of the labour process. Economic management must therefore be centralised, and enterprises must be headed by directors appointed by the Soviet State. Centralised direction by the State and one-man management should be combined with active, conscious participation on the part of the masses in economic life, with various forms of control from below.

"Centralism, understood in a truly democratic sense," wrote Lenin, "presupposes the possibility, created by history for the first time, of full and unhampered development not only of specific local features, but also of local inventiveness, local initiative, variety in the ways, methods and means of advancing to the common goal" (*ibid.*, p. 181).

That was how Lenin defined the Soviet Socialist principle of management.

Large-scale industry is inconceivable without specialists in the various branches of knowledge and technology. The proletariat had no technical specialists of its own at that time, and the bulk of the existing specialists were bourgeois. Lenin taught the Party to be considerate towards the bourgeois experts. He warned it that, owing to their bourgeois way of life under capitalism, not all these experts would be able, at least at first, properly to appreciate the significance of the Socialist revolution. It was necessary to re-educate them patiently, to give them the opportunity of applying their specialised knowledge extensively, to provide them with the best possible material conditions, and not to hesitate to raise their salaries. At the same time Lenin called for persistent effort to discover talented organisers among the people, for bold promotion of organisers with practical experience from among workers and peasants to responsible posts and for assistance to them in mastering the art of State and economic administration.

Lenin paid particularly great attention to developing a new *conscious and comradely* discipline among the workers and all working people generally, and to stimulating their initiative and sense of responsibility. This called for a long and painstaking effort of re-education. Lenin considered that this aim could be achieved by introducing the piece-rate system, the elimination of wage-levelling, organising emulation, and exercising the pressure of public opinion upon idlers and grabbers.

Lenin called for the *consolidation in every possible way of the dictatorship of the proletariat and the development of the Soviet organisation.* The dictatorship of the proletariat is necessary first of all to crush the resistance of the defeated exploiters and all the elements of corruption of the old society (profiteers, grabbers, etc). It is necessary in order to build the new, Socialist society. Only the proletariat, as the most advanced, politically conscious and disciplined class, is capable of winning the support of the majority of the working people, of helping the wavering strata and elements of the population to side definitely with the Soviet power, of crushing the resistance of the exploiters and overcoming the element of petty-bourgeois disorganisation, of directing the reorganisation of society on Socialist lines.

Lenin's work, *The Immediate Tasks of the Soviet Government*, was of enormous historic significance. It concentrated the Party's attention on solving the organisational tasks of the Socialist revolution, on organising the administration of the Soviet State. In it Lenin outlined a scientifically substantiated and concrete plan for reorganising the country's economic system on Socialist lines, and expounded the basic principles of the economic policy of the proletarian State in the period of transition from capitalism to Socialism.

Lenin's theses on the immediate tasks of the Soviet Government were approved by the Central Committee and fully supported by the Party and the working class. On April 29, 1918, the theses were approved by the All-Russian Central Executive Committee.

Lenin's plan was opposed by the Mensheviks and Socialist-Revolutionaries. An incorrect position was also adopted by the "Left Communists," headed by Bukharin. Under cover of "Left" phrases, Bukharin and those who held similar views demagogically claimed that the introduction of discipline and of one-man management in the factories, the employment of bourgeois experts and recourse to State capitalism would mean a return to the bourgeois order. In practice the "Left Communists" proved to be defenders of petty-bourgeois disorganisation and anarchic licence; they were encouraging the kulaks, speculators and idlers. The Party resolutely rebuffed the "Left Communists" and concentrated on establishing nation-wide accounting and control, and organising Socialist production.

The new tasks required the heightening of the leading role of the Party in the Soviet State, and the working out of the right relations between it and the State and other public organisations of the working people. By the spring of 1918, the proletarian State machinery had in the main taken shape. The system of the dictatorship of the proletariat embraced the Party, the Soviets, the trade unions and the other mass organisations of the working people. It was especially important to establish the right relations between the Party and the Soviets. The Party was working out relationships of a kind which gave the Soviets full scope for initiative as organs of State power, while ensuring the Party's leading role in the system of the dictatorship of the proletariat.

e Party was acting as the leading and guiding force of the So-
et State. It determined the policy of the latter and united the
'orts of all the public organisations of the working people in
eir fight to consolidate the Soviet system and reconstruct so-
ety on Socialist lines. The Party exerted political influence
 the Soviets and the trade unions, and carried its directives
to effect through its Communist groups among their mem-
rs.

Problems arising in the building of the Party were decided
 close connection with the requirements of State and economic
velopment. The structure of the leading Party bodies was
rought into line with the administrative division of the
untry then existing (gubernias, uyezds and volosts). From April
 October, 1918, Party conferences were held in most of the
ibernias of the Soviet Republic, and they elected gubernia
arty committees (Gubkoms). Energetic steps were taken to set
p uyezd and volost Party organisations. Thousands of Party
embers were promoted to various posts in the Party apparatus.
he Party devoted much attention to improving its composi-
on, and to drawing up membership rules which would make
 difficult for alien elements to penetrate into it. In raising the
equirements for Party membership, some of the local Party or-
anisations established a term of probation for applicants. Many
arty organisations set up groups of Party sympathisers.

The building of the Party also proceeded in the German-occu-
ied territory. In July, 1918, the Communist Party (Bolsheviks)
f Ukraine held its first congress. This congress demonstrated
ts loyalty to the principles of proletarian internationalism.
ts resolution "On the Party" declared that the Communist
arty (Bolsheviks) of Ukraine was part of the one Russian
Communist Party. In October, 1918, the first congress of the
Communist Party of Lithuania took place illegally in Vilno
Vilnius).

Under the influence of the October Revolution, the youth movement began to develop rapidly in the Soviet Republic. Social-
st youth leagues came into existence throughout the country.
The first All-Russian Congress of Young Workers' and Peasants'
Leagues, which met in October-November, 1918, proclaimed the
establishment of the Russian Young Communist League (Komsomol). In its foundation and activities the Komsomol was guided
from the very outset by the Communist Party, by Lenin. The
Komsomol became a strong bulwark and militant reserve for the
Party.

In the economic field, the Party paid attention primarily to
the organisation of Socialist industry. Central departments and
trusts for managing the nationalised industries were set up within

the framework of the Supreme Council of National Econom
Of great importance in organising the management of indust
and the national economy as a whole was the first All-Russi
Congress of Economic Councils, convened on the initiative of t
Party Central Committee at the end of May, 1918. The congre
declared in favour of the nationalisation of all industry and t
centralisation of its management. On June 28 the Council
People's Commissars adopted a decree on the nationalisation
all large-scale industry. By this decree the nationalisation
large- and medium-scale industry was in the main complete
By June 1 there were a little over 500 nationalised industri
enterprises; by the beginning of September their number e
ceeded 3,000.

The Party's fight to carry out Lenin's plan of Socialist co
struction proceeded in incredibly difficult circumstances. At tl
end of the spring of 1918 a severe food crisis hit the country. Tl
urban population was suffering from hunger, and, as a result, di
content began to spread. Counter-revolution reared its hea
The enemies of the Soviet system tried to throw the blame f
the acute food shortage on the Bolsheviks. But hunger was tl
result of the fact that the grain was concentrated chiefly in th
hands of the kulaks and the rich, who refused to sell it to th
Soviet State at fixed prices, sabotaged the grain monopoly an
engaged in speculation. There were about two million kula
farms in the country. They constituted the main support of in
ternal counter-revolution and of the foreign imperialists. Th
kulaks hated the Soviet power. Lenin wrote that "the kulak
are the most brutal, callous and savage exploiters, who in th
history of other countries have time and again restored th
power of the landlords, tsars, priests and capitalists" (Collecte
Works, Vol. 28, p. 39). In a number of gubernias of the Sovie
Republic the kulaks, along with other counter-revolutionary ele
ments, and with the support of foreign imperialists, raised anti
Soviet revolts. They decided to give battle to the workers' State
on the most vitally important front—that on which the battle
for grain was being waged—and tried to wreck the first Social
ist reforms by means of famine.

It was necessary to suppress the revolts of the kulaks with an
iron hand, to break their resistance, to deprive them of their
grain, so as to preserve the gains of the revolution. The fight
for grain merged with the fight for Socialism. "This seems to be
just a fight for grain," said Lenin, "but in fact it is a fight for
Socialism" (Collected Works, Vol. 27, p. 433). The countryside
at that period was in the throes of a struggle between the poor
peasants and the kulaks. The kulaks were seizing the landlords'
estates and oppressing the poor peasants. The latter put up a

launch fight against kulak domination, but they lacked organisation.

The Central Committee of the Party and the Soviet Government took resolute measures to curb the kulaks and relieve the worst of the hunger. The Soviet Government confirmed that the grain monopoly was inviolable and centralised the food supply service. The Party issued an appeal to the advanced workers to *organise a mass crusade to the countryside,* in order to assist the poor peasants in their fight against the kulaks. Tens of thousands of workers responded to the Party's call. Workers' detachments were formed in the factories. They were headed by Communists. Thousands of such detachments were sent to all parts of the country. By explaining matters to the poor peasants and organising them, these detachments of advanced workers helped to break the resistance of the kulaks, who were concealing their grain surpluses and speculating in grain.

"One of the greatest, and indefeasible accomplishments of the October—Soviet—Revolution," wrote Lenin, "is that the advanced worker, *as the guiding spirit* of the poor, *as the leader* of the toiling masses of the countryside, *as the builder of the State of the working people,* has 'gone among the people.' Petrograd and other proletarian centres have given thousands upon thousands of their finest workers to the countryside" (*ibid.,* p. 361).

On June 11, 1918, the All-Russian Central Executive Committee of Soviets, on Lenin's proposal, adopted a decree to set up *Committees of Poor Peasants* in the countryside. These committees were formed within the framework of the Soviet State system, under the leadership of the local Party organisations. The work of the committees was one of the main questions discussed at the gubernia and uyezd Party conferences held in the summer and autumn of 1918. Committees of Poor Peasants were set up in almost all the villages, and by November, 1918, they numbered about 105,000.

The Committees of Poor Peasants were the strongholds of the dictatorship of the proletariat in the villages. They did an immense job in confiscating grain surpluses from the kulaks and in ensuring foodstuffs for the urban population and the Red Army. Redistribution of the land among the peasants, and the confiscation of draught animals and implements from the kulaks for the benefit of the poor peasants, were carried out through the Committees of Poor Peasants. 125 million acres of land were taken away from the kulaks and placed at the disposal of the poor and middle peasants, which seriously undermined the economic power of the rural bourgeoisie. The confiscation of a considerable portion of the means of production from the rural bourgeoisie did not, however, mean the abolition of the kula[k] as a class. Individual, small-property peasant farming continu[e] to predominate in agriculture.

The organisation of the Committees of Poor Peasants mea[nt] a further development of the Socialist revolution and consol[i]dation of the Soviet power in the countryside. The committe[es] rallied the poor peasants round the working class, they helpe[d] the Soviet State to break the resistance of the kulaks, and the[y] played an important part in winning over the middle peasan[ts] to the side of the Soviet power. The position of the poo[r] peasants improved. Many poor peasants set up their own farms[.] The countryside became increasingly middle-peasant. The Com[-]mittees of Poor Peasants helped to recruit members of the peas[-]ant population for the Red Army.

The first Socialist changes in the countryside were carried ou[t] with the help of the Committees of Poor Peasants. It was thank[s] to these committees that the first agricultural communes an[d] other peasant producers' associations arose; by the end of 191[8] their number exceeded 1,500. During the period when these com[-]mittees existed there began in the countryside a rapid growth of Party groups which drew into their ranks the most advanced and class-conscious section of the poor peasants. At the end o[f] 1918, having completed the tasks set before them, the Commit-tees of Poor Peasants were merged with the volost and village Soviets. The role and significance of the local Soviets in Socialist construction were considerably enhanced.

On July 4, 1918, the Fifth All-Russian Congress of Soviets opened in Moscow. It reflected the growth of the influence and prestige of the Communist Party among the masses. About two-thirds of the Congress delegates were Communists. The influence of the Left Socialist-Revolutionaries among the masses was rap-idly declining. Before the Congress, the Left Socialist-Revolu-tionaries had done their utmost to wreck the Brest Litovsk peace, fought the food policy of the Soviet Government and the Commit-tees of Poor Peasants, and spoke in defence of the kulaks. They prepared an anti-Soviet conspiracy which was timed for the Con-gress of Soviets. During the Congress, on July 6, the Left Social-ist-Revolutionaries assassinated Mirbach, the German Ambas-sador, with the object of provoking Germany to make war with Soviet Russia, and started an anti-Soviet revolt in Moscow. The foreign diplomatic missions secretly supported the rebels. The Soviet Republic was within a hairbreadth of war with Germany.

Thanks to the prompt and decisive action of the Soviet au-thorities, the revolt of the Left Socialist-Revolutionaries in Mos-cow was suppressed within a few hours. The conflict provoked ith Germany was settled. The adventure to which the Left ocialist-Revolutionaries had resorted exposed them completely as an anti-Soviet party which had no support among the working masses. The Fifth Congress of Soviets unanimously endorsed the energetic measures taken by the Soviet Government to suppress the revolt of the Left Socialist-Revolutionaries, and voted for the expulsion of all representatives of the Left Socialist-Revolutionaries from the Soviets.

The Congress adopted the first Soviet Constitution—the *Constitution of R.S.F.S.R.* It gave legislative confirmation to the great achievements of the October Socialist Revolution: the new, Soviet political system, the abolition of private capitalist and landlord property, equality of all the peoples inhabiting Russia, etc. The Constitution provided legislative confirmation of the dictatorship of the proletariat in the form of the Soviet State, guaranteed all the working people of Russia the opportunity to take part in governing the State, and disfranchised the exploiters.

With regard to the disfranchisement of the exploiters, Lenin observed that "the question of restricting the franchise is a nationally specific, not a general, question of the dictatorship. One must approach the question of restricting the franchise through a study of the *specific conditions* of the Russian revolution and the *specific path* of its development" (*Collected Works*, Vol. 28, p. 235).

It would be a mistake, wrote Lenin, to assert in advance that future revolutions in other countries would necessarily result in the restriction of the suffrage for the bourgeoisie. "This is not an *indispensable* condition of the historical and class concept of dictatorship" (*ibid.*).

The Constitution of the R.S.F.S.R. was translated into foreign languages, and met with a wide response abroad. The working people of the capitalist countries saw in it the expression of their own aspirations, and welcomed it warmly. The bourgeoisie, on the other hand, received the Soviet Constitution with hostility. Kautsky and other leaders of the Second International sided with the bourgeoisie. Kautsky maliciously accused the Bolsheviks, who had established the dictatorship of the proletariat, of "violating democracy."

Lenin gave a resolute reply to Kautsky in his book *The Proletarian Revolution and the Renegade Kautsky*. He exposed Kautsky's falsification of Marx's theory of the State and the dictatorship of the proletariat, his gross distortion of the essence of Soviet power and of the experience of the Russian Communists. Kautsky's defence of so-called "pure democracy," in a society divided into antagonistic classes, was branded by Lenin as the empty and lying phrase-mongering of a bourgeois liberal bent on defending bourgeois democracy and duping th workers.

Lenin demonstrated that, as a result of the victory of the Octo ber Socialist Revolution and the establishment of the dictator ship of the proletariat in Russia, a new and *higher* type of de mocracy—*proletarian*, Soviet democracy—had arisen for th first time in the history of the world.

"Proletarian democracy," wrote Lenin, "is a *m i l l i o* *t i m e s* more democratic than any bourgeois democracy; th Soviet State is a million times more democratic than the mos democratic bourgeois republic" (*Collected Works*, Vol. 28 p. 227).

The dictatorship of the proletariat immeasurably extended democracy for the masses of the people. Soviet power was th first governmental authority in the world really to draw the work ing masses into the administration of the State. From the firs day of the establishment of the Soviet power, the labouring classes, the workers and the peasants, began to enjoy all th benefits of Soviet democracy. The strength and stability of So viet power lie in the fact that it combines democracy for the broadest sections of the people with revolutionary dictatorshi against the exploiters.

In his book, *The Proletarian Revolution and the Renegade Kaut-sky*, Lenin showed the epoch-making significance of the ex perience of the Communist Party, which had armed the interna tional proletariat with a new theory, strategy and tactics for Socialist revolution. The Communist Party had demonstrated to the whole world the transformation of the idea of the dicta torship of the proletariat into reality. After crushing the resist ance of the landlords and capitalists and overcoming tremendous difficulties, the workers and poor peasants of Russia had succeed ed, under the Party's leadership, not only in retaining the power they had won, but in consolidating it. in creating a new, Soviet democracy, and in embarking on practical Socialist construc tion. All this enabled Lenin to declare with good reason that "Bolshevism *can serve as a model of tactics for all*" (*ibid.*, p. 270).

BRIEF SUMMARY

The October Socialist Revolution established the dictatorship of the proletariat. The working class became the ruling class, and the Communist Party the governing party. In the difficult con ditions of war and economic dislocation, the Party assumed re sponsibility for the country's destiny. It saved the country om economic and national disaster, freed it from financial ondage and from the threat of colonial enslavement by the nperialist robbers, and led the Soviet people boldly and confid-ntly along the untrodden roads towards the building of So-alism.

Within the short period from November, 1917 to 1918, the ommunist Party roused the broad masses of the working class nd labouring peasantry to revolutionary creative activity, and arried out a number of fundamental democratic and Socialist hanges. All the survivals of medievalism were completely swept way, and full freedom and equality were proclaimed for all the eoples and nationalities of Russia. Landlords' property rights vere abolished for all time. The land confiscated from the land-ords was turned over gratis to the peasants for their use, and all he land in the country was nationalised. The old, bourgeois-land-ord State machinery was broken up and a new, Soviet machinery f State built up in its place. A new, Socialist type of State came nto being. A new and higher, proletarian form of democracy, lemocracy for the working folk, for the vast majority of the peo-ple, was established in the Soviet Republic.

Led by the Communist Party, the working class expropriated the means of production from the bourgeoisie and converted the factories, railways, land and banks into the property of the whole people, into public property. Having established its political rule and smashed capitalism, the proletariat took possession of the commanding heights in the country's economy, laid the founda-tion for the new, Soviet national economy, and created the con-ditions necessary for undertaking the building of Socialism. Lenin elaborated the basic forms and methods of building So-cialism.

The Party exposed and routed the capitulators Kamenev, Zinoviev and their supporters, Trotsky and the group of "Left Communists" headed by Bukharin, who opposed the peace of Brest Litovsk and revolutionary Socialist measures, and strength-ened the unity of the Party ranks. In conformity with the tasks involved in administering the Soviet State, the Party rearranged its organisational structure and strengthened its local organisa-tions.

In the course of the fight to develop the October Socialist Rev-olution and consolidate Soviet power, the counter-revolutionary nature of the Mensheviks and the Right and Left Socialist-Revo-lutionaries was completely exposed; they were isolated from the masses. All these petty-bourgeois parties became anti-Soviet, and took the path of struggle against Soviet power.

The Party rallied the poor peasantry round the proletariat, crushed the furious resistance of the counter-revolutionary kulaks with the help of detachments of advanced workers and the Committees of Poor Peasants, won the middle peasants ov to the side of the proletariat, and consolidated Soviet power the basis of the alliance of the working class and the poore peasantry. The great achievements of the October Socialist Re olution received legislative confirmation in the Constitutic of the R.S.F.S.R. adopted by the Fifth Congress of Soviets.

By its active fight for peace, the Communist Party achieve the withdrawal of Russia from the war, and made the utmos use of the breathing-space obtained to organise the Red Arm and embark on Socialist construction on the basis of Lenin' plan. It roused the masses of the people for the conscious build ing of a new life.

CHAPTER NINE

THE PARTY IN THE PERIOD
OF FOREIGN MILITARY INTERVENTION
AND CIVIL WAR

(1918-1920)

1. The Beginning of Foreign Military Intervention and of Civil War. The Party Organises Resistance to the Interventionists and Whites

It was not for long that the Soviet Republic was able to enjoy its hard-won breathing-space. External and internal enemies of the Soviet State imposed war on the Soviet people, compelling them to interrupt their peaceful Socialist constructive work.

The foreign imperialists could not reconcile themselves to the existence of a country governed by workers and peasants, whose example had a revolutionising effect on the working people of the capitalist countries. The monopolists did not want to lose the thousands of millions of rubles they had lent to the tsarist government and the bourgeois Provisional Government, or the huge profits derived from the factories, mines, etc., which they had owned in Russia.

Russia's withdrawal from the war greatly alarmed the Entente imperialists. They found themselves deprived of the support of the Russian army, which had until then tied down more than half the German forces. Moreover, they feared that Soviet Russia would, by her peace policy, set an example to the working people of other countries of how to put an end to the hated war.

The imperialists of Britain, France, the U.S.A. and Japan had begun to prepare for their predatory attack on Soviet Russia from the very first days after the victory of the Great October Socialist Revolution. In December, 1917, the British and French governments, with the knowledge and consent of the United States, signed a secret agreement dividing spheres of action between them. France undertook to fight the Soviets in Ukraine, Crimea and Bessarabia, while Britain was to deal with them in the Don and Kuban areas and in the Caucasus. After the conclusion of the Brest Litovsk peace, which shattered their hope of strangling the Soviet Republic with the help of the German army, U.S., British and French imperialists landed troops at Murmansk in the spring of 1918. In April, the Japanese landed a force at Vladivostok. They were followed by the British. The Entente used the Czechoslovak corps in Russia against the Soviet Government. This corps, over 40,000 strong, had been formed during the war out of Czech and Slovak prisoners of war and men who had voluntarily gone over from the Austrian army to the Russians. On the conclusion of peace with Germany the Czechoslovaks received permission from the Soviet Government to leave by way of Siberia and the Far East for the Western front in France, where the war against Germany was still on. But the organisers of intervention decided otherwise; they began to incite the Czechs and Slovaks to revolt against the Soviet Republic.

The rank and file were unwilling to take up arms against the Soviet people. Among the Czechs and Slovaks there were Communists. In May, 1918, they held their constituent congress. Many Czech and Slovak prisoners of war joined the Red Army and fought, shoulder to shoulder with Russians, for the land of Socialism, the homeland of the working people of the world.

In secret talks with the corps command, however, the imperialists secured its consent to fight the Soviet Government. The corps command deceived the Czechoslovak soldiers by spreading the provocative rumour that the Soviet Government was going to hand them over to Austria-Hungary. At the end of May, 1918, the Czechoslovaks rose in revolt. The rebels mobilised Czech and Slovak prisoners of war and recruited several thousand volunteers from among the Russian Whites. The rebels made up an impressive force of 60,000 well-armed officers and men.

The action of the Czechoslovak corps raised the hopes of the internal counter-revolution. The defeated exploiting classes started a civil war. The imperialists helped the counter-revolutionaries to organise, and supplied them with arms and munitions. The Cadet, Socialist-Revolutionary, Menshevik and bourgeois nationalist parties made deals with the imperialists. The counter-revolutionaries agreed to cede vast areas of the country to the foreign invaders, to dismember Russia and turn her into a colony, if only they could wrest power from the working people. Anti-Soviet kulak revolts, organised by counter-revolutionaries, began in Siberia, the Urals and the Volga region. Under the influence of the interventionists, and with their help, scattered anti-Soviet actions merged into a single torrent of all-Russian counter-revolution. In the short space of some two months the Czechoslovaks, operating jointly with the forces of internal counter-revolution, occupied a sizable part of Siberia and the Urals, and seized Samara, Kazan and several other Volga towns.

Thus, two counter-revolutionary forces—foreign interventionists and Russian bourgeois-landlord-kulak Whites—joined forces to fight the Soviet Republic.

In the areas overrun by the enemy, the organs of Soviet government were replaced by counter-revolutionary "governments," such as the Siberian "government" at Omsk, the Committee of Members of the Constituent Assembly at Samara, and so on. These "governments" consisted mainly of Socialist-Revolutionaries and Mensheviks, who sought to disguise an outright bourgeois dictatorship by slogans purporting to be democratic.

The interventionists and Whites also attacked other areas of the country. From Murmansk they advanced on Petrozavodsk, threatening Petrograd. British, French and U.S. warships entered the waters of the White Sea and appeared off Archangel. The interventionists seized this town and set up a White puppet government there.

The interventionists who had landed at Vladivostok helped the Czechoslovak corps and Russian Whites to capture the town and occupy the entire Far East. In an attempt to encircle Soviet Russia, the British invaded Turkestan and occupied part of its territory. In Transcaucasia, the British, co-operating with White units, seized Baku. They arrested the Soviet government leaders of Azerbaijan, including some prominent Party workers, such as S. Shaumyan, P. Japaridze, M. Azizbekov, I. Fioletov and Y. Zevin, who were shot, along with the rest of the twenty-six Baku Commissars, on instructions from the British imperialists. The interventionists bolstered up the counter-revolutionary governments of the Mussavatists[4] in Azerbaijan, the Mensheviks in Georgia and the Dashnaks[5] in Armenia.

The capture of Baku closed the enemy ring around the Soviet Republic built up by the Anglo-French, U.S. and Japanese invaders.

The latter owed their military successes to the fact that the Red Army was only just being formed, that it was still small and lacked experience.

Soviet Russia's difficulties were aggravated by the wavering of the middle peasantry. Having received their land from the victorious proletariat, the middle peasants decided that the revolution was over. They did not realise that the landlords and bourgeoisie would not reconcile themselves to the loss of their power, and that land and freedom must be defended against counter-revolutionary attacks. The counter-revolutionaries took advantage of the middle peasants' vacillations.

Furthermore, matters were greatly facilitated for the interventionists by the fact that they were seizing in the main backward, non-industrial border regions where there were few factory workers, or areas inhabited by an ethnically heterogeneous population, where nationalist counter-revolution was very active

But the interventionists and Whites tried to start an anti-Soviet struggle in the heart of the country as well. In July, 1918, on instructions from Noulens, the French Ambassador in Russia, the Socialist-Revolutionaries seized Yaroslavl, and were making preparations for revolt in 20 other towns. The insurrectionary action of the Left Socialist-Revolutionaries in Moscow was one of the links in that conspiracy. But the Moscow venture was dealt with in a matter of hours, and the Yaroslavl revolt quelled in two weeks. In the other towns the conspiracy was discovered in good time, thanks to the vigilance of the working people and the All-Russian Extraordinary Commission. The central areas of the country, where the bulk of the Russian proletariat was concentrated and which had an ethnically homogeneous population, remained an impregnable stronghold of the Soviet State.

The German imperialists, too, had a hand in the criminal attack on the peaceful Soviet State. Although they were committed to non-interference in Soviet Russia's domestic affairs by the terms of the Brest Litovsk peace treaty, they seized Finland and overthrew the workers' government there. They also occupied the Baltic provinces, Byelorussia and Ukraine, took Rostov-on-Don and invaded the Don area. The counter-revolutionaries welcomed the German troops with open arms. The landlords and bourgeoisie suddenly "forgot" that a mere six months earlier they had been calling on the Russian people to fight Germany in order to save the "fatherland." The behaviour of the propertied classes once again went to show that they saw their fatherland wherever they had their investments.

In Ukraine, the Germans put Hetman Skoropadsky, a former tsarist general, in power. By agreement with the Georgian Mensheviks, German troops occupied Georgia. On the Don, the Germans supplied arms to Ataman Krasnov and helped him to raise an army. In the summer of 1918 Ataman Krasnov's White Cossack army marched on Tsaritsyn to block the Volga, help the counter-revolutionaries beyond the river, cut off the famine-stricken country from North Caucasian grain and Baku oil, and advance in a single front on Moscow, the Soviet Russian capital. It followed that Germany was virtually collaborating with the Entente. In the west and south—from the Baltic Sea to the Caucasus—the threat to the Soviet Republic came from the German imperialists.

Soviet Russia found herself in an exceptionally difficult position. A vast part of her territory was occupied by her enemies. The interventionists established an unprecedented reign of terror in the occupied areas. Those who had worked in Soviet government offices were shot. Tens of thousands of workers and peasants were butchered in cold blood for offering the slightest resistance. In the north, the British, French and U.S. invaders set up convict prisons controlled by hangmen brought expressly from the colonies. Unparalleled atrocities and monstrous tortures were the rule in the interventionist prisons on Mudyug Island and in Yokanga in the north.

In the Far East and Siberia, the U.S. monopolies and the United States Government itself supplied arms and munitions to the Russian counter-revolutionaries on a tremendous scale. The United States not only supplied the Russian counter-revolution with arms: her troops took part, along with the Japanese invaders, in military operations against the partisans; they persecuted the civilian population and put many to death. The interventionists plundered national property, removing from the country timber, furs, gold and raw materials, worth enormous sums.

The interventionists cut off the Soviet Republic from its major food and raw material resources. It lost its oilfields and the Donets coalfield, its principal, and at that time almost the only, source of coal. Factories were stopping for lack of fuel. The towns had no lighting, because the power stations were at a standstill. The fuel shortage affected transport, which was unable to cope with freightage. The people were starving. The daily bread ration had dropped to two ounces, and even this was not issued regularly. The starving population fell an easy victim to epidemics. Typhus took a heavy toll of lives. In addition, the interventionists' agents were organising mutinies, sabotage and conspiracies everywhere. One of the conspiracies was contrived in the summer of 1918 by Lockhart, the British diplomatic agent, with Noulens and Francis—the French and U. S. Ambassadors—participating. The intelligence services of all the imperialist Powers were involved. The plan was to arrest the members of the Council of People's Commissars and assassinate Lenin. Official representatives of the imperialist Powers were conducting a vicious slander campaign against the Soviet State.

This was how armed intervention and civil war, which was unleashed by the foreign imperialists with support from the internal counter-revolution and which lasted until the end of 1920, began in Russia.

"Everyone knows," wrote Lenin, "that this war was imposed upon us; we ended the old war early in 1918, and did not begin any new one; everyone knows that the Whites were able to come out against us in the west and south and east only because the Entente helped them" (*Collected Works*, Vol. 29, p. 48).

The Communist Party roused the people to a patriotic war against the foreign invaders and the Whites.

The task which the Party set before the working people was vividly expressed by Demyan Bedny, the proletarian poet, in the following lines:

> *We're in a ring of fire, comrades!*
> *Descending on us is the whole rapacious breed,*
> *Our native land they'd make their chattel.*
> *But two ways out has destiny decreed:*
> *To win, or honourably fall in battle.*

The Central Committee, headed by Lenin, decided all the more important matters concerning the conduct of the war. It drew up strategic plans, took measures to ensure the execution of military operations, to mobilise reserves and to build up and distribute resources.

Main attention was devoted to the organisation of the Red Army. By the summer of 1918, nearly 500,000 had volunteered for military service. It was a force sufficient to crush the landlords and bourgeoisie, but clearly not enough to wage a protracted and difficult war against the allied forces of external and internal counter-revolution. The Soviet Government therefore decided to introduce compulsory military service. Workers and poor peasants joined the Red Army to defend, arms in hand, the gains of the Socialist revolution and the independence of their Soviet country. Red Army units were rapidly formed everywhere. The Party sent its best functionaries to work in the army. They brought with them the spirit of organisation and the ideas of the Communist Party. They combated laxity and strove to create a strictly disciplined regular army. They carried on extensive educational work among the soldiers, exposing the schemes of the interventionists and Whites and showing the just character of the Soviet people's patriotic war. Red Army men went into battle fired by the example of the Communists.

Numerous foreign workers, who had come to Russia to work before the revolution, joined the Red Army. Many prisoners of war volunteered too. International regiments and brigades were formed of former prisoners of war and foreign workers—Chinese, Germans, Poles, Czechs, Slovaks, Yugoslavs, Hungarians, Koreans, Rumanians and others who had adopted Soviet citizenship.

Courses for training commanders from among the workers and peasants were set up in many towns. Many privates and

N.C.O.s of the old army became Red Army commanders. The Communist Party, the working class and the peasantry produced Civil War heroes such as V. I. Chapayev, V. K. Blücher, G. I. Kotovsky, N. A. Shchors, S. G. Lazo, S. S. Vostretsov, A. Y. Parkhomenko, J. F. Fabricius and I. F. Fedko, and outstanding generals such as M. V. Frunze, K. Y. Voroshilov, S. M. Budyonny and others.

Military experts—generals and officers of the old army—were called up for service in the Red Army. They had the knowledge and experience indispensable for building up the new army and directing its military operations. Many of them performed their duties in good faith, for they realised that the Red Army was defending the country and the interests of the people. Among them were S. S. Kamenev, D. M. Karbyshev, B. M. Shaposhnikov, A. V. Stankevich, A. P. Nikolayev. The last two were subsequently taken prisoner by the Whites and hanged for their loyalty to the Soviet Government. But there were aslo many military experts who betrayed their country, gave away military secrets to the enemy and deserted to him.

Army commissars, representatives of the Communist Party and the Soviet power, were introduced into the Red Army. They exercised unremitting control over the military experts and with a firm hand cut short all attempts to weaken the army and help the enemy. Supported by the army Communists, they carried on extensive Party and political work in the Red Army and among the population in the front-line areas, and organised Communist Party nuclei. Selected from among tested and experienced Party members, the army commissars were the life and soul of the Red Army, and rallied and inspired the men and officers to fulfil their revolutionary duty and defend the Soviet Republic. Front, army and divisional political departments were set up to direct Party, political, cultural and educational work in the army.

The Party called on all working people to redouble their defence effort and their vigilance. By decision of the All-Russian Central Executive Committee, adopted in June, 1918, the Right Socialist-Revolutionaries and Mensheviks were expelled from the Soviets for having backed the open enemies of Soviet Russia—the Whites and foreign interventionists.

In the summer of 1918 the Party Central Committee considered the Eastern front to be the decisive front for the Republic, because that was where the latter was faced with the greatest danger. There the revolt of the Czechoslovak corps had merged with anti-Soviet revolts by the kulaks. Furthermore, the enemy had large, well-trained forces there and planned to march on Moscow from that area by the shortest route. In addition, the Czechoslovaks were cutting off important granaries of the country—the Volga region and Siberia—from the central gubernias. Lenin said: "The salvation not only of the Russian but also of the international revolution is on the Czechoslovak front" (*Collected Works*, Vol. 28, p. 65).

In June, 1918, a Revolutionary Military Council and headquarters of the Eastern front were set up. S. I. Gusev, V. V. Kuibyshev, A. F. Myasnikov, P. K. Sternberg and other experienced Party workers were assigned key posts in the armies operating on that front. The Central Committee adopted a special resolution to reinforce the Eastern front. A mass mobilisation of Communists was declared a priority task. The Moscow, Petrograd and other big Party organisations of the country's central areas sent one-fifth of their membership to the front. Those of the Volga region and the Urals sent nearly all their members. By the end of 1918 the number of Communists in the army Party organisations of the Eastern front was close on 25,000. Scattered detachments were reorganised into regular army units and formations. As a result of the organising work of the Party and its representatives on the Eastern front, five Soviet armies were formed within a short two months. A sixth army came into being on the Northern front. Ten more armies were gradually formed on the other fronts. Lenin followed operations on the Eastern front day by day; he saw to it that the troops were reinforced in good time, and gave directions on the work of the commissars and political departments. He personally instructed hundreds of Communists about to leave for the front.

Thanks to the measures taken by the Central Committee and the Party organisations, the Eastern front was strengthened. The Red Army withstood the onslaught of the Czechoslovaks and Whites, and barred the road to Moscow.

Simultaneously the Soviet troops succeeded in repelling attacks by the White Cossack army of the Don, which was trying to force its way into the country's central regions and into the Tsaritsyn area, where Soviet troops were covering the right flank of the Eastern front and preventing the White Cossacks from joining the Czechoslovak corps and the counter-revolutionaries of the Urals and Siberia. The brunt of the defence of Tsaritsyn was borne by the workers' detachments which had withdrawn from Ukraine under the leadership of K. Y. Voroshilov, and by the city's own workers. The Military Council of the North Caucasian District was headed by J. V. Stalin. The defence of Tsaritsyn also relieved the strain on the Eastern front.

Just then the counter-revolution struck a heavy blow at the Soviet people. The Socialist-Revolutionaries made an attempt on the life of Lenin, the great leader of the Party, the founder and head of the Soviet State. On August 30, as Lenin was leaving a meeting at the Michelsohn (now Vladimir Ilyich) Works, he was badly wounded with two poisoned bullets. That same day, the Right Socialist-Revolutionaries assassinated M. S. Uritsky in Petrograd, where shortly before they had assassinated V.V. Volodarsky.

The news that Lenin had been wounded roused a storm of indignation all over the country. The working people pledged themselves to spare no effort to defeat the enemy. Red Army men went into battle eager to avenge the attempt on Lenin's life. The Soviet people closed their ranks around the Party, and helped the Red Army more vigorously than ever.

On September 2, 1918, the Soviet Republic was proclaimed an armed camp. The Soviet State replied to counter-revolutionary terror by introducing Red terror. All persons who had belonged to White organisations, or had been involved in conspiracies or revolts, were liable to be shot. During those days the All-Russian Extraordinary Commission, headed by F. E. Dzerzhinsky, dealt a number of crushing blows to imperialist agents. The Lockhart conspiracy was nipped in the bud.

The Red Army took the offensive on the Eastern front and defeated the combined forces of the Czechoslovaks and Whites. It freed Kazan and Simbirsk in September, 1918, and Samara early in October. This brought about a radical change on the decisive Eastern front. In summing up the experience gained by the Red Army in battle, the Central Committee of the Party wrote: "The military successes achieved on the Eastern front in September were due, first and foremost, to the vigorous, resolute and selfless work which Party members carried out on the Eastern front as commissars, commanders and Red Army privates."

The Party's work to build up the armed forces, and the courageous, selfless efforts of the Communists, ensured the speedy formation of the army. By the autumn of 1918 the Red Army was about one million strong.

2. The Collapse of German Intervention in Soviet Russia. Extended Intervention by the Entente

The German invaders brought untold calamities to the working people of Ukraine, Byelorussia, the Baltic provinces and Transcaucasia. They plundered the occupied regions, and massacred with unheard-of cruelty the patriots who rose to defend their country. They razed entire villages by artillery fire, and shot all persons suspected of taking part in the partisan movement. They were assisted by the bourgeois nationalists, represented by all manner of nationalist parties and the so-called "national governments"

set up with the help of the interventionists. But all the atroci
ties and repressions to which the German invaders and thei
lackeys, the bourgeois nationalists, resorted were powerless i
the face of the rapidly mounting tide of the people's anger. I:
Ukraine, Byelorussia, the Baltic provinces and Transcaucasia
the working people developed a patriotic war under Communis
Party leadership against the German invaders. The partisa:
units grew, underground Party organisations extended and strength
ened their ties with the masses, the prestige of the Communist
grew, and their influence among the people also.

The German Command had to withdraw large forces from the
Western front in order to hurl them against the insurgents. I:
Russia, the German soldiers came to realise that the Soviet Gov
ernment was the government of the working people. They re
turned to the Western front with revolutionary ideas. Thi:
weakened the German armies in the West.

In the autumn of 1918 the armies of Britain, France and the
United States succeeded in breaking the resistance of the German army, which was exhausted by the long war and weakened
by partisan action in the occupied areas and the revolutionary
influence of Soviet Russia.

A soldiers' revolt broke out in Bulgaria in September. It
was followed in October by a revolution in Austria-Hungary
and in November, in Germany. Although the revolution in Germany did not end in victory for the workers and peasants, it
eased the position of Soviet Russia. On November 13, 1918,
the All-Russian Central Executive Committee declared all the
provisions of the Brest Litovsk treaty, and all the commitments
of the Soviet Republic regarding the payment of indemnities
and territorial concessions, to be null and void. Lenin's forecast
that the predatory Brest Litovsk treaty would be short-lived
was fully borne out.

The annulment of the Brest Litovsk treaty and the collapse
of the German imperialists' annexationist policy raised the
struggle of the working people in Ukraine, Byelorussia and
the Baltic provinces against the invaders and bourgeois nationalists to new heights.

The Red Army came to the aid of the insurgents. Pressed by
Soviet troops and partisans, the Austro-German invaders fled
from Ukraine, Byelorussia and the Baltic provinces. The Ukrainian counter-revolutionary bands formed by the invaders were
also defeated. The Soviet governments of Ukraine, Estonia, Latvia, Lithuania and Byelorussia began to function. The Council
of People's Commissars of the R.S.F.S.R. recognised the independence of the new non-Russian Soviet republics, and rendered
them every possible assistance.

But the defeat of the German imperialists had, along with its tremendous positive results for Soviet Russia, serious negative consequences as well, for it enabled the imperialists of Britain, France, the United States, Japan and other countries to use their armies against the Soviet Republic. Gaining easy access to the Black Sea through the Straits, they began to land large forces in the south. French, Greek, Rumanian and other troops appeared in Odessa, Kherson, Sevastopol and Novorossiisk. The Entente also increased the strength of its forces in the north of the Soviet Republic. Over 40,000 British and U. S. soldiers were landed at Murmansk and Archangel. Japan and the United States signed an agreement under which each country was to land 10,000 troops in the Far East. Japan, however, landed close on 100,000. At the same time the Entente requested Germany to leave her troops in the occupied areas of Russia, to prevent those areas from falling into Bolshevik hands. The German bourgeoisie readily accepted the proposal, hoping thereby to secure more advantageous peace terms.

Analysing the history of foreign interference in Soviet affairs, Lenin said:

"The first stage, naturally the more accessible and easier one for the Entente, was their attempt to settle matters with Soviet Russia by using their own troops" (*Collected Works*, Vol. 30, p. 187).

Simultaneously the imperialists increased their aid to the internal counter-revolution. The Socialist-Revolutionaries and Mensheviks cleared the way for open military dictatorship. In November, 1918, the British interventionists installed Admiral Kolchak in Siberia as "supreme ruler." In the south, the Entente had the Don and Volunteer armies unified under General Denikin, whom it began to supply with equipment and munitions. It also helped him by sending him military advisers and in other ways.

In the face of such great danger, Lenin called for the raising of an army of three million men. His proposal to that effect was approved by the joint meeting of the All-Russian Central Executive Committee, the Moscow Soviet and delegates from the factory committees and trade unions held in October, 1918. The resolution adopted on Lenin's report pointed out that the Soviet Republic was threatened with "the onslaught of an immeasurably more dangerous force—that of the international counter-revolutionary bourgeoisie, primarily the Anglo-American and French" (*Collected Works*, Vol. 28, p. 109).

The Soviet Government had repeatedly protested against the intervention, and had offered to conclude peace with the Entente Powers. The Sixth All-Russian Extraordinary Congress of So-

viets, which met at the beginning of November, 1918, once agai
called on the governments waging war against Soviet Russi
to begin peace talks. But the Entente governments ignored th
Soviet proposals. The successes achieved by the Soviet Republi
and the revolution in a number of European countries had great
ly frightened the imperialists. They had decided to overthrow
the Soviet Government in Russia at all costs, and to replac
it by a bourgeois government that would do their bidding.

The Soviet people had to defend the independence of thei
Socialist country in a long and difficult war against foreign and
internal enemies. It was essential to mobilise all the forces o
the Party, the working class and the masses of the people, al
the country's resources, for the defeat of the invaders and Whites
With that aim in view, a Council of Workers' and Peasants
Defence was established, under Lenin's chairmanship, on November 30, 1918. The Council was charged with the task of using
all the industrial and other national resources to fight the invaders and Whites, of organising transport and expanding war industry to the utmost.

The Soviet State had the support of all the working people.
There was a change of heart among the middle peasants, who
were becoming more and more convinced that the policy of the
Communist Party and the Soviet State was correct. Having had
personal experience of the horrors of counter-revolution and
seen that the victory of the enemy was followed by the restoration
of the landlords and the seizure of the peasants' land, as well
as by the loss of the country's independence, the middle peasants
swung over to the Soviet power. The Bolsheviks took due
account of the change in the middle peasants' attitude. In the
autumn of 1918 Lenin was already calling on the Party to pass
from the policy of neutralising the middle peasants to a policy
of stable alliance with them.

Encircled by enemies, the Soviet Republic had to fight single-
handed. Its resources were greatly depleted, and it was necessary
to revise the economic policy of the Soviet State as set out by
Lenin in the spring of 1918 in *The Immediate Tasks of the Soviet
Government*. The war made it imperative to concentrate the industrial effort on defeating the interventionists and Whites.
Step by step, the Soviet Government nationalised not only large-
scale, but also medium-sized and even small industries. Having
taken all the means of industrial production into its own hands,
the Soviet State used them for defence purposes. Industrial management was strictly centralised, so that industry could meet the
requirements of the front as speedily as possible.

Food became a major economic problem in the Civil War,
along with the industrial and transport problems. A law passed

n October, 1918, introduced a tax in kind to be levied on the peasants. But the heavy burden of war prevented its enforcement. t was imperative to supply the Red Army regularly, and to ave the working class from death by starvation. Steps taken in he course of 1918—the introduction of a grain monopoly, the prohibition of private trade and the confiscation of surplus grain— vere supplemented by further measures. In January, 1919, a decree was adopted providing for assessments of the grain and fodder to be requisitioned for the benefit of the State in the pro- ducing gubernias. Under its terms, the Soviet State specified the amounts of grain and fodder it required; these were then ap- portioned among the producing gubernias, and were to be requi- sitioned from the peasants at fixed prices.

"Being in a besieged fortress as we were," said Lenin, "we could hold out only by applying the surplus-requisition- ing system, that is, by taking from the peasants all the surplus produce they had, and sometimes not only the surplus, but also some quantity indispensable to the peasant, in order to maintain the fighting capacity of the army and prevent a complete breakdown in industry" (*Collected Works*, Vol. 32, p. 266).

Universal labour service was introduced during the war. There- by the Soviet State gave effect to the principle: "He who does not work, neither shall he eat." By making physical labour com- pulsory for the bourgeoisie it became possible to release the pro- letariat for work that was more essential to the front.

That was how the economic policy which has gone down in history as *War Communism* came into being. It was introduced gradually, in the course of approximately one year—from the summer of 1918 to the spring of 1919. An economic policy of the working class completely centralising production and distri- bution, it was aimed at mobilising the country's material re- sources and making the best use of them for defence and for the building of Socialism. War Communism was not an inevitable stage in the development of the Socialist revolution. It was of a temporary character, necessitated by foreign military intervention and economic dislocation. In conditions of foreign intervention and civil war, War Communism was the only feasible policy, and it fully justified itself. But it would be wrong to consider that War Communism is the only and the direct way to Social- ism. Afterwards, even while noting that credit was due to the Soviet State for introducing War Communism, Lenin said:

"But it is no less necessary to know the real extent of the service that stands to our credit. We were forced to resort to 'War Communism' by war and ruin. It was not, nor could it be, a policy that corresponded to the economic tasks of the proletariat. It was a temporary measure" (*Collected Works*, Vol. 32 p. 321).

The measures taken by the Party and the Government, and the self-sacrificing support which the working people gave them enabled the Red Army to withstand the interventionist and White attacks.

At the close of 1918 a grave situation arose on the Southern front, then the Republic's main front. In November the Central Committee of the Party, after discussing the situation, called for the strengthening of this front. On instructions from the C.C. experienced military-political workers were sent to the Southern front, along with fresh reinforcements—the Moscow Workers' Division, the Inza, Urals and other units. In the course of December, the Red Army succeeded in checking the advance of the interventionists and Whites in the south, and in January 1919, it launched a counter-offensive. In February the Tenth Army, defending Tsaritsyn, took the offensive. Krasnov's Don Army was smashed by the joint operations of the troops of the Southern front. Bolshevik propaganda and the setbacks at the front prompted many Cossacks to go home.

To foil the Red Army offensive in the south, the Entente struck in the north. Kolchak was instructed to move a sizable force to the northern sector of the Eastern front, in order to effect a junction with the British and American troops in the Perm-Kotlas area, and from there march on Moscow in a united front. The Whites succeeded in defeating the Third Soviet Army and, at the end of December, 1918, in capturing Perm.

Nevertheless, the enemy was unable to carry out his plan. The Soviet troops wore out the White forces in battle. The measures adopted by the Central Committee of the Party enabled the Third Army to take the offensive already in January, 1919. A committee of inquiry appointed by the C.C. R.C.P.(B.), and composed of F. E. Dzerzhinsky and J. V. Stalin, brought to light shortcomings in the organisation of the troops on the Eastern front, and thereby played an important part in strengthening that army and increasing its efficiency. Soviet troops advanced in other sectors of the Eastern front as well. In December, 1918, they freed Ufa. In January, 1919, a combined thrust by the Soviet troops operating from the west and from Turkestan resulted in the liberation of Orenburg. In the southern sector of the Eastern front, the Red Army entered Uralsk.

The Red Army was on the offensive everywhere. In a war against a revolutionary people, the fighting efficiency of the imperialist troops began to decline. They had been sent to northern and southern Russia ostensibly for the purpose of continuing the war against the Germans. But as they did not meet a single German here, the soldiers began to realise that they had been deceived. They saw that the power in Russia was in the hands of the people, that the workers and peasants were building a new society free from exploitation. The underground Bolshevik organisations were carrying on heroic work among the interventionist troops. In Odessa, the Regional Party Committee headed by the fearless Bolshevik I. F. Smirnov (underground name, Nikolai Lastochkin), set up a "Foreign Collegium" for agitation work among the interventionist troops. Many Communists, including I. F. Smirnov, the Frenchwoman Jeanne Labourbe and others, lost their lives at the hands of the interventionist executioners.

The Bolshevik Party's activities in the enemy rear bore fruit. A mutiny broke out in the French fleet operating in the Black Sea. Foreign soldiers began to take action, insisting on being sent home. In the spring of 1919 the invaders were compelled to leave several areas of the Soviet Republic.

"The victory we won by compelling the British and French troops to evacuate," Lenin said, "was the greatest victory we had over the Entente. We deprived them of their soldiers" (*Collected Works*, Vol. 30, p. 189).

3. Founding of the Third, Communist International. Eighth Party Congress

The rising tide of revolution in Western Europe was of great help to the Soviet State. In many capitalist countries mass strikes developed into armed clashes with the bourgeoisie. Soviet Republics came into being in Hungary and Bavaria in the spring of 1919. The colonial peoples began to rise up to fight for their national liberation.

A signal event in the international working-class movement was the founding of Communist Parties in a number of capitalist countries. The constituent congress of the Communist Party of Germany met at the end of December, 1918, and the beginning of January, 1919. The Party was founded by outstanding leaders of the German and international working-class movement— Karl Liebknecht, Rosa Luxemburg, Franz Mehring and Wilhelm Pieck. Liebknecht and Luxemburg were assassinated shortly after by hirelings of the German imperialists. In 1918 Communist Parties were founded in Argentina, Finland, Austria, Hungary and Poland. Communist groups and Left Socialist organisations were formed in many capitalist countries. Finally, it became possible to accomplish the task put forward by Lenin during the first world war, namely, to found a Third, Communist International.

The First Congress of the Communist International took place in Moscow in the early part of March, 1919. It was attended by delegates from the Communist Parties and Left Socialist organisations of 30 countries. Its work was guided by the leader of the world proletariat, Lenin. The Congress resolved to found the Third, Communist International, approved Lenin's theses on bourgeois democracy and the dictatorship of the proletariat, adopted the platform of the Comintern, and addressed a manifesto to the proletarians of the world, calling on them to wage a resolute struggle for the dictatorship of the proletariat, for the victory of Soviets in all countries. The founding of the Comintern was a great victory for Marxism-Leninism over social-reformism. The best of the revolutionary forces of the world proletariat rallied to the banner of Communist internationalism.

From March 18-23, 1919, the R.C.P.(B.) held its Eighth Congress, which represented over 300,000 Party members. The Congress discussed the Central Committee's report, the draft programme of the Party, the military situation and military policy, work in the countryside and questions of organisation.

The Eighth Congress *adopted the new Party programme*, drafted by Lenin. The programme summed up the results of the new stage of the world-wide emancipation movement of the proletariat. More than 15 years had passed since the adoption of the first Party programme. The fundamental task it had set had been performed with the establishment of the dictatorship of the proletariat in the Soviet Republic. The Party was now faced with other tasks—consolidation of the State embodying the dictatorship of the working class, and the launching of Socialist construction.

The new programme defined the Party's tasks for the entire period of transition from capitalism to Socialism. It gave a comprehensive description of Soviet democracy as a democracy of a higher type, and unmasked the class essence and spurious nature of bourgeois democracy.

In the economic field, the new programme considered the development of the country's productive forces in every possible way to be the paramount and decisive task that must govern the entire economic policy of the Soviet State. The programme called for the completion of the process of expropriating the bourgeoisie and the transformation of the means of production and distribution into public property. It put forward as a cardinal task the co-ordination of all the economic activity of the country on the basis of a single State plan. It provided for further extension of co-operation in local and handicraft industry, financial support for it by the State, and its inclusion in the general plan for raw material and fuel supplies. These measures were designed to facilitate a smooth transition from those backward forms of production to a higher, large-scale mechanised industry. The programme pointed out that the Socialist mode of production can be stabilised only on the basis of the comradely discipline of the working people and the maximum degree of initiative, sense of responsibility, mutual control over labour productivity on their part. It assigned the main role in creating a new, Socialist discipline to the trade unions. It provided for extensive development of science and its closer connection with production, as well as for the employment of bourgeois experts under the control of the Soviet Government.

In the sphere of agriculture, the programme recommended that measures be taken to organise large-scale Socialist farming by (1) establishing State farms, (2) founding and supporting societies and associations for collective tillage, (3) State sowing of all uncultivated lands, (4) mobilising all the forces of agricultural science to raise the efficiency of agriculture, and (5) supporting agricultural communes, as completely voluntary unions of cultivators, to conduct large-scale socialised farming.

Seeing that small individual peasant farms would continue to exist for a long time to come, the Party considered it necessary to increase their productivity by supplying the working peasants with improved seeds and fertilisers, disseminating agronomical knowledge, repairing implements at State-owned workshops, setting up centres for the hire of implements and experimental stations, carrying out reclamation work, and so on.

Specific measures were laid down for labour protection and social maintenance, housing, health and public education. They were to secure higher living and cultural standards for the working people of the land of Soviets.

During the discussion of the draft programme, Bukharin and Pyatakov opposed Lenin's proposal for including in the programme a description of pre-monopoly capitalism and simple commodity production in addition to a definition of imperialism as the highest stage of capitalism. Their attitude was in fact a continuation of their struggle against Lenin's theory of Socialist revolution. They held that imperialism was a special social and economic formation, and not a stage in the development of capitalism. Bukharin and his supporters argued that imperialism was incompatible with pre-monopolist forms of economy. It followed from this anti-Leninist theory of "pure imperialism" that in the era of imperialism only a "purely" proletarian revolution was possible, in which the proletariat opposed the bourgeoisie single-handed, and which included neither anti-feudal movements nor national liberation wars. In this attitude Bukharin and Pyatakov were proceeding from the Menshevik-Trotskyist denial of the role of the middle peasantry in the Socialist revolution and in the building of Socialism. In practice, their attitude amounted to depriving the proletariat of its ally, and in the final analysis represented the rejection of the dictatorship of the proletariat.

Lenin vigorously opposed the anti-Bolshevik views advanced by Bukharin and his supporters. He pointed out the political harmfulness of Bukharin's proposal.

"Pure imperialism, without the fundamental basis of capitalism, has never existed, exists nowhere and never will exist," he said (*Collected Works*, Vol. 29, p. 144).

Serious differences arose over the national question during the discussion of the programme. Bukharin and Pyatakov opposed recognition of the right of nations to self-determination up to and including political secession. Exposing the anti-Bolshevik nature of the Bukharin and Pyatakov proposal, Lenin showed the disastrous consequences to which it led. The Party and the Soviet Government had, by their correct nationalities policy, overcome the distrust which the nations felt as a result of national and colonial oppression by the landlords and bourgeoisie, and had laid a foundation for friendship among the peoples. The proposal of Bukharin and Pyatakov would have revived that distrust. It would also have been detrimental to the international influence of the Soviet Republic, for the imperialists would have begun slanderously to allege that the old nationalities policy, a policy of oppression and conquest, was being restored in Soviet Russia.

"And this is what may happen if the principle of the self-determination of nations is denied . . . " said Lenin.

"We cannot refuse to recognise what actually exists; it will itself compel us to recognise it. The demarcation between the proletariat and the bourgeoisie is proceeding differently in each country. Here we must act with utmost caution. We must be particularly cautious with regard to the various nations, for there is nothing worse than distrust on the part of a nation" (*ibid.*, p. 153).

The Congress rejected the anti-Leninist proposals on both points—the nature of imperialism and the national question—and approved Lenin's draft programme.

The attitude to the middle peasantry was one of the most important items on the Congress agenda. The policy of neutralising the middle peasants was the only correct one in the early period of the existence of the Soviet Republic, when the chief task was to suppress the bourgeoisie and firmly establish the dictatorship of the proletariat, when the middle peasants were wavering and Soviet power had not yet been consolidated. But in the new conditions, with the first onslaught of the counter-revolution beaten back, with Soviet power firmly established and the tasks of Socialist construction placed on the order of the day, the policy of neutralisation was no longer suitable. The middle peasant had swung over to the side of Soviet power, he had to be drawn into the work of building a Socialist society. Socialism could be built only in alliance with the middle peasants, who at that time made up the bulk of the peasantry.

"We have entered a stage of Socialist construction," said Lenin, "when we must work out, specifically and in detail, basic rules and directions that have been tested by work in the countryside and that we must follow *if we want to secure a stable alliance* with the middle peasantry . . ." (*ibid.*, pp. 124-25).

On the basis of Lenin's report, the Congress adopted a resolution on changing to a policy of *stable alliance with the middle peasantry while relying on the peasant poor*, for the purpose of combating the kulaks and all the other class enemies of Soviet power, and of continuing Socialist construction. The Congress enjoined all administrative and Party workers to pay proper attention to the needs of the middle peasant, to draw a strict dividing line between him and the kulak, to continue an unrelenting struggle against the kulak, and gradually and steadily draw the middle peasant into Socialist construction, making concessions to him when determining the ways of carrying out Socialist changes.

This Congress resolution was of exceptional importance both for the consolidation of the Soviet State and for the revolutionary movement of the world proletariat. Summing up the experience of the Party in solving the problem of the proletariat's attitude to the middle peasantry after the victory of the Socialist revolution, Lenin assessed the significance of an alliance between the proletariat and the middle peasantry as follows:

"The dictatorship of the proletariat is a specific form of class alliance between the proletariat, the vanguard of the working people, and the numerous non-proletarian sections of the working people (petty bourgeoisie, small proprietors, the peasantry, the intelligentsia, etc.), or the majority of these strata, an alliance against capital, an alliance whose aim is the complete overthrow of capital, complete suppression of the resistance offered by the bourgeoisie as well as of attempts at restoration on its part, an alliance for the final establishment and consolidation of Socialism" (*ibid.*, pp. 350-51).

Lenin enriched the theory of the dictatorship of the proletariat, and developed the theory and policy of the Party on the peasant question.

The Congress decision on an alliance with the middle peasant, with the main mass of the peasantry, played a great part in rallying all the working people for the fight against the interventionists and Whites, for the building of Socialism. Speaking of the establishment of an alliance with the middle peasant, Lenin emphasised at the Congress that "we shall cope with this task, and then Socialism will be absolutely invincible" (*Collected Works*, Vol. 29, p. 191).

The military question held a special place in the Congress deliberations. Although, as Lenin said at the Congress, the country had succeeded in repulsing a furious onslaught from all sides, there was still the danger of fresh Entente campaigns. In fact, the Congress already had information about a new offensive by the invaders and Whites from the east.

By the time the Congress met, a so-called "Military Opposition" had made its appearance. It included "Left Communists" who opposed the Party's policy on the military question as well. But it also included people who had nothing whatever to do with opposition groupings. The "Military Opposition" was against the introduction of iron discipline in the army and against any utilisation of the experience of the old military experts. It advocated the preservation of partisan methods in managing the army and in waging war.

During the discussion on the military question the delegates rejected the proposals of the "Military Opposition." At the same time, they protested against the policy followed by Trotsky, who placed blind trust in the old military experts, among whom there were obvious traitors. The delegates also condemned indiscriminate mobilisations, which did not take into account the class principle of selection and allowed kulaks to be called up as well. This often led to political instability in some units.

Lenin sharply criticised the "Military Opposition." He pointed out that the Central Committee of the Party decided all the more important military matters, planned appropriate measures and verified their fulfilment.

Lenin further noted that without iron military discipline there could be no powerful Red Army, particularly in a peasant country, such as Russia was at the time. While insisting that the achievements of the bourgeois art of war be utilised and the assistance of military experts enlisted, Lenin stressed the need for closer political control over their activity.

The Congress adopted a resolution on the military question unanimously. It condemned the attempt to substitute guerilla units for a well-disciplined regular army under a centralised command.

The resolution laid special emphasis on the role of the army commissars. It noted the heroic work being done by the commissars in the Red Army, and stated that their work was most effec-

ive when it relied on the support of the Communist groups of
heir regiment.

"The army commissars," said the resolution, "are not only
direct and immediate representatives of the Soviet power;
they also, and above all, embody the spirit of our Party, its
discipline, its firmness and courage in the struggle for the attainment of the goal set" (*C.P.S.U. in Resolutions*, Part I,
p. 435).

It was decided to form a Political Department of the Revolutionary Military Council of the Republic, and to entrust it
with the direction of the entire Party political work in the
Red Army.

The practical section of the resolution stated the necessity
of strictly adhering to the class principle of calling up working
people only, and of conscripting kulak and other parasitic
elements into special labour battalions; enlisting the assistance
of military experts and establishing unremitting Party political
control over them through the commissars; extending the
training of commanders of proletarian and semi-proletarian
origin, etc. These provisions were designed to counteract Trotsky's distortions of the Party's military policy.

In its resolution on Party building, the Congress instructed
the Central Committee carefully to watch the social composition of the Party and to see to it, by exercising the utmost discretion in admitting non-workers and non-peasants to Party
membership, that its quality did not deteriorate. As tens
of thousands of Party members were employed in the machinery
of State, the Congress called for a vigorous struggle against the
danger of their drifting away from the masses and becoming infected with a bureaucratic spirit. It was decided to re-register
all Party members, which meant in fact cleansing the Party.
Much attention was given to the strengthening of Party discipline. The situation in the country required the most strict centralisation and rigorous discipline. "The Party at the present
time needs outright military discipline," said the resolution.

The Party organisations in the non-Russian areas acquired
great importance in Party building. Congresses of local Bolshevik
organisations were held in some of these areas, and Communist
Parties were founded with Central Committees of their own.
In the second half of 1918 and the beginning of 1919, Communist
Parties were formed in Turkestan, Ukraine, Lithuania, Byelorussia, Latvia and Estonia. The fundamental question arose of the
principle on which the Party organisations of the non-Russian
areas were to form part of the Russian Communist Party.

Lenin's idea was that all the non-Russian organisations should
be integral components of a single Communist Party of Russia.

The Eighth Congress declared emphatically against a federatio
of independent Communist Parties and firmly stated that a singl
centralised Communist Party, with a single Central Committe
directing the work of the entire Party, was essential. The Centra
Committees of the Communist Parties in the non-Russian Sovie
Republics would enjoy the rights of regional committees unde
the C.C. of the R.C.P.(B.).

In accordance with this decision, the Transcaucasian Bolshe
vik organisations, namely, those of Azerbaijan, Georgia an
Armenia, were transformed in 1920 into the Communist Partie
of Azerbaijan, Georgia and Armenia, and headed the struggl
of the workers and peasants of Transcaucasia for Soviet power
The founding of Communist Parties in the non-Russian Sovie
Republics as integral parts of the R.C.P.(B.) marked a new stag
in the development of the Communist Party of Soviet Russia
on the basis of the Leninist principle of proletarian internationalism. It was a pattern of Party structure in a multi-national
Socialist Republic.

The Congress resolution on the question of organisation ad
ministered a rebuff to the Sapronov-Osinsky opportunist group,
which denied the leading role of the Party in the Soviet State.

The resolution pointed out that the Party "must win undivided
political sway in the Soviets and effective control over all their
activities" through selfless day-by-day work in the Soviets and
the promotion of devoted Communists to all Soviet posts. Party
groups strictly observing Party discipline must be formed in all
Soviet institutions. "The Party seeks to *guide* the activities of
the Soviets but not to supplant them," the resolution said
(*C.P.S.U. in Resolutions*, Part I, p. 446).

The Congress hailed the founding of the Third, Communist
International and declared its unqualified adherence to the platform of the International.

The Eighth Congress of the R.C.P.(B.) was of great importance. The new Party programme which it adopted was a
programme for the building of Socialism. The Congress resolutions helped to consolidate the military and political alliance
of the proletariat and the peasantry, and to strengthen the Red
Army, which ensured the success of the further struggle against
the interventionists and Whites.

The new Party programme armed the workers and peasants
with a clear perspective of Socialist construction. It inspired the
masses of the people to wage a selfless struggle for the triumph
of the new social order.

The programme adopted by the Congress was also of lasting
international significance. It answered the question that interested the working people of the whole world, namely, how the

Socialist revolution had triumphed, why it was inevitable and wherein lay its strength. Speaking of the international significance of the programme of the Communist Party of Soviet Russia, Lenin stressed that

"A simple translation of our programme will best answer the question what the Russian Communist Party, which is a contingent of the world proletariat, has accomplished. Our programme will be very forceful propaganda and agitation material; it will be a document that will entitle the workers to say: 'Here we have our comrades, our brothers. It is here that our common cause is being realised'" (*Collected Works*, Vol. 29, p. 198).

4. The Radical Turn in the Civil War. The Defeat of Kolchak and Denikin

The end of the Eighth Party Congress coincided with the launching of a new campaign by the Entente and the Whites. Protected and aided by the interventionists, the Russian counter-revolutionaries continued to form armies many thousands strong. Their position was particularly strong in Siberia, where all elements hostile to the Soviet power gathered to join Kolchak. Kolchak held the industrial Urals. With support from the kulaks, the Whites forced the peasants to supply them with food. The Socialist-Revolutionaries and Mensheviks backed Kolchak, for whom they had cleared the way. The British, French, Japanese and American imperialists continuously supplied the Whites with arms, munitions and equipment.

Kolchak's offensive was supported by the counter-revolutionary troops in the south, west and north, which had, in their turn, received aid and support from the invaders. The main blow was to be dealt by the Kolchak forces, which intended to push to the Volga and there join Denikin to strike a combined blow at Moscow.

The Kolchak army took the offensive early in March, 1919. The Red Army had to abandon Ufa. The Soviet front was breached. White troops were forcing their way through to the Volga. In the south, General Denikin captured Lugansk and part of the Donets coalfield, with the result that the country was deprived of its coal base. In May General Yudenich took the offensive against Petrograd. In the Baltic provinces, the Whites opened an attack, supported by the British fleet and German troops. A Polish army, formed and equipped by the Entente, invaded Lithuania and Byelorussia. An army under the White General

Miller, and detachments of British, American and French inter- ventionists were advancing from the north. Thus all the forces of counter-revolution took the offensive.

Once again Soviet Russia found herself encircled by enemies. On April 11, 1919, the Central Committee approved the *Theses of the C.C. R.C.P.(B.) in connection with the situation on the Eastern front*, written by Lenin. The theses gave an appraisal of the Republic's military and political situation and under- lined the decisive importance of the Eastern front. The Central Committee called on all working people to do their utmost to defeat the enemies. Over 20,000 Communists were sent to the Eastern front. The Komsomol announced the first country-wide mobilisation of its members, and dispatched upwards of 3,000 of them to the front. The trade unions mobilised over 60,000 workers. The arrival of the Communists, mostly workers from Petrograd, Moscow, Ivanovo-Voznesensk and Tver, raised Red Army morale. They reinforced the Party groups and political departments in the army, and improved the political education of the soldiers.

The working class responded to the call of the Central Com- mittee with labour heroism on a mass scale. In industry, the Com- munists initiated and organised veritable feats of labour. A new form of social labour, known as Communist *subbotniks*, was ini- tiated by the workers. The Party supported it. By decision of a general meeting of Communists and sympathisers in a subdis- trict of the Moscow-Kazan Railway, the first Communist *sub- botnik* took place on May 10. In the second half of 1919, *subbotniks* spread throughout the country.

Lenin described the Communist *subbotniks* as a great initiative. He assessed them as conscious, voluntary and supremely heroic work on the part of the working people, as the actual beginning of Communism. The workers' heroic effort on the home front made it possible to supply the Red Army with all it required, primarily arms and munitions.

On instructions from the Party Central Committee and the Government, the Soviet Command drew up plans for a Red Army counter-offensive. The decisive blow was to be struck by the Southern group of the Eastern front, under M. V. Frunze. V. V. Kuibyshev was a member of the Revolutionary Military Council of the Southern group, which included the V. I. Cha- payev division of legendary fame, with D. A. Furmanov as its po- litical commissar.

At the end of April, 1919, the Southern group began the coun- ter-offensive, and inflicted a shattering defeat on the enemy. Conditions were thus provided for the utter defeat of Kolchak and for the liberation of the Urals and Siberia.

At the decisive moment, when the execution of the plan for defeating the enemy was almost complete, Trotsky, then Chairman of the Revolutionary Military Council of the Republic, proposed to the command of the Eastern front that it should transfer a considerable part of its troops to the Southern front. To do this, the command would have to halt the offensive. This would have enabled Kolchak to restore his army. Lenin had to intervene. He insisted that the Urals be freed without fail before the winter. The Central Committee rejected Trotsky's proposal and directed the Revolutionary Military Council of the Eastern front to proceed with the offensive. The Red troops took the offensive all along the Eastern front. By the summer of 1919 the threat from Kolchak was eliminated as a main danger, although his army was not yet completely destroyed.

In Siberia and the Far East, the partisans were harassing the White troops and the interventionists. They engaged the enemy in bitter fighting, blew up railways, derailed trains, and rescued Red Army men who had been taken prisoner. The partisan movement was led by underground Party committees, which also directed strikes in Kolchak's rear. All these factors contributed to the successes of the Red Army.

In an attempt to frustrate the Red Army offensive on the Eastern front, the counter-revolutionaries delivered a blow in the vicinity of Petrograd. The troops under Yudenich, supported by Finnish Whites and Estonian White units, closed in on the city. The C.C. R.C.P. (B.) decided on defence measures for Petrograd. It called for the mobilisation of Communists, Komsomol and trade union members for the Petrograd front, and revoked an order to send Communists mobilised in Petrograd to the Eastern front. But the Petrograd Defence Committee, which was headed by Zinoviev, did not take all the necessary measures. It ordered the evacuation of factories working for the defence of Petrograd, and even discussed the question of scuttling the fleet in view of the enemy advance. On a proposal by Lenin, the Council of Defence categorically prohibited the evacuation of factories and property from Petrograd. Stalin was sent to Petrograd with full powers from the Central Committee and the All-Russian Central Executive Committee of Soviets.

The White command tried to support its offensive at the front by striking from the rear. A mutiny engineered by Entente agents broke out at the Krasnaya Gorka, Seraya Loshad and Obruchev forts. The mutineers opened fire on Kronstadt. Drastic measures were adopted immediately against the traitors. A unit formed for the suppression of the mutiny attacked the forts with the support of the Baltic Fleet. The mutineers were crushed. Yudenich's offensive against Petrograd was foiled.

In August, 1919, Lenin addressed a letter to the workers an peasants in connection with the victory over Kolchak. He poin ed out the chief lessons of that victory, which had to be learne if the country was to be made secure against a repetition of th Kolchak affair. First, a powerful Red Army was needed. Secon ly, the Soviet State could not maintain an army and the worke unless it had grain, which the peasants must give the State in th form of a loan. Thirdly, it was necessary to maintain revolutio ary order and strictly observe Soviet laws and decrees. Fourth ly, it would be criminal to forget that it was the Mensheviks an Socialist-Revolutionaries who had helped Kolchak appear o the scene and had given him outright support. Fifthly, a stron alliance of the workers and peasants was needed if the enem was to be vanquished. "An implacable fight against capital and an alliance of the working people, an alliance of the peasant and the working class—that is the last and most important lesso of the Kolchak affair," wrote Lenin (*Collected Works*, Vol. 29, p 518).

The nationalities policy of the Soviet Government playe a very great part in defeating the enemies of the Soviet Republic As soon as danger threatened the country there was an intens desire in the independent Soviet Republics to combine their force in the struggle against enemies. The Central Committee of th Party approved this initiative and, on a proposal by Lenin, decidec on the military unity of the Republics. On June 1, 1919, the All Russian Central Executive Committee, at a special meeting ir Moscow attended by delegates from all the Soviet Republics decided to conclude a military alliance and establish a single command, and to amalgamate the councils of national economy the transport system and the commissariats of labour.

The unification of all the forces of the Soviet peoples strength-ened the country, enabling it to fight the invaders and Whites more effectively and to ensure their subsequent rout.

Kolchak's defeat did not stop the imperialists from continuing their intervention. In the second half of 1919 the invaders and the Whites shifted the centre of their struggle against Soviet Russia to the south. This time the main blow was to be struck by the Denikin army.

Churchill, British Minister of War, boasted of having organised a "campaign of 14 Powers" against Soviet Russia.

Once again Soviet Russia found herself in an extremely perilous situation. Although a substantial portion of Siberia, one of the principal grain-producing areas, had been captured by the heroic Red Army, Denikin still held the entire south, which included the main fuel areas—the Donets coalfield and the Grozny oil-fields. Baku was in the hands of the invaders and Mussavatists.

On June 30, 1919, Tsaritsyn fell, and Denikin then ordered his army to march on Moscow. He counted on support from the "National Centre," a counter-revolutionary organisation operating in the Soviet rear. The conspirators were planning to raise a revolt as soon as the enemy troops approached Moscow.

The other forces of counter-revolution took the offensive simultaneously with Denikin, seeking to divert the Red Army troops from the Southern front. The remnants of Kolchak's army launched an offensive in the Tobolsk area. In the north, Miller was advancing on Vologda and Petrozavodsk. Yudenich again broke through to the environs of Petrograd. The troops of bourgeois-landlord Poland captured Minsk.

The Central Committee issued a call to the Party and the country written by Lenin and entitled "All Out for the Fight Against Denikin!" It laid down a concrete programme for rallying the whole people to defeat the enemy. Leading Party and Soviet workers and fresh Red Army forces were dispatched to the Southern front. As a result, the Soviet troops on the Southern front were able as early as the end of July to begin preparations for an offensive against Denikin.

The counter-offensive was to start at the beginning of August, 1919. The plan of the command was to strike the blow from the Tsaritsyn area; that would prevent Denikin from crossing the Volga and making a junction with Kolchak's southern army; secondly, it would be easier to move reinforcements into the Tsaritsyn area from the Eastern front; thirdly, the blow would threaten the flank of Denikin's troops advancing on Moscow, and would enable the Soviet forces to break through into the enemy rear.

But the counter-offensive failed. It began much later than planned, owing to the inefficiency of the war department, which was headed by Trotsky. Denikin, who had his agents in the headquarters of the Southern front, was informed of the intended offensive, and took measures to frustrate it. He was greatly helped in this by a raid of Mamontov's White cavalry into the rear of the Southern front. A number of units had to be withdrawn from the front to counter the raid. Meanwhile, Denikin succeeded in forming a shock group, which he hurled against Moscow by way of Kursk-Orel-Tula. He seized Kursk and Orel, and was threatening Tula. Never before had the Whites drawn so near to the heart of the country as in September, 1919.

Denikin's advance on Moscow made the Southern front the main one. In these critical days the Central Committee of the Party took further measures to reinforce the Southern front. In September a plenary meeting of the Central Committee accepted Lenin's proposal to send the largest possible number of Party workers to the army. The Party developed an extensive political campaign, explaining the situation at the front to the Red Army men. By decision of the Central Committee, the command of the Southern front was removed; A. I. Yegorov was appointed commander and J. V. Stalin a member of the Revolutionary Military Council of the front. The Southern front was divided into the Southern and South-Eastern fronts. A Defence Committee was established for the Moscow fortified area. Additional reserves were moved to the Southern front.

The Central Committee of the Party sent about 30,000 Communists to the front. The Komsomol announced a second country-wide mobilisation of its members, and 10,000 of them left for the front. The Denikinites' hopes of a revolt in the Soviet rear were shattered, for the conspiracy of the "National Centre" was discovered and nipped in the bud.

The Party proclaimed a Party Week, to reinforce its ranks and strengthen its ties with the masses. Over 200,000 workers and peasants joined the Party in the central areas alone. The Party Week was also highly successful in the army in the field whose finest men joined the Party. That was how the working people of Soviet Russia reacted to Denikin's threat to disband the Soviets and hang the Bolsheviks. It was a gigantic political victory for the Party, a victory which showed plainly that the masses were following the Communists. The C.C. R.C.P.(B.) stated in its report: "Under the circumstances, a Party membership card made its holder a candidate, to some extent, for Denikin's gallows. Contrary to all the predictions of our opponents, the Party Weeks everywhere were crowned with a completely unexpected and most brilliant success."

The original plan for delivering the main blow from the Tsaritsyn area no longer met the requirements of the moment. A meeting of the Political Bureau of the Central Committee, held on October 15, took the following decision: "Tula, Moscow and the approaches to them must not be surrendered, and a general offensive must be prepared in the course of the winter. . . . On the South-Eastern front, we must, for the time being, go over to the defensive with the aim of (a) preventing Denikin from joining up with the Urals Cossacks and (b) releasing a part of our manpower to defend Tula and Moscow." As for the other fronts, the Political Bureau directed Headquarters to consider them "from the standpoint of the security of the Moscow-Tula area, first and foremost."

The Red Army struck its main blow along the Kharkov-Donbas-Rostov-on-Don line. A shock group of Soviet troops was assigned to defeat picked White units composed of officer volunteers. In the battles fought in the Kromy-Orel area from October 10 to

30, the shock group routed the Whites. The Red Army freed Orel. Simultaneously Budyonny's cavalry routed the main forces of the Shkuro and Mamontov corps on the approaches to Voronezh, which the Soviet troops liberated on October 24. It was at this time that the cavalry corps under Budyonny was re-formed into the First Cavalry Army, with S. M. Budyonny appointed its commander and K. Y. Voroshilov member of its Military Council.

The successes achieved by the shock group at Orel and by the Red cavalry at Voronezh enabled the Red Army to assume the offensive all along the front. Liberation of Ukraine and the North Caucasus began. Partisans were operating in Denikin's rear. On the occasion of the victories won over Denikin, Lenin addressed a message to the workers and peasants of Ukraine at the end of December, 1919. Pointing out the lessons of the struggle against Kolchak, Lenin stressed that the Soviet Republic would have been unable to win those victories without the alliance of all the peoples of the country. "He who undermines the unity and close alliance between the Great-Russian and Ukrainian workers and peasants is helping the Kolchaks, the Denikins, the capitalist marauders of all countries," he wrote (*Collected Works*, Vol. 30, pp. 271-72).

The victories won on the Southern front inspired the Red Army men fighting at Petrograd. Yudenich's troops were defeated, most of them were taken prisoner, and only a small remnant succeeded in escaping to Estonia.

In December, 1919, the Party convened its Eighth Conference, which played an important part in strengthening the Party and its ties with the masses. The Conference adopted new Party rules, which defined precisely the structure of Party organisations, bringing it into line with the administrative and territorial division of the country established since the foundation of the Soviet State. A provision was included in the rules to the effect that a Party group consisting of not less than three members was the primary unit of Party organisation. A term of probation was established for everyone joining the Party, necessary for the new-comer to familiarise himself with the programme and tactics of the Party, and for the Party organisation concerned to appraise his personal qualities. Another new element of the rules was the section dealing with Party groups in Soviet institutions and other organisations of the working people.

The Conference decisions "On Soviet policy in Ukraine" and "On Soviet power in Ukraine" were of particular importance. A C.C. resolution drafted by Lenin and endorsed by the Conference emphasised: "Unfalteringly applying the principle of self-determination of nations, the C.C. considers it necessary to reaffirm that the R.C.P.(B.) recognises the independence of the

Ukrainian Soviet Socialist Republic" (*C.P.S.U. in Resolutions*, Part I, p. 459).

Pointing out the necessity for a close alliance of all the Soviet Republics in their struggle against imperialism, the resolution said that it was for the Ukrainian workers and working peasants to determine the forms that alliance should take. For the time being, the relations between the Russian Soviet Federative Socialist Republic and the Ukrainian Soviet Socialist Republic were defined as of a federative character.

With regard to carrying out land policy, the resolution recommended that special attention be paid to the interests of the poor and middle peasantry. This should involve: abolishing the landlord proprietorship restored by Denikin; transferring the land to those who have little or no land; setting up State farms strictly within the necessary limits, with due regard to the interests of the peasantry; preventing any coercion in uniting the peasants in communes, artels, etc. The Party insisted that the poor and middle peasantry be drawn more extensively into governing the State, and that all obstacles to the free development of the Ukrainian language and Ukrainian culture be removed.

The Conference resolution on Soviet power in Ukraine was of great help to the Ukrainian Communists, and strengthened the friendship between the peoples of the country.

In December, 1919, the Seventh Congress of Soviets met. It once more addressed to the governments of Britain, France, the United States, Italy and Japan a proposal to begin immediate peace negotiations, jointly and severally. The Soviet Government proposed to the small countries that peace negotiations be held on conditions recognising their independence. Estonia, and later Latvia and Finland, agreed to hold peace negotiations.

Denikin's defeat made it possible to eliminate other links of the counter-revolutionary chain encircling the country. Kolchak, the "Supreme Ruler," was the first to be finished off. His troops were defeated and he himself taken prisoner. He was tried and shot.

The defeat of the enemy on the Southern front also made it possible to complete the liquidation of the Turkestan fronts.

The Red Army victories helped the working people of Transcaucasia in their struggle against the invaders. In the spring of 1920 the Red Army forces operating on the Caucasian front drew near the boundary of Transcaucasia.

As soon as the workers of Azerbaijan got word of the approach of the Red Army, they rose against the Azerbaijanian bourgeoisie. In February, 1920, the C.P.(B.) of Azerbaijan held its first Congress illegally in Baku. It decided on an armed rising against the bourgeoisie. The insurgents asked Soviet Russia for armed aid. On instructions from the Soviet Government, Red Army roops were sent to the assistance of the working people of Azerbaijan. On April 28, 1920, Baku became a Soviet city. G. K. Ordzhonikidze, S. M. Kirov, A. I. Mikoyan and N. N. Narimanov, who implemented the Party's Leninist line, played a leading part in expelling the invaders and crushing the internal forces of counter-revolution, in establishing and consolidating the Soviet power in Azerbaijan. In November, 1920, the workers and peasants of Armenia rose up in arms. Three months later, in February, 1921, the working people of Georgia overthrew the Mensheviks. Transcaucasia became Soviet. The "campaign of 14 Powers" had failed.

Expressing the sentiment of the Soviet people, the poet Mayakovsky derided the ill-fated venture of the interventionists and Whites in the following caustic lines:

> *They came and fought like mad,*
> *They marched on Petrograd,*
> *They got their arms in plenty*
> *From kind old Aunt Entente. . . .*
> *Britons, Frenchmen, Poles,*
> *And brutes like von der Holz,*
> *Mamontov, Shkuro,*
> *They came from high and low.*
> *They came supplied with tanks,*
> *With dollars, pounds and francs,*
> *They came and thought they'd win,*
> *But got their heads bashed in.*

5. Ninth Party Congress. Defeat of the Armies of Landlord-Bourgeois Poland and of Wrangel. The End of Intervention and of the Civil War

By defeating the interventionists and the Whites the Soviet State had gained a temporary breathing-space. The Entente was compelled to call off the blockade. In January, 1920, the Supreme Council of the Entente found it necessary to allow the exchange of goods with Soviet Russia. The Bolshevik Party had succeeded in preventing the isolation of Russia. The conclusion of peace with the Baltic countries and the lifting of the blockade eased the economic situation of the Republic.

The Soviet State immediately set about rehabilitating the national economy, disrupted by the Entente campaigns.

The country's over-all economic situation at that time was very bad. Agriculture was supplying only half of its pre-war output. The railways and industries were short of fuel. Numerous factories had been destroyed. The dislocation of transport, in turn, aggravated the food situation, handicapping food deliveri⌐ to the industrial centres and the front.

The brief respite won enabled the Party to shift more manpow⌐ to economic construction and prepare for the victorious term⌐ nation of the Civil War. With the continuing danger of a ne⌐ armed attack by the imperialists, the Red Army could not ⌐ demobilised. The Party decided to draw part of the army uni⌐ into economic construction. Labour armies were formed in Ukrain⌐ the Urals, the North Caucasus, near Petrograd and in the Midd⌐ Volga region. During the Civil War, thousands of skilled work⌐ ers and Bolshevik organisers had been sent to the Red Army⌐ Now the Red Army began to return part of its manpower for th⌐ rehabilitation of transport, the fuel industry and other priorit⌐ sectors of the economic front. The Central Committee sent 5,00⌐ Communists to work in transport. Army Bolsheviks became organ⌐ isers of the struggle to restore the Donets coalfield and get the reg⌐ ular transportation of Grozny, Baku and Ural-Emba oil under way⌐ The military authorities undertook to supply food to the miner⌐ and oil-workers, and to restore the coal mines and oilfields.

Lenin saw the Soviet system as an inexhaustible source o⌐ strength both for military victories and for overcoming the dif⌐ ficulties of Socialist construction. At the beginning of 1920 h⌐ outlined a bold and strictly scientific plan for the electrification⌐ of Russia within 10 to 20 years.

"It must be provided now," wrote Lenin, "so as to be abl⌐ to present it to the masses in graphic, popular form and⌐ to carry them with us by a clear and vivid (and in principle⌐ perfectly *scientific*) prospect, saying to them: Let us get⌐ to work, and within the next 10 to 20 years we shall make⌐ all Russia, both industrial and agricultural, a country of⌐ *electricity*" (*Collected Works*, Vol. 35, p. 370).

In March, 1920, the Council of People's Commissars set up a⌐ State Commission for the Electrification of Russia (GOELRO)⌐ under G. M. Krzhyzhanovsky. The commission drew up a plan⌐ providing for the construction of 30 large power stations with⌐ a total capacity of 1,500,000 kw.

The prospects of Socialist construction during the new period⌐ of respite were outlined by the Ninth Party Congress, which met⌐ from March 29 to April 5, 1920. The delegates to the Congress⌐ represented more than 600,000 Party members. In the year⌐ which had passed since the Eighth Congress the Party had doubled⌐ its membership, despite the heavy losses sustained in the struggle⌐ against the interventionists and Whites. The growth of membership⌐ in the extremely difficult conditions of civil war was plain evi⌐ dence of the correctness of the Party's policy and of the strength⌐ of its ties with the working class and the masses in general.

The main items on the Congress agenda were the immediate tasks of economic development and the trade unions. Lenin dealt with both questions in the Central Committee report which he delivered. The Congress resolution "The Immediate Tasks of Economic Development" stressed that the basic condition for the country's economic revival was the steady implementation of a single economic plan based on the electrification of the country. The resolution specified the sequence in which the cardinal tasks of the plan should be carried out. They were: (a) first of all, an improvement in the condition of transport, and the delivery and creation of essential stocks of grain, fuel and raw materials; (b) production of machinery for transport, for the extraction of fuel and raw materials and for the production of grain; (c) the intensive development of engineering output for industries producing consumer goods, and (d) the intensive production of consumer goods. The Congress recommended drawing the entire industrial proletariat into production, carrying out mass-scale labour conscription, putting the economy on a military footing and making extensive use of army units on the economic front. Particular attention was devoted to the organisation of emulation. With regard to industrial management, the Congress pointed out the necessity of preserving and further developing centralisation and of encouraging one-man management. On the other hand, it recommended taking into account local features, setting up regional economic boards in the case of large districts far removed from the centre, and distinguished by specific economic conditions, and giving the masses a greater role in industrial management.

As intervention and the Civil War were not yet over, the Congress decision on economic construction was based on the policy of War Communism.

The Party's policy in economic development was opposed by the "Democratic Centralism" group of T. Sapronov, V. Osinsky and V. Smirnov. The "Democratic Centralists" declared against employing the old experts and against one-man industrial management, and advocated unrestricted collective management. The group thereby disputed the Party's basic organisational principle, democratic centralism. Its anti-Party position was supported at the Congress by Rykov and Tomsky, who in their turn opposed one-man management, recognising collective management as the sole principle of administration in industry, from the Supreme Council of National Economy down to the factory management. The Congress rejected these anti-Party ideas.

The Congress resolution on the trade unions stressed the necessity for the working people to take an active part in the economic development of the country. It obliged all Party organisations, with the aid of the trade unions, to carry the spirit of labour enthusiasm which had already begun to show itself into the widest mass of the working people.

In keeping with the decisions of the Ninth Congress, workers throughout the country set about rehabilitating the national economy. Labour discipline in industry improved. Transport began to function more efficiently. The name of the Moscow-Kazan Railway, where the idea of the *subbotnik* had been conceived, was inscribed on a Red Board of Honour. The prospect of transition to peaceful Socialist construction inspired the Soviet people to unprecedented creative effort. This found particularly vivid expression on May Day, 1920, a day which the Ninth Party Congress had set for an All-Russian *subbotnik*. About 500,000 working people came out on the *subbotnik* in Moscow, and nearly 200,000, in Petrograd. Communists were in the lead, and carried the masses with them by their labour heroism. Leaders of the Party and the Government took part in the *subbotnik*. Lenin worked in the Kremlin *subbotnik* and M. I. Kalinin at the Michelsohn Works. In response to the Party's call, tens of millions of working people at the All-Russian *subbotnik* showed their readiness to devote themselves to peaceful labour as selflessly as they had defended their Socialist country at the front.

But the imperialists broke the respite again, interrupting the progress of peaceful Socialist construction. Notwithstanding the failure of its campaigns against Soviet Russia, the Entente resolved to launch a new one, advancing bourgeois-landlord Poland as the chief anti-Soviet force.

Since the beginning of the war against the invaders and Whites, the Soviet Government had repeatedly offered to conclude peace with Poland. It renewed the offer in the early part of 1920. But the Polish imperialists were bent on seizing Soviet territory. The Polish bourgeoisie was completely dependent on the imperialist countries, both economically and politically. The position of the Polish landlords and bourgeoisie was precarious. The masses of the working people, especially the proletariat, rose against the ruling classes more and more frequently. The governing circles of Britain, France and the United States, as well as of Poland, were afraid of the growing revolutionary movement. They saw war against Soviet Russia as a means of diverting the people from revolution. The Communist Party of Poland resolutely opposed the Polish imperialists' war of aggression. It explained to the working people of Poland that war against the Soviet Republic amounted to war against themselves.

The Entente leaders and the rulers of Poland, moreover, regarded the peace proposals of the Soviet Government as a sign of weakness, and hoped to bring about the fall of Soviet power by means of war. On April 25, 1920, the Polish army attacked Soviet Russia and occupied Kiev. The imperialists sent Wrangel's White army, stationed in Crimea, to Poland's aid.

Once again the Soviet Republic was compelled to bend its energies to fight the invaders and Whites. On May 23, 1920, the Central Committee of the R.C.P.(B.) published its theses, "The Polish Front and Our Tasks." Calling on the workers and peasants to rally all their forces to defeat the enemy, the Party and the Soviet Government stressed that Soviet Russia had no designs on the independence and sovereignty of Poland, and that the Polish working people were the masters of their own destiny. "The defeat of the Polish whiteguards who have attacked us *will not in the least change our attitude to the independence of Poland*," the theses said.

The Red Army was reinforced with Communists. Almost half of the Party members, or upwards of 300,000 Communists, were in the army, which also included some 70,000 Komsomol members.

An offensive was started on the Western front in the middle of May. It was unsuccessful, because it had not been properly prepared. True, it tied down enemy forces, thereby easing the situation on the South-Western front. At the beginning of June the First Cavalry Army, which had been moved up from the south, broke through the front of the Polish Whites in Ukraine. Following the Cavalry Army, all the armies of the South-Western front took the offensive, pushing back the enemy. Early in July, 1920, the troops of the Western front also launched an offensive. By the end of July they had entered Polish territory, while the troops of the South-Western front had entered Western Ukraine. The front line drew near to Warsaw, the Polish capital.

The Red Army victories inspired the working class in the West. The "Hands Off Soviet Russia!" movement gathered momentum in Britain, France, the United States, Italy and Czechoslovakia. Workers refused to load arms for Poland, and called strikes.

After the First Congress of the Communist International the Communist movement made great progress all over the world. In May, 1919, the Bulgarian Workers' Social-Democratic Party (Tesnyaks) reorganised itself into a Communist Party.

By 1920 Communist Parties had been formed in the United States, Britain, Yugoslavia, Spain, Turkey and other countries. As a rule, they were founded on the basis of the Left groups that had broken away from Socialist parties. The newly-established parties had as yet no experience of work among the masses, and their activities were handicapped by a certain burden of Social-Democratic tradition and old forms of struggle. On the other hand, there arose within them "Left-wing" groups which rejected all the old methods of struggle employed by the working class, op-

posed the use of parliament and advocated boycotting those trad
unions that were in reactionary hands. Such a policy led to iso
lation from the masses, to sectarianism, to an underestimatior
of the role of the Party. These errors were camouflaged by Lef
phraseology, the "Lefts" trying to represent their tactics as being
revolutionary. These were the growing pains of young partie
that had not yet gone through the school of revolutionary struggle
Lenin described them as a "Left-wing infantile disorder" in Com
munism.

In July, 1920, the Second Congress of the Communist Inter
national was convened. Its fundamental task was to strength
en the Communist Parties ideologically and organisationall
and to direct them towards winning a majority among the masses
Before the Congress met, Lenin wrote his book *"Left-Wing*
Communism, an Infantile Disorder. The main purpose of th
book was to acquaint all Communist Parties with the rich ex
perience of the Russian Communists, with their strategy anc
tactics, in order that the brother parties might be equipped with
that experience. In this book Lenin, who had founded and reared
the Party, summed up the work done. He showed that the Bol
shevik Party had grown, gained strength and become steeled in
the struggle against the principal enemy in the working-class
movement, who remained, indeed, the principal enemy on an
international scale as well, namely, opportunism or Menshevism.
At the same time the Party had grown stronger in combating
petty-bourgeois revolutionism, opportunists "from the Left" and
the Socialist-Revolutionaries and Anarchists.

In his book Lenin explained why the Party, when it became
the governing party, had withstood all trials. The Party had
been able to cope with its titanic tasks thanks to the strictest,
truly iron discipline, to the fact that it was based on the granite
rockbed of revolutionary theory, to its close connection with the
working people, and to the complete and unreserved support it
received from the masses of the people, who had convinced themselves by their own experience of the correctness of the Bolshevik
ideas. In analysing the strategy and tactics which had enabled
the Party to win over the masses of the workers and a majority
of the people, Lenin laid special emphasis on the necessity for
the closest ties with the masses and for working among them
under all circumstances—in a period of revolution and at a time
of retreat, and in all public organisations—parliament, trade
unions, co-operatives, etc.,—that is, wherever the masses are to
be found. Lenin showed the harm caused to the working-class
movement by the absurd "theories" of the "Left," by their refusal to work in reactionary trade unions, in parliament and in
co-operatives. Non-participation of the Communist Parties in the

ork of those organisations led, he pointed out, to isolation from the masses, thereby rendering the greatest service to the bourgeoisie.

"One must be capable of every sacrifice," wrote Lenin, "of overcoming the greatest obstacles, in order to carry on agitation and propaganda systematically, stubbornly, persistently and patiently, precisely in those institutions, societies and unions—even the most ultra-reactionary—in which the proletarian or semi-proletarian mass is to be found" (*Collected Works*, Vol. 31, p. 35).

Lenin taught Communists to master all the forms of struggle. His book summed up the strategical and tactical experience gained by the Communist Party, both during the struggle for the dictatorship of the proletariat and when the dictatorship of the proletariat had been established and Socialist construction begun. Lenin showed that the Russian Marxists' rich experience was not only of national, but also of international significance.

"The Russian model," he wrote, "reveals to *all* countries something, and something very essential, of their inevitable and not distant future" (*ibid.*, pp. 5-6).

Lenin's brilliant book is of vast international significance. Its conclusions formed the basis of the decisions of the Second Congress of the Communist International, which was attended by delegations from 41 countries. The Congress, which heard Lenin's reports and speeches on the tasks of the Comintern, the role of the Communist Party and the conditions of affiliation to the Comintern, passed a resolution on the role of the Communist Party in the proletarian revolution, approved the statutes of the Comintern and adopted the 21 conditions of affiliation to it, based on the Leninist principles of building up a party of a new type.

The Second Congress of the Comintern called on the workers of all countries to defend revolutionary Russia. The revolutionary movement in Germany and throughout Central Europe gained ground. The Polish proletariat was becoming more active from day to day. A Provisional Polish Revolutionary Committee was formed in Bialystok which called on the working people to fight the landlords and capitalists.

The Polish imperialists' defeat brought about a decisive change in the international situation. The capitalist system in Poland and, indeed, the whole Versailles system which the Entente had set up in Europe after the world war, were on the verge of collapse. The Entente took all possible measures to save the bourgeois dictatorship in Poland. Britain and France threatened to begin hostilities against Soviet Russia. France sent enormous quantities of equipment and a large group of officers and instructors to Poland. Britain, seeking to sever Crimea from Russia an[d] create more favourable conditions for a counter-offensive by th[e] Polish gentry, demanded that the Soviet Government shoul[d] halt the offensive of the Soviet troops and conclude an armistic[e] with Wrangel. She offered to mediate in the conclusion of peac[e] between Soviet Russia and Poland.

With Entente aid, the command of the Polish White arm[y] mobilised its reserves and in mid-August, 1920, launched a cou[n]ter-offensive. The Soviet troops had to retreat. The advance o[n] Warsaw had failed.

The reverses on the Polish front in August were largely du[e] to the mistakes made by the Soviet Command. The Soviet offe[n]sive proceeding rapidly, the troops had no opportunity to conso[l]idate the positions they had won, reinforcements lagged behin[d] and munitions were not brought up. The hasty retreat of the Polis[h] Whites was mistaken for a defeat, whereas the enemy was simpl[y] seeking to save his manpower and materiel. "During our offe[n]sive, advancing too fast as we were, almost all the way to Warsa[w] we undoubtedly made a mistake . . . and that mistake was du[e] to our overrating the superiority of our forces," said Lenin (*Collec[t]ed Works*, Vol. 32, p. 149).

But the reverses were due not only to military miscalculation[s.] Part of the Polish workers and other working people had bee[n] deceived. The rulers of Poland had played on the Polish workin[g] people's hatred for tsarist Russia, which had enslaved Polan[d] and had represented the Red Army's liberation struggle as a foreig[n] invasion. The working people had failed to see through the deceit[.]

The Red Army reverses were also due to the fact that Sovie[t] Russia had to fight on two fronts—in the west and in the south[.] Economic dislocation and the disruption of transport also mad[e] themselves felt.

In September reserves were moved up, and the Soviet troop[s] began preparations for striking a blow at bourgeois-landlord Po[-]land. The Polish Government feared this blow, and in Octobe[r] agreed to conclude an armistice, which later became peace. De[-]spite the reverses at Warsaw, the Soviet Republic had gained a[n] important victory. The war had ended, to quote Lenin, "wit[h] a peace more advantageous to us than the one we offered Polan[d] in April" (*Collected Works*, Vol. 31, p. 457).

Nevertheless, the Polish reactionaries secured, with the back[-]ing of foreign imperialists, the annexation of the western re[-]gions of Soviet Ukraine and Soviet Byelorussia.

With the Polish war over, the Soviet Government was abl[e] to mass its forces against Wrangel, the last puppet of the Entente[.] The Party Central Committee addressed a message to all Part[y] organisations, directing them to mobilise Communists for th[e] front and enlist the trade unions and the workers in the struggle against the Whites. In accordance with the directives of the Central Committee and the Government, the Revolutionary Military Council of the Southern front, headed by M. V. Frunze, worked out plans for defeating Wrangel. Numerical superiority was achieved over Wrangel's troops. In response to the Party's call, Party and Komsomol organisations sent more than 10,000 of their members to the Southern front.

As a result of furious fighting, Wrangel was driven into Crimea. In November, 1920, the Red Army, after gallantly storming the Perekop Isthmus, swept into Crimea and cleared it of the enemy.

This was the end of foreign intervention and the Civil War in Russia. It is true that the last groups of invaders and Whites —in the Far East—were completely defeated only in 1922. But the principal forces of the enemy, against which Soviet Russia had had to exert enormous efforts, had been shattered and ignominiously expelled from Soviet soil.

The people had maintained their Soviet power and the independence of their country. The young Soviet State had won the duel with the imperialists of the whole world.

6. Why the Soviet State Was Victorious. Lessons of the Civil War

The chief reasons for the victory of the Red Army over the interventionists and White armies are the following:

1. Russia's workers and peasants, having freed themselves from landlord and capitalist rule, continued, in the Civil War, their struggle for the consolidation of their power and for the establishment of a Socialist society, free from the exploitation of man by man. The Civil War waged by the working people of Soviet Russia was a just war. The policy of the Soviet Government, in whose name the Red Army fought, was a correct policy expressing the interests of the people, and the latter supported it as being their own policy. The Red Army, an offspring of the people, was fighting for the interests of the people, whereas the Whites and the interventionists were fighting against the people. Consciousness of this inspired the masses of the people, though exhausted by four years of an imperialist world war and seemingly incapable of offering resistance, to rally enough strength to bring a civil war of unparalleled difficulty to a victorious conclusion.

2. The principal reason for the Soviet Republic's victory over the interventionists and the Whites was its social and political

system, founded on the stable alliance of the workers and peasants and on friendship among its peoples. The working class and the peasantry formed and consolidated their military and political alliance in the struggle against the landlords, the capitalists and the world bourgeoisie. The economic foundation of that alliance was the fact that the peasant received land and protection against the landlord and the kulak from the workers' State, while the workers received farm produce from the peasants under the surplus-requisitioning system.

The experience of the masses themselves, who had learned all the horrors of intervention and White rule, strengthened the alliance of the workers and peasants.

War puts all the forces of a country to the test. Imperialist wars aggravate class antagonisms which, as the experience of Russia and many other countries has shown, lead to revolution. The liberation war against the invaders and the Whites aroused the patriotic sentiments of the people, and resulted in the internal consolidation of the country. In heavy battles with the foreign invaders and the Whites, who were striving to stifle the revolution and crush the Soviet Republic, the workers and peasants became steeled, their alliance grew stronger and they rallied more closely round the Party. In this was revealed a characteristic and organic feature of the Soviet system: it does not divide the people, but unites them.

3. The correct nationalities policy pursued by the Soviet Government was one of the chief reasons for Soviet Russia's victory. That policy united the working people of the once oppressed nations of all Russia in the struggle against intervention and counter-revolution. Wherever they were victorious, the counter-revolutionaries at once restored the old regime of national oppression. The working people of the formerly oppressed nations learned by experience that the Soviet system was the only reliable guarantee of genuine freedom and national independence for the peoples. The alliance of the working people of various nationalities grew stronger as they fought shoulder to shoulder in the ranks of the Red Army during the Civil War.

4. The partisans operating in the enemy rear greatly helped the Red Army. Organised and led by the Communist Party, they harassed the enemy by disrupting his communications, destroying his manpower and military equipment and wrecking the administrative machinery of the invaders. They helped the Red Army by diverting considerable enemy forces.

5. Soviet foreign policy contributed to the victory of the Red Army. Under the direct guidance of the Central Committee, the Soviet Government consistently pursued a policy of equal rights for all peoples, big and small, made skilful use of the profound

ontradictions among the imperialist countries and of its enemies' miscalculations, and thereby strengthened the position of the proletarian State.

6. The victory of the Red Army was facilitated by the revolutionary struggle of the international proletariat against intervention. The working people of the capitalist countries stopped arms deliveries, and set up "Hands Off Russia!" committees, thus making operations more difficult for the interventionists and helping the working people of the Soviet Republic. Speaking of international solidarity, Lenin said:

"It was precisely this support, it was precisely the sympathy which the working masses—the masses both of workers and peasants, tillers of the soil—showed for us all over the world, even in the States that were most hostile to us, it was just this support and this sympathy that were the last and most decisive source, the decisive reason why all the invasions against us ended in defeat" (*Collected Works*, Vol. 33, p. 119).

7. The decisive condition that made the victory of the Soviet people and the Red Army possible was the leadership of the Communist Party, which was able to rouse, to rally and to organise the proletariat and the vast masses of the working peasantry for the struggle against their enemies.

The Red Army's imposing victories showed what a great force a people can become if it is headed by so experienced a party as the Bolshevik Party. It was the Central Committee of the Party, headed by Lenin, that guided the struggle. It decided all matters relating to the conduct of the war, the distribution of forces, supply and the working-out of strategic plans. The Party resolutely combated all counter-revolutionary machinations and safeguarded the alliance of the working class and the peasantry. While waging a ruthless struggle against all enemies and all counter-revolutionary tendencies, the Party followed a flexible policy with regard to the wavering intermediate, petty-bourgeois strata and parties, winning over to the side of the people all those who recognised Soviet power and were ready to defend it.

At the call of the Central Committee, Communists went into the army. The Party lost not less than 50,000 of its members, who gave their lives for the Revolution. This notwithstanding, its membership doubled during the war. Hundreds of thousands of the foremost workers and peasants joined the Party and went through the school of courageous battle. The Civil War steeled the old cadre of Party leaders, the comrades-in-arms and pupils of Lenin, organisers of the victory of the great Revolution. It also brought up new leaders, on whose shoulders fell the burden of eliminating the consequences of the war and building a Socialist society. Among them were A. A. Andreyev, A. S. Bubnov F. E. Dzerzhinsky, M. V. Frunze, S. I. Gusev, M. I. Kalinin N. S. Khrushchov, S. M. Kirov, S. V. Kosior, V. V. Kuibyshev L. Z. Mekhlis, A. I. Mikoyan, G. K. Orjonikidze, G. I. Petrovsky P. P. Postyshev, Y. A. Shchadenko, N. M. Shvernik, J. V. Stalin Y. M. Sverdlov, K. Y. Voroshilov, Y. M. Yaroslavsky, R. S. Zem lyachka and A. A. Zhdanov.

Everywhere—in the rear, at the front and underground—the Bolshevik Party was with the masses, and leading them; it di rected their titanic struggle, and ensured the Red Army's victory in the Civil War. This is how Lenin appraised the role which the Communist Party played in that war:

"It was only because of the Party's vigilance and its stric discipline, because the authority of the Party united all govern ment departments and institutions, because the slogans issued by the Central Committee were followed by tens, hundreds thousands and finally millions of people as one man, because incredible sacrifices were made, that the miracle could take place which actually did take place" (*Collected Works*, Vol 30, p. 416).

The defeat of the interventionists and the Whites was of tre mendous significance not only to the peoples of Soviet Russia who had maintained their independence and the gains of the Revolution, and could now proceed with their work of Socialist construction interrupted by the imperialists' armed invasion. The lessons of the Civil War in Russia were also of great international significance.

1. The failure of intervention and the outcome of the Civil War in Russia proved to the working people of the world that no forces whatever of internal counter-revolution can defeat a people's power, based on the alliance of the working class and the peasantry and led by the working class. Of course, no defeated class ever surrenders without putting up a fight, without trying all possibilities of resistance. Russia's landlords and bourgeoisie did their utmost to recover their lost power over the people, resorting to savage terror, sabotage, assassination, and bloody revolts. But they proved powerless against a people led by the Communist Party. The foreign imperialists' armed intervention raised the hopes of the defeated exploiting classes, who took up arms against the people and plunged the country into a long and strenuous war. The British, French, U. S., Japanese and German imperialists were to blame for the unparalleled suffering and untold sacrifices the working people of Soviet Russia had to go through.

2. The defeat of intervention in Russia showed all peoples, particularly the dependent and oppressed peoples, that world

imperialism could be defeated and smashed. The victories of the Red Army showed the peoples of the East that, no matter how weak they were and no matter how strong the imperialists with their advanced technique and well-trained armies, the struggle against them was not hopeless and the emancipation of the peoples was feasible. The experience of the Soviet Republic, which had withstood the onslaught of the most powerful countries of the world, inspired the enslaved peoples and stimulated the national liberation movement throughout the world.

3. The struggle against the foreign invaders and their White puppets revealed to the working people of all countries the international character of the Soviet power. The Soviets united all the peoples, all the nationalities of Russia. Fighting for their own interests, Russia's workers and peasants were also championing the interests of the working people of all countries. By fighting the interventionists, the working people of Soviet Russia were diverting the imperialist forces, weakening them, and thus helping the workers in the capitalist countries to fight more successfully against their own bourgeoisie. The world proletariat realised that the Soviet State was fighting for its interests as well: hence the struggle which the world proletariat waged against the interventionists was not only of assistance to the Soviet people, but also a revolutionary war against its own exploiters.

4. During the intervention and the Civil War, the issue of the advantages of Soviet democracy over bourgeois democracy was, to all practical intents and purposes, settled. The working people saw that no country had ever done so much for real freedom and genuine equality as the Soviet Republic, where complete freedom from the exploiting classes, the landlords and the bourgeoisie, had been achieved. Events in Russia brought out the genuinely popular democracy of the Soviet system. In all the capitalist countries, including the most democratic ones, war was attended by a curtailment of democratic liberties, violations or complete disregard of the Constitution, increased use of force against the masses, terrorism and the introduction of military servitude for the workers. The Civil War in Russia was accompanied by a tremendous increase in the activity of the masses who had risen for the fight, and by new sections of the working people being drawn into political activity. Three all-Russian congresses of Soviets, preceded by regular and numerous volost, uyezd and gubernia congresses, were held during the Civil War period alone. The Soviet Constitution was effective throughout this period. Of course, the Soviet State had to resort to force, and in such cases it acted resolutely and sternly, as the dictatorship of the proletariat should. But it used force only against its enemies,

against the accomplices of the interventionists and internal counter-revolution, against the agents and supporters of Kolchak, Denikin and Wrangel.

The defeat of the foreign imperialists and their White agents in Russia demonstrated to the working people of all countries that a people led by a militant, thoroughly revolutionary party is invincible.

"Nobody can ever vanquish a people," said Lenin, "most of whose workers and peasants have come to know, feel and see that they are defending their own Soviet power, the power of the working people, that they are defending a cause the triumph of which will enable them and their children to enjoy all the benefits of culture, all the creations of human labour" (*Collected Works*, Vol. 29, p. 292).

BRIEF SUMMARY

During the imperialists' armed intervention and the Civil War of 1918-1920 the Communist Party came forward as a faithful defender of the achievements of the working people, and the organiser of a patriotic war against the invaders and Russian Whites, who sought to abolish the rule of the people and restore the dictatorship of the bourgeoisie in Russia.

The bourgeoisie and the landlords overthrown in October, 1917, did not lay down their arms, and refused to submit to the authority of the people. Backed by the Socialist-Revolutionaries and Mensheviks, the Anarchists and the nationalists, the classes previously in power resorted to all methods—from subversion, bribery and wrecking to bloody terrorism—in order to overthrow the dictatorship of the proletariat. But they proved to be powerless against the people. Seeking to restore in Russia the rule and property rights of the bourgeoisie and landlords, the counter-revolution did not hesitate to invite foreign troops, to invite armed intervention, to dismember the country and sell its territory.

The foreign imperialists, alarmed by the breach in the imperialist chain effected in Russia, and fearing that the Russian revolution would kindle the flames of revolution in their own rear, attacked the Soviet State, sending their armed forces to Soviet Russia and giving their full support to the Russian counter-revolutionaries. Thus there came into being the united bloc of internal and foreign counter-revolution. For three years the interventionists and the Whites drenched Soviet Russia in blood, destroyed her industry, her towns and villages, and subjected the country to a hunger blockade; but they failed to break the resistance of the people.

The Party rallied the working people for a patriotic war against foreign invasion. It placed all the forces of the country at the service of the war. By its correct policy it strengthened the alliance of the working class and the peasantry, the union of all the peoples of Russia. It created a powerful Red Army, which was inspired by the knowledge that it was waging a just war. The Soviet State appeared before the whole of mankind as a champion of peace, freedom and independence.

Despite the difficult situation created by intervention and the Civil War, the Party adhered to the Leninist standards of Party life. Plenary sessions of the Central Committee and meetings, conferences and congresses were held at regular intervals. During the war years the Party convened two congresses, which dealt with such important matters as the adoption of a new programme, the drawing of wide masses of working people into the building of the Soviet State, the organisation of the armed forces, etc., and which generalised the experience of a party directing, for the first time in history, the building of a Socialist society, an experience that was of importance to the working class of all countries.

The people became convinced that the Communist Party was capable not only of rousing and organising the masses for the overthrow of the anti-popular rule of the bourgeoisie and landlords, but also of organising the defence of the country and the defeat in open battle of the combined forces of internal and foreign counter-revolution. The Socialist-Revolutionaries, Mensheviks, Anarchists and bourgeois nationalists exposed themselves not only as accomplices, but also as active partners of the counter-revolutionaries, as counter-revolutionary parties. The working people of the oppressed nations saw that in the Communist Party they had a real defender of the interests of the people, and in the dictatorship of the proletariat, the only guarantee of the free development of all nations. The proletariat and peasantry of all the peoples of Russia closed their ranks behind the Communist Party.

The heroic struggle of the Soviet people, which diverted considerable forces of the imperialists and weakened them, made it easier for the working people of the West to fight the capitalists of their own countries, and facilitated the national liberation movement of the oppressed peoples against imperialism. The struggle of the working people all over the world and the growth of the national liberation movement, in their turn, were of great help to the Soviet State.

Soviet Russia won the possibility for peaceful coexistence with the capitalist countries and secured the conditions for successful Socialist construction.

CHAPTER TEN

THE PARTY IN THE STRUGGLE TO REHABILITATE THE NATIONAL ECONOMY

(1921-1925)

1. The International and Internal Situation After the Civil War. The Discussion on the Trade Unions

After the interventionists and the Whites had been driven out of the country, the Communist Party and the Soviet people were confronted with the task of developing Socialist construction.

The transition to the peaceful building of Socialism was taking place in a complex international and internal situation. The world bourgeoisie, having lost the fight against the workers and peasants on the battlefields, continued to nurture the design of destroying the Soviet system, this time planning its economic strangulation.

But the realisation of the imperialists' designs encountered obstacles in the shape of the inter-State and class contradictions in the capitalist world. An economic crisis broke out in the capitalist countries in 1920. Factories closed their gates and workers were thrown on the streets. The army of totally or partially unemployed reached 40 million. The crisis accentuated the contradictions between Britain and France, Britain and the United States, the United States and Japan, Japan and Britain. Each of these imperialist Powers sought to emerge from the crisis at the expense of the others, above all at the expense of the Soviet Republic.

Class contradictions, too, became more acute. The world bourgeoisie launched an offensive against the gains won by the working class during the revolutionary upsurge of 1919 and 1920. The workers fought back. In April, 1921, the British miners went on strike against wage cuts. In the same year in Germany (Hamburg, the Mansfeld mining area and a number of cities in Central Germany) the workers rose in revolt, but the rising was crushed

y the bourgeoisie aided by the Social-Democrats. Fierce class
attles were also fought in other European countries.

The positions of the imperialists were weakened by the spread
f national liberation movements in the colonies and semi-
olonies—India, Iran, Turkey, Afghanistan, China and other
ountries.

Lenin characterised the international situation of the
R.S.F.S.R. as a certain equilibrium, which, although an extreme-
y precarious one, nevertheless enabled the Socialist Republic
o exist and develop, despite the hostile capitalist encirclement.

As regards relations with the Soviet State, two basic tendencies
existed among the ruling circles of the imperialist Powers. Some
were anxious to develop economic relations with the Soviet
Republics, though most of them did not relinquish hopes of
the degeneration of the Soviet State and of Russia, Ukraine, the
Caucasus and Central Asia being turned into colonies. Others
held that it was necessary to seize an opportune moment for
renewing armed intervention. According to the political situation in the different bourgeois countries, now one tendency, now
the other grew stronger. The danger of armed attack on the land
of Soviets had not been removed. "It must be remembered,"
said Lenin, "that we are always within a hair's breadth of invasion" (*Collected Works*, Vol. 33, p. 122). Consequently, he added,
to strengthen the Red Army and enhance its military might remained the task of the Party and the Soviet Government.

The country's internal situation was grave in the extreme.
Economically, the Soviet Republic was on the level of tsarist
Russia in the second half of the nineteenth century. This signified
that the rehabilitation and development of the Soviet economy
had to begin from a wretchedly low level. The imperialist and
civil wars and foreign military intervention had reduced the economy to a state of ruin. The interventionists and the Whites had
wrecked rail transport, flooded most of the mines in the Donets
coalfield, wrought havoc in the Baku oilfields and destroyed
many factories. In 1920 the output of large-scale industry was
barely one-seventh of the pre-war volume. The iron and steel
industry was in a particularly bad plight. A mere 116,000 tons
of pig-iron, or roughly 3 per cent of the pre-war output, was
smelted in 1920. The amount of coal brought to the surface was
three times less than before the war, oil output was almost 60 per
cent less, and the output of cotton fabrics had dropped twentyfold.
Shortages of fuel and raw materials had brought most enterprises
to a standstill. Production per head of population was less than
one kilogram (2.2 lbs) of pig-iron and less than one metre (39
inches) of cotton fabric. There was an acute shortage of essential
manufactured goods.

Agriculture, too, was in an extremely bad way. The output of agricultural produce in 1920 was down to 65 per cent of that of tsarist Russia. There was not enough bread and other staple foods. The workers in the industrial centres were starving. Many, seeking to escape hunger, were leaving the towns for the country side. Compared with 1913, the number of industrial workers in 1920 had dwindled by almost half. The working class began to scatter, part of it becoming declassed. This meant a weakening of the social basis of the dictatorship of the proletariat and threatened the very existence of Soviet power, because it is exceedingly difficult to run the State in a petty-bourgeois country with only a thin proletarian stratum. In the conditions of utter economic dislocation then prevailing, the danger from the petty-bourgeois element was particularly great. The petty-bourgeois element Lenin said, was more to be dreaded than all the Denikins, Kolchaks and Yudeniches put together. The exploiting classes of landlords and big capitalists had been abolished. Some two million landlords and capitalists, including the members of their families, had fled abroad, where many of them became imperialist agents. The hostile elements who had not been able to leave the country did their utmost to instigate the peasants against the workers, to undermine the alliance between them and to overthrow the dictatorship of the proletariat. Moreover, one exploiting class—the kulaks—remained in the country. Although its strength had been considerably reduced during the Civil War, this class constituted a great danger to the Soviets.

Early 1921 brought with it, in addition to the economic hardships, serious political difficulties. The surplus-requisitioning system gave rise to discontent among the peasants, for it deprived them of an incentive to produce more. The military-political form of the alliance of the working class and the peasantry that had taken shape during the Civil War and intervention turned out to be inadequate in peace time. The peasants, being small commodity producers, were not satisfied with the surplus-requisitioning system. They wanted freely to dispose of the products of their labour, to sell them on the market and to buy manufactured goods with the proceeds. Peasant discontent was seized upon by the rump of the counter-revolutionary parties—the Cadets, Socialist-Revolutionaries, Mensheviks, Anarchists, and bourgeois nationalists. Taking advantage of the difficulties arising from the country's transition from war to peaceful development, they engaged in feverish activity against the Soviets. In a number of places in the Tambov Gubernia, Ukraine, the Don area and Siberia, they succeeded in inciting peasant revolts.

At the beginning of March, 1921, a mutiny broke out at Kronstadt. The composition of the Kronstadt seamen had changed greatly during the Civil War. The cream of the older seamen had gone to the front to uphold Soviet power. Their place in the navy had been taken by recruits drawn from the countryside, politically quite raw and reflecting peasant discontent with the surplus-requisitioning system. The Socialist-Revolutionaries, Mensheviks, Anarchists and Whites, taking advantage of the weakening of the Party organisation in Kronstadt, conducted frantic agitation against the requisitioning of food surpluses.

After suffering defeat in the Civil War, the counter-revolutionary bourgeoisie did not dare to come out openly against the Soviets, and changed its tactics. The leaders of the Kronstadt mutiny, with a view to deceiving the masses, coined the slogan "Power to the Soviets, not to the parties!" By means of this slogan, the counter-revolutionaries aimed at inducing the people to smash the revolution and destroy the Soviet system. This aim had been formulated in a concealed way by the émigré Milyukov, one-time leader of the Cadet Party, in his slogan "Soviets without Communists!" The counter-revolution sought to remove the Communists from leadership of the Soviets, install a dictatorship of the bourgeoisie and restore the capitalist order in Russia.

The world bourgeoisie in its press hailed the Kronstadt mutiny as a "popular revolution," thereby masking its designs and its activities against the people. It dispatched its agents to Kronstadt, with instructions to turn it into the centre of an all-Russian uprising. It believed that the fortress of Kronstadt was impregnable for the armed forces of the Soviets.

But there were no impregnable fortresses for the Red Army. Neither the hurricane fire from the forts nor the losses sustained when crossing the thin ice were able to halt the advance of the valiant Soviet warriors. The example of valour and heroism was given by delegates of the Tenth Party Congress, headed by K.Y. Voroshilov, who took part in suppressing the revolt. The fortress was taken by storm on March 18, 1921, and the mutiny was crushed.

The events at Kronstadt, in Siberia and elsewhere testified unmistakably to a political crisis in the country. Lenin referred to the crisis in these terms: "We felt the impact of a grave—I think it was the gravest—internal political crisis in Soviet Russia, which caused discontent not only among a considerable section of the peasantry but also of the workers" (*Collected Works*, Vol. 33, p. 383).

Part of the workers, especially those connected with the countryside, gave way to the influence of the petty-bourgeois element. Driven by hunger, these workers voiced their dissatisfaction with the Soviet Government's economic policy, and in some factories even resorted to strikes. Realising how dangerous was the situation that had arisen in the country, Lenin began to devise ways for changing over from a policy which had suited the conditions of the Civil War to a new policy, which would enable the country to engage in peaceful Socialist construction.

The political crisis had repercussions in the Party, too. The gravity of the situation in the Republic at the end of 1920 gave rise to wavering among unstable Party members, including some leading functionaries. This became apparent chiefly on the issue of the role of the trade unions in building a Socialist society.

The trade unions were the medium through which the Party was to rouse the workers to heroic labour. In the Civil War years, however, the unions had been considerably weakened; and the Party was confronted with the task of strengthening them, of enhancing their role and prestige. The work of the unions had to be readjusted to peace-time conditions.

At the Fifth All-Russian Conference of Trade Unions held in November, 1920, the Party posed the question of abandoning military methods of work in the unions for the extension of democracy. Its proposals envisaged the election of the leading union bodies, instead of the practice of co-opting and appointing their members; regular general meetings of union members— which had practically been in abeyance during the war; and reporting back by elected bodies to the membership. Trotsky opposed any extension of workers' democracy in the unions. He wanted instead to introduce there the methods of issuing orders, methods of dictation, such as he had practised in the Union of Rail and Water Transport Workers, when he was leader of its Central Committee. He recognised only one way of enlivening the trade unions—an administrative "shaking up" of all their officials from top to bottom.

The question of the trade unions was, in effect, one of the approach to the masses, of the ways and means of enlisting them in the work of Socialist construction, of the methods of leading the masses. "The real difference" with Trotsky on the trade union question, Lenin said, was "on the methods of *approaching* the masses, of winning the masses, of *contact* with the masses. That is the heart of the matter" (*Collected Works*, Vol. 32, p. 5).

The trade union question was discussed by the Central Committee of the Party, and a commission of five members, of whom Trotsky was one, was appointed to go into the matter. The Central Committee decided that the differences among its members concerning the trade unions should not be made the subject of public discussion.

Trotsky, however, in violation of Party discipline, made the differences in the Central Committee public, and announced his lisagreement and that of his supporters with the line of the Central Committee. He stated that the forthcoming Tenth Party Congress would have to choose one of the two basic platforms—his or Lenin's—and challenged the Party to elect delegates to the Tenth Congress according to platform.

This statement by Trotsky marked the beginning of a factional struggle against the Party.

Trotsky's action in giving publicity to the differences in the Central Committee was condemned at a plenary meeting of the Central Committee in January, 1921. Although it held that the discussion would do harm, the Central Committee, with a view to cutting the ground from under Trotsky's feet, decided to go ahead with it and declared the election of delegates to the Tenth Party Congress according to platforms permissible. It was confident that its decision would help to expose Trotsky and other opportunists.

Thus Trotsky forced a discussion on the Party at an exceedingly critical moment in the life of the country, distracting the Party's forces from the solution of her economic problems.

In the course of the discussion other opposition platforms made their appearance—those of the "Workers' Opposition" group headed by Shlyapnikov, the group of "Democratic Centralists" headed by Sapronov, and the "Buffer" group headed by Bukharin.

The existence of groups and platforms within the Party was due to the influence exerted by the petty-bourgeois element on unstable Party members. By the end of 1920, the Party membership was more than half a million. Its social composition was not homogeneous: workers numbered less than half the total, peasants accounted for about a fourth, while the remainder consisted of professional and office workers and handicraftsmen. Many of the Party members had not yet been tempered as Bolsheviks. Moreover, the Party had been joined by some ex-Mensheviks, Socialist-Revolutionaries, Bundists and Borotbists,[6] who had declared their adoption of the Bolshevik standpoint. It was primarily they who were affected by petty-bourgeois vacillations. When counter-revolutionary revolts broke out in a number of places, these unstable Party members fell into a panic. Trotsky, for example, stated in connection with the Kronstadt mutiny that the end of Soviet power had set in, that "the cuckoo had sung its last note."

On the question of the role and activities of the trade unions, each opposition group advanced its own demands.

The watchword of the Trotskyists was that the unions be immediately "governmentalised." They demanded that the unions be turned into appendages of the State machinery, that they be fused with the State and that as organs of State they be vested with the function of managing production. That was what was meant by governmentalising the unions. The Trotsky platform meant taking away from the unions the function of protecting the material and cultural needs of the workers, and the function of training them in the spirit of Socialism. These, according to Trotsky, were matters for departments of the Soviet Government. Instead of persuasion, Trotsky advocated methods of sheer compulsion, of administrative injunction. He demanded the militarisation of the workers' labour, and the use of military methods in the unions and in industry.

Trotsky's platform, if adopted, would in fact have led to the abolition of the trade unions and would have undermined the dictatorship of the proletariat.

The "Workers' Opposition" demanded that the administration of the national economy be transferred to the unions—to an "all-Russian producers' congress." The group wanted the machinery of the Supreme Council of National Economy to be split up among the respective unions; it opposed the unions to the Soviet State and the Party. In contrast to the Trotskyists, who were all for governmentalising the unions, the "Workers' Opposition" wanted to "unionise" the State, that is, to subordinate the State to the trade unions and reduce the State to nought. This was tantamount to denying the leading role of the proletarian State in the national economy. The views of the "Workers' Opposition" were, in effect, anarcho-syndicalist, for, as against Marxism, anarcho-syndicalism denies the need for a proletarian State during the transition from capitalism to Communism. The anarcho-syndicalists are opponents of a party of the working class and of its leading role in building a Socialist society. They regard the trade unions as the sole organisations of the working class, which, so they claim, are capable of taking over power and of running industry, without the party and the State. The same ideas were at the bottom of the trade union platform of the "Workers' Opposition."

The "Democratic Centralists" advocated that the Presidium of the Supreme Council of National Economy should be nominated by the trade unions, that there should be freedom for factions and groups in the Party, and that candidates nominated by factions and groups should be elected to leading Party and government bodies. The "Democratic Centralists" opposed one-man management and strict discipline in the factories, and centralism in the machinery of administration. They shouted about the trade unions being in a bureaucratic death-grip. Lenin called this group the faction of "loudest shouters," and its platform a Socialist-Revolutionary-Menshevik one.

During the discussion, the Bukharin group put forward a "buffer" platform, so called because Bukharin tried to reconcile Trotskyism with Leninism, and sought to play the role of buffer in the clash between the two platforms—the Leninist platform, which was that of the Party, and the Trotskyist platform, which was that of an anti-Party group. Bukharin concocted his platform by borrowing some formulations from Lenin and some from Trotsky. The Bukharinites demanded that the trade unions should dominate their candidates for posts in the economic administration bodies, and that their nominees should be obligatory for the leading bodies of the Soviets. Lenin characterised this as a deviation towards syndicalism. The Bukharin platform, Lenin said, was "the acme of *ideological* depravity." In effect, Bukharin's 'buffer" platform was a defence of Trotskyism. It was, therefore, no accident that Bukharin soon abandoned his own platform and subscribed to that of Trotsky.

In the platform signed by Lenin, Rudzutak, Stalin and other Central Committee members ("Platform of the Ten"), the trade unions were regarded as a transmission belt from the Party to the masses, as a school of Communism.

Lenin pointed to the highly important role of the trade unions— the organisation of the ruling class embracing the broadest masses —in giving effect to the dictatorship of the proletariat. "But," he said, "they are not organisations of State, not bodies which exert compulsion, they are organisations of education, organisations which attract and train, they are schools, schools of administration, schools of management, schools of Communism" (*Collected Works*, Vol. 32, p. 2).

The trade unions provide a *link* between the Communist Party and the masses. The Party guides the non-Party mass of workers, it enlightens, trains, teaches and educates "first the workers and then the peasants" (*ibid.*, p. 29). By means of its educational work conducted through the trade unions, the Party ensures that every union member becomes conscious of the need to increase the productivity of his labour, and that the productivity of labour of the entire Soviet people is raised. Defining the tasks of the trade unions, Lenin said:

"Following its winning of political power, the principal and fundamental interest of the proletariat lies in increasing the output of products, in tremendously increasing the productive forces of society" (*Collected Works*, Vol. 33, p. 163).

The chief functions of the trade unions in building a Socialist economy are, in Lenin's view, their participation in the planning and economic agencies of the Soviet State, their fight to raise labour productivity and improve labour discipline, the training and promotion of administrators from the ranks of the workers and the working people in general. The activities of the union consist in promoting workers' democracy, fighting against bureau cracy and high-handed methods, educating the union member and encouraging their creative initiative. The unions look a ter the material and spiritual needs of the workers, and are source of personnel for the State apparatus and economic bodie Persuasion is their basic method, while compulsion plays bu a subsidiary role.

In the discussion, which became sharp and widespread, Lenin' view on the unions prevailed. Only in a few Party organisation did the platforms of the opposition groups secure a majority

At a time when the country was faced with enormous difficul ties, was under the increasing pressure of the petty-bourgeois ele ment, and was in a capitalist encirclement, the discussion, a Lenin pointed out, was an impermissible luxury. The enemie of the revolution banked on the inner-Party struggle, on a spli in the Party, and hoped that it would lead to the collapse of So viet power.

In order to govern the country—moreover an essentially petty bourgeois country—and to lead the masses, millions of them, i the work of Socialist construction, the indispensable and deci sive condition was *unity, solid cohesion of the Party, its ideologica staunchness, iron discipline in its ranks, intolerance of opportunis wavering and factions*. Consequently, it was necessary to put a end to the factions and groupings in the Party at all costs. Withou that, it would be impossible to overcome the political crisis i the country, successfully repulse renewed attacks by the imperial ists, and find the right way to build Socialism.

These issues were resolved by the Party's Tenth Congress.

2. Tenth Party Congress. The Transition to the New Economi Policy

The Tenth Congress took place on March 8 to 16, 1921, and was attended by delegates representing more than 700,000 Party members. The agenda consisted of the Central Committee's re port, the question of Party unity, the trade unions, the nationa question, the replacing of the surplus-requisitioning system by a tax in kind, etc.

Lenin delivered the reports on the Central Committee's polit ical work, the replacement of the surplus-requisitioning system by a tax in kind, Party unity and the anarcho-syndicalist devia tion.

The Congress examined the question of passing from Wai Communism to the New Economic Policy (NEP), a problem directly connected with that of the relations between the two principal classes—the working class and the peasantry. The essence of the matter was that, in building Socialism, the working class had *absolutely to go hand in hand with the working peasantry*, who constituted the overwhelming majority of the population. Whereas the landlords and capitalists could be expropriated and ousted, the small producers, which the working peasants were, "*c a n n o t   b e   d r i v e n   o u t*, or crushed; we *must live in harmony* with them; they can (and must) be remoulded and re-educated only by very prolonged, slow, cautious organisational work" (*Collected Works*, Vol. 31, p. 27). So Lenin taught. The working peasants should be helped at first to rehabilitate their farms and then gradually to make the change-over from fragmented petty individual farming to large-scale socialised machine agriculture, which ensures an abundance of products. This problem of Socialist construction, most difficult in itself, was a particularly difficult one in Russia because of the country's backwardness and economic dislocation. But it had to be solved at all costs, otherwise there could be no talk of building Socialism. In tackling it, the traditional ties between industry and agriculture were taken into account.

Over the centuries, the economic tie between town and country had been the exchange of farm produce for manufactures. The exchange had taken place on the market, with money as the medium in buying and selling. During the transition from capitalism to Socialism, when numerous forms of economy existed, the commercial link between State-owned industry and small-commodity peasant farming was an inevitable, objective necessity. It was the sole suitable form of economic contact between town and country. The Soviet Government began to employ this form immediately after the October Revolution. But the Civil War upset this form of contact; the food surplus-requisitioning system had to be substituted for buying and selling.

Lenin taught that the *supreme principle of the dictatorship of the proletariat is the alliance of the working class and the peasantry.* The discontent which had set in among the peasants with the continued requisitioning of food surpluses in peace time threatened to upset this alliance. In order to avoid this danger, it was necessary to conduct a policy that would stimulate the expansion of agriculture and the country's productive forces. Socialist construction could not be developed without first restoring the national economy. A beginning had to be made with agriculture, which, because of its very ruined condition, was unable to meet the needs of the industrial centres for grain and raw materials. And unless this was done, the rehabilitation and development of industry, especially heavy industry—the backbone of a Socialist economy—was out of the question. Thus, the restoration and development of agriculture was at this period the main link on which the entire chain of Socialist construction depended.

The question of the relations between the working class and the peasantry was examined in the political report of the Central Committee and in the report on the substitution of a tax in kind for the surplus-requisitioning system. In these reports, Lenin stressed that only by means of a *New Economic Policy*, which provided for the introduction of a tax in kind, would it be possible to enlist the millions of peasants in the work of building Socialism.

"The essence of the New Economic Policy," Lenin said later, "is the alliance of the proletariat and the peasantry, it is a union of the vanguard of the proletariat with the broad peasant masses" (*Collected Works*, Vol. 33, p. 145).

In the new conditions, this union could rest on an economic basis. The proletarian State, Lenin pointed out, should take not all, but only part of their surpluses from the peasants, in the form of a tax in kind. The remainder should be left at the peasant's disposal, to be sold freely on the market. This would serve as an incentive to the small cultivator. Personal interest in securing the largest possible surpluses for raising his standard of living would encourage the peasant to develop his farm, and this would lead to a rapid improvement in the country's agriculture as a whole. On the basis of this progress it would be possible to rehabilitate and develop State-owned industry, to strengthen the positions of Socialism in the economy of the country and to create the basis for the reconstruction of agriculture along Socialist lines.

But the tax in kind opened the way to free trade. And free trade signified a certain revival of capitalism, the growth of kulak farming, the opening of small private enterprises, and permission of private trade. In a word, free trade meant a life-and-death struggle between Socialism and capitalism.

Did the policy of permitting free trade contain a danger to Soviet power, to the destinies of Socialism? In a way, it did. But the danger was not a very grave one, because the commanding heights in the national economy—industry, the banks, rail and water transport, foreign trade and the land—were in the hands of the State. The growth of the kulak class was held in check by administrative measures from above. Private capital, which would revive during NEP, would be placed under State control, and its expansion permitted only within certain limits. Lenin suggested that private capital should be channelled in the direction of State capitalism.

As one of the forms of State capitalism, Lenin pointed to the possibility of leasing some enterprises as concessions to foreign capitalists for the purpose of securing a supply of manufactured goods. This would make it possible to accelerate the rehabilitation of the country's large-scale industry, primarily heavy industry. Operating under the control of the Soviet State, the State-capitalist enterprises would act as auxiliaries to Socialism. Consequently, there was nothing to fear from a certain revival of capitalism.

Lenin's report on the abolition of the surplus-requisitioning system and its replacement by a tax in kind was unanimously approved by the delegates to the Tenth Congress of the R.C.P.(B.). The Congress instructed the Government immediately to introduce this measure. The Congress also expressed the view that the tax in kind should be considerably smaller than the surplus-requisitioning levies.

The Congress adopted the directive that the poorest peasants should be exempted from some, and in exceptional cases from all, forms of the tax in kind, that privileges be granted to diligent farmers, and that trade in surplus products be permitted within the limits of the local market.

The New Economic Policy ensured a firm economic and political alliance between the working class and the peasantry in building Socialism.

The only correct policy for the Soviet State during the transition from capitalism to Socialism, the New Economic Policy was designed to consolidate the proletarian-peasant alliance, to reinforce the dictatorship of the proletariat, and to develop the country's productive forces in a Socialist direction; it was designed to permit capitalism within certain limits, while retaining the commanding heights of the national economy in the hands of the proletarian State; it envisaged a struggle between the Socialist and the capitalist elements, the triumph of the Socialist elements, the abolition of the exploiting classes, and the construction of Socialism in the U.S.S.R.

In the initial stages the New Economic Policy signified, compared with War Communism, a certain retreat. There are, however, two kinds of retreat. There are times when political parties or armies retreat because they have met with defeat. But there are other times when parties or armies retreat without having suffered defeat. In their victorious advance, they lose touch with their rear lines, a situation that may lead to the failure of the offensive. In such circumstances, the parties or armies fall back on their rear lines in order to establish better contact with them; for a time they pursue the tactics of retreat in order to launch a new offensive later and win the decisive victory. It was this kind of retreat that the Party carried out when it introduced the New Economic Policy.

Lenin said that during the Civil War years we had run too far ahead in our advance to Socialism, and that we were now threatened with losing touch with our rear, that is, with the peasantry. He drew an analogy between the methods of building Socialism during the Civil War and the storming of a fortress. In the period of War Communism, he said, we tried to take capitalism in town and country by storm, that is, "to pass to production and distribution on Socialist lines by the shortest, speediest and most direct way" (*Collected Works*, Vol. 33, p. 69). But experience showed that, for this transition to be successful, a long siege of the fortress of capitalism was necessary. "Not a direct frontal attack," said Lenin, "but the very hard, difficult and unpleasant task of a long siege . . ." (*ibid.*, p. 70).

Hence it was necessary to fall back for a time nearer to the rear lines, to regroup the forces and then launch a new and decisive offensive by the entire mass of working people against capitalism. Given this condition, that is, if the tie with the peasantry was maintained, the rate of the Soviet people's advance to Socialism will be such, said Lenin, as we could not even dream of at present.

The adoption of the New Economic Policy marked a *sharp turn* from the policy of War Communism. The Communists had quickly to find their bearings in the new situation, to adapt their methods of work to the conditions of NEP, to master new methods of management and to learn to trade efficiently. The difficulties of the task were enormous, because, in the underground and in the prisons, nobody had taught the Communists how to manage the economy or how to trade; none had experience in this field and there was no place in which to acquire it, because Socialism was being built for the first time in history. Lenin gave the warning that building Socialism was an incredibly difficult job. But the Party trained by Lenin was not daunted by the difficulties, and boldly began to implement the New Economic Policy, seeing it as the only right road to Socialism.

The adoption of the New Economic Policy by the Tenth Party Congress was an indication of the wisdom of the Communist Party, and of Lenin's brilliant perspicacity, based on a profound knowledge of the laws of social development. Lenin was the first Marxist to substantiate theoretically the economic policy of the proletarian State. The New Economic Policy drawn up by him was an elaboration of those propositions for laying the foundations for Socialist economy which he had set forth in the spring of 1918, in his work *The Immediate Tasks of the Soviet Government*. The experience of the subsequent years of Socialist construction in the U.S.S.R. fully bore out the correctness of Lenin's views and showed how great was his scientific, Marxist foresight.

The New Economic Policy is of international significance. Lenin said that wherever a proletarian revolution took place, socialism would be built by the working class jointly with the peasantry, and that measures characteristic of NEP would inevitably have to be carried out.

NEP was of international significance also in the sense that, by strengthening and developing the land of Soviets, the base and bulwark of the world revolutionary movement, it thereby exerted an influence on the international revolution, on the entire course of world history.

"Now," said Lenin, "we are exerting our influence on the international revolution mainly by our economic policy. . . . The struggle has been transferred to this sphere on a world scale. If we fulfil this task, we shall have won on an international scale for certain and for all time" (*Collected Works*, Vol. 32, p. 413).

The Tenth Congress also discussed the national question, which was of world-wide importance. The correct solution of this problem contributed to the successful building of Socialism in the Soviet Republic, and inspired the peoples of the colonial and dependent countries to fight for national liberation. The national question was part and parcel of the task of restoring the national economy, on the basis of NEP, along Socialist lines. It was, in essence, a peasant question, because the population of the country's non-Russian border regions consisted almost exclusively of peasants. Drawing the economically underdeveloped peoples into Socialist construction meant drawing in the peasants. The New Economic Policy was in keeping with the vital interests not only of the Russian peasantry, but also of the peasantry of all the other nationalities of the country. The latter, however, had their own specific features which called for a special approach. The lines of this approach were set forth by Stalin in his report to the Tenth Congress on the "Immediate Tasks of the Party in the National Question," and in the resolution adopted by the Congress. The problem was to establish proper relations between the working class of the former dominant nation and the peasantry of the former tsarist colonies, in order to combine the efforts of the working people of all the Soviet Republics in building Socialism. Tsarism had kept the peoples of its colonies, especially those of Central Asia and the Caucasus, in ignorance, had preserved their patriarchal-feudal relations and economic backwardness. The productive forces in these colonies were at an extremely low level.

The Communist Party set out to abolish the political, economic and cultural backwardness of the formerly oppressed peoples. The Tenth Congress resolved to raise the backward peoples to

the level of **development** of the advanced nations, *to put an en*
to their actual inequality. Juridical inequality had been abo
ished during the first days of Soviet rule. But the abolition o
actual inequality required considerable time and effort on th
part of the proletariat, and material help from the country'
advanced nations to the lagging brother peoples. To enable th
backward non-Russian border regions to catch up with Centra
Russia, the first thing, as pointed out in the Congress decision
was to establish industries in them, at the very sources of thei
raw materials.

With a view to abolishing the actual inequality of the back
ward peoples as speedily as possible, the Congress considered i
necessary to help them develop and consolidate their Sovie
statehood, their governmental and economic bodies, judiciary
press, schools, theatres, etc., using the native language, and t
accelerate the training of native skilled personnel.

The implementation of the Leninist policy on nationalitie
was hindered by two deviations—dominant-nation chauvinism
and local nationalism. The Congress called for a resolute struggl
against these, and in the first place against dominant-natio
chauvinism. This was the main danger, for it threatened to dis
rupt the unity and fraternity of the peoples that had come togeth
er under the banner of internationalism to fight for the Social
ist revolution.

The Tenth Congress of the R.C.P.(B.) devoted special attention
to Party unity.

The capitalist encirclement and the existence in the country
of a vast mass of petty bourgeoisie fostered the growth of opportu
nism and factionalism in the Party. The Trotskyists, "Workers
Opposition," "Democratic Centralists" and other opportunist
groups, by conducting a factional struggle and demanding freedom of factions and groups, were driving the Party towards a
split. They wanted to reduce the leading role of the Party in the
Soviet State to nought. The Party launched a resolute struggle
against opportunism and against the factional groups in its ranks.

Lenin called upon the Congress to put an end to factionalism
once and for all, to ban factions and groups in the Party. He
taught that unity of will, outlook and action, and iron discipline,
are a law of development for a Marxist party, which rules out
any sort of factionalism and violation of Party discipline.

"Only with such a will on the part of the proletarian
masses," said Lenin, "can the proletariat in a peasant country
carry out the gigantic tasks of its dictatorship and leadership"
(*Collected Works*, Vol. 32, p. 155).

The Congress adopted the resolution moved by Lenin on the
question of Party unity. It read:

"The Congress orders the immediate dissolution of all groups without exception, formed on the basis of a particular platform, and instructs all Party organisations to keep a strict watch to prevent any outbreaks of factionalism. Non-observance of this Congress decision shall entail unconditional and immediate expulsion from the Party" (*C.P.S.U. in Resolutions*, Part I, p. 529).

The Congress empowered the Central Committee to apply, also in relation to members of that body, in the event of their violating Party unity, forming factions or attempting to split the Party, expulsion from the Party as an extreme measure. "The condition for applying this extreme measure (to Central Committee members, alternate members of the C.C. and members of the Control Commission) shall be the holding of a plenary meeting of the Central Committee, to which all the alternate members of the C.C. and all the members of the Control Commission shall be invited" (*ibid.*, pp. 529-30), the measure of the penalty to be decided by a two-thirds vote.

The resolution written by Lenin and adopted by the Congress on the syndicalist and anarchist deviation in the Party expressed severe condemnation of the views of the "Workers' Opposition." These views represented a complete break with Marxism. The Congress pointed out that the views of the "Workers' Opposition" constituted a great political danger to the dictatorship of the proletariat, and described them as anti-Party, a reflection of petty-bourgeois vacillations, syndicalist and anarchist. In practice, stated the resolution, the ideas of the "Workers' Opposition" weakened the consistent leading role of the Communist Party and aided the class enemies of the proletarian revolution. The Congress declared advocacy of these ideas to be incompatible with membership of the R.C.P.(B.).

The decisions of the Tenth Congress on Party unity, and on the impermissibility of factions, became the *unshakable principle* of Party life and Party building. They equipped the Party for its fight against Trotskyism, against deviations on the national question, and all other opportunist deviations from the general line.

The Congress devoted much attention to the problems of Party building, which were closely allied to the unity of the Party and its leading role. Characteristic of Party work during the Civil War were extreme organisational centralism, curtailment of collective leadership, appointment instead of election to posts, and so on. With the coming of peace, the new tasks required a change in the organisational forms and methods of Party work. The Congress pointed to the need for enlivening and extending democracy in the Party, which meant that all leading bodies were

357

to be elected from top to bottom, were obliged to report on thei
work and were subject to control by the membership, and tha
collective leadership must be practised more widely.

The methods employed in Party work were to be those "of broa
discussion of all the most important issues, with complete freedon
of inner-Party criticism, and of the collective working out o
general Party decisions . . ." (*C.P.S.U. in Resolutions*, Part I
p. 520).

These decisions were binding on each member of the Party
and were to be carried out speedily and to the letter. This com
bination of democracy and centralism, freedom of expression and
iron discipline, unconditional fulfilment of collectively worked
out decisions, is the essence of the principle of democratic central
ism.

Seeing that during the years of Soviet power some petty-
hourgeois elements, including ex-Mensheviks and Socialist
Revolutionaries, had joined the Party, elements prone to wavering and ideologically unstable, and that careerists and self-seekers had wormed their way into its ranks, the Tenth Congress
instructed the Central Committee to purge the Party of the non-
Communist elements.

After summing up the discussion on the trade unions, the
Congress adopted Lenin's platform. It condemned the views
of the Trotskyists, "Workers' Opposition," "Democratic Centralists" and other opportunist groups, and defined the basic functions of the unions.

The trade unions, the Congress stressed, were *schools of Communism*, and their chief functions were those of economic organisation
and education. The unions were to devote themselves chiefly to
organising production and rebuilding the country's shattered productive forces. As Socialist construction developed, they would
gradually become auxiliary bodies of the proletarian State.

"The administrative bodies for industry," the Congress
resolution read, "beginning with the enterprise and ending
with the Supreme Council of National Economy, are formed
by agreement between the unions and the respective economic
bodies, on the basis of nominations made by the industrial unions and their associations" (*ibid.*, p. 542).

The function of the trade unions was to concern themselves
with all aspects of the daily life of the working-class masses, to
protect their interests. The unions' basic method of work was
persuasion.

The Congress pointed out that the methods of working-class
democracy, which had been greatly restricted during the Civil
War, should be restored first, and most extensively, in the trade
union movement. The structure of the unions should be based on

the principle of democratic centralism, and their work should be guided by the Communist Party.

These fundamental propositions are the guiding principles in the work of the trade unions throughout the period of the building of Socialism and Communism.

Many working-class members of the Party, the Congress noted, upon taking up jobs in the administration, or leaving for service in the Red Army, had lost direct contact with industry. Many Party members had been killed in action during the Civil War. In view of this, the Congress called for a vigorous recruitment of workers into the Party.

With a view to reinforcing Party unity and raising the Party's prestige, the Congress set up control commissions, whose function was to combat bureaucracy, careerism, abuse of their status in the Party or other bodies by Party members, and violation of comradely relations inside the Party. The Congress elected a Central Committee, headed by Lenin, and a Central Control Commission (C.C.C.).

The Tenth Congress was of historic significance. It charted the path for the transition from capitalism to Socialism, and the ways and means of building Socialism. It stressed with all seriousness the necessity of the worker-peasant alliance for the building of Socialism, and the *decisive role of the Party* in guiding the political, economic and cultural life of the country. It issued the directive to *preserve the unity of the Party as the apple of one's eye* and to wage a relentless struggle against factionalism. It pointed to the need for the closest contact between the Party and the non-Party masses, and specified the forms and methods of leading them.

In his notable work, *The Tax in Kind*, published in May, 1921, Lenin theoretically substantiated the New Economic Policy. The propositions elaborated in this work were a further contribution to the treasure-house of Marxist-Leninist thought.

The historic turn from War Communism to NEP, proclaimed by the Tenth Party Congress, was approved by the Third Congress of the Comintern, which took place in Moscow in June-July, 1921. By the time the Comintern Congress was convened, the number of Communist Parties had grown considerably. The period between the end of 1920 and mid-1921 had seen the founding of Communist Parties in France, Italy, Czechoslovakia, Rumania and other countries. July, 1921, witnessed the birth of the Communist Party of China, with Mao Tse-tung as one of the founders. The Comintern Congress, which was attended by delegates from the Communist and Socialist Parties of 52 countries, heard a report by Lenin on the tactics of the Russian Communist Party (Bolsheviks).

The Congress unanimously endorsed the policy and tactics of the R.C.P.(B.) and called upon the international proletariat to support the Socialist revolution in the land of Soviets.

The Congress noted the temporary lull in the revolutionary struggle in the capitalist countries that had set in, and pointed out that Social-Democracy, the social mainstay of the bourgeoisie, was helping to preserve capitalism and the rule of the bourgeoisie. The Congress put before the Communist Parties the cardinal problem of winning over a majority of the proletariat to their side. It proclaimed the slogan "To the masses!" and the tactics of creating a united working-class front. Unless the proletarian vanguard won over the masses to its side, there could be no question of overthrowing capitalist rule and establishing the dictatorship of the proletariat in any country.

3. First Gains of NEP. Eleventh Party Congress. The Foreign Policy of the Soviet State. Formation of the U.S.S.R.

The Party got down to the job of carrying out the New Economic Policy. Economic questions—the rehabilitation of agriculture, industry and transport, the revival of trade between town and country, and the normalisation of the credit and financial system—now became the focal questions in the work of the Party organisations.

The Party conducted a wide campaign to explain the New Economic Policy, and reorganised its ranks in line with the new tasks. The Central Committee and the Soviet Government headed by Lenin devoted daily attention to the problems of economic rehabilitation and the normalisation of the country's economic life. Many members and alternate members of the Central Committee, and other prominent Party leaders, were directed into the decisive sectors of Party, State and economic work. Felix Dzerzhinsky, while retaining his post as Chairman of the All-Russian Extraordinary Commission-Joint State Political Administration, was appointed People's Commissar for Railways, and later Chairman of the Supreme Council of National Economy. From 1921 to 1926, G. K. Orjonikidze functioned as Secretary of the Territorial Party Committee in Transcaucasia, where he supervised the economic rehabilitation of the Transcaucasian Soviet Republics. From the summer of 1921 onwards, S. M. Kirov worked as Secretary of the Central Committee of the Communist Party of Azerbaijan, where, under his leadership, the economy of the Republic, particularly the oil industry, was being rebuilt. V. V. Kuibyshev was sent into the Supreme Council of National Economy, where he combined the functions of member of the Presidium of that body and head of the Central Power Administration. Later he became Chairman of the Supreme Council of National Economy. L. B. Krassin was appointed People's Commissar for Foreign Trade. V. Y. Chubar worked as Chairman of the Presidium of the Supreme Council of National Economy of the Ukrainian Soviet Socialist Republic and afterwards as head of the Donets coal industry, to the restoration of which Lenin attached great importance.

Thousands of Party members were transferred from the Red Army to economic work. Many commissars, commanders and political workers became factory managers, executives in the State trading organisations, co-operatives, etc.

The Central Committee paid great attention to strengthening the Party groups in the factories. Many Communists were transferred there from posts in Soviet offices with a view to improving the Party's political work among the masses. Communists were sent from economically less important enterprises to those of greater importance. The Party groups were the combat units, as it were, of the Party and exerted an all-round influence on the work of the enterprises; they effected control from below, without, however, interfering with the orders of the management. Their task was to rally the effort of the non-Party workers for the fulfilment of production assignments and for the raising of labour productivity.

In fulfilment of the decision of the Tenth Congress, the Party carried out a cleansing of its ranks. This was done at open Party meetings, at which non-Party factory and office workers and peasants helped in exposing alien, demoralised and careerist elements and in ousting them from the Party. Almost a quarter of the membership was expelled. The result was a considerable improvement in the Party's composition. Discipline was heightened, and the unity and cohesion of the Party were strengthened. The Party's prestige grew, and the confidence of the non-Party masses in it increased. The Party began to lead Socialist construction on the basis of NEP more efficiently.

The Party's measures yielded positive results. The New Economic Policy had an increasingly beneficial effect on the country's economy. The working peasants welcomed the replacement of the surplus-requisitioning system by the tax in kind, and in the spring of 1921 increased their crop area. They actively helped the Red Army in suppressing the kulak uprisings and the political banditry which occurred in some parts of the country. The conditions of the working class improved, and the process of its declassing was arrested. Skilled workers were returning to the factories. Large-scale industry began to revive, and the economy gradually rose from the ruins.

The economic gains of the first year of NEP would have been still greater had it not been for the unprecedented famine which fell upon the country. The root causes of the famine lay in the economic backwardness of the country, especially of agriculture, and in the ruin wrought in the national economy by the interventionists and the Whites. The food shortage was greatly aggravated by the drought which took place in 1920, and which was followed by an even more severe drought in 1921. Thirty-four gubernias, with a population of some 30 million people, were affected by the crop failure.

The Party and the Government took emergency measures to combat the famine. And, grave though the difficulties were, they coped with this very great disaster.

The results of the first year of peaceful Socialist construction under NEP were summed up by the Eleventh Congress of the R.C.P.(B.), which sat from March 27 to April 2, 1922. The Congress, at which more than half a million Party members were represented, discussed the political report submitted by the Central Committee, organisational matters, the results of the Party cleansing, the question of strengthening the Party, and other items.

In the political report of the Central Committee, summing up the results of the first year of NEP, Lenin said that the retreat had ended and the aim had been achieved, that the tie-up with peasant economy was being established, the alliance of the proletariat and the peasantry had grown stronger, and the economic achievements were obvious. The Party was now confronted with a new task—*to regroup its forces for an offensive against the capitalist elements.*

NEP signified a bitter struggle between capitalism and Socialism. The question was: "Who will beat whom?" Would Socialism emerge the victor from this mortal combat, or would capitalism regain its lost positions?

In order to triumph over capitalism, Lenin said, it was necessary to learn the art of management. The past year had shown that the Communists had not yet learnt this art. Lenin called upon the Party members to prove to the people that they could run the economy not worse, but better than the capitalists.

The main problem that confronted the Party at this time was trade. The tie-up of Socialist economy with peasant economy assumed the form of trade. But private capital occupied very strong positions in trade, and possessed, moreover, considerable experience in this sphere. The struggle on the market against private capital was a particularly hard one for the Communists. Trade was an art they had not yet mastered. They had not brought the machinery of trade under their control. Many of them did not appreciate the importance of trade, and tended to treat it with contempt. "Learn to trade" was the slogan put forward by Lenin. The task now, he said, is "to gain the upper hand in competition with the ordinary shop assistant, the ordinary capitalist, the merchant . . ." (*Collected Works*, Vol. 33, p. 246).

In order to be able to manage, to govern the State, to trade efficiently, to oust private capital, and to build Socialism, it was essential to select and place personnel properly. The *heart of the matter*, Lenin said, *lay in people, in selecting personnel and in verifying fulfilment of decisions.*

The policy of the Party and the Government was carried out by people, by competent personnel. Success in any sphere of activity largely depended on the correct placing of experienced, tested and loyal workers. But these workers need supervision and help. The personnel should be verified systematically according to the results of their work; they must be helped, transferred in good time and even removed in the event of their falling down on the job. The selection and placing of personnel and verification of the fulfilment of assignments became focal points of the work of the Party and the Soviet State.

The Eleventh Congress paid considerable attention to strengthening the ranks of the Party. As leader and guide of the masses in solving the titanic problems involved in building Socialism, the Party was in duty bound particularly to see to it that its composition answered to the high demands made on the vanguard of the working class. With a view to reinforcing the proletarian core of the Party and making it more difficult for non-proletarian elements to enter its ranks, the Congress established three categories for new members: 1) workers, and Red Army men of working-class or peasant origin; 2) peasants (excluding Red Army men) and handicraftsmen not exploiting the labour of others; 3) others (office workers, etc.). Special procedure and conditions for membership were established for each category; admittance into the Party was facilitated for the first category but made more difficult for the third.

The Congress was particularly strict towards all manifestations of factionalism. The leaders of the "Workers' Opposition," headed by Shlyapnikov, had ignored the decision of the Tenth Congress, which stipulated the dissolution of factions. They gathered in secret and through conspiratorial channels circulated their decisions aimed against the Party. The Congress sharply condemned the factional activity of this group and warned Shlyapnikov, Medvedev and Kollontai that if they continued their anti-Party activity, they would be expelled. By adopting this decision, the Party re-emphasised that it sacredly guarded its unity and its iron discipline and would in no circumstances tolerate factional groups in its ranks.

The Eleventh Congress was the last Party Congress attended and guided by Lenin. In his closing speech, Lenin said that the Party, thanks to the flexibility of its mind and to its tactics, had raised our revolution to unprecedented heights. He uttered the prophetic words:

"No power on earth, no matter how much evil, hardship and suffering it may yet cause to millions and hundreds of millions of people, can take back the major gains of our revolution, for these are no longer 'our' gains, but world-historic gains" (*Collected Works*, Vol. 33, p. 290).

At the first meeting of the Central Committee elected by the Congress, J. V. Stalin was elected General Secretary.

At this period the Party's work of ideological tempering of its membership and the masses, educating them in the spirit of the Marxist world outlook, had acquired particular importance. The world bourgeois press was waging an ideological offensive against Bolshevism. Inside the country, the Cadets, Socialist-Revolutionaries, Mensheviks and bourgeois nationalists had renewed their activity, taking advantage of NEP. Striving to spread bourgeois ideology among the working people, they engaged in a whispering campaign about the inevitability of a return to capitalism, saying that the question "Who will beat whom?" would be decided in favour of the Nepmen,[7] and that Soviet power would degenerate into bourgeois democracy.

The bourgeoisie who had fled abroad also had big hopes of a degeneration of the Soviet system. What was known as the "Smena Vekh" (Change of Landmarks) trend had the support of part of the émigrés. The name "Smena Vekh" derived from the symposium published under this title in Prague in 1921 by a group of White émigrés, and from the journal of that name which was started by White émigrés in Paris, also in 1921. The Smena Vekh group advocated co-operation with the Soviets, in the hope that the development of the national economy in NEP conditions would take the capitalist road.

As the Smena Vekh trend included a group of émigrés who sincerely wanted to co-operate with the Soviets, the Party called for a positive attitude towards it, and for using the services of those bourgeois specialists who belonged to it. But with regard to those of the Smena Vekh group who co-operated with the Soviets solely for the purpose of covering up their counter-revolutionary activity, the Party called for repressive measures.

The Party exposed the inventions of the bourgeoisie and its agents about the Soviet system degenerating, and explained to the masses that there could be no question of a return to capitalism, and that the Party would lead the Soviet people through NEP to Socialism. The Party inculcated in the minds of the people the proletarian, Marxist ideology, the Marxist world outlook, which alone gives the right interpretation of the laws of social development and shows the way to remaking capitalist into Socialist society.

Lenin's article "On the Significance of Militant Materialism," published in March, 1922, in the journal *Pod Znamenem Marxizma* (*Under the Banner of Marxism*), played a big part in the Marxist upbringing of the Party's cadres and in mobilising them for an uncompromising struggle against bourgeois ideology. Lenin called upon the Communists to propagate Marxist ideology, Marxist materialism, among all sections of the population, and to expose idealism and clerical obscurantism.

It was the duty of Communists, Lenin pointed out, to work in close collaboration with consistent materialists, with representatives of present-day natural sciences who did not belong to the Communist Party. Together with them, and guiding them, the Communists should spread the materialist world outlook among the masses. Lenin called upon all Communists and consistent materialists to spread knowledge of the natural sciences among the masses, to conduct broad atheist propaganda among them on this basis, and help them overcome their religious prejudices. He directed the attention of Soviet natural scientists to the necessity of mastering Marxist dialectical materialism.

"It must be realised," Lenin wrote, "that unless it stands on a solid philosophical ground no natural science and no materialism can hold its own in the struggle against the onslaught of bourgeois ideas and the restoration of the bourgeois world outlook. In order to hold his own in this struggle and carry it to a victorious finish, the natural scientist must be a modern materialist, a conscious adherent of the materialism represented by Marx, i. e., he must be a dialectical materialist" (*Collected Works*, Vol. 33, p. 207).

Lenin warned the Communists against sectarian narrowness, and insisted on utilising all the forces of the old society loyal to the Soviet power for the purpose of building Socialism. To think that Communism can be built by the hands of Communists alone was one of the biggest and most dangerous mistakes. Without an alliance with the non-Party people working in various spheres, he wrote, there could be no question of successful Communist construction.

Lenin called the attention of Communists to the extreme importance of systematically exposing bourgeois "contemporary democracy," especially that of the United States of America. All kinds of "Socialists" worshipped at the shrine of this "democracy," "bowing and scraping" as they lauded it. In reality, this vaunted "democracy" was "nothing but the freedom to preach that which is to the advantage of the bourgeoisie to preach, namely, the most reactionary ideas, religion, obscurantism, defence of the exploiters, etc." (*Collected Works*, Vol. 33, p. 206).

Guided by Lenin's directives and enlisting in the work of building Socialism not only the workers and peasants, but also bourgeois intellectuals, the Party successfully tackled the economic rehabilitation of the country. By the end of 1922 the living conditions of the workers and peasants had improved. Politically, the country was in a stronger position. All the more or less major forces of kulak banditry had been smashed. In the autumn of 1922 the Red Army cleared the Japanese interventionists out of the Far East. On the international arena, the political prestige of the land of Soviets had risen considerably.

Peace was essential for the success of Socialist construction. "Peace and every opportunity to devote all our energies to economic rehabilitation," Lenin said, "is what we hold dearest of all" (*Collected Works*, Vol. 32, p. 94). Taking as its starting-point Lenin's idea of the peaceful coexistence of the two systems—Socialism and capitalism—the Party sought to normalise relations with the capitalist countries. In 1921 the Soviet Government signed a trade agreement with Great Britain, and afterwards with several other countries. In 1921 the All-Russian Central Executive Committee approached the United States, too, with a proposal to establish trade relations. But the U. S. Government, persisting in its interventionist attitude, turned down the proposal. French ruling circles likewise sabotaged the development of trade with Soviet Russia.

In the autumn of 1921 the Soviet Government, with a view to facilitating economic co-operation with the capitalist countries, declared its readiness to recognise the pre-war debts of the tsarist government on certain conditions, and suggested the convening of an international conference to examine the claims of foreign countries against Russia and the Soviet counter-claims, and to draw up a final peace treaty between Russia and her adversaries.

In view of the acute shrinking of markets caused by the economic crisis, the Entente Powers decided to convene, in the Italian city of Genoa, an economic and financial conference of all European States, including Soviet Russia and vanquished Germany, ostensibly for the purpose of "facilitating the economic rehabilitation of Europe."

The conference was held in April and May, 1922. Lenin was appointed head of the Soviet delegation. The workers, however, fearing an attempt on his life, protested against his going abroad. Lenin guided the work of the delegation from Moscow. The functions of head of the delegation to the Genoa Conference were fulfilled by G. V. Chicherin, People's Commissar for Foreign Affairs. Carrying out Lenin's directives, the Soviet delegation publicly roclaimed the necessity of peaceful coexistence of countries with differing social systems. The Soviet Government was anxious to establish broad economic co-operation with the capitalist countries and to ensure lasting peace. The Soviet delegation expressed its willingness to make certain concessions to the capitalist countries. As a condition, however, for recognising the pre-war debts of the tsarist government, it required that Russia be granted a new loan and that de jure recognition be extended to the Soviet Government. The delegation announced the Soviet Government's readiness to grant foreign property-owners definite compensation for their losses in Russia. At the same time, it advanced counter-claims for compensation for the damage caused to the country by the interventionist troops and the Russian Whites who had been supported by the Entente.

But the imperialists had their own plans. They had no desire to co-operate with Soviet Russia on an equal footing, and sought to impose a colonial regime on her by means of economic and diplomatic pressure. They demanded the repayment of all debts and the return of all nationalised property to its former foreign owners. Their brazenness was such that they wanted to establish foreign control over Soviet finances and even over the entire national economy of Russia. The Soviet delegation flatly rejected these claims and exposed their predatory character.

Sharp contradictions became apparent at the conference among the imperialist Powers, chiefly between the victor countries in the first world war and vanquished Germany. In vain did Germany seek from the Entente an easing of the intolerable reparations burden imposed on her by the Versailles Treaty. Soviet Russia, alone among the Powers, denounced this rapacious treaty, and called for the easing of Germany's burden. The more far-sighted members of Germany's ruling circles reached the conclusion that rapprochement with Soviet Russia would strengthen the international position of Germany, help her to gain some concessions from the Entente and, at the same time, open up broad opportunities for trade with Russia.

The Soviet Government, in turn, was interested in preventing the isolation of the Soviet Republics. Thus the possibility of a mutual rapprochement was created. In April, 1922, in Rapallo, a suburb of Genoa, a Soviet-German treaty was signed. Diplomatic relations between the two countries were resumed. Soviet Russia and Germany relinquished all claims against each other—the reparations accruing to Russia under the Versailles Treaty, payments on account of the old debts and compensation for nationalised property.

By signing the Treaty of Rapallo, the Soviet Government made a breach in the front of the imperialist Powers. It skilfully utilised imperialist contradictions in the interests of peace and the security of Soviet Russia.

No agreement was reached with the Entente Powers at Genoa. The talks were continued at the Hague Conference in the summer of 1922, but these too were barren of results.

The Party and the Soviet Government made use of the Genoa Conference to initiate a struggle for disarmament. The Soviet Government suggested that the Genoa Conference should discuss the question of a universal reduction of armaments and the banning of the more barbarous means of warfare—"poison gases, aerial warfare, and others." The imperialist Powers refused to discuss this proposal. The Soviet disarmament proposals opened the eyes of the masses in all countries to the fact that now, for the first time in history, there had appeared a government that sincerely and consistently strove for disarmament.

The Party and the Soviet Government made every effort to establish close contact with the oppressed and dependent nations. In 1921 Soviet Russia signed treaties with Iran, Afghanistan and Turkey, and rendered considerable help to these countries in their struggle for national liberation. Those were the first equal treaties to be signed between countries of the East and a Great Power. The Soviet Government relinquished without compensation all the imperialist privileges and concessions that tsarist Russia enjoyed in these countries.

In 1921 the people of Mongolia, led by the Mongolian People's Revolutionary Party which had been founded in March of that year, and aided by Soviet troops, drove the Whites—agents of the Japanese—out of their country and formed a people's government. Ever since, firm friendship has prevailed between the Soviet and Mongolian peoples.

The year 1922 saw the end of the war between Turkey—battling for her independence—and Greece, behind which stood the British imperialists. Victory was won by Turkey. For the purpose of drawing up the terms of peace, an international conference was convened at Lausanne. The imperialist Powers invited Soviet Russia to take part in discussing only one question, that of the Straits. The Soviet Government defended Turkey's sovereignty over the Straits and demanded unconditional closure of the Straits to all naval craft except Turkish, and complete freedom of mercantile navigation. The imperialists refused permission to the representatives of the Soviet Republic to take part in the discussion of other issues, because they feared that the anti-imperialist stand of the Soviet State, friendly to the nations of the East, would further the development of the national liberation movement in the oppressed countries. Notwithstanding protests by the R.S.F.S.R., the conference adopted decisions whereby the Straits and the Black Sea would be open to the warships of all countries. In this way, the imperialists retained access for their armed forces to the southern borders of Soviet Russia. The decisions of the Lausanne Conference were yet another reminder to the working people of the Soviet Republics of the danger of war from the capitalist countries and of the necessity of always keeping their powder dry.

Constant reminders of this were also the numerous hostile sallies of the imperialist States against the land of Soviets. For example, in 1923, the British Government presented an ultimatum to the Soviet Government, which became known as the "Curzon Ultimatum," after the name of the British Foreign Minister. This ultimatum demanded, among other things, that the Soviet representatives be recalled from Iran and Afghanistan. The Soviet Government, with a view to preserving peace, proposed convening an Anglo-Soviet conference to settle the controversial issues, but it categorically rejected the main demand of the ultimatum—to recall its representatives from the countries named. Following this vigorous rebuff, the British Government retreated. The policy of force in relation to the Soviet State had suffered yet another failure.

Thanks to the firmness, Bolshevik vigilance and wise peace policy of the Party, the Soviet people succeeded in warding off a major war for a period of twenty years—up to 1941.

The task of safeguarding the country's sovereignty, of recovering from the economic devastation, and of building Socialism, insistently called for the closest integration of the economic, political and military resources of the Soviet Republics and of their diplomatic activities.

The need for uniting to form a single entity was appreciated by the working people of all the Soviet national republics. United by the common struggle to establish and consolidate the dictatorship of the proletariat, by joint labour in building Socialism, the Soviet peoples were anxious for State unification as well, for the purpose of upholding the gains of the October Revolution and advancing to Socialism with the greatest speed.

These aspirations were expressed by the Party. The question of unification and the forms it should take was worked out and discussed by the Central Committee.

A plenary meeting of the Central Committee, held in October, 1922, adopted Lenin's proposal for a voluntary, equal union of the Soviet Republics, including the R.S.F.S.R., in a new State formation—the U.S.S.R. Its decision read:

"To recognise the necessity of the conclusion of a treaty between Ukraine, Byelorussia, the Federation of Transcaucasian Republics and the R.S.F.S.R. providing for their unification in a 'Union of Socialist Soviet Republics,' each retaining the right to free secession from the 'Union'."

In October-December, 1922, plenary meetings of the Central Committees of the Communist Parties of Ukraine, Byelorussia, Azerbaijan, Georgia and Armenia declared for the unification of the Soviet Republics in a Union of Soviet Socialist Republics. After these decisions the movement for unification assumed a country-wide scale. The sentiment of the peoples was reflected in the congresses of Soviets of the national republics, including the Tenth Congress of Soviets of the R.S.F.S.R. which took place in December, 1922, and unanimously called for the formation of the U.S.S.R.

The First Congress of Soviets of the Union of Soviet Socialist Republics opened in Moscow on December 30, 1922. It adopted a declaration on the formation of the U.S.S.R., and a Treaty of Union. It elected a supreme legislative body—the Central Executive Committee of the U.S.S.R. M. I. Kalinin was elected Chairman of the Central Executive Committee and V. I. Lenin, Chairman of the Council of People's Commissars of the U.S.S.R.

Thus, under the leadership of the Party, headed by Lenin, a multi-national Soviet Socialist State was created. It was formed on a voluntary basis, with each Soviet constituent republic preserving its national sovereignty.

The formation of the U.S.S.R. was a *triumph for the ideas of Leninism, for the Leninist nationalities policy* of the Communist Party. This development showed to all progressive mankind the way to solve the national question, to abolish the inequality of nations and peoples, the way to unite the peoples into a single fraternal family for the building of Communism.

The first Constitution of the Union of Soviet Socialist Republics was adopted at the Second Congress of Soviets of the U.S.S.R., in 1924.

The Fourth Congress of the Comintern, at which the Communist Parties of 58 countries were represented, was held in November-December, 1922. Lenin delivered a report to the Congress on the subject: "Five Years of the Russian Revolution and the Prospects of the World Revolution." The chief result of these years was the consolidation of the position of Socialism. Had the New Economic Policy helped in this? That, Lenin said, was the principal question, and it was of first-rate importance for all the Communist Parties; for if the reply were in the negative, "we would all be doomed" (*Collected Works*, Vol. 33, p. 384). But the eighteen months' work of the Soviet State on the basis of NEP had proved the absolute correctness of the Party's decision to pass from War Communism to the New Economic Policy.

Lenin's speech at the Fourth Congress of the Comintern was his last address to a congress of that body. In content his report was kind of testament to all the brother Communist Parties—to learn from the experience of the Russian Communist Party how to fight against capitalism and for the dictatorship of the proletariat, creatively applying this experience to the concrete circumstances of their countries.

The Congress of the Comintern noted that for the world proletariat Soviet Russia was a rich treasure-house of revolutionary experience.

Reviewing the international situation, the Congress pointed to the sharpening world economic crisis, the growth of unemployment and the launching, on a world scale, of a capitalist offensive against the gains of the working class. The capitalists sought chiefly to reduce wages and the standard of living of the workers generally. In all countries the proletariat had been forced on to the defensive.

The growing pressure exerted by capital had evoked a spontaneous desire for unity among the workers, and brought them closer to the Communists. The Congress reaffirmed that the basic task facing the Communist Parties was to win over the majority of the working class, and that the struggle for this aim should be based on applying the tactics of the united front. In speaking of the working-class united front, the Communists had in mind the unity of all workers ready to fight against capitalism, including those who followed the Social-Democrats, the Anarchists, syndicalists, etc.

The Congress set the Communists the task of explaining to the workers at large that to avert imperialist wars it was necessary to abolish the bourgeois system.

4. Lenin's Last Articles. Lenin's Plan for Building Socialism in the U.S.S.R.

The consolidation of the external position of the Soviet State and the achievements in Socialist construction gladdened the Party and the Soviet people. But this gladness was darkened by the illness of Lenin. The terrific strain of long years of work had undermined his health. The effects of the wound inflicted by the murderous hand of a Socialist-Revolutionary terrorist also made themselves felt.

In the autumn of 1922, Lenin's illness took a turn for the worse. On November 20, after a slight improvement, he delivered a speech at a meeting of the Moscow Soviet. Referring to the results of the country's development during the last eighteen months, on the basis of the New Economic Policy, Lenin said that difficulties attended the change-over, but these would be overcome. The

Party had registered definite successes: "We have brought Socia ism into everyday life." Amidst loud applause, he conclud his speech by expressing the firm conviction that "NEP Russ will become Socialist Russia" (*Collected Works*, Vol. 33, p. 405

This was the last public appearance of the leader of the Part and the Soviet people.

In December, 1922, his illness took a grave turn.

In January-February, 1923, he dictated his last articles: "Pag From a Diary," "On Co-operation," "How We Should Reorgani the Workers' and Peasants' Inspection," "Concerning Our Re olution," "Better Fewer, But Better." *These articles were the cu minating stage of Lenin's elaboration of the plan for building S cialism in the U.S.S.R.* In a way, they were his political testa ment to the Party.

Lenin put before the Party the problem of industrialising th country, and showed how this should be done. In his articles h proceeded from the point that the main thing in building Socia ism was the development of large-scale industry, particularl heavy industry, as the economic basis of Socialism.

"By exercising the greatest possible economy in the economi life of our State," he wrote, "to use every kopek we save to de velop our large-scale machine industry, to develop electrifica tion, the hydraulic extraction of peat, to complete the Volkho project, etc.

"In this, and this alone, lies our hope" (*ibid.*, p. 459).

On the order of the day, too, was the question of the Socialis reconstruction of the countryside. The proletariat would succee in solving its basic problem only by retaining its leadership of th peasantry and drawing the latter into the building of Socialism Lenin considered the consolidation of the alliance of the workin class and the labouring peasantry to be a decisive condition fo building Socialism in the U.S.S.R. He saw in the co-operative the means by which the peasantry could be drawn into Socialis construction. Under capitalism, the co-operatives bear a capi talist character; they are, as Lenin put it, "collective capitalis undertakings." Under the Soviet system, with power in the hand of the proletariat, with the alliance of the proletariat and the peas antry under the leadership of the working class made secure, and with all the basic means of production, including the land, in the hands of the State, the co-operatives are Socialist undertakings. Gi ven these conditions, co-operation is the way most comprehensi ble for them to unite in large-scale collective undertakings. Co-operation combines the private, personal interests of the peasant with the common interests of society.

"For now we have found," Lenin wrote, "that degree of the combination of private interest, private trading interest, with State supervision and control of this interest, that degree of its subordination to the common interests, that was formerly the stumbling-block for very many Socialists" (*ibid.*, p. 428).

To win the small peasant producer for co-operation is the most ifficult problem after the conquest of power by the proletariat. ; can be solved only on condition of large-scale aid on the part of ie State and the active participation of the peasant masses them-elves. The organisation of the peasants in co-operatives must take lace on a voluntary basis, and in no circumstances by admin-strative measures. With the population of the country organised 1 co-operatives, Lenin wrote, this would be a system of civi-sed co-operators. And such a system in a proletarian country, here the means of production were the property of society, was a ocialist system.

Lenin's teachings on co-operation as the sole possible means of eading the peasantry out on to the path of Socialism were a crea-ive development of Marxism in the new conditions. Lenin out-ined a clear perspective of the building of Socialism in the coun-ryside, of the victory of the Soviet power in solving this vital nd complicated problem.

In establishing and consolidating the co-operative system in the ountryside, as in the entire work of building Socialism, Lenin ttached enormous importance to the cultural revolution. The Par-y and the Soviet Government, he said, must bring about uni-ersal literacy. He suggested that cultural and educational and "patronage" organisations of factory workers should be set up to ielp educate the peasantry, and that regular visits by workers to he villages should be arranged.

In his last articles, Lenin again stressed that the instrument for uilding Socialism was the Soviet State, and that it must con-tantly be improved and strengthened. He proposed that the Work-rs' and Peasants' Inspection and the Central Control Commis-sion should be amalgamated, and the combined body vested with road powers to reduce staffs to the greatest possible extent, and o refresh and cheapen the machinery of State. The Central Commit-;ee of the Party, too, would gain from the amalgamation, wrote Lenin, because through the new body the C.C. would be in closer contact with the masses, would be in a position to solve all the problems of public life better and more correctly. Among the gains, he wrote, "there will also be the advantage that in our Central Committee the influence of purely personal and casual factors will diminish, and this will reduce the danger of a split" (*ibid.*, p. 443).

Lenin was anxious above all to preserve the solid unity of the Party. It was his desire that the Party should always remember the decision of the Tenth Congress of the R.C.P. (B.), which cat-

egorically prohibited all factions and groupings in the Part
A split in the Party, he pointed out, would inevitably lead to
split in the worker-peasant alliance. And that would signify tʰ
end of Soviet power and a return to capitalism. There were ⱡ
grounds in the Soviet system for any split in the worker-peasaⁿ
alliance. Such a split could take place only as a result of blundeʳ
and wrong actions by Party and State bodies. For that reasoⁿ
Lenin put forward as the basic task of the Central Committeᵉ
the Central Control Commission and the Party as a whole, "ᵗ
watch closely the circumstances which may cause a split, and ᵗ
forestall them, for, in the last resort, the fate of our Republic wiˡ
depend on whether the masses of the peasants will march witʰ
the working class and loyally maintain their alliance with iᵗ
or whether they will permit the 'Nepmen,' i. e., the new bouʳ
geoisie, to drive a wedge between them and the working class, tᵒ
split them off from the working class" (*Collected Works*, Voˡ
33, p. 444).

In his last articles, Lenin dwelt also on the international siᵗ
uation. Did the Soviet State possess the strength with which tᵒ
uphold its independent existence against the pressure of the worˡᵈ
bourgeoisie, to safeguard the peaceful labour of the builders ᵒ
Socialism? Would the Soviet country be able to achieve the victᵒ
ry of Socialism?

Proceeding from a scientific analysis of the international siᵗ
uation and of the objective laws of the development of society
Lenin gave a clear and positive answer to these questions.

In the camp of the imperialists, unity and complete agreemeⁿ
were impossible, because in the drive for profits, for dominion oⁿ
the world market, the imperialists were bound to become embroileᵈ
in rivalry. On the other hand, the international policy of thᵉ
Soviet Union was not aimed at seizing foreign territory or unleashᵎ
ing war; its aim was to promote peace, business-like agreementˢ
with the capitalist countries on mutually advantageous termˢ
peaceful coexistence of the two systems—Socialism and capitalᵎ
ism. Lenin said that we must keep a firm hand on the helm
and go our way without succumbing to any provocation oʳ
intimidation on the part of the imperialists. Firmness and steadᵎ
fastness—these were the qualities that the Communists shoulᵈ
display.

Although the victory of the revolutionary movement of thᵉ
world proletariat was slow in coming, this was a temporary matᵎ
ter. "Peace" between the antagonistic classes in the capitalisᵗ
countries was only illusory. The reality was ceaseless class struggle,
which at times smouldered, only to flare up again. Sharpening
of the class struggle in the future was inevitable, just as the victory of the proletariat was inevitable.

An intensification of the national liberation struggle was equally inevitable. As a result of the imperialist world war, and chiefly as a result of the Great October Socialist Revolution, a number of countries of the East—China, India and others—had been drawn into the main stream of the world revolutionary movement. Hundreds of millions of working people in the countries of the East had been reduced by the imperialist exploiters to the last degree of human misery and endurance. And no reactionary forces could stem their revolutionary movement, which would grow with every year. The struggle of the colonial peoples for their liberation would, with incredible force, shake the foundations of capitalism, sap its strength and facilitate the development of the revolutionary movement of the proletariat in the capitalist countries.

Lenin pointed out that the great peoples of the countries of the East—China, India and others—which together with the peoples of Soviet Russia constitute the overwhelming majority of the earth's population, were rapidly being drawn into the national liberation struggle. For this reason, wrote Lenin, "there cannot be the slightest shadow of doubt what the final outcome of the world struggle will be. In this sense, the ultimate victory of Socialism is completely and absolutely certain" (*ibid.*, p. 458).

In his last articles, Lenin substantiated and elaborated his plan for building Socialism in the U.S.S.R. The basic propositions of this plan, which he outlined in his brilliant works written after the October Revolution, are the following:

1. *In the Soviet country there was all that was necessary and adequate for building a complete Socialist society.* The main task of the Party was to revive and develop industry, especially heavy industry, to electrify the country, and to ensure a substantial rise in labour productivity throughout the national economy. In order to build the material and technical basis of Socialism and to increase the defence capacity of the Soviet State, it was necessary to *industrialise* the country and overcome its technical-economic backwardness.

2. The Socialist proletariat should draw the working peasantry into Socialist construction and help it to organise its scattered individual farming into large-scale socialised farming. The best way to draw the peasants into Socialist construction was through *co-operation*. The Communist Party should help the peasantry to establish the co-operative system in the countryside. This should be done gradually, step by step, so that the peasantry might, by its own experience, become convinced of the advantages of collective forms of farming and willingly, without any compulsion, take the path of co-operation. When the peasants became convinced

of the need to go over to collective forms of farming, the rate of their advance to Socialism would be accelerated.

Small peasant farming could be switched to a Socialist path provided agriculture were amply supplied with modern machinery. As early as the Eighth Congress of the Party, in 1919, Lenin said that if we could give the countryside a hundred thousand first-class tractors, the peasantry would declare for Communism. Industrialisation, with priority development of heavy industry, would make it possible to supply the countryside with all the machinery it needed.

3. The development of large-scale industry, equipping the entire national economy with up-to-date machinery, drawing the peasants into co-operation, and the management of the State and the entire national economy called for a sharp rise in the cultural level of the people and the training of highly skilled personnel in sufficient numbers. This required universal literacy, a considerable extension of the network of elementary and secondary schools, higher educational establishments and publishing facilities, and the development of all branches of science. In short, what was needed was a *cultural revolution*. Without this, without training an intelligentsia drawn from the ranks of the people, Socialism could not be built and securely established.

4. The fundamental condition for building Socialism was the *dictatorship of the proletariat*. In the hands of the proletariat, the State was an instrument for building Socialism. For the purpose of enhancing the role of the machinery of State, and also to economise resources, it was necessary to reduce that machinery to a minimum by getting rid of bureaucratic and alien elements, and replenish it with fresh forces drawn from the ranks of the working people. The job of improving the machinery of State, of cutting staffs and reducing costs, should be carried out by the joint organ of the Party and the Government—the Central Control Commission and Workers' and Peasants' Inspection. With the help of the working people, this body would check and improve the work of the Soviet State apparatus, and make it worthy of the new social system.

5. *Socialism could be built only by preserving and strengthening the worker-peasant alliance.* The leading role in this alliance was played by the working class headed by the Communist Party. The Party must closely watch for circumstances that might split the alliance, so as to eliminate them in good time. Unity of the Party was decisive if the alliance between the workers and peasants was to be durable. A split in the Party would entail the destruction of the alliance of the two classes, which would mean the destruction of the dictatorship of the proletariat. For this reason, the Party should tolerate no factions or groupings in its ranks. Only a sol-

idly united Party and its correct policy could guarantee the indestructibility of the worker-peasant alliance and assure the building of Socialism in the U.S.S.R.

6. The building of Socialist society in the U.S.S.R. was wholly assured from the international point of view as well. In the capitalist world the contradictions, both class and inter-State contradictions, were bound to become more acute. Class battles between the proletariat and the bourgeoisie were bound to grow in intensity. The developing national liberation movement in the colonies and semi-colonies, especially in the countries of the East, would increasingly undermine the rule of the imperialists. In their totality, these circumstances would in ever greater measure undermine the foundations of capitalism. Any attempt by the imperialists to destroy the Soviet system would end in failure.

7. Taking into account the capitalist encirclement of the Soviet country and the international situation, the Communist Party and the Soviet Government should conduct a wise foreign policy and seek to avert military clashes with the bourgeois countries. An indefatigable *struggle for peace, for peaceful coexistence and economic competition between the Socialist and capitalist systems,* should be the undeviating policy of the Party. Lenin expressed his unshakable confidence that Socialism would win this competition, that "Socialism contains within itself gigantic forces and that mankind has now entered into a new stage of development, which offers uncommonly brilliant prospects" (*Collected Works,* Vol. 33, p. 456).

Lenin's plan became a most powerful theoretical and practical weapon of the Party in the fight for Socialism. It inspired the working class and the working peasantry to labour exploits for the sake of the victory of Socialism over capitalism.

5. Twelfth Party Congress. The Fight Against Trotskyism. Overcoming the Economic Difficulties. The Death of Lenin. The Lenin Enrolment

The ideas of Lenin's plan for building Socialism in the U.S.S.R. found expression in the decisions of the Twelfth Congress of the R.C.P.(B.). The Congress, at which about 400,000 members were represented, was held on April 17-25, 1923. This was the first Congress after the October Revolution from which Lenin, through illness, was absent.

The reduced membership was due to the Party cleansing which took place on the eve of, and after, the Eleventh Congress.

Items on the agenda included reports by the Central Committee and the Central Control Commission, industry, the national question, tax policy in the countryside, and others.

The resolution adopted on the report of the Central Committee stressed that NEP was creating favourable soil for deviations in the Party. Particularly dangerous and disastrous were those deviations which opposed the Soviet State to the working class and the Party to the State. The Congress categorically warned those who in these matters, so vital to the destiny of the revolution, tried to sow confusion in the Party, divert it from the Leninist path and undermine its unity, that they would be rigorously dealt with, to the point of expelling them from the Party.

The Congress pointed to the need for systematically improving the machinery of State, regarding this as a prime duty of the Party. It stressed that only a really Socialist State apparatus could assure the indissoluble alliance of the workers and peasants.

In pursuance of Lenin's directives, the Congress decided to merge the Workers' and Peasants' Inspection and the Central Control Commission, and charged the new body with improving the State machinery with the help of workers from the bench.

The Congress pointed out the necessity for a precise division of labour between Party and Soviet organisations, for better specialisation of economic and administrative personnel, and for strict adherence to the principle of personal responsibility for the work assigned.

Noting the successes achieved in the national economy and in raising labour productivity in the factories, the Congress called upon the working class to direct its energies to expanding industry, above all heavy industry, "which alone can be a firm foundation for genuinely Socialist construction" (*C.P.S.U. in Resolutions*, Part I, p. 682).

Along with heavy industry, and on its basis, light industry, too, was to be rapidly developed.

The key to success or failure in production was in the factories. The proper organisation of work at each enterprise, in keeping with its particular features, was decisive. The Congress recommended that "everything be done to avoid stifling centralisation, the damping of initiative and arbitrary interference in the work" of enterprises (*ibid.*, p. 697).

The Twelfth Congress underlined that the main responsibility for the work of the economic and State organisations rested with the Party, that on all essentials the Party must determine and supervise this work. *"Still closer to the economy, still greater attention, guidance and help to the economic bodies, this is the Party slogan for the next period"* (*ibid.*, p. 683).

The attention of the Party was directed to organised marketing of manufactured goods. Faulty organisation in this respect was already leading to excessive overhead charges and partly to excess stocking of goods. In order to overcome this, it was essential, in the first place, to build up a network of local trading establishments, so as to ensure contact between industry and the peasant market. It was also necessary to adjust prices, for the prices of manufactures were much higher than those paid for agricultural produce.

With a view to easing the conditions of the peasantry and expanding trade in the country, the recommendation was made that all direct State taxes for which the peasants were liable (tax in kind, household tax in cash, labour and cartage tax), and all local direct taxes, should be replaced by a single direct agricultural tax, and also that part of this tax could be paid in cash. (Subsequently, beginning with 1924, the single agricultural tax began to be computed in gold rubles and was levied wholly in cash.) The main burden of taxation was placed on the richest farms (a manifestation of the policy of restricting the kulaks); some of the poorest peasants were exempted from all tax payments.

At the Congress, attempts were made by the opportunists to divert the Party from the Leninist path. Trotsky called for a rigorous concentration of industry. This was a concealed form of cutting down heavy industry, of closing down a number of enterprises which in the early period were not showing a profit. On the eve of the Congress Trotsky had proposed that some of the biggest plants like the Putilov Works in Petrograd, the Bryansk Works and others should be closed down on the grounds that they were then working at a loss. Actually the closing down of these plants would have caused the gravest injury to heavy industry and would have set the workers against the Party.

Emphatically rejecting Trotsky's proposal, the Central Committee pointed out that its acceptance would be a political defeat and disaster for the entire Soviet Republic. And it was in this same spirit that the Twelfth Congress decision was adopted.

In the theses which he compiled for the Twelfth Congress, Trotsky advanced the slogan of a "dictatorship of industry." As Trotsky employed it, this slogan did not signify emphasis on the leading role of industry in the national economy or on priority development of the production of means of production as against that of consumer goods. In his understanding, it signified the development of industry by exploiting the peasantry. This line would have led to the break-up of the alliance of the workers and peasants, and to the ruin of the Soviet system.

In its decisions the Congress, rejecting the Trotsky slogan, stressed that at the given stage of economic development agriculture was of prime importance to the entire economy of the country.

Before the Congress assembled, Sokolnikov and Bukharin had suggested that the State monopoly of foreign trade should be partly annulled, which, in practice, would have meant its abolition.

These opportunist views were firmly condemned by the Congress.

Some delegates (Krassin and others) put forward the erroneous proposal that substantial economic concessions should be made to the capitalist countries, in return for credits and loans for rehabilitating industry. Their proposal was rejected.

After hearing a report by Stalin on the national question, the Congress called for the speedy elimination of actual inequality among the Soviet nations. The Russian proletariat had to increase its help to the backward peoples of the U.S.S.R. in their economic and cultural development.

The Twelfth Congress of the R.C.P.(B.), like the Tenth Congress, called upon the Party resolutely to combat Great-Russian chauvinism as the main danger, and also local nationalism.

In the conditions created by NEP, bourgeois elements had revived, which resulted in a revival of bourgeois nationalism. It raised its head in all the republics, especially in Georgia. The Georgian deviators (Mdivani, Okujava and others) attempted to pursue a policy of dominant-nation chauvinism in relation to the non-Georgian nationalities inhabiting Georgia. They were also opposed to the establishment of the Transcaucasian Federation and to the entry of Georgia into the U.S.S.R. They demanded that foreign banks be opened in Georgia, which would have paved the way for turning Georgia into an appendage of foreign capital and for the restoration of capitalism there. The Congress vigorously condemned the activity of the Georgian deviators.

The guidance of the national economy improved after the Twelfth Congress. The rehabilitation of agriculture and industry proceeded successfully. Crop areas were extended and annual industrial output increased. The number of workers in large-scale industry, planned by the Supreme Council of National Economy, rose by 14 per cent in 1923 compared with the previous year. But there were also major shortcomings. Labour productivity and the workers' wages were still below pre-war levels. State and co-operative trading organisations were working badly. The directives of the Twelfth Party Congress to close the price gap between manufactured and agricultural goods had not been carried out. By the autumn of 1923 the price gap ("the scissors") had widened enormously. As a result the Soviet ruble became more unstable, and its value was declining.

All these factors, in their totality, had an adverse effect on the living conditions of the workers and peasants and on their purchasing power. Although the quantity of goods manufactured at the time was small, stocks began to pile up. Manufactures piled up in the warehouses. The peasants could not buy them because of the high prices. For example, in order to buy a pood* of nails, the peasant had to sell from 50 to 60 poods of wheat, whereas before the world war the cost of a pood of nails equalled that of 3-3¹/₂ poods of wheat. This price policy gave rise to discontent in the countryside. Among the workers, too, there was grumbling, because overstocking resulted in delays in paying wages. In some enterprises, things went as far as strikes.

The Party Central Committee and the Soviet Government took urgent measures to eliminate the causes of the discontent among the peasants and workers. Prices of consumer goods were lowered. The chervonets,** introduced in October, 1922, was brought increasingly into circulation and became the firm, stable currency unit, in place of the unstable paper money in circulation. The regular payment of wages was resumed. Measures were taken to put trade on a proper footing, squeeze out private traders and vigorously combat profiteering. Agricultural prices were raised and low-interest credits were made available to the peasants for the development of their farms. These cheap credits freed the poor peasants from the necessity of borrowing from kulaks at extortionate rates and of becoming in fact their farm-labourers.

These measures ended the discontent among the peasants and workers and assured the further development of the national economy.

The difficulties on the economic front encouraged a revival of the anti-Leninist elements in the Party.

Taking advantage of the fact that Lenin, the Party leader, was incapacitated by grave illness, Trotsky resumed his fight against the Leninist Central Committee, against the Party. He decided that the country's difficulties gave him a favourable opportunity to realise his designs—to take the leadership of the Party into his own hands and pursue his own line, one that, in the end, would have led to the restoration of capitalism.

At the beginning of October, 1923, Trotsky addressed a letter to the Central Committee in which he vilified the work of that body. Instead of trying to help overcome the shortcomings in the Party through discussion at meetings of the Political Bureau and plenary meetings of the Central Committee, as was and is usual when there are normal relations between the members of leading Party bodies, Trotsky mustered all his supporters for a fight against the Central Committee. Shortly after Trotsky's letter, the Central Committee received a statement, known as the Declaration of the Forty-Six, signed by Trotskyists, "Democratic Centralists"

---

* One pood=40 Russian or 36 English lbs.—*Trans.*
** A bank note, backed by gold and other reliable cover, and equivalent to 10 gold rubles.—*Trans.*

and remnants of the "Left Communist" and "Workers' Opposition" groups. Their number included some members of the Central Committee. Slanderously declaring that the Party apparatus had replaced the Party, they endeavoured to set the membership against the Party apparatus, opposing the latter to the Party. In this Trotskyist crusade against the Party apparatus there spoke a recurrence of Menshevism, which denied the very principle of guidance of Party work. The Trotskyists and the other opportunists demanded freedom for factions and groupings. In other words, they sought to secure the annulment of the Tenth Party Congress decision banning and ruling out factions in the Party, and expressed the aspirations of the Mensheviks, the Socialist-Revolutionaries, and the new bourgeoisie, who, with NEP in existence, were all craving to appear openly on the political scene.

Trotsky's letter and the Declaration of the Forty-Six were circulated by the Trotskyists to the local Party organisations.

The situation in the Party was discussed at a joint plenary meeting of the Central Committee and the Central Control Commission, held in October, together with representatives of the ten biggest Party organisations—Petrograd, Moscow, Kharkov and others. The meeting condemned the action taken by Trotsky and the forty-six as being profoundly erroneous politically and as having assumed "the character of factional activity threatening to deal a blow at the unity of the Party and creating a crisis in the Party" (*C.P.S.U. in Resolutions*, Part I, p. 768).

The decision of the plenary meeting had no effect on Trotsky. He issued a pamphlet entitled *The New Course*, in which he charged the Party leadership with degeneration, compared the old Party leaders with the opportunist leaders of the Second International, and opposed to the old and tried Party members the raw youth—raw in the Party sense—especially the students, flatteringly referring to this youth as the "barometer of the Party."

Trotsky and his followers began levelling charges against the Central Committee at Party meetings in factories and higher educational institutions. Thus once again, as in 1921, the Trotskyists forced a discussion on the Party. A heated discussion began in the Party organisations all over the country. Once more the Party was diverted from the job of rehabilitating the national economy. The Party organisations in Moscow, Petrograd, Ukraine, the Urals, Baku and other big industrial centres crushingly rebuffed the Trotskyist attack. The discussion ended in the utter defeat of the Trotskyists, and rallied the Party round the Leninist Central Committee.

The results of the discussion were summed up by the Thirteenth Conference of the R.C.P.(B.), which took place in January, 1924.

The Conference strongly condemned the factional struggle of Trotsky and the Trotskyists against the Party, and declared that "in the shape of the present opposition, we have before us not only an attempt to revise Bolshevism, not only a direct departure from Leninism, but also a clearly expressed *petty-bourgeois deviation*" (*ibid.*, p. 782).

The latest sally of the Trotskyists reflected the sharpening of the class struggle in the country, caused by the revival of the bourgeoisie and its ideologists in NEP conditions. In the towns, private traders and all kinds of Nepmen intensified their struggle against the proletarian dictatorship, and the kulaks did the same in the countryside. The Trotskyists acted as the spokesmen of these class enemies.

So that Party members might better understand the danger of Trotskyism, the study was organised of the history of the Party, of its struggle against all kinds of factions, groupings and deviations, against opportunism in its ranks, against the agents of the bourgeoisie in the working-class movement. Young Party members learned of the disgraceful struggle waged by Trotsky for many years on the side of the Mensheviks, against Lenin, against the Bolshevik Party. This study, which equipped the Communists with a knowledge of Marxism-Leninism, was aided by the appearance in 1924 of Stalin's *Foundations of Leninism*, which briefly and clearly set forth the basic questions of Leninism, of the theory and tactics of the proletarian revolution, the theory and tactics of the dictatorship of the proletariat, and brought out the new features which Lenin had introduced into Marxism.

Shortly after the Thirteenth Conference the Party, the Soviet people, the world proletariat and all progressive mankind suffered a most grievous loss—on January 21, 1924, Vladimir Ilyich Lenin died. The news of his death evoked inexpressible sorrow among the Soviet people and among the workers and oppressed peoples of the world. An extraordinary plenary meeting of the Party Central Committee adopted an appeal "To the Party, to All Working People." In this appeal, the Central Committee informed the people of the death of the great leader.

"All that is truly great and heroic in the proletariat," the appeal read, "a fearless mind, a will of iron, unbending, persistent and able to surmount all obstacles, burning hatred, deadly hatred of slavery and oppression, revolutionary passion that moves mountains, boundless faith in the creative energies of the masses, vast organisational genius—all found magnificent embodiment in Lenin, whose name has become the symbol of the new world from West to East, from South to North" (*ibid.*, pp. 804-05).

For nearly a week the people took farewell of Lenin. Despite the exceptionally severe frost, they passed through the Hall of

Columns in the Trade Union House day and night to pay a last tribute to the departed leader.

On the day of Lenin's funeral, in every town and village, the Soviet people stopped work for five minutes and in great sorrow bade farewell to their father, teacher and friend. To the mourning sounds of factory and locomotive sirens, which resounded throughout the country, the coffin with Lenin's body was borne to its resting place in the Mausoleum on Red Square. In taking farewell of Lenin, the Party and the people solemnly vowed to carry out his behests.

The great sorrow of the Soviet people was shared by the international proletariat and by the working people of the whole world. On the day of Lenin's funeral workers in many capitalist countries stopped work for five minutes, bidding farewell in thought to the leader of the workers of the world.

The death of Lenin rallied the working class still closer round the Party. During the days of mourning thousands of applications for Party membership were received from workers. Taking into account the large scale of this movement, the Central Committee announced a Lenin Enrolment of workers from the bench to the Party. It addressed an appeal to working men and women, in which it said that the death of the leader had deeply stirred the working class, and that hundreds of thousands of workers had extended a helping hand to the Party.

During the Lenin Enrolment the best, politically advanced workers, those who had been tempered in revolutionary battles, joined the Party. At the open Party meetings, which discussed the applications for membership, non-Party workers, too, played an active part, helping the Party to select the foremost people in industry, those most devoted to the proletarian revolution.

The Lenin Enrolment resulted in over 240,000 workers joining the Party. This was a vivid demonstration of the indissoluble unity of the working class and its Party.

6. Thirteenth Party Congress. Intensification of Party Work in the Countryside. The New Sally by Trotsky Exposed

The unity of the Party's ranks after the death of the leader was demonstrated at the Thirteenth Congress of the R.C.P.(B.) (May 23-31, 1924). Nearly 736,000 members and over 127,000 candidate members were represented. The membership had almost doubled since the Twelfth Congress, the Party's ranks having been replenished mainly by workers. This fact alone testified to the Party's expanding and strengthening contacts with the working people, to the rallying of the masses round the Party and to the growth of its prestige.

The items on the agenda included reports by the Central Committee and the Central Control Commission, trade, the co-operatives and Party work in the countryside, and others.

The Congress noted with satisfaction that although the Party had been deprived of Lenin's direct leadership, its Central Committee, in a difficult and complicated situation, had achieved impressive successes in all spheres. The Congress expressed complete approval of the Central Committee's firmness and uncompromising Leninist stand in the fight against Trotskyism, of its staunch defence of Leninism, and instructed the C.C. to continue, with the same resolution and firmness, to safeguard the unity of the Party and its consistent line against any deviations whatsoever.

The Congress approved the resolution of the Thirteenth Party Conference, which characterised Trotskyism as a petty-bourgeois deviation.

The Congress attached exceptional importance to the Marxist-Leninist education of the Party membership, especially of those who had joined during the Lenin Enrolment, for it regarded them as a reservoir of Party personnel for work in State, economic, trade union, co-operative and other bodies. It laid down that the entire educational work of the Party should be linked up with the "main stages in our Party's history, in view of the exceptional significance in it of the guiding ideas of Comrade Lenin" (*C.P.S.U. in Resolutions*, Part II, p. 21).

The Congress noted the general economic uptrend in the country. The rehabilitation of Socialist industry and transport was making good progress; the working class was growing numerically, and agricultural production was increasing.

On the basis of the successes achieved in the restoration of the coal industry and in transport, the Congress issued the call to extend the struggle for metal, for the expansion of heavy industry and for organisation of production of means of production within the country.

The achievements in agriculture prompted the Congress to stress the need for intensifying the Party's work to win the rural population for co-operation. Bearing in mind that the poor peasants were falling into kulak bondage, the Congress obliged the rural Party organisations to ensure observance of the laws concerning tax exemptions for the poorest peasants and for the protection of their interests, and to see to the strict observance of the tax policy regarding the kulaks, in order to restrict their growth.

In the sphere of trade, the Congress noted that the policy of reducing prices of manufactured goods had completely justified itself. The Congress endorsed the establishment of a People's Commissariat for Internal Trade. The chief task of this commissariat was to secure a dominant position for the State on the home mar-

kct, and in the first place in wholesale trade; to exercise contro
over private capital, and to squeeze it out of trade.

On Party organisational questions, the Congress adopted
the resolution "The Immediate Tasks in Party Building." This
resolution emphasised the need for every effort to draw the main
industrial cadres of the proletariat into the Party. The Lenin
Enrolment had greatly reinforced the Party with workers, and the
number of Party groups in the factories had grown. The Party organisations were instructed to conduct active Party and political
work among the new members, and to do everything to draw them
into Party, State and public life. It was necessary to improve the
work of the factory groups and enhance their role in production,
and to provide them with better guidance.

The Congress also discussed work among the youth and called
for greater Party guidance to the Komsomol. The Lenin Komsomol was the loyal helpmate of the Party. Led by the Party, the
Komsomol had valiantly defended the young Soviet Republic
against its enemies during the Civil War years. It was working
for the restoration of the national economy. The Congress called
upon the Komsomol to take an active part in Socialist construction, in all the public, political and cultural undertakings of the
Party and the Soviets in town and country, in educating the young
people in the spirit of Communism, in training skilled workers
and intellectuals. It called upon them to study and acquire knowledge.

All the decisions of the Congress were aimed at extending Socialist construction, strengthening the bond between the working
class and the peasantry and enhancing the leading role of the Party.

At the Thirteenth Congress not a single open speech was made
by the opposition groups. Whereas at the Seventh Congress the
anti-Leninist opposition on the issue of peace with Germany mustered a quarter of the votes, and at the Tenth Congress it managed
to get one-eighth of the votes, at the Thirteenth Congress not a
single oppositional statement was made. This was an obvious indication of the ideological consolidation of the Party.

Lenin's "Letter to the Congress," which became known as his
testament, was read out to each delegation separately. In this document, Lenin emphasised *the necessity of maintaining the unity
of the Party, of creating a stable Central Committee capable of
averting a split in the Party*. With these aims in view, Lenin suggested that it was essential to bring more people on to the Central
Committee in order to make it a more authoritative body, to improve the work of the Party apparatus and "to prevent conflicts
of small sections of the C.C. from being given excessive importance for the future of the whole Party" (*Collected Works*, Vol. 36,
p. 543).

Lenin's letter contained a characterisation of some members of the Central Committee. About Zinoviev and Kamenev, he wrote that their "October episode" was by no means accidental. He mentioned the "non-Bolshevism" of Trotsky, thereby warning the Party of his extremely dangerous relapses into Menshevism, and added that Trotsky "has too enterprising self-assurance and excessive enthusiasm for the purely administrative side of the work" (ibid., p. 544). Bukharin was characterised by Lenin as scholastic, as a man who "never studied and, I think, never fully understood dialectics" (ibid., p. 545).

Lenin was giving a summing-up of these people, who at decisive moments of the struggle for the victory of the October Revolution had opposed the line of the Party and tried to split its ranks. Only the firmness and uncompromising attitude of Lenin and the Central Committee of the Party in combating the strike-breaking of Zinoviev and Kamenev at the time of the October Revolution, in combating the treacherous and disastrous policy of Trotsky and Bukharin during the Brest period, and their anti-Party line and factionalism during the trade union discussion, had ensured the carrying out of a correct policy by the Party and the solid unity of its ranks, which was the decisive condition for the victory of the October Revolution and the defence of its gains.

In his letter Lenin also expressed his views on Stalin. After noting Stalin's good qualities and pointing out that he was one of the Party's outstanding men, Lenin went on to criticise his failings. "Comrade Stalin," he wrote, "having become General Secretary, has concentrated boundless authority in his hands, and I am not sure whether he will always be able to exercise that authority with sufficient discretion." Lenin suggested that they "think over a way of removing Stalin from that post and appointing somebody else, differing in all other respects from Comrade Stalin by one single advantage, namely, that of being more tolerant, more loyal, more polite and considerate to the comrades, less capricious, etc. This circumstance may appear to be a negligible trifle" but "it is not a trifle, or it is a trifle which can acquire decisive importance" (ibid., pp. 541, 546).

After discussing Lenin's letter, the delegations, bearing in mind the services rendered by Stalin—his uncompromising struggle against Trotskyism and other anti-Party groups—declared for his continuing as General Secretary, on the condition, however, that he paid heed to Lenin's criticism and drew the necessary conclusions from it. The Party took account of the fact that the Trotskyists were concentrating their fire especially on Stalin, who upheld Leninism firmly and consistently. In these circumstances, his release from the post of General Secretary of the Central Committee might be used by the Trotskyists to the detriment of

the Party and of Marxism-Leninism, to the detriment of Social
ist construction in the U.S.S.R.

Lenin's recommendation to increase the membership of the
Central Committee considerably was carried out by the Thirteenth
Congress.

Shortly after the Thirteenth Congress, in June and July, 1924,
the Fifth Congress of the Comintern took place in Moscow. In
the interval between the Fourth and the Fifth Comintern Congresses
the class battles in the West European countries had ended in defeat for the workers. The bourgeoisie had succeeded in beating
off the offensive of the proletariat. The defeat suffered by the working class was due in large measure to the treachery of the leaders
of Social-Democracy, and also to the serious mistakes made by
some of the Communist Parties. The defeatist behaviour of the
Right opportunists who were then in the leadership and were
later expelled from the Communist Parties greatly harmed the
working-class movement and the Communist Parties of Germany
and some other countries.

The year 1924 was the beginning of the period of capitalist stabilisation. But this stabilisation was relative and unstable.

On the strength of its analysis of the international situation,
the Fifth Congress of the Comintern elaborated the tactics of
struggle of the Communist Parties in the new conditions. The absolutely sound tactics of the united front remained inviolate. It
was based on unity of the working masses, unity from below.

The Congress advanced as one of the main tasks the bolshevisation of the Communist Parties of the capitalist countries. This
signified assimilation by the parties of the ideological, organisational and tactical principles of Bolshevism, relentless struggle
against deviations from Marxism-Leninism, skilful combination
of the struggle for the dictatorship of the proletariat with the fight
for the everyday demands of the workers, and the closest contact
with the masses.

The Fifth Congress reviewed the discussion which Trotsky had
forced upon the Russian Communist Party (Bolsheviks), and
condemned Trotskyism. It approved the decisions of the Thirteenth Conference and Thirteenth Congress of the R.C.P.(B.),
which had characterised Trotskyism as a petty-bourgeois deviation in the Party. The Comintern Congress declared the actions of
the Trotskyists to be a threat to the unity of the Party and, consequently, to the dictatorship of the proletariat in the U.S.S.R.

The decisions of the Thirteenth Congress of the Party and the
Fifth Congress of the Comintern inspired the Communists of the
Soviet Union to intensify the building of Socialism. In the factories, they set an example of high labour productivity, and their
example was followed by non-Party workers.

The Communists were improving the trading machinery and securing a dominant position in trade and on the market, squeezing
out the private traders more and more. They organised cultural
"patronage" over the countryside and guided the work of bringing
the working peasantry into all types of co-operatives. Leningrad
workers, for example, assumed "patronage" over 300 volosts,
Moscow workers over more than 200 volosts, Tula workers over
100 villages, and so on.

The Central Committee closely followed what was going on in
the countryside. One of the results of NEP was increased political activity in the villages. The peasantry began to take a more
active part in public affairs. But the kulaks were not dozing either. They began to exert influence on the middle peasants, who
again began to waver. With their support, kulaks were able in some
places to worm their way into the Soviets, where they pursued
a policy of their own. Where this happened, the Soviets distorted the Soviet Government's tax policy in favour of the
kulaks and to the detriment of the poor peasants. In some cases
the kulaks, waging their fight against the dictatorship of the
proletariat, murdered Soviet personnel, village activists and
rural newspaper correspondents who had exposed their anti-Soviet activities. In Guria Uyezd, Georgia, the kulaks actively
supported the Mensheviks, who in August, 1924, raised a revolt
against the Soviet power. The Mensheviks received material aid
from the foreign bourgeoisie, but the working peasantry in Georgia did not support them, and the rising was crushed overnight.

A plenary meeting of the Central Committee, held in October,
1924, discussed immediate tasks in the country side and outlined
measures for combating kulak influence on the middle peasants.
It was necessary to win over the middle peasants from the kulaks
and to strengthen the alliance of the former with the poor peasantry. The C.C. meeting recommended that the activity of the peasantry should be directed above all towards *invigorating the work
of the Soviets*, towards increasing the activity of the co-operatives
and other voluntary organisations. The task of enlivening the Soviets, said the resolution, "is one of the basic and most urgent tasks
of the moment" (*C.P.S.U. in Resolutions*, Part II, p. 102). It was
essential to enliven the rural Soviets in order to isolate the kulaks
politically.

With a view to strengthening contact with the peasant masses,
it was decided to draw the peasants into the administration of the
State on a greater scale. The C.C. meeting recommended that the
number of non-Party peasants on the Central Executive Committees of the Union and Autonomous Republics should be enlarged.
The recommendation was made that the collegiums (boards) of a
number of people's commissariats—for example, the People's

Commissariat for Agriculture, the People's Commissariat fo
Education, the People's Commissariat for Internal Affairs, th
Workers' and Peasants' Inspection, and others—should each b
reinforced by one or two members drawn from the peasantry
Peasants were also brought into the collegiums in the correspondin,
gubernia and uyezd departments, and were elected chairme
of volost and uyezd executive committees of Soviets.

The C.C. plenary meeting thus turned the attention of the en
tire Party to the countryside. On the basis of its decisions, the ru
ral Party organisations changed their methods of work; they be
gan to pay still greater heed to the needs of the peasants.

The carrying out of the decisions of the October plenary meet
ing of the Central Committee strengthened the Party's influenc
on the working peasantry, promoted the political isolation of th
kulaks and reinforced the worker-peasant alliance.

At a time when the Central Committee and the Party as a whol
were straining every nerve to restore the country's productiv
forces as rapidly as possible and to advance further along the roa
to Socialism, Trotsky and his followers made another bid to block
these efforts and to divert the Party from its Leninist course.

In the autumn of 1924 Trotsky once again forced a discussion
on the Party. In an article published under the heading "The Lessons of October," he distorted the history of the Party and slandered Lenin and Leninism. According to Trotsky, Bolshevism became a consistent trend only in 1917, and only after it had bor-
rowed the Trotskyist idea of "permanent revolution." Furthermore,
he claimed that the leading role in the October Revolution had
been played by him and not by the Party, not by Lenin. Thus,
after the death of Lenin, Trotsky made a brazen attempt to substitute Trotskyism for Leninism.

During Lenin's lifetime Trotsky had never dared to parade his
pernicious ideas, which Lenin had long ago exposed as opportunist ideas reflecting the pressure of bourgeois ideology. Now that
Lenin was no more, Trotsky fell back on his old weapon poisoned
with the venom of opportunism—slander of Leninism.

Trotsky opposed the basic concepts of the Party's world outlook,
opposed Leninism. It was essential to refute his malicious slander.
To do so, the Central Committee and all the Party functionaries
were obliged to interrupt constructive work. They opposed Trotsky
in the press and at Party meetings. The Trotskyists rallied to his
support. A discussion began.

A great part in exposing Trotskyism was played by Stalin's works
Trotskyism or Leninism?, and *The October Revolution and the
Tactics of the Russian Communists*. In these works, Stalin upheld Leninism, the Leninist theory of proletarian revolution, and
demonstrated the utterly anti-Marxist essence of Trotsky's theo-

ry of "permanent revolution." This "theory" doomed the working class to passivity, in anticipation of the victory of the Socialist revolution in the leading capitalist countries of Europe and of State aid to the Soviet country by the victorious West European proletariat. Stalin showed up Trotsky as a malignant disrupter, as one who had always attacked the Party and sown panic, as one who had time and again predicted the downfall of Soviet power and tried to obstruct the militant creative effort of the Party and the working people of the Soviet country. Stalin exposed all Trotsky's inventions and his attempts to substitute Trotskyism for Leninism. "It is the duty of the Party," said Stalin, "to *bury Trotskyism as an ideological trend*" (*Works*, Eng. ed., Vol. 6, p. 373).

The joint plenary meeting of the Central Committee and the Central Control Commission (January, 1925), which discussed Trotsky's conduct, warned him in the most categorical terms, insisting that he submit to Party discipline in practice and not just in words, and unconditionally renounce the struggle, in any form whatsoever, against the ideas of Leninism. The meeting removed him from the Revolutionary Military Council of the U.S.S.R., and replaced him as chairman of that body by M. V. Frunze, a loyal Leninist. The meeting decided to consider the discussion closed, but to continue to explain, in Party propaganda, the anti-Bolshevik and petty-bourgeois nature of Trotskyism from 1903 right up to the appearance of "The Lessons of October."

This marked the defeat of yet another attempt by Trotsky and the Trotskyists to divert the Party from its Leninist positions.

Having thus resolutely rebuffed Trotsky's latest sally, the Party, with redoubled energy, went ahead with its historic mission—to guide the building of Socialism in the U.S.S.R.

7. **The Question of the Possibility of Socialism Being Victorious in the U.S.S.R. Fourteenth Congress of the C.P.S.U.(B.). Party Steers a Course Towards Socialist Industrialisation. Defeat of the "New Opposition"**

The heroic labour of the Soviet people under the Party's leadership had borne fruit: the restoration of the national economy was nearing completion. The country was steadily growing stronger. The hopes of the world bourgeoisie that NEP would result in the Soviet system degenerating into capitalism had not been realised. Foreign capitalists were extending their economic connections with the Soviet country. The capitalist ruling circles were beginning to realise that the policy of "non-recognition" of the U.S.S.R. was powerless to prevent its consolidation and its suc-

cess. This policy, moreover, was prejudicial to the capitalis
countries themselves, being a hindrance to the development o
economic relations with the U.S.S.R., which signified good busi
ness for them. Realising this, Britain, Italy, Austria, Norway
Greece, Sweden, Denmark, Mexico and France recognised the So
viet Government, and established diplomatic relations with it in
1924. Diplomatic relations were also established between the
U.S.S.R. and China (the agreement on the occasion was China's
first equal treaty with a Great Power). The example of these coun
tries was followed in 1925 by Japan. Of the Great Powers, only the
United States persisted in its policy of "non-recognition" of the
U.S.S.R.

With the national economy of the Soviet country rapidly approaching the pre-war level, and with capitalist stabilisation proceeding on a world scale, the question arose in all its magnitude: could Soviet Russia, an economically and technologically
backward country, succeed in building Socialism, did it possess
adequate internal forces and resources to accomplish this task in
the conditions of hostile capitalist encirclement?

In their struggle against the Party, the Trotskyists argued that
Socialism could not be built in Soviet Russia without State aid
from a victorious West European proletariat. They were inciting
the working class to capitulate to capitalism.

The Party trenchantly repelled the defeatism preached by the
Trotskyists. The Fourteenth Conference (April 1925) stated quite
clearly: "The Party of the proletariat must exert every effort to
build a Socialist society, confident that this construction can and
will certainly be successful, provided the country is safeguarded
against any attempt at a restoration of capitalism" (*C.P.S.U.
in Resolutions*, Part II, p. 170).

The Party knew very well that the workers and peasants were
unquestionably strong enough to overcome their own bourgeoisie economically. But even if a complete Socialist society were
built the Soviet State would not be guaranteed against intervention on the part of the capitalist countries, against attempts to
restore capitalism in the U.S.S.R.

"The sole guarantee of the *final victory of Socialism*, i.e., the
guarantee against restoration," said the Conference resolution,
"is, therefore, the victory of the Socialist revolution in a number
of countries" (*ibid.*, p. 169).

The decisions of the Fourteenth Conference on the possibility of building Socialism in the U.S.S.R. became a *Party law*, binding on all Party members. They expressed the quintessence of
Lenin's theory that Socialism can be victorious first in one separate country, the quintessence of Lenin's plan for building Socialism in the Soviet Union.

By the end of 1925 the Party and the Soviet people had achieved considerable success in Socialist construction. The national economy had in the main been rehabilitated. Its commanding heights, which were in the hands of the Soviet State, had been consolidated and extended. The worker-peasant alliance had grown stronger as a result of economic progress, and so, consequently, had the dictatorship of the proletariat.

Agricultural output amounted to 87 per cent of the pre-war output. The crop area reached 99.3 per cent of the area sown in 1913. The cattle and pig population was greater than in 1916.

Considerable progress had been made in agricultural co-operation. Between January 1, 1924, and July 1, 1925, the number of peasant farms covered by various types of co-operation rose from 1,740,000 to approximately 5,000,000, i.e., increased almost threefold.

In 1925 large-scale industry was producing at the rate of 75 per cent of the pre-war volume. State and co-operative industry accounted for 81 per cent of the total output, and private industry for 19 per cent. The output of the iron and steel industry, however, was still far below the pre-war level. Pig-iron smelting was approximately one-third, and steel output about half, the pre-war volume. The Party had much to do in the iron and steel industry, where enormous difficulties had to be overcome. The total output of the consumer goods industries was over two-thirds of the pre-war figure. The railways were being rehabilitated, and carried 80 per cent of the 1913 amount of freightage.

Lenin's electrification plan was being carried out successfully. By the end of the restoration period, the Kashira, Shatura, Krasny Oktyabr (Leningrad), Kizel, and Nizhni-Novgorod (Balakhna) power stations had been built. The Shterovka and Volkhov power stations were being completed.

Notwithstanding the impressive gains in industry, unemployment had not yet been abolished. About a million men and women were out of work. These were mostly people who had come to the towns from the countryside, where they had been unable to find jobs. Industry and the other branches of the national economy were not in a position to absorb the flow of people from the villages, though in the course of one year the number of factory and office workers had increased by one and a half million. By the end of 1925 the total number of workers in the country—industrial and agricultural, including the unemployed—was more than seven million.

Considerable headway also had been made in home trade. Total turnover amounted to 70 per cent of the pre-war figure, the State accounting for 50 per cent, the co-operatives for 25 per cent, and private traders for 25 per cent. Thus the Communists were effectively fulfilling Lenin's directive to learn how to trade.

They were successfully ousting the private trader from the market.

The conditions of the working people had improved. Real wages in State-owned industry were higher than before the war. The gap between the rise in labour productivity and the growth of wages had been closed. The consumption of bread, meat, lard, edible oils and sugar by peasant families had increased considerably.

The declassing of the proletariat had come to an end; the class basis of the dictatorship of the working class had thus been strengthened.

Some headway—as yet insignificant, it is true—had been achieved in public education and in cultural development. Literacy among the population had risen from 32 per cent in 1920 to 40 per cent by the end of 1926. More than 22,000 reading-rooms were now functioning in the villages; radio and the cinema were beginning to be introduced into the daily life of the peasant.

During the years in which the national economy was being rebuilt the Party greatly strengthened the State apparatus. Under the leadership of the Party there took shape the system of industrial management based on the Leninist principle of democratic centralism.

The Party achieved successes in planning the national economy, especially industry. In carrying out this work, it never lost sight of the priority role of heavy industry. Thanks to the steady improvement of planning, from year to year, the economy was restored at an unprecedented rate, a rate which the post-war economy of the capitalist countries did not and could not know.

By the end of the rehabilitation period the U.S.S.R. had become still stronger. The years 1924 and 1925 were marked by important measures in policy affecting the nationalities. In Central Asia, the independent Soviet Republics of Turkmenia and Uzbekistan were created, and a few years later that of Tajikistan, all three republics voluntarily joining the Soviet Union as equal members. These developments were accompanied by the formation of Communist Parties in Turkmenistan and Uzbekistan, and then in Tajikistan. The Communist Parties of the Union Republics were confronted with the task of drawing the masses into the work of building Socialism.

By its foreign policy, the Party secured the consolidation of peace and an enhancement of the role of the U.S.S.R. in the international arena. Lenin's principle of peaceful coexistence of the Soviet State and the capitalist countries was being implemented with success.

During this period the Party itself had grown considerably stronger ideologically and had increased its membership. This testified to close contact between the Party and the masses, to the confidence which the masses reposed in the Party, to its incontestable prestige and to the soundness of its policy. The Party was the guide of the more than one-and-a-half million strong Komsomol, the seven-million strong trade unions and the ten million members of various voluntary societies. The work carried on by all these large voluntary organisations was a sign of the growing activity of the masses, of the development of genuine proletarian democracy, and of the tremendous educational work done by the Party; it was a guarantee of the rapid advance of the Soviet people towards Socialism.

The progress made in economic and political life was clear proof that the question "Who will beat whom?", posed by Lenin at the beginning of NEP, was being answered in favour of Socialism. The New Economic Policy had *justified itself*. The Soviet people were advancing steadily along the road to Socialism.

But it was necessary to increase the rate of this advance. This was pointed out by the Fourteenth Congress of the Party, held on December 18-31, 1925. Represented at the Congress were 643,000 members and 445,000 candidate members. The items discussed were reports by the Central Committee and the Central Control Commission, amendments to the Party rules, and other questions.

The Fourteenth Congress approved the political and organisational line of the Central Committee, the carrying out of which had ensured a general advance of the national economy, bringing it close to the pre-war level, and had strengthened the positions of Socialism.

Considering the capitalist encirclement of the U.S.S.R. and the fact that the capitalist countries, headed by Britain and the United States, were forming blocs for a new attack on the Soviet Union, the Congress instructed the Central Committee not to give way to provocation, to fight for world peace, to cement the alliance with the international proletariat and the oppressed peoples and to do everything to strengthen the defensive capacity of the country and the might of its armed forces.

In the economic sphere, the Congress set the target of fulfilling Lenin's plan for Socialist industrialisation. The resolution adopted said: "The Congress holds that the struggle for the victory of Socialism in the U.S.S.R. is the basic task of our Party" (*C.P.S.U. in Resolutions*, Part II, p. 195). Economic development, the Congress pointed out, should aim at transforming the country from an importer of machinery and equipment into a country producing machinery and equipment, an industrialised country fully provided with the latest machinery. The U.S.S.R. must be a sovereign economic entity, not depending on the capitalist world economy.

The important and difficult problems which confronted the Party in connection with the country's industrialisation could be solved only on the condition that absolute unity of will and solidarity prevailed in the Party ranks. The Congress instructed the Central Committee to "wage a resolute struggle against all attempts to undermine the unity of the Party, irrespective of their source or of who is directing them" (*C.P.S.U. in Resolutions,* Part II, p. 201).

One reason for this decision was that by the time the Fourteenth Congress convened, the so-called "New Opposition," headed by Zinoviev and Kamenev—members of the Political Bureau of the C.C.—had taken shape. Whereas previously they had opposed Trotskyism, after the Fourteenth Party Conference they themselves had sunk to a Trotskyist position. At the Fourteenth Conference, they had voted for the resolution which set forth the line of the Party aiming at the building of a complete Socialist society in the U.S.S.R.; but soon after the Conference they had begun to assert that it would be impossible to build Socialism in the U.S.S.R. without a Socialist revolution in the West. This was a relapse into the defeatist attitude adopted by Zinoviev and Kamenev in October, 1917 when, lacking faith in the strength of the proletariat and in its ability to lead the working peasantry, they had opposed the Party line on the Socialist revolution. Trotsky, too, had begun long ago to assert that without State aid from a victorious West European proletariat, Socialism could not be built in Russia. Thus the ideological standpoints of Zinoviev, Kamenev and Trotsky converged on the Menshevik view, which denied the possibility of the victory of Socialism in Soviet Russia.

The question of the possibility of building Socialism in the U.S.S.R. was the *main issue* on which all the opportunists, all the groups and factions, differed from Lenin and the Party. The most bitter opponents of the Leninist theory of the building of Socialism in the Soviet country were Trotsky, Kamenev, Zinoviev and Radek.

Denying the possibility of building Socialism in the U.S.S.R., and opposing the Party's policy of industrialising the country, the "New Opposition" claimed that State industry in the Soviet Union was not Socialist but State-capitalist industry, that NEP was nothing but a retreat, a retreat towards capitalism. The opposition began a struggle against the Party's Leninist line of an alliance between the working class and the middle peasant, a struggle which meant undermining the foundations of the dictatorship of the proletariat. The "New Opposition" calumniated the Party, saying that it was degenerating.

The "New Opposition," whose views were evidence of pressure from the petty-bourgeois strata of the country, became the rallying point for opportunist elements in the Party, for defeatists and sceptics who took fright at the colossal difficulties encountered in building Socialism. The strength of world capitalism sent them into a panic, and the activity of the kulaks frightened them. The "New Opposition" spread the slander that the Party was not fighting the kulaks and was turning a blind eye to the kulak danger.

The Party, however, was waging a struggle on two fronts—against those who exaggerated the kulak danger and underestimated the role of the middle peasants, and against those who ignored the kulak danger. The resolution of the Fourteenth Congress said:

"The Congress emphatically condemns the deviation which underestimates the differentiation in the countryside, which does not see the dangers represented by the growth of the kulaks.

"At the same time the Congress, no less emphatically, condemns the attempts to slur over the cardinal question of Communist policy in the countryside, the question of the struggle for the middle peasant as the central figure in agriculture, and of co-operation as the basic organisational form of the advance of the countryside towards Socialism.

"The Congress particularly stresses the necessity of fighting the last-mentioned deviation" (*ibid.*, pp. 198-99).

In order to cope with the difficulties of building Socialism in the U.S.S.R., it was essential to rid the Party of all opportunist scum, to make it a solidly united body. Since the "New Opposition" had come into being on the Trotsky platform, Trotskyism had to be exposed to the masses and had to be utterly smashed as a variety of Menshevism. Trotsky and the Trotskyists sought to belittle and distort the role of the Party as the leading force in the revolution and in Socialist construction. Advocating the permissibility of factions in the Party, they were seeking, in essence, to disintegrate and destroy the Party, because the existence of factions in its ranks, especially at a time of bitter class struggle, would have doomed the Party to destruction.

The Trotskyists aimed at breaking up the alliance of the working class and the working peasantry, for they regarded the peasantry as a reactionary force fighting against Socialism. The line of the Trotskyists thus meant the destruction of the dictatorship of the proletariat, since Soviet power could not exist without the alliance of the working class and the peasantry, an alliance in which the leading role was played by the working class headed by the Communist Party.

In fighting the Party line of building Socialism in the U.S.S.R., the Trotskyists were sowing defeatist ideas among the workers. From the standpoint of the Trotskyists, there was only one thing for the working class to do—go hat in hand to the capitalists.

Thus, on all the fundamental questions of Leninism, the Trotskyists adopted an anti-Leninist, anti-Party attitude; and hence an end had to be put to Trotskyism at all costs.

Stalin's book *Problems of Leninism*, which appeared in January, 1926, played a great part in exposing the "New Opposition." In this book, Stalin defended Leninism against the attempts of the "New Opposition" to distort it in favour of Trotskyism. This was attempted, in particular, by Zinoviev, who wrote an anti-Leninist book entitled *Leninism*, which substituted Trotskyism for Leninism. Stalin exposed the Trotskyist design to bury Leninism and to substitute Menshevik-minded Trotskyism for Marxism. He conclusively showed that the basis of the struggle waged by the "New Opposition" against the Party was lack of faith in the possibility of building a Socialist society in the U.S.S.R., lack of faith in the strength of the working class and its Communist Party.

Stalin's book helped the Communists in combating distortions of Leninism. It helped the Party to strengthen the faith of the working class in the possibility of building a Socialist society in the Soviet Union with their own forces, without waiting for State aid from the West European proletariat.

The centre of the "New Opposition" was in Leningrad. Zinoviev and his followers managed for a time to conceal their differences with the Central Committee from the Leningrad Communists. They pretended to support the line of the Central Committee, the line of the Party. By this deceit, the members of the "New Opposition" got themselves elected as delegates to the Fourteenth Congress, where they acted as a separate group, determined to give battle to the Central Committee with a view to overthrowing it and taking over the leadership of the Party.

They put up Zinoviev to oppose the Central Committee. In the co-report he submitted, he counterposed the views of the "New Opposition" to the line of the Party on all fundamental issues. Whereas the Leningrad Gubernia Conference had voted confidence in the Central Committee, the "New Opposition" at the Fourteenth Congress voted against confidence in the C.C. Things went so far that the "New Opposition" declared it would not abide by the decisions of the Congress, and, upon returning to Leningrad, began to work in this spirit among the Party members.

In order to expose the leaders of the "New Opposition," the Congress, in a special message to the Leningrad Party organisation, told of their behaviour at the Congress.

After the Congress the Central Committee sent Andreyev, Voroshilov, Kalinin, Kirov, Molotov, Petrovsky and others to Leningrad to explain the Congress decisions and to expose the anti-

Party activity of the "New Opposition." Stormy debates took place at the Party meetings in Leningrad. The members were outraged by the conduct of the "New Opposition." More than 97 per cent of the Leningrad Party members endorsed the decisions of the Congress, and condemned the "New Opposition." The Leningrad Gubernia Conference, held a month after the Congress, removed the Zinoviev leadership and elected a new Gubernia Committee headed by S. M. Kirov.

Thus yet another anti-Party grouping suffered shameful defeat in its attempts to shake Party unity and substitute Trotskyism for Leninism.

The Fourteenth Congress adopted new Party rules, and decided to change the Party's name from Russian Communist Party (B.) to Communist Party of the Soviet Union (Bolsheviks)—C.P.S.U. (B.).

The Fourteenth Congress of the C.P.S.U.(B.) has gone down in history as the *industrialisation Congress*. Its decisions expressed the Leninist line of the Party—the rapid development of heavy industry, large-scale Socialist machine industry capable of equipping the factories and agriculture with up-to-date machinery and reorganising peasant farming along Socialist lines.

"The conversion of our country from an agrarian into an industrial country able to produce the equipment it needs by its own efforts—that is the essence, the basis of our general line," said Stalin at the Congress (*Works*, Eng. ed., Vol. 7, p. 364).

The policy of industrialising the country became possible as a result of economic and political achievements, the consolidation of the Party and the dictatorship of the proletariat, the enhanced prestige and role of the U.S.S.R. on the international arena.

Industrialisation was that *main link* in the chain of tasks of economic development which, when grasped, would enable the country to haul forward the whole chain of Socialist construction and build a Socialist society in the U.S.S.R.

Having repelled repeated attempts by the various opposition groups to divert it from its Leninist path, the Party was passing on to a new phase in its history, solidly united behind its Leninist Central Committee.

BRIEF SUMMARY

The years 1921 to 1925—years of peaceful development—were years of tense struggle by the Party and the people to rehabilitate the national economy and ensure the country's advance towards Socialism.

Having adopted the New Economic Policy as the solely correct policy for the entire period of transition from capitalism to Socialism, the Party by this wise step reinforced the alliance of the workers and peasants, consolidated the dictatorship of the proletariat, and began to develop the Socialist sector of the national economy, thereby ensuring its successful struggle against the capitalist sector.

By its correct, Marxist-Leninist policy towards the nationalities, the Party secured the unity and fraternity of the peoples inhabiting the country, and united them in the unbreakable Union of Soviet Socialist Republics.

The Party boldly and resolutely carried out Lenin's directive to the effect that the Soviet country possessed all that was necessary and adequate for building a complete Socialist society. The question of the possibility of building Socialism in the U.S.S.R. was the fundamental and acute issue over which a bitter struggle was waged against the Party by all the opportunists, all the factional groups, among whom the chief role was played by the Trotsky group. They all tried to divert the Party from the Leninist path, to switch it to another path, the path leading to bourgeois democracy, to the restoration of capitalism in the Soviet land.

The Party decisively defeated these groups. For this it owes an immense debt to the great Lenin, who set the example of an uncompromising attitude towards opportunists and who equipped the Party with a powerful ideological weapon in the struggle for the solid unity of its ranks, for iron discipline and intolerance of factionalism of any kind.

Consistently carrying out Lenin's policy, the Party in this period of NEP won big successes in the course of a bitter class struggle against the capitalist elements. In an extremely brief space of time the working class and working peasantry, under the leadership of the Party, completed the rehabilitation of the national economy. Under the leadership of the Party, a solid foundation was laid for proceeding to a new phase of Socialist construction.

Giving effect to the Leninist principle of coexistence of the two systems—Socialism and capitalism—and working to preserve peace, the Party added greatly to the influence of the U.S.S.R. in the international arena.

Thus, in one of the most complicated periods in its history, the Party passed a difficult test. Its prestige among the working people rose high. The people convinced themselves by experience of the wisdom of the Party, of its able leadership, and saw for themselves that it defended the interests of the working people, that its activity was wholly directed towards the well-being and prosperity of Soviet society.

Having solved the main problems of the rehabilitation period, the Party brought the people up to the threshold of new tasks of immense importance, to a new historical phase—the phase of Socialist industrialisation of the U.S.S.R.

CHAPTER ELEVEN

THE STRUGGLE OF THE PARTY FOR THE SOCIALIST INDUSTRIALISATION OF THE COUNTRY AND THE PREPARATION FOR THE SOLID COLLECTIVISATION OF AGRICULTURE

(1926-1929)

1. The International Situation and the Foreign Policy of the Party and the Soviet State in 1926-1929

The Party started on the Socialist industrialisation of the country in an international situation marked by the relative stabilisation of capitalism. The stabilisation was a precarious and temporary one. It did not, and could not, eliminate imperialist contradictions. Particularly acute at this time were the contradictions between Britain and the U.S.A., which was ousting Britain from her positions on the world market.

The stabilisation of capitalism was everywhere accompanied by intensified exploitation of the working class and all working people. The offensive of the capitalists against the working class inevitably led to fierce class battles by the proletariat against the bourgeoisie. In 1926 a giant strike of British miners broke out; it developed into a general strike of the British proletariat, in which more than five million workers took part. The working class of the U.S.S.R. responded immediately to the strike, and collected considerable funds for the strikers. Despite the opposition of the British Trades Union Congress General Council, the rank and file welcomed the moral and material support extended by the working class of the U.S.S.R. as a vivid example of proletarian internationalism. In July, 1927, the Vienna workers rose against the offensive launched by the capitalists and reactionaries in Austria.

The upsurge of the national liberation movement in the colonial and dependent countries against intolerable imperialist oppression was a powerful blow at capitalist stabilisation. The most important event in the struggle of the oppressed peoples for national liberation was the revolution of the great Chinese people.

In 1924-1927 there raged the first revolutionary civil war in China. The Communist Party of China, basing itself upon the teachings of Marxism-Leninism, and heading the working class, pursued united front tactics aimed at bringing together all the revolutionary forces, and strove to ensure the leading role of the proletariat in the revolution. The initial successes of the Chinese revolution had a powerful impact on the development of the liberation struggle all over the world, particularly in India, Indonesia, Morocco Egypt and other colonial and dependent countries.

The national liberation movement of the peoples in the colonial and dependent countries found a warm response among the Soviet people. The working people of the U.S.S.R. enthusiastically hailed the Chinese revolution. Close friendship sprang up between the U.S.S.R. and the insurgent people of China. The Party was guided by the counsel of Lenin—the great friend of the peoples of the East—who in the historic struggle between Socialism and capitalism attached the utmost importance to the victory of the Chinese people's revolution and to the development of the liberation movement of the other oppressed peoples in the East.

The imperialists in all countries saw a threat to the capitalist system in the development and consolidation of the Soviet Union Relations between the capitalist States and the U.S.S.R. continued to be strained, although the Soviet Union had been recognised by many countries. The imperialists understood that industrialisation would accelerate the advance of the Soviet people to Socialism, consolidate the independence of the U.S.S.R., and add to its defence potential.

They therefore sought to frustrate, or at least to retard, the industrialisation of the Soviet country. They refused to grant it credits, pursued a policy of isolating the U.S.S.R. economically and threatened it with another armed intervention.

The instigator of anti-Soviet policy in those years was the old enemy of the national liberation movement—British imperialism then experiencing very great difficulties. The national liberation movement was gathering particular momentum in the British colonies. The knowledge that the oppressed peoples were deriving inspiration for their struggle from the example and achievements of the Soviet Union prompted the British imperialists everywhere to encourage interventionist acts against the U.S.S.R. Through their agents they organised anti-Soviet provocations in various countries; Soviet embassies and other offices in Peking, London and elsewhere were raided, and the Soviet Ambassador to Warsaw Voikov, was assassinated. The imperialists embarked on subversive activities in the Soviet Union itself. In 1927 British saboteurs threw bombs into a gathering of people in a Party club in Leningrad, wounding about thirty. The British imperialists resorted to every conceivable provocation to impede the industrialisation of the U.S.S.R. They tried to create a solid phalanx of capitalist Powers against the U.S.S.R.

In 1927 the British Conservative government broke off diplomatic relations with the U.S.S.R. and tried to get other capitalist countries to follow suit, the idea being to secure the further isolation of the Soviet Union. But the scheme was a failure: not a single capitalist State followed the example of the British Conservatives.

The foreign policy of peace pursued by the Party and the Soviet Government helped in no small measure to foil the anti-Soviet designs of the British Conservatives. It paralysed their attempts to establish an anti-Soviet front of capitalist States. Britain tried particularly hard to win Germany for the anti-Soviet policy. In those years Germany, aided by U.S. dollars, was rapidly reconstructing her heavy industry, particularly her war industry. In 1925 the German Government signed the Locarno agreements with Britain, France, Italy and Belgium, which signified a step towards setting up a British-led bloc of European capitalist countries against the Soviet Union. But the ruling circles in Germany had no intention of making a complete break with the Soviet Union and of linking themselves wholly with the anti-Soviet front. They continued to think that it was highly important for Germany to maintain normal relations with the Soviet State. In 1926 the U.S.S.R. and Germany signed a neutrality pact which made it difficult for Germany to participate in an anti-Soviet policy. In 1925-1927 the Soviet Union signed treaties of neutrality and non-aggression with Turkey, Afghanistan, Iran and Lithuania. These treaties served to some extent to prevent the capitalist States which signed them from being drawn into an anti-Soviet coalition. This was an important victory for the U.S.S.R.'s foreign policy of peace.

As her attempt to organise another intervention against the U.S.S.R. had failed, and as the disruption of normal trade with it was proving detrimental to her interests, Britain was compelled in 1929 to resume diplomatic relations with the Soviet Union.

But the imperialists did not discontinue their provocations. On their instigation, the Chinese warlords then in control of the north-eastern provinces of China (Manchuria), in the summer of 1929 seized the Chinese Eastern Railway, which belonged to the U.S.S.R. All attempts by the Soviet Government to settle the conflict by peaceful means proved fruitless. Troops of the Chinese warlords and Russian Whites began to make systematic raids on Soviet territory, menacing the security of the U.S.S.R.'s Far Eastern frontier. Retaliatory measures had to be taken against the instigators of war in the Far East. In August, 1929, a Special Far Eastern Army was formed. It soon went into action against the violators of the Soviet frontier and smashed the troops of the Chinese militarists. Soviet-Chinese negotiations followed, and in December, 1929, an agreement was signed which ended the conflict. The status quo was re-established on the Chinese Eastern Railway.

During 1926-1929 the Party and the Soviet Government, anxious to consolidate peace, continued to work indefatigably for disarmament. For this purpose wide use was made of the Preparatory Commission for a conference on disarmament set up by the League of Nations. In November, 1927, the Soviet Government laid before the commission a proposal for total disarmament by all nations. When this proposal was rejected, the Soviet Government advanced another proposal (in 1928)—for partial disarmament. But the imperialists, sabotaging disarmament, turned down this proposal too.

The Soviet Union's fight for peace and its disarmament proposals were most sympathetically received by the international proletariat and all working people. The U.S.S.R.'s prestige among the people in the capitalist countries mounted steadily. This was of tremendous importance for the fulfilment of the Soviet Union's fundamental task—that of building a Socialist society.

Lenin pointed out that it was highly important for the Soviet Union, building Socialism in a hostile capitalist encirclement, to win the support of millions of working people on a world scale.

International proletarian solidarity was a factor of prime importance in preserving peace. The working class in the capitalist countries opposed the predatory plans of the imperialists. The working people of the Soviet Union on their part rendered great assistance to the international working-class movement. Each success won by the Soviet Union strengthened the positions of the working class in the capitalist countries and helped it in the class struggle against capital.

The working class and the working people of the world followed the construction of Socialism in the U.S.S.R. with keen interest. Workers' delegations from Britain, the United States, France, Germany, Austria, Czechoslovakia, Belgium and other countries visited the U.S.S.R. and acquainted themselves with the achievements of Socialist construction. On returning home the delegates told the working people the truth about the first Socialist country; they exposed the slanders spread by bourgeois propaganda. In November, 1927, on the occasion of the tenth anniversary of the Great October Socialist Revolution, a world congress of friends of the Soviet Union was held in Moscow. The decisions of this congress pointed out that the building of Socialism in the U.S.S.R. met the interests of the revolutionary movement in all countries, that it was the vital concern of the proletarians of the whole world.

2. Beginning of the Socialist Industrialisation of the Country. The Party's Fight Against the Anti-Party Bloc of Trotskyists and Zinovievites

The transition to Socialist industrialisation signified a new stage in the struggle for Socialism in the U.S.S.R., a new chapter in the life of the Communist Party and the Soviet people. Having restored the national economy, it was necessary to reconstruct it along Socialist lines, on the basis of modern technology, and this had yet to be created.

Rehabilitation had been carried out in the main on the old technical basis. Compared with the advanced capitalist countries, Russia lagged behind in industrial production. Furthermore, the industry inherited by the U.S.S.R. had been badly damaged by the first world war and foreign military intervention. Despite the tremendous work done by the Party and the Soviet State to restore large-scale industry, its technological and economic level was low, and could by no means satisfy the Party and the people. The Party proceeded from Lenin's counsel:

"The sole material basis possible for Socialism is large-scale machine industry, capable of reorganising agriculture as well" (*Collected Works*, Vol. 32, p. 434).

The expansion of large-scale industry is closely bound up with the electrification of all branches of the national economy. Lenin saw electrification as the key to technological advance.

"If Russia," he wrote, "becomes covered by a dense network of electric power stations and powerful technical installations, our Communist economic development will become a model for the future Socialist Europe and Asia" (*Collected Works*, Vol. 31, p. 486).

Socialism could triumph in the U.S.S.R. solely as a result of the powerful expansion of heavy industry—the backbone of a Socialist economy—which could promote the light industries and the national economy as a whole, reorganise agriculture on Socialist lines, raise living standards, and ensure the defence of the country. A whole series of new industries had to be built, industries which had either not existed in tsarist Russia at all, or had been poorly developed: the iron and steel industry—the basis of industrialisation—the engineering, machine-tool, automobile, chemical, defence, tractor and other industries. It was necessary rapidly to reconstruct the old enterprises and build new factories, mines, and plants turning out means of production. This, basically, was what the Socialist industrialisation of the country meant. The engineering industry was its core.

Large-scale industry had to be developed at a high rate, if the disparity between the most advanced political power in the world and its weak material and technological base was to be eliminated.

Socialist industrialisation was the key to the reconstruction of the entire national economy, a condition for the growth of the working class, the leading force in the country. It was, moreover, fundamental for the further consolidation of the alliance of the working class and the working peasantry in the new forms of the production link between town and country.

The Party set the aim of building a powerful industry in all the Union Republics and the non-Russian regions. This was a step of the greatest importance for overcoming the actual backwardness of the formerly oppressed peoples, for the growth of national cadres and the development of national cultures.

Another most important aim of Socialist industrialisation was to raise the material and cultural level of the working class, of all the working people.

The rapid rate of industrialisation was dictated not only by internal interests, but by external conditions as well—by the fact that the U.S.S.R. was surrounded by a hostile capitalist world. At that time the U.S.S.R. was the only country of dictatorship of the proletariat.

To ensure the economic independence and defensive capacity of the Soviet Union in the difficult conditions of capitalist encirclement, the Party put forward the task of transforming the U.S.S.R. into a leading industrial Power, of overtaking the leading capitalist countries in the shortest possible time and then of outstripping them in industrial and general economic development.

The Soviet people were the first in history to pave the way to Socialism for mankind. Our country had to build a heavy industry without any kind of economic aid from outside. In working to fulfil Lenin's plan to industrialise the country, to build Socialism, the Party faced grave internal and external difficulties. They were caused by technical and economic backwardness, the difficulty of accumulating the vast funds needed for capital construction in industry, and the scarcity of trained industrial personnel. The difficulties were furthermore aggravated by the frenzy with which the capitalist elements in the country and their agents inside the Party resisted Socialist industrialisation. In these conditions, the country's industrialisation and the building of Socialism were a great achievement of the Party and the people. The Socialist method of industrialisation differs fundamentally from the capitalist method. Socialist industrialisation is planned, not haphazard. It does not begin by first developing the light industries, as was the case in the capitalist countries, but by developing heavy industry, which produces means of production.

Large-scale capital construction in industry called for investments of thousands of millions of rubles, but the Soviet Union was not a rich country at that time. The capitalist countries had built their heavy industry by plundering the colonies and semi-colonies, by exacting war indemnities, by ruthlessly exploiting the working people in their own countries. The Soviet Union could not as a matter of principle resort to such means of obtaining funds; they were incompatible with the Socialist system. Foreign loans had played a big part in the industrialisation of the capitalist countries. The Soviet Union could not count on foreign loans, because the capitalist countries refused to grant it any. The funds needed radically to re-equip the old factories and to build new ones had to be found inside the country.

And they were found, thanks to the gains of the Great October Socialist Revolution.

The fact that the main branches of the national economy were now concentrated in the hands of the proletarian State made it possible to mobilise enormous reserves for Socialist industrialisation. The profits from State-owned factories, transport, the banks, and State-controlled home and foreign trade, instead of finding their way into the coffers of capitalists, were now used to expand Socialist industry. Soviet power had freed the country from having to make huge annual payments abroad to the tune of 800-900 million gold rubles in interest on tsarist loans and in dividends to foreign capitalists on their investments in Russia. In the previous phase this had facilitated the rehabilitation of the national economy; it now helped to accumulate the resources for building heavy industry.

The Soviet peasantry, freed by the abolition of landowners' property rights from the annual payment to them of 700 million gold rubles for the lease and purchase of land, could now help the State, by their labour and material resources, to industrialise the country. The peasants were just as interested in this as the factory workers, because they were badly in need of agricultural machinery and manufactured goods.

All these sources of accumulation were in the hands of the Soviet State. All that was needed was to use them efficiently, practice the most rigid economy, put an end to unproductive expenditure, reduce inflated office staffs and invest the savings in industrialisation. It was necessary to raise labour productivity, rationalise production, and cut production costs. These were the economic tasks which the Communist Party tackled vigorously; it mobilised the working class and the whole Soviet people for the creation of Socialist industry.

The fight of the Party and the people for Socialist industrialisation yielded fine results right from the outset. About 1,000 million rubles were invested in industry in the economic year 1926/27, and more than 5,000 million rubles three years later. Work was begun on big undertakings such as the Dnieper Hydroelectric Power Station, the Turkestan-Siberia Railway and the Stalingrad Tractor Works.

Placed on a firm footing, the building of Socialist industry made good progress.

The industrialisation of the country and the growth of agricultural co-operation created the material basis for the elimination of the capitalist elements in the towns and of the only remaining exploiting class—the kulaks—in the countryside. The enemies of Socialism did all in their power to prevent Socialist industrialisation and to uphold the positions of capitalism. The reconstruction of the national economy was carried out in conditions of fierce class struggle.

The sharpening of the class struggle was reflected also inside the Party: various defeatists and opposition elements raised their heads. The chief danger to the Party during the early years of industrialisation came from the Trotskyists and Zinovievites, who had united on an anti-Leninist platform.

The "New Opposition"—Zinoviev, Kamenev and others—having suffered defeat at the Fourteenth Congress of the Party, openly adopted the defeatist positions of Trotskyism. In the summer of 1926 the Trotskyists and Zinovievites joined forces in an anti-Party bloc based on the Trotskyist platform. The bloc was joined by the remnants of all the defeated opposition groups—"Workers' Opposition," "Democratic Centralists" and others—and became in this way the rallying centre for all the opposition elements condemned by the Party; it resembled Trotsky's August bloc of 1912. All these variegated anti-Party elements reflected the interests of the remnants of the capitalist classes in our country, and the dissatisfaction of the urban petty bourgeoisie and the top strata of the bourgeois intelligentsia with the proletarian dictatorship. They were agents inside the Party of the class enemies, mouthpieces of the hostile capitalist encirclement.

Could Socialism be victorious in the U.S.S.R., or not—this was the main issue in the fundamental differences between the Party and the Trotsky-Zinoviev bloc. In its ideological and organising work the Party proceeded from Lenin's view that, given the dictatorship of the proletariat and the steady strengthening of the alliance between the working class and the peasantry, our country had everything that was necessary and adequate for building a complete Socialist society. The Trotsky-Zinoviev anti-Party bloc stubbornly denied the possibility of Socialism triumphing in one country, in the U.S.S.R.

The Party's fight against the Trotskyists and the other defeatists, and to carry out Lenin's plan for building Socialism, was led by the Central Committee and its Leninist core. In this struggle an active part was played by such Party leaders and functionaries as A. A. Andreyev, F. E. Dzerzhinsky, M. V. Frunze, L. M. Kaganovich, M. I. Kalinin, N. S. Khrushchov, S. M. Kirov, S. V. Kossior, V. V. Kuibyshev, A. I. Mikoyan, V. M. Molotov, G. K. Orjonikidze, G. I. Petrovsky, P. P. Postyshev, Y. E. Rudzutak, N. M. Shvernik, J. V. Stalin, K. Y. Voroshilov, Y. M. Yaroslavsky and A. A. Zhdanov. Led by the Central Committee, the Party organisations waged a stubborn and relentless struggle against the enemies of Socialism, and won the people for fulfilment of the plans—plans which required strenuous effort—for the Socialist industrialisation of the country.

The Party unmasked the Trotskyists and Zinovievites as out-and-out defeatists, as people who had abandoned Leninism and renounced the gains of the October Socialist Revolution. They opposed Lenin's plan for Socialist industrialisation, and advanced all kinds of reckless slogans. The Trotskyist proposals to increase the agricultural tax paid by the peasants and to raise prices of manufactured goods were especially dangerous. If carried out, these proposals would have ruptured the Leninist alliance between the working class and the working peasantry and weakened the dictatorship of the proletariat in the U.S.S.R. This defeatist policy of the Trotskyists and Zinovievites would have led in practice to the restoration of capitalism in the Soviet Union.

The Trotsky-Zinoviev anti-Party bloc preached that class conflicts between the working class and the peasantry and a rupture of their alliance were inevitable. The leaders of the opposition contended that peasant farming could not be developed along Socialist lines.

In furtherance of their defeatist policy, the Trotskyists and Zinovievites strove to secure freedom of factions and groupings, and the rescinding of Lenin's resolution on Party unity adopted by the Tenth Party Congress; they set about undermining Party discipline, and sought to discredit the Party apparatus built up over decades of revolutionary work, counterposing it to the membership.

On questions of foreign policy the Trotskyists and Zinovievites sank to the level of asserting that there was no need to defend the U.S.S.R. against imperialist intervention. Blinded by hatred for the Party leadership and the Soviet Government, they were even ready to stab the Soviet country in the back, the moment the imperialists attacked it.

The Trotskyists and Zinovievites embarked on the path of splitting the Comintern. They contacted anti-Leninist factional groups, got in touch with enemies of and traitors to the Communist movement who had been expelled from the Comintern, and with avowedly anti-Communist organisations, groups and individuals fighting against the Comintern.

Such was the defeatist essence of the Trotsky-Zinoviev bloc. The Central Committee called upon the Communists and the entire working class to wage a resolute struggle against the Trotskyist anti-Party opposition, which was undermining the unity of the Party and its leading role in the country. The Central Committee stressed that the Party could ensure the victory of Socialism only if it were united, and only if it were the sole leader of the people and of the proletarian dictatorship. The Central Committee issued a clear warning that unless the anti-Party bloc stopped its factional activities and was dissolved, its members would be expelled from the Party.

The warning, however, fell on deaf ears. In the autumn of 1926 the leaders of the Trotsky-Zinoviev opposition launched an open attack on the Party at membership meetings in the Aviapribor Works in Moscow, in the Putilov Works in Leningrad, and elsewhere. They put up their factional platform for consideration, seeking to impose a new discussion on the Party. The Party members unanimously rebuffed these attacks, and in some places simply ejected the Trotskyists and Zinovievites from the meetings. Completely routed in the Party and among the working class, the leaders of the opposition bloc submitted a statement to the Central Committee in which they condemned their factional work. But this was merely a ruse. In reality, they were secretly banding together an anti-Leninist party with its own discipline, membership dues and illegal printing press. In violation of the Party rules they held clandestine meetings at which they discussed their factional platform and their tactics for fighting the Party and its Central Committee.

The Fifteenth All-Union Party Conference (October-November 1926) was an important landmark in the struggle for the victory of Socialism in the U.S.S.R.

The Conference summed up the results of the 1925/26 economic year. The results proved convincingly, to anyone not blinded by Trotskyist demagogy, that the national economy, overcoming difficulties, was making good progress along the Socialist path. The Conference noted that the hegemony of large-scale industry in the country's economy had been strengthened, that its leading role in promoting the development of agriculture, including agricultural co-operation, had grown. The Conference rallied the Party membership, the working class and the working peasants to fulfil the Leninist plan for the country's Socialist industrialisation.

In a detailed political assessment of the Trotsky-Zinoviev opposition, the Conference qualified it as a Menshevik deviation in the

Party, and warned the opposition members that continued evolution towards Menshevism would lead to their expulsion from the Communist Party. The Conference called on all Communists to wage a determined struggle against the Trotsky-Zinoviev bloc.

The Seventh Enlarged Plenum of the Executive Committee of the Communist International (ECCI) was held during November-December, 1926. This meeting was of outstanding importance in routing Trotskyism ideologically in the international arena, and in purging the brother Communist Parties of Trotskyist and other revisionist elements. The ECCI Plenum endorsed the resolution on the opposition bloc passed by the Fifteenth Party Conference and made it incumbent upon the Communist Parties resolutely to combat all attempts by the Trotskyists to split the international Communist movement. Stalin reported at both the Fifteenth Party Conference and the ECCI Plenary Meeting about the Trotsky-Zinoviev opposition and the action to be taken against it. The decisions of the Fifteenth Party Conference, the Seventh Plenary Meeting of the ECCI and Stalin's reports played an important part in rallying the Party ranks under the Leninist banner, and in exposing the Trotskyists, their defeatism and their disruptive anti-Party activities.

In spite of the fact that the Fifteenth Party Conference and the Seventh Plenary Meeting of the ECCI had condemned outright the Trotsky-Zinoviev bloc, and that the members of the bloc had been decisively rebuffed by the working class, they did not cease their anti-Party activities. In 1927, when the international position of the U.S.S.R. became more complicated in view of the fact that the Conservative government in Britain had severed diplomatic and trade relations with it, the Trotskyists intensified their anti-Party struggle and circulated what they called the "Platform of the Eighty-Three."

It was a mendacious and hypocritical platform, designed to deceive the Party and the working class. In words the Trotskyists and Zinovievites professed to be against splitting the Party, to be in favour of industrialisation and of the collectivisation of agriculture; but in reality, they formed their own illegal party and jeered at the policy of industrialisation and collectivisation. The platform was a hotchpotch of slanderous fabrications such as that the Party and the Soviet Government wanted to abolish the monopoly of foreign trade and to grant political rights to the kulaks. The opposition printed thousands of copies of this utterly mendacious platform on its secret printing press and circulated it among Party members and non-Party people. The Party exposed to the masses this latest slanderous, anti-Party declaration of the Trotsky-Zinoviev bloc as well. Actively engaged in building Socialist industry, the people indignantly rejected the slanderous fabrications of the Trotskyists.

Bent on striking at the unity of the Party and its leadership, the Trotskyist opposition had for years exploited every difficulty encountered by the Party in Socialist construction. They wanted to turn the militant Party, directing Socialist construction, into a debating club.

It was necessary to put an end to the anti-Party activity of the Trotskyists and Zinovievites, completely to lay bare the anti-Leninist, defeatist nature of their platform. By the decision of the joint plenary meeting of the Central Committee and the Central Control Commission (October, 1927), Trotsky and Zinoviev, the ringleaders of the opposition, were expelled from the Central Committee for waging a factional struggle against the Party and its unity. In October, 1927, the Central Committee published theses covering the items of the Fifteenth Congress agenda, and opened a general Party discussion on them. The discussion meetings demonstrated the political maturity of the Party members and their solid support of the Leninist Central Committee: 724,000 Party members voted for the policy of the Central Committee and only 4,000 (or less than one per cent), for the bloc of Trotskyists and Zinovievites. The anti-Party bloc was routed. *The Leninist policy of the Party triumphed.* To mark the tenth anniversary of the Great October Socialist Revolution, the Central Executive Committee of the U.S.S.R., acting on the suggestion of the Central Committee of the Party, adopted a manifesto which proclaimed a seven-hour working day. The manifesto, which won the approval of the people, was opposed by the Trotsky-Zinoviev bloc, an action which revealed their policy as being hostile to the interests of the people.

The more obvious the political bankruptcy of the anti-Leninist Trotsky-Zinoviev bloc and its isolation from the masses became, the lower did this group sink to the depths of anti-Soviet struggle. On the tenth anniversary of the October Revolution the Trotskyists made an anti-Soviet sortie. In an attempt to counter the vast demonstration of the people under the slogans of Leninism, a handful of Trotskyists headed by Trotsky, Zinoviev and Kamenev, in gross violation of Soviet laws, appeared in the streets of Moscow and Leningrad with anti-Party and anti-Soviet slogans. A wave of anger and indignation rose among the people at the action of the Trotskyists.

In November, 1927, the Central Committee and the Central Control Commission, fulfilling the will of the Party, expelled Trotsky and Zinoviev from the Party and removed the other oppositionists from the Central Committee and the Central Control Commission. The question of the opposition as a whole was submitted to the Fifteenth Party Congress.

3. Mobilisation of the Soviet People for the Industrialisation of the Country. Reorganising the Work of the Party and the Mass Organisations

The policy of Socialist industrialisation of the country necessarily involved increasing the political and production activity of the masses and drawing new sections of the working people, first and foremost of the industrial workers, into management of the State.

"Socialism," Lenin pointed out, "is the creation of the masses themselves" (*Collected Works*, Vol. 26, p. 255).

The Party extended and strengthened its contacts with the masses, and increased the activity of its members by developing inner-Party democracy, criticism and self-criticism.

The amended rules adopted by the Fourteenth Party Congress created favourable conditions for the further development of inner-Party democracy and for greater activity and initiative on the part of the membership. The Central Committee saw to it that the Leninist standards of Party leadership were observed and that leading Party committees were properly elected; it fought with determination against manifestations of bureaucracy in Party work, attempts to stifle healthy criticism and other violations of inner-Party democracy. The work of the Central Committee and the local Party organisations was based on the principle of collective leadership and broadening of inner-Party democracy. Plenary meetings of the Central Committee and of Party committees, Party activists' meetings, and Party branch meetings were held regularly. These discussed important questions of Party, State and economic construction. The Central Committee established closer contact with the localities. Between the Fourteenth and Fifteenth Party Congresses the Central Committee, with the participation of local Party functionaries, examined the work of about forty local Party organisations. This helped to enliven and improve Party work in the localities. Fewer directives and circulars were sent out. Live contacts between the Central Committee and local Party organisations assumed more varied forms.

The attention of Party organisations was focussed on rationalising production, raising labour productivity, effecting economies and lowering production costs. An important method of solving these problems was large-scale Socialist emulation. The Central Committee criticised those Party organisations which, immersed in mass political drives, tended to ignore problems of industrial production and practical questions of economic development in general.

It was especially important to improve the activity of the shop Party organisations in the factories, i.e., those closest to the masses. There were 2,000 shop organisations in 1924; by 1927 the number had risen to nearly 4,000. A powerful force of non-Party activists had grown up around them.

During the years of industrialisation the Party's contact with the masses became stronger. Its political influence increased, as could be clearly seen from the growth of its membership by the entry into its ranks of the foremost workers and peasants. The All-Union Party census held in 1927 showed that the Party had 775,000 members and 372,000 candidate members. In three years (1924-1926), over 800,000 people joined the Party, including more than half a million workers.

The Central Committee took steps to improve the social composition of the Party membership, to increase the proletarian core in the Party, this being a paramount condition of its monolithic unity.

In connection with the celebration of the tenth anniversary of the Great October Socialist Revolution, a large-scale enrolment of workers in the Party was announced. Admission to membership was on a strictly individual basis. 108,000 new members were made. This new and considerable working-class reinforcement of the Party enhanced its leading role in Socialist construction. With a view to strengthening the Party organisations in the countryside, the Party set itself the task of drawing into its ranks activists from among agricultural workers, farm-labourers, and poor peasants active in the poor peasants' groups, the Soviets and the agricultural co-operatives.

The industrialisation of the country confronted the mass organisations with new tasks. The work of the local Soviets, the trade unions, the Komsomol and other voluntary organisations had to be reviewed and enlivened. The Party issued the slogan "Production comes first!" addressing it to all the mass organisations of the working class.

The Party continued to improve the work of the machinery of the State through its policy of enlivening the Soviets, with the result that the role of the latter in economic and cultural development was enhanced. Ever larger numbers of the working class and the working peasantry were drawn into the work of administering the State. Groups of non-Party activists were set up to participate in the work of the Soviets. Deputies to the Soviets began to report back to their electors more frequently.

Elections to the Soviets took place in 1926 and 1927, in a situation of increased activity by the working people and a sharpening of the class struggle. The elections showed that the influence of the Party among the working people in town and country had grown, and that the positions of the capitalist elements had weakened; it was obvious that the kulaks were becoming increasingly isolated from the middle peasants. Of great importance in Socialist construction was the Party's campaign to improve the machinery of the Soviet State still further. In keeping with Lenin's counsel, the Party took steps to perfect the governmental apparatus, cut staffs, reduce maintenance costs and waged a systematic struggle against bureaucratic distortions.

Particular attention was paid to improving the management of industry. The policy of industrialisation called for better management of industry, closer contact of the direction of economic construction with local conditions, and the training of key industrial personnel. Industrial management was based on the consistent application of the Leninist principle of democratic centralism. The growth of competent industrial personnel and the experience accumulated in running industry made it possible to free the enterprises from petty tutelage and to increase the responsibility of their managers.

It was necessary to improve the work of the trade unions—the biggest mass organisation of the working class. The working class was growing rapidly: over two million people joined its ranks during the first two years of industrialisation. The switch-over from rehabilitation to reconstruction of the national economy, and the difficulties involved in the latter, called for hard work by the trade unions to educate the masses, particularly the new workers, and to draw them into active Socialist constructive work. Trade union work was improved by developing proletarian democracy. The unions nominated workers for managerial bodies. A most important means of drawing the masses of workers into Socialist construction, the management of production and the battle to raise labour productivity was production conferences, which arose on the initiative of the workers. These conferences, in which the workers took an active part, became widespread; they discussed such questions as the state of production, how to economise and avoid waste, elimination of idle time, reduction of costs, raising of labour productivity, and improvement of discipline on the job. The Central Committee sought to ensure that the progressive methods used in a particular branch of industry or transport and approved at production conferences were extended to other branches. It encouraged all other creative initiative taken by the masses.

During these years the Komsomol—the active assistant of the Party—on which devolved the function of training the young generation of the builders of Communism, played an increasingly important part. Taking an active part in the struggle for the Socialist industrialisation of the country it produced tens of thousands of rationalisers and inventors from among its members.

It was very important to involve women in production and in public life, especially in the non-Russian republics and regions. Delegate meetings of women workers and peasants became widespread. The first All-Union Congress of Women Workers and Peasants was held in October, 1927.

The sharpening of the class struggle in the country made it exceptionally important to increase proletarian influence in the countryside, where a bitter struggle was going on between the working class and the bourgeois-kulak elements for the allegiance of the main mass of the peasantry—the middle peasants. The Party's slogan "Turn to the countryside!" was successfully translated into practice by the Party organisations. Nearly 21,000 Party groups, or over a quarter of a million Communists—such was the Party's outpost in the countryside. At the same time as it sent Party members from the towns to the villages, the Party promoted new cadres who had grown up in the countryside. The role of the Communists in rural public life increased considerably. The results of the elections to the Soviets were eloquent proof of this: every fifth chairman of a village Soviet and half the members of the volost executive committees were Party members.

Proletarian influence was exerted on the peasants also through various urban voluntary organisations, embracing millions of workers. One of the Party's mainstays in its work in the countryside were the trade unions. It should be borne in mind that a considerable section of the workers were connected with the countryside, and had farms there. What is more, over two million trade unionists were employed in the countryside itself, of whom more than a million were members of the Agricultural and Forestry Workers' Union. The Party worked indefatigably to improve the work of the trade unions in the countryside, to get them to take part in rural public life and, in addition, induced workers in increasing numbers to take the countryside under their "patronage." The patronage societies of those years had as many as 1,500,000 members.

In the struggle for the reconstruction of the countryside along Socialist lines, the Party had the support of the working class and of forces that were part of the peasantry itself. But these forces had to be united and organised. The Party focussed attention on groups of poor peasants in the Soviets and the co-operatives. Meetings of poor peasants, in which middle peasants also took part, were held more regularly. Thanks to better organisation, the poor peasants began to exert a growing influence on public life in the villages and actively combated the kulaks.

Loyal helpers of the Party in the countryside were the members of the Komsomol. A million young fighters for a Socialist countryside waged a courageous battle against the kulaks and all anti-Soviet forces, and also against indifference and distrust of the as yet unexplored Socialist path of agricultural development. The peasant press made a big contribution. Every rural district had its wall newspaper, which rallied the peasant masses round the Party and the Soviets. Some 200,000 rural newspaper correspondents boldly campaigned for Socialism, regardless of the danger of getting a kulak bullet in the back. The Party used the Red Army in every possible way to educate the peasants politically. Demobilised Red Army men exerted a powerful influence in the countryside. Half the chairmen of village Soviets and two-thirds of the chairmen of volost executive committees had passed through the school of the Red Army.

As a result of the improved political and organising work of the Party and of the public organisations under its guidance the offensive against the kulaks was intensified. Supported by the poor peasants, the working class strengthened its alliance with the middle peasants. Growing numbers of peasants were drawn into various forms of co-operation. Thirty-eight per cent of the peasant households belonged to consumers' co-operatives, while agricultural co-operatives embraced nearly one-third of the peasant farms. Lenin's co-operative plan was successfully being translated into real life.

The Party was pursuing the policy of extending agricultural co-operation, with the object of preparing for the mass transition from individual peasant farming to the Socialist, collective-farm system.

4. First Successes in Socialist Industrialisation. Fifteenth Party Congress and the Course Towards Collectivisation of Agriculture. Rout of the Trotsky-Zinoviev Anti-Party Bloc

After two years of strenuous effort the fulfilment of the plan for the Socialist industrialisation of the country began to bear fruit. Old factories had been re-equipped and new ones built. By the end of 1927 the gross output of industry and agriculture had surpassed the pre-war level.

Particularly rapid was the rate of development of large-scale Socialist industry, which in the economic year 1926/27 produced 18 per cent more than in the previous year. For the first years of industrialisation this was a record rate of growth of large-scale industry in the U.S.S.R. It was, moreover, many times greater than the rate of industrial growth in the main capitalist countries. In the United States, for example, the average annual growth of industrial output over 29 years (1901-1929) did not exceed 4 per cent. The high rate of industrial growth in the U.S.S.R., especially in heavy industry, testified to the superiority of the Socialist economic system over the capitalist.

The expansion of large-scale industry added to the dominant position of the Socialist sector in the national economy. The share of the Socialist sector in industry at the end of 1927 amounted to 86 per cent, while that of the private sector had fallen to 14 per cent (excluding flour-milling, a considerable part of which was in private hands). Here, then, was the proof of the Socialist nature of the industrialisation taking place in the Soviet Union.

The steady growth of the Socialist sector in industry was linked with the squeezing out of the capitalist elements from trade. The private share in retail trade declined from 53 per cent in 1924/25 to 35 per cent in 1926/27, and in wholesale trade from 9 to 5 per cent.

The national income in the economic year 1926/27 rose more than 11 per cent compared with the previous year. If we bear in mind that the average annual increase of the national income in the United States, Britain, Germany and other highly developed capitalist countries was not more than 2 to 4 per cent, it will be clear how rapidly the economy of the U.S.S.R. was growing. This clearly reflected the advantages of the Socialist economic system over the capitalist, the soundness of the Party's economic policy, and the labour enthusiasm of the masses, particularly of the working class.

Under the leadership of the Communist Party, the country was advancing confidently and rapidly towards Socialism, squeezing the capitalist elements out of the national economy.

But while large-scale Socialist industry was rapidly expanding and the towns were growing, agriculture, the most extensive and vitally important branch of the national economy, lagged very much behind. Whereas the gross output of agriculture as a whole exceeded the pre-war figure, the gross output of its most important branch—grain production—amounted in the 1926/27 economic year only to 95 per cent of the 1913 crop, while the marketed share (that consumed outside the countryside) was but 13.3 per cent, as against the pre-war 26 per cent.

This decline in grain marketed was due to the fact that the October Revolution had abolished the big landlord estates and had considerably reduced the number of kulak farms. Before the war the kulak farms and landlord estates were the biggest growers of grain for the market: the landlord estates accounted for 22 per cent—$4^{1}/_{2}$ million tons—of the grain sold on the market, the kulaks for 50 per cent—$10^{1}/_{2}$ million tons. In 1927 the total grain production of kulak farms was less than one-third of what it had been before the war.

After the October Revolution the small middle- and poor-peasant farms became the main producers of grain. In 1927 they numbered about 24 millions, compared with about 17 millions before the first world war. The middle and poor peasants, freed from their landlords as a result of the October Revolution, and having undermined the strength of the kulaks, were living better. They were now the main holders of grain, producing more than in pre-war days ($64^1/_2$ million tons instead of 40 million tons), but sending only 11 per cent of their total crop to the market.

The share of the State and collective farms in grain production was negligible. They produced only 1.3 million tons, and provided only 6 per cent of all grain marketed.

Grain production, as it was then, could not satisfy the country's needs, which were increasing as a consequence of the growth of the urban population and of the working class.

Big success in the development of Socialist industry and a grave lag in agriculture—such was the economic situation before the Fifteenth Party Congress. The Congress was held on December 2 to 19, 1927. By that time the Party membership was 887,000, with 349,000 candidate members.

The Congress discussed the report of the Central Committee, the report of the Central Control Commission-Workers' and Peasants' Inspection, the directives for a five-year plan, work in the countryside, the opposition, and other questions.

The report of the Central Committee was made by Stalin. The Congress fully approved the political and organising work of the Central Committee. In the sphere of foreign policy it instructed the Central Committee steadfastly to pursue the Leninist line of struggle for peace, to strengthen international ties with the working people of all countries, and to raise the defence capacity of the U.S.S.R. In the sphere of home policy, which had already yielded good fruits, the Congress gave instructions to continue Socialist industrialisation at unremitting speed and to step up the offensive against the capitalist elements, *the objective being their elimination.*

Special attention was devoted to the prospects for the development of agriculture, which was lagging greatly compared with Socialist industry. The reasons for the slow growth of agriculture were brought out by the Congress.

Industry was large-scale and centralised, whereas agriculture was still small-scale and dispersed. Large-scale industry was based on the public, Socialist ownership of the means of production; its expansion was strengthening the positions of Socialism in the national economy and was leading to the elimination of the capitalist elements. Small peasant farming, on the other hand, was based on private ownership of the means of production, apart from the land, which had been nationalised by the Soviet State and handed over to the peasants for their use free of charge. Whereas Socialist industry was conducted along planned lines, small-commodity peasant farming was subject to unplanned market fluctuations. While large-scale Socialist industry received a steady supply of new machinery and developed at a rapid rate according to the principle of extended reproduction, small peasant farming, based on primitive equipment and manual labour, could not make use of modern machinery, developed slowly, and at times failed to ensure even simple reproduction.

By 1927 small-scale dispersed peasant farming had in the main exhausted its possibilities for further raising its productivity. The process of fragmentation of the peasant farms continued. They supplied only a minimum for the market, and this was especially true of grain. Year by year the rate of growth of agriculture slowed down and lagged more and more behind that of Socialist industry. This created difficulties in supplying the urban population with agricultural products, and industry with raw materials. Agricultural produce constituted an insignificant part of exports, and difficulties arose in building up State stocks. The lag in agriculture was holding back all Socialist construction.

The interests of building Socialism and the defence of the country insistently required that an end be put to this lag and dictated the necessity of passing from small-scale privately-owned peasant farming to large-scale Socialist farming.

The Fifteenth Congress, after comprehensive discussion of this question, decided on the *all-out collectivisation of agriculture*, on switching over to large-scale, mechanised Socialist farming. It was decided to *begin preparations for a Socialist offensive along the whole front.*

Without mass collectivisation of agriculture it was impossible to bring the country out on to the broad highway of Socialist construction and rid the millions of working peasants of kulak bondage, misery and ignorance. In this the Party was guided by Lenin's plan for building Socialism in the U.S.S.R., by his brilliant co-operative plan, and his well-known precepts:

"So long as we live in a country of small peasants there is a firmer economic basis for capitalism in Russia than for Communism. This must be borne in mind. Anyone who has carefully observed life in the countryside, as compared with life in the towns, knows that we have not torn up the roots of capitalism and have not undermined the foundation, the basis of the internal enemy. The latter depends on small-scale production, and there is only one way of undermining him, namely, to move the economy of the country, including agriculture, over to a new technical basis, the technical basis of modern large-scale production" (*Collected Works*, Vol. 31, pp. 483-84).

"If peasant farming is to develop still further, we must firmly assure its transition to the next stage as well; and the next stage will inevitably be the gradual unification of small, fragmented peasant farming, the least profitable and most backward, into public, large-scale agriculture" (*Collected Works*, Vol. 32, p. 264).

While recognising the pressing need for the extensive collectivisation of agriculture, the Congress categorically stated that the transition of the peasantry to collective farming must take place in an absolutely voluntary way, with the consent of the working peasants themselves. The Congress at the same time gave instructions to strengthen and develop the State farms.

The Congress emphasised that the only way to abolish the lag in agriculture was to carry out Lenin's co-operative plan. Agricultural co-operation at the time of the dictatorship of the proletariat helped Socialist industry to win over the countryside. The progress already made in the organisation of peasant co-operative societies showed that it was now possible to set the task of drawing all the poor peasants and the bulk of the middle peasants into co-operation in the ensuing period. The Congress assigned to agricultural co-operation the task of helping the poor and middle peasants to free themselves from kulak bondage, by providing service for the weaker farms through a broad network of hiring stations, supplying them with machinery on easy terms for joint cultivation of the land.

The Congress instructed the Party to proceed, jointly with all the poor and middle peasants and on the basis of the strengthened alliance of the working class and the peasantry, to more systematic and insistent restriction and squeezing out of the kulak and the private trader.

The development of Socialist construction and vast, long-term capital investments required a higher level of economic planning. Large-scale Socialist industry, which had grown and gained strength, now played the dominant role in the economy. The Party had accumulated considerable experience in planning, and was now in a position to advance from annual targets to long-term plans for a number of years. This was a major victory for the Leninist economic policy of the Party.

In his last articles, devoted to the plan for building Socialism, Lenin wrote that for the first time in history the Soviet State had the opportunity "of ascertaining the period necessary for bringing about radical social changes; we now see clearly *what* can be done in five years, and what requires much more time" (*Collected Works*, Vol, 33, pp. 441-42).

The Fifteenth Congress adopted directives for the *first Five-Year Plan* of development of the national economy.

The basic economic tasks of this plan were, as the Congress pointed out, steadily to expand large-scale Socialist industry, to use it for bringing about a rapid growth of all branches of the national economy and an increase of the share of its Socialist sector, and to squeeze out the capitalist elements more vigorously, with a view to launching a Socialist offensive against the remnants of capitalism along the whole economic front.

The adoption of directives for the first Five-Year Plan signified a new and higher stage of planning in the Soviet national economy, in the battle to build Socialism. These directives specified the schedules and rates of the great social transformations to take place in the Soviet Union.

Fight to cement the unity of the Party—this was the keynote struck by the Fifteenth Congress. This was seen in the Central Committee's report. The report "On the Opposition," submitted on behalf of the commission elected by the Congress to investigate the anti-Party activity of the Trotskyists, was delivered by G.K. Orjonikidze. The Congress noted that the Trotsky-Zinoviev anti-Party "opposition has broken ideologically with Leninism, has degenerated into a Menshevik group, has taken the path of capitulation to the forces of the international and internal bourgeoisie and has objectively become a tool of the third force against the regime of the proletarian dictatorship" (*C.P.S.U. in Resolutions*, Part II, p. 441). The opposition had become a direct tool of the class enemies in their frenzied struggle against the Communist Party and Soviet power. The Congress declared that membership of the Trotskyist opposition and the propagation of its views were *incompatible with membership of the Party.*

The opposition, the Congress recorded, had transgressed the Soviet law, for from factionalism it had turned to forming an anti-Soviet Trotskyist party. Taking all this into account, the Congress approved the resolution of the Central Committee and the Central Control Commission on the expulsion of Trotsky and Zinoviev, the ringleaders of the anti-Party opposition, from the Party, and expelled 75 active members of the bloc—Kamenev, Pyatakov, Radek, Rakovsky, Safarov, Smilga, I. Smirnov, Lashevich and others. The Sapronov group of 23 members was also expelled from the Party as a patently anti-revolutionary group.

The Congress instructed Party organisations to cleanse their ranks "of all the clearly incorrigible elements of the Trotskyist opposition."

It also instructed the Central Committee and the Central Control Commission to do everything to influence ideologically the rank-and-file members of the opposition in order to get them to renounce the defeatist views of Trotskyism and to take the Leninist path.

The Fifteenth Congress adopted an important addendum to the Party rules: "Members of the Party refusing to give truthful answers to the questions of Control Commissions shall be immediately expelled from the Party" (*ibid.*, p. 491). This addendum was necessitated by the fact that the oppositionists, when summoned to appear before the appropriate Party bodies, refused to give truthful testimony about the anti-Party activity of the Trotskyists, and tried to mislead the Party bodies and to cover up the criminal work of the Trotskyist factionalists.

The Fifteenth Congress of the C.P.S.U.(B.) is known in the history of the Party as the *Congress of collectivisation* of agriculture and of preparation for a Socialist offensive along the whole front. Its decisions, which reflected the new stage in the building of Socialism in the U.S.S.R., and in consolidating the Party's unity, were approved by the Party organisations and by the many millions of workers, by all working people.

Shortly after the Congress, many of the expelled participants in the Trotsky-Zinoviev opposition began to submit applications, breaking with Trotskyism and asking to be reinstated in the Party. Seeing that in the past similar statements by opposition members had usually been followed by fresh anti-Party actions on their part, the Party acted with caution in regard to these applications of the Trotskyists. It made their reinstatement in the Party dependent on the condition of their complete ideological and organisational disarmament, forthright and public condemnation of their views as anti-Leninist, and an undertaking to uphold the decisions of the Party, of its congresses and its Central Committee. A six-months' probationary period was established for those applying for reinstatement. And only after the expiry of this term, having satisfied itself that the behaviour of the ex-oppositionists was in keeping with their undertakings—to observe the rules and programme of the Party and its discipline, and to carry out its general line as laid down in its decisions—did the Party examine the question of the reinstatement of each individual applicant.

The majority of the expelled fulfilled their undertakings and were reinstated in the Party. But, as subsequent events showed, the behaviour of the leaders of the Trotsky-Zinoviev opposition was doublefaced. They returned to the Party with the same provocative aim—to disrupt it from within, to overthrow the Leninist Central Committee, to usurp the leadership of the Party and to frustrate the building of Socialism in the U.S.S.R.

It was the merit of the Party that it completely defeated Trotskyism, equipped the masses of the people with a clear Leninist programme of struggle for the victory of Socialism in the U.S.S.R., and organised that victory.

5. Preparations for the Offensive of Socialism Along the Whole Front. The Party's Fight Against the Right Deviation. Adoption of the First Five-Year Plan. Beginning of the Mass Collective-Farm Movement

In pursuance of the Fifteenth Congress decisions, the Party with renewed force went ahead with Socialist industrialisation and preparations for the mass collectivisation of agriculture based on Lenin's plan for building Socialism in the U.S.S.R.

The Socialist reconstruction of the national economy evoked the stubborn resistance of the capitalist elements inside the country and greatly alarmed the world bourgeoisie. The imperialists and the landlords, the big industrialists and bankers who had fled the Soviet country saw in the Nepmen and the kulaks their mainstay in the bitter struggle to frustrate the building of Socialism in the U.S.S.R. In 1928 the capitalist elements in the country, reduced to 4.6 per cent of the population, still played some role in the economy. Approximately one-fourth of the retail trade and one-sixth of the industrial output were in the hands of the Nepmen. The kulaks grew one-fifth of the grain for the market. And although the share of the capitalist elements in the national economy was steadily declining, their absolute growth could still be observed. They had their roots in petty commodity production—in handicrafts and in individual peasant farming. The capitalist elements, especially the kulaks, still exerted an influence on a certain part of the peasantry, artisans, handicraftsmen and office workers.

The class struggle grew sharper. The capitalist elements tried to take advantage of the grain difficulties encountered by the Soviet State in 1928. On top of the general backwardness of grain production, there came crop failure in southern Ukraine and in the North Caucasus. The gross yield of grain was nearly 5,000,000 tons less than in the previous year. In January, 1928, State grain purchases showed a deficiency of 2,000,000 tons. This shortage brought the export of grain almost to a standstill, and caused difficulties in accumulating the foreign currency needed for the purchase of industrial equipment abroad. Grave difficulties were encountered in supplying the population with bread, and industry with agricultural raw materials.

In this unfavourable situation on the grain front, the kulaks, who had regained ground owing to NEP and held large quantities of grain, refused to sell it to the State at the prices fixed by the Soviet Government. They terrorised the middle peasants who sold their grain surpluses to the purchasing agencies, and tried in every way to weaken and undermine the building of collective farms. They committed acts of sabotage against collective farms, set fire to grain-delivery stations and nefariously murdered Party and Soviet personnel in the countryside.

The Party and the Government, supported by the masses, broke the resistance of the kulaks. Emergency measures were taken against them. Kulak grain hoarders were brought before the courts, by whose decision their surpluses were confiscated. One-fourth of the confiscated grain was turned over to the village poor in the form of loans. In carrying out the grain purchases, the method of self-assessment was used, that is, the peasants themselves were empowered to fix quotas for the different households. In this way the masses of poor and middle peasants were drawn into the battle for grain. They rallied round the Party and Soviet organisations against the kulaks. Elements who were degenerate, corrupt, infected with defeatist ideology and reluctant to "fall out" with the kulaks, and who did not carry out a class policy in the countryside, were expelled from posts in the Soviets and the co-operatives.

All these measures contributed to the success of the grain purchases. By the end of 1928 the State had adequate stocks of grain. The crushing of kulak resistance had strengthened and reinforced Soviet power and the positions of Socialism in the countryside.

The grain-purchasing and sowing campaigns in 1928 and 1929 stimulated the activity of the rural Party organisations and all the State and voluntary mass organisations of the working people. Most of the rural Communists stood the test. Undaunted by kulak threats, they actively fought for fulfilment of the State plan of grain purchases, for a class policy in the countryside. Some Soviet and Party organisations, however, overstepped the mark, applying the emergency measures intended for the kulaks to some of the middle peasants. The Central Committee sharply condemned this distortion of the Party line and remedied the situation.

Solving the grain problem was one of the most important tasks of the national economy. The Central Committee and the Government devoted ceaseless attention to it, applying the Leninist principle of properly combining the interests of the State and the personal interests of the working peasantry. A joint plenary meeting of the Central Committee and the Central Control Commission held in April, 1928, decided to increase the advances to peasant farms supplying the State by contract to 135 million rubles, and to raise the total allocation for agricultural development to 717 million rubles. Additional large State grain-growing farms were established. In five years they were to produce up to 1,600,000 tons of grain annually for the market. The State farms became strong points in the Socialist reconstruction of agriculture. The battle for grain became a component part of the battle for industrialisation, for building Socialism in the U.S.S.R.

The frenzied resistance of the kulaks to the measures taken by the Soviet Government in the countryside encouraged concealed enemy groups in their struggle to restore capitalism in the country. At the beginning of 1928 a big saboteur organisation consisting of bourgeois specialists was discovered in the Shakhty and in other areas of the Donets coalfield (the "Shakhty case"). For several years a group of these specialists and camouflaged Whites had engaged secretly in subversive work aimed at destroying the coal industry in the Donets coalfield, carrying out assignments of the former owners of the mines—Russian and foreign capitalists— and of foreign intelligence services. The saboteurs caused explosions in the mines and flooded them, damaged costly new equipment, set fire to power stations and deliberately misspent the people's money earmarked for capital construction. Members of this subversive organisation purchased abroad equipment for the mines and power stations that was obviously outmoded and useless. Especially dangerous were the wreckers' attempts to worsen the conditions of the miners. They deliberately disorganised the supply of food and consumer goods to the miners and their families, cheated the workers in paying wages, held up housing programmes and infringed safety rules in the mines, which endangered the lives of the miners. The underlying purpose was to cause discontent among the workers and turn them against the Party and the Soviet Government.

The wreckers also aimed at undermining the defence of the country and clearing the way to intervention by the imperialist Powers. Nearly 300 one-time big capitalists and nobles were among the saboteurs exposed in the "Shakhty case."

The "Shakhty case" testified to a blunting of revolutionary vigilance among the Communist managers in regard to the bourgeois specialists, and to bad work on the part of the mass working-class organisations in the Donets coalfield, above all the trade unions, which were deaf to the miners' complaints, and did not encourage criticism from below. Such criticism would have helped to expose the saboteurs sooner.

The "Shakhty case" brought to the fore the question of training a new, Soviet technological intelligentsia drawn from the people and closely associated with them, an intelligentsia abreast of contemporary science and technology. Bolshevik economic executives had to master technology in order really to run industry and to supervise the work of the bourgeois specialists. The training in a brief space of time of a new technological intelligentsia was an extremely complicated and difficult undertaking. But here again the Party was not daunted. It confidently tackled the job of creating a new Soviet intelligentsia, new technological personnel.

The network of technical institutes and technical schools was extended and the numbers of workers and of Communists studying in them was increased. Thousands of Communists ("Party thousanders"), men and women experienced in Party, government, economic and trade union work, were sent to technical institutes. The doors to higher education were opened wide to skilled workers. The system of evening schools and correspondence courses was extended. Front-rank workers from factories and mines, and building projects graduated from the technical institutes and schools, and became worthy representatives of the Soviet technological intelligentsia.

The Socialist reconstruction of the national economy called for unrestricted criticism of shortcomings. A special Central Committee appeal "To all Party members and to all workers," issued in June, 1928, said:

"The slogan of self-criticism '*irrespective of persons*,' *criticism from top to bottom and from bottom to top, is one of the central slogans of the day.*"

For the Party, criticism and self-criticism was not an end in itself, but a means of improving the quality of the work as a whole, of reinforcing unity in the Party's ranks, and of exposing saboteurs, defeatists, bureaucrats and all other alien elements. Criticism and self-criticism served as a means of politically rallying the masses to fight for the general line of the Party. At the same time the Central Committee vigorously opposed any attempt indiscriminately and maliciously to disparage or discredit industrial and Party leaders. In no circumstances could the slogan of criticism and self-criticism be allowed to become an instrument for slandering industrial and Soviet personnel, or be used by anti-Party elements against Party principles and Party discipline.

The difficulties encountered in Socialist reconstruction, and the inevitable sharpening of the class struggle as a result of the Socialist offensive, gave rise to vacillations among the petty-bourgeois strata of the population. There were echoes of this also in the Party. A group of Right-wing defeatists took shape. As early as 1925 Bukharin had proclaimed the slogan "Enrich yourselves!" In practice this slogan signified a policy of support for the kulak farms in the countryside. But when the Party was engaged in combating the Trotskyists and Zinovievites as the main danger, the Right-wingers, carefully concealing their differences with the Party, had been lying low, making a show of fighting against the Trotskyists. But when the Party launched its decisive offensive against the kulaks, the leaders of the Right wingers—Bukharin, Rykov and Tomsky—openly came out against the policy of Socialist industrialisation and the collectivisation of agriculture.

While admitting in words that it was possible to build Social-ism in the U.S.S.R., the Right opportunists in fact resisted the policy of the all-out expansion of heavy industry. They opposed rapid rates of industrialisation.

The Right-wingers opposed the all-out Socialist offensive along the whole front and the liquidation of the capitalist elements in the national economy. They opposed the offensive against the ku-laks. At a time when the capitalist elements were waging a fierce struggle against the construction of Socialism, the Right-wingers propounded the "theory" that the class struggle in the country was subsiding and that the kulaks could peacefully grow into Social-ism. They refused to admit that the broad highway to Socialism in the countryside was, as Lenin taught, the producer co-opera-tion in its highest form—the collective farm. Lenin's co-opera-tive plan could not be put into effect unless the kulaks were elimi-nated as a class. The Right-wingers held that the countryside could be directed along Socialist lines only through the marketing and purchasing co-operatives. They suggested giving "free rein" to spontaneous development of the market and removing all re-strictions on kulak farming. Abandoning Lenin's concept of the class struggle and the dictatorship of the proletariat, the Right-wingers would have the Party and State organisations make direct concessions to the capitalist elements.

Thus, in practice, they denied that Socialism could be built in the U.S.S.R. In the Party they spread the *ideology of defeatism* in the face of difficulties, and sought an *agreement* with the kulak and capitalist elements in town and country. Their stand ultimately meant the restoration of capitalism. The Central Com-mittee rallied the Party and the working class for a decisive strug-gle against the Right-wing defeatists, now the main danger in the Party, the mouthpiece of the anti-Soviet forces in the country and a weapon of the capitalist encirclement.

The work of the Party in building Socialism in the U.S.S.R., and its irreconcilable struggle against deviations and for its gener-al line, were whole-heartedly supported by the international Communist movement. The Sixth Congress of the Communist International, which took place in Moscow in August, 1928, noted the achievements of Socialist construction in the U.S.S.R. These achievements, says the Congress resolution, are strengthening the revolutionary position of the international proletariat and accelerating the growth of the revolutionary movement throughout the world.

The Congress gave a Marxist-Leninist appraisal of the interna-tional situation. The sharpening contradictions between the capi-talist countries and the class contradictions within these countries, the growth of the national liberation movement in the colonies and semi-colonies, the intensification of the contradictions between the capitalist world and the Soviet Union—all were leading to the further undermining of capitalist stabilisation, to the growth of a severe world economic crisis, on a scale unprecedented in the history of capitalism. The capitalists were seeking a way out of this crisis in new wars between the imperialist Powers for a redivision of the colonies, and in war against the U.S.S.R.

The Congress called upon the Communist Parties systematically to explain the danger of new wars, to fight steadfastly for peace and in defence of the U.S.S.R. and its peaceful foreign policy, to support the risings of the colonial peoples against imperialist slavery, and especially the Chinese revolution, which was an event of world-historic significance.

The Congress denounced the counter-revolutionary, Menshevik activity of the Trotskyists in the C.P.S.U.(B.) and in the Comintern, and approved their expulsion from the C.P.S.U.(B.) and from the other Communist Parties. It called upon the Communist Parties to conduct a struggle on two fronts—against the remnants of the masked Trotskyists and against the Right-wing defeatists. The Right opportunists, including the Bukharin group, were slipping into a reformist assessment of capitalist stabilisation. They glossed over the basic contradictions of capitalism, denied the inevitability of a world economic crisis, the rise of a new revolutionary surge forward of the working-class movement in the capitalist countries and of the national liberation struggle in the colonial and dependent countries. The Congress pointed out that Right opportunism in the Communist Parties, which was aligning itself with the reformism of the Second International, had become the main danger in the international Communist movement.

The Sixth Congress adopted the programme and statutes of the Comintern, which played an important part in consolidating and developing the international Communist revolutionary movement. The Congress decisions greatly helped to consolidate the Leninist unity of the Communist Parties, to rally the masses for the fight against capitalism.

The Right-wingers in the C.P.S.U.(B.) and in the Comintern, despite the sharp criticism to which they had been subjected, persisted in their obviously anti-Leninist views. The Right defeatists engaged in factional struggle against the Party; they inspired the anti-Party activity of the top leaders of the Moscow Party organisation (Uglanov and others), intending to counterpose the Moscow organisation to the Central Committee. But this venture of the Right-wingers also ended in complete failure. At the call of the Central Committee, the Moscow Bolsheviks unanimously rebuffed the Right factionalists, who had grossly violated the Leninist unity of the Party and Party discipline.

A plenary meeting of the Central Committee held in November, 1928, called for a decisive struggle against the Right, openly opportunist deviation as the main danger, pointing out at the same time that there must be no relaxing of the fight against Trotskyism either. Irreconcilable struggle against opportunist deviations in the Party *on two fronts and against a conciliatory attitude to them* —such was the directive issued by the plenary meeting of the Central Committee.

The Right-wingers, in the person of Bukharin, linked up through Kamenev with the Trotskyists, and engaged in backstairs negotiations with them with a view to changing the policy of the Central Committee and the Political Bureau. The Right-wing leaders tried to bring pressure to bear on the Central Committee and to compel it to change the policy of the Party in favour of concessions to the kulaks and to the capitalist elements in the towns.

The Party was obliged once more to deal with the question of the Right-wingers. The joint plenary meeting of the Central Committee and the Central Control Commission, and the Sixteenth Party Conference held in April, 1929, condemned the political views of the Right-wingers as being incompatible with the general line of the Party, condemned their backstairs factional talks with the Trotskyists, and rejected the refusal of the Right-wing leaders to perform the work assigned to them as a gross violation of Party discipline. Of great importance in the struggle against the Right opportunists was the speech made by Stalin at the joint plenary meeting of the Central Committee and the Central Control Commission, "The Right Deviation in the C.P.S.U.(B.)." At this plenary meeting, Bukharin and Tomsky were relieved of responsible posts and warned that, in the event of a further attempt to go against the decisions of the Central Committee, they would immediately be removed from the Political Bureau.

But even after this warning the Right-wingers did not take the path of the Party. They began to prepare a new attack against it and its Leninist leadership.

They resisted the Party in reorganising the work of the trade unions and bringing it into line with the tasks of Socialist reconstruction. They ignored the creative activity of the masses in promoting Socialist emulation and the shock brigade movement.

Led by the Central Committee the Party exposed the defeatist ideology of the Right-wingers and their anti-Party activity in the trade unions. With the backing of the activists in the unions, the Party was able to isolate the narrowly trade union and bureaucratic elements in the executive bodies and to have rank and filers who were devoted to Socialism promoted to key trade union posts.

The Central Committee was forced to take more decisive measures against the Rights, who persisted in opposing the general line of the Party. A plenary meeting of the Central Committee held in November, 1929, declared that propaganda of the views of the Right-wing defeatists was *incompatible with membership of the Party*. After discussing the question of the Right-wing leaders—Bukharin, Rykov and Tomsky—the plenary meeting removed Bukharin from the Political Bureau, as the instigator and leader of the Right defeatists, while Rykov and Tomsky received a serious warning.

After this decision of the Central Committee the leaders of the Right defeatists submitted a statement in which they acknowledged their mistakes and recognised the correctness of the general line of the Party. But this was a manoeuvre of double-dealers, for in secret they continued their undermining activity.

Although engaged in a strenuous struggle against the Trotskyists and the Right defeatists over a number of years, a struggle which took up much time and energy, the Party at the same time persistently carried out the decisions of the Fifteenth Congress to accelerate the pace of industrialisation, to build collective and State farms, and to raise the material and cultural level of the masses.

An important part in rallying the forces of the Party and the people for the new advance in Socialist construction was played by the Sixteenth Party Conference, held in April, 1929. The main questions on the Conference agenda were: the Five-Year Plan for the development of the national economy (1928/29-1932/33), ways and means of developing agriculture, the results and immediate tasks of the fight against bureaucracy, the cleansing and verification of the members and candidate members of the Party.

The Conference rejected a "minimum" variant of the Five-Year Plan put forward by the Right-wingers, and adopted the "optimum" variant. Capital investments for the five-year period were fixed at 64,600 million rubles, compared with the 26,500 million invested in the previous five-year period. Output of all industry was scheduled to rise 2.8 times, that of heavy industry, 3.3 times. The share of the Socialist sector in the gross output of industry was to reach 92 per cent by the end of the five-year period. The number of peasant farms united in co-operatives of all types was to be raised to 85 per cent; marketable grain grown by the Socialist sector was to reach 43 per cent. The plan envisaged the collectivisation of approximately one-sixth of all the peasant farms and raising the crop area of the collective farms to 50 million acres.

The first Five-Year Plan was the programme of a full-scale Socialist offensive along the whole front of the national economy. Its purpose was *to lay the foundations of Socialist economy*, and to continue to squeeze out capitalist elements in town and country with a view to their complete elimination. The adoption of the first Five-Year Plan signified that the Party's leadership in building Socialist society had risen to a higher level.

The Sixteenth Conference outlined measures for overcoming the backwardness of agriculture, and for strengthening the new production forms of the link between town and country. Noting the urge towards collective farming not only among the poor strata of the peasantry but also among the middle peasants, the Conference stressed that one of the main shortcomings in the development of the collective-farm movement was the lag in organising the masses of the poor and middle peasantry compared with the scale of the powerful movement from below. It was necessary to do everything to support the peasant masses in switching over to collective forms of farming, to extend material and financial assistance to the collective farms and to supply them with machinery and trained personnel. It was necessary to increase the vigilance of the collective farmers and to organise resistance to the kulak elements who had penetrated into the collective farms, and smash them. Special emphasis was laid on the organisation of big collective farms which could supply the largest amount of marketable produce and make full use of the modern agricultural machinery possessed by the hiring depots and machine-and-tractor stations.

Much attention was devoted by the Conference to the fight against bureaucracy. Lenin had taught that this struggle called for prolonged and persistent effort. It required a high level of culture, universal literacy of the population and the enlistment in every possible way of the working people in the work of the Soviet State apparatus.

Noting certain advances in this sphere, the Conference gave directions to intensify the fight against bureaucracy in the State apparatus and pointed to the need for *"a most resolute, most dedicated, most persistent struggle against the elements of bureaucracy within the Party itself and in the Party apparatus ..."* (*C.P.S.U. in Resolutions*, Part II, p. 603). The decisive method of combating bureaucracy, it was stressed, was to give effect to the slogan of criticism and self-criticism.

The keynote of the Sixteenth Party Conference was the fullest development of the creative activity of the masses in the battle to fulfil the first Five-Year Plan. It adopted a special appeal "To all workers and working peasants of the Soviet Union," calling on them to engage in Socialist emulation, as a mass movement for the fulfilment of the plan.

"Emulation and the *Five-Year Plan,"* said the appeal, "are indissolubly linked. In carrying out these tasks, the proletar-

iat of the U.S.S.R. is continuing the offensive against the class enemies of the proletarian dictatorship" (*ibid.*, p. 619).

The Conference also decided to carry out a general cleansing and verification of members and candidate members of the Party. The chief purpose of the cleansing was to rid the Party of alien and corrupt elements. It was designed to strengthen the Party organisations still further, to raise the vanguard role of the Communists in carrying out the policy of industrialisation and in preparing a mass collective-farm movement.

As a result of the 1929 cleansing, 10 per cent of the members were expelled. These were useless, alien and corrupted elements. The cleansing and verification of members and candidate members was followed by the enrolment of many thousands of new members —the foremost industrial workers, farm-labourers, poor peasants and middle-peasant activists. The Party became still stronger and more united, and its prestige rose.

The year 1929 is known in the history of the Soviet Union as the year of *great change* on all fronts of Socialist construction.

The adoption of the Five-Year Plan evoked a powerful wave of activity among the millions of workers and all working people. Socialist emulation in the factories provided splendid instances of a Socialist attitude to labour on the part of Soviet people. A matter of compulsion under capitalism, labour became more and more a matter of honour, valour and heroism. The famous slogan "Five-Year Plan in Four Years!" was advanced by the working-class masses.

A great role in spreading Socialist emulation was played by Lenin's article "How to Organise Emulation?", published for the first time in *Pravda* in January, 1929.

"Far from extinguishing emulation," Lenin wrote, "Socialism, on the contrary, for the first time creates the opportunity for employing it on a really *large* and on a really *mass* scale, for actually drawing the majority of toilers into the arena of labour of a kind in which they can display their abilities, develop their capacities, reveal their talents, of which there is an untapped spring among the people, and which capitalism crushed, suppressed and strangled in thousands and millions" (*Works*, Vol. 26, p. 367).

New forms of Socialist emulation arose and spread rapidly. The first youth shock brigade was formed in Leningrad in the summer of 1928. This example was followed by members of the Komsomol and young people generally in other enterprises and on building sites throughout the country. In the same year the Komsomol, on the occasion of its tenth anniversary, was awarded the Order of the Red Banner for its courage and valour during the years of the Civil War. This award gave rise to a new wave of labour enthusiasm among the youth.

Socialist emulation became a mass movement of the working class for raising labour productivity, for fulfilment of production plans ahead of schedule and for proficiency in handling the new machinery.

The Party organisations headed the Socialist emulation of the workers. By the end of 1929, 63 per cent of the workers in large enterprises were taking part in various forms of emulation, while 29 per cent were members of shock brigades. The first All-Union Congress of Shock Brigades, held in December, 1929, summed up the results of this powerful movement and charted a programme of struggle to raise labour productivity in all branches of the national economy. The shock brigaders were front-rank members of the working class; under the leadership of the Party they fought for higher labour productivity, for advanced methods of work and for the better organisation of production.

In 1929 labour productivity rose by nearly 13 per cent compared with the previous year, thus exceeding the pre-war level by more than 30 per cent. The best workers broke world records for labour productivity.

By raising labour productivity, practising economy and lowering production costs, the Party and the Soviet State succeeded in solving one of the most difficult problems of industrialisation— the problem of Socialist accumulation. In 1929 industrial investments amounted to 3,400 million rubles—50 per cent more than in the previous year. The rate of growth of Socialist industry exceeded all the planned targets. Output in large-scale industry increased by 25 per cent in one year, and in heavy industry by 31 per cent.

Socialist construction in industry assumed immense scope. Work was under way on the Dnieper Hydroelectric Power Station. Construction was begun of the Novokramatorsk plant in the Donets coalfield and of a heavy engineering plant (Uralmashzavod), the Berezniki and Solikamsk chemical plants and the iron and steel works at Magnitogorsk in the Urals. Heavy engineering works, aircraft, machine-tool, motor and other plants in Moscow and Leningrad were being built or reconstructed. The Moscow automobile plant was under construction. Construction work on the Stalingrad Tractor Works, and on new big agricultural machinery works in Rostov and Zaporozhye was nearing completion. The country's second coal base—Kuzbas—was being extended.

The Party was consistently carrying out Socialist industrialisation not only in the central regions of the country, but also in the backward non-Russian republics and regions. Among the enterprises under construction were the Ridder Non-Ferrous Metal Plant and the Chimkent Lead-Smelting Works in Kazakh-an, and textile mills and other enterprises in Tashkent and shkhabad. The rise of industrial centres in the backward non-ussian areas was of the greatest economic, political and cultural nportance. Industrialisation served as the basis for training mem-ers of the respective nationalities as skilled factory workers. ocialist construction strengthened the friendship of the peoples : the Soviet Union.

In carrying out the Leninist nationalities policy, the Party aged an irreconcilable struggle against manifestations of bourgeois ationalism, against dominant-nation chauvinism and local na-onalism, which were weakening the friendship of the Soviet eoples in the struggle for Socialism, impairing the Soviet State nd undermining the Leninist unity of the Communist Party.

Industrialisation was carried out with a truly Bolshevik élan, ich as the world had never seen before. The working class pro-ided splendid examples of labour valour. The scale and the rate of nstruction in the U.S.S.R. astonished the world. Enemies sserted that the targets planned by the Party would never be eached and foretold the failure of the Soviet plans. The working eople in all countries were gladdened by the successes of the oviet Union.

The vast scale of industrialisation and the heroism displayed y the working class exerted a strong influence on the masses of the orking peasantry. They saw that the Party and the Government, vercoming difficulties, were building factories to make tractors nd new farm machines. Numerous peasant delegations visited he new factories and construction sites, attended workers' meet-ngs and were inspired by their enthusiasm. Upon returning o their villages the advanced representatives of the working peas-ntry took the initiative in setting up new collective farms. he organised workers of industrial enterprises and building ites assumed patronage over rural areas, and sent numerous work-rs' teams to the countryside.

That was how the mass movement for joining the collective farms vas prepared and began, a movement which grew into solid ollectivisation. The peasantry turned to the Socialist path of levelopment, to the collective-farm path. The middle peasants ollowed the poor peasants into the collective farms. In just three nonths, from July to September, 1929, about one million peasant ouseholds set up collective farms—that is, almost as many as luring the twelve years since the October Revolution. During he last quarter of 1929 nearly 2.4 million peasant households ntered collective farms.

The solid collectivisation of agriculture had been prepared y a series of economic and political measures undertaken by he Party and the Soviet State.

The Socialist sector had a planned transforming effect on the rural economy. In the years 1928 and 1929 the contract system (agreements between State and co-operative organisations, an peasant farms) embraced more than a third of all peasant farms. Year by year more and more tractors and other machines were sent to the countryside. The Soviet State helped the working peasant by organising hiring depots, tractor columns and machine-and tractor stations. The economic link between the working class and the main mass of the peasantry acquired a chiefly productive character.

In carrying out Lenin's co-operative plan, the Party persist ently promoted the co-operative movement in the countryside, an did everything to encourage agricultural co-operation. The collec tive farm was the highest form of agricultural co-operation.

The resolute struggle waged against the kulaks during the grain-purchasing campaigns in 1928 and 1929, which greatly undermined the strength of the kulaks and rallied the poor and middle peasants round the Party organisations and the Soviets was of great importance in preparing a mass collective-farm movement.

The swing of the peasant masses towards collective farming was also stimulated by the achievements of the first collective and State farms. Practical experience convinced the peasants of the advantages of large-scale farming and collective labour. The collective and State farms became centres of progressive agron omy. As Lenin had predicted, they helped the neighbouring peasant population with machinery, pedigree livestock, selected seed and so on.

The working class exerted great political influence on the coun tryside. During the years which preceded mass collectivisation nearly a quarter of a million Communists, Komsomol members and non-Party workers were sent to the villages from the towns and industrial centres to help in the sowing and grain-purchasing campaigns.

The plenary meeting of the Central Committee held in the mid dle of November, 1929, summed up the results of the first year of the Five-Year Plan. The main questions on the agenda con cerned collective-farm development. The plenary meeting noted that the decisive turn of the bulk of the peasantry towards So cialism, expressed in the mass collective-farm movement, signi fied a *"new historic phase in the building of Socialism in our coun try"* (*C.P.S.U. in Resolutions*, Part II, p. 621).

Equipped with Marxism-Leninism, and united round the Cen tral Committee, the Communist Party boldly set about solving new problems in Socialist construction.

During the years 1926-1929 the Communist Party, equipped with Lenin's plan for building Socialism in the U.S.S.R., and overcoming immense external and internal difficulties, prepared and embarked upon the Socialist reconstruction of the entire national economy. In all its measures the Party was aided by the creative activity and selflessness of the millions of workers and peasants.

The Party and the Soviet State waged a successful struggle for peace, for peaceful coexistence of the two systems—Socialist and capitalist. As a result, the designs of the imperialists to isolate the U.S.S.R. and to prepare a new intervention were frustrated.

Pursuing the principle of proletarian internationalism, the Party extended and strengthened its contacts with the world revolutionary movement of the working class and with the liberation movement in the colonial and dependent countries, and laid a firm basis for a militant alliance of the U.S.S.R. and the Chinese people's revolution.

At home the Party ensured the victory of the Leninist policy of Socialist industrialisation. The general line of the Communist Party, aimed at abolishing the age-long backwardness of the country and transforming it into a mighty industrialised Socialist Power found widespread support among the masses. In the main, one of the most difficult problems of industrialisation was solved, namely, the problem of accumulating funds for building a heavy industry, the foundations of which were laid during these years. In the battle to fulfil the first Five-Year Plan, the Soviet people, led by the Party, provided remarkable examples of heroic labour, and developed Socialist emulation as a movement of millions of working people in building Socialism. The rate of growth of Socialist industry surpassed anything that the world had ever seen.

In 1929, which has gone down in history as the year of great change, the Party registered the first major successes in the Socialist reconstruction of agriculture. The poor and middle sections of the peasantry swung sharply towards collective farming and a mass movement began for joining collective farms.

The advance of the Soviet Union towards Socialism was attended by a sharpening of the class struggle in the country and by an intensification of the struggle within the Party. The Party mobilised the working class and working peasantry for revolutionary activity against the capitalist elements in town and country. In bitter struggle against the class enemies the resistance of the kulaks and the saboteurs in industry was broken. The alliance of the workers and peasants, under the leadership of the working class, was consolidated. The Party regrouped its ranks, and helped all the mass organisations of the working people to reorganise their work, in keeping with the tasks of the Socialist reconstruction of the national economy.

A vital condition for the success of Socialist construction was the isolation and defeat of the anti-Leninist opposition groups—the Trotsky-Zinoviev bloc, the Right-wing defeatists and the national deviationists. In this struggle the Party became tempered ideologically, and its unity became firmly cemented. The views of the Trotskyists and the Right-wing defeatists were declared incompatible with membership of the Communist Party.

During the years 1926-1929 the Party grew considerably. Hundreds of thousands of the most advanced workers and working peasants joined its ranks; its cadres developed and became steeled in the battle to implement the policy of industrialisation and to overcome difficulties.

Steadfastly upholding the Leninist general line, skilfully guiding the working class and the main mass of the peasantry, battling resolutely against factional groups, the Party prepared the offensive of Socialism along the whole front.

CHAPTER TWELVE

THE PARTY IN THE PERIOD OF THE OFFENSIVE OF SOCIALISM ALONG THE WHOLE FRONT. ESTABLISHMENT OF THE COLLECTIVE-FARM SYSTEM

(1929-1932)

1. The Economic Crisis in the Capitalist World. The International Position of the U.S.S.R. During the Years of the Full-Scale Offensive of Socialism

At the end of 1929 the international situation underwent a considerable change. An economic crisis of unparalleled force and duration shook the whole capitalist world. Its devastating effect on the economy of the capitalist countries was tremendous. The decline in production lasted for almost three years. The volume of industrial output reached its lowest point in 1932. In the U.S.A. it had then declined by almost 50 per cent as compared with 1929, in Germany by more than 40 per cent.

The crisis caused unprecedented unemployment. In the United States alone the number of unemployed reached 15-17 million at the height of the crisis. In Germany in 1932 nearly 44 per cent of all members of trade unions were wholly unemployed. This mass unemployment was of a protracted character, and reduced a considerable part of the working class in all bourgeois countries to a state of extreme destitution.

The crisis put an end to the temporary stabilisation of capitalism, and revolutionised masses of workers. The influence of the Communist Parties grew in many countries. In Germany, for example, the Communist Party polled nearly 6 million votes at the Reichstag elections in November, 1932.

The crisis graphically showed the masses how rotten was the capitalist system. It made them feel the full brunt of the calamities which capitalism brings to the working people.

The crisis undermined the influence of the reformist theories about the possibility of reconciling the class interests of the proletariat and the bourgeoisie, and about the possibility of a crisis-free development of the capitalist economy—theories which had been fairly widespread in the years of the temporary stabilisation of capitalism. Such illusions were spread among the masses of the people by the parties of the Second International.

The successful building of Socialism in the U.S.S.R. was exerting an ever greater influence on the international situation. Ever broader masses of the working people throughout the world were coming to see the superiority of the Socialist system over the capitalist system.

In reactionary capitalist circles the advance of Socialism revived their interventionist inclinations, and their desire to hinder Socialist construction in the U.S.S.R. and to frustrate the fulfilment of the first Five-Year Plan grew stronger. The imperialists did not venture to start a war against the Soviet Union, but resorted to a number of other measures aimed at hindering the building of Socialism. They helped to engineer sabotage in the national economy of the U.S.S.R., and started anti-Soviet slander campaigns in their press. Following a campaign headed by the Pope in support of the counter-revolutionary clergy they began malicious propaganda about alleged Soviet dumping. Then came the lying story about forced labour in the U.S.S.R., and so on. This slander campaign against the Soviet Union knew no bounds. The ruling circles of many capitalist countries (the U.S.A., France, Poland, Belgium) made use of the anti-Soviet propaganda to hamper Soviet exports and to refuse credits to the U.S.S.R. A veritable economic war was waged against the land of Soviets.

At the same time, however, during the crisis years an opposite tendency in relation to the U.S.S.R. was also maintained in the policy of the capitalist countries. In these years the importance of the Soviet market for the industrial output of the capitalist countries grew immensely. The market of the Socialist State acquired particular importance for such important branches of industry as engineering. This was due to the fact that the Soviet market was the only one in the world which was not subject to crises, and which was rapidly expanding when all others were shrinking. Influential business circles were interested in Soviet orders, and this to some extent hampered the anti-Soviet intrigues of the reactionary imperialist forces. The masses of workers, filled with profound sympathy for the Soviet country, resisted the pursuit of a policy inimical to the Soviet Union.

In the years of the economic crisis the international situation continued to be tense. The crisis aggravated to the extreme the struggle of the imperialists for markets and spheres of influence, and intensified contradictions between the imperialist Powers. Many representatives of reactionary ruling circles in the capitalist countries sought a way out of the crisis in war and the seizure of foreign territories.

Japan was the first to embark on the path of aggression. In 1931 the Japanese imperialists, without declaring war on China, seized the Chinese north-eastern provinces (Manchuria). As a result of this aggression, a seat of war arose in the Far East. Soon after the beginning of Japanese aggression the Soviet Government openly declared that the sympathies of the working people of the U.S.S.R. were with the people of China.

Quite a different stand was taken by the Western imperialist Powers. Although Japan's expansionist inroads into China affected their own interests, they in effect encouraged her aggression. In doing so, the Western Powers reckoned on provoking a conflict between Japan and the Soviet Union.

The foreign policy of the Communist Party and the Soviet State continued to be one of peace. During this period, too, the Party succeeded in maintaining peace, and did not allow its enemies to involve the Soviet country in international conflicts. But after the beginning of the Japanese aggression against China the international situation deteriorated sharply. The Soviet Union had to take certain measures to strengthen its defences on its Far Eastern frontiers. The intrigues of the interventionists, the sabotage and subversive activity they organised, the economic pressure of world capitalism on the Soviet Union, and the emergence of a seat of war near the Soviet Far East—all these external factors could not but complicate the work of the Party involved in the solving of tremendous problems in the economic and cultural spheres.

2. The Advance of Solid Collectivisation of Agriculture. Adoption of the Policy of Eliminating the Kulaks as a Class. Sixteenth Party Congress

While the whole capitalist world was in the grip of the economic crisis, the U.S.S.R. was steadily proceeding with Socialist construction. The average annual increase of its industrial output in the first two years of the Five-Year Plan was about 20 per cent.

Along with the rapid growth of industry, the mass collective-farm movement was under way in the country. By the beginning of 1930 the five-year programme of collective-farm development had, in the main, been fulfilled. A number of regions became regions of *solid collectivisation*, when the peasants of whole villages, districts and areas joined the collective farms. In 124 districts more than 70 per cent of all the peasant farms were collectivised. The largest number of districts of solid collectivisation were in the Volga region, the North Caucasus and the steppe part of Ukraine.

The transition to solid collectivisation signified a *radical turn* of the bulk of the peasantry towards Socialism. Prior to the mass collective-farm movement there were 24.5 million individual peasant farms in the U.S.S.R., of which about 8.5 million belonged to poor peasants, 15 million to middle peasants and more than one million to kulaks. The poor and middle peasants together constituted the most numerous labouring class in the U.S.S.R. Though petty peasant commodity economy was not of a capitalist nature, it was essentially of the same type, since it based itself on private property in the means of production and engendered kulak capitalists from its midst. When joining the collective farms, the peasants socialised the basic means of production. The working peasantry was abandoning the old path of development which spontaneously engendered capitalism and led to the enslavement of the poor and middle peasants by the kulaks; it was taking a new, Socialist path, free of kulak bondage and capitalist exploitation. A Socialist, collective-farm system was being established in the countryside.

Furthermore, the transition to solid collectivisation signified a *radical change* in the development of Soviet agriculture. Prior to the organisation of collective farms, each peasant worked on his small farm in isolation. Most of the peasants used antiquated implements. Many of them used wooden ploughs, harvested their crops with sickles and scythes and used flails for threshing. Horses and oxen provided the only traction force. The dwarf peasant farms precluded the use of tractors and other modern machinery. The labour of the peasants was of low efficiency. The swing of the bulk of the peasantry towards collective farming signified a transition from backward small individual farming to advanced large-scale collective, mechanised agriculture. The practical experience of the first collective farms showed that even the mere pooling of the peasants' implements resulted in a considerable increase in labour productivity. But the superiority of the collective farms over the small individual farms became even more evident when the former began to use new agricultural equipment—tractors and other machines. Collective labour, using new agricultural technique, enabled the peasants to extend their crop areas, to increase the efficiency of agricultural production and systematically to raise their material and cultural level.

Thus the advance of the masses of poor and middle peasants to solid collectivisation meant a *profound revolutionary change* in the agriculture of the U.S.S.R. It was based on the transformation of the private ownership of the means of production by the working peasantry into social ownership, on the transition from petty individual agricultural production to collective, large-scale Socialist production. The reorganisation of agriculture on the basis of collective farms signified tearing up the roots of capitalism in agriculture, the establishment of a Socialist system in this highly important branch of the national economy. The main-springs of the restoration of capitalist elements in agriculture were destroyed, since in the collective farms there was no private ownership of the means of production and the basic means of livelihood of the collective farmer was now the agricultural artel and his personal labour in it.

This greatest of revolutionary changes in the countryside was effected on the initiative and under the leadership of the Commu-nist Party and the Soviet Government with the active partici-pation of broad masses of the working peasantry.

On January 5, 1930, the Central Committee of the C.P.S.U.(B.) adopted its historic decision on "The Rate of Collectivisation and State Measures to Assist Collective-Farm Development." In this decision the Central Committee set the Party the task of com-pleting collectivisation in the main by the end of the first Five-Year Plan. Full account was taken of the diversity of conditions in the various territories, regions and non-Russian republics, and of the varying degrees to which the peasants in these areas were ready for collectivisation.

The Central Committee divided the whole country into three groups of areas with different rates of collectivisation. The first group included the principal grain-growing areas, viz., the North Caucasus, the Middle and the Lower Volga, where the process of collectivisation was to be completed in the main by the spring of 1931. These areas were better prepared than the others for solid collectivisation. The Soviet State gave them priority in sup-plying them with large numbers of tractors and other agricultural machinery. Here the differentiation of the peasantry was more marked, the class struggle more acute and the poor peasantry better organised; these areas had the largest number of big State and collective farms equipped with up-to-date machinery; here agricul-tural co-operation was more developed. The Party organisations and the Soviets of these areas had considerable experience in promoting collectivisation. The second group included all the other grain-growing areas of the country—Ukraine, the Central Black-Earth Region, Siberia, the Urals, Kazakhstan—where the plan was to complete collectivisation in the main by the spring of 1932. In the rest of the territories, regions and non-Russian Republics the process of collectivisation was to be completed in the main by the end of the Five-Year Plan, that is, by 1933.

Proceeding from the practical experience of districts with solid collectivisation, the Central Committee of the Party passed a decision that the main form of organisation of the collective-farm movement was to be the agricultural artel, in which only the use of the land and the principal means of production were collectivised, namely, draught animals, agricultural machinery and implements, farm buildings and large cattle. As distinct from associations for the joint cultivation of the land and agricultural communes, the agricultural artel could best combine the personal interests of the collective farmers with public interests; this facilitated the education of the individual peasants of yesterday in the spirit of collectivism.

In view of the growing rate of collectivisation, the Central Committee of the Party took steps to accelerate the construction of plants for the production of tractors, harvester combines, tractor-drawn machinery and complex agricultural machines. The Central Committee emphasised the importance at that stage of the collective-farm movement, of combining mechanical traction with horse traction. The machine-and-tractor stations in all districts of solid collectivisation were fully switched over to servicing the collective farms. State loans totalling 500 million rubles were advanced to the collective farms for the economic year 1929/30. The expense of surveying and demarcation of collective-farm lands was to be borne by the State. A wide network of intensive courses was set up for training skilled collective-farm personnel.

The Central Committee called upon all Party organisations to head the collective-farm movement which was developing from below. At the same time the Central Committee firmly warned the Party organisations against any attempts either to check the development of the collective-farm movement or (and especially) "any attempts whatsoever to 'decree' the collective-farm movement from above, which might lead to the danger of substituting mock-collectivisation for real socialist emulation in the organisation of collective farms" (*C.P.S.U. in Resolutions*, Part II, p. 667).

The decision of the Central Committee embodied the new policy with regard to the kulaks—the policy of *eliminating the kulaks as a class on the basis of solid collectivisation.*

The kulaks were the most numerous exploiting class in the U.S.S.R. When the process of solid collectivisation began, kulak farms constituted about 5 per cent of all the peasant farms in the country. But they still occupied a significant place in agricultural production. In 1927 their crop area under grain was about 25 million acres (the total crop area was 236 million acres); they produced just over 2 million tons of marketable grain (one-fifth of the total).

The kulaks were the bitterest enemies of Socialism. After the elimination of the landlords and capitalists they were the last mainstay of capitalist restoration in the country. They sabotaged all the measures of the Soviet Government, organised anti-Soviet revolts, terrorised rural activists and tried in every way possible to enslave the poor and middle peasants and subordinate them to their influence. Twice—in 1918 and in the economic year 1927/28—the kulaks made desperate attempts to deprive the Soviet State of grain and thereby to frustrate the Government's Socialist measures. The kulaks believed that under the New Economic Policy they would be able to consolidate their position in the country and secure the restoration of the old capitalist regime in the U.S.S.R. The capitalists of all countries who dreamed of restoring capitalism in the U.S.S.R., counted on the kulaks.

Since its Eighth Congress the Party had pursued a policy of restricting the exploiting proclivities of the kulaks, a policy of forcing out the capitalist elements. The Soviet Government by its laws on the renting of land and on the employment of hired labour on private farms had limited the scope of kulak production and the kulaks' opportunities to exploit the working peasants. It had imposed higher taxes on the kulaks, and had required them to sell grain to the State at fixed prices. This policy of restricting the kulaks had only retarded the growth of the kulak class, but did not mean its elimination.

Lenin pointed out that there could be no peace with the kulaks, that the working class must carry on persistent preparatory work to gather the forces for dealing a crushing blow to the kulaks and eliminating them as a class. Lenin said: "We have been, are and shall be in a state of direct civil war with the kulaks" (*Collected Works*, Vol. 29, p. 139). At the Eleventh Party Congress Lenin warned the Party that the near future would witness "the last and decisive battle" against "Russian capitalism, the one which stems from petty peasant farming and which is fostered by it" (*Collected Works*, Vol. 33, p. 248).

In waging this last and decisive battle against the kulak class, the Communist Party and the Soviet Government relied on the major successes of Socialist construction which had been attained by 1930.

The Socialist sector in all branches of the national economy had grown and become consolidated: Socialist industry was rapidly developing, tens of thousands of new collective farms had sprung up in the countryside. The Party and the Soviet Government now possessed a solid Socialist basis both in town and country which made it possible to eliminate the capitalist elements in the U.S.S.R.

The alignment of class forces in the country had changed in favour of Socialism. Socialist industrialisation was accompanied by a considerable growth in the numerical strength of the working class and the enhancement of its leading role in the Socialist reorganisation of the countryside and in the struggle of the working peasantry against the kulaks. The working class was vitally interested in eliminating the kulaks, the remaining exploiting class in the country. The growing mass collective-farm movement involved millions of peasant farms. The middle peasants joined this movement too, and together with the poor peasantry waged a decisive struggle against the kulaks. In their policy of eliminating the kulaks as a class the Party and the Soviet Government could now firmly depend not only on the working class and the poor peasantry, but also on the middle peasants who had joined the collective farms.

Furthermore, by 1930, the Soviet Government had created the necessary material basis for replacing the kulak grain output. In 1929 the collective and State farms had gathered in nearly $6^1/_2$ million tons of grain, of which over 2 million tons were sold to the State. The rapid growth of the collective-farm movement made it certain that in 1930 the collective and State farms would produce not less than $6^1/_2$ million tons of marketable grain, i.e., would exceed the 1927 output of the kulak farms several-fold.

The development of the Socialist sector of the national economy, the new alignment of class forces in the country and the possession by the State of its own grain-producing base—the collective and State farms—enabled the Party to proceed at the end of 1929 from the policy of restricting and squeezing out the kulaks to the policy of eliminating them as a class on the basis of solid collectivisation. The essence of this policy was to *deprive the kulak class of the means of production essential for its existence and development*, namely, the free use of land, the instruments of production, the renting of land and the right to hire labour. This policy was legislatively embodied in a number of decisions adopted by the higher organs of the Soviet State. In districts of solid collectivisation the laws on the renting of land and the hiring of labour on individual peasant farms were repealed.

Solid collectivisation meant that all the land in the area of a particular village passed into the hands of a collective farm. All kulak plots in this land were transferred to the collective farm. Thus the kulaks were deprived not only of the right to rent any land, but also of those plots of land which had been used by them previously. The nationalisation of the land accomplished as a result of the October Revolution made possible such surveying and demarcation of the lands as benefited the collective farms. Lenin pointed out that the nationalisation of the land gave "the proletarian State the maximum opportunity of passing to Socialism in agriculture" (*Collected Works*, Vol. 28, p. 291). The collective farms did not have to make any redemption payments to the peasants for their plots of land, or to recompense them for the lands which were passing into collective use. Thus the absence of private property in land in the U.S.S.R. facilitated the Socialist reconstruction of the countryside and the struggle against the kulaks.

The collectivisation of agriculture proceeded in bitter class struggle with the kulaks, in conditions of a hostile capitalist encirclement. The kulaks carried on malicious propaganda against the collective-farm movement, spread all kinds of provocative rumours, set fire to collective-farm buildings, poisoned the livestock, damaged tractors and other machines, assassinated rural Communists, chairmen of collective farms, rural newspaper correspondents and village activists. They did everything in their power to prevent the peasants from joining the collective farms and to frustrate collectivisation. The entry of the majority of the peasantry into the collective farms on a mass scale was therefore accompanied by a decisive struggle against the kulaks. The peasants demanded the complete expropriation of the kulaks and their expulsion from the villages.

Supporting in every way the struggle of the poor and middle peasants against the kulaks, the Soviet Government lifted the ban on expropriation of the kulaks. Local organs of Soviet power in the districts of solid collectivisation were granted the right to evict the most malicious kulaks to districts far removed from their places of residence and to confiscate all their means of production (cattle, machines and other farm property), transferring them to the possession of collective farms. The kulaks were completely expropriated. This was the only way to deal with the kulaks. These measures fully met the interests of Socialist construction, and ensured the success of the collective-farm movement and the consolidation of the collective farms.

Thus, at the very beginning of the mass building of collective farms the Central Committee of the Party, proceeding from Lenin's teachings on co-operation, gave the Party, the working class and the working peasantry a concrete plan of struggle for the victory of the collective-farm system.

After the adoption by the Central Committee of its decision of January 5, 1930, all Party organisations, particularly in the areas, districts and villages, intensified their work of collectivisation. Rural Communists were the first to join the collective farms, drawing the poor and middle peasants into the collective-farm movement with them. By the spring of 1930 almost 75 per cent of all the rural Communists engaged in agriculture became members of collective farms.

The Party focussed the attention of the Soviets on collectivisation; it put forward the slogan: "The Soviets must turn their face to the collective farms!" The Soviets became the vehicles of the Party's new policy in the countryside. A particularly big part in the movement for collectivisation was played by the village Soviets, more than 70,000 in number. They united something like four million activists from among the poor and middle peasants. These advanced peasants were initiators of the collective-farm movement.

The Party enlisted the active help of the trade unions in building up the collective farms. It supported the growing movement among city workers to take part in the collectivisation of the countryside. In 1930 the trade unions sent 180,000 teams of workers to the countryside to help in organising collective farms and in the repair of agricultural machinery. A particularly important role in the development of the collective-farm movement was played by the *25,000 front-rank workers* who came to work on the collective farms at the beginning of 1930 in response to an appeal of the Party. They were volunteers sent to the countryside by Party and trade union organisations of various plants and factories, by big collectives of workers. Communists constituted about 70 per cent of this body of volunteers.

The Komsomol, too, actively assisted the Party in carrying out collectivisation. By the spring of 1930, 550,000 rural members of the Komsomol—about 50 per cent of the total membership—had joined the collective farms. In the countryside the Komsomol was becoming the organisation of the collective-farm youth.

January and February, 1930, were months of headlong growth of the collective farms. The movement for solid collectivisation embraced ever new regions of the country. During this period about 10 million peasant households joined the collective farms.

But along with real progress in collectivisation, there were also unhealthy signs. There turned out to be certain distortions of Party policy in collectivisation, distortions which caused discontent among the middle peasants.

Above all, the Leninist voluntary principle of forming collective farms was being violated. Not infrequently patient organising and explanatory work was being replaced by mere injunctions and coercion against the middle peasants. Voluntary entry into collective farms was being replaced by compulsion, on pain of being "dekulakised," disfranchised, and so on. In some districts as many as 15 per cent of the peasants were "dekulakised" and from 15 to 20 per cent disfranchised.

The Party's directive concerning the agricultural artel as the chief form of the collective-farm movement was also being violated. In a number of places attempts were made to skip the artel form and pass straight to the commune by collectivising small livestock, poultry, etc. This practice was particularly widespread in the Urals and in Siberia. A great deal of confusion egarding the socialisation of the means of production in the colective farms was caused by the inadequate Model Rules for he Agricultural Artel, which had been approved by the People's Commissariat for Agriculture and the Collective-Farm Centre[8] of he U.S.S.R. and published on February 6, 1930. These Model Rules made no mention whatsoever of the household allotments of the collective farmers, and did not explain on what principles socialisation of livestock should be carried out in the case of households possessing only one cow, some small livestock and poultry.

Carried away by the initial success of collectivisation, some Party organisations infringed the decision of the Central Committee of the Party of January 5, 1930, concerning the rate of collectivisation. In their zeal for inflated collectivisation figures the Party leadership of the Central Black-Earth Region and of the Moscow Region, for example, began to direct the Communists towards completing collectivisation by the spring of 1930, although, according to the Central Committee's decision, the Central Black-Earth Region had no less than two years at its disposal, and the Moscow Region no less than three years.

There were violations of the Party's policy also in the non-Russian districts of the North Caucasus, in Transcaucasia, Central Asia and Kazakhstan. Instead of prolonged preparatory work and patient explanation of the Party's policy in the collective-farm movement to the poor and middle peasants in the non-Russian regions, as recommended by the Central Committee, the Party organisations of these regions set out to complete collectivisation "in the shortest possible time."

The enemies of Soviet power, and above all the kulaks, tried to take advantage of these mistakes and excesses committed by Party organisations. Former Whites, Socialist-Revolutionaries and other hidden anti-Soviet elements raised their heads again. The enemy acted with craft and cunning. Every device was used—from provocation to brutal assassination of Communists and active non-Party people in the villages. The class enemies instigated the peasants to slaughter their animals before entering the collective farms, spreading the rumour that all the livestock would be taken away anyhow. Giving way to this provocation of the kulaks, many peasants slaughtered their cows, pigs, sheep and poultry. In the economic year 1929/30 the number of head of cattle in the country decreased by 14.6 million, pigs by one-third, sheep and goats by more than a quarter. Almost all this livestock was slaughtered mainly in February and March, 1930. As a result of these hostile actions of the kulaks and their toadies, animal husbandry in the U.S.S.R. suffered a heavy loss from which it could not recover for a long time.

The enemies of Soviet power calculated that the excesses and mistakes committed in the process of collectivisation would incense the peasantry and provoke mass anti-Soviet revolts. They hoped to take advantage of the temporary discontent of a certain section of the middle peasants and win them over. Here and there they succeeded in inciting the peasants to anti-Soviet actions.

The Right opportunists likewise attempted to take advantage of the difficulties met with in the collective-farm movement and of the distortions of the Party line towards the middle peasant. They launched new attacks with the object of discrediting all the activity of the Party in the sphere of collectivisation.

The mistakes committed in the process of building the collective farms threatened to discredit the collective-farm movement and to weaken the entire cause of Socialist construction. They tended to divert the Party from the path of alliance with the bulk of the peasantry, the path of consolidating the dictatorship of the proletariat, to the path of a rupture with the peasant masses and the undermining of the dictatorship of the proletariat.

Having received alarming signals of distortions of the Party line in the collective-farm movement and of dangerous signs of discontent among the peasantry, the Central Committee of the Party took a number of steps aimed at rectifying the distortions and mistakes committed. The Central Committee took a decision concerning the procedure for collectivisation in the republics of Transcaucasia and Central Asia, as well as in the non-Russian regions of the R.S.F.S.R. It warned Party organisations against the danger of mechanically transplanting the forms and methods of collectivisation that were being adopted in advanced regions, better prepared for collectivisation, to the non-Russian regions of the country. It stressed the necessity of concentrating on preparatory work, with due regard to the national and economic features of each region.

At the end of February, 1930, the Central Committee of the Party introduced amendments in the Model Rules for the Agricultural Artel. These amended Model Rules were published on March 2, 1930. On the same day, by decision of the Central Committee of the Party, J. V. Stalin's article "Dizzy with Success" was published. The article clarified the Party line on the collective-farm movement and directed the members of the Party towards rectifying the mistakes committed in the process of collectivisation and consolidating the successes already achieved.

On March 14, 1930, the Central Committee adopted its resolution: "Measures to Combat the Distortions of the Party Line in the Collective-Farm Movement." The resolution pointed out that these distortions of the Party line were "the *principal hindrance* to the further growth of the collective-farm movement, and a *direct service* rendered to our class enemies" (*C.P.S.U. in Resolutions*, Part II, p. 670). The Central Committee instructed Party organisations to put an end to the practice of forced collectivisation, and at the same time to continue persistent efforts to draw the peasants into the collective-farm movement on a voluntary basis, to concentrate attention on completing the economic organisation of the collective farms and making them economically successful. Firmly condemning the "Left" distortions in the collective-farm movement, the Central Committee demanded of Party organisations that persons incapable or unwilling to combat distortions of the Party line should be removed from their posts.

The Central Committee helped the Party organisations to take a balanced view of the situation in the countryside and to set about correcting the distortions of the Party line in the collective-farm movement. These energetic measures of the Party to put right the mistakes made set the minds of the peasants at rest. The proper Leninist approach to the middle peasant which had been violated in a number of regions was restored. Thus the schemes of our enemies to utilise the discontent of the middle peasantry against Soviet power were frustrated.

In the course of the rectification of the mistakes committed, the sham collective farms, collective farms formed on paper, fell to pieces, and the wavering elements of the peasantry withdrew from the collective farms. The percentage of collectivisation and the number of collective farms in the country decreased. Only the staunchest elements of the working peasantry remained in the collective farms; they were firmly convinced of the necessity for collectivisation and believed that the collective farms, as the Party and the Soviet Government had explained, would lead the peasants to a new life, free from kulak exploitation and enslavement.

The Party took a number of additional measures to consolidate the success of collectivisation. On April 2, 1930, the Central Committee adopted a decision: "The granting of privileges to collective farms." By this decision the livestock of the collective farms and of the collective farmers was exempted from taxation for a period of two years. By the time of the spring sowing the collective farms had received from the State an interest-free seed loan of close on a million tons of grain. The material and technical basis of Socialist agriculture was being created at an accelerated rate. In June, 1930, the Stalingrad Tractor Works and the Rostov Agricultural Machinery Plant were put into operation. The Zaporozhye Harvesting Machinery Works was re-geared to production of harvester combines. Many other agricultural machinery works were being built and reconstructed. By the spring of 1930 the Soviet State had organised 158 machine-and-tractor stations, their number increasing to 961 by the end of the same year. More than 30,000 tractors were at the disposal of these stations. In addition, the collective farms possessed over 13,000 tractors.

Thanks to the timely and energetic measures taken by the Central Committee the distortions and mistakes committed in the process of collectivisation were rectified by the Party and the success of collectivisation was consolidated. By July 1, 1930, there were about 86,000 collective farms in the country, embracing six million peasant households. Nearly a quarter of all the poor and middle peasants (23.6 per cent) had firmly embarked on the path of collective-farm development. Enemy calculations that the spring sowing would be frustrated fell through; on the contrary, the first collective-farm spring sowing was successful, the collective farmers working with great enthusiasm.

While developing the mass collective-farm movement, the Party was at the same time busily engaged in carrying out the industrialisation of the country. During the first two years of the Five-Year Plan the output of large-scale industry increased almost by 63 per cent, and that of the industries producing means of production by 86 per cent. By 1930, for the first time in the history of the country, the share of industrial output in the national economy predominated over that of agriculture.

The rapid growth of Socialist industry and of Socialist forms of economy in the countryside widened the front of the offensive against the capitalist elements. Before 1929 the energetic offensive against the capitalist elements had been waged chiefly in the towns—in industry and trade. Agriculture remained almost unsocialised. But with the radical turn of the bulk of the peasantry towards collective farming, the offensive against the capitalist elements assumed a general character, developing into an offensive along the whole front, in both town and country.

Such was the situation when the Party held its Sixteenth Congress (from June 26 to July 13, 1930), which has gone down in history as *the Congress of the full-scale offensive of Socialism along the whole front.*

The delegates to the Congress represented 1,260,874 Party members and 711,609 candidate members. During the period between the Fifteenth and Sixteenth Congresses more than 600,000 workers joined the ranks of the Party. Industrial workers at the bench constituted about 50 per cent of the entire membership of the Party. The Sixteenth Congress heard and discussed the political and organisational reports of the Central Committee, the reports of the Central Control Commission and of the delegation of the C.P.S.U.(B.) in the Executive Committee of the Communist International. It also discussed the fulfilment of the Five-Year Plan for industry, the collective-farm movement and the advance of agriculture, as well as the tasks of the trade unions in the period of reconstruction.

The political report of the Central Committee was presented to the Congress by Stalin. The report pointed out that the period since the Fifteenth Party Congress had been a period of a serious test for two opposite economic systems on the world arena—the Soviet and the capitalist system. The Soviet system of economy had successfully stood the test and demonstrated its tremendous superiority. The U.S.S.R. was the only country which had not been affected by the world economic crisis.

The superiority of the Soviet system of economy over the capitalist showed itself most vividly in the high rates of development of Socialist industry in the U.S.S.R. But while it had outstripped all the principal capitalist countries in rates of industrial development, the U.S.S.R. was still far behind them as regards the level of industrial output. In 1929 the U.S.S.R. held fifth place in the world in the output of steel (after the U.S.A., Britain, Germany and France), sixth place in the output of pig-iron and coal, and ninth place in the output of electric power.

Particularly intolerable was the lag in the output of the steel and iron industry. In 1929 the output of pig-iron in the U.S.S.R. was 4 million tons, while in the U.S.A. it was about 43 million tons, in Germany 13.2 million tons, in France 10.3 million tons and in Britain 7.7 million tons. The U.S.S.R. reached and somewhat exceeded the pre-war level of output of pig-iron only in 1930. This lag of the iron and steel industry impeded the development of other branches of industry and of the national economy as a whole; and it compelled the U.S.S.R. to import pig-iron from other countries. In 1930, for example, the U.S.S.R. imported 700,000 tons of pig-iron, and in 1931, 1,600,000 tons. The interests of Socialist construction, of ensuring the country's economic independence and of making good its technical and economic backwardness, urgently required that the rate of development of the iron and steel industry be accelerated.

In its resolution on the report of the Central Committee the Sixteenth Party Congress gave directions to accelerate the speed of development of Socialist industry, especially of metallurgy. The Congress instructed the Central Committee to give priority in the industrialisation of the U.S.S.R. to the development of heavy industry as the basis of Socialist construction; it also adopted a decision to create in the East, in the immediate future, a second coal and metallurgical centre, namely, the Urals-Kuznetsk Works.

The Congress directed the attention of the Party to the importance of developing and reconstructing the country's transport system, which was one of the bottle-necks in the national economy. The Party was also directed to bend every effort to develop the light industries, to provide agriculture with large numbers of tractors and other machinery, to restore and develop animal husbandry. A resolution of the Congress stressed the decisive importance of training leading executive, business and technical cadres.

The rapid rate of Socialist industrialisation proved possible, above all, because the Party was able to organise Socialist emulation on a large scale, to stimulate the labour enthusiasm of millions of workers. By the time of the Sixteenth Party Congress more than two million workers were taking part in Socialist emulation, while over a million workers belonged to shock brigades. The working class was battling for higher rates of Socialist industrialisation. Emulation was developing with the watchword of "The Five-Year Plan in Four Years!" The Sixteenth Congress instructed the Central Committee of the Party "to ensure that the *spirited Bolshevik tempo* of Socialist construction be maintained, and that the Five-Year Plan be actually *fulfilled in four years*" (*C.P.S.U. in Resolutions*, Part III, p. 22).

The Congress defined the tasks of the trade unions in the period of reconstruction. The role of the trade unions in the development of the national economy was to be greatly enhanced. Their main task became that of developing Socialist emulation. The Congress called upon the trade unions to improve the work of the production conferences in the factories, to devote more attention to the training of skilled workers, to encourage the promotion of advanced workers and specialists to executive posts in the national economy, to wage a war against inertia and red tape in industry which were shackling the workers' initiative and creative activity.

The Sixteenth Congress of the Party stressed the great significance of the mass collective-farm movement for the victory of Socialism in the U.S.S.R. The resolution of the Congress, "The Collective-Farm Movement and the Advance of Agriculture," stated:

"While the confiscation of the landed estates was the *first* step of the October Revolution in the countryside, the transition to collective farming is the *second* and, moreover, decisive step, marking a most important stage in the process of laying the foundations of Socialist society in the U.S.S.R." (*ibid.*, p. 60).

By the summer of 1930 collectivisation in the principal grain-growing regions embraced 40 to 50 per cent of the peasant households. The crop area of the collective farms reached 90,000,000 acres. Already in 1930 more than half the grain in the country purchased by the State came from the collective farms. This meant that from now on the future of agriculture in the U.S.S.R. would be decided not by individual farms but by the collective and State farms.

The relative position of the different forms of economy in the U.S.S.R. was undergoing a change. Socialist relations of production which had up to now leaned almost exclusively on Socialist industry, now began to lean also on the rapidly expanding Socialist sector in agriculture. The question of the social basis of Soviet power in the countryside now bore a new aspect. Before the movement for solid collectivisation Soviet power had relied on the poor peasantry, the middle peasant being the ally of the working class in the struggle against the kulaks and for the victory of Socialism. Now, in the districts of solid collectivisation, the whole collective-farm peasantry, as noted by the Sixteenth Party Congress, became "*a real and firm mainstay of Soviet power*" (*ibid.*, p. 52).

By the time of the Sixteenth Congress of the Party certain successes had been attained in the cultural revolution. The Congress, however, considered the rate of cultural construction insufficient, and set the task of introducing, in the immediate future, universal and compulsory elementary education and ending illiteracy throughout the country.

Further, the Congress recorded that the Party had been able to achieve its outstanding successes in the sphere of Socialist construction thanks to the steady implementation of its general line and its determined struggle against Trotskyism and the Right deviation. The Congress stated that *the Trotskyists had completely sunk to the positions of Menshevism and had become an anti-Soviet, counter-revolutionary group.* In conditions of the full-scale offensive of Socialism along the whole front, the Right deviation was the main danger in the Party, since its adherents had objectively become agents of the kulaks in the Party. The Congress summed up the results of the struggle of the Party against the Right deviation and *declared that the views of the Right opposition were incompatible with membership of the C.P.S.U.(B.).*

Noting with satisfaction the growing fraternal co-operation among the peoples of the Soviet Union the Congress drew the attention of the Party to the necessity of waging a persistent fight against deviations on the national question, namely, dominant-nation chauvinism, which was the principal danger, and local nationalism. The Congress called upon all members of the Party to defend the Party's unity and instructed the Central Committee to continue "mercilessly to repulse any *attempts to weaken and undermine iron Party discipline and the unity of Lenin's Party*" (*ibid.*, p. 22).

The Sixteenth Party Congress adopted the policy of reconstructing all branches of the national economy on the basis of modern technology. This reconstruction would put an end to the age-long backwardness of the country, strengthen the economic independence of the U.S.S.R. and raise its capacity for defence. It would enable the Soviet country to overtake and outstrip, technically and economically, the advanced capitalist countries in the shortest period of time.

Technical reconstruction was an indispensable condition for the successful offensive of Socialism along the whole front. It facilitated the reorganisation of the old social and economic system in agriculture, accelerated the amalgamation of the small, individual peasant households in large-scale collective farms and the tearing up of the roots of capitalism in the economy of the U.S.S.R.

The reconstruction of the technical base of industry and agriculture when production was organised on Socialist lines created conditions for a further, still more rapid development of the country's productive forces, rise in labour productivity, increase of output and improvement in the welfare of the working people.

3. The Organising and Political Work of the Party in the Period of the Full-Scale Offensive of Socialism Along the Whole Front

Armed with the decisions of the Sixteenth Congress, the Party continued to develop the offensive of Socialism along the whole front. The main task was to accelerate the rate of Socialist construction.

"We are fifty or a hundred years behind the advanced countries," said Stalin. "We must make good this distance in ten years" (*Works*, Eng. ed., Vol. 13, p. 41).

The first Five-Year Plan period was a period of new construction. Hundreds of big plants, pits, mines, and power stations were being erected on the vast territory of the Soviet Union. New towns and workers' settlements were making their appearance. New main railways were being laid. Thousands of collective farms, State farms and machine-and-tractor stations were being organised. New schools, clubs and hospitals were being built everywhere. During the first Five-Year Plan period there were commissioned *every day*, on the average: one industrial enterprise, two State farms, one or two machine-and-tractor stations, and about 115 collective farms. But this construction was of an unusual nature. The newly-erected enterprises were not ordinary plants or farms; they were enterprises of a Socialist type. Each new plant, collective farm or machine-and-tractor station was a new stronghold of Socialism.

The tremendous scale of new industrial construction and the Socialist reconstruction of agriculture demanded from the Party a higher level of organising work. The Party had in practice to organise the creative activity of tens of millions of people both on a country-wide scale and at each building site. each factory, each collective farm. It was necessary to work out new forms and methods for the practical guidance of Socialist construction, to bring all the levels of the dictatorship of the proletariat closer to the masses, to production. The Party was aware of the increased difficulties of organising work in the conditions of the full-scale Socialist offensive, and understood its significance for the victory of Socialism in the U.S.S.R. It remembered Lenin's words that problems of organisation were the most difficult problems of the Socialist revolution, since it was a question of radically reorganising the entire economic life of the country on Socialist lines, and of remoulding the very foundations of the lives of tens of millions of people.

The Party regrouped its ranks in conformity with the tasks of the Socialist offensive along the whole front.

Fulfilling the decision of the Sixteenth Congress to shift the stress of Party work to the factory shop and the workers' team, the Central Committee carried out in the period between 1930 and 1932 a reorganisation of the Party groups in the factories. As a result of the tremendous growth of the Party, a large number of Party groups in the towns had become big organisations numbering many thousands of Communists. In view of this, the Central Committee of the Party recommended setting up at all industrial enterprises with not less than 500 Communists, factory Party committees, shop Party branches, and Party groups in the workers' teams. This reorganisation improved Party work at the factories and increased the Party's influence among the mass of the workers. The factory Party organisations began to devote more attention to production problems. With a view to improving the guidance of Party organisations, town Party committees were set up in towns with a population exceeding 50,000.

The Party organisations in the countryside were also reconstructed. Most of the rural Party groups had been formed on the territorial principle. By June, 1930, there were about 30,000 Party groups in the countryside embracing 404,000 Communists. Of this number, 263,000 Communists were members of territorial Party groups, 115,000 of collective-farm groups, and 26,000 of Party groups in State farms and machine-and-tractor stations. In districts of solid collectivisation, Communist collective farmers were transferred from village territorial groups to Party groups in collective farms. In big collective farms, machine-and-tractor stations and State farms new Party groups were set up and old ones reinforced. They became the strongholds of Party work in the countryside. Soon after the Sixteenth Congress areas (*okruga*), as administrative and territorial divisions, were abolished while the districts (*rayony*) were reinforced as the main link of Socialist construction in the countryside. The Party leading bodies were thus brought closer to the basic Party organisations, the collective farms and the peasant masses. They became more flexible and efficient.

The Party also took measures to enhance the organising role of the Soviets. The high rates of Socialist construction necessitated smooth and efficient work of the State apparatus at all levels. But quite a number of workers of the Soviet apparatus had become bureaucrats, had lost touch with real life and did not try to understand the new tasks. The Party developed criticism and self-criticism to disclose shortcomings in the work of the Soviet institutions, and organised a cleansing of the State apparatus. Thousands of advanced workers at the bench were promoted to leading Soviet posts. Much work in improving the State apparatus was accomplished by the Central Control Commission-Workers' and Peasants' Inspection and its local bodies. After the Sixteenth Party Congress A. A. Andreyev was appointed Chairman of the Central Control Commission and People's Commissar of Workers' and Peasants' Inspection of the U.S.S.R.

In order to establish closer contact between economic management and enterprise, and the better to ensure the development of the decisive branches of the national economy, some of the People's Commissariats were split up. For example, the Supreme Council of National Economy was reorganised into three People's Commissariats for the Heavy, Light and Timber Industries. A number of leading Party people were placed at the head of the key branches of economic construction: V. V. Kuibyshev as Chairman of the State Planning Commission of the U.S.S.R., G. K. Orjonikidze as People's Commissar for Heavy Industry of the U.S.S.R., A. I. Mikoyan as People's Commissar for Supply of the U.S.S.R.

The trade unions, which numbered 11.5 million members by the time of the Sixteenth Party Congress, were also reorganised. The Party strove for a real turn by the trade unions to the problems of production and for their active participation in Socialist construction. The trade unions cleansed their leading bodies of Right-wing defeatist elements. The Central Committee of the Party reinforced the leadership of the All-Union Central Council of Trade Unions. N. M. Shvernik was elected its First Secretary. On the initiative of the Central Committee the trade unions were subdivided into smaller units. They began to make a more thorough study of the various branches of industry, to give more practical guidance to their local organisations and to give better service to the workers.

The organising work of the Party was directed primarily at accelerating the rate of new industrial construction. The Party sent its best cadres and the best forces of the working class to the construction sites of a number of industrial giants—the Dnieper Hydroelectric Power Station, the Magnitogorsk and Kuznetsk Iron and Steel Works, the Berezniki and Neva Chemical Works, the Urals Heavy Engineering Works, the Novo-Kramatorsk Engineering Plant, the Chelyabinsk and Kharkov Tractor Plants, the Moscow and Gorky Automobile Plants, the Saratov Combine Harvester Plant, and others. The Central Committee of the Party exercised day-to-day guidance of the construction of big enterprises. It sought persistently to ensure the commissioning of every new works, every new power station, by the time fixed.

The new construction projects occupied the main attention of the local Party organisations, especially in Moscow, the Urals, Western Siberia, Ukraine, Kazakhstan, Gorky and Saratov. A tremendous amount of work was done at the construction sites by the Party groups, of which Communists sent from town and factory Party organisations constituted the core. They organised the building workers who were arriving from different parts of the country, mainly from the countryside, pulled together the new collectives of these workers and helped them to work effectively.

The political work of the Party among the masses was geared to the task of ensuring high rates of Socialist construction. The Party explained to the masses the necessity for accelerating the rates of Socialist industrialisation, and did not conceal from them the difficulties involved. It developed the political consciousness of the workers and of the technical personnel, encouraged their creative activity, mobilised them to overcome the difficulties of Socialist construction and to fulfil the five-year plan for industry in four years.

In conditions of the colossal construction during the years of the first Five-Year Plan the country had to put up with many privations and hardships. It was still a poor country. There was a shortage of clothing, footwear, and many other articles of primary necessity. At the construction sites the workers lived in tents and temporary wooden barracks. Foodstuffs and many manufactured goods were strictly rationed. All these difficulties were shouldered primarily by the working class. But the workers realised that, in conditions of a hostile capitalist encirclement, there was no other way of transforming their country into a mighty industrial Power. They understood that industry could be built up only at the cost of sacrifice and the most rigorous economy. Stinting themselves in everything, and tightening their belts, the workers displayed unprecedented labour heroism. The working class and all the working people were firmly convinced of the victory of Socialism in the

U.S.S.R., of the correctness of the policy of the Party; and they advanced unswervingly towards their goal. The unity, high degree of organisation and selflessness of the working class exerted a tremendous moral influence on the poor and middle peasants who were developing the collective-farm movement. Particularly great was the labour enthusiasm of the youth. In response to the appeal of the Party, tens of thousands of young people were sent by the Young Communist League organisations to work in still undeveloped localities, and to construction sites in the Urals, Kuznetsk coalfield, Donets coalfield, Far East and Central Asia.

Mobilising the creative activity of the working class for the fulfilment of the Five-Year Plan in four years, the Central Committee of the Party in September, 1930, addressed an appeal to the workers calling on them to organise Socialist emulation for successful fulfilment of the targets of the third year of the Five-Year Plan. There was not a single enterprise where the workers did not respond to this appeal of the Party. The Socialist emulation movement developed with still greater force throughout the country. The atmosphere of the factories changed, and with it their habitual tenor of life. Workers at kindred construction sites, factories and plants began to exchange their labour experience, while production reviews and competitions for the best shop and workers' team were organised in the individual factories. New indices of the work of advanced workers' teams and shock workers appeared on the boards of honour in factories and at construction sites. The number of heroes of labour steadily grew.

New forms of Socialist emulation originated which were quickly taken up by Party, trade union and Komsomol organisations and spread throughout the country. In the summer of 1930 the workers of the Karl Marx Works in Leningrad, after discussing the target figures of their enterprise for the economic year 1930/31, drew up a counter-plan for output and financial economy exceeding that provided for in the State plan. They called upon all enterprises to follow their example. Soon this movement of counter-planning extended to the majority of factories, and marked the beginning of collective forms of emulation. The workers of the Ilyich Plant in Mariupol (now the town of Zhdanov) took the lead in drawing up shift counter-plans. In the beginning of 1931 the movement of cost-accounting workers' teams originated in Leningrad. By April, 1932, the number of such teams was already 155,000.

The basic form of Socialist emulation during the first Five-Year Plan period was the shock-brigade movement. This movement carried on and developed the splendid traditions of the Communist *subbotniks*. The political work of the Party was concentrated in the shock brigades, which were headed by the most competent and energetic workers, who were most often Communists or members of the Komsomol. Many of these workers attended Workers' Faculties and technical schools without giving up their jobs, and upon graduation became shop managers or directors of factories.

The initiators and organisers of Socialist emulation were Party organisations, Communists and members of the Komsomol. In the period of the first Five-Year Plan every sixth worker was a Communist. By the autumn of 1932 the Party organisations at the biggest industrial enterprises had fulfilled the directive of the Sixteenth Party Congress: almost all the members of the Party and the Komsomol had been drawn into Socialist emulation. The number of Communists in the leading shops and key sectors of the factories markedly increased. Communists became coal-hewers and machine-tool operators, worked at open-hearth furnaces and on the scaffolding at construction sites. Their labour heroism inspired the mass of the workers.

For outstanding services in Socialist construction in the first Five-Year Plan period more than 600 shock workers, engineers, technicians and business executives were awarded the Order of Lenin, which had been instituted in April, 1930; about 400 foremost people in Socialist emulation were awarded the Order of the Red Banner of Labour. The heroes of labour became well known throughout the country; they enjoyed the profound respect of the whole people.

The Party and the Soviet State combined measures of moral encouragement with those which gave the workers a material incentive to raise the productivity of labour. New and improved wage scales were introduced in industry, which provided for differentials reflecting the difference between skilled and unskilled labour, between heavy and light work.

Year after year the Socialist emulation movement became more widespread. By the end of 1932 almost 75 per cent of all the workers were taking part in it. The Soviet intelligentsia too was actively participating in Socialist emulation. The successes attained in Socialist construction and the universal labour enthusiasm beneficially affected the attitude of the old technical intelligentsia, who in their vast majority began to take an active part in Socialist construction. Emulation spread also to the countryside. Following the example of the factory workers, collective farmers and workers at State farms and machine-and-tractor stations started a drive for improved collective and State farm production and for a higher level of labour productivity in agriculture. Socialist emulation and shock work became a nation-wide movement. Soviet people were labouring in the sphere of peaceful Socialist construction with the same enthusiasm and heroism that they had displayed when fighting for Soviet power during the Revolution and the Civil War.

Never before had history known such an upsurge of creative activity of the mass of the people. The enthusiasm of new construction seized upon millions of workers. The mass movement of the workers to raise labour productivity appreciably reduced construction schedules and ensured the fulfilment of the Five-Year Plan ahead of time. At Magnitogorsk and the Dnieper Hydroelectric projects, advanced teams of building workers established new world records in the pouring of concrete. The first turbine of the Dnieper Hydroelectric Power Station was installed in 36 days, instead of the 90 days provided for by the plan. The machine assembly shop of the Moscow Automobile Works assembled 1,200 machine-tools during one month.

New industrial giants came into operation one after another. In 1931 the Kharkov Tractor Works, the Moscow Automobile Works, the Urals Copper-Smelting Works, and the first section of the Urals Heavy Engineering Works were commissioned. At the beginning of 1932 the Gorky Automobile Works and the Saratov Combine Harvester Works were put into service. In February, 1932, the first Magnitogorsk blast-furnace, and in April of the same year the first Kuznetsk blast-furnace, went into operation. The coal output of the Kuznetsk coalfield increased almost threefold in the first Five-Year Plan period. With the commissioning of the first blast-furnaces of the Magnitogorsk and Kuznetsk Iron and Steel Works, and the simultaneous development of the Kuznetsk coalfield, a firm foundation was laid for the creation of a new powerful coal and metallurgical base in the east of the U.S.S.R.

Big towns sprang up around the new industrial giants. Particularly rapid was the growth of the new towns of Magnitogorsk and Stalinsk. At the end of 1929, when the foundation of the Kuznetsk Iron and Steel Works was being laid in distant Siberia, the poet Vladimir Mayakovsky, in verses dedicated to the workers of the Kuznetsk project, wrote:

> That garden
> shall be blooming,
> that city must
> arise
> when Soviet Russia
> has such men
> as those before my eyes.

Indeed, within a short two and a half years after building work began, a big town with a population of more than 100,000 had arisen on what had been a wilderness, and the Kuznetsk Iron and Steel Works began to produce its first pig-iron. Both the town and the plant were the fruit of the labour of Soviet people who were building and at the same time acquiring experience and knowledge. Yesterday's navvies, concreters and assemblers became blast-furnacemen and steel founders. I. P. Bardin, the construction chief, one of the first outstanding engineers who after the October Revolution devoted himself to the service of the people, to building up Soviet metallurgy, became an academician.

The remnants of the defeated exploiting classes and their toadies furiously resisted the victorious advance of Socialism in the U.S.S.R. The hostile forces of the capitalist encirclement in every way possible supported their struggle against Soviet power, seeking to frustrate the fulfilment of the Five-Year Plan and Socialist construction in the U.S.S.R. In 1930 and 1931 three big counter-revolutionary organisations were uncovered: the "Industrial Party," the "Working Peasant Party" and the "All-Union Bureau of the Russian Social-Democratic Labour Party." The "Industrial Party" included the leading group of the old bourgeois technical intelligentsia, which engaged in wrecking activities in industry. The so-called "Working Peasant Party" which had its centre in the People's Commissariat for Agriculture, expressed the interests of the kulak class and sought to frustrate collectivisation. The Menshevik counter-revolutionary group, the "All-Union Bureau of the R.S.D.L.P." was active in the State Planning Commission, the Supreme Council of National Economy, the State Bank, the Central Union of Consumers' Co-operative Societies and in other organisations.

All the participants of these counter-revolutionary organisations were publicly tried, and their crimes against the people and the workers' and peasants' State exposed. The wreckers had been in close touch with Russian capitalists and Whites who had fled abroad. Supported by a number of bourgeois States, they had engaged in wrecking activities and espionage, with the object of overthrowing Soviet power and restoring capitalism in the U.S.S.R.

The criminal activities of these counter-revolutionary groups aroused the indignation of the people. They realised the necessity for the greatest vigilance and firmness towards all enemies who desperately resisted the building of a new society in which there was no place for exploitation and oppression. Big meetings of factory workers and collective farmers were held at which their participants demanded severe punishment of the traitors. The proletarian court passed severe and just sentences on the exposed enemies of the people. In answer to the subversive activities of the remnants of the internal counter-revolution and world imperialism, the workers, collective farmers and intelligentsia rallied still closer round the Communist Party and redoubled their labour efforts and political activity.

The trials of the wreckers showed that the enemies wished for the triumph of the opposition within the Party and hoped for a split in the Party. The Central Committee and the Central Control Commission firmly guarded the unity of the Party, resolutely stopping all attempts of the opportunists to weaken Party discipline, to disorganise the ranks of the workers and peasants and to frustrate Socialist construction. A joint plenary meeting of the Central Committee and of the Central Control Commission held in December 1930 removed Rykov, one of the leaders of the Right opposition, from the Political Bureau. He was also relieved of the post of Chairman of the Council of People's Commissars. V. M. Molotov was elected to this post.

4. The Party's Struggle for the Technical Re-equipment of the National Economy. Further Spread of the Collective-Farm Movement. Organisational and Economic Consolidation of the Collective Farms. Results of the First Five-Year Plan

Re-equipment of the national economy on the basis of up-to-date technique was a most important condition for the victory of Socialism in the U.S.S.R. and a means of accelerating Socialist construction. Lenin stated:

"Only when the country has been electrified, when industry, agriculture, and transport have been placed on the technical basis of modern large-scale industry, only then shall we be fully victorious" (*Collected Works*, Vol. 31, p. 484).

In keeping with Lenin's directions, the Sixteenth Party Congress advanced the task of radically reconstructing all branches of the national economy on the most up-to-date technical lines. But this task called for eliminating the dearth of technique in the U.S.S.R. Thus technique became of decisive importance in the reconstruction period. The national economy could be re-equipped only on the basis of a highly developed engineering industry. It was, therefore, necessary not only to develop Soviet engineering, but to do it in the minimum of time.

The Party energetically set out to build a Soviet engineering industry, and ensured it a higher rate of development compared with the other branches of industry. Machine-tool construction, toolmaking and the manufacture of other industrial equipment, which constitute the basis of engineering, were developed at a particularly accelerated tempo. The reconstruction of old machine-tool plants and the erection of new ones (such as the Moscow Capstan-Lathe Works, the Gorky Milling-Machine Works, and others) were carried out with the greatest possible speed. The stock of machine-tools in operation rapidly grew. More than 50,000 metal-cutting lathes were produced in the period of the first Five-Year Plan. The output of such lathes increased from 2,000 in 1928 to 19,700 in 1932. The successes attained in machine-tool construction and in the production of other new industrial equipment made it possible completely to reconstruct the engineering industry and to create a number of new branches within it, such as heavy engineering, production of tractors and harvester combines, and an aircraft industry. The advanced technique of the capitalist countries was also widely utilised in the technical re-equipment of Soviet industry.

Thanks to the efforts of the Party and of the working class, the Five-Year Plan programme for engineering was fulfilled in three years. Since 1931 engineering has occupied the leading place in the country's industry. By the end of the Five-Year Plan period the gross output of engineering and metal-working had increased fourfold as compared with that of 1928 and sevenfold as compared with that of 1913. Technically, the U.S.S.R. became one of the most advanced countries in the world, ranking second in world engineering after the U.S.A. The task set by the Fourteenth Party Congress—to convert the U.S.S.R. from a country importing machinery into a country producing machinery and other equipment by its own efforts—was in the main accomplished. This was a tremendous victory of the Party in the sphere of the Socialist industrialisation of the country.

The national economy of the U.S.S.R. was being put on a powerful technical basis, which made possible the reconstruction of all its various branches on new, modern technical lines.

First of all, Soviet industry itself was being given firm foundations. All its branches began to be supplied with up-to-date machinery. The bringing into being of a heavy engineering industry was of paramount importance for the technical re-equipment of industry as a whole. In 1931 industry began to turn out powerful machines and equipment for power stations (among them the country's first turbine with a capacity of 50,000 kw.), for the iron and steel industry (including the first Soviet blooming mill), and for the coal industry.

The next step was the reconstruction of the railways which were in a backward state and hampered the development of Socialist construction. In 1931 the question of the railways was discussed twice (in June and in October) by plenary meetings of the Central Committee of the Party. Electrification of the railways was declared the main link in the reconstruction process. In 1931 Soviet industry began to produce diesel-locomotives, and in 1932, electric locomotives. Work was begun on the electrification of railway lines in the Urals and in the Donets and Kuznetsk coalfields, on reconstruction of railway tracks and mechanisation of loading and unloading operations. The output of locomotives and railway cars almost doubled in the Five-Year Plan period.

The supply of new types of machinery to the building industry made it possible to start on the complete reconstruction of a number of old towns and to accelerate the building of new towns. In June, 1931, a plenary meeting of the Central Committee of the Party considered a report on the Moscow municipal economy and the development of municipal economy in the U.S.S.R. It was the first time that the Party discussed this question on such a broad scale. The plenary meeting instructed the Moscow Party Committee and the Moscow Soviet to work out a scientifically grounded plan for the reconstruction of Moscow, which would provide for properly thought-out civic development, in particular for new housing and municipal schemes, for the construction of big heat and power plants, an underground railway, and a canal linking the Moskva River with the Volga. Large-scale reconstruction work was also planned in Leningrad, Kharkov, Baku, Gorky, Dnepropetrovsk, Rostov-on-Don and other cities. New towns were to be built in the Urals, in the Donets, Kuznetsk and Moscow coalfields.

Soviet agriculture too was being completely reconstructed technically. In the first Five-Year Plan its tractor fleet grew to 120,000 tractors with a total capacity of 1,900,000 h.p. The machine-and-tractor stations and State and collective farms received agricultural machinery to the value of 1,600 million rubles. The machine-and-tractor stations and State farms were the principal levers in the technical re-equipment of agriculture. By the end of 1932 there were already 2,446 machine-and-tractor stations in the country with a fleet of tractors exceeding 75,000. The establishment of the machine-and-tractor stations signified a profound technical revolution in agriculture and the abolition of its age-old backwardness.

But with the steady influx of modern machinery into all branches of the national economy, another difficulty arose—an acute shortage of people capable of organising the new branches of production and operating the complex machinery. The newly-erected industrial enterprises equipped with modern machinery needed technically competent administrative and business cadres, engineers and technicians fully answering the requirements of modern science and technology, and skilled workers able to operate the new machines. The Party first encountered this difficulty at the Stalingrad Tractor Works: the plant had been built in record time—11 months—but more than a year was taken up in learning how to run it. Many of the plant's engineers, technicians and workers did not know how to handle the new machinery, how to co-ordinate their work in production line conditions.

This backwardness in mastering the new branches of production and new technique threatened to retard Socialist construction. The biggest danger was that a certain section of Communist business executives underrated the role of technique and did not realise the urgent necessity of raising the level of their own technical knowledge. Among the industrial managers were numerous promoted workers who were good organisers, but lacked special technical training. Many of them continued to hold the old views on technique current in the restoration period, and did not understand that in the new conditions, i.e., in the period of the technical reconstruction of the entire national economy, it was impossible to manage big industrial enterprises without the necessary technical knowledge. Such business executives often fully entrusted the technical management of production to "experts," reserving to themselves the function of "general" direction. At that time the percentage of Communists among the specialists with a higher education was insignificant. Among the technical personnel there were still many old experts, some of whom were politically unstable and even hostile towards Soviet power.

The Central Committee of the Party realised in good time the danger of lagging behind in mastering the new branches of production and new technique. An important part in turning the attention of the Party, trade unions, business executives and the working class to the importance of mastering technique was played by the first All-Union Conference of Managers of Socialist Industry, held at the end of January, 1931, on the initiative of the Central Committee of the Party.

The Party advanced the slogan: "Bolsheviks must master technique!" The struggle to put this slogan into effect was given priority attention by all Party, trade union, economic and Komsomol organisations.

In June, 1931, the Central Committee of the Party convened a conference of business executives which considered the new conditions of industrial development and new methods of management. It defined the most important principles of Socialist management in industry in the new conditions. These were the organised recruitment of labour power, overhauling of the wages system, better organisation of work, better cost-accounting, enlistment of the active co-operation of the old technical intelligentsia in Socialist construction, and the creation of a new working-class technical intelligentsia.

The Party carried out a number of measures aimed at raising the level of technical knowledge of business executives, and training new engineers and technicians. The network of industrial academies, where the leading cadres of Socialist industry were receiving special instruction, was extended. In the first Five-Year Plan period the number of industrial higher educational establishments increased almost tenfold, and that of technical secondary schools fourfold. Preparatory workers' faculties were opened at all technical institutes. Almost 75 per cent of all the students of the technical institutes and technical schools were workers. Every fourth student was a Communist. Large-scale industry received nearly 100,000 engineers and technicians during the Five-Year Plan period. This was a *new, Soviet technical intelligentsia* upon whom Soviet power could fully rely in the colossal work of Socialist construction.

The Party initiated a broad movement among the working class for mastering modern technique. Taking into account the experience of the Stalingrad Tractor Works, the Central Committee of the Party recommended all Party organisations at large construction sites to promote the extensive training of the workers in new trades. The trade unions and the Komsomol actively helped to give effect to this measure. Workers' training centres, technical study circles, schools and courses were started at factories and building sites; regular "technical training days" were held all over the country. Many workers engaged on the building of new factories visited factories already in operation to learn new trades. The number of factory apprentice schools greatly increased. The Party supported another important undertaking initiated by the Komsomol, namely, organisation of technical tests. This movement, originating in 1931, spread to all factories and construction sites. The technical knowledge acquired by the workers helped them to become real experts at their jobs. Hundreds of thousands of the country's unskilled workmen and builders of yesterday became skilled lathe-operators, metal-workers, blast-furnace workers, steel founders, operators of coal-cutting machines, etc. In agriculture, by the spring of 1931, over 200,000 collective farmers had become tractor-drivers and machine operators, and operated the machinery of the machine-and-tractor stations on the collective farms.

The reconstruction of the national economy was accompanied by a cultural revolution. In 1930 the Soviet State introduced universal compulsory elementary education. A nation-wide movement to wipe out illiteracy among the adult population was started. In the period between 1930 and 1932 over 30 million people attended special schools for the liquidation of illiteracy.

Technical reconstruction and the mass movement of the workers to master new techniques facilitated the acceleration of the pace of Socialist industrialisation. The successes attained in industrial production in 1931 made possible the fulfilment of the Five-Year Plan in four years. The Party turned to the task of drawing up a second Five-Year Plan. This question was considered by the

Seventeenth Conference of the C.P.S.U.(B.), held in January-February, 1932.

The Conference approved "Directives for Drawing Up the Second Five-Year Plan for the Development of the National Economy of the U.S.S.R. (1933-1937)." The fundamental political task of the second Five-Year Plan was, according to the Directives, the complete elimination of all capitalist elements and of all causes which give rise to the exploitation of man by man and the division of society into exploiters and exploited. The principal economic task of the new Five-Year Plan was to complete the technical reconstruction of the national economy as a whole. The Directives emphasised that technical reconstruction was indissolubly bound up with producing trained personnel, mastering the new techniques and developing Soviet science and technology. In the sphere of the material welfare of the workers and peasants the Directives provided for a two to threefold increase in popular consumption.

The Party systematically guided the Socialist development of agriculture. The initial successes of collectivisation were consolidated. In September, 1930, the Central Committee instructed Party organisations to intensify their work of drawing new masses of poor and middle peasants into collective farms. A plenary meeting of the Central Committee held in December, 1930, set the task of collectivising in 1931 not less than 50 per cent of all peasant farms in the country; of completing collectivisation in the main in the steppe part of Ukraine, the North Caucasus, the Lower Volga and Middle Volga (the Trans-Volga area); of drawing not less than 50 per cent of all peasant households into collective farms in all other grain-growing regions, as well as in the cotton-growing and sugar-beet-growing regions; and about 25 per cent in the regions of the consuming belt.

Local Party organisations started explanatory work among the peasants still practising individual husbandry, drawing into this work collective-farmer activists.

There began a new powerful upswing of the collective-farm movement. During the year following the Sixteenth Party Congress, more than 7 million peasant households joined the collective farms. In the North Caucasus, the Lower and Middle Volga, Ukraine (the steppe and the parts situated on the left bank of the Dnieper), Crimea and the grain-growing regions of the Urals and Moldavia, collectivisation embraced from 68 to 90 per cent of all peasant farms. Thus, *collectivisation in these regions was completed in the main.* In other grain-growing, cotton-growing and sugar-beet-growing regions more than 50 per cent of all peasant farms were collectivised.

The kulak class was completely eliminated in all districts of solid collectivisation. The kulaks who resisted collectivisation were evicted from their places of residence. From the beginning of 1930 up to the autumn of 1932 altogether 240,757 kulak families, that is, about one per cent of the total number of peasant households, were evicted from the districts of solid collectivisation. The Soviet Government did everything necessary to provide the former kulaks with work at their new places of residence and to create proper living conditions for them. The bulk of the evicted kulaks were engaged in the timber, building and ore-mining industries, and in the State farms of Western Siberia and Kazakhstan. The Party and the Soviet Government re-educated the kulaks, helped them to become equal citizens and active builders of Socialist society.

A very big role in effecting solid collectivisation, in establishing and consolidating the collective-farm system was played by the machine-and-tractor stations. The first machine-and-tractor station in the country was organised in 1928 by the workers of the Shevchenko State farm in the Odessa Region. The peasants of this locality began to cultivate their land in common. Proceeding from the practical experience of the Shevchenko machine-and-tractor station, the Central Committee of the Party considered it expedient to set up an all-Union centre for the organisation and direction of machine-and-tractor stations. Such a centre—the Tractor Centre—was set up in June, 1929. Tractor columns, organised by agricultural co-operatives and by area groups of collective farms, became widespread in 1929 and also helped to promote the collective-farm movement. But they suffered from a number of major defects: they lacked permanent organisational centres, did not have the necessary material and technical base, and did not use the new machinery efficiently.

Soviet industry was from year to year turning out an increasing number of tractors and other agricultural machines. This confronted the Party with the question of how to use them more efficiently when collective farms were being set up on a mass scale. It was necessary to find a suitable form for the technical servicing of the collective farms, a form which would ensure the most rational use of the new machinery. At first, along with the organisation of machine-and-tractor stations, the Soviet State used to sell part of the tractors to collective farms. But practice had shown that this way of using the tractors was unsuitable in the initial period of collective-farm construction. The young and economically weak collective farms lacked the necessary funds for the purchase of tractors and other machines; nor did they have the necessary technical personnel. Besides, Soviet industry was still unable to supply all the collective farms with tractors. The practice of collective-farm development suggested that it was advisable to concentrate the tractors and all the other agricultural machinery in the hands of the State. There was also the highly important political aspect of the question. The machine-and-tractor stations were powerful levers with the help of which the Soviet State could exert its guiding influence on the development of agriculture along Socialist lines and strengthen the alliance of the working class and the peasantry. In the hands of the State they were a means of educating the millions of collective farmers in the spirit of collectivism.

Taking all this into account, the Party considered it necessary to concentrate all agricultural machinery in the State machine-and-tractor stations. After the Sixteenth Party Congress the co-operative tractor columns and the machine-and-tractor stations were transferred to the Tractor Centre, which was entrusted with the further organisation and direction of the machine-and-tractor stations. The Soviet State took upon itself the organisation of the technical servicing of the collective farms and the training of machine-operators for agriculture. The establishment of machine-and-tractor stations was advantageous both to the State and to the collective farms. They ensured a highly efficient use of the new agricultural machinery, served the State as an additional source of obtaining collective-farm grain and raw materials for industry, and helped the collective farms to grow stronger organisationally and economically.

By the summer of 1931 the collective farms embraced 13 million peasant households (52.7 per cent). They became the main producers of grain, cotton, sugar-beet, sunflower and other agricultural crops. Together with the State farms they accounted for more than two-thirds of the country's spring crop area. The collective-farm peasantry had become the leading force in agriculture.

The Party had won a decisive victory in the battle for the collectivisation of agriculture. In 1931 there were already 211,100 collective farms in the country. The principal task now was to strengthen these farms and to draw the remaining individual peasants into them, rather than to organise new collective farms.

Without slackening its work of drawing new individual peasants into collective farms, the Party concentrated its main attention on the *organisational and economic consolidation of the collective farms.*

As large-scale Socialist enterprises, the collective farms offered tremendous possibilities for raising the labour productivity and the material welfare of the collective farmers. But it was a complicated and difficult task to learn how to use these possibilities. Collectivisation meant completely upsetting the age-old tenor of rural life. The peasant who had been accustomed for centuries to work in an individual farm, on the principle of "everyone for himself," could not, upon joining the collective farms, immediately adjust himself to the new and unfamiliar environment. The old habits and customs of individual private farming were still strong with him. The remoulding of the psychology of the individual peasant of yesterday in the spirit of Socialism had only just begun in the collective farms, and the new, social discipline was only just beginning to take shape.

The work of the collective farms therefore suffered from many defects which hindered utilising the advantages offered by large-scale collective farming. The bulk of the collective farmers and the collective-farm leaders were still inexperienced in managing large-scale agricultural production. Work was still badly organised in many collective farms; the collective farmers were often not assigned to definite jobs. Nor was the accounting properly organised. In many cases the income was distributed not according to the work done, but according to the number of mouths to feed in the family. This lowered the collective farmers' incentive to work and slackened their labour discipline; there were many instances of collective farmers shirking work. Harvesting was often dragged out, and large quantities of grain were lost. The absence of individual responsibility for machines, livestock and other property greatly harmed the economy of the collective farms. Former kulaks and other hostile elements penetrated into collective farms, where they stole property, damaged agricultural machines, destroyed horses and productive livestock, often deliberately neglected their duties, and, in every way they could, prevented the honest members from organising a normal collective-farm life.

The creation of a new social discipline in the collective farms required much time and effort. The main difficulty lay in finding the proper form of organisation of the collectively-owned economy and the right material incentives for the collective farmers to develop this economy. The Party still lacked experience in this field. Only the collective farmers themselves could find new forms of labour organisation, new methods of strengthening labour discipline and of applying the Socialist principle of distribution of collective-farm incomes according to work done. These new forms and methods were found.

Collective-farm practice advanced a quite new principle for calculating social labour in the collective farms, namely, *the workday unit combined with piece-work*.

Proceeding from the experience of the best agricultural artels, a plenary meeting of the Central Committee of the Party held in June, 1931, recommended collective farms to organise all their work on the piece-work basis, to calculate work done in workday units, and to distribute the incomes (both in cash and in kind) according to the number of workday units earned.

The Party and Komsomol organisations of the collective farms, supported by district Party activists, headed the campaign to introduce the piece-work system in the collective farms and to organise strict accounting of the work done by the collective farmers. The advanced section of the collective-farm peasantry received with satisfaction the measures taken by the Party to regulate the work in the collective farms and strengthen labour discipline, and actively supported them. In the course of 1931 all collective farms went over to piece-work and the workday unit system.

The next step in the organisation of labour in the collective farms was the formation—in keeping with the experience of the best agricultural artels—of *production teams*, membership of which remained the same over a long period. Definite sections of the land, livestock, machines and agricultural implements were assigned to each production team. In stock-raising teams it was considered advisable to assign definite animals to each milkmaid or pig-tender, and to pay them according to the results obtained.

With the consolidation of the collective-farm system the role of the Soviet State in planning and regulating agriculture markedly increased. The State was now able to influence the development of collective-farm production and to strengthen it.

In May, 1932, the Party and the Soviet Government took a decision to expand collective-farm trade which greatly contributed to the growth of collective-farm production. Obligatory grain deliveries to the State were reduced, and the sale of grain surpluses, remaining after the collective farms had fulfilled the plan of grain deliveries and seed storing, was permitted on collective-farm markets.

At the beginning of 1933 the contract system of State purchases of grain was abolished. Obligatory grain deliveries to the State at fixed prices were introduced for collective farms and individual peasant farms. The grain delivery quotas were calculated per hectare of land to be sown under the sowing plan. Any counter-plans of grain deliveries, exceeding the established per hectare quotas, were forbidden. All grain surpluses left after fulfilment of obligatory deliveries to the State remained wholly at the disposal of the collective farms and collective farmers. The per hectare principle of grain deliveries and the development of collective-farm trade stimulated the collective farms and collective farmers to extend crop areas and to produce more grain for the market.

On August 7, 1932, the Soviet State issued a law for the protection of Socialist property. This law strengthened the foundations of the collective-farm system. Collective-farm property was equated in its importance with State property. Like State property, it was declared sacred and inviolable.

The first All-Union Congress of Collective-Farm Shock Workers, held in February, 1933, in which leaders of the Party and the Government took part, greatly stimulated the activity of the collective-farm peasantry in collective-farm construction. The Party advanced the slogan of making all collective farms Bolshevik and all collective farmers prosperous.

At the beginning of 1933 the glad news spread throughout the country that the first Five-Year Plan had been fulfilled ahead of time—in four years and three months. In January, 1933, a joint plenary meeting of the Central Committee and Central Control Commission of the Party reviewed the results of the Five-Year Plan. It noted the following major results:

The U.S.S.R. had been converted from an agrarian into an *industrial* country. The Socialist system had completely eliminated the capitalist elements in industry and had become the sole economic system. In 1932 the volume of output of large-scale industry exceeded the pre-war level more than threefold, and that of 1928 more than twofold. Its proportion of the total output of the national economy had risen to 70 per cent. The U.S.S.R. had created its own advanced technical basis which had made possible the reconstruction of all branches of the national economy. During the first Five-Year Plan period 1,500 new industrial enterprises had been put into operation. A number of new industries had been built up, such as an up-to-date iron and steel industry, a tractor industry, an automobile industry, a chemical industry, and an aircraft industry. A new coal and metallurgical base had been created in the east, the Urals-Kuzbas base. The output of electric power had increased by more than 150 per cent. The economic independence of the country had been strengthened: the U.S.S.R. had now begun to produce most necessary industrial equipment at its own enterprises. The Soviet Union had strengthened its defence capacity.

In agriculture, as a result of the determined swing of the poor and middle peasants towards Socialism, the collective and State farms had become the predominant force. A *collective-farm system*, large-scale Socialist farming, had been created in the countryside. From a country of petty peasant farming the U.S.S.R. had become a country where agriculture was run on the largest scale in the world. A leap from an old qualitative state to a new qualitative state had taken place in agriculture. The elimination of the kulaks as a class had been carried out on the basis of solid collectivisation. The machine-and-tractor stations, equipped with tractors and the most up-to-date agricultural machinery, had become important levers in reorganising agriculture along Socialist lines. The agricultural artel had become the principal form of the collective-farm movement.

The progress of Socialism in all spheres of the national economy had brought about a *radical improvement in the material conditions of the working people.* Unemployment in the towns, this scourge of the working class of all capitalist countries, had been completely abolished in the U.S.S.R. The collective-farm system had put an end to kulak bondage and to impoverishment of the working peasantry. The poor peasants and the lower stratum of the middle peasants had been raised to a level of material security in the collective farms. The growth of the national income and the improvement of the material conditions of the working people had been accompanied by a marked rise of their cultural level and the rapid growth of a new, Soviet intelligentsia.

The foundations of Socialism had been laid in the Soviet Union. As in the towns, the Socialist form of economy had firmly established itself in the countryside, too. The question: "Who will beat whom?", posed by Lenin, had been settled in favour of Socialism. Radical changes had taken place in the class structure of Soviet society. The capitalist elements in the country had, in the main, been eliminated. The social basis of the dictatorship of the proletariat had been extended and consolidated. The collective-farm peasantry had become the firm *mainstay* of Soviet power. This was already a *new* class, building a new life on the basis of collective ownership of the means of production. The alliance of the working class and peasantry had undergone a change in aspect, and had acquired a new content. Lenin's wise policy of an alliance between the working class and the poor peasants, on the one hand, and the middle peasants, on the other, had helped to draw the bulk of the peasantry into Socialist construction and had ensured victory over the capitalist elements. The alliance of the working class and collective-farm peasantry was being established on a *new basis— the community* of their interests in the building, consolidation and development of Socialism in town and country.

This was an *epoch-making* victory of the working class, working peasantry and intelligentsia of the U.S.S.R., won under the leadership of the Communist Party.

The results of the first Five-Year Plan were of tremendous international significance.

The Soviet Union had demonstrated to the whole world the superiority of the planned Socialist system of economy over the capitalist system, strengthened its economic might and independence and become an important factor in international affairs.

The fulfilment of the Five-Year Plan exerted a revolutionising influence on the working masses of the capitalist countries. The alignment of class forces markedly changed in favour of Socialism. The results of the Five-Year Plan raised the revolutionary spirit of the working class all over the world and strengthened its confidence in ultimate victory.

Even the enemies of the Soviet Union had to admit the success of the Five-Year Plan. The predictions of the world bourgeoisie and its agents about its inevitable failure had proved false. The working class and the working peasantry of the U.S.S.R. had proved that they could manage without landlords, capitalists and kulaks, that they could create a new and better Socialist system, which knew no crises and unemployment and ensured a continuous improvement in their material and cultural well-being.

BRIEF SUMMARY

The period between 1929 and 1932 witnessed the full-scale offensive of Socialism along the whole front.

In importance and complexity of the problems tackled, novelty and profundity of the social and economic processes, rates and scales of Socialist construction, this was one of the most difficult periods in the activity of the Party. In boldness of planning, creative solution of the practical problems of Socialist construction, tremendous scope of the Party's political and organising work, variety of forms and methods of its work, intensive activity and unprecedented selflessness displayed by the working people in the building of Socialism, this was a truly heroic period in the history of the Party and the Soviet people.

In its constructive work the Communist Party was ever guided by Lenin's plan for building Socialism. The Party smashed the remnants of Trotskyism, exposed and isolated the Right defeatists and consolidated its unity. It reorganised its ranks in conformity with the requirements of the reconstruction period, guided the reshaping of the mass organisations of the working people, set up within these organisations strong groups of active workers with initiative, and brought the Party, Soviet, trade union and economic apparatus closer at all levels to the masses and to production. It stimulated tremendous energy in the working people and organised nation-wide Socialist emulation.

Backed by the sweeping labour enthusiasm of the masses, the Party successfully overcame numerous difficulties, and secured an accelerated tempo of Socialist construction and the fulfilment of the first Five-Year Plan ahead of time.

Within an unprecedentedly brief space of time the U.S.S.R. was converted from a backward agrarian country into an advanced industrial Power. A heavy industry, including highly developed engineering, was created in the country. The national economy was given a powerful material and technical basis, which made possible the completion of the technical reconstruction of the whole national economy on the basis of modern technology.

The Party put into practice Lenin's brilliant co-operative plan. The most complex problem of the Socialist revolution, after the conquest of power by the working class, namely, to get the millions of small individual peasant farms to adopt the path of collective farming, the path of Socialism, was solved. This was a real revolution, in the sense that it completely changed socio-economic relations in agricultural production. Collectivisation provided the Soviet State with a firm Socialist basis in agriculture; created the decisive conditions for the building of a Socialist economy; led to the final consolidation of Soviet power in the countryside; reinforced the alliance of the working class and peasantry and raised it to a new, higher level.

The full-scale offensive of Socialism had been completely victorious. The capitalist elements were completely ousted from industry, and the Socialist form of production had become the sole and exclusive form. The last class of exploiters in the country, the kulak class, which had been the mainstay of capitalist hopes of a restoration, was broken up and in the main eliminated on the basis of solid collectivisation. The entire trade turnover was concentrated in the hands of the State, co-operatives and collective farms.

Unemployment in the towns and beggary in the countryside had gone. A veritable cultural revolution was being accomplished in the country. A new, Soviet intelligentsia was making its appearance in large numbers.

These successes of Socialist construction strengthened the internal and international position of the U.S.S.R. and its defensive capacity.

In its struggle to overcome the difficulties of Socialist construction the Communist Party became ideologically tempered, grew organisationally stronger and acquired new experience.

CHAPTER THIRTEEN

THE STRUGGLE OF THE PARTY TO COMPLETE THE SOCIALIST RECONSTRUCTION OF THE NATIONAL ECONOMY. THE VICTORY OF SOCIALISM IN THE U.S.S.R.

(1933-1937)

1. The Beginning of Fascist Aggression. Soviet Foreign Policy in the Conditions of a Growing Menace of War

The international situation in 1933-1937 was characterised by an economic slump in the capitalist world, the further aggravation of all the antagonisms of capitalist society, the establishment of a fascist dictatorship in Germany and the development of fascist aggression.

One of the particular features of the economic situation in the capitalist countries was that the crisis of 1929-1933 was not followed by an upward trend, as had usually been the case before. This time the crisis passed into a prolonged slump that lasted till 1937, when a new economic crisis began in the capitalist countries. From 1929 to 1937 industrial output in the capitalist world hardly increased. Unemployment remained exceedingly high. In the United States, for instance, there were about 10 million unemployed in 1935. Many capitalist and colonial countries were in revolutionary ferment. A new round of big class battles was approaching.

In many countries, the capitalist monopolies considered that they could save their rule by establishing a fascist regime, that is, an open terrorist dictatorship of the most reactionary elements of monopoly capital. They meant to use fascism both to suppress the working-class movement and to start a war for a new redivision of the world.

The situation was particularly tense in Germany. During the years of the temporary stabilisation of capitalism the German imperialists had, with the aid of U.S. credits, restored their economic power. Bolstered up by that power, they were seeking to break the fetters of the Versailles Treaty and seize Alsace, Lorraine, Polish territory, and colonies—in short, all that they had lost in the first world war. Furthermore, they were planning a radical redivision of the world to their advantage. Theirs was a programme setting the course of war. On the other hand, Germany was one of the countries which had been most affected by the economic crisis. Revolutionary feeling was particularly strong among her working class. The German bourgeoisie feared a Socialist revolution.

The fascist party headed by Hitler, and calling itself the National-Socialist Party for demagogic reasons, was openly putting forward chauvinist slogans calling for a war for the supremacy of the German race. It fomented hatred of other peoples and called for ruthless measures against Communists and for the suppression of the working-class movement.

The leading circles of German imperialism decided to put the Hitlerites in power. As a result, in January, 1933, a war party was placed at the helm of the State in one of the biggest countries of Europe.

The Hitler government brutally suppressed all progressive forces in Germany, first and foremost the Communists. It abolished all democratic rights and liberties, and proclaimed the maniacal idea of winning world supremacy for Germany. As they prepared for war, the Hitlerites, in contravention of the Versailles Treaty, restored universal military service and set about arming the country at a frenzied pace. In 1936, again in violation of existing treaties, they marched their troops into the Rhineland. For the first time since the first world war, German armed forces again moved up to the French border. Thus, following the rise of a seat of war in the Far East, a second seat of war arose in the centre of Europe. The Soviet Union had therefore to look to the strengthening of its defences on its western frontiers as well.

The third Power interested in a redivision of the world was Italy, where a fascist regime had been set up as far back as 1922. In 1935 the Italian imperialists began a war to seize Ethiopia. In 1936, Germany and Italy kindled a civil war in Spain, backing a fascist rebellion against that country's Republican government. The German and Italian fascists expected to entrench themselves in Spain so as to be able to threaten France from the rear, and jeopardise the vital lines of communication of Britain and France in the Atlantic and the Mediterranean. The acts of aggression undertaken by the Japanese, German and Italian invaders were a menace to the peoples of Asia, Europe and Africa, and subsequently of America as well.

The three aggressor States were also encroaching, very tellingly, on the imperialist interests of the United States, Britain and France. As a result of the first world war, these victor countries had profited most and had gained a dominant position in the capitalist world. But now Germany and Japan were pressing them hard in world markets. The Japanese militarists, having ousted the U.S. and British imperialists from the north-eastern provinces of China (Manchuria), were preparing to oust them from the rest of Chinese territory, where Britain and the United States had important economic interests. Italy, which had established herself in Ethiopia, was from there threatening British positions in Egypt and on the Red Sea, on the routes to India, and to Iranian and Iraqi oil. But the greatest danger came from Germany, as the most powerful aggressor.

Thus the economic crisis and its consequences, in the conditions of the general crisis of the capitalist system, sharply intensified the imperialist antagonisms between Germany, Japan and Italy, who were preparing a war for a redivision of the world, on the one hand, and the United States, Britain and France, who were holding on to their imperialist positions, on the other.

The Communist Party foresaw not only the end of the relative stabilisation of capitalism and the inevitable aggravation of all its contradictions, but also the imminence of a second world war. This was clearly stated at the Seventeenth Congress of the C.P.S.U.(B.).

The Soviet Union was threatened with attack both in Europe and in the Far East. The Hitlerites were calling for war against the Soviet Union with an eye to seizing Ukraine and other Soviet territories, and also with the object of "destroying Communism." In 1936 Germany and Japan concluded the so-called "Anti-Comintern Pact," to which Italy adhered a year later. It was a bloc of three aggressors. Its signatories did their utmost to advertise its anti-Communist nature. In reality, however, the German-Japanese-Italian bloc was directed not only against the U.S.S.R., but also against Britain, France and the U.S.A. The Hitlerites were clamouring for a "crusade" against Communism. But, under cover of appeals to combat Communism, they were preparing a world war for the redivision of the world in favour of the German monopolies.

In that tense international situation, the Party continued to champion peace. This was indispensable to the interests of Socialist construction, to the interests of the working people of the Soviet Union and to those of the rest of the world. The Party continued its policy of expanding business relations between the Soviet Union and all countries interested in a similar policy towards the Soviet State.

Simultaneously, in view of the development of fascist aggression, the Party directed Soviet foreign policy towards supporting the peoples who had fallen victims to aggression and were fighting for the independence of their countries.

While championing peace, the Soviet Union had to be prepared to repulse an aggressor at any moment. At a time when imperialist aggression was mounting, preparations for a crushing rebuff to any aggressor, or to anyone who violated peace, were the surest means of averting war. The paramount factors in the struggle against aggression were the growing economic and political strength of the Soviet State, the might of its armed forces, friendship among its peoples, and the moral support of the working people of all countries who had a vital interest in preserving peace.

The struggle against fascism and war made it imperative to have unity of action of the working class and to mobilise the forces of peace and democracy, all opponents of war, fascism and reaction. In face of the growing fascist menace among the working class of all countries the pressure grew for it to unite its ranks and to rally all democratic forces around the proletariat.

In the summer of 1935 the Seventh Congress of the Communist International was held. It was attended by delegates from the Communist Parties of 65 countries. It testified to the growth of the revolutionary forces of the world proletariat and to the ideological consolidation of the Communist Parties on the principles of Marxism-Leninism. The anti-Leninist groups in the Communist Parties of the capitalist countries had been ideologically defeated and isolated. A staunch Marxist-Leninist core had formed in the struggle against Trotskyism and Right-wing opportunism within the Communist Parties. In China it was united around Mao Tse-tung; in Germany, Ernst Thälmann, Wilhelm Pieck and Walter Ulbricht; in France, Maurice Thorez and Marcel Cachin; in Italy, Antonio Gramsci and Palmiro Togliatti; in Finland, Otto Kuusinen; in Bulgaria, Georgi Dimitrov and Vasil Kolarov; in the United States, William Z. Foster; in Czechoslovakia, Klement Gottwald; in Poland, Jerzy Leński; in Spain, José Díaz and Dolores Ibárruri; and in Britain, William Gallacher and Harry Pollitt.

The Seventh Congress of the Comintern discussed the main problems facing the international working-class movement in the conditions of the strengthening of fascism and the increasing menace of war. It revealed to the whole world the true nature of fascism and the terrible danger which fascism and the new world war it was preparing, represented for the peoples of all countries. Following a report by Georgi Dimitrov, an outstanding leader of the world Communist movement, and courageous fighter against fascism and war, the Congress proclaimed the aim of fighting for working-class unity and for the establishment of a broad people's front against fascism and war. It called on all the Communist Parties to strive for joint action with the Social-Democratic parties, reformist trade unions and other organisations of the working people against the offensive of fascism and the war danger. It appealed to all peoples to rally their forces in aid of the countries fighting for their independence and against imperialist oppression.

The C.P.S.U.(B.) and the brother Communist Parties fully supported the idea of uniting all the peace-loving, anti-fascist forces.

In some countries, such as France and Spain, a People's Front was established in the course of the anti-fascist struggle. A model of the right strategy and tactics was furnished by the Communist Party of China, headed by Mao Tse-tung, a prominent theoretician of Marxism-Leninism, the leader of the Party and an experienced guide of the masses, who had been elected Secretary of the Party's Central Committee in January, 1935.

But in most countries the Right-wing leaders of the parties of the Second International blocked the establishment of working-class unity and of a People's Front. The split in the working-class movement considerably weakened the forces of the opponents of fascism and war.

In the sphere of the Soviet Union's foreign policy, the C.P.S.U.(B.) considered it necessary to do its utmost to establish a system of collective security against aggression, of collective resistance to the aggressor. In December, 1933, the Central Committee of the Party adopted a resolution envisaging the possibility of the Soviet Union joining the League of Nations and the conclusion of a regional agreement with a large number of European States for mutual defence against aggression. Shortly afterwards the U.S.S.R. was invited to join the League of Nations, and the Soviet Government accepted.

By then the attitude of the League of Nations had changed to a certain degree in view of the changed international situation. Since the beginning of its activity the League had been an instrument of Anglo-French domination in Europe and Asia. But now other imperialist Powers were laying claim to such domination— Hitler Germany in Europe and Japan in Asia. Under those circumstances, Britain and France found themselves on the defensive. In 1933 Germany and Japan withdrew from the League of Nations. These circumstances afforded some possibility of using the League as an instrument, even if an imperfect one, for combating aggression. In the League of Nations, the Soviet Union vigorously defended the peoples of China, Ethiopia and Spain, and later other peoples that had become victims of the imperialist aggressors.

Of the major European countries, France, as an immediate neighbour of Germany, was exposed to the greatest danger of a fascist attack. This circumstance made for a rapprochement between the Soviet Union and France. In 1934 the two countries jointly called for the conclusion of a treaty for collective resistance to aggression. The projected collective security system was to include, besides its two initiators, the countries of Central and Eastern Europe, Germany among them.

The British Government, while professing to be in favour of a collective security system, in reality helped Hitler to foil the organisation of that system. The bourgeois-landlord government of Poland, too, opposed it.

Seeing that it was impossible to reach a broad agreement on the establishment of a collective security system because of the opposition of Germany, Britain and Poland, the Soviet Government in 1935 concluded mutual assistance treaties with France and Czechoslovakia. Under the treaty with Czechoslovakia, the Soviet Union's obligation to render assistance to that country in the event of aggression became operative only provided that similar assistance would be forthcoming from France as well. The treaties with France and Czechoslovakia could have formed the basis on which to administer an adequate rebuff to aggressors.

But that was not to be. The partisans of a policy of collusion with the Hitlerites gained the upper hand in the ruling circles of Paris and Prague, as well as in London. The French and Czechoslovak governments began to sabotage the treaties signed with the Soviet Union, and eventually disregarded them. The governments of the Western Powers were not putting up effective resistance to Japanese, Italian and German aggression. During the German-Italian intervention in Spain the British and French governments, contrary to the national interests of their countries, adopted an attitude of "non-intervention," which in practice meant abetting fascist aggression.

An important political event, testifying to the growth of Soviet influence in world politics, was the establishment in 1933 of diplomatic relations between the Soviet Union and the U.S.A. By that act, the United States acknowledged the bankruptcy of its policy (over many years) of "non-recognition" of a Great Power like the Soviet Union. The ruling circles of the United States were compelled to renounce their discredited policy, first of all, because of their fear of Japanese and German aggression, which threatened their interests and against which they expected to use the Soviet Union, and, secondly, because of their increased need for the Soviet market in view of the long-drawn-out crisis. With normal relations restored between the two countries, Soviet-American trade expanded appreciably.

The establishment of diplomatic relations between the U.S.A. and the Soviet Union was conducive to the maintenance of peace.

But, taken as a whole, U.S. policy actually abetted the fascist aggressors, whom it enabled to enslave unhampered one people after another. In 1935 the U.S. Congress passed a law banning the delivery of American arms to belligerents. This was during the Italo-Ethiopian war, and the law deprived Ethiopia of the possibility of buying from the United States the arms she so badly needed. As for Italy, the aggressor, she was hardly affected by this law. Waging war against a poorly-armed country, Italy did not particularly need American arms. In other words, the law helped fascist aggression.

When the Spanish war broke out, the U.S. Congress passed an amendment extending the law to civil wars. In this instance, too, the American law was to the advantage of the fascist aggressors, since it refused arms to their victim, the lawful government of Spain.

The international situation in the thirties required that the Party and the peoples of the Soviet Union exert every possible effort to increase the country's defence potential.

2. The Struggle of the Party to Strengthen and Develop the Socialist Economy. Increased Party Political Work Among the Masses. Seventeenth Party Congress

After successfully fulfilling the first Five-Year Plan, the Soviet people in 1933 embarked on the second. The U.S.S.R. entered the *period of completion* of the Socialist reconstruction of the national economy.

The conditions of Socialist construction in the second Five-Year Plan period differed in many respects from those that had prevailed in the preceding five-year period. The foundations of Socialism had already been laid in the Soviet Union, where a powerful heavy industry—the basis of the technical re-equipment of all the branches of the national economy—had been created and the collective-farm system had triumphed. A solid base had thus been established for the further growth of Socialism in the Soviet Union.

At the same time, Socialist reconstruction in its closing stage had certain peculiarities and was attended by certain difficulties.

In industry, one of the paramount tasks, along with further capital construction, was the *mastering* of new enterprises. This was much more difficult than using the old factories. Some time was needed to train the required number of engineers, technicians and skilled workers, for them to learn how to use the new machinery, properly to organise the productive activity of the new large bodies of workers that were only just taking shape.

In agriculture, the chief task was the further *organisational and economic consolidation* of the collective farms. In 1931-1932 the Party did a great deal to that end. Experience showed, however, that it was a difficult task. By the beginning of the second Five-Year Plan period, nearly two-thirds (61.5 per cent) of the peasant farms had joined the collective farms. But most of the newly-established collective farms were small and economically weak. Collective-farm property at the time consisted of the means of production collectivised by the peasants, namely, horses, ploughs, harrows and certain outhouses. The most important element of collective-farm property—non-distributable assets—was a mere 4,700 million rubles in 1932, or an average of 22,000 rubles per collective farm. Three-quarters of the collective farms had no cattle departments. The collective farms stood in need of constant help from the Party and the State in organising and developing collective agriculture, equipping it with modern machinery and reinforcing it with experienced personnel.

During the second Five-Year Plan period, the Party tackled the problem of *completely eliminating* the capitalist elements in the Soviet Union. This could not but give rise to desperate resistance on the part of the remnants of the dying exploiting classes. The capitalist elements had in the main been eliminated during the first Five-Year Plan period. But they had not disappeared. The one-time industrialists, merchants, kulaks and their associates were scattered all over the country, infiltrating building sites, factories, railway and water-transport establishments, collective and State farms, government offices and trading organisations. They could no longer act openly—they were powerless to do so. But they did not discontinue the struggle. Nursing their hatred for the Soviet system and the Party, they engaged in wrecking activities, embezzled State and collective-farm property, seeking to undermine the foundations of the Soviet State—public property. It was the most widespread form of the class struggle.

It was essential *firmly to establish* the new Socialist forms of economy in all the branches of production and trade, organise the most strict protection of State and collective-farm property and complete the elimination of the capitalist elements.

During the second Five-Year Plan period the Party was confronted with the task of *overcoming the capitalist survivals* in the minds of Soviet people and making the whole of the country's working population active and politically conscious builders of Socialism. The Party realised that it was a difficult task and would take a long time to accomplish. Marxism-Leninism teaches us that men's consciousness lags behind their position in social production. Over four million new workers and other employees had gone into industry during the period of the first Five-Year Plan. They were people who had had no experience in large-scale production and who, to a large extent, had a petty individualist mentality. Private property habits were particularly strong among the collective farmers. The survivals of the past in the minds of people manifested themselves in a negligent attitude to State and collective-farm property, in pilfering and damaging of this property, in self-seeking tendencies and in breaches of Socialist labour discipline. The remnants of the dying classes and the hostile forces of the capitalist encirclement took advantage of these backward sentiments among Soviet people.

In the new conditions of Socialist construction particular importance attached to Lenin's observations regarding strict adherence to the Socialist principle of the material incentive, proper organisation of labour and the development of a new, Socialist discipline. Lenin considered the re-equipment of agriculture through mechanisation and electrification a most important means of remoulding the peasant psychology.

"The task of remoulding the small farmer," said Lenin, "of remoulding his whole psychology and habits is a task of generations. Only the material basis, technical equipment, the employment of tractors and machines on a mass scale in agriculture, electrification on a mass scale can solve this problem of the small farmer, can cure, so to speak, his whole mentality" (*Collected Works*, Vol. 32, p. 194).

The main preoccupations of Party activity now became the organisation of Socialist production and the education of the working people in the spirit of a politically conscious attitude to labour and to Socialist property. The problems of completing Socialist reconstruction required that the Party increase its political influence on the masses of the working people, improve the organisation and practical leadership of economic construction and perfect its working methods.

The Party strengthened and expanded Socialist production. It concentrated on the decisive sectors of the national economy.

With the collective-farm system firmly established in the countryside, the responsibility of the Party for agricultural progress increased. It now had to render day-to-day assistance to the collective farms and their members in managing collective farming on a planned basis and in using scientific and technological achievements. The Central Committee called the attention of the Party to the necessity of strengthening the collective farms. The *political departments* set up in the machine-and-tractor stations and State farms, in the winter of 1933, by a decision of the January plenary meeting of the C.C. C.P.S.U.(B.) were of exceptional importance in this respect. The Central

Committee sent 17,000 experienced Party workers to the political departments of the machine-and-tractor stations and another 8,000 to the State farms. About 80 per cent of the political departments of the machine-and-tractor stations were headed by Communists who had joined the Party before 1920.

With the organisation of the political departments, the machine-and-tractor stations became centres of *political, economic and organisational* leadership of the collective farms—centres of Party influence on the broad mass of the collective farmers.

The political departments reinforced the ranks of the Communists in the machine-and-tractor stations and collective farms. Between the Sixteenth and Seventeenth Party Congresses, the number of Communists in the countryside almost doubled, reaching 790,000. The reorganisation of rural Party organisations on the production principle was completed. By the autumn of 1933 there were 30,000 Party branches in the collective farms, 20,000 groups of candidates for Party membership, 22,000 mixed Party and Komsomol groups and 38,000 individual Communists working under the direct leadership of the political departments of the machine-and-tractor stations and district Party committees. The Party organisations in the collective farms were becoming genuine organisers of collective-farm production.

The political departments did a great deal politically to educate and build up an active body of non-Party collective farmers. In every collective farm a strong core of activists was formed who, under the leadership of the political departments, took the lead in organising socially-owned production and in improving labour discipline.

The political departments gave effect to Party supervision over the work of the machine-and-tractor stations and the collective farms they serviced. They exposed and foiled the intrigues of the enemies of collective farming, and saw to it that the laws of the Soviet State were strictly observed by the collective farms and their members. The collective farms were cleared of kulaks and other hostile elements that had penetrated into them.

The political departments devoted particular attention to the selection and training of leading personnel for the collective farms. Hundreds of thousands of collective-farm chairmen, stock-keepers, team-leaders, field-crop experts, livestock-breeders and bookkeepers were trained at machine-and-tractor station courses. The political departments selected and promoted to leading positions over 250,000 advanced collective farmers, including about 30,000 collective-farm chairmen. They taught collective farmers to regard the fulfilment of their obligations to the Soviet State as the prime duty of the collective farms.

The workers of the political departments were always among the mass of the collective farmers. They helped the latter to decide practical matters of collective-farm development and inculcated in them an honest attitude to labour and care for collective-farm property. They helped collective-farm leaders to organise the work of the collective farmers.

By setting up the machine-and-tractor station political departments, the Party rendered important aid to the collective farms. They began to grow appreciably stronger; labour discipline improved. In 1933 the spring sowing, harvesting and grain deliveries to the State were carried out more efficiently than before.

The Party continued to pursue with unflagging energy the Leninist general line of industrialising the country. The Central Committee worked persistently for the planned and rapid development of heavy industry; it uncovered shortcomings in good time and overcame the lagging-behind of various industries, particularly the coal industry and railway transport. Industrialisation was accompanied by the growth of new towns and industrial centres, the development of new mineral deposits and the economic opening-up of the country's outlying regions. This increased the demands made of the railways. The railways, in turn, and also the new powerful electric stations and metallurgical plants, required a steady supply of coal and coke. Every year the national economy needed more and more coal.

During the years of the first Five-Year Plan, considerable progress had been made in the technical re-equipment of transport and in the mechanisation of coal mining. Nevertheless, transport and the coal industry were not meeting the requirements of the rapidly growing national economy. The unsatisfactory state of affairs in the coal industry and transport was due chiefly to shortcomings in economic management and to the violation of the principle of material incentives—which made for wage levelling, a constant fluidity of labour, slow mastering and poor use of new machinery and techniques. Party organisations exerted little influence on the work of transport and the Donets collieries.

The Central Committee helped Party and economic organisations to eliminate these shortcomings. The staffs of trusts and central administrations were reduced and their structure simplified; most of the engineers and technicians were sent to work in industry. Remuneration of the labour of miners and railwaymen was normalised by introducing standard rates and by establishing a progressive bonus system for workers in the key trades who mastered the new machinery successfully.

To make the political work of the Party more effective, and to heighten its organising role, the Central Committee in the summer of 1933 established political departments on the railways and appointed Party organisers in the Donets collieries. The political departments in transport and the Party organisers in the coal mines gave effective guidance to Party and political work among the masses, helped managements to organise the fulfilment of production plans and improve labour discipline, and stimulated Socialist emulation among the workers for the mastering of the new machinery and for higher labour productivity.

Thanks to the steps taken by the Party, the increase in coal output in 1933 was 12 million tons, or 50 per cent over that of the previous year.

The political departments, which represented an emergency form of organisation, depended on the strength and prestige of the Party. They were set up in those lagging sectors of Socialist construction which had acquired special economic importance. They proved their worth. Thanks to them, Party leadership in agriculture and railway transport improved, and Party organising work on the spot became more effective. They were very helpful to Party organisations, and Party bodies in other fields of Socialist construction drew on their experience. The leading role of Communists in production increased. The Party achieved a further rise in the labour activity of the working class, the technical intelligentsia, and the collective-farm peasantry.

The Seventeenth Congress of the C.P.S.U.(B.), which met from January 26 to February 10, 1934, was held in an atmosphere of great political and labour enthusiasm. The Party had 1,874,488 members and 935,298 candidate members at the time.

The Congress discussed the reports of the Central Committee, Central Auditing Commission, Central Control Commission-Workers' and Peasants' Inspection, and of the delegation of the C.P.S.U.(B.) to the Executive Committee of the Communist International. It also discussed the draft second Five-Year Plan and questions of organisation (Party and State). J. V. Stalin submitted the C.C. report. It dealt with the radical changes that had taken place in the Soviet Union as a result of putting into effect the Party's Leninist general line. The Soviet Union had become transformed. It had cast off the integument of backwardness and medievalism. From a backward agrarian country it had turned into an advanced industrial and collective-farm Power.

The successes of Socialism in town and country brought fundamental changes in the pattern of the national economy. In industry, the Socialist sector constituted 99.5 per cent of the total, and held undivided sway. In agriculture, the Socialist sector of the area sown to grain crops amounted to 84.5 per cent of the total. As for trade, the capitalist elements had been completely eliminated.

These facts were convincing evidence that capitalist economy had been wiped out in the Soviet Union. *The Socialist economic system, as embodied in public, co-operative and collective-farm property, reigned supreme* in all spheres of the national economy.

A far-reaching cultural revolution was being accomplished in the U.S.S.R. From an ignorant, illiterate and uncultured country, which pre-revolutionary Russia had been, the Soviet Union was turning into a country of advanced culture, covered by a vast network of higher, secondary and elementary schools, with instruction conducted in the languages of the various Soviet nationalities. A new, Soviet intelligentsia was being trained on an immense scale. The number of specialists engaged in the national economy had almost doubled in the years of the first Five-Year Plan. The tremendous scope of cultural construction found vivid expression in an unprecedented expansion of the press, the cinema, radio, and the number of clubs and theatres.

The Congress devoted much attention to questions of ideological and political leadership. It called for steps to raise the theoretical level of the Party and to intensify ideological work in all the sectors of the Party, for vigorous propaganda of the ideas of scientific Communism, educating Communists and non-Party activists in a spirit of internationalism, and boldly criticising deviations from Marxism-Leninism.

The Congress approved a resolution on the second Five-Year Plan for the economic development of the U.S.S.R. and the chief political and economic tasks of the plan, as specified by the Seventeenth Party Conference.

Investments in capital construction in all the branches of the national economy were to total 133,000 million rubles in the period of the second Five-Year Plan, as against a little over 64,000 million rubles invested under the first Five-Year Plan. Total gross industrial output in 1937 was to be approximately eight times as large as in 1913. The Congress directed all Party, State, economic and trade union organisations to concentrate on mastering new machinery and new branches of production, on raising the skills of workers and on training engineers and technicians. In agriculture, the emphasis was on the organisational and economic strengthening of the collective farms, machine-and-tractor stations and State farms, the completion, in the main, of the mechanisation of agriculture and the introduction of agrotechnical methods, and the increasing of the livestock herd and its productivity. Extensive measures were planned for the technical reconstruction of transport and communications. Measures were provided for the further development of science and culture.

The Seventeenth Congress adopted a special resolution on Party and State construction. It called for the raising of the level of organisational leadership to that of the Party's political leadership. The selection of personnel and the verification of the fulfilment of decisions were stressed as being particularly important in organising work. To improve supervision of the fulfilment of Party and Government decisions, the Congress resolved to reorganise the combined Central Control Commission-Workers' and Peasants' Inspection, which had accomplished the tasks set before it by the Twelfth Party Congress, into a Party Control Commission under the C.C. C.P.S.U.(B.) and a Soviet Control Commission under the Council of People's Commissars of the U.S.S.R.

The Congress adopted amended Party rules. The preamble gave a brief definition of the Communist Party, of its role in the struggle of the working class and working people in general for the triumph of Socialism, and its place in the system of the dictatorship of the proletariat. The Party basic groups, which had grown in numbers and organisation, were renamed primary Party organisations. A special section added to the Party rules dealt with inner-Party democracy and Party discipline. It specified that the free and business-like discussion of questions of Party policy was the inalienable right of every member of the Party, a right stemming from inner-Party democracy. At the same time, it stressed that the prime duty of Communists and Party organisations was to preserve Party unity and ruthlessly to suppress the slightest attempts at factional struggle or at a split.

The Party came to its Congress solidly united. There were no opposition groups at the Congress. Zinoviev, Kamenev, Bukharin, Rykov, Tomsky and other former oppositionists, who had been defeated ideologically by the Party, made repentant speeches, extolling the achievements of the Party. But the Congress delegates did not believe in the sincerity of their statements, since they did not back the formal admission of their mistakes and formal agreement with the Party's general line by practical work, by a struggle for the Leninist general line of the Party.

The successes of Socialism made Communists and all working people feel a legitimate pride in their country and strengthened their faith in the complete triumph of Communism. Millions of working people in the capitalist countries rejoiced together with the Soviet people in their historic achievements. Their sentiments were expressed by the foreign Communist Parties in the greetings they sent to the Congress.

In keeping with the Congress decisions, the Party took a number of steps to improve the composition of its ranks.

Party membership had increased by more than 600,000 between its Sixteenth and Seventeenth Congresses. In the course of this mass influx, certain chance elements, careerists and downright enemies had infiltrated the Party. There were also some former oppositionists, who were playing a double game: while paying lip-service to the Party line, they actually obstructed its implementation. The Party had to get rid of such elements, for they weakened its fighting capacity. A mass cleansing was carried out in 1933-1934. The admission of new members and candidate members was suspended for a while. Although grave mistakes were committed in the course of the cleansing, particularly in the way of expelling so-called "passive" members without good reason, still, taken as a whole, it helped the Party to weed out numerous chance elements and careerists. Nevertheless, even after the cleansing, there remained in the Party double-dealers and hostile elements who had managed to escape detection and expulsion.

On December 1, 1934, S.M. Kirov, an outstanding leader of the Communist Party and the Soviet State, was foully murdered in the Smolny, Leningrad, by a revolver shot. The assassin, who was caught red-handed, turned out to be an embittered renegade. He was full of hatred for the Communist Party leaders, who were firmly implementing the Party's general line aiming at the victory of Socialism in the U.S.S.R. He had been connected with some of the former members of the Zinoviev anti-Party group. He was a Party member, held a Party card and had used it as a cover for his heinous crime.

The assassination of Kirov showed that the Party card could be used as a screen for infamous anti-Soviet acts. It was indispensable to safeguard the Party against the penetration of alien elements, to make impossible acts hostile to Socialism and the interests of the Soviet State, whatever the guise under which they might be committed.

One of the first measures towards that end was *the verification of the records of Party members and the exchange of Party cards.* A verification of the records of Party members and of the procedure to be followed in their registration and safekeeping and in the issuance of Party cards had been proposed as early as October, 1934. The C.C. C.P.S.U.(B.) was in possession of numerous facts speaking of irregularities in the matter. The registration of Communists and the safekeeping of Party records—important elements of Party organisation—were often regarded as a purely technical matter. They were therefore often entrusted to technical workers, not controlled by those in authority in the district and regional Party committees. Negligence in the handling of Party files had serious consequences. The misappropriation of Party cards, and the forging of Party records and cards, and erasures in them, assumed a dangerous character. This was the handiwork not only of impostors and rogues, but of downright enemies of the Soviet system, who were bent on wrecking activities.

The verification and exchange of Party cards were carried

out in the course of 1935-1936. On the whole, the measure proved its value. It enabled the Party to rid itself to a very substantial extent of alien and chance elements, to strengthen its ranks and increase its fighting capacity. Order was introduced into the registration of Communists and the keeping of Party records and issuance of Party cards. The leaders of Party organisations established closer ties with the membership.

But certain infringements of the Party's policy with regard to its membership were committed in the course of the verification and exchange of Party cards, as attested by numerous expulsions. As at the time of the last purge, there were instances of unwarranted expulsion of Communists classed as "passive". Many people, though devoted to the cause of Socialism, were declared to be "passive". Those were distortions that could not but affect the situation within the Party.

The Central Committee began to reveal these mistakes even in the course of the verification of the records of Party members and exchange of Party cards. It directed Party organisations to put an end to indiscriminate expulsions and to reconsider the cases of all those expelled as "passive" members. The matter was specially considered at a plenary meeting of the C.C. C.P.S.U. (B.) in June, 1936.

After the verification and exchange of Party cards, admission to membership was resumed on November 1, 1936. The Central Committee reminded Party organisations of the necessity of admitting new members into the Party on a strictly individual basis and of enrolling "people really advanced and really devoted to the working-class cause, the finest people of our country, drawn above all from among the workers, and also from among peasants and working intellectuals tried and tested in various fields of the struggle for Socialism."

Equipping itself ideologically and strengthening its organisation, the Party effectively performed its guiding role in the construction of Socialism. It was leading the Soviet people to fulfilment of the second Five-Year Plan ahead of time, and to the building of Socialist society in the Soviet Union.

3. Fulfilment of the Second Five-Year Plan Ahead of Time. The Victory of Socialism in the U.S.S.R. The New Soviet Constitution

The efforts of the Party and the people to fulfil the second Five-Year Plan ahead of time were marked by further feats of labour.

Overcoming difficulties, the Party was coping successfully with the problem of mastering new industrial undertakings and new machinery. Progress manifested itself primarily in the iron and steel industry. In 1934 the output of pig-iron reached 10,400,000 tons, steel 9,700,000 tons and rolled metal 7,000,000 tons. Compared with 1913, iron and steel output had increased by almost 150 per cent.

The victory of the collective-farm system had promoted a more rapid development of agriculture. By the end of 1934 the collective farms, which embraced about 75 per cent of all the peasant households and 87 per cent of the total sown area, had become a solid and invincible force. The output of grain and industrial crops had increased. Grain deliveries and purchases had assumed a more organised character. That year agriculture supplied the State with sufficient quantities of grain and other produce fully to meet the requirements of the population without rationing, which had been introduced at the beginning of the first Five-Year Plan period.

The November, 1934, plenary meeting of the C.C. C.P.S.U.(B.) decided to abolish the rationing of bread and other foodstuffs. Unrestricted sale of foodstuffs began to supersede centralised distribution everywhere. The result was a substantial improvement in the economic life of the country, a further consolidation of the alliance of the working class and the peasantry, and more successes in Socialist construction.

The consolidation of the collective-farm system enabled the Party to reorganise the political departments of the machine-and-tractor stations into ordinary Party bodies by merging them with the district Party committees. The political departments had performed their task with credit; but now leadership in the collective-farm countryside was becoming a more and more complex matter, and the ordinary Party and Soviet institutions had to be expanded and strengthened, if they were to cope with all aspects of the work in the collective farms— political, administrative, economic, cultural, etc. This measure was added evidence of the Party's flexibility in organisational leadership.

The national economy was receiving more and more machinery as the second Five-Year Plan was fulfilled. During the first two years of that period alone, industry, transport and agriculture were supplied with almost as many machines, machine-tools and other items of technical equipment as they had had during the whole period of the first Five-Year Plan. The solution of the Party's chief economic problem, namely, the completion of the technical reconstruction of the national economy, was thus being assured. At the same time there was a danger that the increase in the number of personnel capable of using the new machinery and techniques skilfully might lag behind technical progress. A disproportion was arising between technical progress and the mastering of modern techniques.

It was necessary to battle still more persistently for the mastering of the new machinery and techniques. This was the decisive link in the development of the country's Socialist economy in those years; and on it depended the further growth of the productive forces of the Soviet Union. The problem of skilled personnel capable of mastering new techniques and using them to the full became decisive. The Party issued the slogan: "*Personnel decides everything.*" This slogan was a logical sequel to the slogan: "Technique in the period of reconstruction decides everything," which the Party had advanced at the beginning of the reconstruction period, when the country needed new machinery and techniques first and foremost. Now that this problem had been solved, it was necessary to focus attention on personnel capable of mastering the new machinery. Nor was it a question of tens of hundreds of thousands but of millions of people capable of putting into operation and making full use of the new machinery in industry, transport, agriculture, and the armed forces—in short, wherever it existed.

When the Party proclaimed the slogan: "Personnel decides everything," it was aware that the new techniques were already being mastered in practice. The foremost workers in industry, transport, agriculture, and other branches of the national economy had launched a movement for the revision of obsolete technical standards.

The movement originated in such industries as coal, iron and steel. The Party had always devoted particular attention to these important branches of the national economy; and not without result. Numerous workers, engineers and technicians began to exceed old technical standards and to show higher labour productivity. In 1934 the Soviet Government awarded the Order of Lenin to Nikita Izotov, a coal-hewer at the No. 1 Pit in Gorlovka, for the excellent results he had achieved as a shock-worker. His example was followed by many other coal-miners.

A movement of shock-workers in industrial production developed all over the country. By the end of 1933 there were about five million shock-workers in industry and transport. The enthusiasm inspired by new building, a sentiment typical of Soviet people in the first Five-Year Plan period, was now supplemented by the enthusiasm for mastering new techniques and achieving high productivity of labour.

In 1935 the movement of the foremost workers for the mastering of new techniques and for the revision of old technical standards was named the Stakhanov movement after Alexei Stakhanov, a hewer who had cut 102 tons of coal during his shift and thus exceeded the standard output 14 times over. Innovators in production came to the fore in all branches of the national economy. Their initiative was given every encouragement by the Party which considered the movement of the foremost workers to be one of vast political importance, and assumed guidance of it.

The innovators' movement for a high productivity of labour was *a new stage in the Socialist emulation of the masses.* Unlike that of previous years, it was now based on new first-class machinery and involved people who knew how to use that machinery. It was a result of the rise in the cultural and technical standards of the working class during the years of the Five-Year Plans. It was an integral part of the establishment of Socialist relations of production in all branches of the national economy, the radical change that had come to pass in the attitude of people to labour, their Socialist attitude to labour.

The All-Union Conference of Foremost Industrial and Transport Workers, held in November, 1935, played a notable part in rallying the working class of the country for the achievement of higher labour productivity. About 3,000 people took part in the Conference. They described their experiences in using new machinery to fulfil high output quotas. This was indicative of the new features of Soviet men and women, who strove, in the interest of the whole of society, to place their personal achievements at the service of all.

The Conference noted that the mass movement of the foremost workers for a more effective use of machinery and better organisation of labour was not merely a routine matter of increasing labour productivity, always indispensable if progress was to be made in industry. Stalin, who addressed the Conference, said that the movement was opening "the path by which alone can be achieved those high indices of labour productivity which are essential for the transition from Socialism to Communism and for the elimination of the antithesis between mental and physical labour" (*Problems of Leninism,* Eng. ed., 1953, p. 667).

The Party and the people had always been guided by Lenin's precept that "Communism is the higher productivity of labour—compared with that existing under capitalism—of voluntary, class-conscious and united workers employing advanced techniques" (*Collected Works,* Vol. 29, p. 394).

The movement of innovators in production was no ordinary movement. It indicated that the Soviet Union had entered *the epoch of Socialism.* It was a movement to organise labour along new lines: proper division of labour in production, the release of skilled workers from secondary or preparatory work, better organisation of the work-place, and higher productivity of labour. New output standards were introduced which in a number of cases topped the productivity of labour of the developed capitalist countries. Conditions were created for rapid growth of the production of consumer goods and cuts in their prices. The wages of workers and office employees were increased considerably. The cultural and technical level of the working class rose.

As it headed the movement of innovators in industry, the Party strove to give it a mass character. Party organisations boldly encouraged every initiative for the mastering of new techniques and for replacing the old, low output standards by new and higher ones, and made it nationally known. Under the guidance of Party organisations, conferences on production and techniques were called to discuss progressive working methods; factories organised exchanges of experience; front-rank workers took under their patronage those lagging behind, and old workers their younger workmates; special schools were set up to promote progressive methods. Communists led the way in acquiring technical knowledge. They steadily raised their technical level at correspondence or evening courses, in secondary specialised schools, technical schools or in higher educational institutions. The raising of the cultural and technical level of the working class, which was the only basis on which the movement of front-rank industrial workers could develop, became a prime task of the Party organisations.

Every new and progressive movement makes headway by combating the old. This was the case with the mass movement of innovators in production. Some workers feared that high production quotas might result in lower piece-prices and hence lower wages. Some engineers and technicians, who were fettered by their old notions of technical standards, proved incapable of supporting the movement and organising it properly. Furthermore, there were among the old experts hostile-minded people, too, who tried to disrupt the innovators' movement. It was primarily the Communists—as exponents of all that was new and progressive—who had to surmount these obstacles. And they coped with their task successfully.

The December, 1935, plenary meeting of the C.C. C.P.S.U.(B.), which discussed the state of industry and transport in connection with the spread of the Stakhanov movement, greatly stimulated the mass movement of innovators in production. The C.C. meeting was attended by nearly three thousand business executives, Party officials, technicians and front-rank workers. It called for more bold and resolute revision of antiquated output standards and for their replacement by new ones, with due regard to the experience of the foremost workers. It laid special emphasis on the need for all working men and women to increase their technical knowledge.

Thanks to the innovators' movement, labour productivity in industry increased by 82 per cent during the years of the second Five-Year Plan, instead of the 63 per cent originally planned. The growth in industrial output during that period was achieved chiefly through the higher labour productivity made possible by the use of new techniques.

While regarding industry as the foundation of the Socialist national economy, the Party did not relax its attention to agricultural production. The development of Socialist agriculture was experiencing difficulties of its own. The collective farms had been formed of small individual peasant farms, and the habits of individual farming told in the work of their members. But the collective farms could produce much more than individual farming. And it was to this aspect of the matter that the attention of Party organisations was directed.

A campaign began in the countryside to improve the cultivation of land, raise the yields of grain and industrial crops, and overcome the lag in livestock farming. There appeared a large number of trained personnel well versed in the technique of agricultural production.

The Second All-Union Congress of Collective-Farm Shock Workers, which convened in February, 1935, was of great importance in consolidating the collective-farm system. It adopted new rules for the Agricultural Artel. The rules were adopted at a time when a certain amount of experience had been gained in the management of large-scale agricultural production. They summed up that experience, and laid down the basic provisions determining the life and activity of the agricultural artel in conditions of the complete victory of the collective-farm system. Their purpose was to promote the further organisation and economic reinforcement of the collective farms.

The rules assigned to the collective farms in perpetual tenure the land cultivated by them. This ensured a solid foundation for the development and consolidation of the collective farms. They indicated how large-scale socially-owned farming should be carried on, and specified the permissible size of individual holdings, having due regard to the interests of collective production and to the necessity of meeting the personal requirements of the collective farmer and his family. The rules envisaged greater democracy on the collective farms and extended the rights of the collective farmers, which stimulated their initiative and ingenuity at work.

The implementation of the collective-farm rules had a beneficial effect on agricultural production, labour discipline and labour productivity. However, it required strenuous efforts by the Party and the people. The Party made intense efforts to place the collective farms on a sound organisational and economic footing, and to assure the continuous growth of agricultural output.

In the years 1935-1937 the Central Committee regularly discussed at its plenary meetings the preparation and carrying out of sowing and harvesting, aid to the still weak collective farms, and State stocking and purchases of grain. The same questions were given constant attention by the regional and district Party committees and by the collective-farm Party organisations.

The district Party committees in the countryside did much in those years to organise labour and its remuneration on the collective farms properly, improve labour discipline, select leading personnel for the collective farms, allocate Communists to the decisive sectors of collective-farm production, reinforce and strengthen collective-farm Party organisations, and organise the individual Communists working at different collective farms. Every advance in this field was a valuable achievement by the Party organisations. Party leadership of the collective farms was improving steadily.

Collective-farm Communists, putting the new rules of the Agricultural Artel into practice, strengthened the socially-owned economy of the collective farms and increased its output. They inculcated a new, Socialist attitude to labour in the collective-farm peasantry.

As it strengthened the collective farms, the Party also created conditions for drawing new sections of the peasantry into them. When the new rules were adopted, there were still approximately four million peasant households outside the collective farms, but towards the end of the second Five-Year Plan period the figure had dropped to about 1,500,000.

The fulfilment of the second Five-Year Plan, especially in its latter years, called for strenuous effort on the part of the working class, collective-farm peasantry and intelligentsia. It was thanks to their selfless labour that the Soviet people succeeded in fulfilling the second Five-Year Plan, like the first, ahead of time, by April 1, 1937, that is, in four years and three months.

In 1937 total industrial output was more than double what it had been in 1932, and eight times as great as in 1913.

The growth of large-scale industry, particularly of engineering, contributed to the technical re-equipment of all branches of the national economy. In 1937 over 80 per cent of the total industrial output was supplied by newly-built factories or factories completely reconstructed in the years of the first and second Five-Year Plans. Substantial successes were achieved in the mechanisation of agriculture. 456,000 tractors, some 129,000 combine harvesters and 146,000 lorries were being used in agriculture in 1937. *The technical reconstruction of the national economy could be considered complete.*

In agriculture, too, the second Five-Year Plan had been carried out successfully. The *collectivisation* of agriculture was *completed.* The collective farms embraced 18,500,000 peasant households, or 93 per cent of the total. Their crop area accounted for more than 99 per cent of the total crop area sown by the peasants.

1937 was a particularly favourable year for grain and industrial crops; its harvest in both respects was greater than in any previous year.

But livestock-farming was still making slow progress. It had suffered greatly in the process of transition from individual to collective farming; and to restore it, a steep rise in grain production, a considerable increase in fodder resources and material incentives to the collective farmers to develop this branch of agriculture were necessary.

The problem of trained personnel was solved in the main in the years of the second Five-Year Plan—an important achievement. The number of experts graduating for the national economy with a higher or secondary specialised education more than doubled compared with the period of the first Five-Year Plan.

The material and cultural standards of the people rose appreciably during the second Five-Year Plan period. The national income of the U.S.S.R. was more than doubled, and the wages and salary fund rose by 150 per cent, the number of workers and other employees increasing by 18 per cent. The money incomes of collective farms increased more than threefold.

The cultural revolution had made immense progress in the U.S.S.R. The number of pupils attending elementary and secondary schools rose by more than 8,000,000 during the second Five-Year Plan period. The number of students in higher educational institutions in 1937 was over 500,000. At the beginning of 1937 the intelligentsia numbered about 10 million.

The second Five-Year Plan period was marked by major achievements in implementing the Leninist nationalities policy. Extensive expansion of industry was effected in the non-Russian republics. Large numbers of the local population were trained as engineers and technicians.

Such were the results of the victory of Socialism in the Soviet Union, of the establishment of Socialist relations of production in all branches of the national economy. *The most difficult problem of the Socialist revolution—that of creating a new, Socialist economy—had been solved.*

The building of Socialism in the U.S.S.R. proceeded in keeping with the plan outlined by Lenin. The Communist Party was the principal, leading force in it. The brunt of the struggle for the victory of Socialism was borne by the numerous Party workers in the republican, regional, district and primary Party organisations. The working class, the working mass of the peasantry and the intelligentsia gave their unqualified support to the policy of the Party and by their heroic labour ensured the triumph of Socialism.

The profound changes in the life of the Soviet Union, and the decisive successes of Socialism in the country's economy and social system found legislative embodiment in the new Soviet Constitution. Soviet citizens took a most active part in the discussion of the draft Constitution, which lasted five and a half months.

In November, 1936, the Extraordinary Eighth All-Union Congress of Soviets met to adopt the new Constitution of the U.S.S.R. Stalin delivered the report on the draft Constitution of the U.S.S.R., giving a vivid picture of the changes that had taken place in the country since 1924.

The Socialist system had won. Social ownership of the means of production had established itself as the unshakable foundation of the new, Socialist system in all branches of the national economy. Hurtful phenomena like crises, poverty and unemployment, which had affected the people so painfully, had been done away with in the Soviet Union for ever. Conditions had been created for a prosperous and cultured life for all members of society.

The class composition of the population had changed. *All exploiting classes had been eliminated.* There remained in the U.S.S.R. the working class, the peasant class and the intelligentsia. But they, too, had undergone radical changes in the struggle for Socialism.

The working class of the Soviet Union, after destroying capitalism and transforming the means of production into public Socialist property, had ceased to be a proletariat in the true or old sense of the word. The proletariat of the U.S.S.R. had become a working class emancipated from all exploitation, a class occupying the leading position in society and directing its development towards Communism. It was an entirely new working class, the like of which the history of mankind had never known.

The peasant class, too, had ceased to be a class of small producers, tied to their small plots of land and exploited by landlords, kulaks, merchants and usurers. With the victory of the collective-farm system, the peasantry had been emancipated from all exploitation. Peasant labour had become co-operative labour based on social ownership. An entirely new peasantry had come into being in the Soviet Union, the like of which the history of mankind had also never known.

The intelligentsia had changed too. It was a new, Socialist intelligentsia, serving the people and free from all exploitation. In its majority it had come from among the workers and peasants. Its interests began to coincide with those of the working class and the collective-farm peasantry, and together with them it was building Socialism. It, too, had no precedent in the history of mankind.

The years of Socialist construction had also witnessed a radical change in the aspect of the peoples inhabiting the Soviet Union. They had taken final shape as *Socialist nations*. Their erstwhile feeling of mutual distrust had given way to one of mutual friendship. They had begun to co-operate fraternally within the system of a single Socialist Union State.

Thanks to the Soviet system, certain peoples, such as the Kazakhs, Kirghiz, Turkmens, Tajiks, peoples of the Far North, Daghestan and others, had passed to Socialism without having to pass through the painful stage of capitalism.

The new Soviet Constitution gave legislative embodiment to the victory of Socialism in the U.S.S.R. It stated that the Socialist system of economy and Socialist ownership of the means of production constituted the economic foundation of the Soviet Union.

The new Constitution introduced into the political system major improvements aimed at the all-round development of Soviet democracy and genuine internationalism in the relations between the peoples of the country. It did away with all remaining restrictions in elections to the Soviets, and replaced indirect elections by direct. Elections to all Soviets of Working People's Deputies were made universal, direct and equal, by secret ballot. All Soviet citizens received the equal right to elect or be elected to the Soviets.

The new Constitution guaranteed the right of all citizens of the U.S.S.R. to work, leisure, education, and maintenance in old age, sickness or disability.

Granting to all citizens rights for which mankind had been fighting for centuries, the Constitution also imposed serious duties on them: strictly to observe the laws of the Soviet State and labour discipline, honestly to perform their duty towards society, to respect the standards of Socialist conduct, to safeguard and build up Socialist public property, honestly to perform their honourable duty of serving in the armed forces of the Soviet State and selflessly defending their Socialist country. The Constitution proclaimed: "To defend the Fatherland is the sacred duty of every citizen of the U.S.S.R."

The rights and duties of the citizens of the U.S.S.R. embody the principles of Socialist democracy for all.

The further democratisation of the Soviet social and political system extended and strengthened the social foundations of the dictatorship of the working class.

The highest type of democracy, *Socialist democracy*, found expression in the new Constitution.

The Constitution emphasised the leading position of the Communist Party in Soviet society as follows:

"The most active and politically conscious citizens in the ranks of the working class, and of other strata of the working people, unite in the Communist Party of the Soviet Union (Bolsheviks), which is the vanguard of the working people in their struggle to strengthen and develop the Socialist system and which represents the leading core of all organisations of the working people, both voluntary and State."

The Constitution of the country of victorious Socialism was the most democratic of all constitutions that had ever existed in the world.

The new Constitution was a powerful encouragement for all those fighting for democracy in the capitalist countries, particularly in the countries with a fascist regime. Therein lay its tremendous international significance.

The adoption of the new Constitution expressed the historic fact that the U.S.S.R. had entered a new stage of development, the stage of the completion of the building of a Socialist society and of the gradual transition to Communism.

BRIEF SUMMARY

In the internal life of the Soviet Union, the years 1933-1937 were characterised by the completion of the Socialist reconstruction of all branches of the national economy and the building, in the main, of a Socialist society. The victory of Socialism in the U.S.S.R. was the greatest historic event after the October Socialist Revolution. The building of Socialism in the U.S.S.R. was the fulfilment of the behests of the great Lenin and a result of the organising and directing activity of the Communist Party, of its wise leadership and of the heroic labour of the workers, peasants and intellectuals, who gave their whole-hearted support to the policy of the Party.

With the fulfilment of the second Five-Year Plan, the Soviet Union became a mighty industrial and collective-farm Socialist Power, supplying its economy with the necessary equipment and its armed forces with the armaments required for the defence of the country. The collectivisation of agriculture was completed.

The struggle to complete the Socialist reconstruction of the national economy required that the Party intensify its political work among the masses and improve its organising work to a considerable extent. The Party concentrated on the more important tasks of Socialist reconstruction, namely, the setting of the new factories into full production and mastery of the new techniques in industry, the organisational and economic consolidation of the collective farms, and the training of large numbers of technical intelligentsia for industry and agriculture.

The victory of Socialist relations of production brought with it changes in the class structure of Soviet society. All the exploiting classes had been eliminated. There remained two friendly classes—the working class and the peasantry—and the working intelligentsia closely connected with them. Friendship and fraternal co-operation among the Socialist nations of the U.S.S.R. grew stronger. Moral and political unity of the people was achieved. It was in these conditions that the Soviet people, on the initiative of the Party, adopted the new Constitution of the U.S.S.R., the most democratic Constitution in the world, which reflected the changes that had taken place in the economic and political life of the country.

With the victory of Socialism the exploitation of man by man was abolished, and the living standards of the working people improved radically. The establishment of the Socialist system in the country's economy created conditions for the rapid and continuous growth of social production on the basis of higher techniques, for the increasing of social wealth and the steady improvement of the standard of life of the working people.

The completion of the Socialist reconstruction of the Soviet Union's national economy proceeded in a troubled international situation. The coming of fascism to power in Germany, and the increasingly aggressive actions of the German fascists in Europe and of the Japanese imperialists in the Far East, increased the threat of war for the U.S.S.R. Therefore, while carrying on peaceful Socialist construction, the Party and the people prepared to defend their country.

The building of a Socialist society in the Soviet Union, in the conditions of a hostile capitalist encirclement and the constant threat of attack from without, was an unparalleled, epoch-making feat of the Soviet people led by the Communist Party.

CHAPTER FOURTEEN

THE PARTY'S STRUGGLE FOR THE CONSOLIDATION AND DEVELOPMENT OF SOCIALIST SOCIETY. STRENGTHENING THE COUNTRY'S DEFENCES

(1937-June 1941)

1. The Fight of the U.S.S.R. for Peace and Security of the Peoples in the Conditions Created by Mounting Fascist Aggression, 1937-1938

The consequences of the economic crisis of 1929-1933 were still in evidence when a new crisis broke out in the capitalist world in the autumn of 1937. Industrial output in 1938 was only 81 per cent of the 1929 level in the United States, and in France only 76 per cent. A distinguishing feature of the 1937 crisis was that it did not affect the aggressor countries—Japan and Germany—which had placed their national economy on a war footing. Compared with 1929, Japan's industrial output in 1938 reached 185 per cent and Germany's, 121 per cent. The industrial boom in these countries was due to war preparations, and was attended by exceptionally brutal exploitation of the workers and impoverishment of the toiling classes, deprived as they were of all democratic rights. Fearing that the crisis would inevitably spread to their countries, the German and Italian fascists and the ruling militarist clique in Japan speeded up their war preparations.

The struggle between the leading capitalist countries for markets and sources of raw material grew ever more acute. The unevenness of economic development stimulated the desire of the aggressor States forcibly to redivide the world by means of war. In 1937 the Japanese imperialists entrenched in the north-eastern provinces of China started a war to conquer the whole of China and reduce her to a colony. In 1938 the German fascists moved their troops into Austria and occupied her. After that they started preparations for the invasion of Czechoslovakia. Italian and German military intervention in Spain continued.

The flames of war enveloped various parts of the world, including such a vast country as China. The aggressive, imperialist Powers were waging wars of aggrandisement; the peoples of Ethiopia, Spain and China, who were the victims of aggression, were fighting just wars for their national liberation. The second revolutionary civil war in China had been going on since 1927, with the revolutionary people, led by the Communist Party, fighting against the forces of domestic and foreign reaction. The intensification of Japanese aggression made it imperative to unite the people in the fight against the imperialist invaders. The Communist Party of China was the only genuinely patriotic force to come out in defence of the country. It put forward the slogan "End the civil war, unite to repel Japan!" It called on the people to give the invaders a decisive rebuff and drive them out. The Chinese Communists headed the heroic resistance of their people to the Japanese imperialists, who threatened to subjugate the whole country.

The flames of war were spreading more and more widely, increasing the danger of a world conflagration.

In the face of mounting fascist aggression, the Communist Party and the Soviet State made fresh efforts to ensure collective security and thwart the aggressors. In March, 1938, after the occupation of Austria by Hitler Germany, the Soviet Government stated that it was prepared to participate in collective action to check fascist aggression and prevent a new world war. The Soviet Government proposed immediate discussion of the appropriate practical measures with other Powers in the League of Nations or outside it. "Tomorrow may be too late," the statement said, "but there is still time today, if all countries, and especially the Great Powers, take a firm and unequivocal stand on the question of joint action for the preservation of peace."

When Hitler Germany began to threaten Czechoslovakia, the Soviet Government in a number of statements reaffirmed its readiness to come to her aid in strict accordance with the stipulations of the Soviet-Czechoslovak treaty of 1935, that is, provided France did the same. The Soviet Government proposed the holding of a conference of military representatives of the U.S.S.R., France and Czechoslovakia to discuss measures necessary for the defence of Czechoslovakia against Hitler's aggression. The Soviet Union was prepared to do even more for Czechoslovakia than it was committed to under the treaty, that is, to come to her aid even without France, provided Czechoslovakia agreed to such assistance and would herself resist the aggressor.

The preservation of peace hinged to a large extent on whether or not the Western Powers would support the Soviet efforts to organise a collective rebuff to the aggressor, as the interests of the peoples demanded. Hitler would not have risked a war against a coalition of the U.S.S.R., Britain, France and the U.S.A., to which many other countries would have adhered.

The ruling circles of the West, however, once again rejected the policy of collective security, although the fascist aggressors were seriously threatening the interests and the very existence of their States. Instead, they chose the policy of concessions to the fascist aggressors in the hope of coming to terms with them. Their aim was to divert the blow from themselves and direct it at the Soviet Union. The reactionary circles of the Western Powers planned to set Germany and Japan on the Soviet Union, in order to destroy the Socialist State and at the same time weaken their rivals, since it was clear that a war against the U.S.S.R. would be no easy matter. By means of this perfidious policy the monopolists of Great Britain, the U.S.A. and France hoped to ensure their dominant position in the world. In September, 1938, when the Hitlerites were preparing for aggression against Czechoslovakia, the heads of government of Great Britain, France, Germany and Italy met in Munich and decided to transfer a number of Czechoslovakia's border regions to Germany. Czechoslovakia was betrayed by the ruling circles of Britain and France. This disgraceful policy of complicity with the aggressors became known as the Munich policy, deriving its name from the venue of the conference. Under the pressure of the Western Powers, the bourgeois government of Czechoslovakia capitulated and decided not to resist the Hitlerites, thus betraying the national interests of the country, although it was fully in a position to defend it with the help of the Soviet Union. Formally, the United States had not been a party to the Munich Conference, but it favoured its convocation and wholly approved of its decisions. The Soviet Union alone condemned the Munich betrayal.

Since France had betrayed Czechoslovakia instead of helping her, the 1935 Franco-Soviet treaty of mutual assistance in fact became null and void.

Under the guise of the so-called "policy of non-intervention," the British, French and U.S. governments also helped fascism to power in Spain, although its victory weakened the strategic positions of the Western Powers themselves. Early in 1939 the Republican government of Spain was defeated. A fascist regime was set up in the country.

The Party and the Soviet Government drew the necessary conclusions from the Munich betrayal by the Western Powers. It became increasingly obvious that they could not be relied upon to co-operate in the struggle against the aggressors.

2. The Party's Political Work in the Conditions of Socialism. Eighteenth Party Congress

The economic and political upheavals of the capitalist world did not affect the Soviet Union. The land of Socialism proceeded with its great constructive job of building a Communist society. The fulfilment of the second Five-Year Plan marked the end of the transition period from capitalism to Socialism. The New Economic Policy introduced in 1921 had served its purpose. The construction of a Socialist society in the U.S.S.R. was in the main completed. The Eighteenth Party Congress pointed out that the Soviet Union had entered the phase of completing the building of a Socialist society and of the gradual transition from Socialism to Communism.

The completion of the building of a Socialist society marks at the same time the gradual transition to Communism, which takes place by the development and perfecting of Socialist relations of production. Full Communism grows out of Socialism, in the process of its stabilisation and development.

"Socialism," said Lenin, "is a society that emerges directly from capitalism. . . . Communism, on the other hand, is a higher type of society, and it can only develop when Socialism comes into its own" (*Collected Works*, Vol. 30, p. 260).

Socialism and Communism are two stages in the development of Communist society. They have a common basis—substitution of the social ownership of the means of production for private ownership, and abolition thereby of the exploitation of man by man. The relations of production are based on the co-operation and mutual assistance of people freed from exploitation. Production is subordinated to the maximum satisfaction of the constantly growing material and cultural requirements of all members of society. The constant growth and improvement of social production proceed on the basis of higher techniques.

These two stages of Communist society differ from each other in the level of development of the productive forces, the mode of distribution of the social product and the degree of political consciousness of the members of society.

Socialism is the lower stage of Communism. Emerging directly from capitalism, it retains certain features of the old society. That is evident both in the sphere of production and in that of distribution of products. A Socialist attitude towards work and social property does not develop in the consciousness of man overnight. The transfer of the means of production to social ownership, and the abolition of the exploitation of man by man, do not in themselves eliminate a certain inequality in distribution. The level of social production is not yet high enough to ensure an abundance of material wealth. Distribution is based on the principle, "From each according to his ability, to each according to his work." Socialism, therefore, implies strict control by society and the State over the measure of work done and the measure of consumption. Under Socialism there still remain traces of social inequality, such as essential differences between town and country, and between mental and manual labour. The experience of the U.S.S.R. shows that there still are two forms of public or Socialist property under Socialism—property of the whole people, and collective-farm and co-operative property. But they are not opposed to each other, for they are two forms of Socialist property serving a common aim—the building of Communism. Socialism also retains money and commodity relations, by means of which the State keeps account of and supervises the amount of work done and the amount consumed, and regulates the distribution of products among the members of society.

Communism represents a higher stage in the development of human society. The further development of science and technology, used for the good of the people, will raise the productive forces of society to a high level. The members of this society, with all-round education and brought up in a Communist spirit, will achieve a high degree of public spirit and will be for ever freed of the survivals of capitalism in man's consciousness. Work will become the prime necessity for man. Under these conditions, "all the springs of co-operative wealth [will] flow more abundantly" (K. Marx, *Critique of the Gotha Programme*, Eng. ed., Moscow, 1954). Society will be in a position to apply the Communist principle of distribution, *"From each according to his ability, to each according to his needs."* Lenin described Communist society as universal prosperity and lasting peace. Communism will know no essential differences between town and country, between mental and manual labour. With the establishment of a single form of public ownership the distinction between the working class and the peasantry will disappear, as will the division of society into classes. All the people will become workers of Communist society.

The building of Communist society requires much effort from the Party and the people. It is necessary both to create the appropriate material and technical basis and to mould the man of the future Communist society. The victory of Socialism marks the beginning of a truly mass, popular movement towards Communism. Socialism has given full scope to the development of the productive forces and the physical and mental abilities of men.

Under Socialism the objective law of the planned, proportionate development of all branches of the national economy began fully to manifest itself. The Soviet State secured greater opportunities for developing the national economy in the interests of building Communist society.

The victory of Socialism in the U.S.S.R. created the moral and political unity of Soviet society. It was the first society in history knit together by the common interests and common objectives of its members, a society closely rallied around the Communist Party, its vanguard. The social basis of the dictatorship of the working class grew broader and stronger. The collective-farm system became a tremendous factor in educating the peasantry in the spirit of Socialism. Further success in the building of the new society now depended largely on the Communist consciousness of the working people and the Party's organising work among the masses.

With the victory of Socialism, the role of the Party in guiding the construction of Communist society became even more important. The Party was confronted with big and complex tasks. The most important of these was to strengthen and develop Socialist relations of production in all branches of the national economy. As before, the Party had to guide the development of social production in such a way as to ensure priority for expansion of the production of the means of production, the key to creating a sufficiency and later an abundance of products in the country. The new, Socialist national economy called for an improvement in the methods of industrial and agricultural management. The Communist education of the working people, particularly the inculcation of a public-spirited attitude towards work and social property, assumed ever greater importance. The Party took greater care to ensure the steady improvement of the people's well-being and cultural standard.

The new conditions required a new approach to Party work, an improvement in organising activity among the masses. With a view to enhancing its leading role in Communist construction and stimulating the political activity and distinction at work of every Communist, the Party began to extend inner-Party democracy further.

In the course of the struggle for Socialism, the Party had grown stronger and accumulated a wealth of experience, both in industrial and agricultural management and in its work among the masses. This enabled the Party to improve its organising and political work among the masses. There were, however, serious shortcomings in the work of the Party organisations, and they were particularly intolerable in the conditions of victorious Socialism and further democratisation of the Soviet system. Some of the Party leaders concerned themselves solely with economic matters; they showed no interest in foreign and domestic affairs and began to drift away from the political work of the Party. A number of Party organisations were breaking the Party rules: co-option was often substituted for election, Party conferences were not held regularly. Leninist standards of inner-Party life, the corner-stone of its strength and vitality, were being infringed. These shortcomings in the work of Party organisations were discussed at the plenary meeting of the Central Committee of the C.P.S.U.(B.) in February-March, 1937. The C.C. plenary meeting pointed out that there could be no durable economic success without success in the political work of the Party. The C.C. called upon Communists thoroughly to assimilate the Leninist principle of Party leadership of economic bodies, which meant strengthening these bodies, helping them systematically and rejecting petty tutelage over them. The C.C. plenary meeting also discussed preparations by Party organisations for the elections to the Supreme Soviet of the U.S.S.R. on the basis of the new Constitution.

The adoption of the new Constitution and the further democratisation of the Soviet electoral system meant a *turning-point in the political life of the country*. The Party had to be adequately prepared for this, and ensure its leadership in the forthcoming elections. But that could be done only if the Party itself was consistent in its democratic practices and in observing fully the principle of democratic centralism, as the Party rules demanded. The C.C. instructed the Party organisations to overhaul their work *along the lines of extensive inner-Party democracy*. The reorganisation included elimination of the practice of co-opting to leading Party bodies, prohibition of voting by lists during elections to them, and introduction of the secret ballot.

In pursuance of the C.C. decision, the Party organisations focussed their attention on work with people. Greater attention was devoted to training and getting to know the personnel, to the political education of Party and non-Party masses. Criticism and self-criticism began to be more widely practised. Elections to Party leading committees in 1937 were held in conditions of much greater activity of the Communists.

The reorganisation of Party work helped the Party to prepare better for the elections to the Supreme Soviet of the U.S.S.R.

The Party entered the elections *in a bloc, in an alliance*, with the non-Party masses, with whom it put up common candidates. The election alliance of Communists and non-Party masses was a logical and natural phenomenon in the country of victorious Socialism. It testified to the moral and political unity of Soviet society and was a vivid reflection of this unity.

The elections to the Supreme Soviet took place on December 12, 1937. 96.8 per cent of the electorate went to the polls, and 98.6

per cent of those who did so cast their votes for the candidates of the Communist and non-Party bloc. The millions of Soviet people thus voiced their confidence in the Communist Party and their endorsement of its policy. The results of the elections graphically demonstrated the successes attained in the building of Socialism under the leadership of the Party. They were evidence of the genuine unity of Soviet society, of the strength and vitality of Socialist democracy embodied in the Constitution of the U.S.S.R.

The victory of Socialism created favourable conditions for the extension of Party and Soviet democracy. But in spite of that, there were direct violations of Party and Soviet democracy resulting from what was later defined by the Party as the cult of Stalin's personality. Stalin began to develop into a law certain restrictions in inner-Party and Soviet democracy that were unavoidable in conditions of bitter struggle against the class enemy and his agents. He began to violate the standards of Party life worked out by Lenin, the principle of collective leadership, deciding many important questions on his own.

In Stalin's actions a discrepancy arose between word and deed, between theory and practice. His printed works contained correct Marxist propositions concerning the people as the maker of history, the role of the Party and its Central Committee as the collective leader, solicitude for cadres, extension of inner-Party democracy, etc. But when it came to practice, Stalin deviated from these Marxist-Leninist propositions. Starting from correct Marxist premises, he warned against impermissible exaggerations of the role of the individual in history, but in practice he encouraged the cult of his own personality.

Stalin rightly stressed the necessity of strengthening the Soviet State in every possible way, of keeping a watchful eye on the intrigues of enemies and, above all, on the machinations of the hostile capitalist encirclement. This held true in the conditions of victorious Socialism as well. It was likewise necessary to be on guard against certain elements from among the routed opposition groups of the Trotskyists, Zinovievites, Right-wingers and nationalists who (especially the Trotskyists) more than once deceived the Party in the course of their struggle against it, violated Soviet legality, and were often in league with counter-revolutionary elements. For this reason the State security organs were compelled to take the necessary measures against them.

On the other hand in 1937, when Socialism was already victorious in the U.S.S.R., Stalin advanced the erroneous thesis that the class struggle in the country would intensify as the Soviet State grew stronger. The class struggle in the Soviet country was at its sharpest stage in the period when the question "Who will beat whom?" was being decided, when the foundations of Socialism were being laid. But after Socialism had won, after the exploiting classes had been eliminated and moral and political unity had been established in Soviet society, the thesis of the inevitable sharpening of the class struggle was an erroneous one. In practice it served as a justification for mass repressions against the Party's ideological enemies who had already been routed politically. Many honest Communists and non-Party people, not guilty of any offence, also became victims of these repressions. During this period the political adventurer and scoundrel, Beria, who did not stop short at any atrocity to achieve his criminal aims, worked his way into responsible positions in the State, and, taking advantage of Stalin's personal shortcomings, slandered and exterminated many honest people, devoted to the Party and the people.

In the same period a despicable role was played by Yezhov, the then People's Commissar for Home Affairs. Many workers, both Communists and non-Party people, who were utterly devoted to the cause of the Party, were slandered with his assistance and perished. Yezhov and Beria were duly punished for their crimes.

The victims of unjustified repressions were fully exonerated in 1954-1955.

The violations of Socialist legality and the mass repressions caused serious damage to the Communist Party. But although the mistakes resulting from the cult of Stalin's personality retarded the development of Soviet society, they could not check it, and still less could they change the Socialist nature of the Soviet system. All the work of Stalin himself was bound up with the great Socialist transformations carried out in the Soviet country. The Soviet people had complete confidence in the Party, was guided by its decisions and pushed ahead with the great cause of Socialism. Socialist construction advanced from success to success.

The victory of Socialism was marked by an influx of new members into the Party and a considerable growth of the Soviet intelligentsia. The young personnel promoted to leading Party, administrative and economic posts often lacked the necessary experience or ideological and political training. It was therefore essential that the Party improve the ideological and political education of the intelligentsia, government and Party personnel.

The C.C. of the C.P.S.U.(B.) adopted a number of measures to improve Party propaganda and agitation. The machinery in charge of the Party's ideological work was reinforced in the centre and in the localities. Schools and refresher courses were set up for Party cadres. *A Short Course of the History of the Communist*

Party of the Soviet Union (*Bolsheviks*) was published in 1938, and the study of the history of the Party was started on an extensive scale. The Party press and the Soviet press generally played an important part in the propagation of Marxism-Leninism. The ideological work of the Party among the masses assumed great dimensions.

The Eighteenth Congress of the C.P.S.U.(B.), held on March 10 to 21, 1939, was an important event in the life of the Party and people who had entered the new phase of Socialist construction. The Congress represented 1,588,852 Party members and 888,814 candidate members.

The Congress heard and discussed reports by the leading Party bodies: it considered and approved the third Five-Year Plan for the development of the national economy and amendments to the rules of the C.P.S.U.(B.).

The report of the C.C. of the C.P.S.U.(B.), presented by Stalin, contained a comprehensive analysis of the international situation and domestic affairs of the U.S.S.R. and of inner-Party life.

The Congress noted that the war unleashed by the fascist States against peace-loving nations constituted a threat to world peace. At that time the war had not yet become a world war, though it had already drawn into its orbit countries with an aggregate population of 500 million.

The Congress exposed the Munich policy of the Western Powers, the policy of concessions to the aggressors. It pointed out that the dangerous political game started by the advocates of the "policy of non-intervention" might end in a serious fiasco for them. This warning soon proved only too true.

After endorsing the foreign policy of the Soviet Government the Eighteenth Congress laid down the following directives: to continue the policy of peace and of strengthening business contacts with all countries; to be on the alert and not allow the Soviet Union to be drawn into conflicts by warmongers accustomed to making a cat's-paw of other people; to strengthen to the utmost the fighting capacity of the Red Army and Navy; to strengthen international ties with the working people of all countries, who were interested in peace and friendship among the peoples.

An exceptionally important question dealt with by the Congress was that of the cardinal economic task of the U.S.S.R.—*to overtake and outstrip the principal capitalist countries in production per head.* This problem was posed by Lenin on the eve of the October Revolution as the perspective in store for a Socialist country. After the victory of Socialism in the U.S.S.R., when the technical reconstruction of the national economy had in the main been completed, it became the immediate practical task of the Party and the entire Soviet people.

The Eighteenth Party Congress noted with satisfaction that the victory of Socialism had further strengthened the Soviet system and consolidated the alliance of the working class and the peasantry and the fraternal ties among the peoples of the U.S.S.R. The victory of Socialism stimulated the growth and development of such *new motive forces* of Soviet society as the moral and political unity of the people, friendship between the peoples, and Soviet patriotism. These motive forces added peculiar strength to the Soviet political system.

The Eighteenth Party Congress also considered some questions of Marxist-Leninist theory which were exceptionally important for the consolidation and development of Socialist society, for the building of Communism.

Marx, Engels and Lenin had elaborated in their works the main principles underlying the building of a Socialist State, showed the fundamental difference between the proletarian State and the bourgeois State, outlined the aims and tasks of the proletarian State and indicated the main paths of its development and later, during the transition to Communism, of its withering away. However, in examining the question of the withering away of the Socialist State, they had confined themselves to general theoretical propositions, for practice had not yet provided adequate material for this question to be answered in full.

The question of the State during the transition period from Socialism to Communism received further development at the Eighteenth Congress.

In his report Stalin formulated the proposition according to which the State will be necessary under Communism also, if capitalist encirclement remains. This emphasised the importance of the Socialist State as the chief instrument in the hands of the workers and peasants in building Socialism and Communism, and in defending the gains of the Soviet people against attacks by imperialist States. Stalin briefly described the development of the Soviet State in its main historical stages and its principal functions. The Soviet State had passed through two major phases in its development. The first covered the period from the victory of the October Socialist Revolution to the elimination of the exploiting classes. The second began with the elimination of the exploiting classes and the victory of Socialism in the U.S.S.R. The functions of the Socialist State in its first phase included suppression of the overthrown classes within the country, defence of the country from external attack, economic organisation, dissemination of culture and education. During the second phase the function of suppressing the exploiting classes ceases because these classes have been eliminated; it is superseded by the function of protecting Socialist property; the functions of economic organisation, dissemination of culture and education develop to the full; the function of military defence of the country fully remains. The change in the functions of the Socialist State after the victory of Socialism does not at all mean the weakening of this State, or its withering away. On the contrary, the withering away of the proletarian State comes through its strengthening, which is achieved primarily by the active participation of the broadest sections of the working people in its activities. For this reason the Party Congress called for the all-out strengthening of the machinery of the State, and above all of those parts of it which had to perform the function of defending the land of Socialism.

The question of the Soviet intelligentsia and the right attitude towards it figured prominently in the report of the Central Committee of the Party. In conditions of victorious Socialism, the intelligentsia had become truly popular in nature, closely bound up with the working class and the collective-farm peasantry, an important force in Soviet society, in its economic and cultural development.

The Eighteenth Congress called upon Party organisations to be tactful and attentive in their attitude towards the Soviet intelligentsia, and resolutely to do away with the still existing distrust of it and with the survivals of old pre-revolutionary views regarding the intelligentsia. The Soviet intelligentsia deserved the complete trust and constant consideration of the Party and the State.

The Eighteenth Congress considered the third Five-Year Plan for the development of the national economy of the U.S.S.R. (1938-1942), which was an important step towards solving the cardinal economic task of the U.S.S.R. It provided for increasing the industrial might of the country, strengthening the collective-farm system, raising the material well-being and cultural standards of the people, and strengthening the defence capacity of the Soviet Union. It was planned to increase industrial output in 1942 to nearly twice the 1937 figure. Capital investments earmarked under the third Five-Year Plan approximated to the sum-total of all capital invested in the years of the first and second Five-Year Plans.

The most important problem of the third Five-Year Plan was to develop the defence industries and create big State reserves of fuel, electric power and other branches of production. It was planned to build duplicates of existing enterprises in the eastern regions of the country—the Urals, the Volga region, Siberia and Central Asia. The plan provided for the expansion of the coal and metallurgical base in the east of the country, creation of an oil base in the area between the Volga and the Urals and a new grain-growing area in the eastern and south-eastern regions of the U.S.S.R.

The Congress devoted considerable attention to questions of organisation. It adopted a resolution on amendments to the rules of the C.P.S.U.(B.), and approved the amended Party rules. In view of the fundamental changes in the national economy and the class structure of the U.S.S.R., the classification of people applying for Party membership in accordance with their social status was abandoned. Common rules and a common probation period were established for all seeking admission to the Party. This, however, did not imply a lessening of demands upon those joining the Party or of the responsibility of the Party organisations for those accepted. As in the past, the task was systematically to improve the composition of the Party, observing the principle of a strictly individual approach in selecting the best people, devoted to the cause of Communism, for Party membership. An addendum specifying the rights of Party members was introduced into the Party rules. It provided that every Communist had the right to take part in free and business-like discussion of practical questions of Party policy at Party meetings and in the Party press; to criticise any Party worker at Party meetings; to elect and to be elected to Party committees; to demand to be present when any decision concerning his activities or conduct was taken; and to submit any question or statement to any Party body, up to and including the Central Committee.

The Congress resolution on amendments to the rules of the C.P.S.U.(B.) condemned a formal, heartless and bureaucratic attitude towards the fate of Party members, and sharply criticised the slanderers and careerists who defamed the Party cadres. The Party rules adopted by the Eighteenth Congress were supplemented by a number of provisions ensuring a careful approach and thorough analysis of the soundness of charges made in deciding the question of expulsion from the Party, or of the rehabilitation of expelled Party members. The rules abolished mass cleansings, which were a means of improving the composition of the Party during the transition period, but were no longer necessary in conditions of victorious Socialism, when capitalist elements had been eliminated. The rules of the C.P.S.U.(B.) reflected the measures taken by the Party to further inner-Party democracy.

The primary Party organisations at productive enterprises, including collective and State farms and the machine-and-tractor stations, were given the right to check and verify the actions of the management. This enhanced the responsibility of the primary Party organisations for the work of such enterprises.

The amendments and addenda to the Party rules adopted by the Congress made for greater inner-Party democracy, greater activity and initiative on the part of Communists, and improved inner-Party work as a whole.

The Eighteenth Congress of the C.P.S.U.(B.) focussed the attention of the Party on solving the tasks confronting the Soviet Union with its entry into a new phase of development, namely, the phase of completing the building of Socialism and the gradual transition to Communism.

3. The Efforts of the Party and the Soviet State to Organise Collective Resistance to Fascist Aggression in 1939. The Beginning of the Second World War

The events which unfolded in the world arena after the Eighteenth Party Congress fully confirmed its assessment of the international situation.

The Western Powers' Munich policy proceeded from the assumption that a war against the U.S.S.R. could iron out the imperialist contradictions between them and the fascist States. Signs appeared, however, that these plans were not feasible, at least not in the immediate future. In March, 1939, the Hitlerites seized the rest of Czechoslovakia without even securing the consent of Britain and France, which they had still considered necessary at the time of the Munich Conference. Having done with Czechoslovakia, the Hitler Government immediately began to prepare for aggression against Poland. The Polish Government was presented with brazen and patently unacceptable demands for territorial concessions, changes in the status of Germans in Poland, etc. At the same time Germany had not the least intention of withdrawing her demands for the return of her former colonies, annexed by Britain and France under the Versailles Peace Treaty. It became clear that the Western Powers had failed, even at the price of the Munich betrayal, to protect their interests and come to a firm agreement with Hitler.

In these circumstances Britain and France announced in the spring of 1939 that they would guarantee the sovereignty of Poland, Greece, Rumania and Turkey, in other words, the countries which were threatened by the fascist aggressor. At the same time they started negotiations with the Soviet Union on how to resist German aggression.

Did all that mean that Britain and France had abandoned the policy of conspiring with Hitler against the U.S.S.R. and had switched to a policy of collectively resisting the fascist aggressor? It soon became obvious that that was not the case.

As a matter of fact, the governments of Britain and France were playing a double game. They continued to seek a deal with Hitler and had merely altered their tactics. Democratic public opinion in these two countries was insistently demanding that their governments establish close co-operation with the Soviet Union. Though not in the least anxious to do so, British and French ruling circles were nevertheless compelled to start negotiations with the U.S.S.R. in order to camouflage their real plans. Moreover, they hoped to utilise these negotiations with the Soviet Government to exert pressure on Hitler, whom they sought to frighten by the prospect of a powerful coalition being created with the participation of the U.S.S.R., and thus to induce him to come to terms with the Western Powers.

The Central Committee of the Party and the Soviet Government took this into account. Nevertheless, the Soviet Government agreed to start negotiations with Britain and France. The Soviet Union did not want to miss a single opportunity, however slight, to organise collective resistance to the aggressor and avert a new world war. The course of the negotiations, however, confirmed that the governments of Britain and France were not really willing to co-operate with the U.S.S.R. to that end.

The original proposals made to the Soviet Union by the British and French governments were absolutely unacceptable. Without assuming any concrete obligations themselves, they sought to impose obligations about taking part in a war only on the U.S.S.R. —to involve the U.S.S.R. in a war with Germany, while themselves remaining outside it.

The Soviet Government rejected the British and French proposals as contrary to the principle of reciprocity. It submitted counter-proposals providing for the conclusion of a mutual assistance treaty between the three Powers. Under this treaty, the U.S.S.R., Britain and France were to assist one another in the event of aggression in Europe against any one of the three States, as well as in the event of aggression against Poland, Rumania, the Baltic countries, Turkey and Belgium. It was also proposed to define precisely the extent and forms of military assistance to be given by each of the three parties to the agreement. The adoption of the Soviet proposals would have meant the establishment of a powerful coalition against fascist Germany, and could have checked the spread of aggression.

The British and French governments would not consent to conclude a treaty providing for reciprocal commitments by all three States. As a result, the negotiations dragged out: started in March, 1939, they continued until August of the same year. In the course of these negotiations, the British and French governments continually submitted new draft treaties, all of them possessing one and the same feature: they were all designed to provoke a Soviet-German war. It was only reluctantly, under the pressure of democratic public opinion, that Britain and France made some concessions. Everything testified to the fact that what the two governments wanted, especially the British, was not to conclude an agreement with the U.S.S.R., but merely to talk about such an agreement, while pursuing other aims.

The unwillingness of Britain and France to form a coalition with the Soviet Union, in the event of Germany launching a war, became finally obvious during the negotiations between military representatives of the three States, held in Moscow, on the initiative of the U.S.S.R., in August, 1939.

At that time, the Soviet Union had no common frontier with Germany. To make contact with the German troops and open hostilities against them, the Red Army had to pass through the territory of Poland which separated them. In the course of the Anglo-Franco-Soviet military negotiations it turned out that the government of Poland was against allowing the Soviet armed forces to cross her territory, and that Britain and France were not doing anything serious to induce the Polish Government to alter its stand. Yet unless it did so, the Soviet Union actually had nowhere to take part in war against Germany. It was clear that Britain and France, starting negotiations with the U.S.S.R., really had no intention of opposing Hitler aggression, arms in hand, together with the Soviet Union. The secret instructions to the British military mission conducting negotiations with the Soviet Command in Moscow expressly said that the British Government did not wish to assume any definite commitments whatever towards the Soviet Union.

While conducting negotiations with the Soviet Union, the British Government started secret talks with the German Government, proposing to Hitler the conclusion of a non-aggression pact and an agreement on the division of spheres of influence on a world-wide scale. This included a truly monstrous proposal—that China and the Soviet Union be among the countries to be divided up. The British Government promised the Hitlerites to break off negotiations with the U.S.S.R. It was likewise ready to withdraw the guarantee of Poland's independence which it had only recently given. In other words, it was ready to betray Poland by surrendering her to Hitler, just as it had done in the case of Czechoslovakia.

The danger to the U.S.S.R. was aggravated by the fact that it was threatened not only from the west but from the east as well. Here the Soviet Union was rendering material and moral assistance to the Chinese people in their struggle against Japanese imperialism, while the U.S.A. and Britain were encouraging the Japanese aggressor and lavishly aiding him with strategic materials. "Since the outbreak of the war against the Japanese invader," Mao Tse-tung wrote, "none of the imperialist governments has given us any real help; the Soviet Union alone has rendered us assistance in the form of aircraft and material resources" (*Selected Works*, Vol. 3, p. 190). Relations between the U.S.S.R. and Japan were deteriorating. In 1938 the Japanese imperialists invaded Soviet territory in the area of Lake Hassan, near Vladivostok. They were intent on testing, with their bayonets, the strength of the Soviet Union and its military preparedness. In the summer of 1939 large Japanese forces invaded the area of the Halhin-Gol River in the Mongolian People's Republic, with which the Soviet Union had been bound by a mutual assistance pact since 1936. Both attacks were repelled with heavy losses for the Japanese.

Thus the U.S.S.R. was already forced to carry on hostilities in the Far East at a time when the Hitlerites were making preparations near the Soviet western borders to attack Poland, and the negotiations with the Western Powers had reached a deadlock through the fault of Britain and France. An extremely unfavourable situation had arisen: the Soviet Union was threatened with war, in conditions of its complete political isolation—and that on two fronts at once, in the west and the Far East.

The country had to be saved at all costs from the danger threatening it. This was a question of life and death not only for the Soviet people and the Soviet Union. The preservation of the first, and at that time the only, Socialist State was in the interest of Socialism throughout the world, in the interest of the working people of all countries.

The Central Committee of the C.P.S.U.(B.) and the Soviet Government were guided by the directive of the Eighteenth Party Congress: to be cautious and not allow the Soviet Union to be drawn into conflicts by warmongers. The Party and the Government proceeded from this directive when, in August, 1939, they adopted the responsible decision to conclude the non-aggression pact with Germany proposed by the German Government. This decision was adopted only when it became absolutely clear that Britain and France, as well as Poland, had no intention of concluding an effective agreement with the U.S.S.R. for a joint struggle against Hitler aggression, and when all other possibilities of ensuring the Soviet Union's security had been exhausted.

When the German Government proposed to the Soviet Union to conclude a non-aggression pact, it did so for reasons of its own and had by no means renounced the idea of an annexationist war against the U.S.S.R. But it reckoned with the enormous difficulties this war would entail; and it therefore planned first to subjugate the West European countries and then, making use of their resources, to attack the U.S.S.R. As for the Soviet Union, by the conclusion of this pact it gained a certain time to prepare its defence and was enabled to ward off the danger of being involved in a war on two fronts in the extremely unfavourable conditions prevailing in 1939, when the Western Powers did not wish to become its allies. The reactionary ruling circles of Britain, France and the U.S.A. sought to isolate the U.S.S.R. and to establish a united front of capitalist Powers against it. Germany and Japan were to play the role of the shock force and to shed their people's blood, so that the three Western Powers could later dictate their terms to the war-weakened countries.

It was impossible to avert war at a time when the U.S.S.R. was alone and encircled by capitalist countries, and the international working class was split by the Right-wing Socialists who had rejected the Communists' call for unity. But the first Socialist country could and had to be saved from war in such adverse conditions. The Soviet Government was in duty bound to its people and the cause of Socialism throughout the world to frustrate the reactionary schemes of the men of Munich. The non-aggression pact with Germany helped to do that.

The Munichites wanted to start a war in such a way that it should begin between the capitalist world and an isolated Soviet Union. But things turned out differently: the war broke out within the capitalist world itself. As a result, the Munichite politicians found themselves in a difficult position, like the one in the popular saying: "He falls himself that digs another's pit." They wanted to involve the U.S.S.R. in a war with Germany and Japan, while they themselves would stand aloof and build up their strength for the time when it would be possible to dictate their own terms to the three countries, exhausted by war. It so happened, however, that they had to fight themselves in difficult conditions.

On September 1, 1939, Germany attacked Poland. The Polish people fell victim to fascist aggression. It offered stubborn resistance, with the Communists, the workers and the other working people who rallied around the Communists, playing a heroic part. But, since the bourgeois-landlord government, committing an act of national betrayal, had rejected the help offered by the Soviet Union, Poland could not withstand the powerful onslaught of Hitler Germany.

After the Hitlerites' attack on Poland, the British and French governments could no longer doubt that, having finished with Poland, Hitler Germany would strike at France, Britain and their vast colonies. The governments of Britain and France therefore declared war on Germany at the beginning of September, 1939.

Thus began the second world war.

Britain and France did not enter the war with Germany for the sake of Poland, and least of all with the object of overthrowing fascism. They did so in order to protect their own imperialist interests and positions, to weaken a dangerous rival, and to maintain their position as Great Powers. That is why they did not raise a finger really to help Poland. The German forces advanced swiftly eastward through Poland, approaching the Soviet frontiers.

The Party and the Soviet Government realised that, while the treaty with Germany enabled the Soviet Union temporarily to stave off war with the Hitlerites, the latter could not be relied upon to observe their obligations for long. It was therefore essential for the country's defence to halt the advancing Hitler troops as far away as possible from the vital centres of the U.S.S.R., and to prevent them from taking up strategical positions farther eastward, nearer to our then frontier, that is, on the immediate approaches to Minsk. Nor could the Soviet Union remain indifferent to the fate of the brother peoples of Western Ukraine and Western Byelorussia, and allow them to fall under the fascist yoke. On September 17, 1939, Red Army units crossed the frontier and soon occupied Western Ukraine and Western Byelorussia. These regions reunited with Soviet Ukraine and Soviet Byelorussia to form single States of the Ukrainian and Byelorussian peoples.

In its early stages, the war that broke out between Hitler Germany and Anglo-French imperialism in 1939 was different in character from the Italo-Ethiopian or Sino-Japanese wars, or the war in Spain. Those had been wars of aggrandisement for one side and of liberation for the other. The war between Germany and Britain and France was in the beginning imperialist on both sides. The Polish people, like other nations that had fallen victim to aggression, were fighting for their independence; but as for the Great Powers, the two sides, both Hitler Germany and Britain and France, were pursuing imperialist aims.

But the situation was that Britain and France found themselves faced with the same enemy as all the nations who had fallen victim to fascist aggression—German fascism. Moreover, as a result of the heavy reverses they suffered at the hands of the Hitlerites in 1940, Britain and France had to think, not so much of achieving their imperialist aims, as of preserving their national independence. At the same time the masses of the people in Britain and France, as well as in the U.S.A., were bringing increasing pressure to bear on their governments to wage an active anti-fascist war, a war of liberation. In these circumstances, under strong popular pressure the nature of Britain's and France's war against Hitler Germany changed in the course of time. In effect, it merged with the war waged by the freedom-loving nations against fascist aggression, and assumed the character of a war of liberation. The liberating character of the war became still more manifest after the Soviet Union's entry, when Britain, France and later the U.S.A. found themselves together with the U.S.S.R. in the anti-Hitler coalition.

In the early phase of the second world war the Munichite elements in Britain and France, as well as in the U.S.A., continued to cherish the hope of switching the war against the U.S.S.R. French and British troops on the Western front were practically inactive, conducting no serious hostilities against Germany. At the same time Britain and France strove to involve the countries bordering on the Soviet Union into a war against it. In Latvia, Estonia and Lithuania the intrigues of the imperialists came to naught. They raised such a storm of indignation among the democratic forces there that the governments of the three States were forced in September and October, 1939, to conclude mutual assistance pacts with the Soviet Union. But anti-Soviet intrigues in the Baltic countries did not stop even after that, and there was a danger of their being involved in fatal imperialist ventures. The working masses of the Baltic countries then demanded the immediate re-establishment of Soviet power, overthrown by the Entente in 1919, and reunion with the Soviet Union. As a result of the pressure brought to bear by the masses, there was a change of government in all the three Baltic Republics in June, 1940. Power was taken over by the progressive forces. For the first time in the history of these countries, parliamentary elections were held in democratic conditions. The newly-elected Parliaments of Lithuania, Latvia and Estonia approached the Soviet Government with a request that their countries be accepted into the Union of Soviet Socialist Republics. In August, 1940, the Supreme Soviet of the U.S.S.R. granted their request and admitted the Lithuanian, Latvian and Estonian Soviet Socialist Republics into the U.S.S.R.

Bessarabia, forcibly severed from Soviet Russia in 1918, and Northern Bukovina, the Ukrainian population of which gravitated towards Soviet Ukraine, were likewise reunited with the U.S.S.R. The reunion of the Baltic countries and Bessarabia with the Soviet Union strengthened its security, for the enemy could have utilised these regions as convenient concentration areas, bringing their troops close to the vital centres of the Soviet Union.

The imperialists achieved a temporary success in Finland. Towards the close of 1939 they provoked the Finnish reactionaries into war against the Soviet Union.

Britain and France wanted to see the U.S.S.R. weakened, and therefore supplied the Finns with arms and planned to send troops to help them, although the Germans had concentrated huge armed forces on the French frontier. It was only the defeat of the Finnish troops that prevented Anglo-French intervention in the Soviet-Finnish war. In March, 1940, that war ended with the signing of a peace treaty in Moscow.

In April, 1940, Hitler Germany invaded Scandinavia and easily overran Denmark and Norway. In May she launched an offensive on the Western front. Hitler armies quickly occupied Holland and Belgium. The British expeditionary forces in France and Belgium were routed. They beat a hasty retreat and embarked for Britain, leaving their arms behind. The French army, defeated by the German forces, retreated into the interior. On June 22, 1940, the reactionary French Government capitulated. The struggle against fascism in France was continued by French patriots, with the Communists in the van. Under the terms of the armistice, a considerable part of France, including Paris, was occupied by Hitler troops.

Such was the deplorable result of the Munich policy: France was defeated, and Britain found herself face to face with Hitler Germany.

The course of the war in Western Europe demanded new foreign policy measures by the Communist Party and the Soviet State. The task was to prevent the further spread of war and fascist aggression. In April, 1940, the Soviet Government warned Hitler Germany against violating Sweden's neutrality, and thereby helped that country to avoid German invasion.

The Soviet Government took various measures to prevent Germany from bringing Finland, Bulgaria, Turkey, and Yugoslavia under her sway. After the defeat of France, however, Hitler Germany became so strong as to make it increasingly difficult to check her aggressive actions. Hitlerite troops were introduced into Finland, Rumania and Bulgaria, and their reactionary governments became Germany's vassals. In April, 1941, the Hitlerites attacked Yugoslavia and then Greece, and occupied these countries.

From the second half of 1940, fascist Germany began direct preparations for war against the U.S.S.R. Her plans were to enslave the peoples of the Soviet Union, destroy it as the world's bulwark of Socialism and democracy, and thus remove the main obstacle to the further realisation of her aggressive aims. Following that she intended to seize the British Isles, which she dared not attack with the Red Army in her rear. Then, in conjunction with Japan, she meant to smash the U.S.A.

The grave danger threatening the Soviet Union called for

redoubled efforts by the Party and the whole Soviet people to enhance the industrial might of the Soviet Union and strengthen its defensive capacity.

4. The Party's Organising Work in the Industrial Sphere. The Strengthening of the Industrial Power of the Country and of Its Defensive Capacity

The Party regarded the third Five-Year Plan for the development of the national economy as another major step towards completing the building of Socialist society and fulfilling its cardinal economic task.

In industry, however, fulfilment of the plan entailed great difficulties. The international situation was becoming increasingly tense. The second world war, started by the fascist aggressors, was a direct menace to the Soviet Union. The people had to be kept in a state of constant readiness against attack by the aggressors, and considerable budgetary, material and manpower resources had to be diverted from peaceful projects to strengthen the country's defence potential.

When it started out on the third Five-Year Plan the Party came up against other difficulties as well. Industry was growing rapidly and required a steady influx of manpower, especially skilled labour, of which there was frequently a shortage. At the same time, available manpower was not everywhere being used properly. The explanation lay in various organisational shortcomings. The organisation of work and wages still had certain defects. The saturation of all branches of industry with modern machinery required improved technical control. But the frequent change of executives in the People's Commissariats and at the factories adversely affected the management of industry and its output. The aim of the Party's organising work in industry was to surmount these difficulties and eliminate shortcomings, and to secure a further uninterrupted advance of Socialist industry.

In its economic policy, the Party sought to distribute the productive forces in the most rational way, accelerate the rate of new construction and develop the production capacity of each enterprise to the utmost.

New industrial enterprises were built as close as possible to sources of raw materials. Particular attention was paid by the Party and the people to the economic development of the eastern regions—the Volga region, the Urals, Western and Eastern Siberia, Central Asia and the Far East. The goal was to achieve the comprehensive economic development of these regions. The production of building materials was organised, power stations, metallurgical works, coal and ore mines were being built, and light and food industries were being developed in each of these regions. A new oil base—known as the "Second Baku"—was being developed between the Volga and the Urals. The Magnitogorsk Iron and Steel Works in the Urals was being enlarged and the construction of the Nizhni Tagil Iron and Steel Works was nearing completion. Big iron and steel mills were going up in the Transbaikal region (the Petrovsko-Zabaikalsky Works) and in the Far East (Amurstal). Duplicate engineering and chemical factories and oil refineries were being built. Co-operation between industrial enterprises was advanced on a bigger scale than heretofore.

The Party saw to it that the strictest economy was maintained. Money, building materials and equipment were allocated, first and foremost, for the completion of the projects that had been started under the first two Five-Year Plans. A new feature in the Party's economic policy was to increase the construction of medium-sized and small power stations, mines and other enterprises. This reduced the time taken in construction and speeded up expansion of production capacities.

Serious attention was paid by the Party and the Government to improving the work of the key industries—coal, iron and steel. This was extremely important because the demand for coal and metal was growing yearly. Large quantities of metal were needed by the defence industries. Yet in 1939, instead of increasing, the output of pig-iron and steel fell somewhat, and there was only an insignificant increase in coal output, especially in the Donets coalfield. This presented a serious threat to the development of the entire national economy, and was quite intolerable in view of the mounting danger of war.

The Party discovered the causes of this lagging behind of the coal, iron and steel industries. It was due mainly to inefficient economic and technical leadership and to the fact that local Party organisations did not pay sufficient attention to the work of the coal mines and the metallurgical plants.

A grave drawback hampering the work of the Donets coal mines was the fluidity of manpower. Frequently the personnel of the mines would change completely in the course of a year, which seriously affected the fulfilment of output plans. Moreover, there were distortions of policy in the organisation of work and in the wages structure in the mines. Output quotas were too low. As a result, in spite of fulfilment and overfulfilment, the actual output of coal fell short of the targets set in the State plan. In many cases engineers and technicians were not assigned to their proper jobs. A large number of engineers and technicians had been trained for the coal industry during the period of the first Five-Year plans, but many of them landed in the offices of trusts and local boards. As a result, mines equipped with the latest machinery were left without adequate technical guidance, new and progressive methods of mining were introduced much too slowly, and labour productivity remained practically unchanged.

There were similar shortcomings in the iron and steel industry. At the Magnitogorsk and Kuznetsk Works and at the iron and steel mills in the south (Makeyevka, Stalino, Zaporozhye), the Party organisations paid insufficient attention to such important problems as the selection and training of men for executive posts, turning out skilled steel-workers, and the correct organisation of their work. Consequently, here, too, equipment was not used at its full capacity. The development of metallurgy was also hampered by delays in the construction of new blast and open-hearth furnaces and insufficient mining of iron-ore.

In the first half of 1940, the Central Committee of the Party adopted several decisions aimed at improving the work of the Donets coal mines and of the iron and steel industry. The Central Committee demanded that Party and economic organisations improve their political work among workers and managements, reinforce the leading sectors of these industries with technical personnel, secure an improvement in the skills of the workers and the correct organisation of their labour, bring system into the wages structure, and accelerate the building of new mines and blast and open-hearth furnaces.

Guided by these decisions, Party organisations began to devote greater attention to the organisation of production, the selection of people for Party and administrative posts and of engineers and technicians, and their appointment to suitable posts in production. While supervising the activities of the management of industrial enterprises, they sought to increase the responsibility of business executives for the fulfilment of Party and Government directives. As a result, the political work of the Party was linked more closely with the achievement of production targets, with the mastering of new technology and with stricter observance of labour discipline.

These measures taken by the Party brought about an improvement in the coal mining and iron and steel industries. In 1940 the coal output increased by 20 million tons, a record in the country's mining industry. By the end of 1940 the average daily output of metal had grown considerably as compared with 1937.

More and more people were drawn into Socialist emulation, which had developed under the leadership of the Party organisations. New forms of this movement came into being, such as the simultaneous tending of many machine-tools, high-speed work methods, the combination of trades, economy of raw materials and power, and the reduction of non-productive costs. Non-Party workers were drawn into this movement by the example of the Communists. On the initiative of Party organisations, conferences to discuss problems of production and technology were held at enterprises. The experience of innovators was pooled, and special schools teaching advanced methods of work were opened.

Of great importance in promoting a substantial expansion of industry in the pre-war years was the change from a seven to an eight-hour working day, a seven-day week and a ban on quitting a job at will. These measures, carried into effect by a decree adopted by the Presidium of the Supreme Soviet of the U.S.S.R. on June 26, 1940, on the request of factory, office and professional workers, were called forth by the urgent need to strengthen the country's defence. They had a positive effect on the work of enterprises: labour discipline improved, the productivity of labour rose and output increased. The important problem of providing industry with skilled manpower was being tackled, under the guidance of the Party, through the establishment of a system of State labour reserves. It was announced that there would be an annual enrolment (mobilisation) of young people for training at trade and factory schools. After finishing these schools the young workers were assigned to work at State enterprises. A constant replenishment of skilled labour for industry and transport was thus secured and this strengthened the country's economic and defensive might. The Soviet Government's law setting up labour reserves was received with great satisfaction by the whole Soviet people, and by young people in particular. They regarded it as a further manifestation of the Party's concern for the rising generation, who in the Soviet Union are given every opportunity of taking part in socially useful labour, acquiring knowledge and advancing science.

Women were playing an important part in industry. By the beginning of 1940 they accounted for 41 per cent of the total number of factory, office and professional workers. Twenty-five per cent of workers employed in building were women. Working women were successfully learning to operate up-to-date machinery. The drawing of women into industrial production was of considerable importance for the country's economy and defence. Having learned men's skills during peace time, they could, in the event of war, successfully replace in industry the men called up to the armed forces.

In the pre-war years, thanks to the efforts of the Party and the working class, Soviet industry was able to surmount its shortcomings and to begin advancing. In 1940 the output of coal amounted to 166 million tons, of pig-iron about 15 million tons, of steel over 18 million tons, and of electric power 48,300 million kilowatt-hours. Such was the Soviet Union's industrial and economic base when it entered upon the Great Patriotic War.

With the uninterrupted increase of the country's industrial power as its goal, the Party never rested content with the successes achieved. In a situation where the threat of war was increasing, the work of industry was the *central* issue of the activity of the Party. It was closely examined at the Eighteenth Party Conference in February, 1941. The Conference discussed the tasks facing Party organisations in industry and transport. It was noted that, from the point of view of economy and technology, modern war was a war of engines and reserves. With this in mind, the Party adopted measures that would raise industry to the level required by the need to reinforce national defence. To achieve this, constant improvement of the management of industry by the People's Commissariats and Party organisations was imperative.

To bring management closer to the factories, many of the People's Commissariats were broken up into smaller units in 1939. New People's Commissariats were set up and put in charge of narrower fields. But this was not enough. There were serious shortcomings in the work of the People's Commissariats. They frequently calculated the fulfilment of the year's plan of output on the basis of over-all, summarised data, while in actual fact the plan was not fulfilled as regards key items of output. Party organisations and regional and town Party committees were still not paying sufficient attention to problems of industry and transport.

The Eighteenth Conference of the C.P.S.U.(B.) again drew the attention of Party organisations to *the needs of industry and transport*. They were given a number of concrete economic and political tasks. These were: to ensure constant supervision of the work of enterprises and their fulfilment of Party directives; to ensure strict stock-taking and maintenance of equipment, materials and all other property in industry and on the railways; to see that correct use was made of equipment and that thrift was exercised in the use of instruments, materials, fuel, and electricity; to introduce exemplary order and tidiness in industrial establishments; to get the latter to work at a steady pace and fulfil their plans in time; to secure the observance of strict discipline in the technological process itself, and ensure that output was of the best quality and in complete sets; to work without cease to improve and make certain of the mastering of new techniques; systematically to secure the reduction of costs, improved accounting methods and elimination of waste.

The Conference demanded consistent implementation of the principle of giving workers and managements material incentives for good work, new emphasis on the one-man management principle at enterprises and improvement of the technical guidance of production. With the purpose of improving Party leadership in industry and transport, posts of secretaries for the key industries and for transport were instituted in town, regional and territorial Party committees and in the Central Committees of the Communist Parties of the Union Republics.

The Conference adopted an economic development plan for 1941 which required an even bigger effort than the plan for the previous year. The purpose of this plan was to achieve a considerable strengthening of the country's defence potential.

The decisions of the Eighteenth Party Conference served as a powerful impetus to a further advance in all branches of the national economy, primarily of industry and transport.

The first six months of 1941 passed in unremitting efforts to attain a high rate of industrial development. By the middle of the year total industrial output reached 86 per cent of the figure envisaged for 1942 by the third Five-Year Plan.

In the conditions of the mounting war danger, the Party and the Government put ever greater emphasis on the development of the *defence industries.*

Prior to the Revolution Russia's war industry bore the stamp of the country's all-round economic backwardness. It lagged far behind the war industries of the developed capitalist countries. This was one of the reasons for the military defeats of tsarist Russia. Soviet power radically changed the situation. A modern defence industry that was a match for the war industries of the leading capitalist countries was built up on the basis of industrialisation. The first Five-Year Plan provided the U.S.S.R. with automobile, tractor, tank and aircraft industries. During the period of the second and third Five-Year Plans the Soviet defence industry was far ahead of the other branches of industry as regards the rate of increase of total output. In the three years of the third Five-Year Plan, the annual increment in volume of production for all industries averaged 13 per cent, while in the defence industry it was 39 per cent.

At enterprises that were of importance for the country's defence there were Party organisers appointed by the Central Committee, to whom they were directly accountable for Party work and who assisted them in their work. The people for these posts were selected by the C.C. from among leading Party workers who had had good technical training, had proved their organising abilities and could properly combine Party work with the settlement of production problems.

Defence enterprises were in a privileged position as regards supplies of raw materials, equipment, fuel, electric power, and so forth.

On the eve of the war, as a result of these efforts by the Party and its tireless concern for the development of the defence industry, the country had a large number of arms factories and other enterprises catering for the country's defence needs, at which during the war it was possible to organise mass production of tanks, aircraft, guns, munitions, and other armaments.

In spite of the undoubted progress of the defence industry, however, there were also serious shortcomings in it. The aircraft industry in the pre-war years fell short of its State targets. Some branches of the defence industry started the mass production of new types of armaments only on the very eve of the war, and this held up the equipment of the Red Army with modern weapons in the early stages of the war.

In the years preceding the war a reorganisation of the Soviet armed forces was carried out. Units and formations built up on the territorial militia principle were reorganised. The Soviet armed forces were now made up wholly of regular troops. The numerical strength of the army was considerably increased. The principle of building up the Soviet armed forces as a regular force was given legal shape in the new law on universal military service adopted by the Supreme Soviet of the U.S.S.R. in September, 1939. The Soviet State could not allow its army to be weaker than the armies of the capitalist States. Defence of the achievements of Socialism, and the success of the struggle for world peace, depended to a large extent on the strength of the Soviet Union and its armed forces.

5. The Party's Efforts to Consolidate the Collective-Farm System and Expand Agricultural Production

Agriculture, and collective-farm production in particular, came next in importance in the country's economy after industry. It was to play a big role in the third Five-Year Plan period in increasing popular consumption, especially the consumption of foodstuffs, 50-100 per cent. The expansion of raw material resources for the development of the light and food industries likewise depended on a further advance in agriculture.

But in the pre-war years agriculture was faced with serious difficulties, caused by the tense international situation and the threat of war hanging over the country. For instance, to complete the comprehensive mechanisation of agriculture, the collective and State farms needed a large number of tractors, harvester combines and other farming machinery. But part of the metal earmarked for the production of tractors and farming machinery had to be diverted to defence needs. During the period of the third Five-Year Plan the annual output of tractors, as compared with the previous five years, fell by 50 per cent.

For all that, the collective-farm system and the work that had been done by the Party and the Soviet Government to provide agriculture with machinery ensured its steady advance even in these difficult conditions. In 1940 the collective farms embraced 96.9 per cent of the peasant households and had 99.9 per cent of the crop area sown by the peasants. They were served by 7,000 machine-and-tractor stations. There were more than 4,000 State farms in the country. Altogether 531,000 tractors, 182,000 grain combines and 228,000 lorries were operating in the fields of the State and collective farms, and more than 1,400,000 tractor, combine and lorry drivers were employed for this huge fleet of machines.

Collective-farm development required the unremitting attention and everyday care of the Party. The prime task of the rural Party organisations was to strengthen the collective farms organisationally and economically. That much was clear to everybody. But not all the leading workers in agriculture had a correct idea of the ways and means of fulfilling this task. The principle of giving the collective farmers a material interest in the results of their work was often ignored, not enough was done to expand and consolidate the socially-owned property of the collective farms, and there was often a conciliatory attitude to self-seeking and individualist, private-property propensities.

All this gave rise to many other mistakes in collective-farm development, and retarded the growth of collective-farm production. To consolidate and develop the collective-farm system, the Party had consistently to implement the principle of giving the collective farmers a material incentive in their work, and to declare war on all self-seeking and individualist tendencies, which harmed the socially-owned economy of the collective farms.

The Party directed agriculture through the Party organisations in the collective and State farms and machine-and-tractor stations. With the development of the collective-farm system the Party organisations in the collective farms grew stronger. By the beginning of 1941 there were 62,300 rural Party organisations. Their responsibility for the development of collective-farm production increased considerably after they were given the right to verify the activity of collective-farm managements. The collective-farm Party organisations rallied round themselves all active collective farmers and drew the rural intelligentsia into their work. The Komsomol, a powerful force in the countryside, which at that time had a membership of more than two millions, was enlisted to help promote collective-farm development. Its organisations drew the rural youth into the work to strengthen the collective farms.

In the pre-war years the Party carried out many important measures to strengthen the foundations of the collective-farm system. One of them was the elimination of certain serious abuses in the use of collective-farm land. A draft decision of the Central Committee of the C.P.S.U.(B.) and the Council of People's Commissars of the U.S.S.R., "Measures to safeguard collective-farm land against squandering," was examined and approved at a C.C. plenary meeting held in May, 1939. The decision cited numerous cases of violation of provisions of the rules of the Agricultural Artel laying down the size of the household plots of the collective farmers, cases where such plots were illegally enlarged and where the collective-farm land had been squandered and alienated.

The question of the use of collective-farm land was inseparably bound up with the question of correctly combining the public and private interests of collective farmers. Enlargement of the household plots over the sizes established by the rules undermined the socially-owned economy of the collective farms and inflated the personal economy of the collective farmers. Frequently the household plot lost its character of a subsidiary enterprise and was turned into the collective farmer's chief source of income. At some collective farms these household plots became in practice the private property of the collective farmers, who disposed of them as they saw fit: leased them or kept them for themselves even if they were no longer working in the collective farm. Many sham collective farmers appeared who were not working in collective farms at all, or did just enough work to keep up pretences, devoting the greater part of their time to their personal subsidiary holdings.

All this hindered the growth of the productivity of social labour in the collective farms, undermined labour discipline and disorganised collective-farm production. Many collective farms began to suffer from an artificial shortage of manpower, although in reality it existed in abundance.

The Central Committee of the Party and the Government called on Party and local government organisations to introduce order into the use of collective-farm land. The socially-controlled land of the collective farms was proclaimed inviolable. The collective farms and collective farmers were forbidden to rent out household plots. Any enlargement of these plots, over and above the size established by the rules of the Agricultural Artel, was also forbidden. All excess land in personal use by the collective farmers was to be returned to the collective farms. After the household plots of the collective farmers and holdings of individual peasants and other citizens had been measured, it was found that there were over 6 million acres of excess land, of which 4¹/₄ million acres were added to the socially-worked lands of the collective farms and the rest turned over to their household allotments funds. In 1939-1940 over 800,000 collective-farm families living in outlying farmsteads moved to collective-farm settlements. An annual minimum number of workday units, depending on the character of agricultural production in the different regions of the U.S.S.R., was laid down for every able-bodied man and woman at the collective farms. The result of all these measures was that the use of collective-farm land improved, labour discipline was strengthened and more and more collective farmers began to fulfil their yearly workday quota.

Another big shortcoming in agriculture in this period was the lagging behind of livestock-breeding. On January 1, 1928, the cattle population was 60,100,000 in the various types of farms, and on January 1, 1939, it was 53,500,000. Effective measures had to be taken to promote livestock-breeding. Its development now depended chiefly on the establishment and enlargement of livestock-breeding departments in the collective farms. Some of the collective farms, however, either bred no cattle at all or kept very small herds. The restoration and development of animal husbandry at the collective farms depended directly on how the principle of giving the collective farms and collective farmers a material incentive to promote this branch of agriculture would be implemented.

In July, 1939, the Central Committee of the C.P.S.U.(B.) and the Council of People's Commissars of the U.S.S.R. adopted a decision on measures to develop socially-owned animal husbandry in the collective farms. This decision aimed at encouraging the development of animal husbandry by introducing a new system of assessing meat deliveries to the State. These deliveries were now assessed not on the basis of the actual herd at the collective farm, as had been the case before, but of the area of land used by the farm. The result was that nearly 200,000 livestock-breeding departments were set up in the collective farms during 1939 alone, whereas during all the preceding seven years 343,000 such departments were established. In 1939-1940 the herd of socially-owned cattle in the collective farms increased from 15,600,000 to 20,100,000 head.

The measures to promote animal husbandry helped to consolidate the collective farms. A collective farm with a developed livestock department was economically stronger than a farm that confined itself to grain production. At the same time these measures helped to solve another urgent problem, that of expanding livestock-breeding and thus ensuring the supply of foodstuffs to the population and of raw materials to industry.

The per hectare system of livestock produce deliveries justified itself. In March, 1940, a plenary meeting of the Central Committee discussed the question of making changes in the policy of deliveries and purchases of agricultural produce, and found it necessary to extend the *per hectare system* to all kinds of state deliveries. The old system, that was based only on the area sown to crops, was thereby abolished. Under the old system, the leading collective farms were at a disadvantage and discouraged from developing the commonly-run economy. The new system put all collective farms on an equal footing. It promoted the expansion of areas sown to various crops and the all-round development of agricultural production. It also created conditions for improving opportunities for the collective farms to plan their production on their own, from below. However, this principle of planning was not fully implemented in those years.

The consolidation of the Socialist system in agriculture enhanced the *planning and regulating role of the Soviet State* in the development of agriculture. The Party and the Soviet Government were now able to introduce a more correct regional distribution of crops, to encourage development of crops needed by the State. The advantages of planned Socialist agriculture were demonstrated by the expansion of the areas sown to industrial crops, which had increased in 1940 more than twofold as compared with 1913 (from over 12 million acres to over 29 million acres).

Cotton production grew considerably too. The area under cotton expanded from nearly $1^3/_4$ million acres in 1913 to over 5 million acres in 1940. The yield increased. While in 1913 the total yield of raw cotton was 744,000 tons, in 1940 it reached 2,237,000 tons. The needs of the Soviet textile industry were now met mainly by home-produced cotton, which was also required by the defence industry. Areas sown to such crops as flax, sunflower and sugar-beet were also considerably enlarged.

The shifting of grain crops from the southern regions to the east (Southern Urals, Siberia and Kazakhstan) also facilitated the expansion of areas sown to industrial crops. In the southern regions land was thus released for industrial crops. There were great expanses of good rich land in the east, including virgin and disused land, which could not be cultivated by the individual peasant. Now some collective farms disposing of a considerable number of agricultural machines began ploughing up these lands. The Central Committee put on record that the eastern regions could and should become one of the chief granaries of the Soviet Union.

The Party emphasised that the basic sector of agriculture was *grain production*, and that its development helped to solve all the other problems of agricultural expansion. The Party and its local organisations strove to raise the yields of grain crops and bring them into conformity with the potentialities of the collective-farm system. Local Party and Soviet bodies showed great initiative in this respect. On the suggestion, and with the active participation, of local officials measures were worked out to combat droughts in the south-eastern regions and to build up a new grain base in the east. On representations by the Central Committee of the Communist Party of Ukraine, the Central Committee of the C.P.S.U.(B.) and the Council of People's Commissars of the U.S.S.R. adopted at the end of 1940 a decision on bonuses to collective farmers for raising the yield of agricultural crops and the productivity of animal husbandry in the Ukrainian S.S.R. The system of bonuses instituted by this decision served as a stimulus for raising the productivity of labour; it was subsequently extended to other regions and districts of the Soviet Union.

Although the measures taken by the Party to raise grain production brought about certain successes, the grain problem in the country was not yet solved. There were quite a few backward regions and collective farms where grain yields were still low, and this told in the total grain harvest in the country. Although the total harvest in 1940 was somewhat higher than that in 1913, the country still needed more grain than was being produced. Grain requirements had grown for a number of reasons: by 1940 the urban population had more than doubled as compared with 1913; the development of animal husbandry also directly depended on grain production. Although intense efforts were made to enlarge State stocking and purchases, the grain procured could not satisfy all the country's needs.

Grain production under the collective-farm system could have developed more successfully had there been a more critical attitude towards the shortcomings in agriculture, above all in grain production. On the basis of the so-called biological estimate of the yield, it was considered that the annual total harvest figure had reached over 113 million tons, but in actual fact much less grain reached the granaries. Far from alerting the people engaged in agriculture and making them strive for higher yields, such exaggeration of the successes of grain production only served to lull them and bred complacency. Expansion of the grain crop area and particularly of wheat was to a certain extent also hampered by an over-zealous application of the lea-farming system in regions where it did not pay. Maize growing was underestimated in agricultural practice, although even in those years it could have added to the country's grain reserves and helped to develop animal husbandry. But the chief obstacle in the way of developing agriculture was the violation over a number of years of the principle of giving collective farmers and all workers in agriculture a material incentive to raise the output of agricultural produce.

However, notwithstanding all the shortcomings and errors in agriculture, the Party and its local organisations did a great deal in the pre-war years to consolidate this major branch of the national economy. That was why Soviet agriculture was able to withstand the severe stresses of the war years, and to provide the army and the country with the necessary quantities of food-stuffs and raw materials.

6. The Rise in Living and Cultural Standards of the Working People. The Growth in Political Power of the Soviet State. The Expansion of Party Membership

The development of material production in Soviet society is aimed solely at improving the welfare of the people and strengthening the power of the Socialist State. This is a law of the economic development of society in the period of building Socialism and Communism.

Now that Socialism was victorious and the exploiting classes had been liquidated, the material standards of the people rose continuously. This rise found expression in the growth of the national income and of the wages of factory and office workers, the bigger incomes of the collective farmers, the development of trade, increased building of houses and in improved amenities in towns and villages. The national income had grown from 96,300 million rubles in 1937 to 128,300 million rubles in 1940. The wage fund in the national economy, over the same years, had grown by 50 per cent. The turnover of State and co-operative retail trade had increased from 126,000 million rubles to 175,000 million rubles.

Incomes of the collective farms and collective farmers, in cash and kind, had also grown. The collective farmers supplemented their cash income considerably by selling their produce at the collective-farm markets.

The cultural standards of the peoples of the U.S.S.R. rose along with the improved material conditions. State allocations for social and cultural purposes in the budget of 1940 exceeded the 1938 figure by 16 per cent. In the 1940/41 school year, general elementary and secondary schools were attended by 35 million pupils, while places of higher education had a student body of over 800,000 (including correspondence students).

The continuous rise of the material and cultural standards of the people served to rally all strata of the population still closer round the Party and the Government, and to strengthen still further the alliance of the working class with the collective-farm peasantry. The political might of the Soviet State was further enhanced.

Soviet patriotism was a powerful source of strength for the Soviet Socialist State. The Party itself was a *genuinely patriotic force* in the country. Its interests lay in constantly serving its people and its country. The idea of serving the country was inseparably bound up with the efforts to build a Communist society.

Love for one's country, pride in its people, the desire to accomplish feats that would bring it glory—all this manifested itself most strikingly in the Soviet Union, especially in the conditions of victorious Socialism. For the first time in history man had a fatherland where he felt he was the complete master of his destiny. How could he not love and glorify it! To strengthen it by one's deeds and defend it self-sacrificingly from foreign attack was the sacred duty of every Soviet man and woman.

Soviet patriotism harmoniously combined the national traditions and interests of all the peoples of the U.S.S.R. with the common vital interests of the multi-national Soviet State—the Union of Soviet Socialist Republics, the common Socialist Motherland of all its peoples. It was the patriotism of new, Socialist nations, forming a single federal State in which all peoples enjoyed equal rights and exploitation of man by man had been abolished. Soviet patriotism went hand in hand with proletarian internationalism. The patriotic deeds of the Soviet people were not aimed at disuniting the peoples but at strengthening their friendship and helping the working people of all countries in their struggle for peace, democracy and Socialism.

In pre-war years, a broad patriotic movement swept the country on the labour front. The Party and the Government gave this national movement every support. In 1938 the title of Hero of Socialist Labour—the highest distinction for achievement in labour—and the medals "For Labour Valour" and "For Labour Distinction" were instituted. A characteristic feature of the patriotic deeds of Soviet people was that by their example they inspired others to perform similarly glorious deeds. For instance, in 1938 the famous woman tractor-driver P. N. Angelina called for a hundred thousand girls to "mount the tractor." About two hundred thousand women responded to her patriotic appeal. Examples such as this could be cited by the thousand.

Soviet people performed heroic deeds in the name of their country. The famous Arctic drift of the ice-breaker *Georgi Sedov*, with its crew of fifteen, lasted for over two years. The long nonstop flights of Valeri Chkalov and other Soviet pilots brought glory to their country. Soviet Polar explorers also distinguished themselves. Ardent patriots were reared in the Red Army and Navy and among the frontier guards, who became heroic defenders of their Socialist country. Under the guidance of the Communist Party the Leninist Komsomol reared many thousands of strong, courageous and staunch patriots.

Correct implementation of the Leninist nationalities policy, and the all-round development of the non-Russian Republics, also served to enhance the might of the U.S.S.R. Under the new Constitution the Azerbaijan, Armenian and Georgian Soviet Socialist Republics, which had made up the Transcaucasian Federation, became Union Republics and individually entered the Union of Soviet Socialist Republics. The Kazakh and Kirghiz Soviet Autonomous Republics were also made Union Republics. Communist Parties of Kazakhstan and Kirghizia were formed. During the years of the third Five-Year Plan, the Socialist nations made great progress. This was facilitated by the economic, political and cultural measures taken by the Soviet State to promote the maximum development of industry, agriculture and culture in the Union and Autonomous Republics. Ukraine, Byelorussia, Transcaucasia and the Republics of Central Asia made great headway in their economic and cultural development. Even peoples who had been the most backward in the past felt the beneficial influence of the country's Socialist industrialisation and the collectivisation of agriculture. They were drawn into the common channel of economic and cultural progress of the peoples of the U.S.S.R. This was seen in the progress made by a number of Union Republics in their industrial development. The total output of large-scale industry had grown between 1913 and 1940 7-fold in the Uzbek S.S.R., 20-fold in the Kazakh S.S.R., 27-fold in the Georgian S.S.R., 153-fold in the Kirghiz S.S.R. and 324-fold in the Tajik S.S.R. Once actual inequality between the peoples of the U.S.S.R. was done away with, friendship between them, a powerful source of might and strength of the Soviet State, was further consolidated.

Other factors that served to strengthen considerably the political, economic and defensive might of the Soviet State and to raise its international prestige, in those years, were the entry into the Soviet Union of new Socialist Republics—Lithuania, Latvia, and Estonia, and the reunification of Western Ukraine with the Ukrainian S.S.R., of Western Byelorussia with Soviet Byelorussia and Bessarabia with Soviet Moldavia. Entry into the great family of free peoples, as represented by the Soviet Union, basically changed the historical development of the peoples of these republics and regions.

Great social transformations in the new republics and regions, aimed at improving the life of the working people, were started immediately after the establishment of Soviet power there. These transformations were carried out under the direct leadership of the Communist Parties of Ukraine, Byelorussia, Moldavia, Lithuania, Latvia and Estonia, with the most active assistance of the central Party and Government bodies of the Soviet Union. The Communist Parties of Ukraine, Byelorussia, Moldavia, Lithuania, Latvia and Estonia started out on a vast programme of ideological education of the working people in these republics, who had freed themselves from capitalist slavery and established Soviet power. A great deal was being done to train leading workers in government, Party and economic affairs from among the local population. The work of the Party apparatus and government machinery was improved.

At the request of the Communist organisations of the new republics, they were incorporated in the Communist Party of the Soviet Union. The Communist Parties of Lithuania, Latvia and Estonia were admitted to the Communist Party of the Soviet Union in October, 1940. In February, 1941, the Moldavian regional Party organisation was reorganised into the Communist Party of Moldavia. Communist organisations were formed in Western Ukraine, Western Byelorussia and Bessarabia after they entered the Soviet Union. Members of the Communist Parties of Poland, Western Ukraine, Western Byelorussia and Rumania who remained on the territory of the Ukrainian, Byelorussian and Moldavian S.S.R., were transferred to membership of the C.P.S.U.(B.).

The victory of Socialism in the U.S.S.R. and the successful achievement of the targets of the first years of the third Five-Year Plan had a beneficial effect on the life of the Party. Its ties with the people grew stronger, and the influx of the best, most advanced members of Soviet society into the Party increased. Between April 1, 1939 and June 1, 1940, 1,127,802 people became candidate members of the Party, and 605,627 joined it as full members.

In their majority, the new members were the best representatives of the working class, collective-farm peasantry and intelligentsia. They were advanced workers in industry and agriculture, innovators and inventors, scientists and technicians, doctors and teachers, workers in culture and the arts, engineers and agronomists, men and officers of the Soviet armed forces.

The establishment of a common procedure for admission to the Party of workers, peasants and intellectuals, and the granting to town and district Party committees of the right to take final decisions in the matter, served to increase Party membership. But this imposed greater responsibility on Party committees and local Party organisations for selecting the best representatives from among the workers, collective farmers and intellectuals. It had to be kept in mind that during a mass influx of new Party members the infiltration of unworthy people was not excluded. Nevertheless, in certain Party organisations the pursuit of numbers was accompanied by violations of the Leninist principles of Party enrolment. There were cases of people who had been accepted without a proper check-up and who turned out to be unworthy of membership. Some town, district and primary organisations adopted the harmful, over-simplified procedure of considering applications in bulk at one sitting, without carefully and thoroughly examining each. The decision on admission to the Party was, in such cases, reduced to a mere formality.

Many regional, town and district Party committees made but a superficial study of those to be accepted, and did not give proper attention to regulating the growth of the Party. It happened not infrequently that there were few workers in the key trades among new members admitted to town Party organisations, and few collective farmers, tractor-drivers and combine-operators in rural organisations.

The Central Committee of the Party proposed a number of measures to ensure the strict implementation of the principle of individual selection of new members. It was demanded that each application be thoroughly examined and carefully verified; that particular stress be laid on enrolling new members from among workers of key trades and among engineers and technicians in industry, and collective farmers, tractor-drivers, combine-operators and intelligentsia in the countryside. Regional and territorial Party committees, and the Central Committees of the Communist Parties of the Union Republics, were required systematically to supervise the growth of Party organisations and regularly to discuss questions relating to the admission of new members.

Party organisations were instructed to pay more attention to the *training in the Bolshevik spirit* of new members, and to attach greater importance to the candidate member's period of probation as a serious test for him. They were to examine the political views and working abilities of the candidates, and to help them study the programme, rules and policy of the Party.

After the Eighteenth Congress, the Party organisations improved the ideological and political education of their members, as well as Party propaganda. The educational work of the Party was based on the study of the decisions of the Eighteenth Party

Congress and the history of the Communist Party. Particular attention was paid to the ideological and theoretical education of leading Party officials. The network of schools and refresher courses for Party workers was considerably enlarged.

The study of the history of the Party heightened people's interest in the classical works of Marxism-Leninism. In view of this the Central Committee took measures considerably to increase the publication of Marxist-Leninist literature.

On the eve of the Great Patriotic War the Party was a powerful organisation of nearly four million members. It directed all spheres of the life and activity of the Soviet State, and was in the lead of the efforts of the Soviet people to complete the construction of Socialist society and begin the gradual transition to Communism.

BRIEF SUMMARY

The period from 1937 to 1941 was the beginning of a new stage in the history of the U.S.S.R., the stage when the construction of Socialism was completed and the gradual transition to Communism began. The features of the international situation of those years were an aggravation of the general crisis of capitalism, an extension of imperialist aggression by the fascist States, the outbreak of the second world war, and an increasing danger of war for the Soviet Union.

The Party, the Government and the Soviet people, working to consolidate and develop Socialist society, tackled the basic economic task of the U.S.S.R., which was to overtake and surpass the most developed capitalist countries in output per head. This found expression in the growth of the country's industrial power, in the development and consolidation of the collective-farm system and in the rise of the material and cultural standards of the peoples of the U.S.S.R.

The Party and the Soviet State did all in their power to avert war. The Soviet Union worked actively to organise collective resistance to fascist aggression. This, however, did not depend on the U.S.S.R. alone, but also on many other States, who did not join in these efforts and did not render the Soviet Union the necessary support. The mounting war danger faced the Party, the Soviet Government and the people with the urgent task of strengthening the country's defensive capacity.

The victory of Socialism brought about an unprecedented upsurge of creative initiative of the whole people. This initiative was aimed at consolidating and developing Socialism in all spheres of life. The Party, guiding the creative activity of the masses, took a number of steps to extend Soviet democracy on the basis of the new Constitution of the U.S.S.R. The leading role of the Party in all spheres of the life of Soviet Socialist society was also considerably enhanced.

The most significant event of this period was the Eighteenth Congress of the C.P.S.U.(B.). It set new targets for Communist construction in conditions of victorious Socialism, rallied the ranks of the Party, and called all Soviet people to fresh efforts to achieve these targets. The Congress evolved new organisational forms of Party work that conformed more closely to the new conditions of the life and activity of the Party. The Eighteenth Congress elaborated some important and urgent problems of the Marxist-Leninist theory of the Socialist State. The Congress considered in great detail the question of the Soviet intelligentsia which was of great political and theoretical importance. The work of the Party to educate its members in the spirit of Marxism-Leninism was improved.

The Party carried out a tremendous programme of consolidation of the Soviet State. The alliance of the workers with the peasants became still stronger, and the friendship between the peoples of the Soviet Union still closer. The formation of new Soviet Republics on the western boundaries of the Soviet State, and their entry into the Soviet Union, signified a new milestone in the historical development of these Republics and served to increase the political, economic and defensive might of the U.S.S.R.

In those years great progress was made in carrying out a cultural revolution in the U.S.S.R.; a large body of Soviet intelligentsia came into being, particularly in the non-Russian Soviet Republics. The practical inequality of the peoples of our country which had previously existed in various spheres of life was done away with.

CHAPTER FIFTEEN

THE PARTY IN THE PERIOD OF THE GREAT PATRIOTIC WAR

(June 1941-1945)

1. Fascist Germany's Treacherous Attack on the Soviet Union. The Soviet People and All the Resources of the Country Mobilised to Repulse the Enemy. Formation of the Anti-Hitler Coalition

On June 22, 1941, fascist Germany, without declaring war or even presenting any claims, attacked the Soviet Union with the object of overthrowing the Soviet system and enslaving the Soviet people. She committed that treacherous act despite the existence of the Soviet-German non-aggression treaty.

The German fascist invaders counted on routing the main forces of the Red Army in a short time, destroying the major industrial centres of the U.S.S.R., paralysing the Soviet people's will to resist, overrunning the territory of the Soviet Union right up to the Urals in six to eight weeks and winning the war before winter came.

The plan of these adventurers for a *blitzkrieg* was based on the supposed weakness of the Red Army and on the assumption that the Soviet social and political system was unstable and so were the alliance of the workers and peasants and the friendship of the peoples of the U.S.S.R. The Hitlerites also counted on isolating the U.S.S.R. internationally and involving Britain and the U.S.A. in the war against the Soviet Union.

Despite its utterly reckless character, the Hitler war plan was fraught with grave danger for the Soviet Union. The Soviet people had to break off their peaceful labour and mobilise all their forces to repulse the enemy and defend their Socialist country. A *new period* began for the Soviet State—*the period of the Great Patriotic War*. It was the most terrible war that the peoples of our country had ever had to experience throughout their long history.

The early war months were a particularly severe ordeal, for the Red Army was sustaining heavy losses and had to retreat deep inland under the impact of superior enemy forces.

The German fascist troops had been massed at the western frontier of the U.S.S.R. well in advance, and had taken up initial positions for the offensive along a vast front extending from the Barents to the Black Sea. Shock enemy troops, which included a large number of armoured and motorised divisions, started the offensive in three main directions: 1) from East Prussia through the Baltic Republics to Leningrad; 2) from the area north-east of Warsaw to Minsk, Smolensk and Moscow; and 3) from the Lublin area to Zhitomir and Kiev, and then on to the Donets coalfield. The first surprise blows of the Hitlerites were borne by the Soviet frontier troops. It was only in some sectors of the border area that the advanced units of regular Red Army troops entered into battle too. The enemy troops, which were superior in strength, were advancing in all the main directions on vital centres of the Soviet Union. By the beginning of July, 1941, they had seized Lithuania, a large part of Latvia, Western Byelorussia and part of Western Ukraine.

How did it come about that the enemy was able to capture a considerable part of Soviet territory during the early weeks of the war?

It cannot be said that the Soviet Union was unprepared for war. In fact, the Communist Party, knowing the habits of the imperialists, and aware of their hatred for the Soviet Union, had taken steps during the years of peaceful construction to strengthen the country's defensive capacity, and had warned the people of the necessity of preparing for defence. Under the pre-war Five-Year Plans, a powerful material and technical basis had been built for the defence of the country, thanks to the Leninist policy of industrialisation and collectivisation. The Party had also concerned itself with strengthening the Red Army, Navy and Air Force. The Red Army had been completely reorganised in the pre-war years; its numerical strength had been increased, its armament and equipment considerably reinforced and its combat training improved.

All that notwithstanding, fascist Germany at the beginning of the war had a number of advantages over the Soviet Union, which accounted for the unfavourable course of military operations for the Red Army. These advantages may be listed as follows:

1. Germany attacked the U.S.S.R. after having seized almost the whole of Western Europe with its economic resources. Her war industry, consequently, had a more powerful material and technical basis at the beginning of the war than the Soviet war

industry. To cite an example, in 1940-1941 the annual output of steel, pig-iron and coal in Germany and the countries she had brought under her sway was more than double the output in the U.S.S.R. Besides, Germany had placed her economy on a war footing long before the war, while the Soviet economy had been serving the needs of peaceful construction. And although the Soviet Union had a powerful war industry, there was no large-scale production of arms. Moreover, certain industries, such as the tank and aircraft industries, were only just mastering the production of new types of armament. All these circumstances gave Germany a numerical, and in the case of some types of weapon a qualitative, superiority in the early period of the war.

2. Fascist Germany attacked the Soviet Union at a time when her land forces in Europe were no longer involved in hostilities, and she was engaged only in naval and air operations against Britain. She was thus able to fling the bulk of her land and air forces against the U.S.S.R. Furthermore, she had the direct support of Italy, Finland, Rumania and Hungary, where reactionary fascist governments were in power. As for the Soviet Union, it had to fight single-handed at first. Besides, it was threatened by Japan, which had massed a large army in Manchuria and Korea in spite of the Soviet-Japanese neutrality treaty concluded in April, 1941. An appreciable Soviet force had therefore to be diverted for the protection of the Far Eastern frontier.

3. Before attacking the Soviet Union, Germany had massed along the western frontier of the U.S.S.R. a huge invasion army totalling 190 divisions, including 153 German divisions that had almost two years' experience in modern warfare, involving the use of large masses of tanks, aircraft and other arms. The Red Army was not concentrated at the frontier, and lacked adequate experience in modern warfare. Its re-equipment had not been completed. It was short of well-trained and experienced officers, a considerable number of them having been unjustifiably relieved of their commands in 1937 and 1938.

4. Lastly, the suddenness of the German attack was an exceedingly important factor.

To be sure, the attack did not come as a complete surprise to the U.S.S.R. The Party, the Government and the Soviet people knew that despite the Soviet-German non-aggression treaty, fascist Germany would start a war against the U.S.S.R. sooner or later. While realising the threat of aggression on the part of fascist Germany, and preparing the country and the armed forces for defence, the Soviet Government abided strictly by the terms of the non-aggression treaty, so as not to give the ruling circles of Germany the slightest pretext for violating the treaty and committing aggression. It was only when large German fascist forces began to concentrate at the western frontier of the U.S.S.R. that the Soviet Government took a number of preventive measures to repel a possible enemy invasion. The neutrality treaty with Japan, signed in April, 1941, enabled the Soviet Government to move some military units from the interior of the country to reinforce the country's western defences. At the same time the Soviet Government drew up and adopted a mobilisation plan to convert industry to war production during the second half of 1941 and in 1942.

But as the very first days of the war showed, these measures proved to be belated and inadequate for beating off the onslaught of the enemy's huge army. One of the reasons for this situation was Stalin's misappreciation of the strategic situation on the actual eve of the war. Stalin, who exercised supreme leadership of the country and the Party, had reliable information on the concentration and deployment of the German fascist troops at the western frontier of the Soviet Union, and of their preparedness for an invasion of the U.S.S.R. But he considered such reports to be provocations. He believed that they were aimed at inciting the Soviet Government to take steps which could be used by Hitler as a pretext for violating the non-aggression pact. The enemy, he thought, would then have started a war against the Soviet Union in a situation unfavourable to it, and would have had grounds for blaming the war on the Soviet Union. To deprive Hitler of any pretext whatsoever for attacking the U.S.S.R., Soviet troops were not instructed to deploy and take up defence positions along the western frontier in anticipation of attack.

Fascist Germany's treacherous attack on the U.S.S.R. gained her a temporary military advantage, but it also had adverse consequences for her, because it exposed her as a blood-thirsty aggressor in the eyes of the whole world. The freedom-loving nations branded the perfidious action of German fascism. The Soviet Union, on the other hand, won the sympathy and support of the whole of progressive mankind. It became the focus of the forces of a powerful anti-Hitlerite coalition. This was a tremendous political gain for the U.S.S.R. and a loss for fascist Germany. But its beneficial effect for the Soviet Union did not tell until much later in the war.

Profiting by the advantages he had gained as a result of his surprise attack and greater military preparedness, the enemy advanced rapidly eastwards. The fascist occupation of a large part of Soviet territory that included major industrial centres, and the destruction or capture by the enemy of a large number of Soviet aircraft on the airfields and of tanks, guns, and arms and munition depots, placed the Soviet Union at a still greater disadvantage in the early months of the war.

In these circumstances the Red Army, pressed by the enemy, had to fall back, abandoning villages and towns. But even as they retreated, the Soviet troops offered stubborn, heroic resistance, inflicting considerable losses on the enemy. The Soviet Command strove to halt the enemy advance at all costs, cover the vital centres of the country, bleed the enemy white, gain time to deploy the armed forces and place the national economy on a war footing, and wrest the strategic initiative from the enemy.

The Communist Party was the organiser, and inspirer of the Soviet people and its armed forces in the war against fascist Germany. It bent all its energies to the armed defence of the Socialist Fatherland, to put up an effective resistance to the fascist aggressors and rout them.

Fully conscious of its historic responsibility for the destiny of the Soviet country and for the cause of Socialism, the Central Committee displayed unflinching courage and Bolshevik skill in overcoming enormous difficulties and mobilising all the forces of the Party and the people, all the country's resources, to defeat the enemy. In the war that had begun, the Party was at the *head of the people*.

On the very first day of the war, the Central Committee of the Party and the Soviet Government called on the Soviet people to close their ranks behind the Party and the Government, and to rise up for a victorious patriotic war against the fascist aggressors, for the honour and freedom of their country.

On June 30, 1941, a *State Defence Committee* was formed by a joint decision of the Central Committee of the Party, the Presidium of the Supreme Soviet and the Council of People's Commissars of the U.S.S.R. Stalin was appointed its Chairman. *All power* in the Soviet Union was vested in the State Defence Committee, which co-ordinated the activities of all State institutions and all Party, Komsomol and trade union organisations, and directed the constructive effort of workers, collective farmers and intelligentsia for the defeat of fascist Germany.

The Party and the Government exposed fascist Germany's criminal plans in the war against the U.S.S.R., defined the tasks of the people and the armed forces in the defence of the Socialist Fatherland, and worked out a programme for resisting and routing the enemy. This programme was laid down in the directive of the C.C. C.P.S.U.(B.) and the Council of People's Commissars of the U.S.S.R. of June 29, 1941, to Party organisations and local government bodies in the front-line areas. It was also set forth and elaborated by Stalin, Chairman of the State Defence Committee, in a radio address on July 3, 1941.

The Party and the Government pointed out that fascist Germany had launched a predatory and unjust war, a war of conquest. The German imperialists were out to destroy the Soviet State, restore the rule of the landlords and capitalists in the U.S.S.R., deprive the free peoples of the Soviet Union of their national statehood and culture, and turn Soviet people into slaves of the German imperialists. The Hitlerites planned to dismember the Soviet Union, to sever Estonia, Latvia, Lithuania, Byelorussia, Ukraine, Crimea, the Caucasus and the Volga region from it and annex them to Germany, or turn them into German colonies. "In the war, against fascist Germany that has been forced upon us," said the directive, "the issue is one of life and death for the Soviet State, of whether the peoples of the Soviet Union shall be free or fall into slavery."

Unlike fascist Germany, the Soviet Union was waging a war of liberation, a just war. The aim of the Soviet people in the patriotic war was to uphold the honour, freedom and independence of their Socialist country, to defend the world's most progressive social and political system—the Soviet system—and the national culture and statehood of the free peoples of the U.S.S.R. Their other aim was to help the peoples of Europe to throw off the tyranny of the German imperialists and restore their national independence.

Underlining the terrible danger created by fascist Germany's attack, the Party and the Government stressed that, in the war that had begun, "everything depends on our ability to organise rapidly and to act without losing a minute's time, or missing a single opportunity in the struggle against the enemy."

To avert the dread danger threatening the country, and then to defeat the enemy, the Party called on Soviet soldiers and all Soviet people:

1. To realise the full gravity of the danger, to forget peacetime sentiments and have done with complacency and carelessness.

2. To fight the fascist enslavers selflessly and courageously, defend every inch of Soviet soil, display bravery and valour and be fearless in battle.

3. To strengthen the rear of the Red Army, and within a short time to put on a war footing the work of all institutions, organisations and factories, start mass production of arms and military equipment, and organise a ruthless fight against all who sought to disrupt the home front—spies, saboteurs, panic-mongers, cowards and deserters.

4. To organise all-round assistance to the Red Army, ensure its intensive reinforcement, the rapid transport of troops and military supplies and the uninterrupted delivery of everything required by the front; and to organise extensive aid to the wounded.

5. In the event of a forced withdrawal of Red Army units, to remove all valuable property or, if that were impossible, to destroy it.

6. To organise partisan units and sabotage groups in the areas seized by the enemy; and to set up in advance underground Party organisations that would direct all the activities of Soviet patriots in the enemy rear.

7. To form, after the example of Moscow and Leningrad, people's volunteer units in every town threatened by enemy invasion.

In the hour of severe trial the Communist Party declared the Socialist Fatherland to be in danger, as it had done in the grim year 1918, and called on the people to rise in defence of the country, to devote all their energies to a selfless struggle against the enemy, to the crushing of fascism.

The people responded whole-heartedly to the Party's call. In the stern times that had come, they showed the greatest confidence in the Party and the Government and gave them their undivided support. They displayed unexampled heroism on the war and home fronts.

The mobilisation of reservists, announced by the Government, proceeded apace throughout the country. Along with the mobilised, thousands of people of different ages and occupations reported at the military commissariats, asking to be sent to the front as volunteers. Communists set an example. Leading Party workers, Soviet executives, men of science, art workers, Party members exempt from military service and even pensioners applied for active military service. On the home front, people were working with redoubled energy at the factories, machine-and-tractor stations, collective and State farms. Their motto was *"All for the front and for victory."* Many hundreds of thousands of people joined civil defence units, and tens of thousands of women volunteered for front-line service as nurses.

Drawing on the economic power of the country, the Party and the Government rapidly reorganised the national economy to meet war-time needs. In compliance with the directives of the C.C. of the Party and the State Defence Committee, the country's resources and reserves were redistributed to supply the armed forces. Many civilian enterprises were switched to war production. Transport was geared to the service of the front and to the speedy evacuation of industrial plants from threatened areas deep into the interior to the Urals and Siberia. Party organisations at the factories rallied the workers, engineers and technicians for a rapid change-over to war production. Key shops were reinforced with Communists and skilled workers. Communists found and quickly put to use all the reserve equipment installed in ancillary shops or kept in storage. A drive was started in industry to save raw materials, materials in short supply and electric power, and to restore discarded tools. It became a patriotic tradition with all those working on the home front not to go home until they had fulfilled their assignment for the day.

The forced withdrawal of the Red Army confronted the country with an extremely difficult and complicated task, namely, that of transferring from the western areas to the east many hundreds of industrial enterprises and the more valuable property of the machine-and-tractor stations, State and collective farms. During the first six months of the war the equipment of more than 1,360 large industrial enterprises, of paramount importance to the country's defence, were removed from the western areas to the east. It was a movement of people and equipment unparalleled in history. In record time the Party organisations of the western districts and regions threatened by enemy invasion organised the dismantling, loading and dispatch of equipment, often under heavy enemy fire. The Party organisations and Soviets of Working People's Deputies in the eastern regions and districts where the evacuated enterprises arrived displayed great ability in installing them on their new sites, starting production and providing tens of thousands of workers and other employees and their families with living quarters.

Thousands of Communists, including those who had arrived with the evacuated plants, went to work at the new construction sites. Tens of thousands of people of the most varied occupations joined them at the call of the Party organisations. The Party's organising and political work at the building sites ensured the development of mass emulation and exceptional labour enthusiasm. Workers did not leave the building sites for days at a stretch, working in rain, frost and blizzard. The result was that many of the evacuated enterprises resumed production very shortly after their arrival at the new sites.

The evacuated plants found themselves cut off from their suppliers and allied enterprises. The Party organisations, working together with the local authorities and economic institutions, rapidly discovered requisite raw materials, semi-manufactured goods and other materials on the spot, ensuring the uninterrupted production of arms and munitions on an increasingly vast scale. They organised assistance by one plant to another to expedite war production.

The war economy plan for the fourth quarter of 1941 and for 1942, adopted by the C.C. of the Party and the Council of People's Commissars of the U.S.S.R. on August 16, 1941, for the Volga region, the Urals, West Siberia, Kazakhstan and Central Asia, was of great importance in organising and starting war production in the eastern areas. The plan provided for a considerable increase in the production of arms, munitions, tanks, aircraft, aircraft engines, pig-iron, steel, non-ferrous metals, oil, electricity and coal, and for the reconstruction or expansion of the main railway junctions, stations and tracks in the eastern areas.

The conversion of many light industry factories to war production, and the occupation of a considerable part of the country's territory by the enemy, led to a sharp drop in the production of consumer goods, including food. On the other hand, war conditions led to an increase in the number of people who depended on the State for supply. The Government was therefore compelled to restrict the sale of foodstuffs and manufactured goods by introducing rationing.

The entire organisational, ideological and political work of the Party was directed towards mobilising the people to defeat the enemy. Outstanding Party and Government leaders, Party and local government functionaries, scientists, cultural workers and propagandists took a direct part in political work among the masses. Every day hundreds of thousands of agitators spoke at factories, collective and State farms, in State institutions and military units, explaining current events. This everyday political agitation at the factories was closely tied up with fulfilment of orders for the front. The agitators' talks were illustrated with graphic posters and short, trenchant slogans.

The Party explained to the people the Leninist doctrine of the nature and character of wars, their relation to the social and political system, the tasks of the war and home fronts in fighting the enemies of the Soviet country, the tasks of the people and the armed forces in defending the Socialist Fatherland. It helped the people to understand the just, liberating character of the Great Patriotic War, to see the advantages of the Soviet social and political system, the decisive role of the alliance of the workers and peasants and of the friendship of the peoples of the U.S.S.R. and of Soviet patriotism in defending the country and achieving victory over the enemy. It imbued Soviet men and women with the spirit of the great ideas of Marxism-Leninism, of the revolutionary traditions of the peoples of our country and the fighting traditions of the Red Army, and inspired them with confidence in victory.

Throughout the war the Party knew no hesitation or differences: it acted as a closely-welded organisation, as a single militant union of like-minded people, united under the banner of Leninism. Thanks to its ideological and organisational unity, the Party was able rapidly to reconstruct its work to meet wartime requirements and to rally all Soviet people under its banner.

At the beginning of the war the Party had a membership of about 3,800,000. There were more than 170,000 primary Party organisations, closely connected with the masses, in factories, in agriculture, in the Red Army and in other institutions. They tirelessly carried on organisational and political work among the masses, ensuring the prompt fulfilment of Party and Government directives to mobilise the whole people in the war effort. They roused the people to feats of labour, and helped the military authorities to carry out mobilisations, train reserves for the front, and arrange for the universal compulsory military training of the working people introduced by the State Defence Committee on September 18, 1941. With the help of the Party organisations, the military authorities formed military units, equipped them with arms, which in many cases were manufactured locally, and sent them to the front.

The central, regional and district committees of the Communist Parties of Ukraine, Byelorussia, Moldavia, Lithuania, Latvia, Estonia, the Karelo-Finnish Soviet Socialist Republic, and of the regions of the Russian Federation invaded by the Hitlerites, helped the Soviet Command in organising the defence of the bigger cities and important defence lines. The Party organisations of Smolensk Region, for example, brought out over 500,000 people for the construction of defences during the battle of Smolensk. They organised the evacuation of industrial enterprises, livestock, and the more valuable property of collective and State farms and machine-and-tractor stations. In accordance with Central Committee directives, they formed underground Party organisations and partisan units in the areas seized by the fascists. The Party organisations in threatened districts and regions arranged in advance for part of the Communists and Komsomol members to go underground, formed sabotage groups and partisan units, and set up arms, munitions and food depots in the forests. Leadership of the underground Party organisations and partisan units was entrusted to the staunchest Party, government and Komsomol workers.

The Party carried out immense work in the Red Army and Navy, to which it assigned its foremost members. Stalin was appointed head of the armed forces of the U.S.S.R. Almost one-third of the members and alternate members of the Central Committee were at the fronts. Prominent Party leaders—N. S. Khrushchov, D. Z. Manuilsky, A. S. Shcherbakov, K. Y. Voroshilov and A. A. Zhdanov were placed in key positions in the armed forces. M. I. Kalinin, President of the Presidium of the U.S.S.R. Supreme Soviet, worked indefatigably to mobilise the people for the defeat of the fascist invaders. A. I. Mikoyan and N. A. Voznesensky, members of the State Defence Committee, A. A. Andreyev,

Secretary of the Central Committee of the Party, and N. M. Shvernik, Chairman of the All-Union Central Council of Trade Unions, headed key branches of the national economy and ensured that the Red Army's requirements were fully met.

By decision of the Central Committee of the Party, about 48,000 leading Party, government, trade union and Komsomol workers were sent in the early war months to reinforce the army and navy. Hundreds of thousands of Communists were called up or volunteered for active service. The members of Party organisations in the front-line districts joined the armed forces almost to a man. By the end of 1941 there were about 1,300,000 Communists serving in the army and navy. Those called up for service under Party mobilisation were sent to the crucial sectors of the front, where the fighting was heaviest and where there was a need for courageous organisers capable of inspiring the men for feats of valour by their own example.

The Komsomol was an active helper of the Party. 900,000 Komsomol members joined the Red Army in the early days of the war.

Front and army Military Councils were set up. They included experienced Party leaders—members and alternate members of the Central Committee, secretaries of the Communist Parties of Union Republics, and of territory and regional Party committees. Among them were L. I. Brezhnev, N. A. Bulganin, N. G. Ignatov, J. E. Kalnberzinš, A. I. Kirichenko, A. A. Kuznetsov, V. P. Mzhavanadze, M. A. Suslov and others. They were in constant contact with the Central Committee of the Party and the State Defence Committee, whose directives they put into effect with the support of the Party organisations in the armed forces. Political departments formed under the Military Councils directed the Party's political work among the troops.

In the middle of July, 1941, the post of military commissar was instituted in the Red Army and Navy. This measure was prompted by the necessity of reshaping the entire political work of the Party in the armed forces so as to organise direct assistance to officers in strengthening military discipline and carrying out combat tasks. Military commissars were all the more necessary because a large number of the army officers came from the reserve, lacking experience in political work in the armed forces and could therefore not cope with their duties. The Party appointed as military commissars experienced Party workers, who in most cases also had the necessary military training. With the support of the Party-political staff and army Party organisations, the military commissars raised the authority of the commanders and helped them to execute combat tasks. They educated the men in the spirit of supreme devotion to and love of the country, and of burning hatred for its enemies. They helped to strengthen revolutionary order and military discipline and raised the morale of the troops. By setting examples of personal valour, the commissars inspired the men with courage and confidence. Great credit is due to them for consolidating the Red Army and raising its fighting efficiency in the early, and most difficult, period of the war.

The Communist Party roused and led the entire Soviet people in a sacred patriotic war. It ensured the building up and reinforcement of the armed forces, and organised work on the home front to supply the needs of the armed forces. It thereby created the most essential internal prerequisites for achieving complete victory over fascist Germany and her satellites.

The wise Leninist foreign policy of the Party and the Government in large measure contributed towards creating an international situation most favourable for winning the war. Of the very greatest importance in this respect was the formation of the anti-Hitler coalition, which resulted in the isolation of the bloc of fascist States.

Fascist Germany's expectations of isolating the U.S.S.R. internationally and drawing Britain and the United States into an anti-Soviet war was shattered in the very first days following her attack on the Soviet Union. On June 22, 1941, the British Government declared its readiness to render assistance to the Soviet Union in the war against Germany, and on June 24, the U.S. Government made a similar statement. Two of the world's biggest capitalist countries thus came to be in the same camp as the U.S.S.R. in the struggle against German fascism.

How did it come about that Socialist and capitalist countries joined forces in the war against Germany? The fact is that the acute contradictions existing even before the war between the bloc of fascist States and the alignment of imperialist Powers consisting of Britain, France and the United States were aggravated in the course of the war. Germany had overrun almost the whole of Western Europe by the time she attacked the U.S.S.R., and now threatened the British Isles with invasion. There was no force in the capitalist world capable of halting the fascist hordes, let alone of defeating them. It was evident to all, including the ruling circles of Britain and the United States, that the Soviet Union was the only real force that could break the backbone of the Hitler army and bar fascist Germany's way to world supremacy. Under those circumstances, it was in the interest of Britain and the United States to ally themselves with the Soviet Union against the common, and extremely dangerous, enemy that fascist Germany represented.

Thus the acute contradictions between the two imperialist

alignments proved to be a peculiar kind of reserve factor in the Soviet Union's fight to rally all progressive forces for the defeat of fascist Germany and her accomplices.

The American and British imperialists did not cease to be enemies of Socialism even though they had joined the anti-Hitlerite coalition. In fact, many of them made no attempt to conceal their hostile attitude to the U.S.S.R. They counted on Germany and the Soviet Union exhausting each other in the war. U.S. Senator Truman, who subsequently became President of the United States, said on the day after fascist Germany's attack on the Soviet Union: "If we see that Germany is winning we ought to help Russia and if Russia is winning we ought to help Germany, and that way let them kill as many as possible." Moore-Brabazon, British Minister of Aircraft Production, expressed similar ideas at the beginning of the war.

The attitude of the governments of Britain, the United States and other capitalist countries was also greatly influenced by the powerful movement in support of the U.S.S.R. started by broad sections of the population all over the world. Big meetings and demonstrations expressing solidarity with the Soviet Union were held in many countries, including Britain and the United States. The masses demanded that their governments should fully support the Soviet Union in the war against German fascism.

Thus by the end of 1941 an anti-Hitlerite coalition, made up of the U.S.S.R., Britain and the U.S.A., had come into being. It was joined by the peoples of Poland, Czechoslovakia, Yugoslavia, France, Belgium, the Netherlands, Norway and other countries occupied by the Hitlerites. It was also joined by China, whose peoples had been waging a heroic struggle against imperialist Japan ever since 1937, and by the British Dominions and several other countries. It was a powerful alliance of nations which had united to fight the fascist invaders, an alliance enjoying the sympathy and support of all democratic anti-fascist forces.

The members of the anti-Hitlerite coalition were pursuing different aims in the war. Unlike the U.S.S.R., and contrary to the interests of the broad masses of their peoples, the ruling circles of Britain and the United States did not aim at defeating German fascism completely. They had no intention of liberating Germany and other countries from the rule of reactionary forces. They were out primarily to eliminate Germany and Japan as dangerous competitors in the world market. But in spite of this, by fighting jointly with the Soviet Union against a common enemy—the bloc of fascist States—Britain and the United States objectively contributed to the victory over fascist Germany and her accomplices.

The war-time foreign policy of the Communist Party and the

Soviet Government served to strengthen the fighting alliance of freedom-loving nations, which intended to defeat the bloc of fascist States and free the European nations subjugated by the German fascists.

2. The Failure of the Hitler *Blitzkrieg* Plan. The Rout of the German Fascist Troops Near Moscow

Already the very first weeks of the fighting on the Soviet-German front made it clear to the German fascist invaders that the war against the U.S.S.R. differed radically from the one they had waged in Western Europe, where they had hardly encountered any serious resistance. Their successes in the West were due not only to the weakness of the West European armies and to the superiority of the Hitlerite army. They were also due to the subversive activities of internal reaction, which, fearing its own people, took the path of national betrayal, siding with the enemy and helping Hitler to establish a fascist regime in Europe. Nothing of the kind happened, nor could happen, in the Soviet Union.

The Great Patriotic War of the Soviet people against fascist Germany was not an ordinary war between two armies or two States. It was a life-and-death struggle between the new social system—Socialism—embodied in the Soviet Union and the most reactionary imperialist State, as embodied in Hitler Germany with her fascist regime. Not only the Soviet people, but the whole of progressive mankind were interested in winning that war.

History had never known of a liberation war in which the interests of the people and the State fighting the enemy had fused so completely as they did during the Great Patriotic War. The civil war waged by Russia's workers and peasants against the interventionists and Whites in 1918-1920 had revealed the close bond between the Soviet State and the masses of the people, who gave their unqualified support to the State of the dictatorship of the proletariat. But at that time there were still exploiting classes in Soviet Russia, and the invaders and Whites were therefore able to engineer counter-revolutionary conspiracies and kulak revolts behind the Red Army lines.

Unlike the Civil War, the Great Patriotic War was waged at a time when Socialism had triumphed in the Soviet Union: there were no longer any exploiting classes in the country, and the enemy had no social basis on which he could rely to organise any revolts in the Red Army's rear. The Socialist system which had firmly established itself in our country assured the moral and political unity of Soviet society. The dread danger threatening the country served still further to strengthen that unity, the alliance of the workers and peasants and the friendship of the peoples of the U.S.S.R. From the very outset the war against fascist Germany became a patriotic war of *the entire Soviet people* against the German fascist invaders.

In the very first weeks of the war, the Red Army proved to be much stronger than the Hitlerites had expected. Wholly devoted to the people, it had the full support of the country, which supplied it with manpower, arms, munitions and food and raised its morale. Despite their early military reverses, the Soviet troops were strong in their staunchness and valour. Realisation of the just nature of this war of liberation and of the vital necessity of defending its Socialist Fatherland, cemented the Red Army and gave rise to heroism on a mass scale.

"In any war," said Lenin, "victory depends in the final analysis on the morale of the masses that shed their blood in the battlefield. The conviction of the justice of the war, and the realisation of the need to sacrifice their lives for the good of their brothers, raises the morale of the soldiers and makes them bear unprecedented hardships" (*Collected Works*, Vol. 31, p. 115).

In the fighting against the German fascist invaders, entire Red Army units displayed exceptional bravery, heroism and resourcefulness. The enemy came up against unshakable staunchness and courage on the part of the Soviet troops. A vivid instance of the patriotic valour displayed by Soviet soldiers in the early war days was the defence of the fortress of Brest. The small Soviet garrison under Captain I. N. Zubachov, Regimental Commissar Y. M. Fomin and Major P. M. Gavrilov was surrounded in the old citadel of the fortress. For more than 20 days, it courageously beat back the furious attacks of an enemy many times superior to it in numbers and armament. "I am dying but not surrendering. Farewell, my homeland!" says one short, moving inscription found in the ruins of one of the barracks in the fortress. When the Hitlerites were already near Smolensk, battles were still raging on the bank of the Western Bug, deep in their rear.

The history of the Great Patriotic War has recorded many similar examples of heroic resistance by individual Red Army units and garrisons. Even those units which found themselves encircled as a result of the swift enemy advance continued to fight valiantly. They either broke out of encirclement or went over to partisan warfare, striking at the German fascist invaders from the rear.

Soviet soldiers also distinguished themselves by many individual acts of bravery in the grim initial period of the war. The exploit of Squadron Leader Nikolai Gastello, a Communist, became a symbol of heroism. In his blazing bomber he dived into a column of enemy tanks and tank-cars. The terrific explosion and ensuing fire destroyed several tanks and their crews.

Heroic deeds became a standard of conduct with most Soviet soldiers.

The resistance of the Soviet troops steadily grew, while the pace of the enemy offensive steadily slackened. More and more often Red Army units launched counter-attacks and dealt the enemy powerful blows.

In the north-western sector the Hitlerites drew near to Leningrad in August, 1941, hoping to capture the city by storm. But troops of the Red Army and the Baltic Fleet, as well as the population of Leningrad, rose in a wall to defend the city. The Leningrad Party organisation directed the defence of the city. At the Party's call, about 160,000 people joined people's volunteer divisions. Nearly 70,000 members of the Leningrad Party organisation went to the front. Their example breathed new strength into the defenders of the city and raised their firmness and courage. Hundreds of thousands of Leningrad people, mostly women, took part in building defences. The factories worked uninterruptedly for the front, despite shelling and air raids. In the middle of September, 1941, the forces of the Red Army and the Baltic Fleet, vigorously supported by the population, halted the enemy on the immediate approaches to the city. The Hitler plan to capture Leningrad and use the troops on his Leningrad front to strike at Moscow was foiled.

Stubborn fighting continued also in the south-western sector. For more than two months the Soviet troops kept superior enemy forces pinned down at the approaches to Kiev, the capital of the Ukrainian S.S.R. It was only on September 20, 1941, when the Hitlerites, after seizing the whole of Ukraine on the right bank of the Dnieper, threatened the Kiev group of the Red Army with encirclement, that Kiev was relinquished by the Soviet forces.

At the beginning of August, 1941, German and Rumanian troops broke through to the Black Sea coast and closed in on Odessa in a semi-circle. Displaying supreme courage and tenacity, units of the Red Army and the Black Sea Fleet repulsed the attacks of an enemy who commanded an overwhelming numerical superiority. The Odessa Party organisation led the population in the defence of the city. About 100,000 people took part in putting up fortification works, and over 10,000 joined the detachments and fighting squads formed in the factories for street barricade fighting. For 68 days and nights battles raged near Odessa. The Soviet troops, repelling the enemy, launched counter-attack after counter-attack, and inflicted heavy losses on the Germans. The Hitlerite troops entered Odessa only after the Red Army and Navy units had withdrawn from the city on the orders of the Supreme Command, and the garrison and part of the population had been evacuated by sea to Sevastopol and the North Caucasus.

In the Crimean sector, the enemy succeeded at the end of September in breaking through the defences of the Perekop Isthmus. He bore down on Sevastopol with all his might. Soviet positions were stormed continuously, the city was bombed from the air and shelled with siege-guns. But the enemy could not break the morale of the city's courageous defenders, who beat off one attack after another. Shoulder to shoulder, soldiers, sailors and civilians, led by Communists, fought the enemy and worked at the defences. Fifteen thousand civilians joined people's volunteer units. Reinforcements flowed steadily from the city to the front. The overwhelming majority of the Communists left for the front line.

In the western sector, German fascist troops sought to cross the Dnieper on the march, capture Smolensk and then strike at Moscow. On July 10 began the battle of Smolensk, which lasted over two months. The stubborn defence and powerful counterblows of the Soviet troops, particularly in the Dukhovshchina and Yelnya areas, cost the enemy heavy losses and foiled his plans of a lightning advance on Moscow. The Hitlerites were compelled to halt 180 miles from the Soviet capital and go over to the defensive in order to regroup their forces.

In this way the valour and staunchness of the Red Army frustrated the Hitlerites' *blitzkrieg* plan. The enemy offensive was halted in all the major sectors.

But the Hitler Command, the heavy losses of its troops notwithstanding, did not give up its gambler's strategy. It wanted to capture Moscow and Leningrad at all costs before winter came, seize the whole of Crimea and reach the Caucasus. With that end in view, the Hitlerites in the autumn of 1941 resumed their offensive in all the principal sectors, aiming their main blow at Moscow. At the close of September some 80 German divisions, including 23 armoured and motorised divisions, were operating in the Moscow sector.

On September 30-October 2 the German fascists began their offensive against Moscow, striking at the flanks and centre of the main group of Soviet armies. The offensive proceeded at a rapid pace at first, and the Soviet forces again had to fall back a considerable distance. The enemy succeeded in breaking through into Moscow Region and reaching the distant approaches to Moscow.

The Soviet Union was now in the greatest danger since the beginning of the war. The enemy had drawn near the capital, and had encircled Leningrad on land. He had occupied Byelorussia, Moldavia, Lithuania, Latvia, Estonia, a large part of Ukraine, Crimea and the Karelo-Finnish Republic. The country was deprived of its iron and steel in the south and of the Donets and Moscow coalfields. A large number of the evacuated plants had not yet started operation. Total industrial output in the second half of 1941 was down to less than half the pre-war level. Transport was operating under a terrific strain. All these factors caused serious difficulties in supplying the armed forces with arms and munitions.

Incredible suffering had fallen to the lot of Soviet people in the areas temporarily occupied by the enemy. The Hitlerites set up a regime of bloody terror wherever they went. They sacked and destroyed towns and villages, factories and collective farms, and removed all valuable factory and machine-and-tractor station equipment, as well as grain and livestock, to Germany. They turned schools, colleges, clubs and libraries into barracks, committed outrages against the civilian population in town and country, tortured and put them to death, introduced convict labour conditions for the working people and deported hundreds of thousands of civilians to Germany.

The Communist Party and the Soviet Government called on the people to defend every inch of Soviet soil to the last drop of blood, halt the enemy at all costs, strike a crushing blow at him on the approaches to Moscow and destroy the shock force of his armies. The Party called on the people to render the fullest assistance to the Red Army units defending the capital.

The appeal of the Party and the Government brought a ready response from the people. The defenders of Moscow displayed matchless heroism in repelling the numerous enemy attacks. The Party organisations in the Volga region, the Urals, Siberia and other areas ensured the continuous operation of the plants and railways that supplied the armed forces. Workers, engineers and technicians began to produce more for the front, collective farmers to deliver more farm produce. Railwaymen accelerated the transport of troops and military supplies to the front. On the initiative of Party organisations in the Urals and Siberia, new regiments and divisions were formed which were joined by worker volunteers, primarily Communists, and hurriedly dispatched to defend the capital.

As the enemy approached Moscow, he met with the growing resistance of the Soviet troops. At the end of October the German fascist troops were halted on the lines they had reached after capturing Mozhaisk and a part of Kalinin and moving up to Naro-Fominsk and Tula.

Moscow put up a stubborn defence. Preparations for resisting the enemy on the approaches to the capital had begun well in advance—in the summer. The Moscow Party organisation did a great deal to strengthen the city's defences. Upwards of 100,000 Party and 260,000 Komsomol members of Moscow and Moscow Region went to the front. A meeting of activists of the Moscow Party organisation, held on October 13, set the Communists the task of grimly defending the capital, of organising and leading its people, and turning it into an impregnable stronghold. One hundred and twenty thousand Muscovites, half of them Party or Komsomol members, went to the front line as people's volunteers. Workers' Communist detachments were formed in Moscow. Local civil defence squads, numbering over 24,000 Moscow volunteers, were on duty day and night, ready to defend factories, institutions and houses. More than 500,000 women, youths and girls took part in building defences on the approaches to Moscow. The city's factory workers engaged in war production worked selflessly day and night, not leaving their machines even during the fascist air raids. On the initiative of Komsomol members at the Stalin (now Likhachov) Automobile Works, the Orjonikidze Works and the Trekhgornaya Textile Mills, Komsomol and youth "front-line" teams were set up which overfulfilled output plans by not less than 100 per cent.

Soviet soldiers were learning to make expert use of their arms in field conditions and were accumulating military knowledge and experience. In the battles on the distant approaches to Moscow, the Soviet Guards units came into being. Using the most advanced methods of warfare, they carried on the finest traditions of the Red Army. The Soviet troops defending the capital were reinforced considerably by well-equipped and trained rifle divisions, tank brigades and artillery regiments sent from the deep rear. On the initiative of local Party organisations, many units were formed of volunteers. The air force was being reinforced too, and air supremacy in the Moscow area was gradually shifting to the Soviet side.

Despite the nearness of the front line, the traditional joint meeting of the Moscow Soviet of Working People's Deputies and representatives of the Party and other public organisations of the capital was held on November 6, 1941. Stalin reported on the 24th anniversary of the Great October Socialist Revolution. He pointed to the increased danger threatening the country. On behalf of the Party and the Government, he called on the people to work selflessly in support of the front; and proclaimed the objective to be to crush the military might of the German fascist armies and exterminate to the last man the fascists who had invaded the Soviet country to enslave its people.

On November 7, the traditional Red Army parade took place in Moscow's Red Square. Addressing the Red Army men, partisans and the Soviet people as a whole, Stalin said:

"The whole world is looking to you as the force capable of destroying the plundering hordes of German invaders. The enslaved peoples of Europe, who have fallen under the yoke of the

German invaders, look to you as their liberators. A great mission of liberation has fallen to your lot. Be worthy of this mission!...

"Under the banner of Lenin, forward to victory!"

The troops, equipped for battle, left the parade to go straight to the front.

In the second half of November the German fascist Command made another attempt to capture Moscow. Flung into the offensive this time were 51 divisions, including 20 armoured and motorised divisions. Heavy fighting broke out in the Volokolamsk and Tula areas, where powerful enemy groups tried to break through the Red Army lines and then encircle and take the capital. The Tula Party organisation roused the population to the defence of the town and the construction of defences. It helped the military command to form detachments of armed workers. Despite overwhelming superiority in strength, the enemy was unable to break the gallant resistance of the Red Army units and workers' detachments defending Tula.

On the near approaches to Moscow, Red Army units fought to the last for their country. The Soviet people will forever remember the feat of a unit of the renowned 316 Rifle Division under General I. V. Panfilov. About thirty Soviet soldiers, under Political Instructor V. G. Klochkov-Diyev, battled against 50 fascist tanks near Dubosekovo, on the Volokolamsk Highway. Almost all of them fell fighting, but they did not let the enemy through.

Powerful reserves of men and military equipment were built up thanks to the selfless efforts of the people and to the immense organising activity of the Party. They were swiftly moved to the front and concentrated on the flanks of the shock enemy forces in the Moscow area.

Great assistance was rendered to the Red Army in the operations near Moscow by the partisan movement organised by the Party. Hundreds of partisan units operated in the enemy-occupied areas. They harassed the fascists' rear, smashed up enemy convoys, destroyed railways and roads, cut communications, destroyed depots and bases and exterminated enemy manpower. They collected information necessary for the Red Army, attacked enemy detachments and annihilated them.

The valiant struggle of the Red Army, supported by the entire people, changed the relation of forces on the decisive sector of the front in favour of the U.S.S.R. and cleared the ground for a Soviet counter-offensive.

The Red Army undertook its first major offensive at the end of November and the beginning of December, 1941, when, after wearing out the enemy and bleeding him white, it halted him along the entire Soviet-German front. Soviet troops struck first of all at the enemy forces threatening Rostov-on-Don and Leningrad. As a result, the enemy's Rostov group was routed and Rostov-on-Don freed at the end of November. The enemy's Tikhvin group, which was threatening a junction with Finnish troops in order to encircle Leningrad completely, was defeated too. Tikhvin was liberated early in December. The victories at Rostov and Tikhvin strengthened the flanks of the Soviet troops and prevented the German fascist Command from transferring part of its forces from those sectors of the front to the vicinity of Moscow.

On December 6, 1941, the troops of the Western, Kalinin and South-Western fronts went over to the counter-offensive before Moscow. Fighting broke out with renewed force on a vast front 500 miles long, stretching from Kalinin to Yelets. By combined blows, the Soviet troops inflicted a heavy defeat on many enemy formations. In the middle of December the troops of the Western front routed the German fascist group threatening Moscow from the north and south and on December 30 freed Kaluga. On the South-Western front, the Soviet troops smashed the Hitlerites' Yelets group, freed Yelets, and pushed on towards Orel. The troops of the Kalinin front completely liberated Kalinin and advanced in the Rzhev sector.

In January, 1942, the Red Army launched a general offensive on a broad front, and in some places advanced more than 250 miles westwards. The Moscow and Tula regions, and dozens of towns and hundreds of villages in other regions, were liberated from the invaders. Simultaneously offensive operations were started in some other sectors of the Soviet-German front, namely, in the areas of the river Volkhov, Lozovaya-Barvenkovo and the Kerch Peninsula. These operations resulted in further enemy defeats.

The Red Army victory before Moscow was of immense military and political significance. For the first time since the beginning of the second world war the German fascist army had sustained a major defeat. In fierce battles the Red Army had wrested the strategic initiative from the enemy and routed his picked infantry and armoured divisions. The enemy air force, too, had suffered heavy losses. A decisive turn was taking place in the course of the fighting on the Soviet-German front. The Red Army had completely upset the Hitler plan of a *blitzkrieg* and exploded the myth of the invincibility of the fascist armed forces. Germany found herself faced with the necessity of waging a protracted war, something which Hitler had not bargained for.

The Red Army victory before Moscow inspired the European peoples enslaved by the Hitlerites to rise and resist the fascists with redoubled energy. The Red Army successes helped to consolidate the anti-Hitlerite coalition.

The victory before Moscow raised the spirits of the people and their armed forces, and inspired them with confidence in the inevitable defeat of fascist Germany. The Soviet people rallied still closer round the Communist Party for the fight until complete victory over the enemy.

3. The Heavy Fighting in the Summer of 1942. The Heroic Defence of Stalingrad

The victory over the German fascist troops before Moscow and the success of the Red Army offensive in the winter of 1941/42 showed that the Soviet Union and its armed forces had grown stronger than they were at the beginning of the Great Patriotic War. But this was not sufficient to break the backbone of the German fascist army and expel it from Soviet soil. The conversion of the entire national economy to war production had not yet had time to yield practical results. Many of the factories evacuated from the western areas were only just starting production. In the areas freed from the German fascist invaders, the factories and collective farms had been destroyed, and hundreds of thousands of Soviet people were left homeless. The art of modern warfare had not yet been acquired by the whole of the Red Army. The enemy was a mere 75 miles from Moscow. He still held strategically and economically important areas. Millions of Soviet people were languishing in fascist captivity. The people of besieged Leningrad were passing through hard times. The enemy continued to bomb and shell the city barbarously, and there was a severe shortage of food and fuel there. A sizable part of the Soviet armed forces had still to be diverted to the protection of the Far Eastern and southern frontiers in view of the hostile policy of the ruling circles of Japan and Turkey.

After the defeat sustained in the winter of 1941/42 fascist Germany and her army had become weaker than in the summer of 1941. But as she had at her disposal the resources of practically the whole of Europe, Germany was able to recover. The Hitlerites achieved a considerable increase in arms production. The fascist armed forces remained a strong and formidable foe, capable of launching a new offensive against the Red Army.

In 1942 the scale of the second world war was greatly extended. On December 7, 1941, Japan attacked Pearl Harbour, the U.S. naval base in the Pacific, without declaring war, and inflicted heavy losses on the U.S. Navy. The United States entered the war against Japan, and later against fascist Germany as well. The war became a real world war. By the beginning of 1942 the antifascist coalition comprised 26 countries, whose population made up the overwhelming majority of mankind. The manpower and material resources of that powerful coalition were considerably superior to those of the fascist bloc.

But even in those conditions the Soviet Union continued to bear the main brunt of the war. It had every right to demand military aid from its allies. Such aid could best be rendered by opening a second front in Europe, which would make it possible finally to change the relation of forces on the fronts in favour of the freedom-loving nations, hasten the defeat of the enemy and spare the lives of millions of soldiers and civilians. But this was not done.

An agreement had been reached between the U.S.S.R., Britain and the U.S.A. on establishing a second front in Europe in 1942. But the ruling circles of Britain and the U.S.A. meant to open such a front in 1942 only in the event of the internal collapse of Germany or an imminent military collapse of the U.S.S.R. In 1942, Britain and the United States undertook no major operations to ease the position of the Red Army, and confined themselves to local operations in North Africa and the Pacific.

Taking advantage of the absence of a second front, the German fascist Command made preparations for a new offensive against the U.S.S.R. By the spring of 1942, it had transferred dozens of fresh divisions from Western Europe to the Soviet-German front. The Hitlerites also obliged their allies to send fresh formations to the Eastern front. As a result there were 237 enemy divisions operating on the Soviet-German front in June, 1942, and as many as 266, including 193 German divisions, by the autumn of that year.

In May, 1942, after heavy fighting, German fascist troops captured the Kerch Peninsula, and prepared for a decisive offensive on the Southern front. A Red Army attempt to foil that offensive by striking a blow south-west of Kharkov ended in a major setback. Early in June, after a long siege, the Hitlerites resumed their assault on Sevastopol. The Red Army made a gallant stand, beating off from 15 to 20 attacks a day. On July 3, 1942, after 250 days of heroic defence, Sevastopol was evacuated on the orders of the Supreme Command. The defence of the city has gone down in the history of the Patriotic War as one of its most glowing chapters.

The Soviet reverses at Kharkov and in Crimea enabled the German Command to achieve a considerable superiority of forces on the southern flank of the front. But the main group of the enemy forces remained in the centre of the front, being spearheaded against Moscow.

Having seized the initiative, the German fascist troops took the offensive late in June. They broke through the Soviet defences in the Kursk-Voronezh sector and reached Voronezh. Coming up here against the stubborn resistance of the Red Army, the bulk of the enemy forces turned south to strike the main blow in the Stalingrad sector. After fierce fighting the Hitlerites crossed the Don and broke through to the Volga. By the middle of September the enemy had reached the outskirts of Stalingrad. There began the famous battle of Stalingrad. Simultaneously the enemy launched an offensive in the Rostov and then in the Caucasian sectors.

Thus in the summer of 1942 the Soviet Union again found itself in an extremely grave position. The enemy controlled a territory in which 45 per cent of the Soviet Union's population had lived before the war, and which had accounted for 33 per cent of the country's total industrial output and 47 per cent of the total crop area.

The Party and the Government instructed the Red Army to halt the enemy at all costs and ward off the danger threatening the Soviet Union. *"Not a step back!"* was the demand of the country, expressed in a Supreme Command order of the day. The officers, political workers and Communists in the armed forces impressed upon the men that there was now nowhere to retreat and that to withstand the blow of the enemy in the next period meant to assure victory. The example of the heroic battle of Moscow strengthened the confidence of the men that the Red Army was capable not only of resisting the onslaught of the invaders, but also of routing them. This required only unyielding tenacity and staunchness, still greater military skill and proficiency in handling military equipment, and iron discipline.

At crucial moments in the battle of Stalingrad, political talks were given and Party meetings held in the front line—in bunkers, shelters and the basements of destroyed houses. The glorious traditions of the legendary defence of Tsaritsyn (former name of Stalingrad) during the Civil War were recalled. At the Party meetings, Communists discussed past battles and experiences, and the latest political developments. These meetings were often broken off by enemy attacks, and the Communists attending them went straight into action at the head of the men.

The people of Stalingrad rendered the Red Army every assistance. When fighting was still going on on the distant approaches to the city, over 150,000 workers and collective farmers, including more than 2,000 members of the Stalingrad Party organisation, worked daily on the construction of defences. Thousands of Party and Komsomol members—Stalingrad factory workers, railwaymen, water-transport workers and students—joined the army at the call of the city's Party organisation. Upwards of 75,000 people of Stalingrad joined the armed forces and over 7,500 fought in people's volunteer units and anti-tank battalions.

The factory workers who remained in the city worked day and night despite the furious air raids, scorning death from enemy bombs. In those grim days the Stalingrad Tractor Works turned out dozens of tanks daily. The tanks started for the front line right from the works. Their crews were often made up on the spot, of the workers who had built them.

Trainloads of arms, munitions and food were sent to the valiant defenders of the heroic city from all parts of the country. This nation-wide assistance raised the men's morale. They defended the city with increasing stubbornness. The enemy advance was checked, and the enemy troops were bled white in fruitless attempts to capture the city.

Stalingrad was defended by the 62nd Army under General V.I. Chuikov. Supported by the 64th and other armies on the Stalingrad front, as well as the Volga Flotilla, the troops of the 62nd Army valiantly battled for every street and every house in the city.

The 13th Guards Division under General A.I. Rodimtsev daily repulsed 12 to 15 attacks by the enemy, who was trying to break through to the Volga. A Siberian division under L. N. Gurtyev beat off 117 attacks in one month. An army group under S. F. Gorokhov, which had been cut off from the main forces of the 62nd Army and pressed back to the Volga, fought heroically. Units of the division commanded by I. I. Lyudnikov, which had been pushed back to the Volga and half-encircled on an area of less than half a square mile, stood their ground and repelled all the attacks of a numerically superior enemy. Gun-boats and floating batteries of the Volga Flotilla helped by their fire to check the furious enemy onslaught. Under incessant fire, boats of the Flotilla transported tens of thousands of troops and thousands of tons of supplies from the left to the right bank of the Volga, and evacuated the wounded from the city. And everywhere Communists inspired the defenders of Stalingrad to heroic feats by their own staunchness and valour.

While the 62nd Army was beating off the attacks of the enemy in Stalingrad, other Soviet armies in the Stalingrad sector were striking blow after blow at the enemy, who was trying to break through to the city. The defence of the Stalingrad area was facilitated by Red Army operations elsewhere, particularly on the Don, South-Western, Western, Kalinin and Volkhov fronts.

By mid-November the German fascist troops, having lost at Stalingrad hundreds of thousands of men in killed and wounded and a large amount of war matériel, were obliged to go over wholly to the defensive. At that time the enemy offensive in the Caucasus had been stopped in the foothills of the Caucasus and on the approaches to the city of Orjonikidze.

A radical change was taking place in the course of the war, thanks to the correct policy and strategy adopted by the Party, its organising work on the home and war fronts, and to the labour and military feats of the Soviet people.

4. The Party Brings About a Radical Turn of the Tide in the Great Patriotic War

As a result of the extensive and complex organising activity of the Party on the home front, an efficient and rapidly expanding war economy was created by the close of 1942 and the beginning of 1943.

The conversion of industry to war production began to bear fruit towards the end of 1942. Thanks to the self-sacrificing efforts of the Party organisations and to the creative initiative and technical ingenuity of Soviet production engineers and workers, great progress was made in gearing factories that had been putting out peace-time goods to war production. Within record time, the metallurgical plants in the eastern regions mastered the production of all the types of ferrous and non-ferrous metals required for the manufacture of war equipment, arms and munitions. Most of the evacuated plants were now producing twice or three times as much war matériel as they had on their former sites.

New munitions, metallurgical, fuel and chemical plants, of decisive importance to war production, went into operation one after another. At Magnitogorsk, the workers led by the Party organisation built Europe's largest blast-furnace in four months. In 1943 and 1944 production was started at new metallurgical plants in Chelyabinsk and in Uzbekistan, at new blast-furnaces in Magnitogorsk and Nizhny Tagil, at an aluminium plant in Stalinsk, at a tractor plant in the Altai region and at other plants. At the same time, as a result of the organising work of the Party, the works in the major industrial centres, and primarily in Moscow and Leningrad, a considerable part of the equipment of which had been evacuated to the east, were also put into operation.

The unprecedentedly rapid reorganisation of Soviet industry, converted to war production within a year, was made possible thanks to social ownership of the means of production, to planned economy, the high technical standard of Socialist industry, the existence of a body of skilled workers, production engineers and technicians, competent organisers of production, and the wise leadership of the Party.

The temporary loss of the Donets and Moscow coalfields gave rise to enormous difficulties in supplying industry with fuel. At the Party's call, hundreds of thousands of people went to the forests to cut wood. Local sources of fuel were put to use. Coal mines were quickly put into operation in the Urals and in Siberia.

In 1942, the Central Committee of the Party took a decision on steps to improve Party work in the Kuznetsk and Karaganda coalfields, with a view to increasing coal output considerably. Simultaneously the State Defence Committee took urgent steps to increase coal output in the Chelyabinsk and Kizel coalfields. The Party organisations in Kazakhstan and in the Novosibirsk, Chelyabinsk and Perm regions carried out extensive organising work to achieve an increase in coal output. Thousands of Party members were transferred to work in the pits. Tens of thousands of collective farmers, housewives, pensioners and schoolboys of the upper grades went to work in the coal mines. Members of the Moscow and Tula Party organisations enlisted the people in restoring the pits in the Moscow coalfield liberated from the German fascist invaders. The result was that the country's coal output in December, 1942, was nearly 25 per cent larger than that of May, 1942.

The Party and the Government did much to supply industry in the eastern regions with power. On instructions from the State Defence Committee, new power stations were built in the Urals and in Siberia, and small factory power stations that had long been disused were restored and set going. The total capacity of the power stations put into operation in 1943 exceeded 1,000,000 kw.

In the spring of 1942, in response to the Party's May Day appeals, and on the initiative of the workers in the foremost works of the aircraft, tank and metallurgical industries, *Socialist emulation on a country-wide scale was started for the best fulfilment of war orders*, mobilisation of internal resources, economy in raw and other materials and lower production costs. The C.C. C.P.S.U.(B.) approved this initiative and, jointly with the State Defence Committee and the All-Union Central Council of Trade Unions, instituted challenge banners for winners in the emulation. The Party organisations at the factories, collective farms, machine-and-tractor stations and State farms headed the powerful patriotic movement. Millions of industrial workers, collective farmers and office and professional workers joined in emulation. The movement of "two-hundred percenters" (workers who fulfilled two production quotas a day—one for themselves and the other for a comrade at the front), which had started in the early war days, was expanding. At the height of the battle of Stalingrad, the foremost workers began to fulfil three to five production quotas a day by using new methods; and there were even those who fulfilled ten or more quotas.

Komsomol and youth "front-line" teams, which had first arisen during the battle of Moscow, became widespread. On the initiative of Komsomol members at the Moscow Ball-Bearing Plant, Komsomol and youth teams in many enterprises started a competition to fulfil production quotas with half the number of workers employed normally.

The devoted effort of workers, production engineers and technicians, combined with improvements in the organisation and technology of production, brought about a continuous increase in labour productivity, lower production costs and greater war output. By December, 1942, the over-all output of aircraft was 3.3 times that of December, 1941, aircraft engines 5.4 times, and of tanks nearly double. In 1943, war production increased, in comparison with 1940, as follows: in the Urals sixfold, in West Siberia 34-fold and in the Volga region 11-fold. Soviet fighting equipment was superior to the enemy's in quality.

Socialist industry owed its achievements largely to the fact that the Party had been able to solve the exceedingly difficult problem of training skilled workers to replace those who had left for the front. Factory and trade schools trained about 500,000 young workers annually. Over 6,500,000 people, who had come to the bench for the first time, were trained in the first two years of the war by the individual or team method, as well as at special courses or short-term schools.

The war confronted agriculture with great difficulties. As a result of the enemy's occupation of a vast territory in the west and south of the country, the whole burden of supplying food to the armed forces and the population and raw materials to industry had to be borne by the collective and State farms in the central and eastern regions. Most of the men—collective farmers, tractor-drivers, combine-operators and skilled workers at the machine-and-tractor stations and State farms—were in the armed forces. Besides, a substantial number of tractors, horses, and other means of traction had been diverted for the needs of the armed forces. The Party's organising work in the countryside was complicated by the fact that, with most of the Communists who had worked at the collective and State farms and machine-and-tractor stations away in the armed forces, the number of rural Party organisations had diminished almost by half, and in some regions even more.

By decision of the Central Committee of the Party, political departments were set up in the machine-and-tractor stations and State farms in the autumn of 1941, to carry on mass political work at the collective farms, machine-and-tractor stations and State farms. These departments, which existed till the summer of 1943, played an important part in raising the political consciousness and labour activity of collective farmers and machine-and-tractor station and State-farm workers. Of tremendous importance in organising agricultural production properly were the decisions adopted by the Council of People's Commissars of the U.S.S.R. and the C.C. C.P.S.U.(B.) at the beginning of 1942. They provided for an increase in the obligatory minimum of workday units which the collective farmers had to earn; material incentives for those who showed the best performance in agricultural production; the staffs and rates of payment, and the establishment of a bonus system in the machine-and-tractor stations; the procedure for mobilising the able-bodied urban and rural population for farm work at the collective and State farms and machine-and-tractor stations; the measures to be taken for the preservation of young livestock and for increasing the collective and State-farm herd. These measures helped to strengthen labour discipline in the collective farms and resulted in higher labour productivity. The annual average number of workday units earned by every able-bodied collective farmer increased by 50 per cent. At the collective farms, machine-and-tractor stations and State farms, hundreds of thousands of women took the place of their husbands, fathers and brothers as tractor-drivers or combine-operators.

In view of the sharp drop in the number of available tractors, Party organisations and local government bodies made use of local resources to cultivate and gather in the harvest from large areas of collective-farm land. The collective farmers' own draught animals were widely used for farm work. The Party organisations at industrial enterprises helped the machine-and-tractor stations to keep tractors and other farm machines in good repair.

Thanks to the all-out effort of the collective farmers and machine-and-tractor station and State-farm workers, the sown area in the regions that had not been occupied by the enemy increased by almost 12,500,000 acres in 1942 as against 1940. In the eastern regions, the area under grain crops increased by 5,750,000 acres in 1942. The Central Asian and Transcaucasian Republics of the U.S.S.R. which had had to be supplied with grain before the war, were not only meeting their own requirements, but were also able to supply grain to the State.

But this was not enough to make up for the enormous loss in food resources which the country had suffered as a result of the seizure of important agricultural areas by the enemy. That is why there was a serious food shortage in the country.

Transport workers moved troops, arms, munitions and goods on an unprecedented scale, and in exceedingly difficult conditions, for the length of railways had diminished by more than 40 per cent and the number of railway engines and trucks, river and sea-going vessels had decreased substantially. A number of important organisational and technical measures, taken by the Party and the Government, contributed to the successful operation of the railways. The traffic capacity of the major railway junctions and sections was increased, and more spur-tracks were laid for the industrial plants newly installed in the Urals, the Volga region and Western Siberia. New railway lines totalling 5,600 miles in length were laid during the war. Martial law was introduced on the railways. This strengthened discipline and helped to operate the railways with a greater efficiency.

Scientists and technologists made a big contribution to the defence of the country. A special commission of the Academy of Sciences of the U.S.S.R., numbering more than 800 scientists and technologists, rendered valuable assistance in making use of the resources of the Urals, Western Siberia and Kazakhstan for the war effort. Engineers and technicians worked out new technological processes and designed new war equipment. Medical workers made notable progress in the treatment of the sick and wounded, so that almost three-quarters of the wounded Red Army men and officers were able to rejoin the ranks on leaving hospital.

Cultural workers, too, did all they could to assist the front. Hundreds of writers worked as war correspondents. Both at the front and in the rear, Soviet people read trenchant political articles, patriotic stories, novels, plays and poems by prominent authors. Army songs by famous Soviet composers were sung in dug-outs and trenches, in workshops and in the fields. Teams of actors and whole theatre companies showed plays and gave concerts at the front line, often under enemy fire. Thus the Socialist culture of the Soviet people served the great cause of victory.

The ties linking the home and war fronts grew stronger, the population rendering increasing assistance to the Red Army. There started a *country-wide movement for the collection of funds to equip the Red Army*. Industrial, office and professional workers and collective farmers built tank columns, air squadrons, batteries and armoured trains with their own money. The working people of the Sverdlovsk, Perm and Chelyabinsk regions formed a Urals Volunteer Tank Corps, and out of their funds supplied it with tanks, arms and outfit. From December, 1942 to April, 1943, the population contributed over 7,000 million rubles to the Red Army Fund, and in four years their voluntary contributions totalled 94,500 million rubles. Workers, collective farmers and the intelligentsia sent their representatives to the front with trainloads of gifts for the defenders of the country. Every day the men at the front received thousands of letters from relatives and friends, who by their messages of love and affection made front life easier for the men and officers, and raised their morale.

Wounded Red Army and Navy men were surrounded with every care and attention. The number of blood donors greatly increased.

They gave over 800,000 litres of blood in the war years, and helped hundreds of thousands of men and officers to return to service.

In those painful days the people rallied round the Party closer than ever. The best Soviet men and women joined its ranks, the influx of new members increasing particularly whenever the situation at the front became critical. Over 198,000 people were admitted to the Party as candidate members, and upwards of 145,000 as full members, between the beginning of the Patriotic War and the end of 1941. In 1942 more than 1,368,000 people were admitted to the Party as candidate members and 573,000 as full members. The applications of those joining the Party testified that the applicants were aware of their increased responsibility and realised that the lofty title of Communist obliged them to be in the forefront of the defence of their Socialist country.

Thanks to the all-out war effort of the population, the fighting strength of the Red Army and its superiority over the enemy in forces and in means of warfare increased continuously. The re-equipment of the Red Army with first-class weapons was completed in the second half of 1942. Large formations of artillery, aircraft and armoured troops were formed. As a result of a series of measures taken by the Party and the Government, the field army steadily received fresh reinforcements of men who had undergone military training in the universal training system, voluntary sports societies or reserve units. The uninterrupted flow of fresh forces and weapons enabled the Supreme Command to build up powerful strategic reserves of troops, officer cadres, arms and munitions.

In hard-fought battles the Red Army commanders gained experience in the art of modern warfare, grew in stature and became seasoned politically. The military commissars carried out tremendous political work: they helped commanders to strengthen discipline, organise the troops more efficiently and carry out combat tasks. They, too, acquired battle experience. Many of them could, if need be, replace a commander at any moment.

When the armed forces had been fully provided with experienced leaders, there was no longer any need for military commissars. In October, 1942, the office of military commissar was therefore abolished and the principle of one-man responsibility re-established in the armed forces. The commanders were charged with all aspects of work among the troops, including political education of the men. The complete restoration of one-man leadership enhanced the authority of the commanders, strengthened discipline and improved the organisation of the troops.

The number of army Party organisations and their role in the strengthening of the Red Army grew steadily. During the first year of the war, the number of Party members in the armed forces increased threefold. In 1942 there were over 2,000,000 Communists, or 54.3 per cent of the total membership of the Party, in the Red Army and Navy.

Helped by its organisations in the armed forces and by officers who had improved their military skill in the course of the war, the Party encouraged all that was new and progressive, and resolutely combated all that stemmed from ignorance, stagnation and complacency on the part of those military leaders who disregarded the peculiarities of modern warfare, preferring to keep to old methods. All obsolete methods were banished from battle practice. Shortcomings in directing the troops, in staff work and in the co-ordination of the various arms of the service on the battlefield were persistently combated. Lulls between battles were generally used to perfect the fighting skill of troops and to master new weapons.

Thus the tremendous organising work of the Party on the home and war fronts, the selfless labour of Soviet people and the heroism of Red Army men helped *to lay a solid foundation for the defeat of the enemy.*

At the height of the defence of Stalingrad, Soviet troops began preparations for a counter-offensive. The Supreme Command massed large forces to the north-west and south of the city. Although the Soviet troops at Stalingrad were not superior to the enemy in numbers, they had gained, for the first time since the beginning of the war, a certain superiority in weapons, specifically in artillery, tanks and aircraft. Soviet troops were concentrated beforehand in powerful shock forces, the enemy's more vulnerable groups as their targets.

On November 19, 1942, the Red Army counter-offensive began at Stalingrad. Fighting hard, the Soviet troops broke through the enemy defences to the north-west and south of the city, routed the enemy's flank groups, and by the end of November had encircled 22 enemy divisions numbering more than 330,000 men. They followed this up by breaking through to the rear of the German fascist troops operating in the big bend of the Don. By skilful actions, the Soviet troops foiled the attempts of the enemy to rescue, from the direction of Tormosino and the middle reaches of the Don, his units encircled at Stalingrad. In December the enemy Command launched an offensive with a large force to the north of Kotelnikovo with the object of breaking through the encirclement and enabling the Stalingrad group to fight its way out. In the heavy fighting that ensued, the new shock group of German fascist troops was routed. The enemy was deprived of the last chance of reaching the troops surrounded at Stalingrad. In January and early February, 1943, the Soviet troops accomplished the task set before them by the Supreme Command, of eliminating the crack enemy forces encircled at Stalingrad.

The complete encirclement and annihilation of so huge an army was unprecedented in military history. It was one of the most outstanding military victories ever recorded. The successes of the Soviet forces and the defeat of the Hitlerites were evidence of the increased military skill of the Red Army and efficiency of its commanders, and of the superiority of the Soviet art of war over that of the German fascist troops.

The Stalingrad victory was a *turning-point* in the course of the Great Patriotic War and the whole of the second world war.

The defeat of the Hitlerite troops at Stalingrad undermined Germany's military might and her European rear, and sapped the strength and morale of her army. Fascist Germany was on the threshold of a grave crisis.

The Stalingrad victory enhanced the international prestige of the Soviet Union and strengthened the anti-Hitlerite coalition. At the same time, it weakened the military prestige of fascist Germany. As a result of the defeat suffered by their armies on the Soviet-German front, the political situation in Rumania, Hungary and Italy deteriorated. Finally, Japan and Turkey were compelled to abandon completely their intention of joining the war on the side of Germany against the U.S.S.R.

Following its counter-offensive at Stalingrad, the Red Army in the winter of 1942/43 launched an all-out offensive on the greater part of the Soviet-German front—from Velikiye Luki to the Caucasus range. It routed the German fascist troops in the North Caucasus and the Kuban area, and dealt the enemy a series of crippling blows in the area between the Don and the Northern Donets. The Hitlerites were hurled back 375 to 430 miles westwards from the Volga and the Terek. The Soviet armies dislodged the enemy from the key areas of Kursk, Rzhev, Vyazma, Gzhatsk, Velikiye Luki and Demyansk. They broke the blockade of Leningrad, and direct railway communication was established between the city and the rest of the country. The Soviet Union recovered economically and strategically important areas of the Caucasus and of the Rostov, Stalingrad, Kharkov and Kursk regions. *The mass expulsion of the invaders from Soviet soil had begun*. Millions of Soviet people were delivered from fascist captivity.

In the course of the offensive Soviet soldiers displayed outstanding valour and heroism, just as they had done earlier in defensive battles. Their heroism was exemplified by the feat of Private A. Matrosov, a Komsomol member. He did not hesitate to sacrifice his life by covering with his own body the gun-port of a pillbox from which the enemy was keeping up a deadly fire at his comrades.

The German fascist troops sustained heavy reverses in the winter of 1942/43. But the Red Army did not win its victories easily. The Soviet troops were worn out by incessant fighting, and it was difficult to maintain an uninterrupted flow of supplies to them in conditions of a winter offensive across territory laid waste by the Hitlerites. New airfields could not be built on time, and the air forces lagged behind the ground troops. Taking advantage of this situation, the Hitlerites in February launched a partial counter-offensive in Ukraine east of the Dnieper and in the Donets coalfield. They succeeded in recapturing Kharkov, which the Soviet troops had freed shortly before. It was in these circumstances that the Red Army stopped its offensive along the whole front at the end of March, and went over to the defensive. Both sides began preparations for the summer battles.

Despite the losses it had suffered, the Hitler Command decided to launch a new offensive on the Soviet-German front in the summer of 1943, this time with a limited force and in relatively small sectors, in the Orel-Kursk and Belgorod-Kursk directions. By that offensive, Hitler hoped to restore the shaken prestige of his armed forces and compel the Red Army to abandon offensive operations. The Soviet Supreme Command was likewise preparing for an offensive, but surmising that the enemy would attack, it simultaneously took the necessary steps to strengthen its defences.

"Total" mobilisation enabled the enemy to reinforce his thinned ranks, and even to form several new infantry and armoured divisions. As in the past, the operations of the German fascist troops on the Soviet-German front were facilitated by the absence of a second front in Europe. In spite of the formal and unqualified commitments assumed by the U.S.A. and Britain, no second front was opened in 1943 either. This enabled fascist Germany to continue transferring to the Soviet-German front divisions reinforced or formed in Western Europe. In the summer of 1943 the enemy massed 257 divisions against the Red Army. In the Orel and Belgorod areas, in the sectors where it was planning to strike its main blows, the Hitler Command concentrated a powerful shock force of 38 divisions, including 20 armoured and motorised divisions. For its strength in tanks, this force was considerably superior to the fascist troops which had advanced on Moscow in 1941 and on Stalingrad in 1942. Moreover, the enemy had a large number of new heavy "Tiger" and "Panther" tanks and self-propelled "Ferdinand" guns, on which the fascist generals pinned great hopes.

Hard as the enemy had tried to keep his plan secret, the Soviet Supreme Command gained information of it in good time. Although it had sufficient forces for an offensive, it nevertheless preferred this time to employ the tactics of active defence, in order to inflict irretrievable losses on the enemy's shock forces in defensive battles, and then to launch a counter-offensive with a view to utterly routing the enemy. Unlike the defensive battles of 1941 and the summer of 1942, the active defence at Kursk was not forced but deliberate, being undertaken in conditions favourable to the Red Army.

The Soviet troops built up a deeply echeloned defence. Large strategic reserves of troops and war equipment were massed to the east of Kursk and Belgorod.

By the time of the battle of Kursk, the Party organisations in the Red Army had been reorganised in accordance with a decision adopted by the C.C. C.P.S.U.(B.) on May 24, 1943. While formerly primary Party organisations had existed only at regimental level, they were now formed in battalions and in other similar units. As a result, Party leadership was brought closer to the company Party organisations and helped to extend Party influence to every individual private and NCO. The large body of Party activists, which had grown since the beginning of the war to more than 500,000, made it possible to cut the number of full-time political workers almost by half. Tens of thousands of political workers were appointed commanders. This strengthened the leadership of the armed forces and heightened its role in the education of the Soviet troops.

Political work among the troops assumed a vast scale. Talks were given on the battles ahead and the difficulties by which they would be attended. The men were reminded that there was still Soviet territory to be freed, where their countrymen languished in fascist captivity, looking to them for help. With the assistance of Party organisations, officers and political workers taught the men how to build trenches better, how to fight the new German tanks and carry on trench battles, to be staunch, cool, and resolute in combat with the enemy.

The German fascist offensive, which started on July 5, 1943, met with a crushing rebuff. The Soviet troops displayed exceptional tenacity and staunchness. The vaunted new tanks did not help the Hitlerites. In defensive battles the Soviet troops wore out crack fascist divisions and bled them white. The enemy offensive was foiled.

On July 12, 1943, the Red Army went over to the counter-offensive to the north and east of Orel. It then launched a counter-offensive in those sectors of the front where the enemy had just been attacking. The enemy, using positions prepared in advance and deeply echeloned, offered desperate resistance, but had to fall back under the pressure of the Soviet troops. The Soviet air force inflicted irreparable losses on the Luftwaffe in fierce air battles and gained complete and final air supremacy.

On August 5, or exactly one month after the beginning of the German fascist offensive, the Red Army liberated Orel and Belgorod. Thereby it exploded the Hitlerite legend that the Soviet troops were incapable of conducting a successful summer offensive.

The Kursk victory of the Red Army was of tremendous importance, for it *completed the radical turn* of the tide in the Great Patriotic War and in the second world war as a whole. The Red Army firmly retained the initiative in military operations. The German fascist Wehrmacht was on the brink of disaster.

The battle at Kursk marked the beginning of a powerful summer offensive, which the Red Army launched on a broad front extending from Nevel to the Sea of Azov. The Soviet troops pushed on, overcoming stubborn enemy resistance. As they advanced, they saw smouldering ruins where towns and villages had once stood, corpses of countless civilians and prisoners of war, whom the fascists had tortured to death or shot. The sight of Soviet people tortured to death by the fascists often gave rise to brief spontaneous meetings in the units. It filled the men's hearts with burning hatred for the enemy, and spurred them on to further feats of valour. The troops continued their offensive with redoubled energy. Among them were many men and officers whose relatives were on the other side of the front line, or had been driven away to hard labour in Germany. They were eager to be in action, and carried the others with them. The advancing troops sometimes came upon letters written by Soviet people languishing in fascist captivity. Those letters stirred the innermost feelings of the men, and aroused in them a compelling desire to press on and to liberate the ravaged Soviet soil and their countrymen from Hitler tyranny as soon as possible.

In the three months of the summer offensive of 1943, the Red Army in some places hurled the enemy as far back as 250 to 280 miles. It freed the Donets coalfield and the Taman Peninsula, and reached the Sivash and the Perekop Isthmus, the gateway to Crimea. It also freed Ukraine east of the Dnieper, Smolensk and Bryansk, and crossed the Dnieper. The Soviet troops displayed remarkable daring, skill and swiftness in overcoming that great water barrier, which the Hitlerites called their "eastern rampart." Over 2,000 men, officers and generals were awarded the title of Hero of the Soviet Union for the Dnieper victory. The Red Army began to rout the enemy on the right bank of the Dnieper, liberating Ukraine and Byelorussia. On November 6 Soviet troops fought their way into Kiev. By then almost two-thirds of the Soviet territory overrun by the enemy had been recovered.

Operations at the front were supported by the systematic blows struck by the partisans at the enemy's rear and communications. The feats of the Red Army inspired Soviet patriots in occupied territory in their struggle against the enemy. The partisan movement spread to ever new areas. The number and strength of partisan units grew steadily, whole Soviet families and even villages joining partisan units. More than 1,000,000 people took part in the partisan movement, which was particularly widespread in the occupied areas of the Leningrad, Kalinin, Smolensk and Orel regions, in Byelorussia and in Ukraine. Hundreds of thousands of partisans fought in the occupied areas of the Russian Federation, in Byelorussia and in Ukraine, and tens of thousands in the Baltic area. The partisans were constantly and selflessly supported by the entire population, which showed them every care and attention, providing them with shelter and food and forewarning them of danger. The partisan movement was a truly nation-wide movement. In its ranks were factory workers, peasants and office workers of all the nationalities inhabiting the country. Partisan warfare on such a vast scale was unprecedented even in the history of the Soviet people, who had a long record of guerilla warfare against foreign invaders.

The partisan movement was directed by the underground Party organisations which had been set up on instructions from the Central Committee in towns and district centres, at railway stations and in other important places occupied by the enemy. The underground organisations were headed by 26 regional and 539 town and district Party committee secretaries. The partisan detachments and brigades were commanded by the finest Party and government workers. Over 16 per cent of the total number of partisans were Party members. The experience gained by the Party in underground work among the masses during the long years of struggle against tsarism and capitalism, the Party's undisputed prestige among the people, fearlessness in the face of danger, utter devotion to the country and clear understanding of the aims of the war, and the people's rich traditions of partisan warfare against foreign invaders—all these factors helped to rouse the masses behind the enemy lines to a people's war against fascist Germany.

The Party organisations operating in the enemy rear did not confine their activities to the formation and leadership of partisan units. They carried on extensive political work among the population, put out newspapers and leaflets, tirelessly exposed the bloody crimes perpetrated by the fascist invaders, gave the true story of developments on the war and home fronts, and strengthened the faith of Soviet people in victory. Despite the fact that the Communists in enemy-occupied territory were constantly exposed to terrible danger, and despite all the difficulties of underground work, the Party organisations in the enemy rear grew steadily, the most devoted and courageous patriots joining them. To cite an example, the membership of the Byelorussian Party organisations operating in the enemy rear increased from 8,500 to 25,152 full and candidate members during the war.

Underground Komsomol organisations, too, operated in the enemy rear under the leadership of the underground Party organisations. The activities of the "Young Guard" in Krasnodon, the "Partisan Spark" in Nikolayev Region, the Lyudinovo organisation in Kaluga Region and the Komsomol organisations in Kaunas, at Obol station in Vitebsk Region and in other enemy-occupied areas were examples of selfless service to the country by the underground Komsomol organisations. Fighting courageously under Party underground leadership against the enemy, Komsomol members carried out sabotage operations, blew up trains, cut telegraph lines, freed Soviet soldiers from captivity and destroyed Hitlerites and traitors.

Direct leadership of the partisan movement and the co-ordination of the military operations of the partisan units and the Red Army were effected by the Central Partisan Staff set up under General Headquarters, on the instructions of the Central Committee of the Party on May 30, 1942. Partisan staffs were also set up in the Union Republics and regions of the R.S.F.S.R. occupied by the enemy. They operated under the direction of the Central Committees of the Communist Parties of the Union Republics and the respective regional Party committees.

At the height of the Red Army offensive in the summer of 1943, partisan units launched vigorous operations on the enemy's communications. They destroyed his headquarters, depots and troops. In the autumn of 1943 partisans in the course of two nights alone blew up over 1,400 miles of rail track. The enemy's railway traffic was disrupted, and freight reduced by 35 to 40 per cent. Partisans often seized river crossings and held them till Red Army units came up. The partisan formations under S. A. Kovpak, M. I. Naumov and others struck powerful blows at the enemy in Western Ukraine by decision of the C.C. C.P.S.U.(B.).

The partisan units diverted large enemy forces. There were partisan territories and Soviet districts in Byelorussia, Ukraine, the Bryansk forests, Leningrad Region and elsewhere.

Soviet prisoners of war in Hitler concentration camps, and Soviet people forcibly deported to the fascist rear, in their turn, continued the struggle against fascism. Under the threat of death, they formed underground anti-fascist organisations, arranged the escape of prisoners from the camps, carried out acts of sabotage, organised anti-fascist actions, and strengthened the bonds of friendship with workers of various nationalities, including Germans, who were fighting against fascism and the war. The Soviet people's struggle against the Hitlerites in their own country sapped the strength of fascism and contributed to the successes of the Red Army.

The national liberation movement in the occupied countries—

Czechoslovakia, Poland, Albania, Yugoslavia and France—grew stronger under the impact of the Red Army victories. In Yugoslavia a powerful partisan movement arose under the leadership of the Communist Party of Yugoslavia. The Yugoslav partisans contributed to the common struggle against Hitlerism by diverting part of the forces of fascist Germany and Italy. The Bulgarian people, led by their Communist Party, rose against the fascist regime. The resistance movement assumed wide scope in Poland, where the partisan Gwardia Ludowa was very active against the Hitlerites. With help from the Soviet people, Polish and Czech patriots formed military units of their own on Soviet territory, and Rumanian prisoners of war opposed to fascism formed a volunteer division to fight Hitler Germany.

The national liberation movement was headed by the Communist Parties. In the countries occupied by fascist Germany, the Communists constituted the chief and genuinely patriotic force waging a heroic struggle against the fascist invaders. They roused the masses of the people to fight against fascist tyranny and for the national independence of their countries and the freedom of all peoples. The Communists of France, Czechoslovakia and other countries made tremendous sacrifices in the great struggle for liberation from the fascist yoke. Thousands of Communists were shot by the fascists, and many more thousands lost their lives in concentration camps. But the unprecedented reign of terror set up by the fascists did not break the Communists. The Communist Parties of the capitalist countries in the anti-Hitlerite coalition vigorously supported the war effort of their countries, and helped to consolidate their fighting alliance, with the purpose of bringing about the speedy and utter defeat of fascist Germany and her accomplices. The Communist Parties of the fascist bloc countries—Germany, Italy, Rumania, Hungary and Finland—steered a course towards the military defeat of that bloc and the overthrow of their fascist governments. In conditions of the most savage terror, they fearlessly and indefatigably rallied the anti-fascist forces of their countries, and roused them to fight for the overthrow of their fascist governments. In Italy and Rumania a partisan movement developed, under the leadership of the Communist Parties.

The leading role which Communists played in the liberation struggle against the fascist invaders, and the heroism and utter devotion to the people's cause displayed by them, greatly increased the influence and prestige of the Communist Parties everywhere and strengthened their ties with the peoples of their countries.

Experience had shown that the unification of the progressive forces and the mobilisation of the masses to fight fascism could best be effected by the Communist Party of each particular country outside the framework of the Comintern. Besides, it was neces-sary completely to refute the calumny of the Hitlerites and their accomplices to the effect that the Communist Parties were alleged-ly acting not in the interests of their people but on orders from outside. Considering all these circumstances and the fact that the Comintern had accomplished its historic task, the Presidium of the Executive Committee of the Communist International decided in May, 1943, to dissolve the Comintern. This decision was approved by all the Communist Parties.

The Communist International had played an important role in history. Credit is due to it for restoring and strengthening the ties between the working people of various countries, ties which had been disrupted by the social-chauvinists during the first world war, for safeguarding Marxism against vulgarisation and distortion by the opportunists, for helping to unite the working-class vanguard in a number of countries into genuine workers' parties, for helping to train revolutionary leaders. Thereby the conditions were created for transforming young Communist Parties into mass working-class parties adhering to Marxism-Leninism.

In July, 1943, when the German fascist troops were sustaining heavy losses and suffering continuous defeats on the Soviet-Ger-man front, and when the Hitler Command was hurling all its re-serves against the Red Army, Britain and the U.S.A. landed troops in Sicily, and then in Italy. A big role in the struggle against the fascist regime of Mussolini and the tyranny of German fascism, and for the liberation of Italy, was played by the guerilla movement of the Italian patriots in whose front ranks the Communists were bravely fighting. Under these favourable conditions for our Al-lies, their offensive against the Italo-German troops in Italy pro-ceeded successfully. At the height of the battle of Kursk, popular revolts broke out in Italy, under the influence of Red Army and Allied victories; they resulted in the overthrow of the fascist re-gime of Mussolini and the dissolution of his fascist party. Defeat-ed militarily and politically, Italy was the first to leave the fascist bloc. She surrendered unconditionally in September, 1943. The bloc of fascist countries began to fall apart.

The wise foreign policy of the Soviet Government, the victories gained by the Soviet armies, the upsurge of the national liber-ation movement in Europe and the successes of the Anglo-Amer-ican troops in Italy strengthened the anti-Hitlerite coalition. At the close of 1943 the three Great Allied Powers—the U.S.S.R., Britain and the U.S.A.—adopted, at a conference in Teheran, a declaration on joint operations in the war against Germany and on post-war co-operation. At the same conference, the Soviet Union's Allies, Britain and the United States, again pledged themselves to open a second front in Europe—not later than May 1, 1944.

5. The Communist Party Organises the Complete Liberation of Soviet Soil from the Fascist Invaders

By the beginning of 1944 the Soviet people had achieved big successes in the war against fascist Germany. The Great Patriotic War had entered a new stage. It was drawing to the final dénouement. The next task was to complete the expulsion of the German fascist invaders from the Soviet Union, and then to do away with the fascist "new order" in Europe. But the difficulties confronting the U.S.S.R. were formidable. The peoples of the Estonian, Latvian, Lithuanian and Karelo-Finnish Soviet Republics were still under the yoke of a cruel enemy. The enemy also still retained his grip on a considerable part of Byelorussia, Ukraine and Moldavia and the whole of Crimea. Enemy troops were still near the western and southern suburbs of Leningrad, from where they continued the barbarous shelling of the heroic city. There was no second front in Europe as yet; the bulk of the enemy forces was still massed on the Soviet-German front. The German fascist invaders, realising their imminent doom, were resisting with the fury of despair.

The Communist Party called on the Soviet people and the Red Army not to rest on their laurels, not to lose sight of the difficulties still ahead, soberly to appraise the enemy's strength, and to remember that the war against the German fascist invaders called for great effort and further feats from the army and the people. The task set the Red Army was to deliver crushing blows to the enemy by skilful and resolute operations and completely to clear Soviet soil of the fascist invaders in the immediate future. On the home front, the tasks were: to increase the output of arms and improve their quality continuously, to build up production capacities, and to restore the national economy in the liberated areas.

These tasks were being fulfilled with credit. In industry, the Party organisations, assisted by business executives, Komsomol members and the foremost workers, were achieving improvements in technologies and production, and popularising the methods used by innovators. On the initiative of the Moscow Party organisation, many factories of the Soviet Union had begun to use conveyor belt production, which led to a substantial increase in the output of arms and munitions with the same equipment and with a smaller number of workers. Thanks to Socialist emulation and to improved technologies and production methods, labour productivity in 1944 increased by 23.7 per cent in the tank industry, and 11.8 per cent in the aircraft industry, as compared with 1943. Production costs in industry continued to decrease. As a result, the State saved about 50,000 million rubles in three and a half years of war.

Metal and coal output, the manufacture of machines, and munitions production all increased appreciably. In 1944 the output of ferrous metals went up almost by one-third as against 1943. The output of heavy machinery increased more than 30 per cent, and coal output registered a similar increase. The successes of heavy industry made it possible to increase arms and military equipment production sharply. During the last three war years, Soviet industry supplied the Red Army with an annual average of more than 30,000 tanks, self-propelled guns and armoured cars, about 40,000 aircraft, some 120,000 guns, about 450,000 light and heavy machine-guns, over 3,000,000 rifles and nearly 2,000,000 submachine guns. This far exceeded the production of weapons in fascist Germany, as well as in Britain and the U.S.A.

The restoration of the national economy wrecked by the German fascist invaders proceeded on a vast scale. Everywhere, in Leningrad, Stalingrad, Rostov-on-Don, Maikop, the Donets coalfield, Kharkov, factories rose from the ruins. In Leningrad, about 1,000,000 square metres of industrial premises were commissioned in 1944. In Stalingrad, the Tractor Works, the Krasny Oktyabr Plant and other enterprises resumed production. In Kharkov, production was re-started at the Turbogenerator, Electrical Engineering and Tractor plants. The restoration of the Donets mines made it possible considerably to increase coal output in 1944 as against 1943. In 1944, production was re-started at some of the largest enterprises in the South, such as the Yenakiyevo, Makeyevka, Stalino and Voroshilovsk iron and steel works, the Novo-Kramatorsk Engineering Works and others. Total industrial output in the liberated areas in 1944 increased more than threefold as compared with 1943. By the end of the war, upwards of 6,000 factories had resumed production in the liberated areas. The power industry, too, was being revived. The Stalingrad Power Station began to generate current again, the first turbine of the Zuyevka Power Station was put into operation, and work was begun on the restoration of the Dnieper Hydroelectric Power Station. In 1944, the Volkhov Hydroelectric Station began to operate at full capacity. As Soviet territory was liberated from the invaders, the railways and bridges on the more important communication lines were restored. About 11,900 miles of rail track were rebuilt in 1943.

Great progress was made in restoring agriculture in the course of applying the resolution "On urgent measures to restore the economy in areas liberated from German occupation," adopted by the C.C. C.P.S.U.(B.) and the Council of People's Commissars of the U.S.S.R. on August 21, 1943. About 900,000 head of livestock were restored to or purchased for the collective farms in the liberated areas. In 1944, about 1,400 machine-and-tractor stations and 1,300 machine-and-tractor repair shops resumed work. In the same year, the sown area increased by 40,000,000 acres over 1943, chiefly as a result of the liberation from the enemy of fertile areas in the Don and Kuban areas and in Ukraine. The total sown area, however, was some 100 million acres less than before the war. The work of the machine-and-tractor stations improved: in 1944 they used tractors on an area 62,000,000 acres larger than in 1943. More grain was harvested in 1944 than in the previous year. The peasants fulfilled the plan for the delivery of agricultural produce on time, and in the decisive period of the war ensured the supply of food to the Red Army and the population and of raw materials to industry without serious interruptions.

The great friendship of the peoples of the Soviet Union stood all tests, and was cemented still further, in the war against the fascist invaders. Every people contributed its share to the supreme struggle for the freedom of their Socialist country. Along with the Russian Federation, the Soviet Republics of Central Asia and Transcaucasia continuously reinforced the Red Army, and uninterruptedly supplied the front with arms, munitions, food and army clothing. Fighting shoulder to shoulder in the Red Army were Russians, Ukrainians, Byelorussians, Moldavians, Letts, Lithuanians, Estonians, Karelians, Georgians, Armenians, Azerbaijanians, Kazakhs, Uzbeks, Tajiks, Turkmens, Kirghiz and members of the country's other nationalities. The national units formed at the beginning of or during the war acquitted themselves honourably in the battles against the German fascist invaders. Despite the monstrous terror and provocation to which the Hitlerites resorted, the people in the occupied Republics, regions and districts intensified, under the leadership of underground Party organisations, their war of extermination in the enemy rear.

At the height of fierce battles against the enemy, the Party Central Committee at a plenary meeting held in January, 1944, took the important decision to reorganise the People's Commissariats for Defence and Foreign Affairs from all-Union into Union-Republican People's Commissariats, and to form People's Commissariats for Defence and Foreign Affairs in the Union Republics.* The tenth session of the Supreme Soviet approved this decision and enacted appropriate laws. The decision of the C.C. C.P.S.U. (B.) and the Supreme Soviet of the U.S.S.R. was added evidence of the might of the Soviet multi-national State, the indestructible friendship of the peoples of the U.S.S.R. and the maturity of the

---

* The transformation of the all-Union People's Commissariats for Defence and Foreign Affairs into Union-Republican ones meant that such People's Commissariats were established in all the Union Republics as well.—*Trans.*

Soviet Republics. The extention of the rights of the Union Republics, made possible by the co-operation of the peoples of the U.S.S.R. during the Patriotic War and by the entire history of the Soviet State, enhanced the military might of the Soviet Union and its fighting forces.

In 1944 the Red Army continued to gain strength. It was joined by tens of thousands of Soviet people liberated from fascist captivity. Its armaments were improving steadily. Its technical equipment fully met the requirements of the new stage of the Patriotic War, both in quantity and in quality. Since the beginning of the war the fire-power of its artillery had increased more than fivefold, the number of modern-type tanks fifteenfold and that of military aircraft fivefold. The supply of combat equipment to infantry units and formations had been augmented. The number of Red Army divisions had grown fourfold. Its fighting cadres had grown and acquired military experience. They had learnt to make the fullest and most competent use of their tremendous resources in arms and combat equipment, and skilfully to lead troops in the battlefield.

The increased might of the Red Army and the maturity and efficiency of its personnel fully manifested themselves at the decisive stage of the Great Patriotic War, when the Soviet armies delivered a series of increasingly powerful blows at the enemy.

The Red Army offensive began in January, 1944, with the rout of the German fascist troops at Leningrad and Novgorod. Smashing his powerful permanent and widely-ramified system of fortifications, the Red Army hurled the enemy back to the Baltic region. Leningrad was completely freed from the enemy blockade, and the barbarous shelling ceased. The enemy was driven out of the Leningrad and Kalinin regions. The Red Army entered the territory of Soviet Estonia. From February to April it routed a strong enemy group in the Korsun-Shevchenkovsky, Krivoi Rog and Nikopol area, threw back the German fascist troops beyond the Dniester, cleared Ukraine on the right bank of the Dnieper and entered the territory of Soviet Moldavia. Between April and May, the Red Army, by skilful and swift operations, crushed the enemy's powerful defences in Crimea, and inflicted irreparable losses upon him. By May 12 the Crimean Peninsula had been cleared of the invaders. Following closely on the heels of the Hitlerite troops and their Rumanian allies, the Red Army in April entered the foothills of the Carpathians, reached the State frontiers of the U.S.S.R. with Czechoslovakia and Rumania on a stretch of over 260 miles, and transferred military operations to Rumanian soil.

In the course of these and subsequent offensive operations, in 1944, the Red Army skilfully demolished the enemy's fortified zones, and swiftly pursued, encircled and annihilated enemy forces.

Its actions were marked by the close co-ordination of all arms of the service and by high skill in manoeuvring. The Soviet Command brought the enemy to battle wherever it was to the advantage of the Red Army. While Soviet troops advanced in some sectors, the next blow was being prepared in others. As a rule, the enemy was struck a new blow where he least expected it, often many hundreds of miles away. More and more enemy divisions were put out of action. The surprise blows dealt by the Red Army in various sectors compelled the fascist Command to keep changing its plans and frequently transferring reserves from one sector to another, over the entire length of the vast front. The Red Army, displaying swiftness and determination, furnished unsurpassed examples of large-scale offensive operations that ended in the encirclement and annihilation of strong enemy forces, as was the case in the Korsun-Shevchenkovsky area, in Byelorussia, at Kishinev and at Jassy.

The Party political network of the Red Army accumulated rich experience in conducting political work in any conditions—when the troops were resting or training, or at the height of the fighting. When an offensive was in preparation, political work among the troops was geared to inspiring the men in the coming battles, to firing their élan, their determination to smash the enemy in the impending encounter. The units were alerted for action, and their Party and Komsomol organisations reinforced with Party and Komsomol members from rear units. As soon as the order of battle had been received before an offensive, short Party and Komsomol meetings, and meetings of the men and officers, were held. Often these meetings took place around the unit's banners, when shelling and air bombing had already begun preparatory to the attack.

In the course of the advance slogans, brief reports on the first success, on battle feats and the decoration of those who had distinguished themselves in action, were passed down the line—by word of mouth or in writing. Visual aids were used extensively for political propaganda. In the liberated towns and villages, on motor vehicles, roadside posters, buildings and fences the Soviet soldiers read slogans calling on them to pursue and destroy the enemy relentlessly. These measures, combined with the examples of bravery set by Communists, stiffened the morale of the armed forces, and welded the troops together in a common desire to crush the enemy.

The exceptionally high moral and political make-up of front-line Communists can be seen from a letter by G. P. Maslovsky, who died the death of a hero in fulfilling a battle task. "The glorious city of Lenin, the cradle of the Revolution, is in danger," he wrote to his son. "Its future welfare depends on the fulfilment of the task assigned to me. For the sake of that great happiness, I will do my duty to my last breath, to my last drop of blood.... What helps me perform an act of valour? Military discipline and obedience to the Party. Those who say that it is but one step from discipline to heroism are right. Always remember that, son.... When you grow up you will see what I mean, and you will hold your country dear. It is a good thing, a very good thing, to love one's country!"

The Red Army's successes showed plainly that the Soviet Union was capable of routing fascist Germany single-handed and liberating the West European countries enslaved by the German fascists. Fearing such an outcome of the war, and severe punishment of the reactionaries by the peoples of the West European countries, the U.S. and British governments began to prepare vigorously for an invasion of Western Europe. On June 6, 1944, the American-British Command landed a major force in northern France, thus finally opening a second front in Europe. But even after the landing in the north of France, Churchill, then head of the British Government, advocated directing the main thrust of the Anglo-American troops against the Balkans. Instead of reinforcing the Allied armies already landed in France, he proposed landing, in the Istrian Peninsula, a force that would advance into Austria and Hungary through the Ljubljana Pass.

In the summer and autumn of 1944, Soviet troops inflicted further crushing blows on fascist Germany. In June they began an offensive in Karelia, routed a large Finnish army group, liberated Viborg and Petrozavodsk, and reached the Soviet-Finnish frontier. In the autumn of 1944, the Finnish Government, realising that resistance was hopeless, signed an armistice with the U.S.S.R. and declared war on Germany. In June and July the Red Army utterly routed the central group of German fascist armies in Byelorussia, completely liberated that Republic, and ejected the invaders from the greater part of the Lithuanian Soviet Republic. The Soviet forces drew near the frontiers of Germany. In July and August the Red Army smashed the German fascist troops at Lvov, pushed them beyond the San and the Vistula, liberated the whole of Western Ukraine and opened the road to the southern regions of Poland. The summer operations of the Soviet armies culminated in the defeat of German and Rumanian troops in the Kishinev-Jassy area in August, 1944. The Moldavian Soviet Republic was completely liberated from fascist occupation. Developing their rapid advance, the Soviet troops took a number of strategic points covering the way to central Rumania. In September and October the Red Army defeated the Baltic group of Hitlerite armies at Tallinn and Riga and liberated the Estonian, and the greater part of the Latvian, Soviet Republics. In the autumn the Red Army routed large German fascist forces in Poland, Rumania, Bulgaria, Hungary, Yugoslavia and northern Norway. In September, 1944, Soviet troops crossed the frontier of East Prussia and entered German territory for the first time since the beginning of the war.

The year 1944 was one of decisive victories for the Red Army over the German fascist forces and their allies. Its offensive was supported by the Soviet people living in the areas being freed from the enemy. The liberation of Soviet soil from the invaders had been almost completed. There remained only a small portion of the territory of the Latvian S.S.R., to which an enemy force, pressed to the sea, still clung. *The Soviet frontier had been restored along its whole length*, from the Barents Sea to the Black Sea.

The Party organisations of the Soviet Republics freed from the enemy were confronted with the complex tasks involved in restoring the towns, villages, factories, collective and State farms and machine-and-tractor stations destroyed by the Hitlerites. It was necessary to improve political work among the population.

The fascist invaders had planned to foment, with the help of nationalists, hatred for the Russian people among the peoples of Western Ukraine, Western Byelorussia, Bessarabia, the Estonian, Lithuanian and Latvian Soviet Republics, to disrupt the fraternal unity of the peoples of the Soviet Union, stir up national discord among them and provoke a fratricidal war.

But the peoples of the Soviet Republics and regions occupied by the enemy had remained loyal to their Socialist country. The enemy had been able to use only negligible groups of traitors and enemies of the Soviet system—remnants of the defeated exploiting classes and declassed elements. As he withdrew from Soviet territory, he had left behind, in some regions of the Baltic Republics, Western Byelorussia and Western Ukraine, armed bands made up of nationalist scum and common criminals to disorganise reconstruction work, carry on anti-Soviet propaganda and terrorise the population. The Soviet authorities and Party organisations in the areas liberated from the enemy had to tackle the major task of combating banditry and improving organisational, political and ideological work among the masses.

As soon as Western Byelorussia, Western Ukraine, Bessarabia and the Baltic Republics were liberated, the Soviet State restored to the farm-labourers, peasant poor and middle peasants who owned small plots all the land that the fascist invaders had taken away from them and turned over to the landlords and kulaks. It supplied the peasants with farm implements and livestock. In accordance with instructions from the Central Committee of the Party, the Communist Parties of Ukraine, Byelorussia, Estonia, Latvia, Lithuania, Moldavia and Karelia extended their work of ideological and political education of their membership, and the population at large, in a spirit of uncompromising opposition to bourgeois nationalist ideology, of proletarian internationalism and friendship among the peoples of the U.S.S.R. Banditry was soon liquidated with the vigorous assistance of the people. Broad sections of the population took an active part in State, economic and cultural development.

6. The Victorious Conclusion of the Great Patriotic War. Liberation of the Peoples of Europe from Hitlerite Tyranny. The End of the Second World War

The task of the Red Army was not confined to the expulsion of the enemy from Soviet territory. The Red Army had to consummate its liberating mission—completely to crush the Wehrmacht, help the peoples of occupied Europe to break the chains of fascist slavery and regain their freedom and independence, and, in the case of the German people, to destroy the fascist regime in Germany.

In the second half of 1944 the Red Army, pursuing the enemy, rendered the peoples of Europe tremendous assistance in their struggle for liberation. In the summer of 1944, Soviet troops entered Polish territory. Units of the Polish Army fought side by side with the Red Army for the liberation of their country. On the liberated Polish territory the people, led by their Workers' (Communist) Party, set up a people's government in the form of the Polish Committee for National Liberation.

The Soviet Union's tremendous successes in the war against fascist Germany inspired the Rumanian people to start a liberation struggle, which assumed an increasingly broad and militant character. With Soviet troops advancing rapidly on Rumanian territory, Rumania's patriots, led by the Communist Party, rose in armed revolt on August 23, 1944, and overthrew the Antonescu fascist government. The Rumanian Army turned against the German troops, and sided with the Red Army. Patriotic detachments and units of the Rumanian Army drove the Hitlerites out of the capital. There began the expulsion of Hitlerite troops from the other parts of the country. The Red Army, continuing to rout the fascist troops, entered Bucharest on August 30. Everywhere the population hailed the Soviet forces as their friends and liberators. The Red Army in concerted action with Rumanian troops drove the German fascist hordes out of Rumania. The Rumanian forces fought jointly with the Red Army up to complete victory over fascist Germany. Rumania began to build a new life on democratic lines.

The victorious Red Army offensive contributed to the liberation movement in Bulgaria. The fascist government of Bulgaria, though not officially in a state of war with the Soviet Union, rendered direct aid to fascist Germany by making bases available to German troops on Bulgarian territory. In view of this the Soviet Union on September 5, 1944, broke off diplomatic relations with the fascist government of Bulgaria and declared war on it. Soviet troops entered Bulgaria. This was a decisive factor in the liberation struggle of the Bulgarian people against their oppressors. Rising in armed revolt even before the arrival of Soviet troops the Bulgarian people on September 9, led by their Workers' Party, overthrew the monarchist-fascist dictatorship. A government of the Patriotic Front was formed in Sofia. The Bulgarian people enthusiastically welcomed the Soviet army as their liberators. The Hitlerite troops hastily retreated under the blows of the Red Army. Bulgaria declared war on Germany. On September 16, Soviet troops entered Sofia.

In October, 1944, Soviet troops, pursuing the Hitlerites on Yugoslav soil, met with the Yugoslav People's Liberation Army, which, under the leadership of the Communist Party of Yugoslavia, had been valiantly fighting the German fascist invaders for three years. By co-ordinated action, Soviet and Yugoslav troops expelled the invaders from the towns and villages of Yugoslavia and on October 20, 1944, liberated her capital, Belgrade. The population met the Red Army with acclaim.

At the end of October, 1944, the Red Army routed the German fascist troops in northern Finland, entered Norway and liberated her northern part.

In the same month, striking at the German fascist forces between the Tisza and the Danube, Soviet troops drove a wedge deep into Hungarian territory, in December encircled Budapest, where there was a large force of German fascist troops, and cleared four-fifths of the country's territory from the enemy. A Provisional National Government was formed on the territory liberated by the Soviet troops from the German invaders, and it declared war on Germany.

In October, 1944, Red Army forces, operating jointly with Czechoslovak units formed on Soviet territory, crossed the Carpathians and began to liberate the peoples of Czechoslovakia from the yoke of German fascism.

As the Red Army advanced westwards to liberate the European peoples from Hitlerite tyranny, important problems of the restoration of their political, economic and cultural life came up. The policy of the Communist Party and the Soviet Government on these problems remained unchanged throughout the war. The Soviet people set as their object:

1. To liberate the peoples of Europe from the fascist invaders and help them to rebuild their independent national States.

2. To grant the liberated peoples of Europe absolute freedom in deciding what form of government they were to have.

3. To ensure that the chief war criminals, those responsible for the war and the suffering of the peoples, were severely punished for their crimes.

4. To establish in Europe an order that would utterly preclude the possibility of new aggression on the part of Germany.

5. To establish lasting economic, political and cultural co-operation among all the peoples of Europe, based on mutual trust and mutual assistance, for the purpose of restoring the economy and culture in the countries that had been occupied and plundered by the Hitlerites.

In connection with the entry of Soviet troops into the territory of other countries, the Soviet Government reaffirmed the invariable principles of its peaceful foreign policy and its respect for national sovereignty. It stressed that it did not seek to seize foreign territory or change the social systems existing in other countries, and that the entry of Soviet troops into the territory of other countries was dictated solely by the military situation and continued enemy resistance. As soon as the liberated regions ceased to be zones of direct military operations, the Soviet Command transferred all civil government to the local national authorities. The Soviet Union helped the liberated countries with food and otherwise.

The success of the Red Army offensive also created favourable conditions for the liberation struggle in those countries whose territory it had not entered. In November, 1944, the Albanian People's Liberation Army, led by the Albanian Communist Party, drove the German fascist invaders out of the country.

The Greek patriots intensified their fight against the German fascist invaders. The People's Army, formed by the National Liberation Front headed by the Communist Party of Greece, routed the German fascist troops and in the autumn of 1944 freed the country from the enemy. This fact alarmed the British imperialists. The British Government, with the approval of the ruling circles of the U.S.A., moved its troops into Greece and, together with the local reactionaries, wreaked bloody reprisals against the Greek patriots. The British invaders restored the old, reactionary order in Greece, and lorded it in the country as if it had been their colony.

In the second half of 1944 the American-British troops in Western Europe achieved considerable successes. Having landed in Normandy and southern France, they launched an offensive at the end of July. They were helped by the French patriots, who fought valiantly under the leadership of the French Communist Party against the invaders. The French patriots freed Paris on the eve of the arrival of the American-British troops. Continuing their offensive, the latter liberated nearly the whole of France, Belgium, and part of the Netherlands by the end of 1944. But the Germans checked their further advance at the so-called Siegfried Line. And although the strength of the enemy in the West was insignificant, the American-British forces were unable to break through his defences, and stopped in their advance, without completing the rout of the enemy.

In the liberation struggle against fascism, the friendship of the freedom-loving peoples grew stronger, and the international prestige of the Soviet Union as the bulwark of peace, democracy and Socialism grew. Under the blows of the Red Army and the peoples who had risen against German fascism, the bloc of fascist States fell to pieces. Fascist Germany lost her European Allies; she found herself isolated and directly threatened with utter defeat.

Crossing into Germany and Hungary, the Soviet armies at the beginning of 1945 took up initial positions for the decisive advance on Germany's life-centres. The task of the Red Army was to crush fascist Germany by a swift assault, finish off the fascist beast in its own lair in joint action with the Allied troops, and end the war in Europe with the complete victory of the freedom-loving nations. The Soviet armed forces had yet to overcome powerful defences hundreds of miles in depth between the Vistula and the Oder. Germany still kept her main forces on the Soviet-German front. She had massed 204 divisions, including 180 German divisions, against the Red Army. As for the Western front, less than 70 divisions confronted the Anglo-American troops there.

Despite their comparatively small numbers on the Western front, the German fascist forces took advantage of the pause in the American and British advance and in December, 1944, started successful operations in the Ardennes area (Belgium), where they broke through the Allied front. The Anglo-American troops found themselves hard pressed, and retreated. In view of this, the British Prime Minister Churchill on January 6, 1945, asked Stalin, the Soviet Supreme Commander, for immediate assistance. This assistance was extended: the Soviet offensive, set for January 20, 1945, began instead on January 12.

Soviet troops struck at the enemy a blow of unprecedented force along the entire front from the Baltic to the Carpathians, and pierced his defences on a line 745 miles long. The Hitler Command was compelled to transfer further dozens of divisions to the Soviet-German front, denuding whole sectors of the Western front. This enabled the American-British armies to take the offensive in the West. By the spring of 1945 the Red Army had captured East Prussia—the seat of German militarism—Silesia, Pomerania and the greater part of Brandenburg, entered Austria and pushed forward to Berlin. Thanks to the skilful operations and humane attitude of the Soviet troops, many German towns and villages escaped destruction.

Poland, Hungary, the eastern part of Czechoslovakia, a considerable part of Austria and her capital, Vienna, were completely liberated from the German fascist yoke. Landing on the Danish island of Bornholm, Soviet troops forced its German fascist garrison to surrender, and helped the Danish people to liberate their country from the fascist invaders.

At the height of the Red Army's winter offensive, in February, 1945, the three Allied Powers—Britain, the U.S.A. and the Soviet Union—met in conference in Crimea. The Conference outlined a plan for the final defeat of Germany and worked out the terms of her unconditional surrender. At the instance of the U.S.S.R., the Conference approved the fundamental provisions for the demilitarisation and democratisation of Germany. The governments of the three Great Powers stated their firm resolve to destroy German militarism and Nazism and to create such guarantees as would prevent Germany from violating peace in the future. The Conference decisions were directed against fascism, and not against the German people. Moreover, they emphasised that "only when Nazism and militarism have been extirpated, will there be hope for a decent life for Germans, and a place for them in the comity of nations." For the purpose of maintaining peace and international security, the Crimea Conference adopted a decision to found a United Nations Organisation.

The decisions of the Crimea Conference dealt a blow to the plans of the German imperialists and Anglo-American reactionaries, who would have liked to conclude a separate peace with fascist Germany behind the back of the Soviet Union.

However, Churchill, the head of the British Government, continued his perfidious policy towards the U.S.S.R. He held that the decisive practical task of Anglo-American strategy and policy should be, not the total defeat of Germany, but the slowing down of the rapid advance of the Red Army, so that U.S. and British troops could enter the German, Czechoslovak and Austrian capitals before the Red Army did. When the imminent defeat of fascist Germany became obvious, he ordered Field-Marshal Montgomery to collect the arms of the surrendering German fascist troops and be prepared to return them to the Hitlerites for a joint struggle against the Soviet Union.

On April 16, the Soviet forces began an all-out offensive in the Berlin sector. Officers and political workers, Party and Komsomol members explained to the men the historic importance of the last blow being delivered to the enemy. The Military Councils of the First Byelorussian and First Ukrainian fronts called on the men to smash the enemy on the immediate approaches to Berlin, capture the capital of fascist Germany and hoist the Soviet Victory flag over it. Neither natural obstacles and powerful fortifications, nor the desperate resistance offered by the Hitlerites, could check the advance of the Soviet troops. Soon they entered the Berlin suburbs on three sides. Bitter fighting raged in the streets of the city for 10 days. On April 30, Soviet troops broke into the Reichstag building. Two intrepid scouts— Sergeant Yegorov and Sergeant Kantaria—hoisted the Soviet Victory flag on the Reichstag's dome. On May 2, 1945, the Berlin garrison laid down its arms.

The defeat of the Berlin group sealed the fate of the enemy forces on the other fronts. Under the powerful blows of the Red Army and the armies of France, Britain, the U.S.A., Czechoslovakia, Poland, Yugoslavia and Albania, as well as of the forces of Rumania and Bulgaria and units of the Hungarian army which had joined them, the German fascist State collapsed. Germany admitted defeat. On May 8, 1945, she signed the act of unconditional surrender. On May 9, Soviet troops routed the large German fascist force encircling the Czechoslovak capital, Prague, and entered the city, which had already been freed of the invaders by the population risen in revolt.

The war in Europe was over. The heroic deeds of the Red Army on the war front and the selfless effort of Soviet people on the home front were crowned with complete victory over fascist Germany.

The future of Germany and the post-war settlement in Europe were discussed at the Berlin (Potsdam) Conference of the Heads of Government of the U.S.S.R., the United States and Britain, held on July 17-August 2, 1945. Agreement was reached on the political and economic principles of Allied policy on Germany. The agreement was based on the decisions of the Crimea Conference. The Allies undertook to be guided, during the occupation period, by political principles aimed at destroying fascism and democratising Germany. The leaders of the three Powers agreed on ensuring that Germany would never again be able to threaten peace. With this end in view, it was decided to disarm Germany, abolish the German war industry, disband the Nazi Party and the organisations connected with it, and make all fascist and militarist activity impossible. The Berlin Conference decided on the transfer of Königsberg and the adjacent area to the Soviet Union. Thanks to the consistent efforts of the Soviet delegation in the interests of the Polish people, the Conference took the decision to restore to Poland the ancient territories belonging to her and to establish the new Polish frontier along the Oder and Neisse. On the proposal of the Soviet delegation, the Conference resolved to expedite the trial of the chief fascist war criminals.

The complete defeat and surrender of Hitler Germany did not mean that the second world war was over. The war had terminated in Europe, but in the Far East aggressive Japan continued hostilities against China, the U.S.A. and Britain. The Soviet Union could not stand aloof from the war against Japan. The security of its Far Eastern frontier and its obligations towards its Allies required its intervention. During the Great Patriotic War Japan had maintained a hostile attitude to the Soviet Union despite her obligations under the Soviet-Japanese Neutrality Treaty. Large Japanese forces were massed in Manchuria and Korea, close to the Soviet frontier, threatening an attack on the U.S.S.R. They tied down a considerable number of Soviet troops. Furthermore, Japan had rendered substantial assistance to fascist Germany in gross violation of her treaty obligations. The Soviet Government therefore informed its Allies at the Crimea Conference that it would enter the war against Japan two or three months after the termination of the war against Germany. The Soviet Government denounced the Soviet-Japanese Neutrality Treaty on April 5, 1945, within the term envisaged by the treaty for the possible renunciation of treaty obligations by either party.

In fulfilment of its obligations as an ally, and actuated by the desire to end the suffering caused the Chinese people and the other peoples of the Far East by Japanese aggression, and save the Japanese people from the ruinous consequences of the war as speedily as possible, the Soviet Union declared war on imperialist Japan on August 8, 1945. It aimed to safeguard the security of the Soviet State in the Far East, help the Chinese people in their struggle against the Japanese invaders and end the second world war as early as possible.

On August 9, 1945, Soviet troops began to advance on Manchuria from the Transbaikal, Blagoveshchensk and Primorye areas. The Mongolian People's Republic joined the Soviet Union in the war against imperialist Japan. The People's Liberation Army of China, led by the Communists, likewise took the offensive against the Japanese invaders. In 11 days—from August 9 to 19—the Red Army routed the Kwantung army, Japan's main striking force. The Soviet troops drove the Japanese out of the north-eastern provinces of China (Manchuria), the towns of Dalny (Dairen) and Port Arthur, Southern Sakhalin, which had belonged to Russia from of old, and the Kurile Islands, and freed North Korea.

At the close of the war against Japan, on August 6 and 9, the U.S. air force dropped two atomic bombs on the Japanese cities of Hiroshima and Nagasaki. The use of atomic weapons against the civilian population was completely unwarranted from the military standpoint. It could not, and did not, have any decisive effect on the outcome of the war. What brought about the speedy termination of the war in the Far East was not America's employment of atomic weapons against the civilian population, but the defeat of the main group of Japan's land forces in Manchuria by the Red Army.

On September 2, 1945, Japanese government and military representatives signed an act of unconditional surrender. Japan admitted defeat and laid down her arms. The plans of the Japanese imperialists to establish their supremacy in Asia had utterly collapsed. The hotbed of aggression in the Far East was destroyed. *The second world war was over.*

7. The Historic Significance and the Sources of the Soviet Union's Victory in the Great Patriotic War

The Soviet Union played the decisive role in the victorious conclusion of the second world war, and above all in the annihilation of the most dangerous hotbed of fascism and aggression—Hitler Germany. The Soviet people bore the brunt of the most terrible war against fascist Germany and her accomplices.

In grim battles against their enemies, the Soviet people victoriously defended their Socialist achievements, the most progressive social and political system, and the freedom and independence of the U.S.S.R., and strengthened the security of their State frontiers.

By their heroic war effort the Soviet people saved the peoples of Europe from the yoke of German imperialism. The Red Army, assisted by the peoples of Europe, expelled the German fascist invaders from Poland, Czechoslovakia, Yugoslavia, Bulgaria, Rumania, Hungary, Austria, Denmark and northern Norway, fulfilling with honour its liberating mission.

The second world war aggravated the general crisis of capitalism. This was most strikingly manifested in the weakening of the world capitalist system, which suffered a serious blow from the breakaway of Czechoslovakia, Poland, Bulgaria, Rumania, Albania, Hungary and Yugoslavia.

By smashing German fascism, which represented the interests of the most reactionary and aggressive imperialism, the Red Army helped the German people as well. The foundation was laid for the establishment of a peace-loving German Democratic Republic. The defeat of the Japanese imperialists and the liberation of China from the Japanese invaders paved the way for the victory of the people's revolution and people's democratic system in China, North Korea and Vietnam.

A major result of the second world war was the sharpening of the crisis of the entire colonial system of imperialism, which found expression in a powerful upsurge of the national liberation movement of the masses in the colonial and dependent countries.

The second world war greatly aggravated the basic contradiction of capitalism, namely, the antagonism between the working class and the bourgeoisie. The struggle against German fascism contributed to the growth of the class consciousness of the proletariat and enhanced the influence of the Communist Parties.

The victory of the Soviet State in the war against fascist Germany, the most reactionary imperialist State, was a logical outcome of the solidity and vitality of the new, Socialist social and political system, of its great advantages over the moribund capitalist system.

The Soviet State, based on the indestructible alliance of the working class and the peasantry and on friendship among the peoples of the U.S.S.R., proved to be the world's most stable and firm State. The Soviet system proved to be not only the best form for organising the country's economic and cultural progress during the years of peaceful development, but also the best form for mobilising all the forces of the people to repel the enemy in war time. The Soviet Union did not find itself unarmed in the face of the enemy, and of the danger of military defeat, for the Party had long before the war rejected the rotten and harmful theory, advanced by the enemies and vulgarisers of Marxism, of the withering away of the State of the dictatorship of the proletariat. In the pre-war years the Party had, as in the past, done everything to strengthen the Socialist State, its armed forces, penal organs and intelligence service, as well as the mass organisations of the working people in town and country, and primarily the local organs of authority, that is, the Soviets of Working People's Deputies.

In economic development and organisation, in the experience, skill and morale of its forces, and in the endurance and unity of its people, the Soviet Union proved in the course of the war to be stronger than its enemy precisely because State power in the U.S.S.R. belonged to the workers and peasants, and because the Soviet economy was based on Socialist ownership of the means of production. The war demonstrated that the economy of the Soviet Union was more virile than that of fascist Germany or any other bourgeois country. And although the Soviet Union had to develop its war economy in incredibly difficult conditions, being compelled to evacuate many factories from the west to the east, when the enemy had seized important industrial and agricultural areas of the country, Soviet arms production in the end, both in quantity and in quality, surpassed that of such capitalist countries as Germany, the U.S.A. and Britain.

One of the major sources of the strength and might of the Soviet Union is the friendship and fraternal co-operation of its peoples. This friendship withstood all hardships and trials, and was still further cemented in the war against the fascist invaders. The Russian people played an outstanding role in the Great Patriotic War, and their great services earned them the universal recognition of the other peoples of the U.S.S.R. The boundless confidence of the peoples of the Soviet Union in the Communist Party and the Soviet Government ensured the historic victory over the enemy. The Soviet ideology of the equality of all races and nations, the ideology of friendship among peoples, triumphed completely over the fascist ideology of brutal nationalism and racial hatred.

The Soviet social and political system constituted the basis on which the indestructible alliance of the working class and the peasantry, the moral and political unity of Soviet society, the friendship of its peoples and Soviet patriotism grew and matured during the Patriotic War. The war brought out the supreme patriotism of the Soviet people, their deep devotion to and infinite love of their country. The selfless efforts of all Soviet people —of the workers, peasants and intelligentsia—on the home front has gone down in history, along with the heroism of the Red Army, as an unexampled feat.

Great were the services of the All-Union Leninist Young Communist League—the Komsomol—in the defence of the Socialist country. A loyal helper of the Party, the Komsomol fought heroically for the freedom and independence of its country on the war and home fronts and in the enemy-occupied areas. It roused the Soviet youth to fight the enemy, and educated them in a spirit of Soviet patriotism, fidelity to the behests of Lenin and devotion to the Communist Party and the Soviet State. Hundreds of thousands of Komsomol members displayed the greatest heroism and valour on the battlefield. At the factories, machine-and-tractor stations, State and collective farms, Komsomol members initiated many patriotic deeds to assist the Red Army. In the areas seized by the enemy, they joined partisan units *en masse*. The people will never forget Zoya Kosmodemyanskaya, Alexander Chekalin, Liza Chaikina, Oleg Koshevoi, Parfenty Grechany, Dasha Dyachenko, Vladimir Morgunenko, Frosya Zenkova, Zinaida Portnova, Juozas Aleksonis, Hubertas Boris, Alfonsas Čeponis, Alexei Shumavtsov and their companions-in-arms.

During the war years the Soviet people displayed their great spiritual strength. They emerged victorious from the severest trials because they were conscious of the just aims of the patriotic war they were waging and knew they were fighting for their Socialist country, for a happy present and a still more radiant future.

The war revealed in all their greatness the basic features of the Red Army, an army of a new type, an army of workers and peasants, of the emancipated peoples of the U.S.S.R., an army educated in the spirit of proletarian internationalism. The Red Army is inseparable from the people. The valour of the Red Army embodied the spiritual strength of the Soviet peoples, and their moral and political unity. The Soviet soldiers knew that they were defending the independence of their Socialist country and the freedom of the peoples of Europe and Asia. This inspired them to heroic feats, and led to victory over the enemy army, an army educated in the spirit of racial hatred for other peoples, an army that had no lofty aims. The fearlessness and bravery of the Panfilovist Heroes of the Soviet Union led by V. Klochkov-Diyev, of N. Gastello, V. Talalikhin, A. Matrosov, Y. Smirnov and many other Soviet soldiers, symbolised the heroism of millions.

In the war years the Party promoted and trained many gifted officers and generals. Outstanding qualities were displayed in the battlefield by I. K. Bagramyan, S. S. Biryuzov, S. M. Budyonny, I. D. Chernyakhovsky, V. I. Chuikov, L. A. Govorov, A. A. Grechko, I. S. Konev, R. Y. Malinovsky, K. A. Meretskov, K. S. Moskalenko, F. S. Oktyabrsky, I. Y. Petrov, K. K. Rokossovsky, P. S. Rybalko, V. D. Sokolovsky, S. K. Timoshenko, F. I. Tolbukhin, B. M. Shaposhnikov, A. M. Vasilevsky, N. F. Vatutin, N. N. Voronov, K. Y. Voroshilov, A. I. Yeremenko, G. K. Zhukov and other prominent military leaders. Educated in the ideas of Marxism-Leninism and well versed in the advanced Soviet science of war, our commanders inculcated high moral and soldierly qualities in the men. They combined personal courage and bravery with the art of leading troops in action. The professional training, battle experience and political maturity of the Red Army's and Navy's commanding personnel were important factors in achieving victory over fascist Germany and imperialist Japan.

Great services were performed by the Soviet partisans—the people's avengers—in defeating the enemy. Partisan warfare brought to the fore A. F. Fyodorov, A. V. German, M. A. Guryanov, S. A. Kovpak, I. A. Kozlov, V. I. Kozlov, M. I. Naumov, P. K. Ponomarenko, S. V. Rudnev, K. S. Zaslonov and many other outstanding commanders and organisers.

The Soviet Union won the Great Patriotic War under the leadership of the Communist Party and its Central Committee headed by Stalin. During the war the Central Committee was the militant leader of the Party and the people. Its members performed important functions on the home and war fronts. The Central Committee worked out the plan of the defeat of fascist Germany. The Party inspired the Soviet people and their soldiers for a just Patriotic War; it united the efforts of Soviet people, directing them towards a common goal, that of routing the enemy. By the beginning of 1945 there were 3,325,000 Communists, or nearly 60 per cent of the total Party membership, in the Red Army and Navy. Both on the war and the home fronts, Communists were in the front line, and led the masses. Whenever it was necessary to attack under enemy fire, Communists were the first to go forward. If, in times of reverse or defeat, it was necessary to rally the men, to infuse courage in them, it was the Communists who did it. The Party organisations in the factories, machine-and-tractor stations, State and collective farms roused Soviet people to feats of labour. The Party was the organiser and inspiration of the powerful partisan movement.

With every day of the war, the Party's ties with the masses of the working people grew stronger, and its prestige grew in all sections of the Soviet people. Striking evidence of this was the rapid growth of its membership, especially in the crucial period of the war. Over 5,000,000 people joined the Party during the war as candidate members and about 3,500,000, as members. They were the finest men and officers of the Red Army and Navy who had fought valiantly on the war fronts, advanced workers, collective farmers and intelligentsia who had worked selflessly on the home front.

The solid unity of the Party, and of the entire Soviet people, under the Party's Leninist banner—this was the decisive factor in winning the Great Patriotic War.

BRIEF SUMMARY

The Great Patriotic War of the Soviet people against fascist Germany and imperialist Japan was a part, and the decisive element, of the second world war. The second world war was unleashed by the bloc of aggressive States comprising Hitler Germany, Italy and Japan. But these States merely constituted the most ferocious and predatory detachment of world imperialism, which as a social system was responsible in its entirety for the death of tens of millions of people in the war, for the incalculable suffering of hundreds of millions of working people, for their tears and blood, for the destruction of tremendous material and cultural values created by the labour of many generations.

The Great Patriotic War started as a result of the sudden attack on the Soviet Union by Hitler Germany, owing to which the German fascist troops were successful at the early stage of the war. The temporary success of the Hitlerites was also due to the superior numerical strength of the fascist army and air force. The enemy captured a vast territory of the U.S.S.R., which included important industrial centres. The Red Army and the Soviet people sustained heavy losses.

The Communist Party pointed out to the Soviet people the mortal danger threatening the country, and roused them to a Great Patriotic War. It defined the tasks of the people and the armed forces in the struggle for the freedom and independence of the Socialist Fatherland, inspired Soviet people to feats of valour on the field of battle and for selfless labour on the home front, and organised a powerful partisan movement in the enemy-occupied areas. The correct policy and strategy of the Party, its ideological and organising work on the home and war fronts, and the mass heroism of Soviet people ensured the victory of the Soviet people and their armed forces over the bitterest enemies of the country.

Backed by the moral and political unity of the Soviet peoples, the Party transformed the whole country into one armed camp. It made effective use of the advantages of the Soviet social and political system, organised a well-co-ordinated war economy, developed war production, and ensured the Red Army's superiority over the enemy in armaments, military equipment and the art of warfare.

All these factors led to a turning-point in the war in favour of the Soviet Union, and later to the defeat of the German fascist armed forces, followed by the defeat of the armed forces of Japan.

The war against the Soviet Union, engineered by international imperialism and unleashed by fascist Germany, produced results totally unforeseen by the imperialists. The imperialists had expected that the land of Socialism would be destroyed; but actually it was the capitalist system that suffered enormous and irretrievable losses. A number of European and Asian countries fell away from this system; they established a people's democratic system and, together with the Soviet Union, formed a single powerful Socialist camp.

Yet one more imperialist attempt to do away with the State of workers and peasants, the land of Socialism, thus came to an inglorious end.

Reared by the Communist Party, the Red Army saved the peoples of Europe from fascist enslavement. Thereby the Soviet people demonstrated in deed their international solidarity and proletarian internationalism. Progressive mankind saw for itself that there was no champion of the free national development of the peoples more staunch than the Communist Party, nor a more dependable bulwark in the struggle for democracy and peace, than the Soviet Union, the country of victorious Socialism.

The Great Patriotic War showed the immense moral and material forces in the possession of a people who, under the leadership of their Party, have assumed power in their country and built a Socialist society. The people's solid unity behind the Communist Party, their readiness to go through all privations and sacrifices in defence of their Socialist achievements and their Socialist Fatherland, were the decisive factor in winning the Great Patriotic War.

Under the leadership of the Communist Party, and under the Party's Leninist banner, the Soviet people emerged victorious from the Great Patriotic War. Under the leadership of the Party, the Soviet people, even while the war was still on, set about restoring the national economy in the areas freed from the enemy. It was the beginning of a great national effort to repair the ravages wrought by the fascist invaders and to advance the national economy, complete the building of Socialism, and pass gradually to Communism in the Soviet Union.

CHAPTER XVI

THE PARTY'S STRUGGLE FOR THE RESTORATION AND DEVELOPMENT OF THE SOCIALIST NATIONAL ECONOMY AFTER THE WAR

(1945-1953)

1. Radical Changes in the International Situation After the Second World War. Formation of Two Camps

After the Great Patriotic War, the Soviet people turned all their efforts to the restoration and further development of the national economy, the completion of the building of Socialism and the gradual transition to Communism. The Party's domestic and foreign policy measures were all bent to achieving these aims.

The main foreign policy aim of the Party was to secure a stable and lasting peace, to strengthen Socialism's positions in the world arena, to help the nations that had broken away from capitalism to build a new life. One of the most significant features of the international situation was the radical change that had taken place in the balance of forces in the world arena, in favour of Socialism and to the detriment of capitalism.

The Soviet Union bore the brunt of the war. It had sustained heavier material and manpower losses than any other State. But it emerged from the war politically stronger than it had been at the beginning. The unity of the people, the Party and the Government was stronger, the authority and moral and political prestige of the Soviet State were greater and its international influence had grown. No major world political issue could now be fully settled without the participation of the U.S.S.R.

The Soviet State took a more active part in international affairs and extended its ties with other countries. The Party devoted more attention to foreign policy problems in its work.

Developments in the capitalist countries followed a different course. As a result of the war the capitalist system sustained enormous losses and became weaker. *The second stage of the general crisis of capitalism set in,* manifesting itself chiefly in a new wave of revolutions. Albania, Bulgaria, Eastern Germany, Hungary, Czechoslovakia, Poland, Rumania and Yugoslavia broke away from the system of capitalism. The revolutions in these countries were governed by the general laws of development, yet they had their specific features, engendered by different social and economic conditions. The people's governments established in these countries carried out a number of important democratic reforms: the people acquired extensive democratic rights and liberties, an agrarian reform was carried out in the countryside, landlord property rights, where they existed, were abolished, and the peasants were given land.

As democratic measures were pushed to their conclusion, the working class in these countries passed to Socialist changes in political and economic life. The new people's governments everywhere confiscated the property of the German and Italian imperialists and of the people who had collaborated with the enemy. The bourgeois elements were smashed in a bitter class struggle. The question of power was thus settled. The dictatorship of the proletariat, in the form of people's democratic republic, triumphed in the countries of Central and South-East Europe. Industry, the banks and transport were nationalised. The economy began to develop along the Socialist path.

The rapid victory of the masses of the people in these countries over the bourgeoisie was achieved thanks to the correct policy of the Communist Parties and the leading role of the working class. A great factor in the liberation struggle of these peoples was the assistance rendered by the Soviet Union.

In their relations with the People's Democracies the Communist Party and the Soviet Government strictly adhered to the principle of non-interference in their internal affairs. The U.S.S.R. recognised the people's governments in these States and supported them politically. True to its internationalist duty, the U.S.S.R. came to the aid of the People's Democracies with grain, seed and raw materials, although its own stocks had been badly depleted during the war. This helped to provide the population with foodstuffs and also to speed up the recommissioning of many industrial enterprises. The presence of the Soviet armed forces in the People's Democracies prevented domestic counter-revolution from unleashing a civil war and averted intervention. The Soviet Union paralysed the attempts of the foreign imperialists to interfere in the internal affairs of the democratic States.

Major breaches were made in the imperialist chain in Asia too. After years of armed struggle against the landlords, the compradore bourgeoisie and foreign imperialists, the Chinese people, headed by the working class and under the leadership of the Communist Party, overthrew the Kuomintang government and took power into their hands. The People's Republic of China was established in October, 1949, on the basis of the alliance of the workers and peasants, with the working class playing the leading role. The bourgeois-democratic revolution developed into a Socialist revolution. The establishment of the dictatorship of the proletariat opened the way to the Socialist development of China.

The victory of the Chinese people was the most outstanding post-war development. In the history of the world liberation movement, the Chinese Revolution was second to the October Revolution in significance and influence on the destinies of mankind. It dealt another powerful blow at capitalism, especially at its colonial system, and altered the alignment and balance of forces in the world arena still more in favour of Socialism.

After a long struggle, the Socialist path of development in Asia was also taken by the Korean People's Democratic Republic (K.P.D.R.) and the Democratic Republic of Vietnam (D.R.V.).

Eleven States in all, with an aggregate population of more than 700 millions, broke away from the capitalist system after the second world war. This radically changed the international position of the Soviet Union. For many years the Soviet Union was the only Socialist country in the world. This period was now over. International Socialism entered a new phase of development.

Before the second world war, the Socialist system accounted for 17 per cent of the world's territory and about 9 per cent of its population; after the war the figures were 26 per cent and about 35 per cent respectively. The sphere of capitalist exploitation dwindled considerably.

Another most important feature of the second stage of the general crisis of capitalism was the mighty sweep of the national liberation movement, the steady disintegration of imperialist colonial domination. The October Revolution started a profound crisis in the colonial system; after the defeat of the fascist aggressors it began to disintegrate. Besides the People's Republic of China, the Democratic Republic of Vietnam and the Korean People's Democratic Republic, which broke away from the capitalist system and set out to build Socialism, the path of independent development was taken by India, Burma, Indonesia, Ceylon and many other countries, which had been under the colonial yoke for centuries. A liberation struggle flared up in the African countries. The imperialists were left with less possibilities for colonial exploitation.

The growing national liberation movement weakened the imperialist forces, strengthened the front of the peoples' liberation struggle and consolidated the positions of the supporters of peace and democracy, and also the position of Socialism. The disintegration of the colonial system was accelerated, above all, by the growing prestige and influence of the Soviet Union and the consolidation of the position of Socialism on a world-wide scale. The U.S.S.R. consistently defended the rights of nations to choose their own way of life, and in close co-operation with the People's Republic of China and the other Socialist countries, restrained the aggressive actions of the colonialists: in a number of cases it prevented military suppression of the liberation movement. The Soviet Union rendered moral and political support to the national liberation movement everywhere and promoted friendship with the peoples that had thrown off the colonial yoke.

Still another manifestation of the second stage of the general crisis of capitalism was the intensification of the uneven economic and political development of the capitalist countries. Their economic life acquired a still more contradictory and unhealthy character, and the signs of decay and parasitism became still more pronounced. The economy of Italy, Japan and West Germany remained disorganised for a long time. France no longer played the role she used to play. The British Empire began to disintegrate. There began the decline of British imperialism. Industrial production in Britain and France long remained stagnant, whereas the economic and military potential of the U.S.A. rose sharply. The U.S.A. actually became the economic, financial and political centre of the capitalist world.

The war was followed by mass unemployment in the capitalist countries. In 1949 there were over 40 million unemployed, that is, more than during the 1932 crisis. The capitalist world staggered under heavy economic blows.

The U.S.A. decided to take advantage of the economic and political difficulties in the other leading capitalist countries and bring them under its sway. Under the pretext of economic aid the U.S.A. began to infiltrate into their economy and interfere in their internal affairs. Such big capitalist countries as Japan, West Germany, Italy, France and Britain all became dependent on the U.S.A. to a greater or lesser degree. The peoples of Western Europe were confronted with the task of defending their national sovereignty against the encroachments of American imperialism.

It took five to six years after the end of the second world war for the capitalist countries to overcome their economic difficulties to some extent. The pre-war level of production was surpassed and the number of unemployed decreased. The capitalists, however, failed to solve the more acute economic contradictions and achieve stabilisation. Industrial output rose on an unsound and unstable foundation. The growing unevenness of economic development in the capitalist countries still further aggravated the problem of markets. The struggle between the capitalist Powers for spheres of influence and sources of raw material intensified with each passing year. The contradictions between the imperialist States grew sharper.

The second stage of the general crisis of capitalism was distinguished, lastly, by further exacerbation of the contradictions between the monopoly capitalists, on the one hand, and the working class, the working people generally, on the other. This led to the narrowing of the social basis of monopoly capitalist domination and to the further decay of bourgeois democracy. The reactionary nature of the monopoly capitalists became more pronounced in all the imperialist countries. They threw overboard the banner of democratic liberties and set out openly to establish their dictatorship.

Further sharpening of the contradictions between the people and the monopoly capitalists found expression also in the intensification of the class struggle and in the growing political consciousness and degree of organisation of the working class. The prestige and influence of the Communist Parties grew. Before the war, the Communist Parties in the capitalist countries had a membership of about 1,724,000; in 1946, the figure was approximately 5,000,000, although the number of these countries had decreased.

Some of the Communist Parties, formerly not strong numerically, became mass parties. In a number of countries (Italy, France) the Communist Parties became the most influential parties among the masses. Wide non-proletarian sections of the working people began to rally around the working class. New weak links appeared in the capitalist system. The working people in Italy, France, Greece, Malaya, Indonesia, Burma, the Philippines and other countries launched an active struggle against reaction, for genuine freedom and people's government.

In most of the capitalist countries the monopoly capitalists proved incapable of independently checking the revolutionary tide of the popular masses. The ruling circles of these countries thereupon began to unite their forces and build up reactionary international alliances for a joint offensive against the working class and all the working people, for the crushing of the liberation movement and for the struggle against democracy and Socialism.

The capitalist world headed by the U.S.A. turned with all its strength to the task of reinforcing its weakened links and retaining them in the system of imperialism. To suppress the revolutionary movement it resorted to armed force, economic pressure and direct interference in the internal affairs of other countries. In 1947-1949, the combined forces of international reaction crushed the popular movement in Greece and dealt heavy blows to the liberation struggle waged by the working people of Italy, France and other countries. The monopoly capitalists of the U.S.A., France, Italy and Britain embarked on a large-scale political offensive, with the object of destroying democracy and crushing the working-class movement in their countries. A crusade was organised against the forces of democracy, fascist tendencies in political life became more pronounced and there began the unbridled persecution of Communists. The attacks of the fascist and semi-fascist forces, however, were in the main beaten off and the proletariat retained its most important positions. In some countries the Communists preserved their influence among the masses, in others they even extended it. The strike movement grew in scope and became more militant. The proletariat became better organised and politically more conscious.

The radical changes that took place after the second world war substantially altered the political map of the world. There emerged *two* main *world* social and political camps: the *Socialist* and democratic camp, and the *imperialist* and anti-democratic camp.

The Socialist camp included the U.S.S.R. and the People's Democracies in Europe and Asia. It was actively supported by the entire international working-class movement and all the Marxist-Leninist parties.

The C.P.S.U. did much to expand its ties with the Communist Parties of other countries. The Communist Parties exchanged experiences, jointly discussed important problems of the political and ideological struggle and worked out a common point of view. The forms of these ties varied in accordance with the prevailing conditions. In 1947, the Communist Parties of the U.S.S.R., of a number of People's Democracies, and of France and Italy set up an Information Bureau. It was entrusted with the task of organising the exchange of experience and, whenever necessary, of co-ordinating the activities of the Communist Parties on a basis of mutual agreement. It had its newspaper *For a Lasting Peace, for a People's Democracy*. The Communist Party of the U.S.S.R. maintained ties with other brother parties through bilateral contacts.

Social forces and groups in the capitalist countries actively fighting for national independence and democratic freedoms began to gravitate towards the camp of Socialism.

The forces of this camp are consistently battling for peace and against the threat of new wars, are defending democracy and the national independence of the peoples. They seek to strengthen and extend the positions of Socialism and to ensure a bright future for mankind.

The core of the reactionary imperialist camp was made up of the bloc of leading imperialist States headed by the U.S.A. It was joined by all the reactionary classes, all the anti-democratic forces in the other capitalist countries. The imperialist camp aims at strengthening the positions of capitalism and suppressing the Communist movement, breaking the will of the peoples for national independence, and restoring capitalism in China, in the other People's Democracies and in the Soviet Union.

The ruling circles of the U.S.A., striving for world supremacy, openly declared that they could achieve their aims only from "positions of strength." The American imperialists unleashed the so-called cold war, and sought to kindle the flames of a third world war. In 1949, the U.S.A. set up an aggressive military bloc known as the North Atlantic Treaty Organisation (NATO). As early as 1946, the Western States began to pursue a policy of splitting Germany, which was essentially completed in 1949 with the creation of a West German State. Subsequently they set out to militarise West Germany. This further deepened the division of Germany and made her reunification exceptionally difficult. A dangerous hotbed of war began to form in Europe. In the Far East the United States strove to create a hotbed of war in Japan, stationing its armed forces and building military bases on her territory.

In 1950, the United States resorted to open aggression in the Far East. It occupied the Chinese island of Taiwan, provoked an armed clash between the Korean People's Democratic Republic and South Korea and began an aggressive war against the Korean people. The war in Korea was a threat to the People's Republic of China, and Chinese people's volunteers came to the assistance of the Korean people.

The military adventure of the U.S.A. in Korea sharply aggravated international tension. The U.S.A. started a frantic arms drive and stepped up the production of atomic, thermonuclear, bacteriological and other types of weapons of mass annihilation. American military bases, spearheaded primarily against the U.S.S.R., China, and the other Socialist countries, were hastily built at various points of the capitalist world. Military blocs were rapidly knocked together. The threat of a third world war with the use of mass destruction weapons increased considerably.

In those conditions the question of peace became one of paramount importance. Defence of peace everywhere became the most important task facing the people, a task of national significance, the crucial point in the struggle for human progress. A democratic peace movement developed throughout the world. It was joined by people of different classes and parties, different political views and religious beliefs. The peace movement is the biggest social and political movement in the history of mankind. It by no means infringes the social and economic systems of States. But it helps to expose and isolate the most aggressive imperialist circles and thus undermine and weaken the position of reaction in general.

The struggle for peace was the main link in all the activity of the Communist Party and the Soviet State in the sphere of foreign policy. Consistently pursuing a policy of peaceful coexistence of countries with different social systems, the Soviet Union proposed settlement of outstanding international issues through negotiation, reduction of conventional armaments and armed forces, prohibition of atomic weapons, and the institution of effective control over the observance of all disarmament measures. The U.S.S.R. took the initiative in the all-round promotion of international trade and cultural relations.

The Soviet Government repeatedly proposed the reunification of Germany on a democratic basis with the participation of the Germans themselves and the conclusion of peace with a united democratic Germany. In the Far East the Soviet Union upheld the independence of Japan and strove to conclude a just peace and establish good-neighbourly relations with her. It worked for a peaceful solution of the Korean question and for an end to the war in Vietnam, waged by the French colonialists with direct support from the U.S.A.

The Party's consistent peace policy found expression in a series of practical measures. After the war, the U.S.S.R. withdrew its troops from China, Korea, Norway, Czechoslovakia and Bulgaria, which they had entered pursuing the German and Japanese aggressors. The greater part of the armed forces was demobilised. Soon after, they were reduced to the pre-war level of 1939. Actively participating in the peace movement, the Soviet people unanimously signed the Stockholm Appeal for the prohibition of atomic weapons. In 1951, the U.S.S.R. Supreme Soviet passed a law proclaiming war propaganda a grave crime.

In the struggle for peace and a just solution of international issues, the U.S.S.R. attaches definite importance to the United Nations Organisation (UNO) and actively participates in its work. Notwithstanding all the shortcomings and defects of the U.N., arising from the fact that the U.S.A. has knocked together a big group of small States, mostly Latin American, ready to do its bidding, the Soviet Government regards the activity of UNO as a definite factor in international co-operation and in the fight for peace.

The consistent peace policy of the Communist Party and the Soviet State accords with the interests of all the peoples of the world, all progressive strata of society. In its fight for peace, the U.S.S.R. has many allies in the capitalist countries. Led by the Communist Party, the Soviet people have established close ties with all peace supporters and, together with them, have been waging an active struggle against attempts by aggressive elements to unleash another world war. The Soviet people need peace in order to accelerate their advance to Communism.

2. The Party's Work for the Restoration and Further Development of the National Economy. Fulfilment of the Fourth Five-Year Plan Ahead of Schedule

The war and the temporary occupation of a part of Soviet territory by the Hitlerite forces inflicted colossal losses on the peoples of the U.S.S.R. The Hitlerites annihilated millions of the civilian population in the Soviet Union. Millions of men were killed at the front. In the temporarily occupied areas the fascists destroyed or plundered tremendous wealth. They pillaged and laid waste 1,710 towns, and reduced to ruins or burned down more than 70,000 villages. They destroyed—completely or partially—close on 32,000 industrial enterprises and 40,000 miles of rail track, plundered 98,000 collective farms, 1,876 State farms and 2,890 machine-and-tractor stations, and demolished many hospitals, schools, colleges, and libraries. The material values plundered or destroyed amounted to 679,000 million rubles (in pre-war prices). This was approximately as much as was spent in the U.S.S.R. during the four Five-Year Plan periods on building new factories, railways, mines, power stations, State farms, machine-and-tractor stations and other enterprises. But that was not all. The Soviet Union had to expend vast resources on reorganising the economy for war purposes and on the conduct of the war. Furthermore, it suffered great losses through being deprived of its supplies from the invaded areas, which before the war had accounted for a third of the Soviet Union's industrial output. All this damage is estimated at about 1,900,000 million rubles (in pre-war prices).

The material losses sustained by the Soviet people as a result of the looting of wealth by the enemy, war expenditure and the loss of supplies from enterprises in the occupied territory totalled nearly 2,600,000 million rubles. No country had ever suffered such enormous losses and destruction in any war. The war held up the Soviet Union's advance towards Communism for more than ten years.

Losses such as these would have thrown back any capitalist country a long way, and it would have fallen into dependence on stronger Powers. But no such thing happened to the Soviet Union. The Socialist system, the heroic effort of the Soviet people and the leadership of the Communist Party ensured the rapid restoration and further development of the national economy.

One of the cardinal tasks of the Party and the Soviet State was to reconvert the country's economy to peace-time production. In the capitalist countries, the change-over to peace-time economy was an unplanned and exceedingly painful process. Many factories were closed down. Millions of workers were left without jobs. The entire burden of reconversion fell on the shoulders of the working people.

In Socialist conditions the transition to a peace-time economy likewise entailed great difficulties, and required time and sacrifices. But the Socialist system made it possible to reorganise the economy without setbacks, on a planned basis.

All factories and plants were given plans for peace-time production. Manpower and raw and other materials were redistributed accordingly. In the course of this reorganisation, new proportions as between the different branches of the national economy came into being. Investments in the national economy were increased considerably by cutting military expenditures. A large part of war industry was switched to peace-time production. The Party ensured the financing of the national economy, primarily by running industrial enterprises more profitably.

The methods of management and the organisation of work were changed. At the factories, work returned to normal. Compulsory overtime was abolished, and factory and office workers began to get their holidays regularly. Reconversion of the economy to peace-time conditions was, in the main, completed in 1946. This made it possible to enlarge the scale of restoration work.

In mobilising the masses to restore and further develop the national economy, the Party clearly indicated the supreme goal of the people's effort—to build Communism. When the war ended, the country re-embarked on the fulfilment of the programme worked out by the Eighteenth Party Congress for the completion of the building of a Socialist society and for the gradual transition to Communism. Greater attention began to be paid to theoretical problems of Communist construction. The theory of the building of Communism was further developed in a number of Party and government documents of that period, and in speeches and articles by Party leaders. The Party's immediate and long-term tasks in the political, economic and ideological fields were specified.

In defining the concrete ways for the gradual transition from Socialism to Communism the Party proceeded from the fact that the first phase of Communist society with its characteristic features had, in the main, been achieved in the U.S.S.R. But certain features of Socialism had not yet manifested themselves in full. The productive forces had not yet reached a degree of development making it possible to create a sufficiency of consumer goods and meet the people's housing requirements. There were still great difficulties in consistently applying the Socialist principle of distribution. This was particularly evident during the first post-war years; rationing had to be continued, there was a big difference between the low prices of rationed and high prices of unrationed goods, and prices in the collective-farm market were still higher. The goods shortage diminished steadily as progress was made in restoring the economy and expanding the productive forces. But there was still a shortage of some products, and the difference between the prices in State and co-operative trade and those in the collective-farm market remained.

The Party directive for the completion of the building of Socialism and the gradual transition to Communism meant that, first and foremost, the unresolved tasks of the first phase of Communism had to be carried out and Socialism consolidated still further, which would provide the basis for the further advance to the higher stage of Communism.

In the sphere of production, it was first of all necessary to restore the national economy as speedily as possible, considerably surpass its pre-war level, strengthen the country's might still more and guarantee it against all eventualities. For a longer period ahead, a great goal was fixed—solution of the basic economic problem of overtaking and surpassing the leading capitalist countries in output per head of the principal products, reaching higher labour productivity than in the capitalist countries and thereby securing the complete economic victory of Communism over capitalism.

In the sphere of economic relations, the task was to develop and improve Socialist production relations as the productive forces grew; to strengthen the role of public property, and consolidate collective ownership of the means of production; to put an end as soon as possible to all departures from the Socialist principle of distribution in accordance with the quantity and quality of the labour expended; to abolish levelling and other irregularities in remuneration for work, to increase real wages and to abolish all food rationing.

In the sphere of ideology and culture, the tasks were to start a resolute struggle against survivals of bourgeois views, morals and customs; to overcome completely the pernicious influence exercised by the reactionary culture of the imperialist West; to make all Soviet citizens politically conscious patriots, to raise still higher the cultural level of the working people, to publish more books, newspapers and magazines, and to produce more motion pictures. As a long-term objective, the Party aimed at ensuring the all-round physical and spiritual development of Soviet people, eliminating the survivals of capitalism in their minds, raising the cultural level of the workers and peasants to that of engineers and agronomists, overcoming the negative consequences of the division of labour, and turning all citizens into active, conscious builders of a Communist society.

It was recognised that it would take several five-year periods to complete the building of a Socialist society and effect the transition from Socialism to Communism. The *fourth Five-Year Plan*, adopted by the Supreme Soviet of the U.S.S.R. in 1946, was a major contribution towards accomplishing this task.

The principal economic and political aim of the fourth Five-Year Plan was *"to restore the ravaged areas of the country, to reach the pre-war level of industry and agriculture, and then to exceed that level considerably."*

First and foremost, it was planned to restore and further develop heavy industry and rail transport, without which there could be no question of a rapid and successful restoration of the entire national economy. It was planned, on this basis, to secure the expansion of agriculture and the consumer goods industries; to reach the pre-war level of consumption and surpass it; to promote large-scale trade and systematically reduce prices; to restore and enlarge the network of schools and institutions of higher education; to develop housing construction on a wide scale; to improve the health services.

In 1946, the Central Committee took a decision on agitation and propaganda work in connection with the adoption of the fourth Five-Year Plan. This decision defined the duties of the Party organisations in explaining the objectives of the post-war Five-Year Plan to the working people, organising Socialist emulation and mobilising Soviet citizens to fulfil and overfulfil the fourth Five-Year Plan.

The Party encouraged the holding of production conferences at factories, which was very important as a means of stimulating the activity and initiative of the masses. Nearly four million production conferences were held in the country in 1946 at which more than five million suggestions for improvements in the work of industrial enterprises were made. The number of production conferences and of the improvement proposals considered by them increased steadily. Upwards of six million production conferences were held in 1950 and over nine million improvement proposals tabled at them, of which more than seven million were carried into effect.

In mobilising the people to carry out the fourth Five-Year Plan, the Party organisations devoted particular attention to promoting mass Socialist emulation. With the aim of improving the organisation of this movement, the Central Committee checked up on its progress at a number of enterprises, and brought to light serious shortcomings, such as elements of formalism and bureaucracy, and an underestimation of the importance of political work among the masses. Similar defects were discovered by local Party bodies.

As these shortcomings were eliminated, the Socialist emulation movement rose to a new stage characterised by increased activity on the part of the masses, a fuller content and greater diversity of forms.

A country-wide Socialist emulation movement, aimed at fulfilling and overfulfilling the fourth Five-Year Plan, was started in 1946 on the initiative of the steel-workers in the town of Makeyevka and the workers of a number of factories in Moscow and elsewhere. It was headed by the Party organisations, and Communists were in the van. Following the example they set, hundreds of thousands of workers took personal commitments to fulfil the annual plans, and the Five-Year Plan as a whole, ahead of schedule. The Party organisations came forward as the initiators of the advance from outstanding achievements by individual workers to highly productive work by whole teams, shops and entire factories. A movement for high-speed work methods began in 1946. Turners employing high-speed methods increased cutting speeds from 70-80 metres to 1,000-1,500 metres a minute. On the initiative of the Communists, these methods became widespread in metallurgy, oil-well boring, and mining. High-speed workers were popularly called men who were outpacing time. Leningraders initiated close co-operation between scientists and workers at the bench. This movement spread swiftly to other towns. A movement to economise raw materials was started at the Kupavna (Moscow Region) Fine Cloth Mill. Through the efforts of Party organisations, this movement was joined by hundreds of thousands of the foremost workers in other enterprises. Workers in Moscow started a country-wide drive to raise the profitability of industrial enterprises, increase accumulations over and above plan and accelerate the turnover of circulating funds. This enabled Soviet industry to manufacture more than 20,000 million rubles' worth of additional goods in 1949 alone. The workers at the Krasnokholmsky Worsted Mill in Moscow started a movement for manufacturing only excellent quality goods.

Popular initiative spread rapidly. As a result of the large-scale activity of Party organisations the emulation movement was joined by increasing numbers of workers. In 1946, the movement embraced more than 80 per cent of the workers, and in 1950, 90 per cent. Factory competed with factory, Donets miners with the miners of the Kuznetsk coalfield, Baku oilworkers with those of Bashkiria.

A movement of inventors and production rationalisers began throughout the country. Workers made hundreds of thousands of suggestions, and saw to it that they were carried into effect. An annual average of over 400,000 inventions, technical improvements and rationalisation suggestions speeding up production and yielding a big saving, were put into effect in the fourth Five-Year Plan period.

The Party organisations put before the working people outstanding examples of heroic labour; they perseveringly gathered the experiences of the foremost workers, and popularised them among the masses. Party technical conferences for the study and application of progressive work methods became widespread; advanced workers representing different industrial enterprises and towns met to exchange experience.

The Party directed all the energy of the working people towards the economic restoration of the war-ravaged areas. Komsomol members helped the Party to heal the wounds inflicted by the war. They assumed "patronage" over the restoration of fifteen of the oldest Russian towns, including Voronezh, Pskov, Novgorod and Orel. Tens of thousands of Komsomol members helped to restore the Donets collieries, the Dnieper Hydroelectric Power Station and the Zaporozhye Iron and Steel Works. Factories, towns and villages were raised from ashes by the heroic labour of the Soviet people. The ore mines in Krivoi Rog and the collieries in the Donets coalfield, the iron and steel mills in the South and the engineering works at Kharkov and Stalingrad, the oil wells at Maikop and Grozny, all the power stations, including the Dnieper Hydroelectric Power Station, and thousands of other industrial enterprises destroyed by the Hitlerites were put back into operation. An important feature distinguishing post-war reconstruction was that the rebuilt factories were equipped with the most up-to-date machinery.

Under the leadership of the Party organisations the working people performed miracles of labour heroism, that were reminiscent of the feats of the war years. Hundreds of thousands of volunteers went to the building sites. The workers and engineers displayed much ingenuity and resourcefulness. For example, at the Azovstal Works, blown up by the Hitlerites, Blast-Furnace No. 4 had been badly damaged. It sagged and leaned over. It was thought that the furnace should be dismantled and a new one built in its place. But on the initiative of the Party organisation, the technicians and workers decided to restore it. The furnace, which weighed 1,300 tons, was straightened out, put upright and moved back into place. This operation took only six weeks, and the furnace was commissioned four months ahead of schedule. At the Dnieper Hydroelectric Power Station, the workers employed an unprecedented method of closing the tunnels at the base of the dam, and expedited its reconstruction considerably. The Donets miners pumped 650 million cubic metres of water out of the flooded pits in record time. In its volume, this was equivalent to draining a lake 27 square miles in area and 33 feet deep. The miners restored more than 1,500 miles of mine workings choked with rock. This was approximately equal to cutting and securing a tunnel from Moscow to Paris at a depth of 600-2,200 feet. The Donets coalfield once again became one of the Soviet Union's major coalfields.

In restoring the national economy of the Republics and regions laid waste by the war, the Party and the people were assisted by the industry of the Urals, Siberia, Kazakhstan and Central Asia. The industrial capacity of these areas had grown considerably during the war years. Large numbers of highly efficient machines and other equipment were sent to the liberated areas from the eastern regions of the country. Kazakhstan and the Central Asian Republics, which had eliminated their backwardness with the help of the working people of the R.S.F.S.R., Ukraine and Byelorussia, now rendered the war-ravaged areas tremendous assistance in the way of skilled personnel and equipment. This was a vivid expression of the great strength of friendship among peoples, one of the sources of strength of the Soviet system.

In 1948 total industrial output in the U.S.S.R. reached the pre-war level and even *exceeded it.* Industry was restored within an exceptionally short space of time. After the Civil War it had taken the country six years to restore its economy. The tremendous losses suffered during the Great Patriotic War were unparalleled. Nevertheless, industry was restored in under two and a half years.

While organising economic reconstruction in the liberated areas, the Party did not overlook industry in the other Republics and regions, and continued improving the distribution of the productive forces of the country. The productive capacity of the metallurgical industry of the Urals and Siberia grew appreciably during the years of the fourth Five-Year Plan. On the initiative of the Party new centres of the ferrous metals industry arose in Central Asia and Transcaucasia. The building of a metallurgical base was started in the north of the European part of the U.S.S.R. Coal output grew steadily in the Kuznetsk coalfield, Karaganda and the Urals. The output of oil increased rapidly in the Urals-Volga Basin. The building of new thermal and hydroelectric stations (Gorky, Kama and others) was begun on a big scale. Construction was started on the Volga and Stalingrad hydroelectric stations on the Volga. The engineering and chemical industries made considerable headway.

The Party made important progress in equipping the national economy with modern machinery. Economic competition between Socialism and capitalism required rapid technical development. This was the only way in which higher labour productivity than under capitalism could be achieved. The problem of technical progress acquired paramount political importance. The Party headed the drive of scientists, engineers and innovators seeking new paths in science and technology, and organised the application of technical achievements in production.

The Party's efforts to promote science and technology were crowned with signal successes. The chief of these was the harnessing of nuclear power, the employment of which in production heralded the beginning of the deepest-going technical revolution in human history. It was the opening of a new era in industrial development.

During the fourth Five-Year Plan period electrification made rapid progress, electronic machines began to be introduced, labour consuming work was mechanised on a big scale in the iron and steel industry, the mechanisation of coal-mining was completed, and the production of turbodrills, the world's best oil-well-sinking machinery, was begun. Production lines became widespread in the engineering industry. Automatic production lines were introduced, and an automatic factory making automobile engine pistons was built. Engineers designed more than a thousand different kinds of highly efficient machine-tools, automatic and other machines, and put them into mass production.

Nevertheless, many problems of technical progress remained unsolved. In some branches of industry and agriculture, the newest achievements of science and technology were put to use much too slowly. The designing of highly efficient machinery did not receive adequate attention. At some factories the equipment had grown obsolete, the technologies were inefficient, and antiquated types of machine-tools and other mechanical equipment were being produced. The timber and coal industries were not making satisfactory use of the latest machines and mechanisms. Complacency, and even stagnation and routine, reigned at many industrial enterprises. Having achieved some success in mastering new machinery, the heads of these works were lulled into complacency, and stopped fighting for technical progress, for the replacement of new machinery by the newest. The result was that technically some branches of industry lagged noticeably behind world science and technology. The struggle for technical progress remained a prime and vital problem for the Party and the people.

Thanks to the heroic labour of the workers and the correct leadership of the Party, the fourth Five-Year Plan was fulfilled ahead of schedule in industry. During this period the country restored, built anew or put into operation more than 6,000 industrial enterprises (not counting small ones), or almost as many as were built in the period of the first and second Five-Year Plans. An average of over three enterprises went into production daily. The industrial targets of the fourth Five-Year Plan were reached in four years and three months. In 1950, total industrial output exceeded the pre-war level by 73 per cent; the plan had called for a rise of 48 per cent. The output of pig-iron was over 19 million tons (29 per cent more than in 1940), steel over 27 million tons (49 per cent above the pre-war level), coal over 261 million tons (57 per cent more than in 1940), oil approximately 38 million tons (22 per cent more than in 1940) and electric power over 91,000 million kw-h. Compared with 1940, labour productivity in industry had risen by 37 per cent.

Difficult problems had to be solved, under the leadership of the Party, in agriculture, which had suffered tremendous losses during the war and also during the drought of 1946. The Party organised the restoration of collective farms, State farms and machine-and-tractor stations in the liberated areas, and ensured the consolidation of collective-farm property.

The Soviet peasantry, which had through personal experience become convinced of the advantages of collective work, restored the collective farms under the leadership of the Party organisations as soon as the fascists were driven out. The Government extended State aid to the restored collective farms in the shape of machines, livestock and seed. Socialist mutual aid assumed great proportions; collective farms in the eastern regions of the country sent large numbers of livestock and big quantities of seeds and farm implements to the collective farms that were being restored.

Practical measures to restore agriculture and a number of proposals aimed at promoting its development were outlined in a series of decisions taken by the Central Committee, in particular at its February, 1947, plenary meeting. The organisational and economic consolidation of the collective farms was of prime importance for increasing agricultural production at that time. The resolution of the Soviet Government and the C.C. C.P.S.U.(B.) "On measures to put an end to violations of the rules of the Agricultural Artel in collective farms," adopted in the autumn of 1946, and the decisions of the February, 1947, plenary meeting of the C.C. laid bare serious shortcomings in the life of the collective farms (the squandering and misappropriation of the land in common usage and collectively-owned property, the incorrect allocation of workday units) and mapped out ways of eliminating these shortcomings.

The Central Committee set the Party organisations the following tasks: to put an end to all violations of the Agricultural Artel rules, prevent the squandering and misappropriation of the land in common usage and collectively-owned property of the collective farms, stop the incorrect allocation of workday units, put an end to violations of the democratic principles of collective-farm management, do away with the absence of personal responsibility for the utilisation of land, implements and means of traction, abolish levelling in remuneration for the work of the collective farmers and in distributing collective-farm incomes according to workday units, render the collective farms greater assistance in agronomy and livestock-breeding, and improve the training of specialists in collective-farm production at courses and refresher courses.

In accordance with the decisions of the Central Committee, the local Party organisations carried out a number of important measures. Collective-farm lands, livestock and other material values which had been used by various organisations and institutions, or illegally turned over to collective farmers or other persons, were returned to the collective farms. The managing staffs of the collective farms were reduced and this saved a considerable number of workday units. The activity of the collective farmers rose noticeably in the course of the fulfilment of the C.C. decisions. But many major shortcomings in the organisation of collective-farm production and in the management of collective farms were not brought to light at that time, and this seriously handicapped the development of Socialist agriculture.

The material and technical basis of agriculture was substantially strengthened, thanks to the efforts of the Party. A large number of machines and great quantities of fuel and fertilisers were sent to the countryside. In 1949, the collective farms, State farms and machine-and-tractor stations received two and a half to four times as many tractors and agricultural machines as in 1940. There were more tractors in agriculture than before the war. The electrification of collective farms, State farms and machine-and-tractor stations was started.

The consolidation of the material and technical basis of collective-farm production and the supply of large numbers of the latest agricultural machines to the machine-and-tractor stations made it imperative to improve the social sector of production in the collective farms. There were many small collective farms in the country, with small land areas and uniting from 10 to 30 households. Machinery was used badly at these small farms, and management expenses were very high. Collective farms such as these hampered the rise of productivity in agriculture.

Proposals to amalgamate collective farms began to come in from many parts of the country. In 1950, Communists initiated a broad movement among the collective farmers *to amalgamate small collective farms into big ones*. Amalgamation was effected on a strictly voluntary basis, and only if all the collective farms concerned favoured the measure. There were 254,000 small collective farms in the country, but after amalgamation, towards the close of 1953, there were 93,000 large collective farms.

This amalgamation was of great economic significance, for it opened up vast prospects for progress in agriculture. Large collective farms could make fuller use of highly efficient machinery, and had greater opportunities for growing big harvests and raising the productivity of livestock husbandry.

Another major social and economic step taken in agriculture after the war was collectivisation in the western regions of Ukraine and Byelorussia, in Moldavia, Estonia, Latvia and Lithuania. In these regions and Republics, which had become part of the Soviet Union on the eve of the war, agriculture was based on individual, petty commodity economy. The Party organisations of these Republics and regions carried out a big campaign among the individual peasants. They showed them the advantages of large-scale collective farming and helped them to take that path. The collectivisation of agriculture in these areas was, in the main, completed in 1949-1950.

Rural Party organisations were strengthened considerably in the post-war period. Many Communists, demobilised from the armed forces, went to the countryside. Communists were also sent to the villages from district centres and towns. The number of Communists in the countryside increased and the network of Party organisations grew accordingly. In 1947 there were 110,800 primary Party organisations in the countryside, and in 1950, their number exceeded 148,000. They united about 1,500,000 Communists.

Through mechanisation, the organisational and economic consolidation of the collective farms, the promotion of Socialist emulation and the use of the experience of innovators, the Party organisations achieved some success in reaching the targets of the fourth Five-Year Plan for agriculture.

Under the leadership of the Party organisations and with the assistance of the entire Soviet people, the collective farmers and machine-and-tractor station and State-farm workers made good most of the enormous losses that had been inflicted on agriculture by the war. In the main, agricultural production reached the pre-war level. However, the opportunities which the collective-farm system offered for increasing agricultural production were not used to the full. For that reason, agriculture did not meet the growing food requirements of the population and the raw material requirements of the light and food industries. The grain problem remained unsolved. Although the grain crop area had increased by 20 per cent during the five-year period, it still fell short of the pre-war level. The crop yield continued to be low. There were big shortcomings in the development of livestock-farming. The number of cows and pigs was smaller than before the war. Livestock productivity remained low. Many collective farms made inadequate use of machinery. There were many collective farms and districts that lagged behind the others.

This state of affairs was due in large measure to serious defects in the management of agriculture, restriction of the initiative of local personnel, and violation of the principle of giving the collective farms and their members a material incentive to produce more. On a suggestion by J. V. Stalin, certain uncalled-for measures were carried out after the war, measures which had an adverse effect on the development of agriculture.

On the basis of the rapid growth of industry and of certain successes in the development of agriculture, the Party was able to secure a rise in the material and cultural standards of the Soviet people. At the end of 1947, the Central Committee of the Party and the Soviet Government abolished rationing, and replaced it by extensive State and co-operative trading. At the same time a currency reform was carried out and the prices of consumer goods were reduced. The population benefited immensely thereby. Between 1947 and 1950, the prices of consumer goods were cut three times. In 1950, the incomes of industrial, office and professional workers and peasants were substantially greater than in 1940.

There was a rise in consumption by the working people of the U.S.S.R. But its further rise was hampered chiefly by the lagging behind of agriculture. In some localities there were difficulties in supplying food to the population. Some towns were short of meat, butter, milk, vegetables and fruit.

Restoration of the housing destroyed by the Hitlerites and the construction of new houses was started on a big scale. In the course of the five-year period more than 1,000 million square feet of housing was restored or built in towns and industrial communities, and 2,700,000 houses were built in the countryside. But the need for housing was still very great, and the housing problem remained the most acute problem of all. The number of medical establishments and sanatoria was considerably increased, and the network of holiday homes, clubs, theatres and libraries was enlarged.

Great difficulties were encountered in fulfilling the fourth Five-Year Plan. Not all of them were surmounted. On the whole, however, the fourth Five-Year Plan period was marked by major achievements in Communist construction. It was an important step towards creating the material and technical basis of Communism.

3. Organising and Ideological Activity of the Party. Nineteenth Congress of the C.P.S.U.

During the fourth Five-Year Plan period the Soviet people achieved signal successes in the economic and cultural fields thanks to the tireless organising activity of the Party, the efficient and rapid readjustment of the Party ranks for work in peace-time conditions, improved Party leadership and a higher ideological standard of social, cultural and scientific activity.

With the war over, the Central Committee set about strengthening the local Party organisations and enhancing their prestige and leading role. The Party strove to ensure that its organisations exercised effective supervision over the activities of the State and economic bodies and fulfilled their political and organising role among the masses.

Between 1946 and 1948 the Central Committee adopted a number of important decisions on questions relating to Party life. In carrying out these decisions, Party organisations spared no effort to improve their work and raise the standard of the leadership they gave to State and economic institutions and voluntary organisations.

Further extension of inner-Party democracy was of decisive importance for improving the efficiency of the Party organisations. During the war, the work of the Party had its positive features and its peculiarities. But inner-Party democracy was somewhat restricted. Continuation of this practice in peace time would have led to a lessening of the activity and initiative of Communists, and would have created the danger of the Party becoming isolated from the masses.

After the war, the first step towards restoring inner-Party democracy was the regular holding of Party meetings and committee plenary meetings, and reports and elections of Party committees at the times laid down by the Party rules.

District and town Party conferences were held in 1945-1947, and regional Party conferences met in 1947 and early in 1948. Congresses of the Communist Parties of the Union Republics were convened at the close of 1948 and in 1949. From then on, local Party committees reported on their work, and were elected, at regular intervals. Meetings of the Party activists began to be held systematically. Plenary meetings of Party committees began to play a bigger role as organs of collective leadership.

At the same time the Party applied a number of measures aimed at effectively combining its political and economic activity. District, town and regional Party committees that had relaxed or neglected their organising, ideological and political work were criticised in decisions of the Central Committee and Party conferences. Such Party committees had assumed functions that did not come within their competence; they occupied themselves with current economic questions, including minor ones, bypassing local government and economic institutions. They had accustomed the heads of collective and State farms, machine-and-tractor stations and factories to refer all business matters solely to the Party committees and to receive instructions only from them. The role of the local Soviets of Working People's Deputies was greatly diminished. Many district and town committees, and departments of regional committees, took up requests with higher authorities on behalf of business executives. The result was that some of the local Party leaders unwittingly began to change from political leaders into officials of the departmental type, and some Party committees began to change from militant, active political organisations into a peculiar kind of administrative and managerial office. Such Party organisations were not always able to oppose parochial, narrow-departmental actions. Absorbed in routine affairs, they lost sight of important, long-range questions of economic development, and underrated organising and political work among the masses. The Central Committee also brought to light cases of Party workers losing their independence and becoming dependent on economic institutions.

These irregular, non-Bolshevik practices began to be eliminated on the initiative of the Central Committee. The harmful practice of tutelage and administration by mere injunction was uprooted step by step. The district, town and regional Party committees became more exacting in their attitude to the workers in local government and economic institutions. Strict Party supervision was established over their activities. As the methods of work improved, Party organisations began to play a bigger role as political leaders. They were enabled to concentrate on fundamental questions of economic and cultural development. They became more active in mobilising the masses to solve the major problems of Communist construction.

Party organisations which clung to the external, ostentatious side of Party work, disregarding its content and effectiveness, were seriously criticised in Central Committee decisions and at Party conferences and plenary meetings of Party committees. Such organisations carried out Party measures without proper preparation. They adopted declarative, general decisions, and neither organised nor verified their putting into effect.

The activity and initiative of the Party rank and file and the efficiency of Party organisations rose to a higher level as they took determined steps to eliminate these shortcomings. Party organisations began to play a much greater organising and guiding role in State, economic and cultural development, and in the political education of the masses.

This period, however, did not witness the complete elimination of the essential shortcomings in Party work. In some cases inner-Party democracy was restricted. Party work retained elements of administration by injunction, and the principle of collective leadership was violated. The Party's political work fell short of the growing requirements of the masses. These facts had an adverse effect on the work of Party organisations and on the activity of Communists.

In the post-war period educational and ideological work occupied an important place in the activity of the Party. Lenin taught that Communism is the result of the conscious historic creative effort of the masses. The continuous growth of the conscious creative activity of the masses is a law of the progressive development of society and an absolute condition for the transition from Socialism to Communism. In the course of Socialist construction the educational work carried out by the Party brought about radical changes in the minds of Soviet people. The characteristic features of the moral aspect of man in Soviet society are lofty principles, unbounded faith in the cause of Communism, the attitude to labour as a matter of honour and valour, the desire to augment Socialist property, Soviet patriotism, and appreciation of the fact that public interests come before all others. But survivals of a private-owner psychology and of a bourgeois type of morality, servile admiration for the reactionary culture of the West, manifestations of nationalism and other survivals of capitalism still lingered in the minds of part of the Soviet people.

The completion of the building of Socialism and the gradual transition to Communism logically made the ideological activity of the Party the *basic* form of struggle against the survivals and traditions of the old exploiter system. The time came when capitalism had to be driven out of its last refuge—the sphere of ideological relations. Only when the remnants of the traditions and morals cultivated for centuries by private property relations have been completely eliminated will it be possible to say that "the last nail" has been driven "into the coffin of capitalist society, which we are burying" (V. I. Lenin, *Collected Works*, Vol. 27, p. 379). With every step forward, practical experience brings up questions of Communist education, and they acquire increasing importance.

There were certain other circumstances in the post-war years that made it imperative to give greater attention to educational, and ideological work. During the war tens of millions of people had lived in territory temporarily occupied by the enemy. Millions of people had been deported to Germany by the Hitlerites. Many Soviet servicemen had been prisoners of war. The Hitlerites had subjected all these people to assiduous propaganda. During the liberating anti-fascist drive of the Soviet troops to the West, part of them found themselves on the territory of capitalist countries, and reactionaries tried in various ways to influence them. In the western regions of Ukraine and Byelorussia, and in the Baltic Republics, bourgeois nationalist groups left behind by the Hitlerites carried on anti-Soviet propaganda among the population.

A pernicious ideological influence was exerted on Soviet people through these and other channels. The mass of the people scornfully rejected the reactionary bourgeois views that were thrust on them. But a section of the population showed ideological instability, and took an uncritical view of the capitalist régime.

It should also be borne in mind that ideological work was underrated in many Party organisations, and propaganda and agitation work was neglected. For a long time a part of the leading Party cadres did nothing to improve their knowledge of Marxism-Leninism. The result was that, as a whole, ideological work lagged behind the tasks which the Party was carrying out, and behind the scale of the Communist construction going on.

Taking into consideration the general requirements of Communist construction and the specific circumstances of the post-war period, the Party launched an *offensive* on the ideological front.

The success of the Party's educational work depended primarily on the ideological level of the Communists. The Party membership had changed considerably during the Great Patriotic War. It continued to grow rapidly in the first post-war years. In 1946 the Party had close on six million members, of whom more than half had joined during the war. A sizable section of the Party membership had not had time to receive the necessary theoretical training. There was a certain discrepancy between the Party's quantitative growth and the level of the political education of its membership. To overcome this discrepancy, the Central Committee decided not to press the further growth of the Party ranks but to organise Party education on a large scale.

Party organisations began to select new members more carefully, and devoted greater attention to the political education of Communists. A ramified system of Party education was again established. It included political literacy schools, circles for the study of the history of the Party, political economy and philosophy, district Party schools and universities of Marxism-Leninism. Many Communists studied theory on their own. Between 1946 and 1952 the bulk of Party and government workers went through refresher training.

The higher ideological level achieved by Communists made it possible to extend educational work among the masses. Party organisations sought to bring political education to all sections of the population, special attention being paid to repatriates.

To improve the political education of the masses, the Central Committee of the Party took steps to raise the level of its agitation. The level of agitation activity was checked up on in several

Party organisations, and major shortcomings were laid bare. The general scope of agitation and its ideological level did not meet the tasks facing the people and the Party. In many cases, mass agitation lacked a militant spirit, and was inadequately used to raise the political consciousness of the working people and mobilise them for a more rapid development of the national economy. Many Party organisations underestimated the role of political agitation, and reduced it to talks on production and technical subjects. Carrying out the decisions of the Central Committee, the local Party organisations considerably improved agitation among the masses.

On the ideological front, the Party directed the main blow at the survivals of bourgeois views and ideas, at uncritical appraisals of the reactionary bourgeois culture of the West, and at departures from Marxism-Leninism in science, literature and art.

A major task of the Party in its ideological work was to expose and completely eradicate all manifestations of grovelling before the reactionary culture of the bourgeois West on the part of a section of the Soviet intelligentsia. The aim of the Party organisations was to make every citizen of the U.S.S.R. a conscious Soviet patriot, an active fighter for Communism. By showing the epoch-making significance of the successes achieved by the U.S.S.R. in building Socialism and of the advantages of Socialism over capitalism, the Party strengthened the patriotic Socialist pride of the Soviet people and their sacred feeling of love for their Socialist Fatherland. It encouraged them to have faith in themselves and in their ability to build Communism. The Party paid special attention to the education of the youth, so that they might grow up ideologically well-tempered, spiritually robust and optimistic, full of creative energy and prepared to work selflessly for the cause of Communism.

The propagation of Soviet patriotism played an outstanding role in the spiritual development of the Soviet people building Communism. Their ideological level rose, their faith in their own capacity grew still stronger, and their activity increased. At the same time, however, certain mistakes were made in propagating Soviet patriotism. The press frequently portrayed all life in the capitalist world as being a mass of corruption. The activity of the progressive forces was underrated and achievements in science and technology abroad were ignored. This hindered the speedy utilisation of major discoveries made in science and technology abroad, limited creative contacts between Soviet and foreign scientists and engineers, and impeded the establishment of close ties with the democratic, progressive sections of the people in the capitalist countries.

In order correctly to define the immediate tasks in the ideological field, the Central Committee adopted a number of important decisions: in 1946, "On the magazines *Zvezda* and *Leningrad*," "On the repertoire of drama theatres and steps to improve it" and "On the film *A Great Life*"; in 1948, "On the opera *A Great Friendship*, by V. Muradeli."

The Central Committee decisions and the Party press noted the achievements of Soviet culture, at the same time laying bare serious shortcomings in the development of literature and art. Certain writers and artists had begun to preach that art should be shorn of ideological and political content. There were cases of a truthful picture of life being distorted and realistic traditions discarded. Certain magazines were printing insipid, ideologically harmful works, sometimes imbued with depression and disillusionment, scepticism about the future. Theatres had included in their repertoires cheap, unartistic, banal plays by foreign bourgeois playwrights. Formalistic vacillations were in evidence in music. These facts indicated that there was a certain danger of the work of some writers, composers and artists losing touch with the vital interests of the people, the policy of the Communist Party.

The Central Committee took serious steps to eliminate these shortcomings, emphatically condemning all attempts to divorce art from politics.

"The vitality of Soviet literature, the most progressive literature in the world," said a resolution of the C.C. C.P.S.U.(B.), "lies in the fact that it has not, and cannot have, any interests other than those of the people and the State. Soviet literature must help the State to educate the youth properly, to meet their requirements, and to bring up a healthy young generation that believes in its cause, is undaunted by difficulties and is prepared to surmount all obstacles" (*C.P.S.U. in Resolutions.* Part III, p. 487).

The Central Committee's decisions on literature and art further developed the fundamental Leninist principles of Soviet culture: service to the people, recognition of the lofty social role of art, its links with the political tasks of the present day and with the life of the people, and realism in art. The Central Committee showed in all its magnitude the significance of Lenin's principle of the Party spirit in art, the role of the Marxist-Leninist outlook in giving a truthful portrayal of Socialist reality. In its decisions the Central Committee worked out a programme of struggle for the creation of works that combine lofty ideological content and perfect artistic form. They also contained a profound criticism of erroneous, formalistic tendencies.

The Central Committee's decisions on literature and art

were discussed by all literary and art organisations. Many regional and city Party committees held special conferences with workers in literature and art. Hundreds of thousands of people took part in the discussions. The result was that the people as a whole became much more exacting towards workers in art and literature, and took an uncompromising stand on ideological vacillations.

At the same time, as a resolution of the Central Committee on May 28, 1958 pointed out, the C.C. decision on the opera *A Great Friendship* contained some unjust and unwarrantedly sharp criticisms of the work of a number of talented Soviet workers in art. This was a manifestation of the negative features that were characteristic of the period of the personality cult. In carrying out these decisions of the Party, the press and the organisations connected with literature and art had committed errors and distortions. They had sometimes substituted mere injunction for a constructive discussion of problems of art and, in appraising books, music and films, had levelled unfounded criticism at some works while giving undue praise to others.

As it developed its offensive on the ideological front, the Party also discovered serious shortcomings in the development of science. Many theoretical works had no connection with reality, with the actual experience of the millions of people building Communism. This fostered dogmatism. Works appeared written in an objectivistic spirit, which constituted a concession to bourgeois ideology. Un-Marxist concepts were infiltrating into the natural science as well.

On the initiative of the Central Committee, discussions were held on philosophy (1947), biology (1948), physiology (1950), linguistics (1950), and political economy (1951).

Serious shortcomings in the elaboration of Marxist-Leninist philosophy were revealed and criticised during the discussion of philosophical problems. These shortcomings were disregard of Party principles, attempts to gloss over the contradictions between Marxism-Leninism and philosophical trends alien to it, isolation from urgent problems of the day, and manifestations of scholasticism. The discussion mapped out ways of reorganising the front of philosophical science.

The economic discussion dealt with the features distinguishing the economic development of modern capitalism, the basic laws governing the Socialist reorganisation of society, and the ways of effecting the gradual transition from Socialism to Communism. Subjective and voluntarist views of all kinds were condemned. The advocates of these views denied the objective character of economic laws and alleged that under Socialism economic laws could be made, transformed or abolished at will. This point of view led to an arbitrary approach to economic management and to adventurism in politics. The discussion revealed the serious consequences of the prolonged isolation of the economic sciences from the actual development of Socialist society.

The discussions held in various fields of science on the initiative of the Party helped to remove a number of ideological distortions, strengthened the Party principle in science and raised the standard of scientific research. However, under the influence of the Stalin personality cult, these discussions had negative consequences as well. In some cases the clash of opinions was narrowed down and scientific forces were divided. In the social sciences, elements of dogmatism remained in evidence, as was the divorce of theory from practice.

In spite of some negative aspects resulting from the personality cult, the decisions and measures taken by the Central Committee of the Party on ideological questions were of signal importance to the ideological life of the Party and the people, and to the development of Soviet culture. They greatly stimulated creative thought in science. Questions concerning the progress of Soviet literature and art began to be regarded as matters of national importance. The discussions on ideology brought scientists, art workers and the people still closer together; the people began to show a greater interest in questions concerning culture and science, and to exert a stronger influence on the creative work of writers and artists. Lack of principle, objectivism, cosmopolitanism and other manifestations of bourgeois ideology were dealt crushing blows during the ideological offensive. The ideological level of Soviet culture rose considerably, which made it possible to raise the political consciousness and cultural level of the Soviet people to a higher stage.

The Nineteenth Congress of the C.P.S.U. was held in October, 1952. It represented 6,013,259 members and 868,886 candidate members. It summed up the results of the struggle and achievements of the Soviet people over a period of more than 13 years.

The principal results, confirming the correctness of the policy pursued by the Communist Party, were the historic victory in the Great Patriotic War, the rapid restoration and high rates of further development of the national economy, the rise in the material and cultural standards of the Soviet people, the further consolidation of the Soviet social and political system and the gathering of all the forces of the camp of peace and democracy around the Soviet Union. The Congress approved the political line and practical work of the Central Committee of the Party.

The Nineteenth Congress defined the Party's new tasks in

furthering the country's economy and culture. It approved directives for the Five-Year Plan of economic development of the U.S.S.R. for 1951-1955. The new plan envisaged further progress in all branches of the national economy, through the priority development of heavy industry and a rise in the material and cultural standards of the people. It laid down high rates of development for the metallurgical, coal, oil and engineering industries and electrification, as the basis for large-scale technical progress in all branches of the national economy. It called for a general increase during the five-year period of 70 per cent in the industrial product, an increase of 80 per cent in the output of the means of production and a 65 per cent increase in the ouptut of consumer goods. The output of the engineering and metal-working industries and the capacity of the power stations were to be nearly doubled in the five-year period, and the capacity of the hydroelectric stations in particular was to be trebled.

In agriculture, the task set was to increase the yield of all crops, to increase the number of livestock owned by the collective farms and, at the same time, to raise its productivity considerably, and to increase the total and marketable output of crop and animal husbandry. But these targets were not backed with the necessary economic and organisational measures, with the result that for a long time agricultural production made no headway.

The directives provided that labour productivity should increase roughly 50 per cent in industry and 55 per cent in building. The national income was to grow by 60 per cent. It was planned on this basis to achieve a substantial rise in the material and cultural standards of the people.

The Nineteenth Congress adopted a decision to change the name of the Party. It resolved that the Communist Party of the Soviet Union (Bolsheviks)—C.P.S.U.(B.)—should thenceforth be named the Communist Party of the Soviet Union—C.P.S.U. The double name of our Party ("Communist" and "Bolshevik") had arisen historically, as a result of the struggle against the Mensheviks, and its purpose had been to draw a clear line between itself and Menshevism. As the Menshevik party had long since left the stage in the U.S.S.R., the double name of the Party had lost its point, all the more so that the concept *Communist* expressed most precisely the content of the Party's main task—the building of a Communist society.

The Congress discussed N. S. Khrushchov's report on changes in the Party rules, and amended the latter. The new rules generalised the vast experience accumulated by the C.P.S.U. in Party development since the Eighteenth Congress. They contained a short definition of the C.P.S.U. as a voluntary militant union of like-minded people, Communists, drawn from the working class, the working peasantry, and the working intelligentsia.

The rules recorded the principal tasks of the Communist Party of the Soviet Union as set by the Nineteenth Congress:

"To build a Communist society by means of a gradual transition from Socialism to Communism, continuously to raise the living and cultural level of society, to educate the members of society in the spirit of internationalism and fraternal ties with the working people of all countries, and to strengthen to the utmost the active defence of the Soviet Motherland against aggressive actions on the part of its enemies" (*C.P.S.U. in Resolutions*, Part III, p. 579).

The rules most fully and concretely expressed the main tasks of the Party, and the duties and responsibilities of the Party organisations and of all Communists at the present stage of Communist construction.

The question of the leading role of Communists in Soviet society had acquired special importance in the new conditions. This was reflected in the clauses of the rules defining a Communist as an active fighter for the fulfilment of the Party's decisions, and about the duties and rights of a Party member, which were defined more fully and concretely. The rules emphasised the duty of the Communist to "do his utmost to guard the unity of the Party as the chief condition of its strength and might."

The demands made of Communists by the rules of the C.P.S.U. are of great political and educational importance. They heighten the role of each Party member as an active, conscious and selfless fighter for the cause of Communism. They are indicative of the increased activity of Party members through the broad development of inner-Party democracy.

In full conformity with the principles of democratic centralism, the Congress introduced a number of changes into the structure of the central Party bodies. It was considered advisable to discontinue the practice of convening all-Union Party conferences, because basic questions of the Party's policy and tactics should be examined in good time by Party Congresses. The Political Bureau of the Central Committee was reorganised as the Presidium of the Central Committee, established to direct the work in the intervals between plenary meetings of the Central Committee. This reorganisation was in keeping with the functions that were actually being carried out by the Political Bureau. Practice had shown that it was advisable to concentrate the Central Committee's organising work of an executive nature in a single body, the Secretariat of the Central Committee; hence there was no longer any need for the Organisational Bureau of the Central Committee. With a view to enhancing the role of Party control bodies in preventing violations of Party and State discipline by Communists, the Party Control Commission was reorganised into a Party Control Committee under the Central Committee of the C.P.S.U.

J. V. Stalin spoke at the closing session of the Congress. He stressed the importance of mutual support between the C.P.S.U. and the Communist Parties of the other countries in the attainment of their supreme goal. He showed the immense significance of the struggle for democratic liberties and national sovereignty in the liberation movement. The monopoly capitalists, the chief enemy of the emancipation movement, had become more reactionary than ever. They had trampled the principle of equality of people and nations underfoot, and had thrown overboard the banner of national independence and of bourgeois-democratic liberties. These banners could and should be raised and carried forward by the Communist and democratic parties, if they wanted to be patriots of their countries and to become the leading force of their nations.

Delegations from 44 brother Communist and Workers' Parties attended the Congress as guests. The Congress also received greetings from the Communist and Workers' Parties of a number of capitalist countries whose representatives had been unable to come to the U.S.S.R. because of persecution by their governments.

Inspired by the decisions of the Congress, Party organisations began to work for the fulfilment of the fifth Five-Year Plan and for the further economic and cultural progress of the country.

On March 5, 1953, soon after the Congress Joseph Vissarionovich Stalin died. The enemies of Socialism counted on confusion breaking out in the ranks of the Party and in its leadership, and on vacillation appearing in the conduct of home and foreign policy. But their hopes were dashed. The Communist Party rallied still closer round its Central Committee, and raised the all-conquering banner of Marxism-Leninism higher than ever. The Leninist Central Committee successfully led the Party and the entire people forward, along the road to Communism.

4. The Role of the C.P.S.U. in Strengthening the Community of Socialist Countries. Formation of the World System of Socialism

The emergence of Socialism from the bounds of a single country confronted the Communist Party of the Soviet Union and the Communist Parties of the other Socialist countries with a new important task, namely, that of *establishing international rela-*

tions of a new type, the community of Socialist countries. Such a task had never been set or resolved by anyone in history. Formerly, in its foreign policy, the U.S.S.R. had proceeded from the fact that it was dealing only with capitalist countries. But now it was necessary to build up inter-State relations with Socialist countries as well.

The general principles of Socialist foreign policy—complete equality of countries, non-interference in each other's internal affairs, mutual respect for territorial integrity, defence of peace—which determined the content of its relations with the capitalist countries, also became the basis of the Soviet Union's relations with the other Socialist countries. But relations between the Socialist Powers could not be confined to this, especially as the young People's Democracies stood in need of political support, economic aid and an exchange of experience in Socialist construction.

International relations *of a new type* took shape between the U.S.S.R. and the People's Democracies of Europe and Asia. The content of Soviet foreign policy became richer and more varied. The international character of the dictatorship of the proletariat gave rise to a fundamentally new, hitherto non-existent function of the Socialist State—*the function of aiding other countries in the building of Socialism* and of establishing international Socialist relations.

There were objective economic, political and ideological grounds for establishing new, Socialist relations between the nations which had overthrown capitalism. In all the Socialist countries, power was in the hands of the people led by the working class, which was headed by its vanguard, the Communist Party. Social ownership of the means of production determined the community of economic interests of these countries. It determined the interest of each country severally in promoting the economy of the Socialist camp as a whole and of its individual members. All the countries which had overthrown capitalism were in their social and economic development moving towards a common goal —Socialism and Communism—and were equally interested in defending the revolutionary gains and national independence of their peoples. They were guided by the same ideology, Marxism-Leninism. It was on this basis that qualitatively new, Socialist relations were established between peoples who had thrown off the yoke of capitalism. The features distinguishing these relations were fraternal co-operation, mutual aid and sincere mutual support in the struggle for Communism on the basis of proletarian internationalism.

The Communist Party of the Soviet Union took an active part in creating and strengthening the community of Socialist countries. As the guiding force of the first country to have built Socialism, it shared, and continues to share, its experience of building a new life with the brother Parties, on a footing of equality.

To find the forms and methods of building Socialism that would be best suited for their countries, the brother Communist and Workers' Parties carefully studied the experience of building Socialism accumulated by the C.P.S.U. and of all the aspects of its activity since it came to power. "The work we have to do," said Mao Tse-tung, "is difficult and our experience is insufficient. We must therefore study the advanced experience of the Soviet Union." In his speech at the Nineteenth Congress of the C.P.S.U., Klement Gottwald said: "We come to you to learn how to build Socialism."

The Communist and Workers' Parties, as well as the governments of the Socialist countries, sent Party and government officials, trade union leaders, economic executives, engineers and technicians, scientists, workers and peasants to the Soviet Union to study Soviet experience. The Central Committee of the C.P.S.U., the Soviet Government and local Party and Soviet organisations did their best to facilitate the study of the experience of Socialist construction in the U.S.S.R. They gladly received these delegations and opened all doors to them. The envoys of the friendly countries visited towns and villages, factories, collective and State farms, machine-and-tractor stations, scientific and educational establishments, Party organisations and State institutions. In studying Soviet experience, the brother Parties compared it with their own experience and that of other Socialist countries, and creatively applied it in their own countries, choosing the forms and methods of building Socialism best suited to the specific conditions obtaining in their countries.

The extensive joint theoretical and practical activity of the C.P.S.U. and the brother Communist and Workers' Parties of the People's Democracies produced the only correct, scientific view of the significance of the experience of Socialist construction in the U.S.S.R. This view expresses the general laws governing the Socialist transformation of society.

The path travelled by the Soviet people is the highroad of Socialist development for the working people of all countries. The main features and laws of development of the Socialist revolution and of the building of Socialism in the U.S.S.R. are not of local, specifically national, significance; they are of international importance.

The Communist Party of the Soviet Union established close cordial political co-operation between the U.S.S.R. and the other Socialist countries. Bilateral treaties of friendship and mutual

assistance were concluded, which strengthened the national independence of the People's Democracies. The Soviet Union and
the People's Democracies co-operated in the struggle for peace.
The U.S.S.R. rendered the Socialist countries friendly assistance
in setting up a new State machinery. At the request of their governments, the U.S.S.R. sent these countries advisers on various
questions.

Through the joint efforts of the C.P.S.U. and the brother Communist Parties, a new type of economic co-operation, based on
full equality, mutual benefit and comradely mutual assistance
was set up between the U.S.S.R. and the People's Democracies,
and the forms of this co-operation worked out. As the Socialist
countries developed and grew stronger, relations between them
embraced ever new spheres of economic life.

At first the basic form of economic co-operation was foreign
trade. It was conducted not on the basis of competition and ruthless suppression of the weak, as is the case under capitalism, but
on the basis of complete equality and mutual benefit, without
any selfish motives. The volume of trade grew year after year.
A world Socialist market came into being.

Later, this economic co-operation became more varied. Aid
by means of credits acquired great importance. In the post-war
years (up to and including 1952), the U.S.S.R. extended to the
People's Democracies long-term credits totalling close on 15,000
million rubles. These credits were given on the most favourable
terms possible.

Mutual assistance in the sphere of production and technology
increased from year to year. The Soviet Union helped the People's
Democracies to design, build and operate new industrial enterprises. Scientific and technical co-operation got under way. The
U.S.S.R. helped the Socialist countries to build many industrial
enterprises, and handed over to them a large number of designs
for industrial and cultural projects, complete sets of blueprints
for new machines and equipment, technological specifications
and calculations. Extensive assistance was rendered in training
personnel and in mastering technology. Thousands of specialists
from the People's Democracies were trained at Soviet higher
educational institutions. Many workers from a number of the
fraternal countries mastered the latest techniques at Soviet
factories. In its turn, the Soviet Union received production and
technical assistance from the People's Democracies.

The need for a special body to co-ordinate economic relations
was felt more and more acutely as economic co-operation developed. A Council of Mutual Economic Assistance was set up by
the U.S.S.R. and the European People's Democracies early in
1949. Its aim was to arrange exchanges of experience in economic

management and to organise mutual aid by supplying raw materials, foodstuffs, machines, and so forth.

The co-ordination of economic plans was the highest form of economic co-operation and mutual assistance. In the early years it was sporadic. The first steps to co-ordinate the national economic plans were taken during the period of the fifth Five-Year Plan. Inter-State specialisation, and the co-ordination of production among the factories of the Socialist countries, began to be organised. This ensured the most favourable conditions for the development of the productive forces and the best opportunities for utilising production and raw material resources, accelerated the rate of Socialist construction and strengthened the economic independence of the People's Democracies.

As relations between the Socialist countries developed and the Socialist mode of production took root in the People's Democracies, there came into being a *Socialist system of world economy*, of which the world Socialist market is a component. The world system of Socialism represents the sum-total of the Socialist economies of independent and sovereign States, and develops in accordance with economic laws inherent in Socialism. It includes the gradually shaping international division of labour among the Socialist countries, and is distinguished by specialisation and co-ordination of production. Its important distinguishing features is comradely co-operation and mutual assistance. These factors ensure the rapid and planned economic development of each country, and of the world economic system of Socialism as a whole.

Certain difficulties were encountered and some mistakes were made in establishing and developing friendly co-operation between the Socialist countries. The Central Committee was greatly concerned about relations with the Communist Party of Yugoslavia and relations between the U.S.S.R. and Yugoslavia. Whereas the C.P.S.U. and the Communist Parties of the People's Democracies were building up relations between themselves in a spirit of Marxism-Leninism, the attitude adopted by the leadership of the Communist Party of Yugoslavia on a number of fundamental questions ran counter to Marxism-Leninism. Step by step, the C.P.Y. leadership departed from the principles of proletarian internationalism, and slid towards nationalism. In 1948 the Information Bureau of the Communist and Workers' Parties, of which the Communist Party of Yugoslavia was a member, examined this question, and adopted a resolution "On the situation in the Communist Party of Yugoslavia." All the basic points of this resolution were correct. It contained Marxist-Leninist, principled criticism of the mistakes made by the leadership of the C.P.Y., and was approved by all the Marxist-Leninist Parties. The C.P.Y. leadership refused to take part in the work of the Information Bureau and rejected all criticism, declining even to examine it on its merits. The differences became acute.

While an effort was being made to overcome these differences, J. V. Stalin committed a grave error. Instead of developing comradely criticism in principle of the wrong views and actions of the C.P.Y. leadership and showing their incompatibility with the fundamentals of Marxism-Leninism, he took the path of interrupting normal State and diplomatic relations between the U.S.S.R. and Yugoslavia. All relations between the C.P.S.U. and the C.P.Y. were broken off. Under the influence of the hostile activity of Beria and his accomplices, certain unfounded charges were made against the leaders of the C.P.Y. Subsequently, the Communist Party of the Soviet Union, on its own initiative, took steps to restore normal relations between the U.S.S.R. and Yugoslavia.

The policy of friendship and mutual assistance, pursued by the C.P.S.U., triumphed. The mistakes made occasionally in the relations with fraternal countries were of a secondary, accidental character. The essence of these relations was genuinely Socialist, and accorded fully with the principles of proletarian internationalism. The C.P.S.U. directed all its efforts to strengthening friendship with People's China and the other People's Democracies, and this policy was entirely successful. The joint activities of the C.P.S.U. and the other Communist Parties standing at the helm of their respective States, resulted in the establishment of a fraternal community of Socialist countries, and no amount of intrigue on the part of their enemies could, or can, shake their solidarity and unity. This unity is a source of the strength of the Socialist camp.

The establishment of international relations of a new type, and of the world system of Socialism, was a great and historic gain of the peoples. The important progress made by the Socialist countries in their economic and cultural development would have been impossible without comradely co-operation and mutual assistance.

The relations of friendship and mutual assistance that have arisen between the Socialist countries successfully combine the interests of each country with the interests of the Socialist camp as a whole. The problem of relations between the Socialist countries was, for all its complexity and novelty, successfully solved in the interests of each country and of the entire Socialist camp.

The victorious termination of the Great Patriotic War against the fascist aggressors enabled the Party and the Soviet people to resume their peaceful, creative labour and set about completing the building of Socialism and starting the gradual transition to Communism.

The most important post-war task of the Party and the Soviet people was to restore the national economy as quickly as possible and to ensure its further uninterrupted development. The Party rallied the working people for the fulfilment of this task, and organised mutual assistance between the different republics and regions. It achieved the rapid restoration of the liberated areas along with the further expansion of industry in the east of the country, the technical re-equipment of the economy and greater profitableness of industry.

In the conditions obtaining after the war, the Party raised the standards of Party leadership, and considerably improved its political and ideological work. The restrictions on inner-Party democracy that had existed during the war were gradually removed, though they were not completely eliminated, and criticism and self-criticism developed to some extent. The role of the Party organisations as political leaders was enhanced thanks to proper combination of the Party's political and economic activity. In the course of the ideological offensive the Party dealt crushing blows to all manifestations of lack of principles, cosmopolitanism, objectivism and other expressions of bourgeois ideology.

Victory over the fascist aggressors consolidated the position of the Soviet Union and raised its international influence and prestige. The relation of forces in the world arena changed radically in favour of Socialism, to the detriment of capitalism.

The Party made effective use of the post-war changes in the world arena to create favourable international conditions for the building of Communism.

The emergence of the People's Democracies ushered in a new stage in the development of Socialism. A world system of Socialism came into being. The U.S.S.R. ceased to be the only Socialist country encircled by capitalist States. It now occupied the position of the leading country in the Socialist world. A new sphere of activity opened up before the C.P.S.U., that of rendering assistance to the brother Parties of the People's Democracies in Socialist construction, promoting mutual assistance and co-operation with them. This mutual assistance benefits the Soviet Union, each one of the Socialist countries separately and the Socialist camp as a whole.

The Party made use of the Soviet Union's immense prestige to preserve and consolidate peace and to combat the Anglo-American war-mongers. Consistently implementing Leninist policy of peaceful coexistence of countries with different social systems, the Party developed economic competition between the U.S.S.R. and the capitalist countries, being confident that Communism would win a decisive, epoch-making victory in this competition.

CHAPTER SEVENTEEN

THE PARTY'S STRUGGLE FOR A POWERFUL UPSWING OF THE NATIONAL ECONOMY, FOR THE COMPLETION OF THE BUILDING OF SOCIALISM

(1953-1958)

1. The International Situation in 1953-1958. The Efforts of the Party and the Soviet State for a Relaxation of International Tension

The period from 1953 to 1958 was marked by momentous events in the life of the Soviet Union, in the activity of the Party, in its struggle to build a Communist society in the U.S.S.R. and to preserve peace.

The international situation had become extremely tense. The successes of Communist construction in the U.S.S.R. and of Socialist construction in the People's Democracies, the greater unity of the Socialist countries, the growth of their international influence and the further weakening of the positions of capitalism, the exacerbation of all the contradictions of capitalism and the accelerated break-up of the colonial system, increased the fear of the ruling imperialist circles of losing their supremacy and intensified their hatred for the forces of democracy and Socialism. The policy of the leading imperialist Powers, primarily the U.S.A., became still more aggressive, particularly after the North Atlantic military bloc was formed and war unleashed in Korea by the U.S. imperialists.

Peace was preserved thanks to the consistent peace policy of the Soviet Union, the Chinese People's Republic and the camp of Socialist countries as a whole; but it could not be regarded as durable. The threat of a third world war loomed over mankind.

To save the world from a nuclear war of extermination, the U.S.S.R. had to make fresh efforts, pursue a still more active peaceful policy and extend its relations and contacts with peace-loving forces abroad. True to Lenin's principle of peaceful coexistence, the Soviet State started, under the leadership of the C.P.S.U., an energetic and purposeful *struggle to achieve a relaxation of international tension.* Relying on its own steadily growing might and on the fraternal support of the other Socialist countries and the international working class, the U.S.S.R. took a series of important steps aimed at consolidating peace.

To bring about a lessening of international tension, it was necessary, first and foremost, to stop the bloodshed in Korea and Indo-China.

The Soviet Union actively supported the Chinese People's Republic and the Korean People's Democratic Republic in their efforts to end the war in Korea. For two years the U.S. aggressors kept disrupting the armistice talks. The armistice was finally signed in 1953. The war in Korea, which had been fraught with serious international complications, ended on the lines from which the American aggression had started. The predatory plans of the U.S. imperialists in this area were frustrated. One hotbed of war was extinguished.

In 1954, the Democratic Republic of Vietnam and the Democratic forces of Cambodia and Laos succeeded, with the active assistance of the Soviet Union and the Chinese People's Republic, in reaching an agreement with France on a cease-fire in Indo-China despite bitter resistance on the part of the American imperialists. This victory of the forces of peace met the interests of the peoples of Vietnam and Laos and also the interests of the French people. Another hotbed of war was extinguished.

The Soviet Union also took steps to reduce tension in Europe. On the initiative of the Soviet Government, the Austrian problem was finally settled in 1955 on the basis of the permanent neutrality of Austria. On the initiative of the Soviet Government, diplomatic relations were established between the U.S.S.R. and the Federal Republic of Germany.

The Central Committee of the C.P.S.U. and the Soviet Government took the initiative in settling the conflict between the U.S.S.R. and Yugoslavia. Relations between the two countries were improved in 1955.

The Party considered that a stable and lasting peace could be achieved by establishing a system of *collective security*, a collective security system based on the joint efforts of all the States of a particular area of the globe to maintain peace, and which would be the very antithesis of the imperialist system of military blocs, which divide countries into restricted opposing alignments.

In 1954, the Soviet Government proposed a draft All-European Treaty on Collective Security to the countries of Europe and to the United States. This Soviet initiative was vigorously supported by the masses of the people. The Western Powers, however, rejected the Soviet proposal, for they had entirely different plans in view. In October, 1954, they signed agreements providing for the remilitarisation of West Germany and her involvement in the North Atlantic military bloc.

The U.S.S.R., like the other Socialist countries, could not ignore these acts, which constituted a grave threat to world peace. In the new situation that had arisen in Europe, the Soviet Union, jointly with the governments of the People's Democracies, worked out new measures to ensure peace and security. In May, 1955, a treaty of friendship, co-operation and mutual assistance was signed in Warsaw between the U.S.S.R. and the European People's Democracies. The signatories to the treaty undertook, in the event of armed attack on any one of them, to come to the immediate assistance of the country attacked with all the means at their command, including the use of armed force. The Government of the Chinese People's Republic declared its complete solidarity with, and support of, the decisions adopted.

The Warsaw Treaty became an important stabilising factor in Europe. It is a defensive measure taken by peace-loving countries, and serves the security of the peoples of Europe and the maintenance of peace throughout the world. Unlike the military treaties of the imperialist Powers, the Warsaw Treaty is open to any State that may desire to accede, irrespective of its social system. The Warsaw Treaty loses its validity in the event of a collective security system being set up in Europe.

Meanwhile, militarism was being restored in West Germany. Former Hitler generals were put in command of the armed forces of the Bonn government. Propaganda of revenge steadily increased. All this raised big obstacles to the settlement of the German question. The Soviet Union, however, persevered in its efforts to achieve such a settlement speedily. It proposed the conclusion of a peace treaty with Germany and the withdrawal of all foreign troops from her territory. It supported the aspirations of the German people for the national reunification of both parts of their country on peaceful and democratic lines. But since there were two independent German States with totally different social systems on the territory of Germany, this reunification could not be achieved by mechanically joining one part of Germany to the other. It could be brought about only by the German people themselves, through negotiation between the German Democratic Republic and the Federal Republic of Germany. The Soviet Government supported the proposal of the Government of the G.D.R. to establish a confederation of the two German States as a first step towards the restoration of Germany's national unity.

By restoring militarism in West Germany and rejecting the

proposals for negotiations between the Germans of the two parts of Germany, the governments of the U.S.A., Britain and France, and also of the F.R.G., closed the doors to a settlement of the German question. They preferred to keep Germany split indefinitely.

In the fight for peace and a relaxation of international tension, the C.P.S.U. and the Soviet Government paid unflagging attention to disarmament. They called as before for a reduction of armaments and armed forces, the prohibition of atomic and hydrogen weapons and the banning of tests, and for the establishment of strict international control over the implementation of all these measures. In an effort to facilitate reaching an international agreement on disarmament, the Soviet Government accepted a number of the proposals made by the Western Powers, although it would have preferred more radical decisions being taken on the disarmament question. For example, at an earlier date the U.S.S.R. had proposed that the Great Powers reduce their armed forces by a third, but in 1955 it accepted the proposal of the Western Powers that the U.S.A., the U.S.S.R. and China reduce their armed forces to 1,000,000-1,500,000 men, and Britain and France to 650,000 men.

But whenever the Soviet Government accepted any of the proposals of the Western Powers, the latter either hastened to go back on them and renounce them altogether, or to complicate matters by making numerous reservations. In this way the Western Powers revealed that their aim was to frustrate disarmament. Behind talk about disarmament, they were deceiving the peoples and continuing the arms race.

It was obvious that the U.S.A., Britain and France had no intention of adopting a radical decision on disarmament as suggested by the Soviet Union. The Soviet Government sought every opportunity to break the deadlock in the disarmament talks, and put forward a series of proposals for settling the problem by stages. But here again the Soviet Union came up against sabotage on the part of the Western Powers which blocked all its steps towards genuine disarmament.

It became increasingly clear to the peoples that the Soviet Union and the other Socialist countries were the only sincere advocates of disarmament, that they alone were seeking to rid the working people of all countries of the burden of armaments and of the threat of a nuclear war.

A major achievement of the peaceful foreign policy of the U.S.S.R. was the extension of relations between the Soviet Union and the peoples of Asia and Africa who were upholding their independence against imperialism. The visits by Soviet leaders to the countries of the East and the visits of numerous political leaders of those countries to the Soviet Union greatly helped to strengthen ties with those nations. Contacts with the peoples of Latin America expanded too.

During the period 1953-1958 the crisis of the colonial system of imperialism became most acute. The national liberation movement was in full tide. A large number of countries in Asia and Africa freed themselves from the colonial yoke and became independent national States. Following Syria, the Lebanon, India, Burma and Indonesia, which gained their State independence in the post-war years, freedom was won by Egypt and Iraq, which had been dependent on British imperialism, by former colonies like Sudan and Ghana, and a number of other countries. The peoples who won their independence had to defend it not only against the old colonialists, Britain and France. More and more often they were compelled to defend themselves against U.S. colonialism, now the chief bastion of the colonial system of imperialism, the chief exponent of colonial and racial oppression.

In their struggle against the colonialists, the peoples of the East found a staunch champion in the U.S.S.R. The bonds of friendship and co-operation between the U.S.S.R. and the Asian and African countries working for peace, grew steadily stronger. The Soviet Union's tireless struggle against imperialism and aggression was of immense help to the oppressed and dependent peoples in their struggle for political emancipation, and later in defending the State independence they had won against numerous encroachments by the colonialists.

The countries that had won political independence also received all possible assistance from the Soviet Union in their struggle to achieve economic independence. This aid was given on principles of full equality, non-interference in internal affairs, and without political or military strings attached. The character of this aid was the exact opposite of the onerous terms on which the U.S.A. and other colonial Powers extended their so-called aid. Thanks to the Soviet Union, the economic position of the underdeveloped countries was strengthened as against the imperialist oppressors, and the colonialists' possibilities of imposing onerous terms on these countries were limited. All this helped to raise the international role of the countries of Asia and Africa who stood for peace.

Relations between the Soviet Union and the neutral European countries that were not members of military blocs likewise developed and grew stronger.

The Communist Party and the Soviet State time and again took the initiative for the improvement of relations with the U.S.A., Britain, France, Italy and other capitalist countries. The U.S.S.R. strove to secure mutual trust in international relations, to promote foreign trade, to remove all discrimination, and expand contacts and co-operation in the fields of culture and science. To quote N. S. Khrushchov: "Our country would like to have good relations with all countries that are against war and favour peaceful coexistence, and we are doing all we can to establish such relations" (*Forty Years of the Great October Socialist Revolution*, Eng. ed., p. 69).

The steps taken by the Communist Party and the Soviet Government to consolidate peace had a beneficial effect on the international situation. A certain lessening of tension was achieved in international relations. In the summer of 1955 it became possible to convene a conference of the Heads of Government of the U.S.S.R., U.S.A., Britain and France in Geneva. As a result of the exchange of views, the Heads of Government of the four Powers announced their desire to contribute towards a relaxation of international tension. However, the Soviet Union was the only country to back up its declaration with practical steps to strengthen peace.

After the Geneva Conference, the Soviet Government made still more active efforts to bring about a détente and extend co-operation between States, thereby once again furnishing convincing proof of its good will. It took important steps radically to improve its relations with the U.S.A., as well as with Britain and France. These efforts of the Soviet Government met with no response from the reactionary ruling circles of the Western Powers. But in spite of the obstacles put up by them, the Soviet Government achieved a considerable expansion of international business and cultural contacts. Diplomatic relations were restored with Japan. Graphic evidence of the Soviet Union's resolve to cut armaments was the reduction of its armed forces in 1955 by more than two million men.

The peace initiative of the Soviet Union was a most important factor in world politics. It exerted increasing influence on the entire course of international relations. The peace forces grew and united their ranks. The aggressive imperialist circles found themselves in ever greater isolation. The peoples felt more hopeful that war could be averted. This was a major victory of the forces of peace. The Soviet Union's prestige and influence increased immensely.

However, any real prospect of a further détente and consolidation of peace ran counter to the interests of the ruling imperialist circles. For the monopolies, peace meant smaller profits. Peaceful economic competition between the two social systems benefited Socialism. The relation of forces in the world arena was changing continuously to the detriment of capitalism, as a result of the rapid economic and cultural growth of the Soviet Union, China and the other People's Democracies, and of the consolidation of their unity. The crisis of the colonial system was weakening the position of imperialism.

The ruling circles of the imperialist countries had always opposed a détente, but at the time of the Geneva Conference they tried to disguise their policy of intensifying the cold war and preparing for aggression. They soon discarded their peace mask and again openly reverted to their "positions of strength" policy. They had not abandoned their intention of restoring capitalism by force of arms in the countries that had taken the path of Socialist construction, and of re-establishing colonial oppression where the peoples had overthrown colonial rule.

As it worked for a détente and for peace, the C.P.S.U. was ever aware of the fact that the reactionary imperialist forces had not laid down their arms, and were capable of engaging in all kinds of adventures, and that unremitting vigilance was therefore necessary.

In the autumn of 1956, Britain, France and Israel made an armed attack on Egypt in order to reimpose a colonial regime on her.

Almost at the same time, reactionary imperialist circles, chiefly of the United States, organised a counter-revolutionary revolt in Hungary. The imperialists intensified their subversive activities against the other Socialist countries as well. They made feverish attempts to disunite the Socialist countries and viciously attacked the policy of the Soviet Union, doing their utmost to discredit it. No means were too low for them to use, if only they could discredit the ideas of Socialism. The danger of war loomed large again. The forces of reaction at the same time intensified their fight against the Communist Parties in the capitalist countries. They placed great hopes on undermining these parties from within by reviving the activity of revisionist elements.

With the war danger growing, the Soviet Union once again came forward in defence of peace, relying on its own economic and military might, on the support of the other Socialist countries and on the warm sympathy of all the peace-loving peoples. It emphatically demanded that the aggression against Egypt be stopped. Faced with this demand, and coming up against the heroic resistance of the Egyptian people and the indignation of democratic opinion throughout the world, the British, French and Israeli governments were compelled to cease their aggression and withdraw their troops from Egypt. The forces of peace headed by the U.S.S.R. thus helped the Egyptian people to uphold their independence.

At the request of the Hungarian Government and in fulfilment of its internationalist duty, the Soviet Union rendered the brother

Hungarian people effective assistance in putting down the counter-revolutionary uprising. Thereby it prevented the restoration of capitalism and fascism in Hungary and her conversion into a spring-board for imperialist aggression in the heart of Europe.

The U.S.S.R. frustrated the plans of the aggressors, and they had to retreat. It was a great and historic victory. It showed the significant shift that had taken place in the relation of forces between the advocates of peace and the advocates of war in favour of the former, and opened up further prospects of preventing aggression.

The imperialists' insidious plans to drive a wedge between the Socialist countries completely failed too. Adhering strictly to the principles of proletarian internationalism, the Soviet Government in a declaration published on October 30, 1956, advanced a programme for the promotion of friendly relations with all the People's Democracies on the basis of complete equality, respect for territorial integrity, State independence and sovereignty, non-interference in internal affairs, fraternal co-operation and mutual assistance. In the joint struggle against the onslaught of reaction, relations between the Soviet Union and China and the other People's Democracies became still closer and friendlier than before. The fraternal co-operation of the Socialist countries and their mutual assistance in the economic, political and cultural fields developed successfully. The unity of the Socialist camp is a reliable guarantee of the national independence and sovereignty of each Socialist country.

Victorious in the struggle against imperialist aggression in Egypt and Hungary, the U.S.S.R. continued to champion peace. It resolutely opposed the renewed threat of aggression in the Middle East. When the U.S.A. organised a conspiracy against the independence of Syria and set Turkey and other countries against her, the Soviet Union helped Syria to stave off the danger threatening her. In 1958, the Soviet Union prevented American and British aggression spreading to Iraq and other countries of that area, and helped the peoples of the Lebanon and Jordan to get rid of the American and British troops that had invaded their countries. The peoples saw the U.S.S.R. as the most dependable bulwark of their independence.

In the latter half of 1958, a dangerous situation arose in the Far East, in the area of Taiwan and the Straits of Taiwan, as a result of aggressive acts undertaken by the U.S.A. against the Chinese People's Republic. War threatened to break out. The Chinese people were prepared to give a fitting rebuff to the aggressors. True to its duty, the Soviet Union declared that an attack on the Chinese People's Republic, the Soviet Union's great friend, ally and neighbour, would be regarded as an attack on the U.S.S.R. and that it would come to the assistance of People's China if the U.S.A. committed an act of aggression against her. This had a sobering effect on the high-handed American aggressors. The peaceable policy of the Chinese People's Republic prevented a further complication of the situation in the Taiwan area.

The setbacks suffered by the imperialist aggressors were evidence of the growing might of the Socialist camp and of other peace forces. There was now a real and increasing possibility of averting war, of preventing the imperialist aggressors from plunging the peoples into fresh military adventures. But if the great cause of peace was to succeed, all the forces opposing war had nevertheless to be vigilant and ready for action: they had to act in a united front and not relax their struggle.

The struggle for peace, for an international détente and for the promotion of friendship among nations had been, and remains, the corner-stone of the foreign policy of the U.S.S.R. and the other Socialist countries. This idea runs through all the proposals made by the Soviet Government on various international issues.

In March, 1958, the Supreme Soviet of the U.S.S.R. took a further initiative in the matter of disarmament. It decided on the unilateral cessation of atomic and hydrogen bomb tests by the Soviet Union. The Soviet Union called upon the other nuclear Powers to take similar steps. It warned them, however, that unless the other nuclear Powers did stop tests, it would have no choice but to renew its own. The Soviet proposals for a peace treaty with Germany and for giving West Berlin the status of a free city, as well as for averting surprise attack, were all aimed at strengthening peace and relaxing international tension. The Soviet Government did, and continues to do, all in its power to have outstanding international issues settled by negotiation. It proposed a meeting of the Heads of Government as the best means of lessening international tension.

These steps of the U.S.S.R., motivated by humanism and love of peace, were acclaimed by broad sections of world opinion. Nevertheless, the governments of the U.S.A., Britain and France persisted in their refusal to respond to the call of the peace forces and take the road to a détente.

One of the major results of the activity of the Party and the Soviet Government in the field of foreign policy between 1953 and 1958 was the extension of the Soviet Union's international relations. The Soviet Union was visited by a large number of people representing all sections of the population in capitalist countries. They were able to see for themselves the peaceableness and good will of the Soviet Union, and its great historic achievements. In their turn, many Soviet citizens visited foreign countries. This helped to expose the slanderous anti-Soviet propaganda carried on by imperialist reaction, and convinced wide circles abroad that the Soviet people sincerely wanted peace; it exploded the slanderous assertion of hostile propaganda about "Soviet aggression." The attempts of imperialist reaction to impose on public opinion a distorted picture of the situation in the U.S.S.R. came to nothing. The C.P.S.U. did much in those years to spread the truth about the U.S.S.R., the first land of Socialism. The result was that considerably more people throughout the world came to appreciate the advantages of the Socialist system over capitalism. The number of the Soviet Union's friends grew, and so did the social forces supporting its policy. The lying story that the U.S.S.R. wanted to shut itself off from the capitalist world by an "iron curtain" was destroyed.

In 1953-1958, the Communist Party and the Soviet Government developed the greatest activity in the fight for peace, to prevent aggression and to consolidate the international position of the U.S.S.R. Consistently adhering to the Leninist general line in foreign policy, the Party took into account all that was new in the international situation, and found ever new methods and means of implementing its peace policy in keeping with the changing conditions. This period was characterised by the tremendous constructive initiative displayed by the Party in foreign policy. The Party's wise activity raised the Soviet Union's international prestige and increased the possibility of repelling aggression. Aggressive circles found themselves in greater isolation.

The Communist Party and the Soviet Government combined their consistent policy of peace with a further strengthening of the Soviet Union's defensive capacity. The growing might of the U.S.S.R. was the most dependable guarantee against the threat of war, and a powerful peace factor throughout the world.

2. The Reorganisation of Party Work in Line with the Leninist Standards of Party Life. Rectification of the Errors and Shortcomings Produced by the Personality Cult. The Measures Adopted to Achieve a Steep Rise in Agriculture and to Promote Technical Progress in Industry

In 1953-1958, Soviet society entered a period in its internal development when the tasks of Communist construction became *immediate practical tasks* of the Party and the people. Under the leadership of the Party, the people carried out important political and economic measures aimed at further consolidating the Soviet social and political system, promoting the development of industry, primarily heavy industry, on a big scale, achieving a steep rise in agriculture and improving the living conditions of the people. In these years the Party came out against the personality cult, and eliminated its consequences from all spheres of Soviet life. In the process of eradicating these consequences, the Party, in full keeping with the new historic tasks, ensured the reconstruction of the work of Party organisations, State institutions and voluntary associations in accordance with tried and tested Leninist traditions, and enhanced its role as leader.

The Party resolutely eradicated everything that impeded the forward movement of Soviet society and was incompatible with Leninist traditions. It did not merely restore the Leninist principles, but creatively applied them to the new historical conditions. It worked out new forms of leadership which while fully conforming with the spirit of Leninism, took account of the new situation and the wealth of experience accumulated. Such were the most salient features of the new period in the life of Soviet society, and the features distinguishing the Party's activity in those years.

In mobilising the masses to carry out the tasks of Communist construction, the Party boldly laid bare serious shortcomings in Party, State and economic activity. It critically appraised the situation in agriculture and industry, and set out to eliminate these shortcomings and achieve a further rapid growth of Socialist economy.

A major irregularity in Party life had been the violation of the Leninist standards of Party life and the principles of Bolshevik leadership, as a consequence of the personality cult. For a long time there had been no collective leadership, or proper criticism and self-criticism, in the activity of the Central Committee and its Political Bureau.

Serious mistakes had also been made in the management of the national economy, in particular of agriculture, where a grave situation had arisen as a result of departure from the principles of Socialism. The output of agricultural produce was lagging far behind the country's growing requirements. The Leninist principles of administration were not fully complied with in industrial management. As a result of excessive centralisation of economic management and planning, and of underestimation of the importance of economic incentives, the actual possibilities for increasing production, and the untapped resources, were not fully taken into consideration, while the creative initiative of the masses was not given sufficient scope. Little was done to stimulate the interest of factories in the development of technology. The result was that in a number of industries technical development was below world standards.

There were gross violations of Socialist legality and the democratic rights of Soviet citizens.

There were other mistakes and distortions as well, arising from the cult of Stalin's personality, a phenomenon that was utterly alien to the spirit of Marxism-Leninism, and that had become widespread in theory and practice. The Party could not reconcile itself to these negative features, which were particularly intolerable in the new conditions.

The eradication of the consequences of the personality cult from all spheres of the activity of the Party and the State became a major political task of this period, and the main condition for strengthening the leading role of the Party, further reinforcing the Soviet social and political system and reorganising Party and administrative work.

On the initiative of N. S. Khrushchov, the Party and its Leninist Central Committee laid bare the harm caused by the cult of Stalin's personality and the mistakes and shortcomings arising from it, and began energetic efforts to eliminate them.

The exposure of Beria, a political adventurer and a sworn enemy of the Party and the people, was of great importance for the consolidation of the Soviet system, the promotion of Socialist democracy and the elimination of the harmful consequences of the personality cult. As head of the State security service, Beria tried to place it above the Party and the Government and use it against the Party and its leadership, against the Government of the U.S.S.R. Pursuing hostile aims, he trumped up charges against honest people and grossly violated Soviet law.

The Central Committee put an end to the criminal activities of Beria and his associates. Having rid itself of these dangerous agents of the class enemy, the Party considerably strengthened its ranks and consolidated the Soviet State still further.

At its plenary meeting in July, 1953, the Central Committee of the Party approved the resolute measures that had been taken to end the criminal activities of Beria and his accomplices. The plenary meeting took steps to strengthen Party guidance at all levels of the State machinery, and to ensure effective supervision over the work of all agencies and departments, including the State security service.

The Central Committee adopted a firm policy of restoring and developing the standards of Party life, primarily the principle of collective leadership, that had been worked out by Lenin and tested in practice. The decision of the July plenary meeting stated that proper leadership of the Party and the country, the unshakable unity and cohesion of the Party membership and the successful building of Communism could be ensured only by the collective political experience of the entire Party and by the collective wisdom of the Central Committee, which in its work draws on Marxist-Leninist theory and on the initiative and activity of the Party leaders and rank and file.

The Central Committee greatly extended inner-Party democracy through the consistent implementation of the principles of democratic centralism. Leninist methods and style of leadership, based on a thorough and detailed knowledge of life, on close ties with the masses, on a careful consideration and use of their experience, and on the encouragement of the creative activity and initiative of the working people, were introduced into the work of the Party organisations, State institutions and voluntary associations.

The reorganisation of the work of the Party's central bodies was of paramount importance. The principle of collective leadership was restored in the work of the Central Committee, after a long period of disuse. Plenary meetings of the C.C. began to be held regularly, in accordance with the Party rules. The Central Committee of the C.P.S.U., the supreme directing body of the Party in the interim between congresses and the centre of ideological, political and organisational leadership, began to play a more important role. Once again the Central Committee became a standing collective body.

The structure of the leading bodies of the C.C. C.P.S.U. was reshaped to the new conditions. Instead of two bodies, the Presidium and the Bureau of the Presidium, it was decided to have only one, the Presidium of the C.C. C.P.S.U. as established by the Party rules. It was found advisable to institute the post of First Secretary of the Central Committee. N. S. Khrushchov was elected to this post in September, 1953.

The principle of collective leadership began to be consistently implemented in local Party organisations as well. Methods of management by instructions were resolutely uprooted in the work of the Party. The number of Party activists grew and their role was enhanced. Basic questions of Party and economic life began to be submitted more regularly for broad discussion by Party activists and Party meetings. To encourage inner-Party democracy, the C.C. abolished the post of C.C. organiser in industry and elsewhere, and the political departments on the railways, in the river and maritime fleets and in the fishing industry. Greater responsibility for the work of these enterprises and organisations was assumed by the local Party organisations. The Party apparatus was reduced. The C.C. began systematically to invite rank-and-file Communists to help work out Party policy through a broad discussion in Party organisations of the fundamental questions of Communist construction.

The Party did everything possible to promote the creative

activity and initiative of local Party and government bodies and of the broad masses of the working people. It brought about a bigger participation of the trade unions, the Komsomol and the co-operative, scientific, cultural and other organisations of the working people in the political life of the country.

When investigating and eliminating the flagrant violations of Socialist legality, the C.C. looked into the so-called "Leningrad case" and established that it had been trumped up by enemies and careerists with the purpose of weakening the Leningrad Party organisation and discrediting its leaders. All the other doubtful cases, fabricated in 1937-1938 and other years, were re-examined. Honest Party and government workers, military men and business executives, who had been declared to be enemies of the people and convicted, were exonerated. This act was a further indication of the Party's political courage, fidelity to Marxism-Leninism and devotion to the interests of the people.

Distortions of the Leninist policy on nationalities, committed during the Great Patriotic War, were eradicated. The national autonomy of the Balkars, Kalmyks, Chechens, Ingushes and Karachais was re-established and they were thus enabled to develop unhampered in the fraternal family of peoples of the U.S.S.R. The friendship and Socialist internationalism of the Soviet peoples benefited thereby.

The Party and the Government took resolute steps to have the standards of Socialist legality strictly observed in all spheres of the life and activity of the Soviet State. The State security service, the courts and the Procurator's offices were reinforced with tested personnel; Party supervision over the work of these bodies was restored. The Party put an end to all violations of the constitutional rights of Soviet citizens, and did all that was necessary to ensure Soviet citizens a tranquil life and the benefits of Soviet socialist democracy.

The restoration and development of the Leninist standards of Party life, and the reorganisation of the work of the Party and the State on this basis, enabled the Party to increase efficiency in its ranks, broaden its ties with the masses and enhance its leading role.

The Party did much to remedy the consequences of the personality cult and overcome serious shortcomings in the economic field.

The Party devoted special attention to eliminating the lagging-behind of agriculture. This had given rise to a disproportion in Socialist economy between industry and agriculture, a disproportion that could become a major obstacle to the country's development and retard the growth of the national economy and the well-being of the people, and the country's advance towards Communism.

A plenary meeting of the Central Committee of the C.P.S.U.,

held in September, 1953, thoroughly examined the situation in agriculture and mapped out measures to improve it. It pointed out that the most urgent and important economic task at the moment was to achieve a steep rise in all the branches of agriculture while continuing vigorously to develop heavy industry. The plenary meeting was a *turning-point* in the development of agriculture. Agriculture was also discussed at the February-March and June, 1954, and January, 1955, plenary meetings of the Central Committee, with N. S. Khrushchov reporting. The Central Committee held a series of zonal meetings with the participation of leading Republican, territorial and regional officials and the foremost workers in agriculture. These meetings worked out concrete measures for securing a *steep* rise in agriculture in the areas concerned.

In their decisions, the plenary meetings of the C.C. critically appraised the state of agriculture and established both the objective and the subjective reasons for its lagging behind. The objective reasons were that formerly it had been impossible simultaneously to maintain a high rate of development of heavy industry—the foundation of Socialist economy—of agriculture and of the light industries. The considerable damage done to agriculture by the war also told.

The subjective reasons had their roots in inefficient leadership. Little had been done over many years to study the situation in agriculture. The actual state of affairs in some branches of agricultural production was being presented in unwarrantably rosy colours. Inadequate use was being made of machinery. Many collective farms, machine-and-tractor stations and State farms lacked competent leaders and specialists. Undue centralisation of planning fettered local initiative and impeded the development of agricultural production. Great damage was done to agriculture as a result of violations of the Leninist principle of giving the collective farmers a material incentive to increase agricultural output. The fixed delivery and purchasing prices of many agricultural products did not always correspond with the outlay of labour, and hence did not properly stimulate the output of these products. At many collective farms, payment for workday units was low. The principle of calculating fixed deliveries to the State on a per hectare basis was distorted. The commitments to the State that were not fulfilled by the more slack collective farms were being shifted to the more advanced and efficient collective farms.

The Central Committee outlined and carried out a series of measures to effect a rapid rise in agriculture.

First and foremost, the Party and the Government saw to it that the collective farms and collective farmers were given a greater material incentive for increasing output. They were guided in this by Lenin's well-known proposition that Socialist tasks can be successfully carried out "not directly relying on enthusiasm, but aided by the enthusiasm engendered by the great revolution, and on the basis of personal interest, personal incentive . . ." (*Collected Works*, Vol. 33, p. 36).

Fixed delivery and purchasing prices for the main agricultural products were raised considerably. The size of compulsory deliveries of grain, potatoes, vegetables and oil seeds by the collective farms, and of livestock products by the collective farmers was reduced. An end was put to the impermissible practice of placing almost the entire burden of deliveries to the State on the more efficient collective farms. New and progressive forms of material incentives were introduced. Monthly and quarterly advance payments to the collective farmers, which helped to increase labour productivity and improve discipline, became widespread. In 1956, such advance payments were already being made in two-thirds of the country's collective farms.

The Government began to allocate substantially larger sums for the pressing needs of agriculture. In 1954-1955, State investments in agriculture totalled 34,400 million rubles, which was 38 per cent more than in the whole period of the fourth Five-Year Plan. The technical basis of agriculture was enlarged. In 1954-1955, the collective farms, machine-and-tractor stations and State farms received 404,000 tractors (in terms of 15 h.p. units), 227,000 lorries, 83,000 grain combines and a large quantity of other machinery. New progressive methods of cultivating the land and tending crops, such as the square-pocket method of planting potatoes and sowing maize and the square method of sowing vegetables, began to be applied in agriculture.

One of the most important measures taken in those years was the reinforcement of the collective farms, machine-and-tractor stations and State farms with specialists and managerial personnel. In 1954-1955, at the call of the Party, more than 20,000 Communists living in towns went to the countryside, recommended as collective-farm chairmen.

The Central Committee saw to it that specialists in agriculture were used to the best advantage. Of the more than 350,000 specialists with a higher or secondary school training who were employed in agricultural agencies at the time, only 18,500 were working directly in collective farms. By decision of the Party and the Government, more than 120,000 agricultural experts working in towns and district centres were assigned to collective farms, machine-and-tractor stations and State farms.

Continuing to do everything to promote the initiative of the collective farmers in making the most of local conditions and potentialities, the Central Committee and the Government revised the system of agricultural planning. The collective farms were permitted themselves to plan the size of their crop areas, the yield of certain crops, the number of livestock and the productivity of animal husbandry. State bodies retained the right to specify the amounts of produce to be delivered or sold to the State by the collective farms. The State retained supervision over the output of staple products in the quantities required by towns and industrial centres and necessary for foreign trade and for the accumulation of stocks. The new system of planning helped to eliminate bureaucratic abuses in agricultural management and gave full scope to the creative initiative of the collective farms.

The Party paid special attention to expanding grain farming, the basis of the whole of agricultural production. A sharp increase in grain output was the most pressing task of the day.

The chief means of increasing the output of grain in that period was the development of virgin and disused land, which very soon yielded good results. The original plan was to plough up 32 million acres of virgin lands in Kazakhstan, Siberia, the Volga region, the North Caucasus, and other areas. But in view of the immense labour enthusiasm and initiative shown by the people, the Party and the Government adopted a decision to develop a minimum of 70 to 75 million acres of new lands by 1956.

The Communist Party started extensive political and organising work. The Central Committee appealed to the youth to take an active part in developing the virgin and disused lands in Kazakhstan and Siberia. Hundreds of thousands of people, including more than 350,000 young men and women, responded to the Party's call. The labour valour displayed by them was worthy of the builders of Communism. More than 200,000 tractors (in terms of 15 h.p. units) and thousands of other machines and implements were sent to the new land-development areas in 1954-1955. A total of 425 State farms were set up in these areas, a large number of machine-and-tractor stations, State storehouses and elevators were built and thousands of miles of motor roads and railways were laid. Close on 90 million acres of virgin and disused lands were developed in three years.

There were enormous difficulties hindering the rise in livestock-farming, which had been lagging behind for many years. The development of livestock-farming was held up mainly because fodder resources were inadequate. The Party took steps to increase these resources; the maize area was enlarged. This made it possible to improve the situation in livestock-breeding within a short time.

To increase labour productivity in crop-farming and animal husbandry, the Party organisations widely popularised the achievements of agricultural science and advanced experience.

The Party radically improved agricultural management. Big changes took place in the work of the Party organisations and local government institutions connected with the countryside, particularly the district Party committees and the district executive committees. The Party reinforced them with well-trained and experienced personnel. New blood was infused into the ranks of Party workers. Bureaucratic methods and red tape were gradually eradicated from the leadership of the collective farms, machine-and-tractor stations and State farms. Party workers got down to studying the economy and techniques of agricultural production, which enabled them to guide the collective farms, machine-and-tractor stations and State farms more competently.

Party and Komsomol organisations in the collective farms began to play a bigger role in the countryside. At the beginning of 1941 there were Party organisations in only 12 per cent of the collective farms; in 1956, the figure had risen to 93 per cent. Between 1954 and 1958 the number of Communists in the collective farms increased by more than 230,000.

Working for the fulfilment of the Party's decisions for the improvement of agriculture, the rural Communists headed a mass Socialist emulation movement in the collective and State farms. There began a patriotic movement to undertake obligations for increased output of grain, milk, butter, meat and other agricultural produce. The co-operation of a great mass of collective farmers and machine-and-tractor station and State-farm workers was enlisted in working out and implementing concrete measures to increase production.

The important steps taken by the Party and the Government to bring about a rapid advance in agriculture, the energetic assistance rendered to the countryside by the Socialist towns, and the selfless labour of the collective farmers and machine-and-tractor station and State-farm workers, soon yielded positive results. Before long thousands of previously slack collective farms had moved into the front ranks. Total grain output increased in 1954, despite the drought that affected many areas. The grain deliveries plan was carried out ahead of schedule. Thus the way was paved for all the branches of agriculture to forge ahead and the disproportion in Soviet economy to be bridged.

To secure a steady rise in the standard of living, the Party put forward the aim of supplying the population with greater quantities of manufactured goods, in addition to foodstuffs. The Central Committee and the Government took decisions to increase the output of consumer goods and improve State trade. The output of consumer goods began to grow steadily.

Aiming to achieve the balanced development of all branches of the national economy, the Party steadfastly followed Lenin's policy of giving priority to heavy industry. It did much to increase the capacity of the metallurgical, coal, power, engineering and other industries turning out the means of production.

The decisions adopted by the July, 1955, plenary meeting of the C.C. C.P.S.U. played a big part in improving the work of all industries, primarily heavy industry. The plenary meeting and conferences attended by leading industrial executives, innovators, engineers and technicians, outlined measures to ensure a further powerful expansion of industry through better organisation of production and the introduction of the latest achievements of science and technology.

Technical progress in industry was an important means of speeding up the country's economic development, raising labour productivity and providing a material and technical basis for Communism. The Soviet Union achieved major successes in scientific and technological development. New techniques were introduced into the national economy. The change-over to automation in the power, iron and steel and engineering industries was accelerated. The Soviet Union was the first country to use atomic power for peaceful purposes. The building in the U.S.S.R. of the world's first atomic power station marked the beginning of the new and greatest scientific, technical and industrial revolution in history, a revolution which is in keeping with the requirements of the epoch of Communist construction.

Along with these notable achievements, the plenary meeting of the Central Committee recorded that some industries were lagging behind in their technical development. Many executives were doing little to introduce new techniques, lacked perspective and purpose in their technical policy. They forgot that technology must develop continuously, that the old must be replaced by the new, and the new by the latest. Soviet scientific achievements were frequently not used or simply shelved, and the successes of science and technology abroad were ignored. This had an adverse effect on technical progress.

The plenary meeting demanded that the executives of Socialist industry put an end to complacency and conceit, make a systematic and thorough study of the achievements of science and technology at home and abroad, and steadily move technology forward. The main trend in the development of industry was to be *steady technical progress with the course set towards improved technology* and a further rise in labour productivity on that basis.

The plenary meeting adopted decisions on other urgent questions of improving industrial production. It called for promoting specialisation and co-operation in industry in every possible way, and outlined measures to improve labour organisation and the system of remuneration, raise the quality of output and reduce costs.

To improve industrial management, the Central Committee and the Government introduced changes into the structure of the State and economic machinery so that it could meet the requirements of industry better. Parallel economic departments and offices that were not needed were closed down. In 1954 and 1955, administrative, economic, State purchasing and other staffs not engaged in production were reduced by almost 750,000 people.

Party organisations extended their political work in industry and strove to do away with formalism in Socialist emulation. A movement for the fulfilment of the fifth Five-Year Plan ahead of schedule, initiated in 1954 by the workers of leading industrial enterprises in Moscow and Leningrad, stimulated the drive to achieve greater labour productivity. Emulation spread to promote technical progress and to make fuller use of production premises, equipment, raw materials and other inner potentialities. The spreading of technical knowledge was improved, and the experience of the best workers more extensively popularised, in the factories.

Enthusiastically supported by the Party and the Soviet people, the bold initiatives of the Central Committee led to big successes in industry and agriculture. The Party overcame the resistance of conservatively inclined executives who were blind to the new demands posed by reality, persisted in their outdated dogmatic views of the tasks of Communist construction, hindered reorganisation and clung to the old methods of work.

True to its Leninist principles, the Party and its Central Committee combated everything that hindered progress. They raised and confidently solved problems of Communist construction posed by practical experience, and were always in search of the new. An outstanding role in formulating the new tasks and in creatively developing the basic problems of the Soviet Union's home and foreign policy was played by the Twentieth Congress of the C.P.S.U.

3. Twentieth Party Congress and Its Historical Significance

The Twentieth Congress of the C.P.S.U. was held in February, 1956. The delegates represented 6,795,896 members and 419,609 candidate members of the Party. Delegations from the Communist and Workers' Parties of 55 foreign countries attended the Congress as guests.

The Congress discussed the reports of the leading Party bodies and directives for the sixth Five-Year Plan of economic development of the U.S.S.R. (1956-1960).

The report of the C.C. C.P.S.U., delivered by N. S. Khrushchov, contained a comprehensive analysis of the Soviet Union's international and domestic situation, summed up the results of the Party's activity since the Nineteenth Congress, and outlined the prospects of Communist construction.

In a detailed resolution, the Congress unanimously approved the political line and practical activity of the Central Committee and mapped out the Party's tasks for the next few years.

The Congress laid special emphasis on the fact that the main feature of the present era was the emergence of Socialism from the bounds of a single country and its transformation into a world system. This had given rise to new conditions for the solution of internal and international problems.

The C.C. report gave a vivid description of the results of the development of two opposite world social systems—Socialism and capitalism. The interval between the two congresses had been marked by a further rapid increase in the economic might of the U.S.S.R. and the other Socialist countries. A distinctive feature of the economic growth of the U.S.S.R., China and the other Socialist countries was their all-round development and general peaceful trend. In the Socialist countries, the advantages of the Socialist system and the correct policy of the Communist Parties ensured high rates of industrial development, far exceeding those of the capitalist countries. This was a real guarantee that Socialism would achieve further successes in its economic competition with capitalism. The industrial basis of Socialism was becoming more and more powerful. The steadily increasing share of the Socialist countries in the world's industrial production was a material expression of a progressive historical process: the contraction of the sphere of capitalist exploitation and the expansion of Socialism's world positions. A major result of the development of the Socialist camp in the period under review was the expansion of economic ties and the establishment of still closer friendship between the Socialist States. All this showed that Socialism was advancing triumphantly.

In the capitalist countries, events were developing in the opposite direction. The economy of world capitalism had become still more unstable, developed still more unevenly, and the decay of the capitalist system was deepening. The problem of markets was growing more acute from year to year and the contradictions between the imperialist countries were increasing. The workers and working people in general were waging an ever more active and resolute struggle against imperialist oppression. In the capitalist countries there was taking place a further realignment of forces, leading to still greater isolation of the reactionary, aggressive circles. The positions of world capitalism were growing steadily weaker.

The Twentieth Congress of the C.P.S.U. profoundly analysed and drew scientific general conclusions from the latest phenomena in the world arena, and advanced a number of new propositions on fundamental problems of international development that enriched Marxist-Leninist theory.

The Congress developed Lenin's principle of the peaceful coexistence of countries with different social systems in its application to the present age, when two opposed world camps existed. Peaceful coexistence meant competition of countries with different social systems in the economic and cultural fields. A tense struggle was developing between them in the ideological field.

Marxism taught that Socialism would triumph inevitably in all countries: but victory would come, not as a result of the "export" of revolution, which was impossible and had nothing to do with the Marxist concept of history, but as a result of the development of internal contradictions and class antagonisms in each capitalist country.

The confidence of Communists in the victory of the Socialist mode of production in competition with capitalism was based on the decisive advantages of the Socialist system over the capitalist system.

The Twentieth Congress of the C.P.S.U. drew the conclusion that there was *a real possibility* of averting wars in the present-day international conditions. Lenin formulated his thesis about the inevitability of wars in the epoch of imperialism, at a time when, first, capitalism was the only, and all-embracing, world system and, secondly, when the social and political forces that had no interest in and were opposed to war were weak, poorly organised and hence unable to compel the imperialists to renounce war.

It stood to reason that so long as imperialism existed, the economic basis for the outbreak of wars would remain, and this made it imperative for all the forces of peace to be vigilant. But in the new conditions, when a powerful Socialist camp had arisen, when nation-wide peace movements were gaining momentum in all countries, when in addition to the Socialist countries there existed other peace-loving States, there were real possibilities of preventing the imperialists from unleashing another world war. If, however, they attempted to start another war, there were powerful social and political forces capable of dealing the aggressors a crushing rebuff, frustrating their reckless plans and defeating them. And that would be the decisive blow at the entire capitalist system. The peoples would no longer tolerate a system which brought them so much suffering and exacted such sacrifices from them.

Drawing general lessons from the experience of the world working-class and Communist movement, the experience of the U.S.S.R. and the People's Democracies, the Twentieth Congress of the C.P.S.U. developed and deepened Lenin's proposition on the diversity of the forms of transition to Socialism in different countries and on the possibility of the Socialist revolution developing peacefully. The radical changes that had taken place in the world, the existence and consolidation of the mighty camp of Socialism, the growth of its power of attraction, the growth of the working-class and national liberation movement, and the weakening of the capitalist system had created a new, more favourable situation for the transition to Socialism in those countries where capitalism still held sway. Moreover, while Lenin spoke of the possibility of the peaceful development of revolution as an exceedingly rare exception, in present-day conditions the possibility of such a development had *increased*. Later on the specific forms of transition of the various countries to Socialism would be more diversified.

In a number of capitalist countries, the working class, led by its vanguard the Communist Party, had a real opportunity of uniting under its leadership the working peasantry, large sections of the intelligentsia and all patriotic forces. Supported by a majority of the people and resolutely repulsing the opportunist elements that were incapable of renouncing the policy of compromise with the capitalists and landlords, the working class could defeat the reactionary, anti-popular forces, win a solid majority in parliament and turn it from an instrument serving the class interests of the bourgeoisie into a genuine instrument of the people's will, that is, into an instrument serving the working people. Thus, conditions could be created for carrying out radical political and economic changes peacefully.

In those capitalist countries where the bourgeoisie possessed a strong military and police apparatus, and where the exploiting classes, supported by the militarists and a reactionary bureaucracy, resisted the will of the working people to the point of imposing an armed struggle on them, the working class and all working people would be compelled to overthrow the power of the bourgeoisie by armed force. The degree of intensity which the class struggle might assume, and the use or non-use of violence during the transition to Socialism, would depend not so much on the proletariat as on the stubbornness with which the reactionary circles resisted the will of the overwhelming majority of the people, on whether these circles would resort to violence at any stage of the struggle for Socialism.

For all the diversity of the specific forms of transition to Socialism, the decisive and indispensable condition for successful

Socialist construction was the political supremacy of the working class, led by the Communist Party, that is, the dictatorship of the proletariat.

The Twentieth Congress of the C.P.S.U. emphasised that the Communists' recognition of the possibility of a peaceful transition to Socialism, including the conquest of parliamentary institutions by the proletariat, must not be confused with the views of the reformists, who rejected the dictatorship of the proletariat, substituted petty reforms for revolutionary transformations of society and who, in fact, were opposed to the abolition of the capitalist system and the seizure of political power by the working class. The reformists must be vigorously combated as advocates of the capitalist system.

The basic propositions of the Twentieth Congress regarding present-day fundamental international problems were of great theoretical and practical significance. Being a creative elaboration of Marxism-Leninism, they provided the answer to problems of vital interest to the masses, and opened up before the Communist Parties new ways and means of preserving and consolidating peace, new prospects of the revolutionary transformation of capitalism into Socialism. They extended the possibilities of uniting all progressive forces under the leadership of the working class, and establishing unity of action and working contacts between the Communist and Socialist Parties, as well as other parties which really wanted to uphold peace, to fight against imperialist oppression and to defend democracy and the national interests and independence of their peoples.

The results of Communist construction in the U.S.S.R. since the Nineteenth Congress were summed up in the Central Committee report. The fifth Five-Year Plan (1951-1955) had been carried out in four years and four months, as regards total volume of industrial output. That signified another major victory of the Soviet people in building up the economic and defensive might of the U.S.S.R. and in its further advance towards Communism.

Compared with 1950, the total industrial product during the last year of the fifth Five-Year Plan had increased by 85 per cent, output of the means of production going up 91 per cent. As regards consumer goods, the Five-Year Plan was overfulfilled, prewar output being more than doubled. Agriculture made successful headway.

The real wages of industrial, professional and office workers had increased and so had collective farmers' incomes. More than 1,500 million square feet of housing space had been built in towns and industrial settlements in the five-year period. Towards the end of that period the country's institutions of higher education had a student body of almost two million, or more than double the number in all the capitalist countries of Europe put together.

The Congress issued the directive persistently to continue to carry out, in peaceful competition, *the basic economic task of the U.S.S.R.*, *namely*, *to overtake and surpass* the more developed capitalist countries *in output per head of the population within a historically very short period*. The advantages of the Socialist system of economy and the level of social development attained in the U.S.S.R. had made it practically possible to carry out this historic task successfully.

The Twentieth Congress pointed out the following principal ways for the speedy fulfilment of this basic economic task:

to continue to give priority to the development of heavy industry—ferrous and non-ferrous metallurgy, the oil, coal, chemical and engineering industries;

consistently to put into practice Lenin's behests regarding the country's electrification, to ensure the growth of electric power capacities ahead of production capacities and the further expansion of the use of electric power in industry, and to proceed with the electrification of transport and agriculture on an increasing scale;

to develop and improve in every way the building industry, so that it might meet all the requirements of capital construction in industry, of housing construction and the building of cultural and other amenities;

to make the most effective use of the country's rich natural resources, to tap new sources of raw materials, fuel and electric power, and, within the next 10 to 15 years, to establish in the eastern regions of the country a major coal and power base, a third great iron and steel base with an output capacity of 15 to 20 million tons of pig-iron a year, and also new engineering centres;

to work persistently to accelerate technical progress: by introducing in industry the latest achievements of science and technology, as well as highly efficient equipment and improved technologies, by speeding up mechanisation, by making extensive use of automation in the production process, by making fuller use of atomic energy for peaceful purposes, by vigorously developing new branches and new types of production, and by technically modernising railway transport;

to perfect the organisation of production through greater specialisation and co-ordination of factories;

to speed up the rate of production of consumer goods and to increase to a maximum the output of artificial and synthetic fibres, plastics and other synthetic materials for the manufacture of garments, footwear and household goods;

to continue unremittingly to advance agriculture, to complete the comprehensive mechanisation of the whole of agricultural production within the shortest possible time, to make extensive use of the achievements of agronomy and the experience of the more efficient farms, to reduce the outlay of labour and materials per unit of agricultural output, and sharply to increase the yield of all crops and the productivity of livestock-breeding;

to achieve a further rise in the people's living standards: to increase the real wages of industrial, professional and office workers, primarily of the low-paid groups, to increase the incomes of collective farmers, gradually to shorten the working day of industrial, professional and office workers without reducing wages, to increase pensions, and to carry out other improvements in the social services;

to encourage in every way the creative effort and initiative of the people in increasing labour productivity, steadily to raise the cultural and technical level of the working class and the collective-farm peasantry, to improve the training of specialists by establishing a close link between instruction and work in production and to bring instruction in the schools closer to life;

systematically to improve the work of local government institutions and trade union and Komsomol organisations, and to enhance their role in the country's economic life.

The guarantee for the successful performance of all these tasks, the Twentieth Congress emphasised, was improvement of all the organising work of the Party in the economic sphere.

"Party organisations must turn their attention to problems involved in the concrete guidance of economic development; they must make a closer study of the technical operation and economic management of industrial enterprises, collective farms, machine-and-tractor stations and State farms in order to give efficient and competent leadership" (*Resolutions of the Twentieth Congress of the Communist Party of the Soviet Union*, Eng. ed., pp. 23-24).

The Congress adopted directives for the sixth Five-Year Plan of economic development of the U.S.S.R. for 1956-1960.

The question of overcoming the personality cult, alien to Marxism-Leninism, and of eliminating its consequences, occupied an important place in the proceedings of the Twentieth Congress. The Congress approved the immense work done by the Central Committee to restore the Leninist standards of Party life and promote inner-Party democracy. It criticised, from the standpoint of principle, the mistakes brought about by the cult of Stalin, and planned measures to eradicate its consequences completely.

In criticising the personality cult, the Party was guided by the well-known propositions of Marxism-Leninism on the role played in history by the masses, parties and individuals, and on the impermissibility of the cult of the personality of a political leader, no matter how great his services.

The Party was aware that open criticism of the errors stemming from the cult of the personality would be used by enemies for anti-Soviet purposes. Nevertheless, it decided on that step, which it regarded as a matter of principle and prompted by the interests of Communist construction. It proceeded from the fact that, even if its criticism gave rise to some temporary difficulties, it would indisputably yield positive results from the point of view of the interests of the people and of the ultimate goal of the working class. The personality cult had to be denounced above all in order to provide sure guarantees that *phenomena of this kind would never again arise in the Party and the country*, that Party leadership would be based on the collective principle and on a correct, Marxist-Leninist policy with the active, creative participation of millions of people. The criticism of this cult was of tremendous importance for the consolidation of the Party, the creative development of Marxism-Leninism, the extension of Socialist democracy, and also for the whole of the international Communist movement.

In the Congress decisions, and in the resolution of the C.C. C.P.S.U. of June 30, 1956, "On overcoming the personality cult and its consequences," the Party clearly explained the causes that had given rise to the personality cult, its manifestations and consequences.

The cult of Stalin arose in definite, concrete historical conditions. Incredible difficulties had attended the building of Socialism in a relatively backward, agrarian country, ruined by an imperialist and a civil war and surrounded by hostile capitalist States, in conditions of the constant threat of attack from without. The complicated international and domestic situation called for iron discipline, a high degree of vigilance and the strictest centralisation of leadership. In conditions of bitter attacks by the imperialist States, Soviet society had to make certain temporary restrictions of democracy. These restrictions were removed as the Soviet State grew stronger and the forces of democracy and Socialism developed throughout the world. The triumph of Socialism in the U.S.S.R. was an epoch-making feat that the Soviet people accomplished under the leadership of the Communist Party.

In those years Stalin held the post of General Secretary of the Central Committee of the Party. Together with the other leaders of the Party and the State, he actively fought to carry out Lenin's behests. His work was bound up with the achievement of great Socialist changes in the U.S.S.R. As an outstanding theoretician and organiser, he led the fight against the Trotskyists, Right-wing opportunists and bourgeois nationalists, against the intrigues of the capitalist encirclement. He rendered great services not only in ensuring the victory of Socialism in the U.S.S.R., but also in developing the world Communist and liberation movement. This naturally earned him great prestige and popularity. However, as time went by, all the successes achieved by the Soviet Union under the leadership of the Party began to be ascribed to him. The cult of his personality was gradually built up.

The development of this cult was, to a very large extent, facilitated by certain negative personal qualities of Stalin, to which Lenin had called attention. The successes achieved by the Communist Party and the Soviet people, and the praises addressed to Stalin, turned his head. Excessively over-estimating his role and services, he came to believe that he was infallible, and began to encourage people to extol him. His words began to be more and more at variance with his deeds. During the last years of his life, the cult of his personality caused particularly great damage to the leadership of the Party and the State.

The errors and shortcomings it engendered impeded the progress of Soviet society, caused it great damage, and stood in the way of the creative initiative of the masses. But, contrary to falsehoods spread by the enemies of Socialism, they could not change the thoroughly democratic and genuinely popular character of the Soviet system. The policy pursued by the Party was a correct one, and it expressed the interests of the people.

The Party criticism of the personality cult was essentially aimed at eliminating the harmful consequences of this cult and thereby strengthening the positions of Socialism, and was *not* a sweeping denial of the positive role played by Stalin in the life of the Party and the country. Under the leadership of the Communist Party and its Central Committee, in which Stalin played a leading role, the Soviet Union made tremendous, epoch-making progress. Stalin did much for the Soviet Union, for the C.P.S.U., and for the entire international working-class movement. "We," said N. S. Khrushchov, "see two sides to Comrade Stalin's activities: the positive side, which we support and value highly, and the negative side, which we criticise, condemn and repudiate. . . . Our Party and all of us resolutely condemn Stalin for the gross errors and distortions which seriously injured the cause of the Party, the cause of the people" (*Pravda*, August 28, 1957).

As it worked to eliminate the consequences of the personality cult, the Party opened up great opportunities for the activity and creative initiative of the masses. In a short time it achieved substantial successes in advancing Soviet economy and culture, and greatly strengthened the position of Socialism in the world

671

arena. This was another striking expression of the Party's Leninist training.

The Twentieth Congress noted the substantial consolidation of the Soviet social and political system, the moral and political unity of Soviet society and the friendship between its peoples, and, with due regard to pressing requirements, marked out the course for the further development of Socialist democracy.

"The majestic tasks of building Communism," stated the Congress resolution on the C.C. report, "require further development of the creative activity and initiative of the people, wider participation of the masses in the administration of the State and in every aspect of its organisational and economic activity. This calls for maximum development of Soviet democracy, persistent efforts to improve the work of all governmental organisations, central and local, and bringing them into closer contact with the people" (*Resolutions of the Twentieth Congress of the Communist Party of the Soviet Union*, Eng. ed., p. 21).

The Congress decisions contained fundamental directions on questions of nationalities policy. Approving the measures taken by the Central Committee to extend the rights of the Union Republics, the Congress recommended further steps in the same direction. In the new conditions, when the economy of the Republics had developed and grown stronger, and when a large number of local personnel had been trained, it was becoming more and more obvious that new forms of economic management by the State had to be devised, such as would properly combine centralised leadership and the initiative of the Republics, take account of the common interests of the peoples in building Communism and their national distinctions and specific features, and would promote further friendship among the peoples.

The Congress adopted an extensive programme for cultural development and for the Communist education of the people. It stressed the necessity of greatly improving the entire system of training and education of the rising generation by bringing education closer to productive labour.

Important measures were decided on to strengthen the Party ranks, raise the Party's leading role in the Soviet State and improve its organising work.

There was sharp criticism at the Congress of shortcomings in ideological work, and primarily of its lack of connection with the practical tasks of Communist construction, of dogmatism and quotation-mongering. It set the task of overcoming these shortcomings, of radically improving all ideological work and closely linking theoretical activity, propaganda and agitation with the vital requirements of the struggle for Communism.

In its decisions the Congress emphasised the duty of workers on the ideological front and of Party organisations to cherish, as the apple of one's eye, the purity of Marxist-Leninist theory, to wage an uncompromising struggle against all manifestations of bourgeois ideology and to improve the Marxist-Leninist training of cadres.

The Congress introduced partial amendments in the Party rules, prompted by the experience of Party development, and passed a resolution on the drafting of a new Party programme.

The Twentieth Congress of the C.P.S.U. was a momentous historic event, that marked the beginning of a new and important stage in the life of the Party, in the development of the Soviet Union and in the international Communist and working-class movement. It defined practical tasks involved in building Communism in the U.S.S.R., and mapped out ways of developing and strengthening the Soviet system. The Congress posed from a new angle, and resolved, a number of fundamental problems relating to contemporary international development, problems which determined the course of current events and the prospects for the future.

The Congress drew scientific generalisations from the new phenomena at the present stage of history, and was an example of a creative approach to Marxism-Leninism, enriching revolutionary theory with new conclusions and propositions in the sphere of the Party's home and foreign policy. The Congress demonstrated that the Party and its Central Committee were not only a collective political and organisational centre, but also a collective centre of development of Marxist theory.

The Congress decisions had a tremendous effect on the life of the Party and on the advance of Soviet Socialist society to Communism.

4. The Development of Socialist Democracy. The Raising of the Leading Role of the Party and the Consolidation of Its Unity. The Reorganisation of the Management of Industry

The historic decisions of the Twentieth Congress of the C.P.S.U. were unanimously approved by the entire Party and met with the warm support of the Soviet people. The masses saw in them an inspiring programme of struggle for further successes in developing Socialist economy and culture and in raising the living standards of the people. The masses began a heroic movement to carry out the Congress decisions as speedily as possible.

The people became more active—and this found expression in the further spread of Socialist emulation. On the initiative of the workers at several industrial enterprises in Moscow and Moscow Region, an emulation movement to fulfil the industrial plan of the first year of the sixth Five-Year Plan ahead of schedule started on a country-wide scale. The countryside vigorously set about increasing the output of grain and other agricultural produce. A broad movement to overtake and surpass the U.S.A. in the output per head of milk, butter and meat in the near future was started early in 1957 under the leadership of the Party.

The rapidly growing activity of the masses and the increased scale of Communist construction necessitated a further extension of Socialist democracy, more effective Party leadership and better work on the part of State, economic, trade union and Komsomol organisations. The Party held that, in keeping with the requirements of society, its task was to extend its organising and educational work among the masses, and to improve the old and find new forms of direct participation by the masses in the economic, organising, cultural and educational work of the State.

The Party began to carry out this task by increasing the activity of Communists and the efficiency of Party organisations, improving Party leadership and all the methods of work of the Party organisations. A new and most typical feature in the life of the latter was that their activity was based on a profound and concrete knowledge of economics and on ability to make use of advanced practical experience and achievements of science and technology. Party officials successfully studied economic processes and established the dominant trends in the economic development of collective and State farms, districts, regions and Republics. This helped them to find and to utilise new production potentialities.

Special attention was devoted by the Central Committee to district Party organisations, since the success of the efforts to achieve a steep rise in agriculture depended largely on the level of their work. The leadership at district level was reinforced with experienced, capable people who were well grounded in economic affairs and showed initiative as organisers of the masses. The Central Committee achieved a considerable improvement in the work of district Party committees.

In carrying out the decisions of the Twentieth Congress, the Party improved the ideological and political education of Communists and reorganised the system of Party education. It resolutely began to overcome the harmful isolation of propaganda from the practical work of building Communism. There was a noticeable and fruitful livening up of the theoretical activity of the Party. Dogmatism, which reduces living and continuously progressing Marxist-Leninist theory to a collection of petrified formulas, detaches theory from practice, hinders the creative development of theory and impedes the scientific elaboration and practical solution of major problems of Communist construction, was a considerable danger to the proper education of Party personnel in the new conditions, and to a scientific substantiation of Party policy. The Party launched a consistent struggle against dogmatism in theory and practice, and against manifestations of revisionist views among individual Party members. It ensured the creative development of Marxist-Leninist theory, inseparably linking it up with reality.

Persistently and tactfully, the Party cleared up the ideological confusion among certain workers in the field of culture. Some writers, who had not understood the essence of the Party's criticism of the personality cult, had begun to look only for mistakes and the seamy sides of Socialist construction, and to deny the need for the Party to play the leading role in the ideological sphere. Voices made themselves heard opposing any Party spirit and ideology in science, literature and art, against linking them up with the urgent tasks of Communist construction. Attempts were made to question the basic method of Soviet literature and art, that of Socialist realism.

The Party and its Central Committee did much to explain the essence of Marxist-Leninist ideology to workers in science, literature and art. The Party once again showed that Soviet culture could flower only if it kept in touch with reality, if it served the cause of the people, the cause of building Communism.

In accordance with the decisions of the Twentieth Congress, the Party organisations reorganised their educational and propaganda work among the masses, and linked it up more closely with the tasks of Communist construction. The Party further strengthened its ties with the working class, the collective-farm peasantry and the intelligentsia, and began more fully to study, and draw general conclusions from their experience. On this basis, the Party and its Central Committee theoretically substantiated and carried out a number of important political and economic measures of programme significance, determining the ways by which Socialism would grow into Communism.

The Party took steps to improve the work of local government institutions. In its resolution, "On improving the activity of the Soviets of Working People's Deputies and strengthening their ties with the masses" (January, 1957), the C.C. C.P.S.U. defined the basic tasks of the Soviets in the new conditions to be: to enhance the part played by the local Soviets in economic and cultural development and improve their activity, to strengthen their ties with the masses and to draw the largest possible number of working people into the work of the commissions of the Soviets and the latter's other channels for mass voluntary activity. The C.C. recommended that Party organisations and government institutions of the Union Republics should take practical steps to extend the rights of the local Soviets, first and foremost in economic planning, in the production and distribution of the output of the local and co-operative industries, in organising housing schemes, in the building of cultural institutions, public amenities and roads, in expanding the production of building materials and fuel and in deciding financial and budgetary questions.

The Soviets of Working People's Deputies began to play a more active part in economic and cultural development. This referred above all to their elective bodies, which began to exercise more effective control over the activities of economic, cultural and other local government organisations. The deputies to the Soviets began to work more actively. The political and economic work of the Soviets became more varied, and their importance as organisers of the masses increased.

One of the biggest economic and political measures carried out by the Party was the reorganisation of the management of industry and the improvement of the Socialist principles of economic management.

The Party bent its efforts to provide, by its policy and appropriate measures in the economic sphere, the greatest scope for the operation of the economic laws of Socialism in all spheres of production. As it studied the organisational forms of management, the Central Committee came to the conclusion that the system of managing the national economy through specialised central Ministries and Departments had served its purpose, and no longer corresponded to the level and scale achieved by industry. There were more than 200,000 industrial enterprises and over 100,000 building sites in the country. A few all-Union Ministries and Departments could no longer give concrete and efficient guidance to such a large number of industrial enterprises and building jobs— scattered, moreover, all over the country. It was impossible for a single centre fully to take account of all the peculiarities of the various areas, enterprises and building projects and to settle questions arising in their work with due regard to those peculiarities.

The need arose to organise management of industry in a way that would be most appropriate to the requirements of the country's developing productive forces and allow the fullest possible use of the potentialities of Socialist industry.

Taking into account these pressing necessities, the Party considered the problem of a radical change in the forms and methods of management of industry. The matter was dealt with specially by the February, 1957, plenary meeting of the C.C. C.P.S.U., which adopted a decision, "On the further improvement of management in industry and building."

The C.C. specified the principal lines along which industrial management was to be reorganised. It stated that the new system of management should be based on the combination of centralised State guidance with the extension of the rights of Republican and local government and economic bodies, and with still more active participation by the broad masses of the working people in the management of industry. The national economy would continue to be developed under a single State plan, but the centre of gravity of day-by-day management was to be shifted *to the localities*, that is, to the *economic councils* to be set up in the country's principal economic administrative areas. The existence of a great number of trained and experienced personnel there would make it possible to effect this change.

In view of its great importance to the State, the question of reorganising the management of industry was submitted for country-wide discussion. More than 40 million people took part in the discussion at meetings and in the press.

In May, 1957, the Supreme Soviet of the U.S.S.R. enacted a law embodying the measures worked out by the C.C. C.P.S.U. and approved by the people.

Under the guidance of the Party, the reorganisation of the management of industry was carried out quickly and efficiently. Economic administrative areas were rapidly established, and economic councils set up and staffed with trained personnel. The economic councils took the direct management of industry into their own hands.

The reorganisation of the management of industry was an important revolutionary step. Its significance lay in the fact that it *drew management closer* to production, made it more specific, efficient and flexible, and gave *full rein to the initiative* of local executives, enabling them to draw greater numbers of working people into directing economic development. This reorganisation still further enhanced the role of the Union Republics, local Party organisations and local government institutions in the guidance of industrial enterprises and opened up big opportunities for the comprehensive development of the economic areas and for better specialisation and co-ordination in the national economy.

This reorganisation represented a creative development of the Leninist principle of democratic centralism in the economic field. In the new historical conditions, the new form of management was the best combination of centralised planning with democratic methods of guidance. It made possible the achievement of the greatest efficiency in managing the national economy, by making fuller use of the advantages of the Socialist economic system and by greater participation of the working people in industrial management.

A major economic and political undertaking, aimed at heightening the activity of the masses and giving them a greater part in managing public affairs and production, was the right granted the collective farms and their members to introduce amendments and additions to the collective-farm rules. The resolution of the Central Committee and the Council of Ministers of the U.S.S.R. on the rules of the Agricultural Artel, and on the further encouragement of the initiative of the collective farmers in organising production and managing the affairs of the artel, noted that the countryside now had vast material and technical resources and ample experience in organising and conducting collective farming. The political consciousness of the collective-farm peasantry had grown. The collective farms now had experienced and politically mature personnel capable of running a socially-owned economy properly. Thereby the necessary conditions had been created for increasing the independence of the collective farms in organising production and managing their own affairs—in settling matters of collective-farm life on the basis of a correct combination of the public interest with those of the collective farm. The Party and the Government advised the collective farmers to introduce amendments and additions to the rules adopted by their collective farms, proceeding from the main task—the achievement of a steep rise in crop farming and animal husbandry—and with due regard to local conditions.

This measure was an important step in developing collective-farm democracy, in extending and strengthening Socialist democracy. It was of great economic and political importance, for it gave scope to the initiative of the collective farmers, gave them an incentive to run their farms properly, economically and efficiently, and created new opportunities for expanded agricultural production.

In pursuance of the course set by the Twentieth Congress to enlist the assistance of the masses in managing industry and the State, the Party took important steps to improve the work of the trade unions. A number of Party documents, above all the decisions of the December, 1957, plenary meeting of the C.C., explained the need for the trade unions to play a steady bigger part in the building of Communism, specified the forms of their participation in the solving of political, economic, cultural and educational problems, and suggested ways of reorganising the work of the trade unions in the new conditions.

Soviet trade unions had great obligations—those of drawing the masses into the management of industry, further improving the Socialist emulation movement, mobilising the workers, at the bench and elsewhere, for the fulfilment and overfulfilment of State plans, raising labour productivity and improving the methods of management in industry. The Party pointed out that production conferences were the best method of drawing large numbers of people into the management of industry. It was found desirable to convert production conferences into standing bodies, composed of representatives of workers, office employees, management, Party and Komsomol organisations, and scientific and technical societies, which would carry on their work with the active participation of workers, engineers, technicians and office employees.

To increase the part they played in the building of Communism, the functions of the trade union organisations were extended. They were accorded the right to participate in drawing up the industrial and financial plans of factories, settling questions concerning output rates and the wages system, and supervising the observance of labour legislation. They were empowered to demand the removal of business executives who systematically violated labour laws and evaded fulfilment of their obligations under collective agreements, and to express their opinion about those nominated for executive posts. Thenceforward no worker, manual or otherwise, could be dismissed without the consent of the works or office trade union committee concerned.

The trade unions improved their work on the basis of the decisions of the Party. They began to play a bigger role in economic development; the level of their work of organisation and their political and educational work rose to a higher level. Trade union democracy was expanded, and trade union members became more active.

Under the guidance of the Party, big changes also took place in the activity of the Komsomol and its organisations. Their work was enlivened considerably; it acquired a new content and became more purposeful. The decisions of the Twentieth Congress inspired the youth and opened before it broad vistas for creative endeavour and daring feats. Komsomol organisations actively helped the Party in the execution of its decisions, in all its undertakings. They assumed "patronage" over the more important and difficult building projects of Communism. In response to the call of the Party, Komsomol organisations sent hundreds of thousands of volunteers to develop the virgin and disused lands and to build mines, blast- and open-hearth furnaces, power stations and chemical plants. In the countryside, Komsomol members became more active in collective-farm production. The Party helped the Komsomol to develop the initiative of its members, to uproot formalism, ostentation and sensationalism, and to improve educational work among young people.

The labour enthusiasm aroused among the masses by the development of Socialist democracy, and the improvement of the activity of Party, government, economic, trade union and other voluntary organisations ensured the successful fulfilment of economic plans. More than 1,600 large industrial enterprises, including the Lenin Hydroelectric Power Station on the Volga, one of the biggest in the world, were put into operation in 1956 and 1957. There was a considerable increase in industrial output. The output of industries producing the means of production rose by 24 per cent. Major successes were achieved in agriculture. The total grain harvest in 1956 was bigger than in all the preceding years. This enabled the State to purchase over 53 million tons of grain. In 1957, despite unfavourable weather conditions in a number of regions, the State purchased over 4 million tons of grain, nearly 10 million tons of milk and other dairy produce and 1,450,000 tons of meat more than in 1953.

After the Twentieth Party Congress important measures were taken further to improve the living and cultural standards of the people. The working day on Saturdays and on the eve of holidays was shortened by two hours, maternity leave was lengthened, the working day for adolescents was reduced by two hours and some industries had their working day reduced to seven or six hours. Tuition fees were abolished in the senior grades of secondary school, in the special secondary schools and in the institutions of higher education. Old age and disability pensions were substantially increased.

While the Party, under the leadership of the C.C., was implementing the decisions of the Twentieth Congress and making important progress in economic development and in raising the living standard still higher, there were some people who came out against the line of the Party. They were G. M. Malenkov, L. M. Kaganovich and V. M. Molotov, who formed an anti-Party group within the Presidium of the Central Committee.

This anti-Party group opposed the Leninist line of the Twentieth Congress of the C.P.S.U. in domestic and foreign policy, and aimed at changing the Party's political line and frustrating its measures.

The members of the anti-Party group were against the extension of the rights of the Union Republics in economic and cultural development, and resisted the measures that the Party was taking to reduce the State apparatus and combat bureaucracy. They sought to frustrate the reorganisation of management in industry.

The anti-Party group did not consider it necessary to give the collective-farm peasantry greater material incentive to expand agricultural production. It opposed the replacement of the old system of agricultural planning by a new one, and the abolition of compulsory deliveries of farm produce from the household plots of the collective farmers. It was against the movement to overtake and surpass the U.S.A. in the output of milk, butter and meat per head of population in the near future—a movement which had been started by the collective farms and vigorously supported by the Party. One of the group, Molotov, resisted the extremely important undertaking—the development of the virgin and disused lands—which, tested in practice, proved of tremendous economic significance. The anti-Party group opposed the Party's foreign policy, which pursued the aim of relaxing international tension, consolidating peace, promoting co-operation and strengthening friendship among nations.

Malenkov, Kaganovich and Molotov opposed the Party's measures to eradicate the consequences of the personality cult. This was not accidental. They had held key positions in the Party and bore their share of responsibility for the errors engendered by the personality cult.

The Presidium of the C.C. and the Central Committee persistently combated the errors of the anti-Party group and corrected them, hoping that they would draw the necessary conclusions from the criticism levelled at them and move into step with the entire leadership of the Party. But they slid further down to anti-Party, non-Leninist positions, and took the path of factional struggle against the Party leadership. They united on an anti-Party basis and resorted to intrigue, conspiring against the Central Committee. Employing factional methods, Malenkov, Kaganovich, Molotov and Shepilov, who had joined them, sought to change the leading bodies of the Party, so as to alter the Party's policy and restore in the Party the incorrect methods of leadership condemned by the Twentieth Congress.

N. A. Bulganin was in effect one of this factional group. By his perfidious anti-Party behaviour he did much to encourage the anti-Party group to venture upon opposition to the Party's Leninist line.

A stubborn and bitter struggle began against the anti-Party group in the Presidium of the Central Committee in June, 1957. In the course of that struggle N. S. Khrushchov, members and alternate members of the Presidium, secretaries of the Central Committee A. B. Aristov, N. I. Belyaev, L. I. Brezhnev, Y. A. Furtseva, A. I. Kirichenko, F. R. Kozlov, A. I. Mikoyan, N. A. Muhitdinov, P. N. Pospelov, N. M. Shvernik and M. A. Suslov, as well as members of the Central Committee N. G. Ignatov, O. W. Kuusinen, D. S. Korotchenko, J. E. Kalnberziņš, A. P. Kirilenko, A. N. Kosygin, K. T. Mazurov, V. P. Mzhavanadze, N. V. Podgorny, D. S. Polyansky and others resolutely opposed the anti-Party group and gave a crushing rebuff to their bitter attacks on the Leninist line of the Party and its Central Committee.

The question of the anti-Party group was examined by a plenary meeting of the Central Committee in June, 1957. All the members and alternate members of the Central Committee and the members of the Central Auditing Commission unanimously condemned the behaviour of the splitters. The speakers proposed that the sternest Party measures be applied to them. The plenary meeting unanimously adopted a resolution condemning the factional activity of the anti-Party group.

The plenary meeting pointed out that the anti-Party group had violated the Party rules and the decision of the Tenth Congress on Party unity, drafted by Lenin. The members of the group were entrammelled by old notions and outmoded methods of work. They had lost touch with the life of the Party and the country, and were blind to the new conditions, to the new situation that had arisen. They displayed conservatism, adhered to dogmatic views on Communist construction, and clung stubbornly to forms and methods of work that were outdated and no longer met the interests of the advance towards Communism. That was the basis of their anti-Party stand. They tried to drag the Party back, rejecting everything new engendered by reality and prompted by the interests of the development of Soviet society, by the interests of the whole Socialist camp.

"Both on domestic and on foreign policy," the decision of the C.C. plenary meeting stated, "they are sectarians and dogmatists; they display a dogmatic, unrealistic approach to Marxism-Leninism. They do not see that, in present-day conditions, living Marxism-Leninism in action and the struggle for Communism manifest themselves in the application of the decisions of the Twentieth Congress of the Party, in the persistent application of the policy of peaceful coexistence and friendship among nations, in the policy of strengthening the Socialist camp in every possible way, in improving the management of industry and in working for an all-round rise in agriculture, for an abundance of food, for big-scale housing construction, for an extension of the rights of the Union Republics, for the flowering of national cultures and for the utmost encouragement of the initiative of the popular masses" (*Pravda*, July 4, 1957).

The June plenary meeting of the C.C. found the activity of the anti-Party group incompatible with the Leninist principles of the Communist Party. In the face of the incontrovertible facts brought to light at the plenary meeting of the C.C., the members of the anti-Party group admitted the harmfulness of their factional, anti-Party activity and undertook to submit to the decisions of the Party.

The plenary meeting removed Malenkov, Kaganovich, Molotov and Shepilov from the Central Committee and the Presidium of the C.C.

N. A. Bulganin was severely reprimanded and warned. He promised to rectify his gross mistakes and vigorously to uphold the Party line. However, the course of events showed that he did not keep his promise and did not live up to the trust that had been placed in him as a member of the Presidium of the C.C. For that reason the Central Committee at a subsequent plenary meeting relieved him of his duties as a member of the Presidium of the C.C. C.P.S.U. Prior to this, he had been relieved of the office of Chairman of the Council of Ministers of the U.S.S.R.

In view of the fact that M. G. Pervukhin and M. Z. Saburov had taken up an incorrect, vacillating position during the struggle against the anti-Party group and had admitted their mistakes and dissociated themselves from the group only at the plenary meeting of the Central Committee, Pervukhin was demoted from member of the Presidium of the C.C. to alternate member of the Presidium and Saburov was removed from the Presidium of the C.C.

The exposure and condemnation by the Central Committee of the factional, anti-Party activity of the group of Malenkov, Kaganovich, Molotov, Bulganin and Shepilov, who had joined them, still further strengthened the Leninist unity of the Party and was a new victory for the Party's general line, for creative Marxism-Leninism. The decision of the plenary meeting of the C.C. was unanimously approved by the Party and the Soviet people as a whole. Communists and non-Communists alike emphatically condemned the members of the anti-Party group, who found themselves isolated individuals, having lost all contact with the Party and the masses. Communists and all Soviet people rallied still closer round the Leninist Central Committee for the successful fulfilment of the historic decisions of the Twentieth Congress of the C.P.S.U.

As it combated the departures from Marxism-Leninism and all violations of the Leninist principles of leadership, the Party came across serious shortcomings in the political work conducted in the Soviet Army and Navy. It was found that G. K. Zhukov, in his capacity of Minister for Defence, had violated the Leninist principles of leadership in the armed forces of the U.S.S.R. He had sought to restrict the work of the Party organisations, the political apparatus and Military Councils, to do away with the guidance and supervision of the armed forces by the Party, its Central Committee and the Soviet Government. With Zhukov's personal participation, a cult of his personality had begun to be implanted in the Soviet Army, and his role in the Great Patriotic War excessively extolled. Thereby the true history of the war was being distorted and the all-out war effort of the Soviet people, the heroism of the armed forces, the role of the Communists and political instructors, the military skill of Soviet army leaders and the guiding and inspiring role of the Communist Party, were belittled.

In a resolution, "On the improvement of the Party's political work in the Soviet Army and Navy," a plenary meeting of the C.C., held in October, 1957, condemned the gross violations of the Leninist principles of leadership that had been committed in the armed forces and removed Zhukov from the leading bodies of the Party.

The plenary meeting stressed the decisive importance of the Communist Party's leadership for the country's armed forces. The Soviet Army and Navy, the decision of the plenary meeting pointed out, owed their might, above all, to the fact that they were organised, trained and led by the Communist Party. Besides the commanders, an important role in strengthening the armed forces was played by the Military Councils, political bodies and Party organisations in the army and navy, whose mission was to carry out the policy of the Communist Party firmly and consistently. The plenary meeting decided on measures to improve political work in the Soviet Army and Navy.

A Bureau of the C.C. was set up for the Russian Federation to give more concrete guidance to the work of the Republican, regional and territorial Party organisations, local government institutions and economic bodies, and to ensure the prompt decision of questions relating to economic and cultural development in the Federation.

The steps taken by the Central Committee to strengthen the Party and to reorganise Party and government activity were the development of Lenin's teaching on the Party, and an expression of its steadily growing role as the leading and guiding force of Soviet society. The growing role of the Party as the leading force in the economic, political and cultural life of the country was a natural development of Socialist society, which became more marked as Communist construction made headway.

In the conditions of transition from Socialism to Communism, when the importance of the subjective factor, the conscious guidance of society, increases, the Party, equipped with the theory of Marxism-Leninism, is called upon to direct the creation of new economic and political relations on the basis of the principles of Communism.

As the most organised and politically conscious section of the Soviet people, the Party, through its indefatigable organising and political activity, rallies the masses and ensures the unity of will and action of the entire people, whom it inspires for the building of a Communist society. Enjoying as it does immense moral and political prestige, the Party ensures the solution of the most difficult and complex problem of the present stage of Communist construction, namely, the education of all the members of society in a Communist spirit, the complete eradication of the survivals of capitalism from the minds of men, and the continuous growth of the political consciousness and activity of the masses.

The Party is the authoritative and influential force which strengthens the ideological and political links between the peoples of the U.S.S.R. and unites them in the struggle for Communism.

The C.P.S.U. is the leading and directing force of the Soviet State. The Party alone can successfully lead the voluntary organisations (trade union, youth, etc.), whose sphere of activity is widening and whose influence on the life of society is increasing. The Party directs their work into the common channel of Communist construction.

5. The Results of Forty Years of the Party's Activity at the Head of the Soviet People. The Growing Solidarity of the Communist Parties and of the Ties Between Them

In November, 1957, the Soviet people, the working people of all countries, and the whole of progressive mankind celebrated the fortieth anniversary of the Great October Socialist Revolution. Besides the deputies and representatives of the Soviet public, the jubilee session of the Supreme Soviet of the U.S.S.R. was attended by foreign guests—Party and Government delegations from all the Socialist countries, representatives of 64 brother Communist and Workers' Parties, numerous delegations from public, cultural and scientific organisations of various countries, and representatives of the biggest international trade union, youth and women's organisations.

In a report to the jubilee session, N. S. Khrushchov summed up the epoch-making results of the great changes that had taken place in the Soviet Union and showed the impressive economic and cultural progress made by the country over forty years. The tremendous successes achieved in all fields of economic and cultural life in the U.S.S.R. were graphic evidence of the great advantages of Socialism over capitalism. The Soviet Union had shown the whole world that the creative abilities of the people receive full scope only under Socialism.

Socialism had emerged from the confines of a single country and become a world system. This was a great victory for the international Communist and working-class movement. It was a result of the heroic struggle of the working class and the working peasantry, of the leadership of this struggle by the Communist and Workers' Parties, and of their ability to apply Marxism-Leninism creatively in the specific conditions obtaining in their countries. The world Socialist camp represented a tremendous and steadily growing force.

The jubilee session of the Supreme Soviet of the U.S.S.R. adopted a Message to the peoples of the Soviet Union and another Message to the working people, political and public leaders, men of science and culture, to the parliaments and governments of all countries.

The documents and other records of the jubilee session, in which the Party and the Soviet people summed up the results of the effort and achievement of the Soviet Union, unfolded to the world a majestic picture of the social, economic and cultural changes effected on the basis of Socialism.

The great results of forty years of the activity of the Communist Party of the Soviet Union may, in the main, be listed as follows:

1. The working class of the land of Soviets, under the leadership of the C.P.S.U. and in alliance with the working peasantry, took State power into its own hands for the first time in human history. The Party was well aware that the working people needed a *strong* and *durable* State of their own if they were to consolidate their victory, curb the exploiters, preserve the country's independence and build a new society. The Party set about creating such a State, at a time when it had neither experience in governing the country nor trained personnel. But it coped with the task brilliantly.

The Party gave a scientific definition of the class content of the new authority—the dictatorship of the proletariat—and of its social foundation—the alliance of the working class with the peasantry. Drawing general lessons from the revolutionary experience of the masses, the Party advanced a new form of political organisation of society, expressing the essence of the dictatorship of the proletariat—a republic of Soviets. The old State machinery was smashed and a new one established in its place, one that carried out the will of the people.

The Party worked out the mechanism of the dictatorship of the proletariat, that is, the system of State bodies (Soviets) and voluntary (trade union, co-operative, youth and other) organisations which most fully express the interests of the people. Through the Soviets it ensured real and direct participation by every working person in governing the country.

The establishment of the dictatorship of the proletariat began the era of the downfall of bourgeois democracy, the era of genuine people's rule, of Socialist democracy.

2. Following the establishment of the dictatorship of the proletariat, the entire energy of the Communists was directed to carrying out Lenin's plan of building a new, Socialist society. This task would have been an exceedingly difficult one for any country, and in the case of Russia the difficulties involved were many times greater.

The world revolutionary movement had no previous experience in building Socialism, and knew of no form for organising society on the new foundation, or of methods of running a Socialist economy. Socialism had existed only as a theory, as ideas. The first time Socialism had to be built was in an economically backward country with a predominantly small-scale commodity production. In its level of industrial production, Russia was 50 to 100 years behind the developed capitalist countries. Moreover, as a result of the imperialist and the civil war she was in a state of appalling ruin. She had to build Socialism without having the necessary trained personnel, and with the culture of the population at a low level. The overthrown exploiting classes furiously resisted Socialist construction. The difficulties were aggravated by the fact that Soviet Russia was the only Socialist country in the world and was encircled by capitalist States. The imperialist Powers refused to reconcile themselves to the victory of the working people, and endeavoured to overthrow the people's power by military force, economic blockade, diplomatic pressure, blackmail and slander. All this intensified the class struggle in the country and increased the vacillations of the petty bourgeoisie. The Trotskyists and other opportunists within the Party denied the possibility of building Socialism in Russia and hampered the building up of a new society.

The Communist Party boldly led the people along an absolutely new, unexplored path of social development. It radically reshaped all aspects of social life. The political and economic system, the class structure of society, the State machinery, law, morals, and the views of people—all were remoulded in keeping with Marxist-Leninist theory.

The political, social and economic relations which had been born of private property in the means of production thousands of years ago, and which therefore seemed everlasting and immutable, were replaced, in 15 to 20 years, by Socialist relations founded on social ownership of the means of production. A Socialist society was built in the U.S.S.R. The exploiting classes were abolished once and for all. In the Soviet Union there are two friendly classes—the workers and the peasants—and an intelligentsia that has come from them. The entire wealth of the country is the property of the people. No one can appropriate the fruits of another man's labour. Labour has become the only source of material and cultural well-being. The sacred principle, "He who does not work, neither shall he eat" has been firmly established. From an age-old dream, from a scientific prevision by Marx and Engels, Socialism has for the first time in the history of social development become *a reality, the sum and substance of the life of the masses.*

The building of Socialism in the U.S.S.R. was the greatest achievement of the Communist Party and the Soviet people. It was a real triumph of the Party's policy and ideology, the result of its wise leadership of the masses.

3. The Party won political and economic supremacy for the working people, real *people's rule.* Genuine freedom, equality and fraternity were established in the relations between men and peoples, and a truly happy life was secured for the entire people. In capitalist society, economic relations are basically contrary to true democracy. In no bourgeois country do, or can, the people enjoy genuine rights and liberties. In capitalist countries, parliamentary elections are organised in such a way that only representatives of the bourgeoisie win seats in parliament, or are assured an overwhelming majority. In the U.S. Congress, for example, there is not a single worker or farmer. It is a legislative body of industrialists, financiers and their henchmen.

Socialist democracy not only proclaims, but actually assures to all citizens of the Soviet Union real freedom of speech, press and assembly, meetings and demonstrations, and guarantees the right of every citizen to work, to rest and leisure, to education and to social maintenance.

The Soviet people is the sole master of its country, the lord of its destiny. All power both in the country as a whole and in the Republics, regions, towns, districts and villages belongs to the Soviets of Working People's Deputies. The Soviets are elected on the basis of universal, equal and direct suffrage by secret ballot. All deputies to the Soviets are working people. In the Soviet Union, the working people are guaranteed real participation in the management of the national economy, something which the most democratic bourgeois republic neither has nor can have.

4. When preparing to take over power, the Party promised the people that it would transform the poverty-stricken and weak country into a mighty Socialist Power. The bourgeois politicians

mocked at this promise of the Bolsheviks. They maintained that Bolshevism was incapable of creating anything, that it brought nothing but destruction in its wake. Even among those whose sympathies lay with the Soviet Union there were people who doubted the feasibility of the Bolshevik plans, regarding them as utopian. But the Communist Party by its deeds disproved these fabrications and doubts.

The period of constructive work by the Party was not long—only 40 years. In those 40 years (actually 22, since 18 years were spent on the wars imposed by the imperialists and on subsequent rehabilitation) the Soviet Union made such economic progress as had taken the capitalist countries a whole century to achieve.

The Soviet Union made a gigantic leap from backwardness to industrial prosperity. In volume of industrial output, it moved into first place in Europe and second place in the world. In 1957, its total industrial product was 33 times as large as in 1913 and 46 times as large as in 1917, the output of the means of production rising nearly 75 times compared with 1913.

In 1913, Russia produced 29,100,000 tons of coal. In 1957, the Soviet Union's coal output amounted to 463,000,000 tons. The capitalist countries of Europe, taken together, required almost 65 years to achieve such an increase. In 1913, Russia produced 4,200,000 tons of pig-iron. In 1957, the U.S.S.R. was putting out 37,000,000 tons. To achieve such an increase, the capitalist countries of Europe combined had required something like 75 years.

In 1913, Russia produced 4,200,000 tons of steel. In 1957, steel output in the Soviet Union exceeded 51,000,000 tons. Today the U.S.S.R. is producing as much steel as Britain, France, Japan and Sweden taken together.

The U.S.S.R. achieved its first victory in economic competition with the capitalist countries by emerging to second place in the world in volume of industrial output. Today the Soviet people, led by the Party, are carrying out another great task, that of overtaking and surpassing the most developed capitalist countries in output per head within the shortest possible space of time. In this respect, Russia's backwardness had been truly disastrous. In 1913, Russia's industrial output per head was 13 or 14 times less than in the U.S.A. This gap was substantially reduced through the efforts of the Party and the people. In 1957, industrial output per head in the U.S.S.R. was only 2.6 times less than in the U.S.A.

5. The Party solved the peasant problem: by effecting a change-over from individual to collective farming it, for the first time in history, *brought the peasants a happy life.*

The peasant question was among the "eternal," and most difficult, problems engendered by a society based on exploitation. Under capitalism, the rural proletarians and semi-proletarians, borne down by the conditions of petty individual farming, poverty and the entire mode of rural life, disunited and unorganised, are wholly in the power of the landlords, kulaks and capitalists.

The lot of the peasants of tsarist Russia was particularly appalling. The primitive, unproductive forms of farming and exceedingly brutal exploitation made the life of the peasant one of back-breaking toil. The elimination of the landlord class, the nationalisation of the land and its transfer for use to the peasants changed the position of the toiling people of the countryside. But that did not completely settle the peasant question.

The Party found the only possible way of ensuring the peasants a prosperous life, free from exploitation—the way of producers' co-operation. The multitude of small peasant households using primitive implements gave way to large collective farms set up through the voluntary association of peasants. The wooden plough and the wooden harrow, which predominated in the individual peasant households, were replaced on the collective farms by tractors, lorries, grain combines and other complex agricultural machines.

The antithesis between town and country, which had been engendered by a society based on exploitation and had existed for centuries, was eliminated. The alliance of the workers and the peasants became indestructible.

In the course of social transformation the mode of rural life changed radically. The age-old foundations of peasant life, with its petty proprietor customs and manners collapsed, and a revolution took place in the consciousness and psychology of the peasant. An entirely new type of peasant—the collective farmer—came into being. Free from exploitation, literate, and with a broad outlook, he has become complete master of his destiny.

The Communist Party led the Soviet peasantry on to the high-road of Socialism.

6. The Party smashed the chains of national oppression and, for the first time in human history, solved the problem of *relations between peoples*, establishing fraternal friendship between them.

National oppression had existed for a long time, intensifying as class relations developed. Many States founded on force, on ruthless exploitation and oppression, on the enslavement of nations deprived of all rights, sprang up under capitalism, especially in the imperialist epoch. The overwhelming majority of the peoples were ruthlessly enslaved. Such also was the lot of many of the peoples inhabiting tsarist Russia. The national question had become one of the most vital and pressing issues.

The Communist Party worked out and implemented altogether new, just principles in the national question. It united the numerous peoples of the country into a friendly family on the progressive principles of equality, national independence and mutual assistance. The Union of Soviet Socialist Republics, uniting dozens of peoples, was established. In the U.S.S.R., each people is guaranteed complete national freedom and political equality, as well as actual economic equality, which is the material basis of all equality.

The Party pursued the policy of accelerating the development of peoples who had been in the past the most backward. In 1957, industrial output in the Armenian Republic was 49 times as great as in 1913; the Kirghiz and the Kazakh Republics showed a 46-fold and a 40-fold increase respectively. In industrial development, the Soviet Republics in Transcaucasia and Central Asia have far outstripped neighbouring Turkey and Iran.

The Party ensured the all-round development of culture that is national in form and Socialist in content. The culture of each people influences that of other peoples, and shares in the common process of creating a Soviet Socialist culture.

The result of the radical changes which had taken place in the life of the peoples was that in the Soviet Union the old, bourgeois nations were transformed into Socialist nations. New nations, shaped as Socialist nations from the very beginning, came into being on the basis of existing nationalities and ethnographic groups. Nations drew steadily closer together, enriching each other. The material, political and ideological foundations uniting all the peoples of the U.S.S.R. into a single whole have been laid and are developing in the country.

7. Under the leadership of the Party, a cultural revolution, the most deep-going and impressive of changes in the spiritual relations between man and man, was carried out in the U.S.S.R. in an exceedingly short time.

The Party brought knowledge to the people. The greater part of the population of tsarist Russia could not read or write. Prior to the Revolution, only a fifth of the children and adolescents went to school. Secondary, to say nothing of higher, education was within the reach of only the well-to-do. Books, newspapers and magazines were unknown to the mass of the people. During the first fifteen years of Soviet power illiteracy was liquidated, in the main, and universal four-year and, later, seven-year education was made compulsory. An average of more than 50 million people study in the U.S.S.R. every year. Tens of thousands of libraries and thousands of clubs and cinemas have been opened in Soviet years, and hundreds of thousands of portable film projectors are in use. The annual printing of books has increased more than 10-fold, and the circulation of newspapers has grown 18-fold. In its level of culture and literacy of the population, the Soviet Union has outdistanced all the capitalist countries of the world.

An entirely new intelligentsia has been created, an intelligentsia coming from the people and bound up with the people by common interests and tasks. The pre-revolutionary intelligentsia was numerically small, and for the most part served the landlord-bourgeois classes. In 1913, there were 136,000 specialists with a higher education engaged in Russia's national economy. In 1957, the number of such specialists in the U.S.S.R. was 2,805,000, that is, 21 times as many. It took the capitalist countries nearly 100 years to create a technical intelligentsia. In the Soviet Union, this task was carried out in 15 to 20 years. For the scale on which it trains engineers, the Soviet Union has long since overtaken all the capitalist countries of the world.

A totally new, Socialist culture, signifying a higher stage in the modern cultural development of mankind, has been created. It is distinguished by a truly humane and progressive character and by the fact that it is of the people and for the people. The working class carefully selected all that was valuable, progressive and truthful in the cultural heritage of the past, critically reworked it and used it as a foundation for building up a new and genuinely people's Socialist culture. At the same time it discarded everything reactionary, unscientific and unartistic. No other class had, or could have, carried out a transformation on so vast a scale.

The Party created conditions for colossal progress in science. Soviet science now leads the world in many respects. The antithesis between brainwork and manual labour, engendered by a society based on exploitation, has been eliminated. The labour of millions of people has assumed a conscious, creative character; it is the masses who are creating a Socialist culture.

The greatest forces of social development—the people and culture, the masses and scientific and technical knowledge— which had been fenced off from each other for thousands of years, were brought together as a result of the transforming activity of the Party. This substantially accelerated the progress of Soviet society.

8. The Party aimed at creating a social system in which the material and cultural requirements of each person would be met to the full and where the all-round, harmonious development of the individual would be assured. All the manifold activities

of the Party are subordinated to the achievement of this great goal. Concern for the well-being of the people has always been, and remains, the chief goal of the Party's existence, the *supreme law* of its activity.

By its very nature, capitalism cannot give the working people a happy, prosperous life. The social revolution carried out in the U.S.S.R. under the leadership of the Communist Party has given the working people inexhaustible benefits. Socialism ensures a steady rise in the living standard of the people. Unemployment, that terrible scourge of the workers in town and country, has been done away with for all time. Every Soviet citizen has a job and is confident of the morrow. Every year sees Soviet people eating better food, dressing better, and enjoying all the benefits of culture. Taking into account the fact that unemployment has been done away with and the working day shortened, the real wages of workers increased almost fivefold between 1913 and 1956, and the real incomes of the peasants increased sixfold. The prices of consumer goods are being cut systematically. Tuition is free in the elementary, secondary and higher schools. Moreover, a considerable number of the students in technical schools and higher educational institutions receive stipends.

The health of the people is protected by numerous medical institutions. There are 17 doctors per 10,000 people in the U.S.S.R. as against 12 in the U.S.A., 10 in Japan, 10 in France, 9 in Britain, 3 in Turkey and 1 in Iran. Medical services and treatment are free in the Soviet Union. Every year millions of people receive medical treatment at the country's numerous sanatoria, or spend their holidays at its innumerable holiday homes and tourist stations, free of charge or for a small fee. Millions of children annually spend part or the whole of the summer in Young Pioneer camps or children's health homes.

A decreasing death rate is an important index of the improvement in the life of a people. In pre-revolutionary Russia, the death rate was more than twice as high as in the U.S.A. and Britain, and half as much again as in France. In recent years the death rate in the Soviet Union has been the lowest in the world, and its population has been growing at a higher rate than in the overwhelming majority of the capitalist countries. In 1955-1956, the mean expectancy of life in the U.S.S.R. was more than twice as long as in pre-revolutionary Russia.

The U.S.S.R. has the best system of social insurance in the world. Citizens of the U.S.S.R. are guaranteed social security in old age, in the event of sickness or disability.

Large sums of money are spent annually on the maintenance of schools and hospitals, free tuition, free medical treatment and social maintenance. In 1957, the State spent more than 200,000 million rubles for these purposes, or approximately a third of the budget allocations.

In the past 40 years millions of people have moved into new, comfortable flats. In the Soviet Union, rent (including municipal services) is the lowest in the world. It makes up from four to five per cent of the budget of a working-man's family.

The Party is leading the Soviet people to a full sufficiency to be followed by an abundance of consumer goods.

9. A major achievement of the Party's transforming activity has been the upbringing of a new man, a man with *new spiritual features*. For thousands of years the exploiting system had crushed and strangled popular talents, corrupted people, and spread brutal, misanthropic customs, morals and manners in their mutual relations.

In the course of radical social and economic changes, as a result of the Party's persistent and purposeful educational work, profound revolutionary changes have taken place in the mentality of Soviet people, in their morality, and in their attitude to the community and to one another. The characteristic features of Soviet man are lofty ideals, unbounded devotion to Communism and the Socialist Motherland, an awareness that public interests come first, a conscious attitude to labour and to Socialist property, great humanism, an internationalism that is inseparably bound up with patriotism, deep respect for all peoples, big and small, and recognition of the inviolability of their national independence. For many people, labour has ceased to be only a means of subsistence. It has become the substance of their lives, a source of joy and delight. With many Soviet working people, their daily routine work has become a source of heroism and inspired creative effort, for its aim is to build a Communist society for the good of all.

In forty years of Soviet power the creative endeavour of the Soviet people, led by the Communist Party, has conclusively refuted the reactionary legend of the exploiters about the mental poverty and political inferiority of the working people.

With the passing of power into the hands of the people and the organisation of material production on the basis of social ownership of the means of production, the masses were enabled directly to influence all aspects of social relations. And in this lies an inexhaustible source of the amazingly rapid rates of social, economic and cultural progress under Socialism.

10. The Communist Party did away with the most terrible of social calamities, one that had existed for thousands of years—

social oppression of man by man and the use of force by the exploiting class against the exploited class.

The enemies of progress like to portray Socialism as a society of violence, arguing that the transition from capitalism to Socialism requires great sacrifices. In reality, violence is an organic feature of capitalism, whose everyday, "peaceful" existence exacts incomparably greater sacrifices of mankind than the Socialist revolution which is inevitable in the progressive development of society. The events of the past forty years have conclusively borne this out.

Capitalism breeds wars which bring the peoples the greatest suffering and privations and exact colossal sacrifices. The forty years after the victory of the October Revolution witnessed the last battles of the first world war, and also the second world war—the most sanguinary man has ever known. Between these two wars, and after the second world war, hotbeds of war kept flaring up now in one area of the globe, now in another. More than 40 million people were killed in the two world wars alone. But this figure will grow many times over if we include those who were killed in other wars and during the suppression of revolutionary and national liberation movements by the capitalists, and those who died from wounds and starvation.

Socialism, by its very nature, precludes wars. Contrary to the capitalist countries, the U.S.S.R. has never started a war on its own initiative. All the military operations ever conducted by the Soviet people—against the interventionists and internal counter-revolution, the Japanese militarists, and the German fascist invaders and their satellites—were provoked and imposed on them by the imperialists. *Socialism brings peace to the peoples*, it rids them of bloody wars. Had the proletariat of the big capitalist countries succeeded in taking power after the first world war, the peoples would not have known the horrors of the second world war and of many other wars.

The experience of the Soviet Union shows that the peoples must put an end to capitalism if they want to do away with social oppression and violence, to avert the sacrifices it entails.

11. The Communist Party and the Soviet Government worked out and proclaimed, and consistently implement, entirely *new principles of relations between countries*: mutual respect for national sovereignty and territorial integrity, non-interference in the internal affairs of one another, equality and mutual benefit, renunciation of war as an instrument of foreign policy, and peaceful coexistence of States with different social and economic systems.

The first legislative act of the Soviet Socialist State born in 1917 was the Decree on Peace. Ever since then, the Soviet Union has consistently and steadfastly been championing peace, seeking to curb the militarists and working persistently for a reciprocal reduction, and afterwards abolition, of armed forces.

The new principles of international relations proclaimed by the Soviet Union, principles that are the very antithesis of the aggressive, predatory policy of the imperialist States, are of vital importance to the destiny of mankind. The foreign policy of the U.S.S.R. is a powerful factor in preventing another world war, in defending peace.

The ruling circles of the imperialist countries reject the peaceful principles of Soviet foreign policy; they are pursuing a policy of aggression and military adventures. That is why the Soviet State, working vigorously for peace, is constantly strengthening its defensive capacity as a guarantee of the country's independence and of Communist construction.

In the course of forty years the Soviet Union, led by the Communist Party, has demonstrated its defensive might. In 1918-1920, the Soviet people defeated the foreign interventionists and won for themselves the possibility of engaging in peaceful Socialist construction. They delivered an even more crushing blow to the German fascist invaders, who had dared to raise their hand against the Socialist gains of the Soviet people.

Headed by the Party, the Soviet State has built up powerful armed forces that are provided with the latest military equipment and are capable of repelling any aggression.

12. By their transforming activity within the country in the forty years that have passed since the triumph of the October Revolution, the Communist Party and the Soviet people have exerted *a tremendous influence on the entire course of world history*, on the destiny of mankind. Faithful to the principles of proletarian internationalism, the Communist Party and the Soviet people have always regarded themselves as an integral part of the international Communist liberation movement. The Soviet Union influences historical development chiefly by its social and economic changes and its economic achievements. The progressive solution of pressing social problems and the tremendous rate of economic development show the advantages of Socialism over capitalism, increase the attractive power of Socialism, weaken the positions of capitalism, and accelerate the progressive development of mankind. The U.S.S.R. has pioneered the highroad to Socialism for other countries.

The defeat of the German fascist invaders in the second world war was one of the greatest victories of the Communist Party and the Soviet people, a victory of epoch-making significance. The U.S.S.R. thereby rendered humanity a great service. By inflicting a military, moral and political defeat on fascism, the

Soviet people, led by the Communist Party, not only upheld their own independence and Socialist gains, but also freed the peoples of Europe, Asia, Africa and America from Hitlerite slavery or the threat of fascist enslavement. They saved millions of people from annihilation, and the achievements of human culture from destruction.

The relation of forces in the world arena changed in favour of Socialism and to the detriment of capitalism. This provided favourable conditions for revolutionary changes in other countries, for the victory of the working people of China and of a number of countries in Europe and Asia, where people's democratic republics were established. The victory of the forces of progress in the war aggravated the crisis of the colonial system of imperialism, which began to break up under the blows of the oppressed peoples.

Such were the main results of the activity of the Party and the people in forty years of Soviet power.

In reviewing the path travelled by the Soviet Union during those forty years, Communists may say with legitimate pride that the undertakings in the programme of the Party have been, and are being, carried out with credit. During those years far-reaching social changes were carried out in the Soviet Union under the leadership of the Communist Party, changes of world significance, and which constitute an immortal service to history by the Soviet people and the Communist Party. The forty years' experience of the C.P.S.U. showed convincingly and incontrovertibly that *the path of Socialism is the only correct path for the whole of mankind.*

A most important source of the strength of the Soviet people, who have won fame as a people of creators, a people of heroes, is that their struggle for freedom and happiness, for Communism, is headed by the Communist Party, founded by the great Lenin and steeled in battle. The Soviet people won their historic victories thanks to the correct policy of the Party, to its revolutionary energy and organising activity.

"The experience of the Soviet State during the past forty years shows that without a Party united and solid as a rock, without a Party armed with a knowledge of the laws of social development, without a Party faithful to the great principles of Marxism-Leninism, the working class, the working peasantry, and our people as a whole would not have been able to win power, smash their enemies, build a Socialist society and successfully begin the gradual transition to Communism" (N. S. Khrushchov, *Forty Years of the Great October Socialist Revolution*, Eng. ed., p. 36).

A vivid indication of the Party's growing prestige among the people, and of its growing ties with the masses, is the striving of Soviet people to link up their destinies with the Party and to fight under its banner. On the eve of the Great October Socialist Revolution, the Party had 240,000 members. Forty years later the Communist Party of the Soviet Union had become a party of many millions. In 1958, it had a membership of over 7,800,000. The Party is doing everything necessary to extend and strengthen its ties with the masses.

The celebration of the fortieth anniversary of the October Revolution strikingly demonstrated the unity of the Soviet people around the Communist Party, which they regard as the spokesman of their interests, as their recognised and tested leader and guide.

The celebration of the fortieth anniversary of the October Revolution vividly demonstrated the great unity and cohesion of the Socialist countries, of all the Communist and Workers' Parties. The speeches delivered at the jubilee session by the leaders of the delegations from the foreign Communist and Workers' Parties, and from the international voluntary organisations, testified to the increased solidarity of the working people of the whole world. Mao Tse-tung, who led the Party and Government delegation from the Chinese People's Republic, stated in his speech that the very fact that representatives of the working class and of the broad masses of different countries were present at the jubilee session of the Supreme Soviet of the U.S.S.R. spoke of "the great unity of the peoples of the world, and symbolises the upsurge and development of the international Socialist movement" (*Pravda*, November 7, 1957).

The delegations from the Communist and Workers' Parties that took part in the celebration of the fortieth anniversary of the October Revolution decided to use their visit to Moscow to meet and discuss questions that were of moment to all the brother Communist and Workers' Parties. A conference of representatives of the Communist and Workers' Parties of the Socialist countries was held on November 14-16, 1957, and a conference of representatives of the Communist and Workers' Parties of more than 60 countries met on November 16-19. These were the most representative conferences in the history of the Communist movement, in whose ranks there were more than 33 million Communists in 1957. After an exchange of views on urgent questions of the international situation and the world Communist movement, the conference of representatives of the Communist and Workers' Parties of the Socialist countries adopted a Declaration, and the conference of the representatives of 64 Communist and Workers' Parties addressed a Peace Manifesto to the workers and peasants of all countries, to men and women throughout the world, to all people of good will.

The Declaration fully supported the conclusions and propositions of the Twentieth Congress of the C.P.S.U. on the major fundamental issues of international development. It drew broad theoretical conclusions from the vast practical experience of the struggle for Socialism and peace, and thereby made an important collective contribution to the creative development of Marxism-Leninism. It contained a Marxist analysis of the international situation and of the basic changes that had taken place in the recent period in the alignment of forces in the international arena, and emphasised that at the present time the most important international task was to fight for peace and against the preparations being made by the imperialists for another world war. It pointed out that today the cause of peace was being defended by powerful forces, by forces capable of averting war.

The Declaration reaffirmed the Communist and Workers' Parties' unity of views on the basic questions of Socialist revolution and Socialist construction. Pointing to the diversity of the forms and methods of building Socialism arising from the specific historical conditions obtaining in each country, the Declaration generalised the principal common features of the struggle for Socialism and the laws governing it. These common features and laws were: leadership of the working masses by the working class, whose core is the Marxist-Leninist Party, in carrying out a proletarian revolution in one form or another and establishing the dictatorship of the proletariat in one form or another; an alliance of the working class with the bulk of the peasantry and other sections of the working people; the abolition of capitalist property and the establishment of social ownership of the basic means of production; the gradual Socialist transformation of agriculture; the planned development of the national economy, with the aim of building Socialism and Communism and raising the standard of life of the working people; the accomplishment of a Socialist revolution in ideology and culture, and the creation of a numerous intelligentsia devoted to the cause of Socialism; the abolition of national oppression and the establishment of equality and fraternal friendship among the peoples; the defence of the gains of Socialism against attack by external and internal enemies; solidarity of the working class of any particular country with the working class of other countries, that is, proletarian internationalism.

The Declaration pointed out that these main features and laws were characteristic of the development of all the countries that had taken the path of Socialism, and that it was necessary to apply these basic principles of Communism correctly, in conformity with the historical conditions and national peculiarities of each country concerned.

The Declaration dealt the opportunists a crushing blow. Indicating the need for resolutely overcoming revisionism and dogmatism in the ranks of the Communist and Workers' Parties, it stressed that in present-day conditions the main danger was revisionism, as a manifestation of bourgeois ideology that paralysed the revolutionary activity of the working class and demanded the preservation or restoration of capitalism.

Addressing millions of people of good will in all countries, the representatives of the Communist and Workers' Parties called upon them to redouble their efforts in the struggle for peace.

"Peace," the Peace Manifesto said, "can be preserved only if all to whom it is dear combine their forces, sharpen their vigilance in relation to the machinations of the instigators of war, and become fully conscious that their sacred duty is to intensify the struggle for peace, which is threatened."

The unanimity with which the conference of the Communist and Workers' Parties adopted the Declaration and the Peace Manifesto signified a major ideological and political victory of the world Communist movement. This unanimity was all the more important because international reaction had made every effort to split the Communist movement. The November conferences of the Communist and Workers' Parties dealt a shattering blow to the plans of reaction.

All the Communist and Workers' Parties of the world supported and approved the two programme documents—the Declaration and the Peace Manifesto—drawn up by the conferences.

Only the leaders of the Communist League of Yugoslavia disagreed with the propositions of the Declaration recognised by all Communists, and set themselves against the international Communist movement. The delegation from the Communist League of Yugoslavia refused to attend the conference of representatives of the Communist and Workers' Parties of the Socialist countries or to sign the Declaration adopted at the conference. The leaders of the Communist League of Yugoslavia thereby showed that they had not discarded their anti-Leninist views and that they ignored the good will of the C.P.S.U. and the other Marxist parties, which were striving to normalise relations with the League of Communists on the basis of Marxist-Leninist principles. This apostasy from Marxism-Leninism found full expression in the programme adopted in 1958 by the Seventh Congress of the Communist League of Yugoslavia. All the Communist and Workers' Parties of the world qualified that programme as revisionist. In an effort to help the leaders of the Communist League of Yugoslavia to see and rectify their erroneous views, the Communist Party of the Soviet Union offered comradely criticism of the non-Marxist propositions laid down in the programme.

This criticism, made in the interests of the world working-class movement, in the interests of the triumph of Marxism-Leninism, was unanimously supported by all the brother parties. But the leaders of the League of Communists rejected it. Moreover, they made new hostile declarations against the C.P.S.U. and other brother parties, and found themselves isolated in the ranks of the international Communist movement.

The Declaration was a powerful ideological weapon for the Communist and Workers' Parties of the Socialist countries; it inspired the masses in the struggle for the triumph of Socialism.

The constructive activity of the working people of the People's Democracies was headed by their militant Marxist-Leninist parties: in the People's Republic of Albania by the Albanian Party of Labour (first secretary of the Central Committee E. Hoxha); in the People's Republic of Bulgaria by the Bulgarian Communist Party (first secretary of the C.C. T. Zhivkov); in the Chinese People's Republic by the Communist Party of China (chairman of the C.C. Mao Tse-tung); in the Czechoslovak Socialist Republic by the Communist Party of Czechoslovakia (first secretary of the C.C. A. Novotný); in the German Democratic Republic by the Socialist Unity Party of Germany (first secretary of the C.C. W. Ulbricht); in the Hungarian People's Republic by the Hungarian Socialist Workers' Party (first secretary of the C.C. J. Kádár); in the Korean People's Democratic Republic by the Korean Party of Labour (first secretary of the C.C. Kim Il-Sung); in the Mongolian People's Republic by the Mongolian People's Revolutionary Party (first secretary of the C.C. Y. Tse-denbal); in the Polish People's Republic by the Polish United Workers' Party (first secretary of the C.C. W. Gomulka); in the Rumanian People's Republic by the Rumanian Workers' Party (first secretary of the C.C. G. Gheorghiu-Dej); in the Democratic Republic of Vietnam by the Working People's Party of Vietnam (chairman of the C.C. Ho Chi Minh).

The November, 1957, conferences of the Communist and Workers' Parties and the documents adopted by them, as well as the criticism of the revisionism of the Yugoslav leaders by the brother parties, were a vivid demonstration of the unbreakable unity, cohesion and close co-operation of the Communist and Workers' Parties on the ideological basis of Marxism-Leninism, an expression of the great ideological and political upsurge in the international Communist movement. The conferences opened up new vistas for the development of the world Communist movement, for the further strengthening of the mighty forces of the Socialist camp, for the struggle of all the peoples for peace, democracy and Socialism.

6. The Party Efforts to Speed Up Fulfilment of the Basic Economic Task of the U.S.S.R. Measures Taken to Develop the Collective-Farm System. Working out the Problems Connected with the Gradual Transition to Communism

On the basis of the successes achieved by the Soviet people in the past forty years of Soviet rule, the Party steadfastly continued on the course set by the Twentieth Congress towards a sweeping advance in the country's economy and culture. Now that the U.S.S.R. had achieved major successes in these fields, the building of a Communist society had become the immediate practical task of the Party and the people.

Taking into account the country's resources and potentialities, the Party came to the conclusion that there was a real possibility of *gaining time and shortening the period* needed to carry out the basic economic task of the U.S.S.R. It steered a course towards accelerating the fulfilment of the basic economic task, which was necessitated by the internal requirements of Soviet society, the interests of world Socialism, and the struggle for peace. Only with highly developed productive forces, and having overtaken and surpassed the most developed capitalist countries in output per head of the main industrial and agricultural products, would it be possible to win in the competition with capitalism, sharply raise the living and cultural standards of the people, provide first a sufficiency and then an abundance of consumer goods, and create the conditions for the transition to Communism. The growth of the Soviet Union's economic might and the progress of its science and technology accelerate the tempo of development in all the Socialist countries, raise the prestige and influence of Socialism in the world arena, strengthen its position and reinforce the attraction of Socialism for millions of people. The might of the Soviet State, which is part of the great camp of Socialist countries and possesses first-class armed forces, is a reliable guarantee of durable and lasting peace. That is why the whole of progressive mankind is interested in rapid economic progress in the U.S.S.R.

In conformity with these requirements and tasks, the Party proceeded to draw up a new programme for the country's economic development and defined the main directions and scale of the growth of production for the next fifteen years.

During this period it was planned to increase industrial and agricultural output very considerably, to ensure an annual output of 75-85 million tons of pig-iron, 100-120 million tons of steel, 650-750 million tons of coal, 350-400 million tons of oil, and 800,000-900,000 million kw-h of electric power.

In organising the masses for the accomplishment of these great plans, the Party sought to make proper use of the country's material resources, steadily to improve techniques, and distribute the productive forces rationally. It gave special attention to the development of the industries that increase man's power over nature, greatly raise the productivity of labour, improve technological processes, ensure the fullest use of raw material resources, and accelerate the creation of the material and technical basis of Communism.

Of primary importance in this respect was the rapid expansion of the chemical industry. The application of chemistry leads to a tremendous acceleration of technological processes and makes it possible to increase the intensity of production substantially. Development of the chemical industry was a most essential condition for the creation of the material and technical basis of Communist society.

At a plenary meeting in May, 1958, the C.C. C.P.S.U. outlined a number of measures to advance the chemical industry, particularly the production of synthetic materials and articles made from them, in order to meet the demand of the national economy and the requirements of the population. More than 250 enterprises of the chemical and allied industries were to be built or reconstructed in seven years. Over 100,000 million rubles were appropriated for capital construction in the chemical industry.

The Party shows constant concern for the well-being of the people. It was decided to meet in sufficiency the requirements of the population for fabrics, garments, footwear and other items of general consumption within the next five or six years. This was a realistic plan. The economic progress made in the U.S.S.R. had provided all the requisites for increasing the output of consumer goods at a much higher rate, especially through the development of the chemical industry, without detriment to the priority growth of heavy industry and the strengthening of the country's defensive capacity.

An important step was taken towards solving the housing problem. Soviet society inherited very little housing from the ruling classes of tsarist Russia; moreover, a large part of that housing was in bad repair. Tens of millions of people lived in barracks, and many simply in mud huts. After the Revolution a large number of houses was built in the U.S.S.R. and the situation improved somewhat. But housing again became an acute problem as a result of the war. The Hitlerites had destroyed hundreds of towns and thousands of villages, leaving nearly 25 million people homeless. It took much effort to make good this loss; whole towns and thousands of villages had to be built anew. Nevertheless, there was still a serious housing shortage in the U.S.S.R. Thanks to the rapid growth of the Soviet Union's economic might, the country was now in a position to solve the housing problem. The Party and the Government drew up an extensive housing programme. It provided for doing away with the housing shortage within the next 10 to 12 years. Beginning with 1960, there was to be an annual increase of 100 million square metres of housing.

The Party took very important steps to achieve a steep rise in agriculture and to carry out the task of overtaking and surpassing the U.S.A. in agricultural output.

Thanks to the correct policy of the Party, its extensive organising activities and the selfless work of the collective-farm peasantry in 1953-1957, economic conditions in the countryside had changed. The collective-farm system had entered a new stage of development, which was distinguished by the following main features:

The collective farms had become big, economically strong Socialist units, making wide use of modern equipment, science and advanced experience.

The amalgamated collective farms had acquired varied modern machinery, and many of them had built power stations and industrial enterprises.

They had trained numerous skilled field-crop experts, livestock-breeders, electricians, machine-operators, building experts, and leaders and organisers of collective-farm production.

The incomes of the collective farms had grown substantially and the living standards of their members had improved. In 1949, for example, the cash income of a collective farm averaged 111,000 rubles, whereas by 1957 it had risen to 1,250,000 rubles.

The new situation in agriculture necessitated a major reorganisation of collective-farm production and management. A plenary meeting of the C.C. C.P.S.U. held in February, 1958, adopted a resolution, "On the further development of the collective-farm system and the reorganisation of machine-and-tractor stations."

The plenary meeting noted that the machine-and-tractor stations had played a historic part in setting up and consolidating the collective-farm system, in providing agriculture with technical equipment and in strengthening the alliance of the working class and the peasantry.

In the new conditions, this form of productive and technical service had begun to hinder the further development of the collective farms and to fetter the initiative of both the collective farms and their members. The negative consequences of two Socialist enterprises—the collective farm and the machine-and-tractor station—cultivating one and the same piece of land began to tell more and more. This situation often led to the absence of personal responsibility for the organisation of production and the use of machinery, reduced the responsibility of both the collective farm and the machine-and-tractor stations for raising yields, and gave rise to big and unnecessary expenditure on maintenance of parallel links in the administrative apparatus.

This state of affairs made it imperative that the existing form of productive and technical service to the collective farms be changed. The plenary meeting of the C.C. C.P.S.U. found it advisable to reorganise the machine-and-tractor stations into maintenance and repair stations, and to sell their machinery to the collective farms, at different dates, depending upon the area concerned. Those collective farms which were unable to purchase tractors and other machines or, more important still, could not handle complex machinery properly, were for the time being to go on using the productive and technical services of the machine-and-tractor stations.

The measures proposed by the plenary meeting of the C.C. were submitted for nation-wide discussion. Close on 50 million people took part in it. The measures worked out by the Party and approved by the people were given the force of law by the Supreme Soviet at its session in March, 1958.

At that session N. S. Khrushchov, on the recommendation of the Central Committee of the C.P.S.U., was appointed Chairman of the Council of Ministers of the U.S.S.R. by a unanimous decision of the deputies to the Supreme Soviet. The C.C. C.P.S.U. also decided that N. S. Khrushchov should retain his post as first secretary of the Central Committee.

The reorganisation of the machine-and-tractor stations was an important revolutionary step. After the victory of the collective-farm system it was *the biggest and most significant event* in the development of Socialist agriculture. The land, assured to the collective farms for their use in perpetuity, and the agricultural machines were now concentrated in the same hands—in the hands of the collective farms. This opened up tremendous additional possibilities for rapidly increasing agricultural output.

The changes in productive and technical service to the collective farms called for new forms of economic relations between the State and the collective farms. First and foremost, it was necessary to change the system and conditions of purchasing agricultural produce. The June, 1958, plenary meeting of the C.C. C.P.S.U. thoroughly examined the existing system, and noted the great stimulating importance of the principle of delivering agricultural produce to the State on a per hectare basis. As a whole, however, the existing system was complicated and cumbersome; it consisted of many stages, with numerous forms of purchase and a wide range of prices. This system frequently clashed with the economic laws of Socialist society. The June plenary meeting of the C.C. decided to abolish the multiplicity of forms of purchasing agricultural products and to change over to a single system of State purchasing with uniform, economically sound prices differentiated according to the different zones of the country.

In determining the level of the new purchasing prices, account was taken of the need to reimburse the expenses of the collective farms in accordance with the average zonal conditions of production, the growth of labour productivity, reduction of costs, and the creation of the necessary accumulation for extended reproduction.

The reorganisation of the machine-and-tractor stations and the change in the system and conditions of purchasing agricultural produce were *important* political and economic measures, expediting the advance of Soviet society towards Communism. They further strengthened the alliance of the working class and the peasantry and made it possible to develop collective-farm production and the whole of the national economy at a higher rate. The reorganisation helped to enlarge the non-distributable assets of the collective farms, consolidated the basis of collective-farm-co-operative property and created the conditions for bringing it increasingly closer to national property. The expansion and strengthening of non-distributable assets was one of the major requisites for the gradual development of collective-farm-co-operative property into national property.

The resolutions of the February and June plenary meetings of the C.C. gave a profound theoretical analysis of the prospects for further advancing the collective-farm system and enhancing its role in Communist construction, of the ways of raising collective-farm property to the level of national property and creating a single Communist form of ownership.

Parallel with the tasks of economic development, the Party tackled urgent problems of the Communist education of the people, particularly of the rising generation. The reorganisation of public education was of immense importance for the material and spiritual progress of Soviet society towards Communism.

The Soviet school had trained millions of educated, cultured citizens, active participants in Socialist construction. It had trained excellent specialists in all spheres of economy, culture and science. But, all these achievements notwithstanding, the work of the general schools and places of higher education was not meeting the requirements of Communist construction and had serious shortcomings. The main shortcoming, brought to light by the Central Committee of the Party, was that the school, while giving a general theoretical knowledge, did little to prepare the rising generation for practical activity, did not give it work training and did not do enough to accustom it to work in material production. This gap between instruction and life was at variance with the tasks of Communist construction and could no longer be tolerated.

The Party raised the question of reorganising secondary and higher education. The basic propositions on the reorganisation of the schools were expounded in a memorandum submitted by N. S. Khrushchov to the Presidium of the C.C. C.P.S.U. and then in the theses of the C.C. C.P.S.U. and the Council of Ministers of the U.S.S.R.: "On establishing closer links between school and life and on the further development of public education in the U.S.S.R."

The reorganisation of public education affected the interests of the entire Soviet people, and the question was therefore submitted for nation-wide discussion. The theses of the C.C. C.P.S.U. and the Council of Ministers of the U.S.S.R., which were published in the press, evoked widespread response and were warmly approved by millions of citizens. Soviet public opinion recognised reorganisation of education to be a pressing matter. The main points of the theses, approved by all Soviet people, were embodied in a law passed by the Supreme Soviet of the U.S.S.R. at its session in December, 1958.

The reorganisation of education was based on the principle of linking instruction with productive work, with the practice of Communist construction. The chief task of the school was to prepare the rising generation to take its place in life, for socially useful work, to raise the level of general and polytechnical education, to train highly educated people with a sound knowledge of the fundamentals of science, to bring up the youth in a spirit of profound respect for the principles of Socialist society, in the spirit of the ideas of Communism. Participating in socially useful activity, the younger generation of builders of a Communist society should be accustomed to the most varied forms of physical work for which it was fitted.

In keeping with these requirements, universal compulsory eight-year education was substituted for universal compulsory seven-year education. Educational work in the eight-year school was to be reorganised in such a way as to combine the study of the fundamentals of science with polytechnical instruction and education in labour, and widely to draw pupils into various forms of socially useful work compatible with their age. At the next stage young people were to engage in socially useful work, and all their further training (in schools for young workers and peasants, secondary general-educational polytechnical schools with instruction in production, technical schools and other special educational establishments) was to be linked up with productive work in industry or agriculture.

Factory schools, the vocational, railway, mining, building, and agricultural mechanisation schools of the Labour Reserves Training Board, professional-technical, factory apprenticeship and other vocational schools under the Economic Councils and government departments were to be gradually transformed into urban and rural vocational-technical schools. These schools would enrol young people taking up work after finishing the eight-year school, and their educational work would be based on the active and systematic participation of their pupils in productive work, in close co-operation with industrial enterprises, building projects, and State and collective farms.

Places of higher education were to enrol people who had received a full secondary education. They were to train specialists by combining instruction with socially useful work. The specific forms of combining instruction with practice, with work, would be determined according to the speciality of the establishment in question, the composition of the student body and also the specific features of the nationalities and localities concerned. It was considered necessary to do everything possible to improve and extend evening and extra-mural instruction, promote university education and improve the theoretical and practical training of students.

The reorganisation of the secondary and higher school system through the establishment of close links with material production and productive work was inspired by the Party's concern for the upbringing of the rising generation, for the expansion and improvement of education in the country, for the shaping of the new man, a citizen of all-round development, harmoniously combining mental and physical labour in the single process of social work. The reorganisation of the general school and higher education was therefore to play a great role in removing the essential distinction between physical and mental labour, and creating the conditions for the country's transition to Communism.

The political and economic measures put into effect by the Party shortly before and after the Twentieth Congress are of great and historic importance in the struggle of the Soviet people to build Communism, to carry out their basic economic task. In five years (1954-1958) the Soviet Union made big strides forward in its economic and cultural development, in improving the well-being of the masses.

The new and most important feature of the peaceful competition between Socialism and capitalism was the fact that the U.S.S.R. had outstripped the most advanced capitalist country, the U.S.A., not only in the rate of development but also in the absolute increase in the output of such important industrial products as iron-ore, coal, oil, pig-iron, steel, cement and woollen fabrics.

From 1953 to 1957 the average annual increase in industrial output was: iron-ore, 6.1 million tons in the U.S.S.R., while in the U.S.A. it decreased by 3 million tons; pig-iron, 2.4 million tons in the U.S.S.R. and 0.8 million tons in the U.S.A.; steel, 3.26 million tons in the U.S.S.R. and 0.3 million tons in the U.S.A.; all kinds of coal (in terms of hard coal), 30.6 million tons in the U.S.S.R. and 6.2 million tons in the U.S.A.; cement, 3.2 million tons in the U.S.S.R. and 1.2 million tons in the U.S.A.

In 1958, total industrial output in the U.S.S.R. was 70 per cent greater than in 1953. During the same period the output of pig-iron, steel, rolled metal and metal-cutting machines increased almost 50 per cent, of coal more than 50 per cent, of oil more than 100 per cent, of electric power 73 per cent. In 1958, the productivity of labour was 40 per cent higher than in 1953.

Outstanding successes were achieved in agriculture. The results of its development during the five years (1954-1958) were summed up at the December, 1958, plenary meeting of the C.C. C.P.S.U.

The plenary meeting was unanimous in noting that the period which had elapsed since the September, 1953, plenary meeting of the C.C. was of historic significance. The implementation of the measures worked out by the Party enabled the country swiftly to make good the lag in agriculture and to strengthen the economy of the collective and State farms, and of the Socialist system as a whole.

In that five-year period the output and purchases of agricultural produce increased considerably. In 1958, grain output totalled 137 million tons, or 69 per cent more than in 1953. The grain deliveries plan was overfulfilled. In 1953, the State granaries received less than 31 million tons of grain, while in 1958, it received 56 million tons. It was an all-time record.

There was a big increase in the total harvest and marketable output of industrial crops and vegetables. In the period under review, the gross yield of sugar-beet increased more than 100 per cent, flax fibre more than 150 per cent, vegetables 40 per cent (potatoes 20 per cent) and raw cotton 20 per cent.

The implementation of the measures planned by the Party over this period resulted in the elimination of the long-standing lag in livestock-breeding, a vital branch of agriculture. This was a major success achieved by the Party, by the entire Soviet people. In 1958, the 1953 figure for cattle was exceeded by 24 per cent, for pigs by 41 per cent and for sheep by 29 per cent. Livestock productivity rose sharply. Compared with 1953, the output of milk in 1958 was 60 per cent higher and that of meat (reckoning the increment in the herd), 40 per cent higher. The increase in socially-owned livestock surpassed the average increase in the country's total livestock. The share of the collective and State farms in the total deliveries of livestock products rose considerably. The collective and State farms became *the decisive force in supplying the State with livestock products*. This was an outstanding achievement of agriculture and of Communist construction.

The basic economic task was being successfully carried out in agriculture as in industry. As a result of the measures taken by the Party, the U.S.S.R. surpassed the U.S.A. in the rate of growth of total agricultural output. During the four years from 1950 to 1953 the annual increase in agricultural output averaged 1.6 per cent in the U.S.S.R. and 1.7 per cent in the U.S.A. But in the next five years (1954-1958), the annual growth of agricultural output averaged more than 8 per cent in the U.S.S.R. and less than 2 per cent in the U.S.A. The Soviet level of output of a number of agricultural products came close to the U.S. level, and for some of the more important products exceeded the U.S. level. The U.S.S.R. had already overtaken the U.S.A. for the total output of milk and butter. The U.S.S.R. was producing twice as much wheat as the U.S.A., four times as much sugarbeet, 130 per cent more wool and a considerably greater quantity of potatoes.

Appraising the headway made in agriculture, N. S. Khrushchov said in his report to the plenary meeting:

"The significance of the five years that have passed since the September meeting of the Central Committee lies in the fact that, thanks to the steps taken by the Party, the forces of the collective-farm system have developed, its potentialities were put to use and a realistic foundation was laid for creating an abundance of farm produce and achieving a higher labour productivity in the country's agriculture. This is of invaluable importance for the cause of Communist construction and for further improving the well-being of the people."

Summing up the results achieved in agriculture in the past five-year period, the plenary meeting of the C.C. noted that the general successes must not screen the shortcomings in the work of individual regions, territories and Republics, and the lagging-behind of some collective farms and even of whole districts. The plenary meeting sharply criticised shortcomings in the work of some local Party organisations. It emphasised that the successes achieved should serve as a stimulus for a further, still steeper rise in agricultural production. The local Party organisations, enriched by the experience of the preceding five years, were called upon to display still greater energy in organising those engaged in agriculture, and the whole of the Soviet people, in the struggle to achieve a greater increase in agricultural output.

The C.C. plenary meeting drew up a programme for the further development of agriculture, and approved agricultural targets for 1959-1965 as State assignments. Under that programme, the total output of grain was to rise in 1965 to 160-177 million tons, of meat (dead weight) to 16 million tons, and of milk to 100-105 million tons. There was to be a considerable increase in the output of other agricultural products.

The December, 1958, plenary meeting of the C.C. stressed that the collective and State farms had every opportunity not only of fulfilling, but also substantially overfulfilling these assignments. The progress made in agriculture made it possible for the U.S.S.R. to overtake and surpass the U.S.A. in the output per head of staple agricultural products within the next few years.

The decisions of the plenary meeting pointed out that agricultural output in the coming seven years must be increased by raising the crop yield and the productivity of livestock-breeding, and by considerably raising labour productivity through further mechanisation and electrification. The main thing was to secure the maximum quantity of produce with the minimum outlay of labour and resources. All the reserves and potentialities of Socialist agriculture were to be mobilised for the purpose of increasing the output of grain, meat, milk, butter and other agricultural products. It was the task of local Party organisations to help each collective and State farm to draw up its own seven-year development plan, providing for the fullest use of the above-mentioned resources.

The December plenary meeting of the C.C. was an important event in the life of the Party and the country. Its proceedings, which were the Party's political report to the people on the situation in agriculture, found a warm response among all working people. The plenary meeting's decisions constituted a powerful appeal to organise a nation-wide struggle for further achievements in agriculture and for the creation of an abundance of agricultural produce.

The efforts of the Party and of the whole people to achieve a steep rise in industrial and agricultural output had a favourable effect in further improving the Soviet people's standard of life, now steadily rising year by year. The real wages of factory, office and other workers, and the incomes of the collective farmers, increased considerably.

The Soviet Union made outstanding progress in culture, science and technology. It was the first in the world to build a 5,000 kw. experimental atomic power station. Construction was started on a number of big atomic power stations. The first section of a 600,000 kw. atomic power station under construction was put into operation. The Soviet Union developed an inter-continental ballistic missile, capable of reaching any set target. It built an atom-powered ice-breaker, powerful jet airliners, and the world's biggest machine (proton synchrotron) for the study of the atomic nucleus. The crowning scientific and technical achievement was the creation and successful launching of artificial earth satellites and an artificial planet of the solar system.

Such were the principal results of the efforts of the Soviet people to develop economy and culture in the five-year period under review.

These achievements were the result of the selfless constructive labour of the Soviet people and of the immense political and organising work of the Communist Party and its Central Committee. In the successful solution of the problem of building Communism, a major role was played by the leading Party bodies of the Union Republics, territories, regions, and districts and by the primary Party organisations, which, guided by the Central Committee, led the masses in the struggle to achieve a steep rise in the national economy and culture. The Central Committee persistently introduced the Leninist style and method of work in all Party, government and other public bodies.

Possessing profound knowledge and experience, understanding the new demands posed by practical experience, and conscious of their responsibility for the work entrusted to them, leading Party workers imparted Bolshevik fervour to the work, devoted all their strength and knowledge to the good of the people and by their tireless and selfless activity ensured the implementation of the Party's Leninist general line.

The sweeping changes that the Soviet people brought about under the leadership of the Communist Party, and the vast achievements in economic and cultural development, created the necessary requisites and opportunities for the U.S.S.R. to enter a new, and most important period in its development—the period of the full-scale construction of a Communist society.

BRIEF SUMMARY

The period from 1953 to 1958 was a new and significant stage in the life of the Communist Party and in its struggle to increase the might of the Socialist Motherland, to build a Communist society, to ensure world peace. In the significance of the political and economic measures carried out, in the scale of the Party's creative activity and in the level of the activity of the masses, it was one of the most important periods in the history of the Communist Party of the Soviet Union.

In the decisions of the Twentieth Congress, the C.C. resolutions and other documents, the Party unswervingly applied Lenin's principles in giving a profound and comprehensive appraisal of the situation in the country and of the specific features of international relations at the time. While noting the Soviet people's tremendous achievements in all the fields of economy and culture, the Party uncovered serious shortcomings in Party, government, economic and cultural activity, outlined ways of eliminating these shortcomings, drew up an extensive, economically substantiated programme for the gradual transition from Socialism to Communism, and has been successfully putting this programme into effect.

The Party resolutely swept aside everything that was alien to the spirit of Leninism. It openly and severely criticised the personality cult and the mistakes and negative phenomena engendered by it, and started a consistent struggle to eliminate the consequences of the personality cult and the shortcomings arising therefrom. It broke down outdated conceptions and boldly discarded everything that had become outmoded and was hindering the advance of Soviet society. The leading cadres of the Party, Communists educated in the spirit of Lenin's immortal theory, worked vigorously completely to restore and further develop Lenin's traditions, which in these years manifested themselves with renewed strength in the activity of the Central Committee and the Party as a whole.

The Party reorganised its work through consistent implementation and creative elaboration of the principle of democratic centralism, collective leadership, self-criticism and other tested Leninist standards of Party life. Violations of inner-Party democracy were stopped and Party organisations and Party members were given full scope to display their initiative. The Central Committee collectively examined and took decisions on all the major issues of home and foreign policy. The participation of Communists and of Party organisations in the discussion of economic and political problems and in working out Party policy increased to a tremendous degree. Extensive work was done to reorganise and improve the methods and style of Party leadership. Party organisations began to take a deeper interest in the state of affairs in definite fields of Communist construction, to give more competent and effective leadership, to raise in concrete terms and to solve the basic problems of political and economic life.

The Party did away with the shackling influence of the personality cult in the ideological field. It upheld and steadfastly carried into effect the line of creative Marxism. It restored and consolidated the organic unity of theoretical and practical activity which was a key feature of Leninism, but which had been violated in the period of the personality cult. New opportunities were opened up for the rapid development of Marxist-Leninist thought, for the theoretical generalisation of the experience of the masses and for the scientific elaboration of the major problems of building Communism.

By reorganising Party and government work in the spirit of Leninist principles and by overcoming the consequences of the personality cult, the Party increased its efficiency, established still closer ties with the masses and strengthened the unity of its ranks. It came to play a greater guiding and leading role in the administrative, economic and cultural life of the country.

The Party and its Central Committee theoretically elaborated and, with nation-wide support, put into effect a number of highly important political and economic measures which bore the character of a programme. These measures were a big step forward in the development of Marxist-Leninist theory. In its decisions, the Party theoretically substantiated and defined the practical ways of building a Communist society.

Management in industry was completely reorganised, and economic planning improved. The ways of speeding up technical progress, and of perfecting specialisation and co-ordination in production were defined.

The Party developed a nation-wide struggle for a steep rise in agriculture. The Socialist principle of giving the collective farms and their members a material incentive was consistently carried out, the machine-and-tractor stations were reorganised, the system of agricultural deliveries was altered, and the material and technical basis of the collective farms was strengthened. Experienced personnel was sent to help the collective farms. The period between 1953 to 1958 witnessed the biggest changes in agriculture since the period of collectivisation. They led to a considerable increase in the productive forces of agriculture, to the consolidation of the collective-farm system and to the improvement of the living standards of the collective-farm peasantry.

Important measures were taken in the political sphere as well. The rights of the Union Republics and local Soviets were extended, and local government institutions came to play a more active part in the life of the country. The violations of Socialist legality connected with the personality cult were eliminated, and steps were taken to guarantee the observance of the constitutional rights of citizens. The work of the trade unions was reorganised and they were assigned a bigger role in the management of the State and of industry. Further steps were taken to extend collective-farm democracy. The working people began to take a greater share in working out the policy of the Soviet State and in managing it. The political consciousness and cultural standards of the Soviet people rose to a higher level. These measures were not only of practical importance; they were also of theoretical significance. They determined the concrete ways of developing Socialist democracy in the process of the transition to Communism, and were a big step forward in working out more effective forms of the participation of the masses in the building of Communism.

The measures carried out by the Party provided broader scope for the creative initiative of the masses, for using untapped resources to increase production, and led to outstanding achievements in industry, agriculture, science and technology. A vivid indication of this was the launching of the Soviet earth satellites and the artificial planet of the solar system, which opened a new era in the history of world science and technology.

On the basis of great successes in developing the national economy, the Party achieved an improvement in the living conditions of the people: the real wages of the workers rose, and so did the incomes of the collective farmers; the working day was shortened and pensions were considerably increased.

As a result of these measures, a further big step forward was made along the road of the gradual transition from Socialism to Communism, and a solid foundation was laid for the rapid expansion of all the branches of the national economy, for the speedy fulfilment of the basic economic task and for creating a sufficiency, and then an abundance, of consumer goods.

In the process of carrying out its economic measures, the Party gave scientifically grounded and practically tested answers to the most important questions related to the building of Communism: how to create the material and production basis of Communist society, at what rate to carry out the basic economic task, what were the principal directions of technical progress, what were the prospects for the development of the collective-farm system in the process of the transition to Communism, how to bring about a sufficiency, and then an abundance, of foodstuffs, and what should be the organisational forms of increased participation of the masses in the management of industry. The Party's decisions and the measures implemented under its guidance enriched the theory and practice of the building of Communism.

In these years the C.P.S.U. achieved outstanding successes in its foreign policy. Faithful to the behests of Lenin, the Party set splendid examples of a creative approach in settling the most complex international issues. It ensured a considerable heightening of the activity of the Soviet State in the sphere of foreign policy, for which it found new forms and methods that meet present-day requirements more fully.

The Communist Party of the Soviet Union made a valuable contribution to the consolidation and development of the community of Socialist countries on the basis of the ideas of Marxism-Leninism and of consistent observance of the principles of proletarian internationalism. Together with the brother parties, it developed new Socialist principles of international relations, of economic, political and cultural co-operation and mutual aid between the Socialist States. The policy pursued by the C.P.S.U. jointly with the brother parties helped to accelerate the development of the productive forces, the growth of labour productivity and to raise living standards in the Socialist countries still higher. It helped further to increase the economic and political might of the Socialist countries, and the economic and political strength of the Socialist camp as a whole. Friendship between the Socialist countries was still more firmly cemented.

The correct home and foreign policy of the Soviet Union and the tremendous successes scored in building Communism had a most beneficial effect on the development of the international working-class and Communist movement. The scientific generalisation of the experience of the world liberation movement today provided by the Communist Party of the Soviet Union enriched the Marxist-Leninist theory of the laws governing the transition from capitalism to Socialism.

During all the changes in the complex international situation, the Party firmly followed the Leninist general line in the sphere of Soviet foreign policy—to ensure the peaceful coexistence of countries with different social and economic systems. The Party and the Government steadily increased their activity and initiative in the struggle for peace, for ending international tension and for the establishment of good-neighbourly political and economic relations with all countries.

As a result of this policy, the number of peace supporters increased considerably and friendly relations were established with many States. Truthful information about the Soviet Union's foreign policy and about the situation inside the country spread far beyond the borders of the U.S.S.R.

The imperialist aggressors were exposed and the process of their isolation developed swiftly. This made it possible to stamp out the flames of war they had kindled (in Korea, Indo-China, Egypt, the Lebanon) and to maintain peace. The peoples of all countries became more confident that peace could be preserved. The Soviet Union's steadfast struggle for world peace and security enhanced its prestige and influence in the international arena.

In the course of fulfilling its important and historic tasks, the Party came up against the opposition of the anti-Party group of Malenkov, Kaganovich, Molotov, Bulganin and Shepilov, who opposed the Party's Leninist line. They took an incorrect stand on major issues of home and foreign policy, opposed the implementation of political and economic measures worked out by the Party and approved by the people, took the path of factional, splitting activity and hampered the Soviet Union's successful advance towards Communism. The Party exposed them and swept them off the historic path along which the Soviet people were advancing.

The Party's home and foreign policy, carried out in the spirit of tested Leninist traditions, had the whole-hearted support of all Soviet people, who were carrying it out more and more actively.

The Communist Party of the Soviet Union displayed the advantages of Socialism over capitalism more fully, and won the esteem and admiration of the broadest sections of world public opinion. This attracted ever new millions of people to the side of Socialism, and strengthened its position in the world arena.

Having achieved great successes, the Soviet people turned to new tasks, firmly confident of the complete triumph of their cause.

CHAPTER EIGHTEEN

THE U.S.S.R. ENTERS THE PERIOD OF THE FULL-SCALE BUILDING OF A COMMUNIST SOCIETY. TWENTY-FIRST PARTY CONGRESS

1. The Seven-Year Plan of Economic Development—a Component Part of the Programme of Building Communism in the U.S.S.R.

In carrying out the decisions of the Twentieth Party Congress, the Soviet people made outstanding progress in economy, culture and science. The inexhaustible potentialities of the Socialist economic system for accelerating the rate of industrial development and improving the living standards of the people became more manifest than ever. The level achieved in the development of the productive forces showed that the U.S.S.R. possessed the necessary requisites for the transition to a higher stage in the building of Communism.

The Party took timely account of the beginning of a new period in the development of the Soviet Union. The Twentieth Congress of the C.P.S.U. had put forward the problem of drawing up a long-term plan of economic and cultural development covering several five-year periods. At the session of the Supreme Soviet of the U.S.S.R. dedicated to the 40th anniversary of the Great October Socialist Revolution, N. S. Khrushchov outlined the principal tasks involved in developing the country's productive forces within the next fifteen years. During this period, the key industries were to more than double or treble their output. The long-term, fifteen-year plan of economic development is the economic programme for building Communism in the U.S.S.R.

On the basis of the resolutions of the Twentieth Party Congress and subsequent decisions of the Party and the Government, and in line with the programme for the development of the Soviet Union's productive forces set forth at the jubilee session of the Supreme Soviet of the U.S.S.R. on November 6, 1957, the Central Committee of the C.P.S.U. and the Council of Ministers of the U.S.S.R. drafted targets for the economic development of the U.S.S.R. for 1959-1965. The draft seven-year plan was worked out with the participation of the Councils of Ministers of the Union Republics, the Ministries and Departments, the Academy of Sciences of the U.S.S.R. and other scientific institutions, and the Economic Councils. Very great work in this connection was done by local Party committees, government and economic bodies and by Party, trade union and Komsomol organisations. The draft plan took account of numerous suggestions that were advanced by workers, collective farmers and intellectuals. The November, 1958, plenary meeting of the C.C. C.P.S.U. approved the draft theses of N. S. Khrushchov's report, "Control Figures for the Economic Development of the U.S.S.R. for 1959-1965," to be submitted to the Twenty-First Party Congress, and resolved to publish them in the press for wide pre-Congress discussion.

The discussion of the draft seven-year plan developed into a mighty demonstration of the unbreakable ties between the Party and the masses, of the Soviet people's solid unity around the Communist Party. More than 968,000 meetings were held throughout the country, attended by over 70 million people, and 4,672,000 of them spoke in the discussion. In addition, more than 650,000 letters and articles were received by newspapers, magazines and radio and TV stations. About 300,000 of them were published.

A nation-wide Socialist emulation movement for the pre-schedule fulfilment of State plans and assignments was started in honour of the Twenty-First Congress of the Communist Party. It strikingly reflected the new upsurge of labour enthusiasm of millions of people. The Komsomol initiated a new patriotic movement for the formation of Communist work teams. This movement assumed a big scale, and its motto became: "Learn to live and work in a Communist way."

The Extraordinary Twenty-First Congress of the Communist Party—*a congress of builders of Communism*—was held on January 27-February 5, 1959, in an atmosphere of nation-wide enthusiasm. The delegates to the Congress represented 7,622,356 members and 616,775 candidate members.

The Twenty-First Congress met at an important period in history, at a period when the Soviet Union, as a result of far-reaching changes in all spheres of social life on the basis of the victory of Socialism, had entered a new period of its development, *the period of the full-scale building of a Communist society.*

The Congress heard and discussed the report on "Control Figures for the Economic Development of the U.S.S.R. for 1959-1965," submitted by N. S. Khrushchov, first secretary of the C.C.

C.P.S.U. and Chairman of the Council of Ministers of the U.S.S.R.

N. S. Khrushchov's report and the relevant Congress resolution summed up the great achievements of the Soviet people, defined the Party's tasks for the next seven years, set forth the plan of economic development in the U.S.S.R. for 1959-1965, dealt with important theoretical problems of the transition from Socialism to Communism, and showed the international significance of the Seven-Year Plan.

The Congress noted that the period that had elapsed since the Twentieth Congress had been one of the most important in the history of the Communist Party and the Soviet State. The Congress approved the activity of the Central Committee and the important measures it had taken, in domestic and foreign policy, to ensure the Soviet Union's successful advance towards Communism, to increase the might of the Soviet State and to raise its international prestige.

Under the leadership of the Party, the Soviet people had continued to advance confidently along the path indicated by Lenin and had won epoch-making victories in the building of Socialism. The U.S.S.R. had become a mighty Socialist Power with a highly developed economy and advanced science and culture. In 1958, the total industrial product was 36 times greater than in 1913, the output of the means of production having increased 83 times and the output of the engineering and metal-working industries 240 times. In 1958, the Soviet Union produced about 55 million tons of steel, 113 million tons of oil, 496 million tons of coal and 233,000 million kilowatt-hours of electric power. There were splendid achievements in Socialist agriculture. The Soviet Union had never harvested so much grain and industrial crops, never produced so much livestock products and the State never purchased so much agricultural produce, as in 1958.

The country's social wealth had increased. In the years of Soviet power, the national income per head of population had risen 15 times. The Soviet people's standard of living had improved considerably. Compared with 1940, the real incomes of factory and office workers had almost doubled by 1958, while the real incomes of the collective farmers per working farmer had more than doubled. Multi-national Socialist culture in the U.S.S.R. was thriving as never before. The Soviet Union was heading world scientific and technological progress, and blazing the trail into the future. The world's first artificial earth satellite was the Soviet sputnik. The first artificial planet of the solar system was made in the Soviet Union.

The measures taken in recent years by the C.C. C.P.S.U. and the Soviet Government had still further strengthened the Soviet

State, consolidated the alliance of the workers and peasants, and cemented the friendship between the peoples of the Soviet Union. The community of countries of the world Socialist camp had grown stronger.

Summing up the great gains of the Soviet people, the Congress noted with pride that the Soviet Union, which had blazed the trail to Socialism for mankind, had reached a level in productive forces, Socialist production relations and cultural development that made it possible to begin building a Communist society on a broad front. The principal tasks of the period of the full-scale building of a Communist society were the creation of a material and technical basis for Communism, the further strengthening of the Soviet Union's economic and defensive might and, at the same time, the fuller satisfaction of the growing material and spiritual requirements of the people. This period must witness the accomplishment of the Soviet Union's historic task of overtaking and surpassing the leading capitalist countries in output per head.

In a unanimously adopted resolution, the Congress approved the theses and the report submitted by N. S. Khrushchov, and the control figures for the economic development of the U.S.S.R. for 1959-1965. The Seven-Year Plan of economic development of the U.S.S.R. was a most important part of the Party's programme for building a Communist society, the decisive stage in the creation of the material and technical basis of Communism. The fundamental task of the Seven-Year Plan was to make the most of the time factor in Socialism's peaceful economic competition with capitalism.

The Congress defined the Party's tasks in the coming seven years as follows:

in the economic field—all-round development of the country's productive forces and, on the basis of the priority development of heavy industry, the achievement of such a level of production in all branches of economy as would make possible a decisive step forward in establishing the material and technical basis of Communism, and in ensuring the victory of the Soviet Union in peaceful economic competition with the capitalist countries. The increase in the country's economic potential, further technical progress in all economic spheres and the continuous growth of the productivity of social labour, must bring about a substantial rise in the living standard of the people;

in the political field—further consolidation of the Soviet Socialist system, strengthening of the unity and solidarity of the Soviet people, development of Soviet democracy, of the activity and initiative of the broad masses of the people in building a Communist society, extension of the functions of voluntary organisations in settling questions of State importance, raising of the organisational and educational role of the Party and the Socialist State, and all-round consolidation of the alliance of the workers and the peasants and of the friendship of the peoples of the U.S.S.R.;

in the ideological field—intensifying the ideological and educational work of the Party; raising the level of Communist consciousness of the working people, particularly of the rising generation, inculcating in them a Communist attitude to labour, Soviet patriotism and internationalism, eliminating the survivals of capitalism in the minds of men, and combating bourgeois ideology;

in international relations—a consistent foreign policy aimed at preserving and consolidating international peace and security, on the basis of Lenin's principle of peaceful coexistence of countries with different social systems; implementation of a policy aimed at ending the cold war and relaxing international tension; the strengthening in every way of the world Socialist system and the community of fraternal peoples.

The Seven-Year Plan of economic development envisaged a big upswing in the economy, culture and living standards of the people. In the "Control Figures for the Economic Development of the U.S.S.R. for 1959-1965," it was stated: "The principal target of the Seven-Year Plan of economic development of the U.S.S.R. for 1959-1965 is to effect a further steep rise in all branches of economy on the basis of a priority growth of the heavy industry and a substantial increase in the country's economic potential with the purpose of ensuring a steady improvement of the standard of living" (*Theses of N. S. Khrushchov's Report to the Twenty-First Congress of the C.P.S.U.*, Eng. ed., p. 27).

The Seven-Year Plan provided for a high rate of development and a large absolute increase of output in all branches of the national economy. Prime importance was attached to the development of industry, particularly of heavy industry, the foundation of Socialist economy. In 1965, total industrial product was to be 80 per cent greater than in 1958; output of the means of production was to rise by 85-88 per cent and the output of consumer goods by 62-65 per cent. The average annual increase in industrial output in 1959-1965 would be 8.6 per cent.

The Congress gave directions to accelerate progress and considerably increase output in the key branches of heavy industry —the metallurgical, chemical, fuel, power and engineering industries. The target for 1965 was to raise the output of pig-iron to 65-70 million tons, steel to 86-91 million tons, rolled metal to 65-70 million tons, marketable iron-ore to 150-160 million tons, oil to 230-240 million tons, gas to 150,000 million cubic metres, coal to 600-612 million tons, and electric power to 500,000-520,000 million kw-h. In the seven-year period the output of the chemical industry was to be approximately trebled and the output of the engineering and metal-working industries doubled.

The output of consumer goods was to grow considerably on the basis of the rapid expansion of heavy industry and the further rise in agriculture. In the seven-year period, the total output of the light industries was to increase 50 per cent, and that of the food industry 70 per cent. There would be a sufficiency of fabrics, garments, footwear and some other commodities.

In agriculture, the chief task for the seven-year period was to attain a level of production that would make it possible to provide an abundance of staple food products for the population, sharply to increase the supply of agricultural raw materials and to meet all the other requirements of the State in agricultural produce. It was planned to carry out this task by substantially raising the yield of all farm crops, increasing the livestock herd and further expanding the productivity of socially-owned animal husbandry. The emphasis in crop farming would continue to be laid on the utmost expansion of grain-growing as the basis of all agricultural production.

The control figures envisaged a 70 per cent increase in total agricultural production in the seven-year period. Output of the staple products was to be increased as follows: grain, to 160-177 million tons; sugar-beet, to 76-84 million tons; raw cotton, to 5.7-6.1 million tons, meat (dead weight), to not less than 16 million tons; milk, to 100-105 million tons, and potatoes, to 147 million tons.

The volume of State capital investments in the national economy in 1959-1965 would amount to 1,940,000-1,970,000 million rubles. This was nearly equivalent to the total investments made in the national economy in all the preceding years of Soviet power. The plan provided for the most effective use of the investments so that production capacities could be augmented, output increased and labour productivity stepped up with the least expense. Therefore, parallel with the construction of new enterprises, large sums were earmarked for the reconstruction, expansion or technical re-equipment of undertakings already in operation, and for the renovation and modernisation of plant. A further extension of industrial methods of building was envisaged, to ensure the timely fulfilment of the projected volume of capital construction.

Huge sums were allocated for other branches of the national economy. In agriculture, investments by the State and the collective farms would amount to about 500,000 million rubles. The sum of 209,000-214,000 million rubles was to be spent on the development of transport and communications; 375,000-380,000 million rubles, on housing and municipal construction; more than 80,000 million rubles, on the building of schools, hospitals and other cultural institutions, public amenities and medical establishments.

The Congress approved the Seven-Year Plan provisions for the territorial distribution of the country's productive forces. With a view to ensuring the successful fulfilment of the colossal programme of Communist construction, the country's richest and economically most advantageous natural resources were to be drawn into economic use; industry was to be brought closer to the sources of raw materials and fuel; more rational use was to be made of all types of transport; specialisation and comprehensive economic development of the Union Republics and the big economic areas were to be effected, and the fullest possible use was to be made of manpower resources. Primary attention was to be given to the development of the country's eastern regions— the Urals, Siberia, the Far East, Kazakhstan and Central Asia— with their enormous natural resources. More than 40 per cent of the Seven-Year Plan investments were to be directed into those regions.

The Seven-Year Plan of economic development envisaged further all-round economic and cultural progress in all the Union Republics. In each Republic, priority was to be given to industries for which it had the most favourable natural and economic conditions. The rapid expansion of the economy of all the Soviet Republics represented the further application by the Party of the Leninist nationalities policy at the present stage, a policy aimed at promoting unbreakable friendship among the peoples of the Soviet Union enjoying equal rights and united by a common will to advance steadfastly to Communism. *"The Leninist national policy,"* N. S. Khrushchov said in his report to the Congress, *"which provides ample opportunities for the all-round economic and cultural progress of all peoples, finds vivid expression in our plans"* (Control Figures for the Development of the U.S.S.R. for 1959-1965, Eng. ed., pp. 49-50).

Greater labour productivity through extensive use of the latest achievements of science and technology in all branches of the national economy was the decisive factor in the growth of Socialist production and the improvement of the people's standard of living. Under the Seven-Year Plan, labour productivity was to rise 45-50 per cent in industry, 60-65 per cent in building, 34-37 per cent on the railways, 60-65 per cent in the State farms, and about 100 per cent in the collective farms. By a steady rise in labour productivity, costs were to drop by not less than 11.5 per cent in industry. The Congress defined the main directions for raising labour productivity in the period of the full-scale building of Communism: electrification of the national economy, the extensive introduction of new machinery in production, comprehensive mechanisation and automation of industrial processes, specialisation and co-ordination in all the branches of the national economy, and promotion of the cultural and technical level of the people.

The Twenty-First Congress of the C.P.S.U. pointed out that thanks to the tremendous progress that had been made in industry and agriculture there was every opportunity in the U.S.S.R. for the Soviet people to live still better in the immediate future, and to satisfy more fully their material and spiritual needs.

The material and cultural standards of life in the U.S.S.R. were to be raised very substantially in 1959-1965. The Seven-Year Plan provided for:

a 62-65 per cent increase in the national income in 1965, compared with 1958; a 60-63 per cent rise in the volume of consumption; a rise of 40 per cent per working person in the real incomes of the factory and office workers; an average rise of not less than 40 per cent in the real incomes of collective farmers, and the abolition, within the next few years, of taxes levied on the population;

completion of the process of normalising the wages structure, and raising the wages of the low-paid groups of factory and office workers from 270-350 to 500-600 rubles a month in the next seven years;

a rise in the minimum old-age pension from 300 to 400 rubles a month in towns, and from 255 to 340 rubles for pensioners permanently residing in rural localities and connected with agriculture; a rise in the minimum disability pensions and pensions paid to families losing their breadwinner;

a considerable improvement in trade and in personal services; extension of the network of public catering establishments and reduction of the prices of the food they supplied; an approximately 62 per cent increase in the volume of State and co-operative retail trade;

an extension of the network of nurseries, kindergartens, boarding-schools, and homes for the aged;

the building, within the next seven years, of housing with a total floor space of 6,500-6,600 million square feet, or 15 million flats, in towns and factory housing estates; the building, with the resources of the collective farmers and the rural intelligentsia, of about 7 million houses in the countryside;

the completion in 1960 of the transfer of factory and office workers to a seven-hour working day, and workers of leading trades in the coal and ore-mining industries and those engaged in underground work, to a six-hour day; the introduction in 1962, for factory and office workers with a seven-hour day, of a 40-hour week; the gradual reduction of working hours, starting from 1964, of workers engaged in underground work and in work involving harmful labour conditions to a 30-hour week, and for the rest of the working people to a 35-hour week, with two days off a week and a six- or seven-hour day. The working day and week in the U.S.S.R. would be the shortest in the world.

The measures envisaged by the Seven-Year Plan were striking evidence of the constant concern displayed by the Party and the Government for the well-being of the Soviet people. Implementation of these measures would represent another great gain by the working people of the Soviet Union.

The Congress pointed out that it was of exceptional importance for the building of Communism to raise the political consciousness and activity of the masses, to educate the working people in a Communist spirit. At the present stage emphasis in Communist education was laid on the moulding of the new man, on the education of politically conscious workers of Communist society. The task of the Party and the State in the ideological field was to develop new qualities in Soviet people, to educate them in the spirit of collectivism and industriousness, Socialist internationalism and patriotism, and in steadfast observance of the lofty principles of Communist morality.

Special importance was attached to the Communist education of the rising generation. Active participation in Communist construction and the linking up of study with productive work were the best school for the education and training of the Soviet youth. The Congress called on Party and government organisations to carry out all the measures connected with the reconstruction of secondary and higher education, and to ensure that the Soviet school should closely link study with production, with Communist construction, and should bring up citizens with an all-round culture who would be politically conscious builders of Communism.

Under the Seven-Year Plan, far-reaching measures were to be taken to promote public education, science and culture.

In 1959-1965 there was to be a change-over from seven-year to eight-year universal compulsory education; the number of urban and rural schools offering secondary education without interrupting work was to be increased; the training of specialists with a higher and secondary special education would be extended and improved. In 1959-1965, the institutions of higher education were to graduate 2,300,000 specialists, and more than 4 million people were to be trained at secondary special schools.

The Seven-Year Plan ensured a still more rapid development of all branches of Soviet science. Scientists were provided with the necessary conditions for engaging in important theoretical research and making important new discoveries. An extensive programme was drawn up for research and for the concentration of scientific forces and resources on investigations of particular theoretical and practical importance. Paramount importance was attached to research in physics, chemistry, mathematics and biology, since the development of kindred sciences and of the national economy depended on successful progress in these fields. Scholars in the sphere of the social sciences, especially economics, were confronted with the task of producing fundamental works, generalising the laws governing social development and the experience of Socialist construction, and of elaborating problems connected with the gradual transition to Communism. They were called upon tirelessly to fight for the purity of Marxist-Leninist theory and to expose bourgeois ideology.

Socialist culture was to make further progress. There was to be a considerable increase in the number of cinema units, public libraries and clubs, TV centres and stations, and radio-receivers. Books and magazines were to be published in larger editions. The task of workers in literature, the theatre, the cinema, music, sculpture and painting was to raise still higher the ideological and artistic standards of their art, to establish closer ties with the life of the people and to continue as active assistants of the Party and the State in the Communist education of the working people, in the propaganda of Communist morality and in promoting multi-national Socialist culture.

The Seven-Year Plan of economic development was the embodiment of the Party's Leninist general line in the contemporary stage of the building of Communism. It was a majestic programme of the further powerful rise in the economy, culture and living standards of the people. It had no precedent in history for its gigantic scope.

The Twenty-First Party Congress marked the entry of the Soviet Union into a new period of its historical development. The full-scale building of a Communist society in the U.S.S.R., and the new balance of forces between Socialism and capitalism in the world arena, confronted the Communist Party of the Soviet Union and the international Communist movement with a number of important theoretical problems.

The report delivered by N. S. Khrushchov and the resolution adopted by the Congress gave a scientific analysis of the tasks of building Communism in the U.S.S.R. at the present stage, and dealt with important theoretical problems of the transition of the Soviet Union from Socialism to Communism, of the struggle for the triumph of Socialism and Communism.

The development of Soviet society had confirmed the Marxist-Leninist doctrine of the two phases of Communism, of the development of Socialism into Communism. Led by the Party, the Soviet people had achieved Socialist gains in every field of economic, social and political life that enabled them to enter the period of the full-scale building of a Communist society. In his report N. S. Khrushchov noted that the experience of Communist construction in the U.S.S.R. makes it possible to draw a number of important conclusions concerning the nature of society's forward movement towards Communism. First, the transition from the Socialist stage of development to the higher stage—Communism—was a *law-governed* historical process which could not be violated or bypassed. Society could not pass straight from capitalism to Communism without going through the Socialist stage. Second, the transition from Socialism to Communism was a *continuous* historical process. Notwithstanding all the difference between Communism and the Socialist stage, there was no wall between them. Communism would grow out of Socialism, and was its direct continuation. Third, the gradual transition to Communism must not be understood as a slow movement. On the contrary, it was a period of *rapid growth* of society's productive forces.

The growth of Socialism into Communism could be accelerated through the all-round development of material production. The chief practical task of the Soviet Union at the present stage, therefore, was to create the material and technical basis of Communism, to secure a further powerful expansion of the productive forces. Building the material and technical basis of Communism implied, first and foremost, a highly developed modern industry; total electrification of the country; scientific and technical progress in every branch of industry and agriculture; comprehensive mechanisation and automation of all production processes; maximum utilisation of new sources of power, the rich natural resources of the country, new synthetic and other materials; higher cultural and technical standards of the working people; further improvement in the organisation of production, and higher productivity of social labour.

"Communism," stated the resolution of the Congress, "can be achieved on the sole condition that we surpass the production level of the developed capitalist countries and attain a higher productivity of labour than exists under capitalism" (*Decisions of the Twenty-First Extraordinary Congress of the Communist Party of the Soviet Union*, Eng. ed., p. 24).

Full-scale Communist construction must, along with material plenty, provide for a genuine flowering of spiritual culture and an ever fuller satisfaction of the requirements of the people, the further development of Socialist democracy and the upbring-

728

ing of politically conscious workers of a Communist society. With the growth of the productive forces, Socialist social relations, based on the principles of comradely co-operation, friendship and mutual assistance, would be improved. In step with technical progress in all branches of economy, and as education became more closely linked with production, the cultural and technical standards of the working people would rise and the essential distinctions between mental and physical labour would gradually be effaced. A shorter working day, and steady improvement in working conditions through the comprehensive mechanisation and automation of production, would facilitate the transformation of labour into a vital necessity for all-round cultivated man.

At the Socialist stage of development of society there were two forms of property: public and collective-farm-co-operative. In Communist society there would only be Communist property. The collective-farm-co-operative form of production relations fully accorded with the present stage of Communist construction. Property forms could not be changed at will. They developed in accordance with economic laws, and depended on the nature and level of development of the productive forces. The measures carried out by the Party and the Government in recent years to advance agriculture and strengthen the collective-farm system had revealed the tremendous potentialities of that system. The collective-farm system served, and for a long time to come could still continue to serve, the development of the productive forces in agriculture. However, collective-farm-co-operative property would in the future inevitably merge with national property. This would take place, not by dispensing with co-operative property, *but by raising its level of socialisation* with the assistance and support of the Socialist State.

In the course of Communist construction the productive forces of agriculture would develop continuously, the degree of socialisation of collective-farm production would be increased, collective-farm-co-operative property and national property would be brought closer together and the line dividing the two would gradually be obliterated. This process would take place along lines that have already taken shape: expansion of the non-distributable assets of the collective farms, fuller entry of socialised collective-farm production into all branches of agriculture, a widespread expansion of joint production by groups of collective farms, and the electrification, mechanisation and automation of agricultural production.

Through technical progress in agricultural production and the drawing of collective-farm-co-operative and national property closer together, agricultural labour would gradually become a variety of industrial labour, and the essential distinction between town and country would gradually disappear.

The advance of Soviet society towards Communism had brought to the fore the problem of the distribution of material and spiritual values among all members of society. Under Socialism, material wealth was distributed on the principle: "From each according to his ability, to each according to his work." At the Socialist stage of development and at the present stage of Communist construction, this was the only reasonable and just principle of distribution. Equalitarian distribution was incompatible with Socialism. Distribution according to work done served to promote Socialist production: it gave people a material incentive to increase production and stimulated the growth of the productive forces, furthered the raising of proficiency among working people and made for better production techniques. It also played a big educational role: for it made labour universal and obligatory, and taught people to treat public property with care and to observe Socialist labour discipline. It developed moral stimuli to labour and fostered labour enthusiasm. As the political consciousness of the working people of Socialist society grew and the principle of the material incentive was consistently applied, labour would become more and more a habit, a vital necessity for millions of people.

The principle "from each according to his ability, to each according to his needs" would be applied at the higher stage of Communism. The transition to distribution according to needs was a gradual process. It would take place as the productive forces developed. This transition would be effected when there was an abundance of all the necessary consumer goods and when all people, voluntarily and irrespective of their share of material benefits, would work according to their ability, knowing that this was necessary for the common weal.

As Soviet society progressed towards Communism, the social aspect of human life would reveal itself more fully, and society would take increasing care of the welfare of the individual. The individual requirements of each person would be met parallel with the growth of the material and cultural wealth of society, not only through increased wages, but also through socialised funds, the role and importance of which would rise steadily. A really *Communist way of improving the well-being of the people*, of creating the best conditions for the life of society as a whole and for each of its members, had taken distinct shape in the U.S.S.R. This was seen in the comfortable homes being built for the people, the organisation of public catering, the improvement of the amenities provided for the people, the extension of the network of children's institutions, the improvement of public education, organising rest and recreation, improvement of the medical services, the building of cultural facilities, and so on.

At the present stage of Communist construction, the greater part of material and cultural benefits was distributed among people according to the labour they contributed to social production. Factory and office workers received wages, and collective farmers received incomes from their socially-owned economy. At the same time, in Soviet society a substantial and ever-growing portion of the material and cultural product was even now being distributed gratuitously in the form of pensions, stipends for students, grants to mothers of many children, and funds for the building and maintenance of schools, hospitals, children's establishments, boarding-schools, and also of clubs, libraries and other cultural institutions. This share of the social consumption fund would increase, which was a highly important ' prerequisite for the gradual transition to the Communist principle of distribution.

In addition to problems of economic development, N. S. Khrushchov's report dealt with problems of the political organisation of society, the State system and administration in the period of the full-scale building of Communism. Marxism-Leninism taught that in a Communist society the State would wither away. This withering away of the State was a question of the development of the Socialist State system into self-government by Communist society. In Communist society, too, there would remain certain public functions, similar to those now performed by the State. Their nature, and the methods by which they would be exercised, would be different from those obtaining in the present stage. The chief trend in the development of the Soviet State was the all-round promotion of democracy: the drawing of all citizens into the management of economic and cultural affairs, the enlistment of large sections of the population in the management of all public affairs, the raising of the role of the Soviets as mass organisations of the working people. Many of the functions now performed by State agencies would gradually pass over to voluntary organisations. They included cultural services, health, physical culture and sports. The functions of maintaining public order and protecting the rights of citizens would be performed to a growing extent, along with the State agencies, by the people's militia, courts of honour and other volunteer public bodies.

The transfer of certain functions from State agencies to voluntary organisations did not in any way signify a weakening of the role of the Socialist State in the building of Communism. On the contrary, it would broaden and strengthen the political foundations of Socialist society, ensure the further development of Socialist democracy and strengthen the Soviet system. The Soviet Socialist State would be able to give more attention to its economic and organising functions, to its functions of supervising the measure of labour and the measure of consumption, protecting Socialist property, and the further development of the function of organising co-operation with the other Socialist countries.

It was a major function of the Socialist State to safeguard peace and ensure the defence of the country. As long as there was an aggressive imperialist camp, the Socialist State must strengthen and perfect its armed forces. The State security service, whose activity was directed primarily against agents smuggled into the U.S.S.R. by imperialist States, must be strengthened in every way. The function of defending the Socialist country, now performed by the Soviet State, would wither away only when the threat of imperialist attack had been completely eliminated.

Radical changes had taken place in the Soviet Union's international position. The time was past when the Soviet Union was the only Socialist State, a State encircled by hostile capitalist countries. Today there were two world social systems—capitalism and Socialism. Capitalism was living out its day. Socialism, full of vitality, was growing and flourishing. It had the moral support of the working people of all countries. There was now no force on earth that could restore capitalism in the U.S.S.R. or crush the Socialist camp. The balance of power in the world today was such that any imperialist aggression against the Socialist countries was doomed to failure. The danger of capitalist restoration in the Soviet Union was ruled out. "And this means," N. S. Khrushchov said in his report, "that *the triumph of Socialism is not only complete, but final*" (*Control Figures for the Development of the U.S.S.R. for 1959-1965*, Eng. ed., p. 131).

The Twenty-First Congress of the C.P.S.U. elaborated the ideas of scientific Communism and enriched Marxist-Leninist theory with new, important conclusions. The theoretical propositions in N. S. Khrushchov's report on the ways of transition from Socialism to Communism had the importance of a programme. The road leading Soviet society to Communism is illumined by the bright light of the theory of scientific Communism.

2. The International Significance of the Twenty-First Congress of the C.P.S.U.

The Twenty-First Congress of the Communist Party of the Soviet Union, the decisions adopted by it, and the Seven-Year Plan of economic development of the U.S.S.R. are of vast international significance. Successful fulfilment of the Seven-Year Plan by the Soviet people will strengthen the position of the Soviet Union and the world Socialist camp; it will lead to a further growth of the peace forces and to a weakening of the forces of war. The successful fulfilment of the Seven-Year Plan in the U.S.S.R. will have a tremendous effect on the working masses of the capitalist countries, and attract millions of new supporters to the side of Socialism.

The Seven-Year Plan opens a new and decisive stage in the economic competition between Socialism and capitalism. Under the leadership of the Communist Party, the Soviet people have raised Socialist economy to so great a height that they can now successfully compete with the United States in the economic sphere, win this competition and outdistance that leading capitalist Power.

The Seven-Year Plan will be a decisive step in carrying out the basic economic task of the U.S.S.R., that of overtaking and surpassing the most advanced capitalist countries in output per head within a brief span of history. In the absolute volume of output of some key industrial products, the Soviet Union will, towards the end of the Seven-Year Plan period, have exceeded, and in the case of other items have approached, the present level of industrial output in the U.S.A. Within the same period, the output of key agricultural products in the U.S.S.R., in the aggregate and per head, will exceed the present level of the U.S.A.

The confidence of the Party and the Soviet people in the success of economic competition with the United States rests on the high rates of economic development in the U.S.S.R. and on the relatively greater absolute average annual increase in the output of a number of key items (steel, pig-iron, iron-ore, oil, coal, cement, woollen fabrics) than in the U.S.A. It will take the Soviet Union about another five years after completing the Seven-Year Plan to catch up and outstrip the United States in industrial output per head of population. By that time, or possibly sooner, the Soviet Union will rank first in the world both in the absolute volume of production and in production per head of population. This will be a *world historical victory for Socialism* in its peaceful competition with capitalism.

Towards the close of the Seven-Year Plan period there will be a decisive shift in world economy in favour of Socialism. The superiority of the world Socialist system over the world capitalist system in material production, that decisive sphere of human endeavour, will thereby be assured.

Economic competition is in progress in the world arena between the two systems, Socialism and capitalism. The economy of the Socialist countries is developing at rapid rates. High rates of production growth are a general law of Socialism, confirmed by the experience of all the Socialist countries. The world Socialist system has already overtaken the world capitalist system in industrial output per head of population. The Socialist countries, where close on a third of the world's population is concentrated, account for more than *a third* of the world's industrial product, nearly half the world output of grain and 43 per cent of the cotton. As a result of fulfilling and overfulfilling the Seven-Year Plan of economic development in the U.S.S.R. and also as a result of carrying out the economic development plans in the People's Democracies, the world Socialist system will by the end of the seven-year period be producing *more than half* the world's industrial output. This will be added evidence of the superiority of Socialism over capitalism.

New economic laws of development, the application of which ensures the rapid development of all the Socialist countries, are characteristic of the world Socialist system of economy.

The distinctive feature of the economic development of the Socialist countries is that the growth and development of each Socialist country leads to the strengthening of the world Socialist system as a whole. Conversely, under capitalism the growth of output in one particular country aggravates the contradictions between countries, worsens their relations, intensifies competition and leads to conflicts between them.

A new law of economic development, never known to mankind in the past, operates in the world Socialist system. Drawing on the experience of other Socialist countries and benefiting by mutual assistance and co-operation with them, the Socialist countries that were economically backward in the past are rapidly making up for lost time as they raise their economic and cultural levels. In this way, the general economic and cultural progress of all the Socialist countries is levelling up. Under imperialism, on the contrary, there operates the law of uneven economic and political development of the different countries. The course of development in the capitalist world is such that some countries forge ahead at the expense of others. The countries that have moved ahead do all they can to protect their privileged position and to keep the other countries in subjection and dependence.

The law of balanced, proportional development operates in the Socialist system of economy. All the Socialist countries unite and mutually accommodate their production efforts, co-ordinate their economic plans. The international division of labour, particularly in its higher forms—specialisation and co-ordination —plays a big part in the development of the Socialist countries.

This offers new additional opportunities for the rapid expansion of production in the Socialist camp as a whole, and in each of the Socialist countries in particular. The Soviet Seven-Year Plan takes these possibilities into account.

The Socialist countries are advancing in a united front. Some of the People's Democracies have already entered the period of the completion of Socialist construction. In the course of the further growth and consolidation of the world Socialist system, all the Socialist countries will develop with increasing success, and conditions will be gradually created for their advance from the first to the second phase of Communism. The time is drawing near when these countries will, like the Soviet Union, start the building of Communist society. Consequently, all the Socialist countries will pass to the higher phase of Communist society more or less simultaneously. As this takes place, account will be taken of the different conditions obtaining in the different countries. Different ways, methods and forms of accomplishing the transition to Communism will inevitably arise. But as Marxism-Leninism teaches, the determining factor in the progress of all countries towards Communism will be the laws common to all countries, and not their specific manifestations.

The resolution of the Twenty-First Party Congress stated that the Soviet Union considered it to be one of its primary tasks to continue to promote the unity of the Socialist countries, the further development of close economic and cultural ties between them and still greater unity of the fraternal family of free peoples, on the basis of the great ideas of Marxism-Leninism and the principles of proletarian internationalism.

The Seven-Year Plan, adopted by the Congress, was a source of inspiration for the peoples of the Socialist countries, and served to strengthen their unity. The thoughts and feelings of the peoples of the Socialist countries, their admiration for the great plan of Communist construction in the U.S.S.R. and their approval of it, found vivid expression in the speeches made at the Congress by representatives of the brother Communist Parties.

The Twenty-First Congress of the C.P.S.U. strengthened the confidence of the peoples in the possibility of delivering mankind from world wars. The conclusion drawn by the Twentieth Party Congress that war was not fatally inevitable had been fully justified. All imperialist attempts in recent years to settle international issues by war had failed completely. The peace-loving nations had upheld peace. The mighty Socialist camp was a stronghold of peace. It had placed the whole of its economic might and all its achievements in science and technology at the service of international peace and security. An aggression of imperialist

States against the Socialist camp could have only one outcome—the downfall of capitalism.

Fulfilment of the economic plans of the Soviet Union and of the other Socialist countries offered still more favourable conditions for solving the cardinal problem of our time—the preservation of universal peace. When the U.S.S.R. became the world's foremost industrial Power, when the Chinese People's Republic became a mighty industrial Power and all the Socialist countries together produced more than half the world's industrial output, the international situation would change fundamentally. The economic potential attained by the Socialist countries would tip the scale in the balance of power on the international scene definitely in favour of peace. The successes of the Socialist countries would serve to increase and strengthen the peace forces still more. An increasing number of countries would align themselves with the states working for a lasting peace. The idea that war is inadmissible would take ever firmer root in the mind of man. Backed by the might of the Socialist camp, the peaceful nations would then be able to compel the bellicose imperialist groups to abandon their plans for new wars. Thus, even before the complete victory of Socialism in the world, with capitalism still extant in a part of the globe, there would be a real possibility of excluding world war from the life of society.

The Seven-Year Plan was a further manifestation of the Leninist peace policy of the Soviet Union. It was imbued with the spirit of peace. The Soviet people wanted to preserve peace, and were doing all in their power to make it really possible to eliminate war from the life of society. However, the danger that the imperialists might start a war still existed, and must not be under-estimated.

The report and concluding speech by N. S. Khrushchov at the Twenty-First Congress, and the Congress resolution, dealt with pressing issues of the international situation, pointed to the principal sources of the war danger and international tension, and defined the foreign policy tasks of the Party and the Soviet State at the present stage.

The Congress pointed out that a task of vital importance to international peace and security was the proper solution of the German problem and the conclusion of agreements between countries on the cessation of nuclear tests, the complete prohibition of nuclear weapons, disarmament and ending the cold war. The aggressive policy of U.S. imperialism remained the main source of the war danger. The North Atlantic military alliance was the principal aggressive alignment of the imperialist States. The ruling circles of the United States, as well as of West Germany, Britain, France and other member countries of the aggressive

North Atlantic bloc were persisting in their refusal to settle international problems peacefully; they were stockpiling nuclear weapons and provoking armed conflicts. The role of the main shock force of the North Atlantic alliance had been assigned to West Germany, which was being turned into the main nuclear and rocket base of the alliance. Militarism and revenge-seeking had reared their heads in West Germany, and constituted a threat to the peaceful nations. Imperialist aggression threatened the peoples in the most different regions of the world. The imperialists were provoking armed conflicts in the Middle East and in the Pacific area. They were carrying on military operations against the peoples of Africa fighting for their freedom, and were constantly threatening armed intervention in the domestic affairs of the Latin-American countries.

The aggressive policy of the imperialist States was opposed by the peace policy of the Soviet Union, a policy which raised insuperable obstacles to the imperialist aggressors. Thanks to the firm stand of the Soviet Union and the other Socialist countries, and of the peace-loving countries of the East, dangerous hotbeds of war in the Middle and Far East were extinguished in their incipiency, and other attempts by imperialist aggressors to start a war were frustrated. The Soviet Union was persistently working to improve the international climate and to have pressing international issues settled peacefully.

The Twenty-First Party Congress unanimously approved the Leninist peaceful foreign policy of the Soviet Government and the timely and correct steps it had taken to safeguard international peace and security. The Congress instructed the Central Committee and the Soviet Government to continue to be guided by Lenin's principle of coexistence, to persevere in their efforts for a relaxation of international tension and the establishment of mutual trust and co-operation between countries irrespective of their social systems, and to expose and frustrate the schemes of imperialist aggressors. The Congress stressed the special importance of the expansion of world trade, cultural exchanges, and personal contacts between statesmen and public leaders. Better relations between the United States and the Soviet Union, the two Great Powers bearing special responsibility for the destiny of world peace, could make for a healthier international atmosphere. A peace treaty with Germany and the settlement of the Berlin question would go a long way towards improving the international situation, ending the cold war and bringing about disarmament.

The Congress called on the Soviet people, the peoples of the other Socialist countries and all peace forces to be highly vigilant, and to intensify the struggle for peace. *"We call on all peo-*

ples," said N. S. Khrushchov at the Congress, "*to work harder to maintain and promote peace. For our part, we shall do everything in our power to assure universal peace*" (*Control Figures for the Economic Development of the U.S.S.R. for 1959-1965*, Eng. ed., p. 100).

The Twenty-First Congress was a vivid demonstration of the growth of the strength of the international Communist movement, of the unity of all the Marxist-Leninist parties. There were Communist and Workers' Parties in 83 countries, and they united more than 33 million people. This was a great achievement of the working class, of Marxism-Leninism. The Twenty-First Congress of the C.P.S.U. was attended by delegations from 72 Communist and Workers' Parties. The envoys of the foreign brother parties extended cordial greetings to the C.P.S.U., confidently leading the peoples of the U.S.S.R. to Communism. The Communist and Workers' Parties that were unable to send representatives sent friendly messages of greeting.

The Congress materials contained a profound analysis of the contemporary international working-class movement. In the capitalist countries there were sinister signs that reaction was launching another offensive against the gains of the masses. This offensive showed itself in the reactionary bourgeoisie's recourse to open dictatorship and in a revival of fascism. The most reliable barrier to the fascist threat was the unity of the democratic forces, above all of the working class. The Soviet Union's successful advance towards Communism, the progress made by all the Socialist countries in Socialist construction, the increased degree of organisation of the working class and the great experience of struggle against reaction were opening favourable prospects for working-class unity of action on both an international and a national scale. The Congress expressed the hope that, in the course of the class struggle, the broad masses of Social-Democratic workers and their organisations in the capitalist countries would more and more realise the need for unity of action, and would join other groups of the working class and other democratic sections of the people in barring the road to fascism and war.

The Twenty-First Congress of the C.P.S.U. noted with satisfaction that the meetings of representatives of Communist and Workers' Parties in November, 1957, had demonstrated the complete unity of views of the brother parties. The Declaration of the meeting was unanimously approved by all the Communist and Workers' Parties, and had become a militant programme of action for the world Communist movement. It condemned revisionism as the chief danger, and also dogmatism and sectarianism. The course of events had proved the conclusions of the Declaration to be correct. After the November meetings there was a further consolidation of the Communist and Workers' Parties, and of the international Communist movement as a whole, on the ideological basis of Marxism-Leninism. The revisionist programme of the League of Communists of Yugoslavia had been criticised from positions of principle and unanimously condemned by all the Marxist-Leninist parties. Revisionism was dealt a crushing blow by the Communist movement. The revisionists had failed to split the international Communist movement, and to divert any one of the brother parties from the Marxist-Leninist path.

The views and policy of the Yugoslav revisionists were criticised, and their unworthy methods of struggle exposed and condemned, in the report by N. S. Khrushchov, in the Congress resolution and in the speeches of the delegates and representatives of the brother Marxist-Leninist parties. The Congress pointed out that the theory and practice of the Yugoslav leadership amounted to a departure from the position of the working class and from the principles of international proletarian solidarity. The Twenty-First Congress declared that the Soviet Communists and the whole of the Soviet people cherished friendly feelings for the brother peoples of Yugoslavia and for the Yugoslav Communists, that the Soviet Union would continue to work for co-operation with Yugoslavia on all questions of the struggle against imperialism and for peace in which the positions of the Soviet Union and Yugoslavia coincided.

The Congress declared that, together with the other Communist Parties, the C.P.S.U. bore responsibility for the destinies of the Socialist camp, the destinies of the world Communist movement. The Congress resolution stated that the C.P.S.U. would continue "to follow faithfully the great international teaching of Marx, Engels and Lenin, combat revisionists of all hues, uphold the purity of Marxism-Leninism, and work for new successes of the world Communist and working-class movement" (*Decisions of the Twenty-First Extraordinary Congress of the Communist Party of the Soviet Union*, Eng. ed., p. 35).

The Twenty-First Congress of the C.P.S.U. was an epoch-making event. The Seven-Year Plan of economic development of the U.S.S.R., adopted by the Congress, received universal international recognition. The working and progressive people of the whole world realised that the Soviet Seven-Year Plan served peace, democracy and Socialism. The plan caused confusion in imperialist circles. Bourgeois leaders and the bourgeois press were, however, compelled to admit the feasibility of the Seven-Year Plan and the successes of Communist construction in the U.S.S.R.

3. The Communist Party as the Leading and Organising Force of the Soviet People in the Struggle for the Triumph of Communism in the U.S.S.R.

The Twenty-First Congress of the C.P.S.U. demonstrated the solid unity of the Party, the high degree of activity of the Party organisations and of all Communists, and the Party's ability to accomplish the great tasks involved in the building of a Communist society. Speakers at the Congress included representatives of the Party organisations of all the Union Republics, many Autonomous Republics, territories and regions, foremost workers in industry and agriculture, scientists, engineers and cultural workers. The delegates' speeches showed a desire further to strengthen the unity of the Party. All the delegates expressed their full approval of the great plan of Communist construction, and in their speeches made many valuable suggestions, the implementation of which would speed up the fulfilment of the Seven-Year Plan.

The Congress approved the decisions of the June, 1957, plenary meeting of the Central Committee, which exposed and ideologically routed the anti-Party group of Malenkov, Kaganovich, Molotov, Bulganin and Shepilov. The plenary meeting's decisions were unanimously supported by the Party and the entire people. Resorting to the vilest methods of factional struggle, the group had sought to destroy Party unity and divert the Party and the country from the Leninist path. It had opposed implementation of the decisions of the Twentieth Party Congress. The resolution adopted by the Congress emphasised that the Central Committee had been right in resolutely condemning and casting aside the despicable group of factionists and disrupters. Having exposed and ideologically routed the anti-Party group, the Party closed its ranks still more firmly around the Central Committee, under the banner of Marxism-Leninism.

The Twenty-First Congress of the C.P.S.U. reflected the increased prestige of the Communist Party and the close unity of the Soviet people around the Party. The boundless faith which the people had in the Communist Party found striking expression in the growth of its membership. More than a million of the finest representatives of the working class, the collective-farm peasantry and the intelligentsia had joined the Party in the period between the Twentieth and Twenty-First Congresses. While the Congress was in session, it received numerous telegrams, messages of greeting, and reports of labour achievements from factories, building sites, State and collective farms, military units and voluntary organisations. The Soviet people regard the Communist Party as their tested leader and guide.

The experience of the struggle for the triumph of Socialism and Communism confirmed the truth of one of the most important conclusions of Leninism, namely, that in the process of the building of a Communist society the role of the Party grows steadily.

The role of the Communist Party was growing, first and foremost, as the vanguard of the Soviet people building Communism. The progress of Socialist society towards Communism posed ever new problems. It was only a party armed with Marxist-Leninist theory and capable of applying the principles of Marxism-Leninism creatively that could correctly show the way to Communism. At its plenary meetings, the Central Committee regularly examined urgent questions of Communist construction and outlined the prospects of the country's forward movement. The decisions of the Twenty-First Party Congress and the major problems of the transition from Socialism to Communism dealt with by the Congress were a new vivid expression of the leading role played by the Party at the present stage of Communist construction.

The Communist Party was playing a bigger role as the leader and organiser of the country's economic activities. This found expression, above all, in the Party's drafting of the plans of Communist construction. It was only a party armed with a knowledge of the economic laws of Socialism that could direct the development of Socialist economy towards Communism. In the State plans, the Party defined the principal problems of Communist construction and the ways of solving them. The Seven-Year Plan of the U.S.S.R., adopted by the Twenty-First Congress of the C.P.S.U., was further striking evidence of the growing role of the Party as leader in economic development in the period of the transition from Socialism to Communism. The national economy had expanded tremendously in Soviet times, particularly in recent years. Fulfilment of the plans of Communist construction would signify a further increase in the scale of production. This called for constant improvement of the forms of economic management. The reorganisation of the management of industry, the establishment of Economic Councils in the economic administrative areas, the extension of the rights of the Union Republics, local government bodies and industrial enterprises and the introduction of a new system of planning had increased the leading role of the Party in economic development, and had raised the responsibility of local Party organisations for the condition and successful development of the economy in the Union and Autonomous Republics, territories, regions, industrial enterprises and State and collective farms.

The Communist Party was playing a bigger role in the education of the working people. The problem of bringing up all-round developed members of a Communist society—the men of the future —would have to be solved in practice in the period of the full-scale building of Communism. The Communist education of tens and hundreds of millions of people, of the entire Soviet people, was a complicated and difficult process. Communist views were taking root in the course of struggle against the survivals of capitalism, against bourgeois influence and alien views and customs that found their way among Soviet people. Only the Communist Party, which had mastered the theory of Marxism-Leninism, could educate the people in the spirit of Communism, mould their Communist world outlook and resolutely combat bourgeois ideology. The Twenty-First Congress called on the Party to raise the standard of its ideological and political work, to use all the media of ideological work to solve successfully the problems of Communist construction, to explain to the people what Communism was and what benefits it brought to society.

The Communist Party was playing a bigger role as the highest form of organisation of the working class, of all working people. In carrying out the decisions of the Twentieth Congress of the C.P.S.U., the Party became more intimately linked with the people, it extended and strengthened its ties with the masses. The submission of draft laws on major questions of State, economic and cultural development for discussion by the whole nation, the calling of conferences of workers engaged in different branches of the national economy, science and culture, and appeals to the working people on questions vital to the country, had become a regular part of Party work. The development of the Socialist State in the direction of the maximum expansion of democracy was accompanied by an extension of the rights of the Union Republics and local bodies in the management of economic and cultural development, the raising of the part played by the Soviets, the trade unions and the Komsomol, the establishment of new voluntary organisations of the working people for the maintenance of public order and the protection of the rights of citizens, an increase in the activity of the masses and the drawing of large sections of the people in the management of public affairs. It was important at the same time that all voluntary organisations, too, should strictly observe the interests of the State, and that all manifestations of parochialism, self-centredness and lack of co-ordination should be nipped in the bud. At the present stage of Communist construction there was a greater need than ever for an authoritative and influential directing organisation capable of co-ordinating the activities of all the other voluntary organisations. Such an organisation was the Party. The Communist Party gave guidance to all voluntary organisations and directed their activities into the single channel of Communist construc-. tion.

Between congresses, all the activities of the Party are guided by the Central Committee. The everyday work of the C.C. is directed by its Presidium and Secretariat, elected at plenary meetings. Full members of the Presidium of the C.C. C.P.S.U. are: A. B. Aristov, L. I. Brezhnev, Y. A. Furtseva, N. G. Ignatov, N. S. Khrushchov, A. N. Kosygin, F. R. Kozlov, O. W. Kuusinen, A. I. Mikoyan, N. A. Muhitdinov, N. V. Podgorny, D. S. Polyansky, N. M. Shvernik and M. A. Suslov; alternate members: J. E. Kalnberzinš, A. P. Kirilenko, D. S. Korotchenko, K. T. Mazurov, V. P. Mzhavanadze, M. G. Pervukhin and P. N. Pospelov. Secretaries of the C.C. C.P.S.U. are N. S. Khrushchov (first secretary), F. R. Kozlov, O. W. Kuusinen, N. A. Muhitdinov and M. A. Suslov. The Central Committee of the C.P.S.U. guides the work of all the central government bodies and public organisations.

The main task of the Communist Party and the Soviet people now was to ensure the fulfilment of the Seven-Year Plan without fail.

The Congress pointed to the need of raising the organising role of the local Party directing bodies and primary Party organisations. The restoration and further development of the Leninist standards of Party life and the principles of collective leadership, consistent pursuance of the policy of developing inner-Party democracy, criticism and self-criticism, had increased still further the efficiency of the Party organisations and the activity of the Party membership. The success of the Seven-Year Plan would be decided in the factories and on the building sites, the State and collective farms and in the scientific institutions. The task of the Party organisations was to rally and organise the masses for the fulfilment of concrete production assignments, to acquaint all the working people with the plan's targets, to organise and direct the efforts of every collective unit of the working people for the attainment of those targets and resolutely to eradicate shortcomings and overcome difficulties. An atmosphere of constructive effort and labour enthusiasm must be developed at every factory, collective and State farm, at every office and institution, so that the organised working folk who were employed there, by their labour, should actively help to fulfil and overfulfil the Seven-Year Plan.

The ideological work of the Party was subordinated to the successful building of Communism. At the present stage, the Party placed special emphasis on the education of Soviet people in the spirit of collectivism and industriousness and the development of a Communist attitude to labour. The Congress made it incumbent upon Party organisations to establish the closest possible connection between ideological work and the fulfilment of practical tasks, to be concrete and clear of purpose in their educational work, to give every encouragement to Communist forms of labour, and to get every working person to make the most of his machine, lathe, installation, tractor, harvester combine, and employ the most advanced methods of work.

The Twenty-First Congress of the C.P.S.U. pointed out that leading personnel in the Party and the State had a role of paramount importance to play in Communist construction. The task of Party organisations was to improve the allocation of personnel, more boldly to promote young people, reinforce lagging factories, collective farms, State farms and districts with competent personnel, educate leading personnel and all Communists to be exacting to themselves and to appreciate their responsibility for the job entrusted to them, to imbue them with the spirit of loyal service to the people, to the Communist cause, and systematically to raise the level of their theoretical knowledge and Marxist-Leninist training.

The Congress expressed the firm conviction that the entry of the U.S.S.R. into the period of the full-scale building of a Communist society would increase the activity of local government, trade union and Komsomol organisations and give rise to a new and powerful wave of labour enthusiasm among the working class, the collective-farm peasantry and the intelligentsia for fulfilment and overfulfilment of the Seven-Year Plan of economic development of the U.S.S.R.

The Communist Party is leading the Soviet people to the radiant summits of Communism along the tested Leninist path, under the great, all-conquering banner of Marxism-Leninism. Mankind's most daring dream, the dream of Communism, is coming true in the U.S.S.R. Blazing the trail to Communism, the Soviet people are advancing in close unity with the peoples of the other Socialist countries; they are supported by the mighty Socialist camp, by the working class and the working people of all countries.

"The Seven-Year period we have now entered," said N. S. Khrushchov in his concluding speech to the Congress, "is a new important and, we might say, a decisive height on our path in history. The Communist Party and all our people are fully confident that they will be able to scale this height as well and will emerge on to a broad plateau. Then new vistas will open and it will be easier to march on" (*Control Figures for the Economic Development of the U.S.S.R. for 1959-1965*, Eng. ed., p. 149).

CONCLUSION

What are the principal results of the historic path travelled by the Communist Party of the Soviet Union? What are the basic laws governing its development and struggle? What does the history of the C.P.S.U. teach us?

1. The history of the Party teaches us that the working class can achieve victory, and carry out the historic tasks of establishing the dictatorship of the proletariat and building Socialism and Communism, *only under the leadership of the Communist Party*, a party revolutionary in its attitude towards the bourgeoisie and its State power, uncompromising towards conciliators and capitulators, and free from opportunism.

The C.P.S.U., which was founded by the great Lenin, is a party of a *new type*. Unlike the reformist and Social-Democratic parties, parties of the old type that follow a policy of compromise and reconciliation of the proletariat with the bourgeoisie, the Communist Party expresses the fundamental interests of the proletariat as a class fighting for the triumph of Socialist revolution, for the abolition of the exploiting system, for the creation of a Socialist and a Communist society.

The C.P.S.U. is the organised, Marxist-Leninist vanguard and political leader of the working class and all the Soviet people. Leninism teaches, and history confirms this, that the Party wins and consolidates its role of vanguard of the working class, of leader of the masses, by fighting selflessly for the vital interests of the working people at all stages of the revolutionary movement and the building of Communism.

"It is only the Communist Party," wrote Lenin, "provided it is really the vanguard of the revolutionary class, provided it comprises all the finest representatives of this class, provided it consists of thoroughly class-conscious and devoted Communists educated and steeled by the experience of tenacious revolutionary struggles, provided it has succeeded in linking itself up inseparably with the entire life of its class and, through its class, with the entire mass of the exploited, and in winning the unqualified trust of this class and this mass— it is only such a party that can lead the proletariat in the last, most ruthless and resolute struggle against all the forces of capitalism. On the other hand, it is only under the leadership of such a party that the proletariat is able to deploy the full might of its revolutionary onset and reduce to nought the inevitable apathy and partly the resistance of a small minority—the working-class aristocracy, old trade union and co-operative leaders and others, who have been spoilt by capitalism—is able to deploy its full strength, which is immeasurably greater than its share of the population, by virtue of the very economic system of capitalist society" (*Collected Works*, Vol. 31, pp. 163-64).

The existence of such a party and its leadership of the masses was a most important condition for the victory of the Great October Socialist Revolution. The leadership of the Party ensured the establishment in the U.S.S.R. of the world's first Socialist society in difficult and complicated international and domestic conditions. It ensured the defence of the country against hostile imperialist forces and its successful advance towards Communism.

A law of the development of Soviet society is the steady raising of the Party's role in Communist construction, in its political and ideological leadership of society, and in the economic and cultural life of the country.

2. The historical experience of the C.P.S.U. has confirmed one of the most important conclusions of Marxism-Leninism, that the transition from capitalism to Socialism and the successful building of Communism are possible only on the basis of the *dictatorship of the proletariat*, that is, of the political, State, leadership of society by the working class.

The dictatorship of the proletariat is necessary primarily for the purpose of crushing the resistance of the overthrown exploiters and of all anti-Socialist class forces within the country, and for safeguarding the gains of Socialism against attack from without.

The dictatorship of the proletariat is not pure force, not even predominantly force.

The dictatorship of the proletariat is a special form of class alliance between the working class and millions of working people, above all, the working peasantry, with the purpose of establishing and consolidating Socialism.

In the Socialist epoch, the development of this alliance has led to the moral and political unity of society.

A most important function of the dictatorship of the proletariat is to give effect to State leadership by the working class of the working masses of the peasantry, the non-proletarian sections of the working people in the towns and the intelligentsia, to strengthen the alliance with them for the purpose of drawing them into the building of Socialism and re-educating them.

With the victory of Socialism in the U.S.S.R., the exploiters have disappeared and, in consequence, the need to suppress them; but the dictatorship of the working class remains. It carries out the functions of defending the country against attacks by the imperialist camp and its agents; it is necessary in order to lead the Soviet people in their further advance, on the basis of the gains of Socialism already achieved.

The dictatorship of the proletariat expresses and defends the interests of the working people. It is a new and higher form of democracy as compared with bourgeois democracy. Under Socialism in the U.S.S.R., democracy has become a universal, Socialist democracy.

The history of the C.P.S.U. teaches us that the dictatorship of the proletariat cannot be put into effect without the Communist Party. "The dictatorship of the proletariat," Lenin said, "is possible only through the Communist Party" (*Collected Works*, Vol. 32, p. 176). Only a Marxist-Leninist Communist Party, marching at the head of the masses, can organise the working people, educate them politically, show them the road to Socialism and Communism, and inspire them to heroic feats.

The Communist Party is the leading force in the system of the dictatorship of the proletariat. It was under its leadership that the machinery of the new State power and the principles of its activity were established and tested in practice. The system of the dictatorship of the proletariat consists of: *Soviets* of Working People's Deputies, which are the direct expression of the dictatorship of the proletariat; *trade unions*, which are the biggest organisations of industrial, professional and office workers; the *Komsomol*, which unites broad sections of advanced youth; *co-operatives* of all types; other *voluntary organisations*; the *Party*, which is the vanguard of the Soviet people, the political leader of all the organisations of the working people.

"Thus, on the whole," wrote Lenin, "we have a formally non-Communist, flexible and relatively wide and very powerful proletarian apparatus, by means of which the Party is closely linked up with the *class* and with the *masses*, and by means of which, under the leadership of the Party, the *dictatorship of the class* is exercised" (*Collected Works*, Vol. 31, p. 30).

The Party's leading role in the system of the dictatorship of the proletariat has received nation-wide recognition. The

Communist Party, the Constitution of the U.S.S.R. states, is the "leading core of all organisations of the working people, both voluntary and State."

The working class of the U.S.S.R. exercises its dictatorship through the Soviets. But experience shows that the dictatorship of the proletariat can also take other forms. A new form of the dictatorship of the proletariat, *people's democracy*, arose after the second world war.

3. The history of the C.P.S.U. teaches us that the Party would not have been able to secure the historic gains of Socialism in the U.S.S.R. if it had not been guided in all its activity by the *theory of Marxism-Leninism*.

"Bolshevism," wrote Lenin, "arose in 1903 on the very firm foundation of the theory of Marxism" (*Collected Works,* Vol. 31, p. 9).

Marxism-Leninism is an integral and consistent dialectical materialist world outlook, and the theory of scientific Communism. It is the science of the laws of development of society, the science of the Socialist revolution and the dictatorship of the proletariat, the science of the building of Socialist and Communist society. From Marxist-Leninist theory the Party draws its strength and its confidence in the triumph of Communism. This theory enables the Party to ascertain the laws governing social life, to find the right orientation in any situation, to understand the inner connection of events and the trend of their development. It helps to find the answers to the basic questions posed by the revolutionary struggle and Communist construction.

The absolute demands which the Communist Party makes on theory are:

(a) fidelity to Marxism-Leninism, defence and support of its principles, an uncompromising attitude towards any kind of deviation from it, and a determined struggle against all attempts to revise it;

(b) a creative approach to theory; the mastering of theory; its development in keeping with the changing conditions of the life of society and the tasks confronting the Party at different stages of the struggle for the triumph of the proletariat and the building of Communism; a resolute struggle against dogmatism, against divorcing theory from practice, from the Party's revolutionary struggle;

(c) the indissoluble connection of theory and practice; organic unity between theory and practice in the Party's entire activity.

Throughout their entire activity, Lenin and his comrades-in-arms, the Party as a whole, carried on a resolute struggle against overt and covert opponents of Marxism, and against revisionists of all hues both in Russia and in the international arena. As a result of this struggle the revolutionary theory of Marx and Engels triumphed, in spite of bitter attacks, spread throughout the world, and today serves as a powerful ideological weapon in the building of Communism in the U.S.S.R., and in strengthening and developing the world Socialist system and the international liberation movement. The history of the Party is the history of uncompromising struggle for the purity of Marxist-Leninist theory, both against open revisionism and against dogmatism.

The struggle of Lenin and his followers for the purity of Marxist theory went hand in hand with a *creative* elaboration of this theory. Mastering Marxist theory does not at all mean learning its various conclusions and propositions by heart. Marxist theory must not be regarded as something set and fossilised, as a collection of dogmas. Like any other science, it develops, advances and is enriched with new experience, new knowledge, new conclusions and propositions. Mastering Marxist theory means assimilating its essence and learning to apply it in solving practical problems of the revolutionary movement and Communist construction. The Communist Party's fidelity to the spirit of Marxism has ever been combined with the replacement of some of its obsolete propositions and the elaboration of new fundamental theoretical propositions conforming to the changes that have come about in the life of society, and to the requirements of the practical struggle for the interests of the working class, for the cause of Socialism and Communism.

Proceeding from the essence of Marxist theory, Lenin made a number of brilliant discoveries, and drew new conclusions that are of decisive importance for the proletariat and its revolutionary Party in the new conditions of the epoch of imperialism and Socialist revolution.

An example of the creative development of Marxism, and the replacement of obsolete propositions by new ones that meet the requirements of the political struggle of the proletariat, is the theory of Socialist revolution worked out by Lenin.

Marx and Engels, who discovered the laws of capitalism in its pre-monopoly stage, arrived at the conclusion that Socialist revolution could not triumph in one country, taken singly, that it would triumph simultaneously in all or most of the capitalist countries.

This conclusion, which was correct in the period when capitalism was on the ascent, became a guiding principle for all Marxists. But the situation had changed radically by the beginning of the twentieth century: capitalism had grown into imperialism, which intensified all the contradictions of capitalism to the utmost and brought mankind to the threshold of the transition to Socialism; ascendant capitalism had turned into moribund capitalism. The proposition of Marx and Engels that Socialism could not triumph in one country taken singly no longer corresponded to the new situation, and Lenin did not hesitate to revise it. Analysing capitalism at its new stage, he showed that the uneven development of capitalism becomes especially marked in the epoch of imperialism, and that this development assumes a spasmodic, catastrophic character. He arrived at the conclusion that in the conditions of imperialism, Socialism cannot triumph simultaneously in all the capitalist countries and that, on the contrary, the world imperialist chain can be broken at its weakest link, that Socialism can triumph at first in one capitalist country taken singly.

The Party upheld this brilliant discovery of Lenin's in its struggle against the opportunists. It became a guiding principle for the whole of revolutionary Marxism, enriched the revolutionary struggle, opened up new prospects for it and unfettered the initiative of the proletariat in its revolutionary onslaught against its own bourgeoisie in each particular country. The victory of the Great October Socialist Revolution and the building of Socialism in the U.S.S.R. furnished irrefutable proof of the correctness of the Leninist theory of Socialist revolution.

Had Lenin not made his brilliant discovery in time, had he not had the courage to replace one of the obsolete propositions of Marxism by a new proposition, and the only correct one for the new historical situation, and had the Communist Parties not mastered and adopted this proposition as a guiding principle, the revolutionary initiative and activity of the proletariat of the various countries would have been fettered, and they would not have had a clear perspective or confidence in the success of their revolutionary undertaking.

Another instance of the creative elaboration of Marxism was Lenin's discovery of Soviet power as a State form of the dictatorship of the proletariat, now firmly established in the U.S.S.R. Had Lenin not discovered the Soviet form of the dictatorship of the proletariat, the Republic of Soviets, the Party would have groped in the dark, the proletariat would have lost, the bourgeoisie would have won and Marxist theory would have suffered a severe setback.

Still another illustration of the creative development of Marxism is the discovery by Marxists-Leninists of a new form of the dictatorship of the proletariat, in the shape of People's Democracy. Only one form of the dictatorship of the proletariat, the Soviets, was known before the second world war. The experience of the Soviet Union, which acquired all the more significance as a result of the establishment of a Socialist society and the victory of the U.S.S.R. in the second world war, attested the vitality of the Soviets. However, taking into account the international situation during and after the second world war and the actual course of revolutionary development in the countries where a people's revolution was unfolding, and drawing upon the Leninist proposition that different forms of the dictatorship of the proletariat were possible and upon the experience of the masses, Marxists-Leninists advanced a new form of the dictatorship of the proletariat—People's Democracy. It was applied in the Chinese People's Republic and in all the Socialist countries that came into being after the second world war.

The decisions of the Twentieth Congress of the C.P.S.U. serve as a vivid example of creative development of the theory of Marxism-Leninism. N. S. Khrushchov's report and the Congress decisions were a development of Lenin's doctrine of the peaceful coexistence of the two social systems, and contained the theoretically and politically important proposition as to the possibility of averting wars in our epoch. They dealt with the forms of the transition to Socialism in a number of capitalist countries and with the ways of establishing working-class unity in the capitalist countries.

The Twenty-First Congress of the C.P.S.U. made a further contribution to the theory of scientific Communism. Its decisions and N. S. Khrushchov's report theoretically substantiated and elaborated, on the basis of Marxism-Leninism, major problems of the new stage of Communist construction in the U.S.S.R.— the laws governing the development of Socialism into Communism, the ways of developing and bringing closer together the collective-farm and nationally-owned forms of Socialist property; the distribution of material values among the members of society, the political organisation of society, the State system and administration in the period of the full-scale construction of Communism. The Congress stated that in the U.S.S.R. the victory of Socialism was not only complete but final. Of tremendous importance is the conclusion drawn by the Twenty-First Congress that the successes of the Socialist countries, the growth and strengthening of the peace forces throughout the world, will make it really possible to exclude war from the life of society even before the complete victory of Socialism on earth, with capitalism still existing in a part of the world.

The decisions of the Twenty-First Congress and the report delivered by N. S. Khrushchov were an example of the creative application and elaboration of Marxism-Leninism. The propositions elaborated by the Congress are of immense theoretical and practical importance to the activity of the C.P.S.U., and to all the brother Marxist-Leninist parties.

Leninism teaches us that he who takes no account of the changes in the development of society, ignores concrete historical conditions, defends obsolete propositions and conclusions, and substitutes a simple repetition of old Marxist formulas for a scientific analysis of new historical conditions and a theoretical generalisation of new experience in the class struggle of the proletariat, remains true only to the letter of Marxism, distorts its revolutionary substance and, in fact, deviates from Marxism.

The Communist Party has never dissociated theory from revolutionary practice. The invincibility of the Communist Party lies in the organic unity of its theory and practice.

The Communist Party has always been guided by the proposition of Marx and Lenin that Marxism is not a dogma but a guide to action.

4. The history of the C.P.S.U. teaches that *unity of the working class* is an essential condition for victory in the Socialist revolution, and that such unity cannot be achieved unless the petty-bourgeois parties are exposed and isolated from the masses, unless they are routed ideologically.

The Socialist-Revolutionaries, Mensheviks, Anarchists, and nationalist and other petty-bourgeois parties, styling themselves Socialist and revolutionary parties in order to deceive the masses, called upon the working class not to fight against the bourgeoisie but to compromise with it, not to abolish capitalism but to preserve it. They denied the leading role of the working class in the revolutionary struggle of the masses, did not recognise the dictatorship of the proletariat, tried to convert the working class into a subsidiary of the bourgeoisie. The policy of reconciling the class interests of the proletariat with those of the bourgeoisie, the policy of agreement between them, led the petty-bourgeois parties to a betrayal of the interests of the working class and of all working people, and in the end landed them in the camp of the counter-revolution.

The Communist Party hammered out the militant unity of the working class of Russia, and by its uncompromising struggle against the petty-bourgeois parties, by its able and flexible tactics of winning the masses over to the side of the vanguard of the proletariat, safeguarded the working class against compromise with the bourgeoisie, against chauvinism, against nationalist enmity.

At the same time, the history of the C.P.S.U. shows that the proletariat, led by the Communist Party, could fulfil its role of leader of the masses in relentless, selfless struggle against all parties representing the interests of the landlords and bourgeoisie—the monarchists, Octobrists and Cadets. The Communist Party won over the peasant reserves from the Cadets and Social-

influence on unstable elements. This may find its reflection in the ranks of the Party as well. Hence it is one of the Party's prime tasks to pay constant attention to the *ideological training* of Communists, to Marxist-Leninist propaganda among the broad mass of the working people, and to work steadfastly to further strengthen the unity of its ranks.

Unity of the Communist Party, based on the ideological principles of Marxism-Leninism, always has been, and remains, the principal condition for the stability of the Soviet system, the cementing factor in the moral and political unity of Soviet society and an earnest of the triumph of Communism in the U.S.S.R.

6. The historical path travelled by the C.P.S.U. shows that the Party can effectively lead the struggle of the working class for power, for the establishment of Socialism and Communism, only if the internal life of the Party is highly *organised*, if all of its organisations and all its members have *one* will, if they act as a *solid* force, if there is *iron discipline* in its ranks. The methods of Party work and the forms of Party organisation depend on concrete historical conditions; but the basic principles of organisation, which were worked out and substantiated by Lenin, and are now an integral part of Bolshevism, are immutable.

The Party consistently applies the Leninist standards of Party life and the principles of Party leadership. The guiding principle in the organisational structure and internal life of the Party is *democratic centralism*. The merit of this principle, tested by more than half a century of Party history, is that it combines the strictest centralism with broad Party democracy, the indisputable authority of the leading Party bodies with their electivity and accountability to the Party membership, Party discipline with the creative activity of the Party masses. Lenin taught that democratic centralism is needed in order that "the *organising* role of the proletariat (and that is its *principal* role) may be exercised correctly, successfully, victoriously" (*Collected Works*, Vol. 31, p. 27).

It is not accidental that the enemies of Marxism-Leninism, and revisionists of all shades, oppose the Leninist principle of democratic centralism, advocating federalism, anarchic autonomism and other similar petty-bourgeois principles.

Party democracy and discipline are indivisible; the internal life, the strength and militancy of the Marxist-Leninist party, and the firmness of its ties with the masses, depend on this unity. Inner-Party democracy can be successfully extended only by strengthening Party leadership and discipline. In this is revealed the interrelation of democracy with centralism and Party discipline, freedom of discussion with the duty of all Party members to carry out Party decisions implicitly.

The Leninist principle of *collective leadership*, which stems from the very nature of the Party built on the lines of democratic centralism, is of utmost importance in the life and activity of the Party. The Party cannot, as Lenin pointed out, carry on its political struggle, organise the revolutionary forces and discipline them "without working out, by collective effort, certain *forms and rules of managing its affairs*" (*Collected Works*, Vol. 4, p. 199).

Collective leadership safeguards the Party against unilateral decisions, against grave mistakes, and if such mistakes have been committed, it enables the Party to rectify them promptly. The collective experience of the entire Party and the collective wisdom of its Central Committee ensure the unshakable unity and cohesion of the Party ranks, correct leadership of the country and the successful building of Socialism and Communism.

The experience of the Communist Party shows that with the advance towards Communism, inner-Party democracy expands and Communists display increasing activity and creative initiative in resolving questions of the country's political and economic life.

7. The history of the C.P.S.U. teaches us that the strength and invincibility of the Marxist-Leninist party lie in its *close, indissoluble connections* with the working class, with the mass of the people. The strength of the people lies in their *solid unity* around the Party.

A party can really lead the people only if it is the conscious spokesman of the aspirations of the masses, if it marches at the head of the masses, illumining the road to victory for them with the theory of Marxism-Leninism.

A party can perform its role of vanguard only if it does not shut itself off from the masses, including the backward sections of the working people, and works with them day after day, is able to convince them that it is right and to raise them to the level of advanced fighters for the Communist cause.

Sectarian isolation from the masses and *opportunist adaptation* to backward sentiments are alike alien to the Marxist-Leninist party.

Leninism teaches us, and the experience of the C.P.S.U. confirms this, that a party is invincible if it is able to draw close to the broadest sections of the working people, if it is able to link itself closely with the life of the working class and working people in general.

A party loses its role of vanguard of the working class if it shuts itself up in its narrow party shell and turns into a sect, into a purely propagandist organisation.

A party is invincible if it not only teaches the masses, but also learns from them, if it attentively studies the creative work of the people, solicitously cultivates the shoots of the new, resolutely eliminates bureaucratic obstacles standing in the way of creative endeavour, vigorously supports every manifestation of initiative on the part of the working people in the revolutionary transformation of society, and critically tests its decisions by the experience of the development of social life.

8. The history of the C.P.S.U. teaches us that *bold criticism* of its own shortcomings, weaknesses and mistakes is a major condition for the successes of a party. The activity of the C.P.S.U. provides brilliant confirmation of Marx's idea that constant criticism and self-criticism are a distinctive feature of the proletarian revolution, that they constitute a law of its development.

A party cannot perform its role as leader of the working class and all working people if it ceases to notice its own shortcomings, if it is afraid to acknowledge its mistakes openly and honestly, if it cannot correct them in good time.

A party, Lenin teaches us, is invincible if it is not afraid of criticism and self-criticism, if it does not gloss over the mistakes and defects in its work, if it teaches and educates its personnel not only on the achievements, but also on the mistakes in Party work and State administration, if it is able to show up and correct its mistakes in good time.

A party loses its prestige if it conceals its mistakes from the masses, if it glosses over sore problems, covers up its defects by pretending that all is well, is intolerant of criticism and self-criticism, gives way to self-complacency and is ready to rest on its laurels.

"The attitude of a political party towards its own mistakes," Lenin wrote, "is one of the most important and surest ways of judging how earnest the party is and how it *in practice* fulfils its obligations towards its *class* and the toiling *masses*. Frankly admitting a mistake, ascertaining the reasons for it, analysing the conditions which led to it, and thoroughly discussing the means of correcting it—that is the earmark of a serious party, that is the way it should perform its duties, that is the way it should educate and train the *class*, and then the *masses*" (*Collected Works*, Vol. 31, p. 39).

The Party's frank statement about the serious consequences of the Stalin personality cult, about the grave mistakes committed by Stalin in the latter period of his life, may serve as an example of bold self-criticism. The Twentieth Congress of the C.P.S.U. criticised these mistakes from positions of principle, and took the necessary steps to eliminate them. This resolute self-criticism was fresh evidence of the strength and stability of the Communist Party and the Soviet Socialist system.

"We Communists criticise the personality cult as being alien to the spirit of Marxism-Leninism, as something intolerable in a Communist Party, in a Socialist society. The Party is doing this to strengthen its positions and consolidate the Socialist system, so that such things shall never occur again. But we cannot agree with those who try to use the criticism of the personality cult for attacks against the Socialist system, against the Communist Party" (N. S. Khrushchov, *Forty Years of the Great October Socialist Revolution*, Eng. ed., p. 33).

9. The historical path travelled by the Communist Party testifies to the fact that it is this party, a Marxist-Leninist party, that acts as the *genuinely patriotic force*, that expresses and upholds, consistently and fully, the interests of its people, the interests of its country.

The C.P.S.U. came to power in a country which the ruling classes and their political parties had reduced to a state of utter decline and general ruin, and which was faced with the threat of partition by the imperialist Powers. Assuming responsibility for the country's destiny, the Communist Party aroused, organised and inspired the masses for the struggle against backwardness, ruin, and the threat of enslavement by foreign Powers, for the struggle to build Socialism.

Under the leadership of the Communist Party, the country's productive forces were unshackled and unprecedented progress was achieved in economy and technology, science and culture. Within an extremely short time, the Party led the country to signal historic victories, transformed it into a mighty Socialist Power, and ensured the prosperity and greatness of the Soviet Motherland.

The Party ensured the victory of the Soviet Union in two patriotic wars, saved the country from the threat of enslavement by foreign imperialists, and successfully upheld the independence and sovereignty of the Soviet State. By its correct policy, which expresses the interests of the people, the Communist Party raised the country to heights it had never reached in all its history.

Although all the other political parties that had been active on the Russian political scene had advertised their "love" of Russia, they had in fact championed not the interests of the people and the country, but the selfish interests of the capitalists and landlords. They had doomed Russia to backwardness and stagnation, and would readily have placed her under the yoke of foreign imperialists.

The people tested all the political parties in Russia by their own experience, and entrusted the leadership of the country to the Communist Party. They rejected all the other political parties —the monarchists, Octobrists, Cadets, Socialist-Revolutionaries and Mensheviks and the numerous nationalist parties. The political evolution of these parties, which entered the service of the foreign imperialists, showed that they were not only anti-Socialist, but also anti-popular and anti-patriotic. They came out against the national interests of the country.

Leninism teaches us, and historical experience confirms this, that Marxist-Leninist parties act as a genuinely *patriotic* force. This is a law for the party of the new type.

10. The most rich experience of the C.P.S.U. teaches us that it has achieved historic successes in the struggle for the triumph of Socialism and won tremendous prestige among the masses in the U.S.S.R. and foreign countries because, in its theory as in practice, it has invariably been guided by the principle of *proletarian internationalism.*

On Lenin's proposal, the Party was, from the very beginning, built up as a single organisation of workers of all the nationalities of Russia. The Party grew up and became steeled in the struggle against dominant-nation chauvinism and local bourgeois nationalism. It advanced the historic slogan of self-determination of nations. All the nations forming Russia were given the right of freely seceding and forming independent States. By its selfless struggle against dominant-nation chauvinism and for the freedom of the peoples, for Socialism, the Russian proletariat won the confidence of all the working people of the nations oppressed by tsarism. A multi-national State, founded on the voluntary union of all the nations of the country and their equal participation in Socialist construction, was created for the first time in history. The very difficult historical problem of putting an end to the economic and cultural inequality of the formerly oppressed peoples was successfully solved in the course of Socialist construction.

True to its international duty, the Communist Party consistently cements the friendship among the peoples of the U.S.S.R. and unites them for the great common cause of building a Communist society.

The Marxist-Leninist concept of proletarian internationalism is the very opposite of that of the parties of the old type, that is, the parties of the Second International. Recognition of internationalism in words and its replacement by vulgar nationalism in deeds, Lenin pointed out, is a usual phenomenon among the parties of the Second International. Petty-bourgeois nationalism declares recognition of the equality of nations to be internationalism, leaving national egoism intact. Proletarian internationalism, Lenin teaches, demands indivisibly linking up the interests of the proletarian struggle in one country with the interests of this struggle in other countries, with the interests of the international working-class movement as a whole.

By upholding the principle of proletarian internationalism, the C.P.S.U. has discharged, and continues to discharge, its duty to the international proletariat. The programme, strategy and tactics of the Leninist Party, and its entire practical activity, are permeated with the spirit of proletarian internationalism.

Regarding themselves as a detachment of the international army of labour, the Communists have always participated actively in the struggle for Marxism in the ranks of that army. In 1914-1919, the Bolshevik Party, headed by Lenin, helped to prepare and organise, within the Social-Democratic parties, the Left internationalist groups and trends that subsequently formed the basis of the Communist Parties.

Following the victory of the Great October Socialist Revolution, the chief international duty of the Communist Party and the Soviet people as a whole was the struggle to build Communism in the U.S.S.R., which is of tremendous international significance. The building of Socialism and Communism in the U.S.S.R. signified above all effective aid by the C.P.S.U. and the Soviet people to the international working class, and the liberation movement of the peoples. For their part, the Communist Parties and the working class of the capitalist countries supported the first Socialist country in the most diverse ways. Regarding the Soviet Union as its shock brigade, the international proletariat considers its prime duty to be defence of the world's first Socialist State, the bulwark of progressive mankind. This reciprocal aid is an expression of proletarian internationalism.

Proletarian internationalism was strikingly manifested during the second world war. The war waged by the Soviet Union against the fascist troops was not only a war for the land of Socialism; it was also a struggle for the freedom of the peoples of Europe and Asia, for the deliverance of the whole of humanity from the threat of fascist enslavement. In the bourgeois countries, the working people, all patriotic forces, among which the Communist Parties were in the forefront, fought selflessly against the German, Japanese and other imperialist invaders, thus facilitating the Soviet Union's struggle against fascism.

In the period of the formation and development of the world Socialist system, a major requirement of proletarian internationalism is the struggle to preserve and consolidate this system, to educate the masses in a spirit of friendship and fraternal co-operation and mutual aid. The relations between the Socialist countries are built up on new international principles—fraternal friendship, all-round co-operation and mutual assistance. The unity and fraternal co-operation of the Socialist countries are based on the community of interests of the Communist and Workers' Parties and of the peoples of these countries, on their striving for one and the same goal—the building of a Communist society.

The Socialist countries strictly observe democratic principles in relations between peoples. These principles are complete equality, respect for territorial integrity, State independence and sovereignty, and non-interference in the internal affairs of other countries.

The working people of the capitalist countries and the oppressed peoples regard the world Socialist camp, and the great Soviet Union, as the bulwark of international peace and friendship.

"Capital," Lenin wrote, "is an international force. To vanquish it, an international workers' alliance, an international workers' brotherhood, is needed.

"We are opposed to national enmity, to national discord, to national exclusiveness. We are internationalists" (*Collected Works*, Vol. 30, p. 268).

Throughout the history of its heroic struggle, the C.P.S.U. has consistently implemented the principle of proletarian internationalism, guided by the appeal of the *Communist Manifesto*: "Workers of all countries, unite!"

The victorious activity of the Communist Party in the period of the struggle for the overthrow of tsarism and capitalism, as well as in the period of the building of Communism, is a graphic illustration of the mighty force of proletarian internationalism, of the international solidarity of the working people.

11. The experience of more than half a century of social development has proved that the C.P.S.U. was right in the historic argument and struggle against the parties of the Second International, against the ideology and policy of Social-Democracy.

Guided by the theory of Marx and Engels, which was developed further by Lenin, the Bolshevik Party took the path of Socialist revolution. It called on all the parties active in the international working-class movement to take the same path. But the Social-Democratic parties chose a different, a reformist path. The international proletariat and the oppressed peoples now have the opportunity of comparing and appraising the results of the development of the parties and countries moving along these two different paths.

The C.P.S.U. has ensured the epoch-making victories of Socialism, which have been acknowledged by the whole of progressive mankind. It has achieved the transformation of the Soviet Union into a mighty Socialist Power, into a stronghold of peace, democracy and Socialism. It is leading the people on to Communism, which is the goal of the Socialist movement of the working class.

The experience of the Social-Democratic parties shows entirely different results.

In the past 30-40 years, the parties of the Socialist International have frequently been in power in many countries. During the years from 1918 to 1958, the Social-Democratic and Socialist parties of Germany, France, Belgium, Denmark, Norway, Sweden and the Netherlands, and the Labour parties of Britain and Australia, were ruling parties or took part in governments in coalition with the bourgeois parties. Enjoying the trust and support of the working class, they had the opportunity of leading their countries along a different, non-capitalist path and of carrying out what their programmes proclaimed. Being in power, these parties could have taken steps to abolish the capitalist system, which engenders the exploitation of man by man, poverty, unemployment and destructive wars. But as everyone knows nothing of the kind happened. Countries where the reformists, who call themselves Socialists, held power for many years remain capitalist.

In a number of the above-mentioned countries, the working class, with the assistance of the Social-Democratic parties, secured some improvement in their economic conditions and won certain rights and democratic liberties within the limits of the dictatorship of the bourgeoisie. But the working class paid a high price for all that—the retention of power by the bourgeoisie, the preservation of an exploiting society, the preservation and intensification of the danger of war, ruinous crises, unemployment, and attendant hardships for the mass of the people. Moreover, whenever there is a serious complication of the economic situation, the ruling classes of exploiters deprive the working people of the material benefits they have gained and throw back the masses for whole decades.

A major reason why the capitalist system was preserved in the countries where the Social-Democratic parties were or are in power are the theoretical principles and views of these parties, which are contrary to Marxism-Leninism, and their opportunist practice. Both in theory and in practice, the Social-Democratic leaders have invariably proceeded from their basic proposition, that it is possible to reconcile the class interests of the proletariat and the bourgeoisie, that the revolutionary overthrow of bourgeois rule is impermissible, that the dictatorship of the proletariat is unnecessary, and that a coalition of bourgeois and Social-Democratic parties should be formed instead. In due course the Social-Democratic parties drifted further and further away from Marxism, and many of them eventually repudiated it openly.

A comparison of the results of the two ways chosen by different detachments of the international working class convincingly shows the bankruptcy of Social-Democracy, and the immense significance of Marxism-Leninism in the struggle of the working class for the triumph of Socialism and Communism throughout the world.

* * *

Thus the history of the Communist Party of the Soviet Union and the great victories achieved under its leadership are graphic evidence of the invincible force of the ideas of Communism and of the creative power of the working class, which has performed its historic mission of transforming capitalist society into Socialist society.

In close co-operation with the brother parties of other countries, the C.P.S.U. is marching in the van of the struggle for world peace. The Communist Party embodies the "intellect, honour and conscience of our epoch" (*Lenin*).

The Soviet people, united around the Communist Party and backed by imposing achievements in all spheres of life, have entered the period of the full-scale building of Communism.

Backed by the victories won and by its vast experience, the Communist Party is directing the mighty forces of the Soviet people towards fulfilment of the inspiring task of building a Communist society, on whose banner are inscribed the words: "From each according to his ability, to each according to his needs."

NOTES

[1] **Zemsky Nachalnik**—in pre-revolutionary Russia an official with administrative and magisterial powers over the peasantry, appointed from the noble class.

p. 20

[2] **Zemstvo** — so-called local self-government body which was dominated by the nobility. It was set up by the tsarist government in 1864 in several gubernias in the European part of Russia. The Zemstvo wielded very limited rights and was controlled by the tsarist authorities.

p. 88

[3] **Tesnyak Socialists** (Tesnyaks) — Revolutionary Social-Democratic Workers' Party of Bulgaria, founded in 1903 after the split in the Social-Democratic Party. D. Blagoyev was the founder and leader of the Tesnyaks. In subsequent years the Tesnyaks were headed by Blagoyev's disciples: G. Dimitrov, V. Kolarov, and others. The Tesnyaks opposed the imperialist war of 1914-1918. In 1919, they joined the Communist International and thenceforth called themselves the Communist Party of Bulgaria.

p. 132

[4] **Mussavatists** — members of a counter-revolutionary bourgeois-landlord nationalist party in Azerbaijan formed in 1912. They were enemies of the fraternal unification of the Azerbaijan people with the Russian and other peoples of Russia. During the Great October Socialist Revolution and in the period of foreign military intervention and the Civil War in Soviet Russia they represented one of the principal counter-revolutionary forces in Azerbaijan. With the support of the Turkish, and later the British, interventionists they were in power in Azerbaijan in 1918-1920.

p. 299

[5] **Dashnaks**—members of an Armenian counter-revolutionary bourgeois-nationalist party that arose in the early nineties of the last century. After the victory of the October Revolution the Dashnaks, together with the Georgian Mensheviks and Azerbaijan Mussavatists, set up a counter-revolutionary bloc and with the help of the foreign interventionists wrested Transcaucasia from Soviet Russia. In 1918-1920, the Dashnaks, then at the head of the bourgeois government in Armenia, brutally oppressed the workers and peasants, incited Armenians against Georgians and Azerbaijanians. They reduced Armenia to a state of utter ruin. In November, 1920, the

Dashnak government was overthrown and Soviet power was established in Armenia.

p. 299

[6] **Borotbists** — Left wing of the Ukrainian Socialist-Revolutionaries, which formed an independent party in May, 1918. The Borotbists took their name from their central organ **Borotba (Struggle)**. In March, 1920, in view of the growing influence of the Bolsheviks among the peasant masses, the Borotbists were obliged to disband their party, and joined the Communist Party (Bolsheviks) of Ukraine. The Fourth Conference of the C.P.(B.)U. decided to admit the Borotbists into the Party, all newly-accepted members being re-registered. Subsequent years showed, however, that many of them were double-dealers, that they headed the anti-Soviet struggle of the counter-revolutionary, bourgeois-nationalist elements in Ukraine. They were exposed as enemies of the people.

p. 347

[7] **Nepman** — a private trader or manufacturer in the early period of the New Economic Policy.

p. 364

[8] **Collective-Farm Centre** — All-Union Council of the collective farms which existed from 1927 to 1932. The Centre provided organisational guidance to the collective farms.

p. 449